The Official History of
Yorkshire County Cricket Club

THE OFFICIAL HISTORY OF
YORKSHIRE

COUNTY CRICKET CLUB

DEREK HODGSON

With a Foreword by
the Viscount Mountgarret,
President of the Yorkshire County Cricket Club

THE CROWOOD PRESS

First published in 1989 by
THE CROWOOD PRESS
Ramsbury, Marlborough
Wiltshire SN8 2HE

British Library Cataloguing in Publication Data

Hodgson, Derek
The official history of Yorkshire County Cricket Club.
1. Yorkshire. County cricket. Clubs. Yorkshire County
Cricket Club, to 1988
I. Title
796.35'863'094281

ISBN 1-85223-274-9

Printed and bound in Great Britain by
Butler & Tanner Ltd, Frome and London

This History is dedicated to
the Reverend R.S. Holmes, A.W. Pullin, J.M. Kilburn, Peter Thomas
and every small boy or girl who ever aspired to wear
the White Rose.

Contents

List of Player Portraits

Tom Marsden
Harry Sampson
James Dearman
Andrew Crossland
George Anderson
Isaac Hodgson
Roger Iddison
Billy Slinn
Lascelles Hall
John Thewlis
George Atkinson
Joe Rowbotham
Edwin Stephenson
George Freeman
Luke Greenwood
Tom Emmett
George Pinder
Ephraim Lockwood
Allen Hill
George Ulyett
Louis Hall
Billy Bates
Ted Peate
George Harrison
Martin Hawke
Joe Preston
Ted Wainwright

Saul Wade
David Hunter
George Hirst
Bobby Peel
David Denton
Frank Mitchell
John Tunnicliffe
F.S. Jackson
Ernest Smith
Bobby Moorhouse
Lees Whitehead
J.T. Brown
Frank Milligan
Schofield Haigh
Wilfred Rhodes
T.L. Taylor
Irving Washington
Alonzo Drake
Major Booth
Arthur Dolphin
Roy Kilner
Edgar Oldroyd
Rahley Wilson
Percy Holmes
Herbert Sutcliffe
Emmott Robinson
Abraham Waddington
George Macaulay

Maurice Leyland
Arthur Mitchell
Arthur Wood
Wilf Barber
Cyril Turner
Bill Bowes
Hedley Verity
Frank Greenwood
Brian Sellers
Frank Smailes
Len Hutton
Paul Gibb
Ellis Robinson
Norman Yardley
Alec Coxon
Arthur Booth
Vic Wilson
Ted Lester
Gerald Smithson
Ron Aspinall
Don Brennan
Johnny Wardle
Brian Close
Frank Lowson
Fred Trueman
Bob Appleyard
Willie Watson
Jimmy Binks

Billy Sutcliffe
Ray Illingworth
Doug Padgett
Byron Stott
Ken Taylor
Ronnie Burnet
Don Wilson
Philip Sharpe
Brian Bolus
Harold Bird
Tony Nicholson
Geoffrey Boycott
John Hampshire
Richard Hutton
Chris Old
David Bairstow
Richard Lumb
Phillip Carrick
Graham Stevenson
Bill Athey
Kevin Sharp
Jim Love
Martyn Moxon
Paul Jarvis
Neil Lloyd
Ashley Metcalfe
Richard Blakey

Foreword

Forty years ago Mr J.M. Kilburn, a distinguished cricket correspondent of the *Yorkshire Post* for more than thirty years, wrote the third volume of the original *History of the Yorkshire County Cricket Club*, covering the years 1924 to 1949. That was the last of the volumes to be completed and now all three are, sadly, long out of print.

It is therefore a particularly great honour for me to have been invited by Derek Hodgson to write a short introduction to this new work that embraces the years covered by the previous three volumes and brings the Official History up to date, to the winter of 1988. Coincidentally it was in 1949 that Derek Hodgson became a member of Yorkshire at the start of a journalistic career that embraced cricket reporting, home and abroad, for several national newspapers; since the foundation of *The Independent* he has been the Northern Sports Correspondent. It can be safely said that there is no one better qualified to report on the momentous years of Yorkshire's history, aided by the superb records that have been faithfully maintained over the years by Mr Roy Wilkinson.

Momentous mainly because of the slide of Yorkshire's greatness in the field of cricket through time-consuming internal quarrels and controversy. Derek Hodgson discusses the many troubles that beset Yorkshire with a distinctive flavour and fairness.

So much change has occurred in the field of cricket during these years, ranging from the influx and dominance of first-class cricket by overseas players to the introduction of one-day cricket, the covering of pitches, and the host of things that have made these changes which have had their knock-on effect on Yorkshire. It is said that we in Yorkshire do not play cricket for fun, and we take our game pretty seriously. For this reason there will be much in this book which will give rise to interesting debate for years to come, and the arguments put forward by Derek Hodgson will surely remind all Yorkshiremen, good and true, that at the end of the day it is only a game.

I thoroughly commend this book to all cricket-lovers, but especially, of course, to every Yorkshireman.

Viscount Mountgarret
President, Yorkshire County Cricket Club

Acknowledgements

The major sources for this History are recorded elsewhere. The author is also grateful to the following: Charles Burgess and Philip Shaw of *The Independent* for a benevolent attitude towards writing time; Kathleen Rainford, Bill Bridge and David Hopps, the Librarian, Sports Editor and Cricket Correspondent of the *Yorkshire Post*; John Featherstone, Editor of *The White Rose*; the Reverend Malcolm Lorimer, the Yorkshire-born Curator and Librarian of Lancashire County Cricket Club; John Callaghan, Cricket Correspondent of the *Yorkshire Evening Post*; David Warner, Cricket Correspondent of the *Telegraph and Argus*, Bradford; Robert Mills, Cricket Correspondent of the *Hull Daily Mail*; Anthony Woodhouse, Curator to the Yorkshire County Cricket Club; Roy Wilkinson, Consultant Editor, the Yorkshire CCC Yearbook; Richard Streeton; Edward Sheard; J.B. Daffern, Lascelles Hall CC; Paul Dyson; Alan Thompson; Tom Naylor; Jeremy Lonsdale; Prior Timothy Ratcliffe, Blackfriars, Oxford; Andrew Barker; Roger Mann; Peter Pickup; Peter Davy; Henry Norris; Mark Graham; Jack Sokell; A.D. Oates; Mick Pope; N. Pearn; Sir Leonard Hutton; Jean Ough; N.W.D. Yardley; the late Bill Bowes; David Bairstow; Constance Whitworth, Margeret Thomas, Moira Banks and certainly not least, the editor, Graham Hart.

DEREK HODGSON
May, 1989

The Author and Publishers are grateful to the following for permission to reproduce photographs:

All-Sport Photographic Ltd: 177
Bert Butterworth: 209, 213
Colorsport: 139
Irving Fairhurst: 92 (bottom)
John Featherstone: 216, 219 (top), 219 (bottom), 234
The Guardian: 103, 124, 191, 201
Jack Hickes, Leeds: 205, 210
Ken Kelly: 46, 50, 63, 70, 115, 125, 148, 157, 194
Malcolm Lorimer: 20
Photopress (Leeds) Ltd: 163, 187
The Press Association: 15, 166, 179, 190, 195, 198, 211
Sporting Pictures (UK) Ltd: 221
Walkers Studios Ltd, Scarborough: 121, 134
Yorkshire Post: 31, 37, 38, 43, 53, 54, 57, 67, 74, 84, 88, 92 (top), 97, 105, 106, 109, 123, 130, 140, 144, 153, 154, 156 (top), 156 (bottom), 167, 173, 181

Introduction – God's own county

Yorkshiremen are religious in the catholic sense, resentful of central authority, lovers of music, particularly choral and brass, disputatious and often simply bloody-minded. Convinced of the justice of a cause they are stubborn last-ditchers, loyal to a fault; wary of hard times they are careful with their money. They have an innate belief in their own superiority and when they hear the phrase "God's Own County" it would never occur to them that it might carry a derisive implication; to them it is no more than the truth.

When they were known as Brigantes they gave the Romans so much trouble that a fortress city had to be established at Eboracum and a Legion posted there; even an Emperor, Septimus Severus, had to be proclaimed in York. Had the northern earls Edwin and Morcar reached Harold in time there might have been no Norman Conquest. Enraged at the intractability of the men north of the Humber, the Conqueror brought fire and sword and laid the land waste, thus inserting antipathy to London's edicts into the genetic memory.

Richard, Duke of Gloucester was a much admired administrator of the North before he was translated into a wicked uncle and the crook-backed Richard III. His device of the white boar and white rose is still worn proudly by many Yorkshiremen more than 500 years after the Tudors won the last battle and wrote the history. Henry VIII's dissolution of the monasteries, at a time when Yorkshire boasted 28 abbeys and 26 priories, brought the county's last armed rising (so far) against central government, the Pilgrimage of Grace. No English king was safe unless his man held York.

The Industrial Revolution brought steel to the south, textiles to the west, shipbuilding to the east and coal just about everywhere through the Ridings. Strong backs, hearty lungs and nimble fingers were needed by the new overlords, the master at the mill or the mine. The chapel took hold on Sundays, proclaiming a simpler, more fundamental faith whose preachers thundered against sin and strong drink, advocated unity as strength, rehearsed "The Messiah" and formed Sunday-school cricket teams.

The story follows; what needs to be mentioned in this introduction is the line of administrators whose strength of purpose first persuaded the recalcitrant parts to come together in a county club, who ensured, once the club was founded, there would be no fissures serious enough to bring it down, and whose diligence took the club prosperously into its second century.

Each of these men appears within the context of this History but deserves further mention, starting with Michael John Ellison, the Sheffielder who could see beyond Hallamshire. As Peter Thomas wrote: "Each milestone in the early history of Yorkshire county cricket is a milestone in the endeavour and generosity of the white-bearded Ellison."

He was forty-four when he first urged the setting up of the club's fore-runner, the Public Match Fund Committee, and two years older before the club was actually formed. He took on the arduous role of President-Treasurer and it is accepted that when the Committee prevailed upon him to accept a refund of some of the money he had spent to keep the club afloat the amount (£400, probably worth around £40,000 today) was only a token repayment of the full debt. Another of South Yorkshire's institutions, Sheffield United, also owe Ellison a debt for he guaranteed the rent of Bramall Lane to his employer, the Duke of Norfolk.

J.E. Wostinholm

Ellison's son Michael succeeded his father as Treasurer in 1894, a post he surrendered to Charles Stokes in 1899. Michael had played full-back for Sheffield United while Stokes, a dentist and an accomplished violinist, was regarded as the enthusiast who put the United Football Club on its feet. Stokes was a member of the Yorkshire Committee for thirty-six years.

Joseph Beckett Wostinholm was the Secretary of the Club from 1864 to 1902 and ruled it during the formative years at Ellison's right hand. Originally paid ten per cent of all subscriptions, he was then paid a fixed £10 from 1870 to 1882, at which point the Committee felt he was worth £25 per annum.

Significantly, when the "perfect Tartar" as Hawke described him did retire, the club was forced to offer the huge salary of £350 in order to replace him and it was not until he had gone that the Committee felt able to move the club offices from Sheffield to Leeds, another indication of Wostinholm's influence and prestige. He was as intimately connected with Sheffield United for forty years. Wostinholm was presented with a portrait in oils, several silver articles and a testimonial of £200 by the club.

Frederick Toone, Wostinholm's successor, had made his name with Leicestershire where, in five years, he had lifted the membership from 500 to 1800 and on his arrival in Leeds in 1903 he was equally successful. In his twenty-seven years of office he raised the membership figure by 100 per cent to 6000, revised many of the club rules, organised players' benefits and insisted, as the County Secretary, of taking charge of the county's matches wherever they were played in Yorkshire.

His reputation for management won him appointment to England's tours of Australia in 1920, 1924 and 1928 and on his return from the third tour he was knighted for his services to cricket. He was, in Warner's words, "the perfect manager" and *Wisden* described him as "the organiser supreme". It was Toone who revised and edited that other Yorkshire cricket institution, the Yearbook, in a style that has not greatly altered to this day. In 1923 he was appointed by the Government to the "Crowds Committee", set up to enquire into the safety of spectators at sporting events, a sequel to the Bolton-West Ham FA Cup Final when the crowd overflowed on to the pitch and were marshalled to safety by one policeman on a white horse.

Hawke wrote of Toone in 1924: "It is remarkable that our office is run by one secretary and a boy."

That boy was for many years John Henry "Jack" Nash, appointed Assistant Secretary in 1922, succeeding Toone in 1931 to serve in that office for the next forty years. Nash had a classical Yorkshire cricket background, born in Farsley and educated at Pudsey Grammar.

Toone's death occurred when Nash was only twenty-five and several of the Committee, including Hawke, had misgivings about appointing so young a successor; but Nash had been well trained and the office continued

Sir Frederick Toone

smoothly; he was rewarded in 1950–1 when he managed the England tour of Australia.

A church organist, Nash was regarded by some, especially among the enlarged and encroaching media, as a rather distant and aloof man and it is doubtful if he ever considered what is now called "public relations" as part of his duties. A small but memorable kindness might be recorded: the author, when a National Serviceman in 1949, wrote to Nash asking if he could be proposed for membership, apologising for the lack of a proposer and seconder, his father having resigned on moving to Bedfordshire in 1932. Strictly against the rules as they were at that time, Nash arranged for the eighteen-year-old aircraftsman to be elected and took the trouble to write a terse but welcoming note to Royal Air Force Hospital, Ely.

Yorkshire's fifth Secretary, succeeding Nash, Joseph Lister, had another exemplary York-

shire background. Born in Thirsk and related to George Macaulay, he was educated at Cheltenham, played hockey for Yorkshire and as a right-hand bat played twenty-four first-class matches between 1951 and 1959, although only twice for Yorkshire.

After becoming Secretary of Worcestershire he was the obvious candidate to replace Nash in 1971 and felt the full force of the gale of change that swept through cricket in the ensuing years, a long trial that tested his strength. The County Secretary today has tasks and pressures undreamed of in Wostinholm's time. The most efficient form of administration for a county cricket club that promotes Test matches has still to be devised but it is significant that Lancashire, the nearest comparison, employ a Secretary, two Assistant Secretaries, a commercial and public relations manager, a team manager and a team coach, with a full secretarial staff to service each office.

In the Treasurer's chair, an honorary position, Stokes was followed by the Heselton father and son who served the club for a total of forty-nine years, the son Wyndham becoming one of the first honorary life members in 1946. Principals of a firm of Bradford accountants, they gave life service to both Yorkshire and the Bradford club and the father did most to raise the funds necessary to purchase the Park Avenue ground.

Michael Grove Crawford, who succeeded in 1963, was a right-hand bat who was educated at Shrewsbury and Cambridge (a soccer blue) and a contemporary of Joe Lister's in the Yorkshire second team, making one first-team appearance in 1951. Crawford is the only Treasurer to become Chairman of the General Committee (a post created in 1971 to ease the President's duties), an office he filled capably during a stormy four years until it became clear that as a moderate he was a target for both sides of the then controversy.

David Welch, from Rotherham, Treasurer from 1980–4, was another forced out by the continuing political battles although he returned to serve the General Committee, Peter Townend taking office in 1984 and becoming one of the club's few officers to command the confidence of all factions.

Hawke apart – and he was President for forty years – the holder of the club's premier office preferred to play the gentle helmsman and it was not until Sir Keith Parkinson's term (1974–81) that the President became involved in the raging arguments over policy. Sir Keith, who was also chairman of the *Yorkshire Post*, and his successor, the greatly respected Norman Yardley, tried but failed to restore unity and it was not until the Viscount Mountgarret was elected in October 1984 that a new force appeared.

A descendant of the Butler Earls of Ormonde, whose titles had been won while pacifying Ulster, Mountgarret came into office with a background of the Irish Guards and Eton and no preconceived attitudes nor loyalties. He conceded, from the start, that he would have to learn by trial and error but he was the fresh new strength the club needed and he exercised his influence and power like no one President since Hawke, forcing through a new constitution, strengthening the central government of the club and rallying support by, in effect, asking one simple question of the members: "I will always put the good of the club first. Will you?"

Mountgarret could not be accused of place-seeking, nor social climbing, nor self-glory. The early success he needed came when Philip Carrick's team won the Benson and Hedges Cup in 1987.

Mountgarret's rise inevitably diminished the

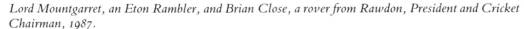

Lord Mountgarret, an Eton Rambler, and Brian Close, a rover from Rawdon, President and Cricket Chairman, 1987.

office of Chairman of General Committee that had been occupied, since 1971, by the able Arthur Connell from Sheffield, by Crawford and then, by the overthrow of the General Committee in March 1984, by Reg Kirk of Hull. Kirk, in his eighteen months of office, was able to fulfil one promise in that he did open up his office, and the Committee generally, to the members and the public and the club's administration, since Kirk, has been seen to be more immediately accessible. All General Committee members are now much more aware of their responsibilities to their constituents.

When Kirk stood down the General Committee turned to Brian Walsh QC, from Leeds, a brilliant speaker who, when allowed by his busy schedule, was able to put the club's argument forcefully and wittily whether at Lord's or in a working man's club. While the members and the public could not be said to accept all the club's policies with rapturous agreement, Yorkshire did enter the last twenty years of the twentieth century with a reasonably unified administration capable of making firm decisions.

1

The Beginnings 1750–1880

If Thomas Lord, vintner, speculator and entrepreneur, is the first Yorkshire cricketer known to history, founding as he did the most famous ground in the world, he had a contemporary who, but for international circumstances, might have stolen some of his thunder. Francis Osborne, 5th Duke of Leeds, was enough of a Yorkshireman to insist upon being buried at Harthill in the old West Riding. His Grace's full connections with cricket are undetermined, but he did have the foresight, as Secretary of State for Foreign Affairs, to appoint a cricketing devotee, the Duke of Dorset, as His Majesty's Ambassador to the Court of Louis XVI.

The Times, in its second year of publication, recorded in May 1786 a match played in Paris on 16 April: ' . . . by some English gentlemen, in the Champs Elyses [sic]. His Grace of Dorset was, as usual, the most distinguished for skill and activity. The French, however, cannot imitate us in such vigorous exertions of the body; so that we seldom see them enter the lists.'

Dorset, vaguely rumoured to have been a lover of Marie-Antoinette, invited a Surrey team to play an exhibition match in the Bois de Boulogne a little over three years later. The tourists had reached Dover when they were met by the Duke, who had sagely concluded that the storming of the Bastille was not the most conducive of climates for the launching of the game upon the French. Any claim the Duke of Leeds might have presented to have promoted the first Test match therefore went up in smoke and flame. However, Dorset did return to England with one predilection of the Bourbons – an interval for tea – duly adopted at his matches.

After the Napoleonic wars English lace-makers spread the game throughout northern France, and clubs are mentioned in Paris, Dieppe, Calais and Boulogne. Teams from Nottingham went on tour across the Channel, having the usual impact on Anglo-French relations, according to one verse:

> That England has no rival
> Well know the trembling pack,
> Whom Charley Brown by Calais Town
> Bowled out behind his back

The French, in turn, obstinately refused to have such wonders thrust upon them. In 1867 a Frenchman observed to a touring Englishman, a Butterfly: 'I cannot understand why you do not engage a servant to field for you.' At about the same time the French made an attempt to describe the game: 'The bowler, grasping the ball in the right hand, watches for a favourable moment when the attention of the batsman is distracted and then launches it at him with incredible force; the batsman, however, is on the alert; he strikes it to an enormous height and immediately runs.'

Napoleon III, watching a match between Bickley Park and Beckenham, was so impressed by the taking of a spectacular catch that he despatched an aide to request that the fielder repeat the feat. The last French emperor also intervened when the Paris CC was in danger of being suppressed as dangerous, a batsman having tripped and broken his arm during the course of a game.

One reason for this emphasis on cricket's French connection is that the word 'crice' (a 'staff') is one possible etymological source of the name of cricket. The same language also contributes 'criquet', a stick used in bowls. An illustration, depicting two men playing with a bat and a ball, can be seen in a mid-thirteenth-century French book named as *Chronique d'An-*

gleterre. The Bodleian Library possesses a manuscript showing monks engaged in some sport that involves fieldsmen; and Guildford Corporation records refer to 'crickett' in 1597.

Cricket in Yorkshire probably derived from several different sources. Stool-ball, in which a stool, known in some parts as a 'cricket', was turned on its side and defended like a set of stumps, is one; in a later form the stool is turned upside down and a comb placed across two of the legs – a primitive wicket with a bail. Then, too, there was knurr and spell, a ball or stone being propelled from the ground and hit by a bat or stick while in flight, the hitter scoring 'runs' while the ball was retrieved. A catch was 'out'. Several public schools played variations of bat and ball games; rounders is yet another development, a branch that an American Civil War general, Abner Doubleday, turned into baseball in 1839.

There is historical record of cricket in Yorkshire by 1751 when Sheffield engaged professionals to 'amuse the populace and draw them from cock-fighting'. In the same year the Earl of Northumberland's XI defeated the Duke of Cleveland's XI at Stanwick, near Richmond. Six years later, in Leeds, the Church burgesses paid fourteen shillings and sixpence to cricketers to entertain the local population on Shrove Tuesday, 'to prevent the infamous practice of throwing at cocks'. A more refined occasion occurred on Chapeltown Moor in 1776, as the Colonials were revolting in New England, when the Married Men played the Bachelors for five guineas and a dinner, the single men winning by 6 runs. Another four years and a Leeds theatre was advertising, on the bill for a night's entertainment, 'a new dance called The Cricketers, or the Sports of Chapel-Town'.

By then cricket was becoming organised. A club was formed in York in 1784. In October 1786 the Gentlemen of York defeated the Gentlemen of Doncaster, reputedly for a hundred guineas – a vast sum and one that must be treated with caution, for it was common practice to advertise matches for great prizes when in fact no money was at stake. Wetherby, too, was playing matches as the nineteenth century neared, meeting Scruton over two days in 1797, and by 1802 there occurred what today might

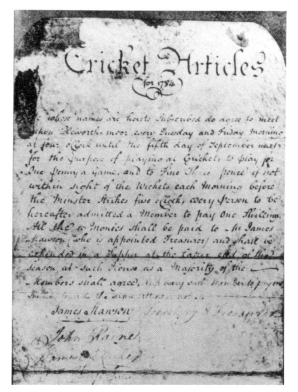

The constitution of the York Cricket Club, drawn up in 1784, with signatures of 31 founder members.

be called a sponsors' match – Smiths and Co. defeating Goodman and Co. in Sheffield.

While Britain fought Napoleon, the game of cricket advanced dramatically. Scores, notched on a stick, gave way to the scorebook in which individual accounts were kept, enabling clubs to publish proper records. The strong Ripon club, who played as far afield as Nottingham in 1816, were showing the way towards standardisation by publishing, in 1825, the 'Laws of Cricket as Approved by the Mary-le-Bone Club'.

The first glimmering of a Yorkshire county identity, certainly unrecognised at the time, came with the opening of a custom-made (to use the modern term) cricket ground at Darnall, Sheffield in 1822, and it was fitting that the southern city should have seen the first major establishment, for Sheffield is the true birthplace of Yorkshire county cricket.

Darnall, as represented on a contemporary illustration, consisted of a field in front of a fairly substantial mansion, the balcony apparently providing a view for ladies of quality, with the crowd gathered around a seemingly unmarked boundary upon which were stationed a few tents and at least one hut, where two handsomely dressed ladies and a Regency buck appear to be taking wine or tea. The umpires, in polished knee boots, wine-dark dress coats and top hats, have an air of authority far beyond that possessed by today's more humble arbiters. The players, all in white and tight breeches, wear dark caps; the bats are straight, the stumps are three and the bowler is about to deliver, under-arm. The whole ambience is one of enjoyment and not a little wealth, suggesting that our Georgian and Victorian forefathers may have experienced hard times but never lost their enormous capacity for enjoying themselves.

Darnall opened at a momentous point in the game's history. Since 1750 the under-arm bowler had reigned without challenge to his method, but as pitches improved batsmen began to assert an increasing advantage, leading bowlers, in the natural course of things, to strive to make the method of delivery more potent. In trying to increase the pace without jerking the ball, which was illegal, bowlers began to deliver the ball further away from the body.

There is another theory, adopted by romantics, that round-arm stemmed from the inability of that formidable lady Mrs Grace, the Doctor's mother, to bowl under-arm in a hooped skirt. Whatever the circumstances, the bowling of William Lillywhite and Jem Broadbridge of Sussex was causing concern and MCC, who had paid their first and only visit to Darnall in 1825, instituted a series of three 'test' matches in 1827 between England and Sussex to judge the new style of bowling, with Darnall, confirming its rank among cricket grounds, being chosen for the first of these trials.

Sussex won that first experiment by seven wickets, and it was the exposure of so many high-class cricketers in the county that fired the imagination of Yorkshiremen with enormous enthusiasm for the game. Over the next fifteen years cricket clubs are recorded at Bedale,

The cricket ground at Darnall, near Sheffield, 1822.

Dalton, Thirsk, Beverley, Bradford, Otley, Rotherham, Mexborough, Harrogate, Keighley, Scarborough, Redcar and Barnsley.

But it was to Sheffield that all Yorkshire clubs rightly deferred, for cricket was so well established among the grinders that its eventual displacement by soccer in the city remains to this day something of a mystery. (The Wednesday began as a cricket club, and Sheffield United's title was 'Cricket, Football and Athletic Club', reflecting the enormous interest of much of the population.) There was another reason for Sheffield's status, however: it had pioneered out-of-county games against Nottingham, thus attracting a partisan interest.

Nottingham's lacemakers, like the weavers of Huddersfield and Sheffield's grinders, needed a happy marriage of hands and eye to be successful in their work. They were mostly self-employed on a piece-work basis, and they, too, cheerfully embraced cricket. Between 1771 and 1860 the players of Sheffield and Nottingham met twenty-six times, Nottingham winning fourteen of the matches and being regarded as the superior side, for Sheffield were sometimes offered odds. In 1800 Sheffield played twenty-two such matches, in 1822 fifteen, in 1857 and 1860 sixteen, and in later matches Sheffield were assisted by Leicester and Durham.

Sheffield, nevertheless, had what would today be called the 'Man of the Series' in the doughty Tom Marsden. Three three-figure scores were recorded in these inter-city contests, Marsden making two of them (227 in 1826 and 125 in 1828), and he was the only player to carry his bat in the series. In this period of the game's formation it should also be

Tom Marsden *Sheffield's Pride*

The most famous man in the city's history, Marsden had poems written of his prowess, which he regarded highly enough for him to challenge, for a side-stake of £50, any man in England in 1828 to a single-wicket match (with a further £10 offered for travelling expenses). For five years no one was bold enough to take him on until, in 1833, Fuller Pilch who, ironically, had Sheffield connections, routed him by an innings and 70 at Norwich.

Such was Sheffield's faith in her twenty-eight-year-old champion that 20,000 crowded the Darnall ground to watch the return, only to see Pilch triumph again, this time by 127 runs. The Sheffielder's reputation was such, however, that Pilch went on to advertise himself as the man who had defeated 'Marsden the Champion'.

Marsden stood 5 feet 8 inches, batted left-handed and bowled fast under-arm, occasionally switching to round-arm medium. His 227 for Sheffield and Leicester against the mighty Nottingham club side of 1826, scored in eight hours, was only the third double-century in history, and the first by a Yorkshireman. He was then twenty-one and the innings included one hit of more than 130 yards and over a 45-foot-high wall; such was the crowd's enthusiasm that a collection for him, perhaps the first in the county, was organised. As he also took six wickets, he clearly deserved his reward.

Marsden may also have been the first Yorkshire cricketer to have had too many hospitable friends. Famous at twenty-one, he had achieved most of his great performances by twenty-five and was only thirty-eight when he died. Holmes described him as 'a rollicking sort of fellow', citing a match played against a G. Jarvis, Marsden promising to pull down the sign on his inn 'The Cricketers' if he lost; he didn't. The professions of inn-keeping and cricket are ill suited. There is no direct evidence that Marsden's career was affected by over-indulgence, but such were his popularity and fame that his well-wishers were legion.

Two years after Marsden's death the Treasurer of the Leeds club, a Mr Clarke, was presented with a gold breast-pin, subscribed for by the members, as a token of respect for his two years in office. The pin was composed of a bat, stumps and a ball and, adds Holmes, 'instead of a chain were two links of the late Tom Marsden's hair'. Such a gesture might today smack of voodoo, but in 1845 when photography was still rare any memento of the renowned was treasured. 'At cricket he's nature's perfection,' writes an unknown poet of Marsden's skills, and to him must be given the major credit for advertising the game and its attractions throughout the county.

Harry Sampson   *The Landlord*

Even if Harry Sampson had not been a formidable cricketer in his own right, he would have a place in this history if only because he was for twenty years the landlord of the Adelphi Hotel in Sheffield, birthplace of both the Yorkshire County Club and of Sheffield Wednesday Football Club. He was described as a small, stout man who as a batsman was a back player of very high quality and as a bowler was renowned for his accuracy.

Marsden was the first Yorkshireman to be chosen for the Gentlemen against the Players in 1827, then a fixture bearing much more prestige than a modern Test match, and Sampson was the second, selected in 1841. This followed his appearance for The North against The South at Lord's the previous year, and after his appearance for the Players he was appointed a ground bowler and coach to the MCC, opening his first hostelry in 1842, in Reading. Mr Sampson did not allow the grass to grow under his feet.

It was at about this time, in 1841, that Sampson, a member of the United England XI, met the now declining Marsden in a single-wicket match at the Hyde Park ground, Sampson proving his right to the succession with a substantial victory by an innings and 50 runs. Marsden was bowled twice for 19 and 9, and in the second innings of what sounds a very tense affair Sampson bowled 446 consecutive deliveries, conceding over 7 wides.

Harry Sampson was also a fine long-stop, a passionate fisherman, and even today holds one world record: playing for Wednesday against Sheffield Town on 8 February 1841, he scored 162, on ice.

remembered that players thought nothing of starting a match at 9 a.m., nor of playing on into November if weather permitted.

From this Sheffield–Nottingham series came Yorkshire's first county fixture, an all-Sheffield venture on the Hyde Park ground, home of the Wednesday club, in 1833. The origin of the match is not clear, although it may have arisen from the need to raise a team to match the status of the first opponents, Norfolk. Three gentlemen, or amateurs as they were to become known, were in that first Yorkshire team, hinting at a different organisation from that at Darnall, but as the side included two of the city's great professionals, Marsden and Samp-

son, the result was never in doubt, despite the appearance for Norfolk of three Pilches, including Fuller.

While Fuller Pilch was Norfolk-born, he was a member of the Wednesday club, and had assisted Sheffield against Nottingham and The North against The South. This first county fixture was won by Yorkshire by 120 runs, Marsden and Dearman contributing 93 of the second-innings total of 196 and taking eight of the twenty Norfolk wickets (four batsmen were run out).

Further fixtures between the two counties followed in 1834 and 1836, but as Fuller Pilch had departed to play for Kent, at the enormous annual salary of £100, in the intervening year, Norfolk's strength, and therefore its attraction as an opposition, had declined to such an extent that further meetings could no longer be considered viable. Pilch's aggregate in the five matches was 385 runs at an average of 48, a tremendous contribution.

Having now developed the taste and the organisation for county matches, this Sheffield-based Yorkshire then set about enlarging the fixture list. Sussex were met in 1835 and 1855, Manchester three times in 1844–5, and the first Roses match was played in 1849, with Kent also providing the opposition for the first time in that year. Surrey joined the list in 1850. From 1846 William Clarke's famous All-England XI, founded the previous year, began fixtures against various Yorkshire combinations of between fourteen and twenty-two players. Their great rivals, the United All-England XI, played a Yorkshire fourteen in 1853.

Yorkshire's fielding, on the rough surfaces of the time, must have been worth watching. In one of the early matches, in 1835, six Sussex batsmen were run out in the two innings, Sussex thereupon conceding victory with Yorkshire needing 21 and an innings to play!

The spreading strength of cricket in the county can be judged from a series of fixtures between Sheffield and Yorkshire in 1849–50. The city won three of the four matches, but the fact that the rest of the county could even raise a team to match the experts was as remarkable as it was encouraging. Such was the enormous interest in South Yorkshire that by 1855 a third cricket ground had been opened in Sheffield.

Darnall, as mentioned earlier, was regarded as one of England's premier grounds. 'It is much to be regretted that the Darnall Ground is so far from London and other principal places where the noble game is played, as it may justly be considered the finest in the kingdom,' was the opinion of one southern newspaper.

In fact, there were two Darnall grounds on the Glossop Road. The first, opened on 26 August 1822, saw Sheffield engage Nottingham and during the match a stand gave way, two spectators were killed and more than fifty injured. George Steer, the owner, was unde-

terred by this tragedy, and set about building a more substantial ground in the same district which opened in 1824 and passed into the management of William Woolhouse, a noted Sheffield left-handed amateur batsman who married Steer's daughter Mary. At one end a terrace was built to accommodate 8000 spectators, and upon that terrace a handsome brick pavilion stood upon stone pillars. It was sad, then, that such a well-appointed ground should house top-class cricket for only five years.

Darnall was three miles from the city centre, so that when the Hyde Park ground opened in 1826, costing £4000, at only half that distance, the crowd, almost all of whom would be walking, naturally preferred the shorter journey. Darnall passed to James Dearman and then to his wife, who was reported to have promoted rabbit coursing on the 'Old Cricket Ground'. Andrew Crossland was another famous name at Hyde Park.

On high ground, Hyde Park became known for its splendid views and rapid draining and drying, and Woolhouse was astute enough to bring it into his orbit. Hyde Park's five and a half acres enabled it to be used for massed cricket, like Parker's Piece or the Maidan in Bombay. In September 1830 Pierce Egan's *Book of Sports* noted that upwards of two hundred cricketers could be seen at work. It was at Hyde Park that Yorkshire played their first match, against Norfolk in 1833, and when All England played Sheffield in 1846 Hyde Park housed an astonishing 16,000. As for Woolhouse, Peter Thomas wrote the perfect epitaph when he described him as 'the Thomas Lord of Sheffield'.

But, as with Darnall, the early promise failed to flourish. The ownership passed to a landlord who thought he might make greater profits from sports other than cricket, making it impossible after a while for the game to be played there. The Hallamshire Volunteers took over Hyde Park as their drill ground, and in this century the site has been used for high-rise community flats.

The fulcrum of Yorkshire cricket then moved to Bramall Lane, even more central and as handsome a ground, enclosed by a ten-foot wall with 'beautiful stands and refreshment

James Dearman *Brave Little Jimmy*

The last Yorkshireman to challenge the rest of England to a single-wicket match, Dearman came from a cricketing family of many talents. He was a Sheffield filesmith who bowled fast round-arm, and in 1838 he issued his challenge, £100 a side. Fuller Pilch accepted but was pressed to fit the contest into a busy schedule, so Alfred Mynn, the 'Lion of Kent', agreed to deputise, the match being arranged for Town Malling on 2 August 1838.

About 5000 spectators attended, Mynn appearing, according to a witness, in 'a close-fitting jersey bound with red ribbon, a red belt around his waist and a straw hat with a broad red ribbon'. As a study in scarlet it was far too much for little Jimmy, who conceded 34 and 89 runs, scoring only 3 and 8 in reply, but the courage of the diminutive Dearman displayed against the strong 6 feet 2 inches of Mynn won him much praise and applause. It was suggested that the kindly Mynn fed him a few easy deliveries until, near six o'clock, there were shouts of 'Finish him off, Alfred,' the witness adding: 'I have a vision of middle stump flying up in the air and spinning like a wheel.'

The return match was in September in Sheffield where Dearman lost his bails to a ball of 'lightning speed', but there, at least, the margin was only 20 runs. Dearman played regularly for North against South and for the infant Yorkshire XI, retiring to take over the inn and ground at Darnall, his wife following as 'mine hostess'. He is known to be buried in the Attercliffe cemetery but he was never given a tombstone.

Andrew Crossland *Exceedingly Well*

Crossland was the most famous product of Dalton, another Huddersfield village that, around mid century, almost rivalled Lascelles Hall for cricketing prowess. Born two years after Waterloo, he was regarded as Yorkshire's best bowler (right-arm round) for many years and a batsman of great tenacity, once batting on a Hyde Park flier for 150 minutes to make 8 runs.

In one surviving photograph he is seen to be a handsome man wearing a cap not greatly dissimilar in style to the one sported by Geoffrey Boycott a century later. He played for and against the All-England XI, the equivalent of Test-match status today, taking twelve of their wickets at York in 1854 and four for 11 against them at Hull, the city in which he died at the ripe age of eighty-five.

His batting style was much remarked upon, *Scores and Biographies* noting that 'he got much off his ground to play the ball'. What he took as a batsman he could also dish out, once having Julius Caesar caught 'from a ball that rose as high as his head'. He made 24 on his debut at Lord's on a rough pitch against Grundy and Wisden, *Bell's Life* reporting: 'Each day the teams were invited to Mr Dark's house where they partook of old English fare of roast beef and plum pudding, which we imagine many of the visitors would have been glad to get a sight of.' The press, presumably, were not sponsored.

Crossland's obituary read: 'He could bat, bowl and field exceedingly well.'

13

rooms for visitors', according to a Sussex player whose team met Yorkshire in the first principal match on the ground in 1855. The cricketers, too, had perhaps learned a lesson from their experiences of private management at Darnall and Hyde Park, for Bramall Lane was leased by the Sheffield United club from the Duke of Norfolk for ninety-nine years, provision of the annual rent of £70 being the responsibility of Michael Ellison, the Duke's agent, who became one of the founder members of the county club. After Ellison's death in 1898 Sheffield United bought the freehold for £10,300, the Duke's stipulation being that it could not be resold for any purpose other than recreation for the next twenty-one years.

Another £6000 was spent on rebuilding the pavilion, and throughout Yorkshire's formative years Bramall Lane was the county club's home. The Reverend Holmes, in 1904, asserted it to be the most attractive of all enclosures, mentioning the Sheffield crowd's reputation for knowledge and fairness: 'The crowds all together there seem to have the genuine sporting instinct – a love of the game for its own sake. Where else in the country is the accommodation so ample? No less than 60,000 persons can see every ball, most of them from comfortably-seated terraces.'

For 120 years Bramall Lane was to keep at least some part of that fame and reputation until it, too, was sacrificed for ambitions of a different kind and slipped into second-class anonymity.

Cricket was so much a part of the life of Sheffield from 1820 to 1860, and an interest that crossed the divides of a class-ridden society, that it seems in retrospect surprising that it should have taken until 1861 before an attempt was made to establish a county club on a properly representative basis. Nevertheless, on 7 March 1861 a meeting was called at Harry Sampson's hotel, the Adelphi, on the site of what is now the Crucible Theatre famous world-wide as the venue for the World Snooker Championships. The purpose was to set up not a county club, but a 'Public Match Fund Committee', and it was resolved that such a committee should consist of the Bramall Lane Management Committee with the addition of one representative from each club willing to contribute not less than £1 to the Fund.

The Wednesday club, founded in the same hotel and whose football section was also to be established there six years later, and the clubs of Pitsmoor and Hallam, also from Sheffield, paid up immediately, but a year passed before an outsider, Scarborough, forwarded their money. M.J. Ellison was elected President and Treasurer; W. Whittles was the first Secretary. A match between the first eleven and the next sixteen was arranged, and the Secretary was instructed to seek home and away games with Surrey. Players were to be sounded out as to their terms for playing against Surrey.

Two dozen 'books' were printed seeking financial support from noblemen and gentlemen of the county, but the Fund was soon in trouble, apparently being unable to convince the rest of the county that it was not merely another Sheffield grouping. Lack of funds prevented matches being played against Lancashire at Manchester in 1862, yet of Yorkshire's cricketing prowess there was no doubt, for although Yorkshire lost to England's strongest county team at The Oval, they were able to take their revenge against Surrey at Bramall Lane.

As a London journalist pointed out, Yorkshire possessed cricketers of the calibre of Atkinson, Hodgson, Slinn, Iddison, Stephenson, Anderson, Rowbotham and Luke Greenwood, and 'in a year or two Yorkshire could be second to none in England'. So another attempt was made to launch a county club, and on 8 January 1863 it was resolved 'that a county club be formed', the membership to be unlimited, the minimum subscription 10s 6d. The stated object was to provide funds for the playing of first-class matches 'either in Sheffield or in any other towns of the county according as arrangements may be made'.

The mayor of Sheffield, T.R. Barker, was elected the first President, despite his Derbyshire birth, according to the minutes; George Padley was first Secretary, and with Ellison as Treasurer, Joseph Wostinholm became Secretary after the first year. No record, according to the Reverend Holmes, was ever made of Mr Barker's attending a meeting, and no minute has been found of Ellison's translation to the

George Anderson *The Ramrod*

'Old Ebor's' affectionate portrait of George Anderson in 1898 begins:

> It is a snug room in a comfortable house in Aiskew, Bedale. Two striking portraits assist in embellishing the walls and mark the old cricketer's dwelling; the original of each sits in his cosy armchair and chats pleasantly . . . The two portraits show George Anderson in two stages of his career; now he has passed into his seventies, no longer perhaps as erect as when he wore the white flannel and red spots of the All-England Eleven but still commanding presence . . . .
>
> The earlier portrait was sketched in 1853 by N. Felix. George Anderson appears as a young man of seven and twenty under Felix's brush and pigments. The other was drawn in Melbourne ten years later and shows the matured cricketer at the height of his career.

The quotation illustrates both the affection and respect with which Anderson was regarded through his seventy-six years (he died in 1902). He played alongside all the great men: Felix, Pilch, Mynn, Clarke, Parr, Wisden, Box, Caffyn, Sampson, Willsher and Julius Caesar. He played for Yorkshire for twenty years (captain for four) and for All England for twenty-one, and he was the first Yorkshireman to score a thousand runs in a summer, in 1862.

His height, over six feet, is often remarked upon, as were his military bearing and hitting power. In 1903 he was judged to have been Yorkshire's hardest hitter, and in the days when all scores had to be run out he hit an eight at The Oval in 1862, declaring afterwards that it would have been nine had not his partner Carpenter, from Cambridgeshire, been 'dead beat'. He must have been a ferocious driver, his style comparing with George Ulyett's.

'We were not in the habit of letting balls go by on the off side. If we had stood at the wicket and allowed balls to go by, as some modern [1898] batsmen do, we should have been hooted, and properly so,' he told 'Old Ebor'.

Anderson was a member of the second England team to tour Australia, under George Parr's leadership, in 1863–4. The voyage out took sixty-one days, leaving the Mersey on 14 October, and the tour began in Melbourne on New Year's Day before a crowd of 14,000. Sixteen matches were played, all against teams of twenty-two; ten were won, none was lost. Anderson's diary recorded a dreadful trip out, with seasickness day after day, but his Victorian spirit was unflagging.

Despite being a county captain and prominent player, Yorkshire did not reward this popular man with a benefit until he was in his sixty-ninth year, and Anderson himself had no doubt that this was because of his leadership of the 'strike' that stemmed from John Lillywhite's no-balling of Edgar Willsher at The Oval in 1862.

Lillywhite was standing in his first match, Surrey *v* All England, and warned the Kent bowler Willsher that his arm was getting high. Two overs later Lillywhite called seven balls in succession, and the bowler flung down the ball and walked off the field, followed by the team's nine professionals who included Anderson and three other Yorkshiremen. Anderson said later that the professionals had been convinced that Surrey had prompted Lillywhite to call Willsher, and as a result he declined to play against Surrey again.

That decision – and he was recognised as a stubborn man – cost him good years, and he did not appear for Yorkshire again until 1867, declining to captain the team in 1865 because it meant he would have to play against Surrey. The controversy grew until it became a rift between the northern and southern professionals that led, in 1865, to the formation of a United South of England XI that competed in touring fixtures with All England and United England.

Anderson scored 114 not out at the age of fifty, for Constable Burton against Darlington, and then decided to retire. He remembered as a sixteen-year-old playing against W. G. Grace in Sheffield and recalled W. G.'s famous mother, the lady it was said who invented round-arm bowling: 'I think the mother was a better player than the father. She was the only lady I ever saw who could throw a ball. She could throw it 60 or 70 yards.'

He was very proud of his north-country origin, nostalgically recalling when there were four Bedale men in the All-England XI. By that Aiskew fireside he told 'Old Ebor': 'I was born in Bedale, have lived there all my life and hope to die there.'

presidency, but according to official accounts Michael Joseph Ellison was President from the foundation meeting until 1898, and to him must go the major credit for steering the club through some difficult formative years.

Ellison was, in fact, the first of the benevolent dictators who have built Yorkshire cricket. Lord Hawke, hardly a populist himself, described Ellison as 'a jolly old autocrat', adding later that Ellison and Wostinholm 'ran it for years'. What will never be known is how much of the fledgling club's financial burdens were borne by the President. As mentioned earlier, Ellison guaranteed the rent of the Bramall Lane ground to his employer, the Duke of Norfolk. In 1884, twenty-one years after foundation, the Committee voted to refund to the President 'the money expended by him from his private purse in supporting first class and county cricket during the years preceding the founding of the county club in 1863'. The sum granted was £400, and the suspicion is that this was only a fraction of the money spent on Yorkshire cricket during Ellison's thirty-five years in office.

In his youth Ellison was a useful enough batsman to open the innings for Sheffield against Leeds at the latter's Victoria ground, and it was said that for seventy years he never failed to shoot his grouse on 12 August (he died at the age of eighty-one). In an undated photograph he is shown as a man of sturdy build, balding, with a long white beard, steady of eye, wearing a thick tweed suit, with watch-chain, and assuming a pensive pose leaning upon a mantelpiece.

Ellison may have been a difficult man to cross, but he was also an able administrator and rock-like in his principles. It was he who laid down that only Yorkshire-born players should be selected, yet when it was pointed out that the young Martin Bladen Hawke, of an old Yorkshire family, had actually been born in Lincolnshire, he took a Nelsonian attitude: 'Don't tell me, then, and let me have a convenient memory.'

It was also Ellison, supported by C.W. Alcock of Surrey, who campaigned for the admission of Derbyshire, Essex, Leicestershire, Warwickshire and Hampshire to the first-class

M.J. Ellison

list in 1894–5. *Wisden* attacked him for overextending his players with the additional fixtures, but Ellison believed the game had to be expanded to a national basis. He also insisted, at Lord's meetings, that umpires 'should not be allowed to stand for the counties for whom they had played'.

Ellison and Wostinholm, when they began, were among friends and colleagues, for the first County Committee consisted of twelve Sheffield men who decided, among other resolutions of those early days, that 'a central or any fixed ground shall not be considered requisite'; recommendation of young players was 'earnestly invited', while clubs were asked to apply for county fixtures.

The response was disheartening. York, as the county capital, were willing to bid to share fixtures with Sheffield but could rely on only a £50 attendance. Bradford were interested but independent, and in the end Yorkshire county cricket settled into Sheffield for thirty years. Bradford, in fact, tried to go it alone, arranging matches against Nottinghamshire, while York still felt they had rights, too. A mystified Kent cancelled fixtures in 1864, the Secretary declaring he had doubts as to 'who were the proper parties to get up Yorkshire matches'. Yorkshire (Sheffield) wrote to explain, but Kent changed their minds only so far as to play Yorkshire at Bradford.

In 1886 *The Cricketers' Companion* summed up the claimants, describing York as 'the gentleman's club', and Bradford as boasting 'a most energetic Committee and a liberal subscription list'. But Horton Lane was described as 'too confined' for first-class cricket, while the *Companion* asserted that Bramall Lane was '. . . a splendid area. Except Nottingham there is no town in England where the spectators are so numerous or enter so thoroughly into the spirit of the game.'

Modern histories tend to regard Sheffield's supremacy in Yorkshire county matters as unchallenged, whereas there were at least two major attempts to unseat what many, especially in the North Riding, regarded as a dictatorship. As early as November 1863, ten months after the Sheffield launch, a meeting was called at Harker's Hotel, York for the purpose, said *Bell's Life*, of 'forming a cricket club for the county of Yorkshire'.

The Hon. G.E. Lascelles took the chair over representatives of Bradford, Leeds, Huddersfield, Wakefield, York, Middlesbrough, Doncaster, Sheffield, Hull, the Vale of Derwent, Harewood, Boroughbridge, Bedale and Redcar. Earl Fitzwilliam was named President and the Lords Londesborough, Feversham and Wenlock agreed to join, which made for an impressive start. However, the structure had no sooner been assembled than it fell apart. Not one but two clubs emerged from the meeting: one for amateurs, the Gentlemen of York, which survived, and a county club, which didn't. Sheffield, of course, had the best ground by far and, at that time, almost all the players and thus the public appeal.

Eleven years later, after the first season of Championship cricket, another rebellion flickered, again centring on York. This time the meeting, on 28 January 1874, was called at Abbott's Railway Hotel with Lord Londesborough in the chair, and was more overtly

North Riding with representatives of Malton, York, Leeds, Scarborough, Bedale, Hull, Hornsea and Middlesbrough. Among the delegates were, interestingly, two great names – Roger Iddison and George Anderson. It seems that Nottinghamshire were not above stirring this particular pot, their Secretary writing to advise the meeting that 'for a successful county policy one ground only be used and that be York'. From this meeting emerged the Yorkshire United club which, under Londesborough's leadership, regularly called upon leading Yorkshire players to play a fixture list that never attained first-class recognition.

Londesborough tried once again, in 1884. After the demise of the United club, he formed the North Riding of Yorkshire XI, a team that were totally crushed when they met the full power of the county eleven, scoring 162 and 41 for 3 in reply to 530. Another four years and Londesborough became President of the North and East Ridings XI, Lord Derwent succeeding him the following year, but that, too, failed to capture public interest.

All this would seem to make William Henry Forester Denison, Earl of Londesborough, a malcontent, when in fact he was a great benefactor to the early game. His enthusiasm and support brought into being the Scarborough Festival; he greatly assisted the foundation of Hampshire cricket by taking teams to Lyndhurst; and his generosity to old professionals was legendary. He offered to pay for specialist treatment for Harry Dewse's battered hands. Said Dewse: 'When I found it would cost him £50, and as I had no pain, I declined to go.'

Londesborough became President of the MCC in 1876 when his carriage became a familiar sight at both Lord's and Scarborough, where his wife would also attend, showing equal enthusiasm for the game. The Countess, in fact, loved listening to the repartee and broad accents of the old cricketers. One Yorkshireman, angry at being caught in the deep at Lord's by the Gentlemen, brought a peal of laughter with his irate explanation of how he came to be out to such a ball: 'Ah ment to put t'bugger over t'pavilion.'

Somehow, Yorkshire did manage to take the field with a fully representative eleven in that

Isaac Hodgson   *Ikey*

The first of Yorkshire's great slow left-arm spin bowlers, 'Ikey' Hodgson was born in Bradford and with Billy Slinn formed the first of the county's famous bowling partnerships. Both men began their careers playing for travelling teams at fairs and feast days. Hodgson's style was reported to be similar to that of Wilfred Rhodes, although he was also renowned for a variation of pace that suggests he might also have been compared to Derek Underwood,

Hodgson won fame by attaching himself to the various sides of twenty-two which met the All-England XI, and it was said that when a local club met to organise a side to meet the Englanders then Hodgson's was the first name to be put down, with Slinn's as the second.

In six seasons he took 475 wickets against All England, an astonishing figure, with his greatest feat coming in, of all places, Glasgow. All England, containing Daft, Caesar, Alfred Clarke, Hayward, Anderson, H. H. Stephenson and Tinley, needed 49 to beat a Caledonian twenty-two. Hodgson, sensing that the 'cracks' would expect him to push the ball through on a pitch deadened by rain, instead, warning the Scots to watch their catching, held it back and took seven for 8, All England being dismissed for 20.

He played only twenty-eight matches for Yorkshire, but still managed 139 wickets. He was a cheerful, popular performer, known for his 'good-natured grin', but like many of his generation his health was poor and he died aged only thirty-nine.

summer of 1863. Captained by Iddison (Bedale), the team read: Thewlis (Lascelles Hall), Berry and Dawson (Dalton), Iddison and Anderson (Bedale), Atkinson (Ripon), Hodgson (Bradford), Rowbotham, Stephenson and Slinn (Sheffield). At The Oval on 5 and 6 June Surrey raised a then huge 315, to which Yorkshire replied with 257 and then bowled out Surrey in their second innings for 60, with Ikey Hodgson taking nine wickets and Billy Slinn six in the match.

By 1865, however, the club was plunged into its first player crisis by the refusal of five senior players – Anderson, Atkinson, Iddison, Rowbotham and Stephenson – to play against Surrey. The dispute was not of Yorkshire's making but arose from the no-balling of Kent's Edgar Willsher when playing for the All-England XI against Surrey at The Oval in 1862. AEE players suspected that Surrey had put up umpire John Lillywhite to no-ball Willsher and when, in 1864, Iddison failed to appear in a North *v* South match at Islington, the Southern players, thirteen in all, seceded from the AEE and the United England XI to form the United South of England XI, whose red, white and blue blazer was soon to be worn by a prodigious young player from the West – William Gilbert Grace.

In 1865 Anderson, offered the Yorkshire captaincy, declined, saying he would 'not play against those who have combined to sweep us from the cricket field altogether if they could' – in other words, most of the Surrey XI. The Committee thundered that they 'cannot help reminding you that every professional player is bound to play for his county when called upon to do so'.

Anderson had support, however, and with the backbone of the side gone Yorkshire did not win a match in 1865 and cancelled fixtures for the following year. The other four strikers did play against Cambridgeshire at Bradford in the year of the strike, and it was in that match that the first of Yorkshire's indisputably great bowlers appeared: George Freeman, taking four wickets for 29 on his debut.

Early in April 1867 the Committee, having had a long winter to think things over, decided to seek a rapprochement, announcing that they would select those players who had refused the previous summer 'on their expressing regret for what had happened before'. All five apologised although Anderson, the ringleader, never appeared for Yorkshire again. Writing almost thirty years later, the Reverend Holmes was able to conclude: 'Ever since that year there has reigned the most perfect harmony between the Committee and the cricketers of the Yorkshire County Club.'

Roger Iddison *First captain*

A jovial Bedale man, also given to flashes of temper, Iddison was one of the early organisers of professional cricket in the North. A shrewd judge of the game, its players and its commercial possibilities, Iddison was the obvious choice to lead Yorkshire into their first county match in 1863.

Typical of the professionals of his day he could both bat and bowl 'crafty, insidious lobs' according to the Reverend Holmes, and, in the loose affiliations of the time, he played for both Lancashire and Yorkshire and ran what was called a 'cricket depot', in Manchester. As a batsman he was considered to have a curious stance, moving the left leg while awaiting delivery, and he was also famous as a fielder at point.

In fact Lancashire's first century in county cricket was Iddison's 106 against Surrey in 1866, and the following year he played for both the Roses counties. With Ned Stephenson he was the first Yorkshireman to tour Australia where his lobs wreaked havoc, taking twenty-two wickets against a twenty-two of Victoria, and he returned with a tour aggregate of 103 at an average of 6.59.

But Iddison had other connections with the game. He was Secretary to the Yorkshire United club, joint Secretary of North of England United, and regularly organised teams for Lord Londesborough. It was this very partisanship that led him into the North–South schism of 1864 when he failed to arrive to play in a match at Islington, sending his brother, a much lesser player. Iddison claimed that he had never agreed to turn out, but ill feeling rumbled on for several years.

Roger Iddison (left) and George Anderson.

Together with Anderson, Atkinson and Hodgson, Iddison was the backbone of the first Yorkshire team and his popularity never declined in the North, not even when he grew to seventeen stone of ruddy corpulence. He was held in such esteem that the great George Freeman came out of retirement in order to play in Iddison's benefit match. He led Yorkshire for their first ten years.

Billy Slinn

A Sheffielder, Slinn bowled fast right-arm to complement Hodgson in Yorkshire's first county attack. A tall man, he was described as having a classical action in the days when round-arm was still widely practised. His great gift seemed to be his ability to win extra life from any pitch, often with a good length ball, and this, combined with excellent direction, made him a formidable bowler.

Like Hodgson, Slinn earned his money playing for selected teams against the great touring elevens. He took all ten All-England wickets at Scarborough in 1862 (and six for 23 in the second innings) and did the hat-trick against another All-England XI at

Bramall Lane. The great Tom Hayward once faced him for forty minutes without being able to score.

Slinn was also compared to Hodgson in the mediocrity of his batting, even managing a duck in his benefit match against All England in 1863. The rise of Emmett and Freeman brought his retirement at the age of thirty-eight, but in the following decade he was employed by Cambridge University as a coach and practice bowler.

Although Yorkshire had no official fixture list in 1866, three matches were played of considerable historical implications, two against Nottinghamshire, one against Cambridgeshire, all at Bradford. Freeman played in two and sadly surprised his admirers by not taking a wicket; Billy Slinn having retired in 1865, this was Ikey Hodgson's last summer and there must have been a few Yorkshire cricket followers who could not visualise the team without both Slinn and Hodgson. However, in compensation for Hodgson's departure and Freeman's apparent failure there did arrive from Halifax one Tom Emmett who, against Nottinghamshire, took six for 55.

If the county's first four years had been clouded, 1867 burst through into brilliant sunshine, all seven matches being won, Surrey being beaten twice (once by an innings), Lancashire three times (twice by an innings) and Cambridgeshire twice. The difference was, of course, the arrival in harness of Freeman and Emmett, the former taking 51 wickets at an average of 7.4, the latter 30 at 5.2. Opposing batsmen were simply swept aside and such was Yorkshire's confidence – perhaps almost arrogance – that they accepted challenges to play elevens of Surrey and Nottinghamshire, Middlesex and Cambridgeshire and of Sussex at a stake of £1000 per match. Perhaps fortunately for Yorkshire pockets, the matches never took place.

Lascelles Hall

While Sheffield provided Yorkshire's earliest cricketers of reknown, the village of Lascelles Hall, three miles from Huddersfield, near the Kirkheaton birthplace of Hirst and Rhodes, followed with a record of producing cricketers of high class that can be surpassed in the world only by Hambledon.

Between 1820 and 1860 the club from the village on the hill was strong enough to defeat, among others, All England, Yorkshire, Sheffield, Yorkshire Gentlemen, Surrey and any number of clubs and public schools. The village contributed six players to the county eleven at one time, and it was said there

were up to twenty-three professional cricketers living there, six in one row of cottages. Certainly a list exists of twenty-one village cricketers who appeared for Yorkshire.

Alan Thompson, who did much research into the beginnings of the club and published his findings in a booklet (1952), discovered that the village revolved around five families: Lockwood, Pollard, Redfearn, Hill and, most famous of all, Thewlis. Thompson identified thirty-five Thewlises who played cricket, many of them professionally, and so confusing was their ubiquity in so small an area that identification

was reduced to such names as 'young Jack t'youngest'.

Thompson believed there were two distinct clans of Thewlises, who were cousins to the Lockwoods, who in turn were related to the Eastwoods and the Bateses. The most famous Lockwood, Ephraim, married the niece of the most famous cricketer of his day, Fuller Pilch. In 1866 the Thewlises fielded not only an entire eleven against Chickenley at Lascelles Hall, but the gateman, scorer and umpire were all named Thewlis too. The Family were dismissed for 250, Chickenley having made 37 for 2 when rain ended the match.

So much extraordinary proficiency in one area is explained by Thompson. West Riding villages were all concentrated on cottage industries before the mechanical loom was invented, the children being trained in hand-loom weaving as soon as they were able.

In those days the textile industry was beginning to profit from the inventors but before the new machinery arrived the men at Lascelles Hall used to throw the shuttle from hand to hand to weave their 'single-width' cloth. That needed a very sharp and accurate eye for if the shuttle was dropped the cloth had to be pulled back, a process which lost time and in turn lost money for payment was by the piece; not often, then, was the shuttle dropped.

The loom could be worked in the dark, by the light of a 'farthing dip' during the evenings or in bad weather. When the weather was fine the village lads could turn such co-ordination of hand and eye to the development of other skills, notably cricket. In the mid nineteenth century there were few other distractions for the poor.

The Lascelles Hall club was founded in 1825 when the village consisted of grey stone cottages around a gentleman's residence and an inn. Several boys were caught playing in the grounds of the Hall and two of them, named by A. A. Thompson as George Jessop and John Hudson, were said to have gone to see the squire, a Mr Joseph Walker, to 'beg off'. Mrs Walker is said to have intervened, saying to her husband: 'These lads are fond of cricket. Why not give them a try?'

They practised first in a quarry and then in a small field known as the Croft, which had a stone wall down one side, the reason, it is said, why so many of the Hall's batsmen were fine off-side players. Practice took place in every minute of fine weather, each batsman received forty balls and no more, and, while awaiting the next man in, the fielders always flicked the ball from man to man, hand to hand.

A permanent ground was opened in 1866 when the club boasted ninety members, each of whom contributed work and money until the ground was completed – this was at a time, after the American Civil War, when many weavers had no work. John Lockwood, Eph's cousin, was one of the early groundsmen, later taking charge of The Oval.

The full list of players provided to Yorkshire by the club reads: John Thewlis, Luke Greenwood, Ephraim Lockwood, David Eastwood, Andrew Greenwood, Henry Lockwood, Allen Hill (born in Kirkheaton but who moved to the Hall as a boy) and, of course, Billy Bates. Had Hill not had a minor accident in 1874 the Yorkshire team playing Gloucestershire would have contained seven men from the village. Subsequently new technology, in the shape of the power loom, destroyed the village's pre-eminence.

If times were hard and poverty and illness never far away, there were happy times too. Thompson unearthed a provisions list of 1882 for matches against Harrow Wanderers and Uppingham: 'Half-gallon Scotch whisky, gallon brandy, half-gallon rum, nine boxes ginger beer, 30 lbs beef, 2 hams, 12 dozen pies – for the first day'.

No wonder then, that when Sir Stanley Jackson was visiting Huddersfield his first words, on passing through that imposing entrance to the railway station, were the enquiry: 'Which would be the road to Lascelles Hall?'

That such contests should be contemplated confirms that county cricket was still loosely organised and that such towns as Bradford, especially, and occasionally Middlesbrough, Dewsbury and Hunslet continued to promote their own county fixtures for a decade. Not until 1873 was the county club's authority recognised and accepted.

The following year, too, had its great moments, even if the level of success could not be maintained. In 1868 John Thewlis scored the first century for Yorkshire, 108 at The Oval, the match in which his country cousin Ephraim Lockwood made his famous debut. Freeman and Emmett were again irresistible, bowling unchanged against Lancashire and hitting the stumps eighteen times, the Red Rose being humiliated at Holbeck for 30 and 34.

Yet in an incredibly hot summer (so intense was the heat that play against both Lancashire and Surrey had to be stopped for an hour) Yorkshire won only four of their seven matches. The costume of the time would not have helped: striped or coloured shirts with separate collar and tie, a heavy belt with a metal buckle (braces having been slowly phased out) and brown boots.

In 1869 Rowbotham scored centuries against Surrey and Nottinghamshire, the first Yorkshireman to compile two three-figure scores in one year. Rowbotham was awarded £5 for his innings against Nottinghamshire, Iddison £5 for a 112 against Cambridgeshire, and the latter was also given a silver cup for his batting in that match. Yet there was no doubt that the star of that summer was Emmett. Against Cambridgeshire, who were dismissed for 40 and 46, he took sixteen wickets for 38 runs, nine in the

John Thewlis   *'Think dead; if not, Manchester'*

Those five words, in reply to an enquiry as to the whereabouts of Thewlis, aged seventy, from A. W. Pullin ('Old Ebor' of the *Yorkshire Evening Post*) are as meaningful as any ever uttered in the cricketing world. So stirred was Pullin at the old cricketer's plight that he straight away pitched into Yorkshire and cricket administration generally, his message winning great public sympathy and bringing into being such unheard-of reforms as winter pay. That estimable body, the Professional Cricketers' Association, might one day think of honouring 'Old Ebor'.

Pullin had started to write a series of winter articles on old Yorkshire cricketers for the *Evening Post* in 1898, in the course of which he not only produced one of the most valuable source books on Victorian cricket but also discovered how desperate were the circumstances in which some of these old heroes lived – none more so than Thewlis, the most distinguished cricketer of all that great Lascelles Hall clan.

Thewlis was yet another born in Kirkheaton (along with Hill, Hirst, Rhodes) who, like Hill, went into hand-loom weaving at the Hall. He never attended school, being sensitive about his shock of white hair, but he taught himself to read and write and was playing cricket with his pals as soon as he was able. Before he reached the Lascelles Hall XI he was practising on the ground one day when the visiting team arrived. Asked if he was to play against them the lad replied that he wasn't good enough. The visitors' reaction is recorded: 'They thought the others must be very good for they declined to play.'

When young John did join the first team, his hair turning light brown then black as he grew older, he wore a coat when batting in his first away match. The crowd called for him to take it off but the boy refused, being too ashamed to show the holes in his shirt.

He was thirty-two before he broke out of local cricket, Luke Greenwood recommending him to George Parr as a batsman of redoubtable defence on the rough tracks of the day, who could also hit fiercely when required. At thirty-five he was opening for Yorkshire and he continued playing until he was forty-eight. He was, of course, responsible for bringing his nephew Ephraim Lockwood into first-class cricket wth that marvellous debut at The Oval.

Thewlis's recollection of that famous occasion began when he met his nephew at King's Cross.

> Going on a bus to The Oval I said to him 'If tha does well in this match it'll be a rare good thing for thee.' I can remember hearing people around asking 'Who's yon farmer that Thewlis has brought?' Ephraim must have made his mark in due time but it was just a toss up whether or no he should have his chance at the time he did.

John Thewlis was a good enough player to have once taken on Eleven Landlords of Chickenley, all runs to be scored in front of the wicket, at Dewsbury Savile. The Landlords dismissed Thewlis for 1 in the first innings but couldn't get him out on the second, so the match was left drawn.

Lascelles Hall could in time field a whole team of Thewlises, and the fact that they were related to the Lockwoods and Greenwoods makes Thewlis's later misfortunes somewhat mysterious. He received about £350 from his benefit in 1875, and might have expected the support of such a large family. However, when Pullin set off for Manchester to find the old man he discovered that he was living in Failsworth, making a meagre living carrying baskets of laundry the four miles into Manchester.

When Pullin found him he was anxious to get back to earn a few more coppers carrying coal. The old man said he was well and could still manage his twenty miles a day: 'I have had to cease going to matches because I could not see what was taking place at the wicket. I have lost my teeth but perhaps it is as well for there hasn't been much for them to do lately.' Pullin commented:

> The moral responsibilities of cricket managers, so far as a player is concerned, should surely not end with the termination of his active career. He ought not to be cast aside like an old shoe . . . .
>
> It is necessary therefore to protest strongly and publicly against the way in which a few old Yorkshire cricketers have been allowed to sink into oblivion and even into poverty. One would have thought that the kindly remembrance of past services would at least have enabled the Yorkshire County Club to know whatever old players were under the sod or above it.

The story had a happier ending. Pullin's bitter words stirred consciences and old John Thewlis got a job that following summer (1898) as groundsman at the Greenfield Club. Yorkshire, in turn stirred by Lord Hawke, gave the old man a 'winter allowance'.

A year later, in December 1899, old John went home to Lascelles Hall to spend Christmas with his clan. He had a jolly night or two with old friends and players in the Tandem Inn but was then taken ill and died on 29 December. Billy Bates struggled out of a sick bed to attend the funeral on an icy day, caught a chill and died himself ten days later.

John Thewlis junior, who played for Yorkshire in three matches as a batsman in 1879, was a nephew and not, as *Wisden* reported at the time, old John's son.

George Atkinson *Windmill*

George Atkinson was the first of Yorkshire's line of deadly accurate right-arm medium to fast bowlers. When the mayor of Keighley, in an excess of pride, said that Ripon's Atkinson could pitch on a sixpence, the bowler commented, with straight face: 'That statement is not far wrong.'

He had an unusual approach and action, as an amateur of his time described:

> As he delivered the ball with his right hand his left arm swung round with a similar action. You thus might have thought he was going to deliver the ball with his left hand. He came sailing up to the pitch with both arms swinging like a windmill.

Odd he might have been, but there were plenty to testify to his accuracy and efficacy. On his first visit to Lord's, in 1859, playing against the mighty All Englanders for the United XI, he took five for 17 in 36 overs; four years later he took six for 18 for The North against Surrey at The Oval. His own preferred performance was seven for 19 against Surrey at The Oval in 1868 (Ephraim Lockwood's debut).

Born in Ripon, he moved to Leeds where his father combined butchery with the management of a public house. Young George was apprenticed to a glass-blower but 'couldn't stand that game so I went and followed cricket'. He was dutiful enough to develop a pleasant tenor voice with the Leeds parish church choir and had something of a reputation as a singer, but when the family moved back to Hunslet young George found a much more congenial occupation making cricket bats from old oak barrel staves.

There he could mix with cricketing professionals, becoming one himself in time, travelling all over the North and making one mysterious allusion: 'I wish I had never seen Middlesbrough. The reasons for this statement will be known to some old cricketers.'

He later coached at Marlborough and Rossall and tells of a match between the latter school and Preston Garrison in 1880. The soldiers' side being short, he persuaded a well-known Lancashire bowler to enlist for the day, playing him as Private Jones. The boys, unaware of the ringer, scored 398, one reaching 205 not out, and 'Jones' departed grumbling that he would never soldier again.

Atkinson coached, among others, A. G. Steel and Lord Tennyson, and was proud to have received from his Lordship's father, the Poet Laureate, a book in appreciation. In a happy career Atkinson had only one disappointment when in 1863 eight Yorkshire players threatened not to turn out against Surrey if Atkinson were chosen. Yorkshire had lost to Nottinghamshire by a narrow margin and blamed Atkinson for not turning up, although he claimed that he had never agreed to play. In the end the other eight did appear against Surrey, Atkinson did not, but the matter was smoothed over.

Like all old cricketers he became very critical of his juniors. 'Old Ephraim Lockwood would have given these modern off-bowlers some pepper,' he declared at the turn of the century. 'Men are now frightened of being caught in the slips.' A final word on his legendary accuracy: he angrily denied that he had once bowled two wides in a match. 'I only remember bowling one wide in my life.'

second innings, completing a remarkable match by catching another off Freeman. Such a feat, however, won him no extra rewards for, in the prevailing conditions, it was runs rather than wickets that were valued. As the Reverend Holmes commented: 'No wonder that certain promising young bowlers became batsmen.'

Yorkshire's record in 1869 – won four, lost one – was bettered the following year when six of the seven matches played were won, and although no championship existed there is no doubt that Yorkshire were England's premier county team. Freeman had another summer of devastation, taking 50 wickets for 327 runs in what, sadly, was his last full season for the

county. He and Emmett were aided by the appearance of George Pinder behind the stumps for, valuable as Ned Stephenson had been, Pinder proved to be a brilliant keeper against fast bowling. As the Second Empire fell to the Prussians, the Yorkshire pair were the Lillee and Thomson of their day.

Pinder was the first to stand up to the wicket (with Rowbotham initially behind him at long stop), a move to make any batsman apprehensive facing Freeman's pace and Emmett's movement of the surfaces of those days. Freeman's increasing business commitments meant that he played in only three of Yorkshire's seven matches in 1871, but he did leave cricket

Joe Rowbotham   *Old Tarpot*

Joe Rowbotham was Yorkshire's second captain, following Roger Iddison to lead the county in 1874 after a long and thoroughly professional career. Born almost next door to Bramall Lane, his home overlooked the Sheffield Milton ground, and as his father was described as 'a bit of a cricketer' the boy was encouraged in the time he had free from his trade as a sawmaker.

'A fine punishing bat in front of the wicket', Rowbotham also attracted attention for his brilliant fielding, especially at long stop which was regarded as a difficult and dangerous position in the days of unprepared pitches and outfields.

Like Allen Hill, young Rowbotham was taken on the staff at Old Trafford as a twenty-one-year-old, then became a temporary professional with Rochdale and while there was spotted by George Parr, travelling and playing with the All England team for the next decade. Joe was always pleased to recount how he played in the opening match at Bramall Lane in 1855 and in Yorkshire's first match in 1863, but he was thirty-eight before he reached real renown, scoring 101 against Surrey at The Oval in 1869 and 100 against Nottinghamshire at Bramall Lane, the first Yorkshireman to score two centuries in one season – an indication of how valued was a three-figure score at that time.

Rowbotham toured America with Edgar Willsher's team in 1868, only he, the captain and George Griffith of Surrey not being ill on the voyage. Indeed, Joe's ability to eat a meal whatever the weather, no matter how rough the sea led Ted Pooley of Surrey to say that he 'stuck to everything

he ate so well we nicknamed him "Old Tarpot"'.

Rowbotham's own account of that voyage concerned the death of an old lady and the birth of a boy 'to a female steerage passenger. We collected about £5 for her and gave her also the proceeds of a concert which we got up on board. The ship was the *City of Baltimore* and the mother said she would christen the child "Baltimore".'

He was an abstemious man, as his financial accounting of that tour reveals. The players were given £50 as travelling expenses and seven and a half dollars a day once in American waters, and Rowbotham proudly reported that he had 'made' £100 on the trip.

His captaincy coincided with George Freeman's virtual retirement, Rowbotham himself giving way at the age of forty-four 'as I had got too stout and could not run'. In fact he did make two further appearances for the county, one as late as 1883, by which time he had become a first-class umpire and had clashed with the great Doctor. He gave Grace out caught at the wicket at Trent Bridge. W. G. asked the umpire what he thought he was doing, scratching his forearm. Joe replied: 'I've given you out and I shall do it again if it happens.'

There was no ill-will. Rowbotham's benefit in 1873 was against Gloucestershire at Bramall Lane. Nottinghamshire wanted Grace at Trent Bridge and Rowbotham travelled up to London to ask the 'Champion' what he would do. 'Joe, I will play for you and no one else on that day as I promised.'

Joe Rowbotham also kept the New Inn in Eccleshall Road, Sheffield for more than thirty years.

Edwin Stephenson *Merry Ned*

From Hallam, Sheffield, Ned Stephenson was Yorkshire's first wicket-keeper/batsman who could also bowl useful round-arm when allowed. He played thirty-six matches for Yorkshire and, mostly to the bowling of Slinn and Hodgson, collected 57 victims, 27 stumped and 30 caught.

One of his stumpings, against Surrey in 1864, was off fast bowler Slinn, and against Nottinghamshire that same season he stumped five, four off Iddison's lobs. As a batsman he was renowned for his tenacity, and it was this all-round ability that undoubtedly won him a place on the first tour of Australia.

Stephenson was, in William Caffyn's words, 'quite a character, always saying something to put a roomful into a roar of laughter'. He was a notorious prankster and enjoyed jokes played upon him, and it was possibly his joviality and sense of companionship that brought him troubles in later life, when he was said to be 'heard of at the Plough Inn, Hallam, any night'. According to *Wisden*, 'in his later days he unfortunately fell into very poor circumstances'. He died at the age of sixty-six.

George Freeman *Meteor*

Although he played county cricket for only five years, Freeman in action was a meteor, acknowledged by all his contemporaries as the best fast bowler of his time and, indeed, up until the advent of Trueman, accepted as Yorkshire's greatest fast bowler. Born in Boroughbridge and coached assiduously through boyhood by a cricket-mad clergyman (who would keep wicket and discreetly signal to the boy as to which delivery he should next bowl), Freeman had a dazzling career ended only by his opening of a successful business as an auctioneer in Thirsk.

At his peak Freeman stood a handsome 5 feet 10½ inches, weighed fourteen stone and wore a rich black beard. Handsome is as handsome does, and while he was regarded as a highly intelligent and affable man, he was always a formidable prospect on the field. A natural bowler, like Statham, he took a run of only a few steps, but according to Eph Lockwood 'he used to make the ball come back six inches, whipping like lightning from the pitch. It was all done with a remarkable whip of the wrist.'

He was also credited with being able to bowl a shooter at will, and if this seems hardly credible it was J. M. Kilburn who pointed out that Freeman, on poorly prepared pitches, would deliver the ball with an action that would appear low today but was then regarded as suspiciously high. W.G. and Richard Daft both regarded him as the best bowler they had faced, and Grace considered a hit on the leg from a delivery by Freeman as 'being cut with a knife'. Daft said the insides of his legs were often black and blue after facing Freeman. One of Freeman's deliveries once uprooted all three stumps of a Gloucestershire batsman.

Freeman made his debut for Yorkshire in 1865, on Billy Slinn's retirement, taking four for 29 against

Cambridgeshire at Bradford, and was joined in attack the following season by Emmett, Yorkshire not surprisingly winning all their seven matches, Freeman taking 51 wickets at an average of 7.4. Surrey and Lancashire were both beaten by an innings.

Freeman took 209 wickets for Yorkshire in only thirty-two matches, and his early retirement might have been hastened by a muscle strain in his elbow that must have affected the famous 'whip'. It was never more deadly than in Yorkshire's first match against MCC at Lord's in 1870 when, on a poor pitch, Freeman and Emmett made the ball fly dangerously, taking nineteen wickets between them. Grace made 66, an innings regarded as marvellous by everyone who saw it, the Yorkshire pair reporting afterwards that 'it was a marvel that the doctor was not either maimed nor unnerved for the rest of his days or killed outright'. Grace's partner, the Essex amateur C. E. Green, was supposed to have carried a livid bruise over his heart, caused by Freeman, for the rest of his days.

So accurate was Freeman that batsmen felt that if he did not hit their legs he would certainly hit the stumps, and he terrorised local twenty-twos when playing for the United North – as for instance when a Tadcaster twenty-two lost seven wickets to his first

nine deliveries. As Peter Thomas pointed out, bowlers of that era aimed at the stumps because they could not trust the judgement of many umpires, especially the local ones.

As one of Willsher's American tourists in 1868, Freeman took 104 wickets, bowling 74 of his victims. From New York he wrote home: 'Today we played a match at baseball and were again defeated. It is a fool to cricket, still the Yankees think otherwise.'

Freeman's career was unusual for another reason. He might have been the first professional to be invited to become a 'Gentleman'. Four years after his retirement he was invited by MCC to appear against the Players at Lord's but, according to 'Old Ebor', had to decline for an undisclosed reason, possibly business. 'Old Ebor' is certain that Freeman was asked to play for the Gentlemen of England against the Australians at The Oval in 1882, the year after he finished with Yorkshire, and would have played had he not been a witness in a criminal trial at the Old Bailey. His wife would jokingly assert afterwards that George was afraid of what the Colonials might do to his bowling.

A successful life came to a sadly premature end, for George Freeman died at the age of fifty-one after two years of suffering with Bright's disease.

Luke Greenwood *One Wide*

Job Greenwood was the first cricket professional to come out of Lascelles Hall. His brother Luke was the first Lascelles Hall professional to play for Yorkshire, and his son played in the first two Test matches for England.

Luke, in fact, opened many gates. At twenty-four, clean-shaven except for short goatee beard, he was engaged as a bowler (right-arm, medium to fast) by the Duke of Sutherland in Staffordshire, then followed Roger Iddison to Broughton, Manchester and was there when recruited for George Parr's All-England XI. He made his debut for Yorkshire in 1861 and for the Players (W.G. appearing for the first time for the Gentlemen) in 1865, and a year later added 114 with Alfred Shaw for the Players' ninth wicket, having been chosen for his bowling.

He introduced John Thewlis to the All-England XI and subsequently to Yorkshire. His views on bowling remain fascinating.

> There is nothing that beats a batsman better than a good length straight ball. There is a length which the batsman cannot play and it is the business of a good bowler to find that length. Modern bowlers

[he told 'Old Ebor' in 1898] have an advantage compared with those of our day. If we bowled above our shoulder we were no-balled. Now they can bowl as high as a mill chimney and they ought to come down much straighter than from a round-arm delivery.

He was with Alf Shaw one day at Nottingham when they were both asked how many wides they had bowled for their counties. 'One,' replied Greenwood, explaining apologetically that it had happened in a thunderstorm at The Oval. 'None,' replied Shaw.

After serving Yorkshire as an all-rounder for their first thirteen years, he became an umpire – 'the Australians always behaved like gentlemen to me' – and then, like many of his old comrades, fell upon hard times. As an umpire Luke Greenwood was perhaps not enamoured of the great Doctor.

In the Oval Test of 1882 Spofforth told how he deliberately 'drew' W.G.'s front leg down the pitch and then sent him a perfectly straight ball on the leg stump. 'Howzat?' he asked umpire Greenwood. As the finger went up and W.G. departed grumbling and growling, Greenwood told him: 'I can't help it, no, not if you was the Prince of Wales himself.'

In the Australian second innings Murdoch and Jones took a quick single while Lyttleton, keeping wicket, fielded the ball down the leg side and threw it to Peate, described as short-slip. The batsmen were home and Peate made no attempt to throw the ball, whereupon Jones left his crease to pat the pitch. According to Greenwood, at the bowler's end, Grace then walked across, collected the ball and broke the wicket, appealing to umpire Bob Thoms at square, who agreed that Jones was out. Murdoch snapped,

'That's a very sharp practice, W. G.' and Greenwood concurred, commenting that he would not have allowed the appeal, believing the ball to be dead.

As an older man Greenwood was poor but loved his cricket enough to walk from his Ossett home to watch Yorkshire at Leeds, Bradford and Huddersfield. He set out one Sunday night to walk to Sheffield where Sussex were playing, but on hearing that Ranji was not included he turned back. For all his penury, he never complained: 'They [Yorkshire] always behave to me like a gentleman and send me a card every year.'

with an immortal testimonial from W.G.: 'the finest fast bowler I ever played against'. Ten years later Freeman was persuaded to return for one match, and at the age of thirty-seven he took nine wickets against Lascelles Hall and was also Yorkshire's top scorer with 60 runs.

Freeman's departure did open a door for another great fast bowler, Allen Hill, whose twelve for 57, all bowled, against Surrey must have hit county cricket like a thunderclap. The success of these years began to be reflected in the balance sheet, a healthy profit enabling the Committee to grant Bramall Lane £50 for the repair and improvement of seating.

It was the custom then for the ground authority to award prizes and marks of distinction, a function now taken over by sponsors, and it was Yorkshire who awarded talent money to the Surrey brothers Tom and Richard Humphrey for their 140 out of 165 at Bramall Lane. That particular match ended in some controversy for, with neutral umpires standing for the first time, Surrey walked off the field after one over of the second innings, deciding for themselves that the light was too bad for batting. Then, without waiting to see if there would be any improvement, Surrey dressed and left Sheffield.

That year Yorkshire won only three of their seven matches, also losing three – an indication of changing strengths, for worse was to follow in 1872. The programme was increased to ten matches of which no less than seven were lost, the Reverend Holmes adding that the toss was lost in 'nearly every match'.

A new power had arisen in the West: the Gloucester of the Graces. Six years later Francis Thompson captured some of the glitter and splendour of that team when he wrote, of a match at Old Trafford:

> The champion of the centuries, he cometh up
> against thee,
> With his brethren, every one a famous foe,
> The long-whiskered Doctor, that laugheth
> rules to scorn
> While the bowler, pitched against him,
> Bans the day that he was born.
> And G.F., with his science,
> Makes the fairest length forlorn,
> They are come up from the West, to work thee
> woe.

W.G. Grace had appeared in Sheffield in 1869, scoring 122 out of 173 for The South against The North. He returned for the county fixture in 1872, a match that was also Iddison's benefit, with Freeman also reappearing to mark this special occasion. W.G. and T.G. Matthews batted through the first day and were not separated until the first wicket had raised 238, W.G. contributing 150. Bramall Lane now boasted turnstiles.

The search for greater competition was illustrated by a combined Nottinghamshire–Yorkshire fixture against England and the first realisation in Yorkshire that a reserve strength was needed. Two matches, Seniors v Juniors and a Yorkshire XI v a Colts XI, were played this summer, the Juniors beating the Seniors (including Iddison, Rowbotham, Anderson, Thewlis and Atkinson) by seven wickets, a result that must have heartened a Committee perhaps disappointed by the earlier happenings of the season.

Dissatisfaction with the laxity of the qualification requirements stirred Surrey into calling a meeting of the counties then considered first-class (Surrey, Derbyshire, Gloucestershire, Kent, Lancashire, Middlesex, Sussex and Yorkshire, Nottinghamshire being ranked but not represented), and on 11 December 1872, at 15 Hanover Street, London, a set of regulations was approved that would still be regarded as liberal today. Because there were some discrepancies between these regulations and another draft, prepared earlier by MCC, another meeting was called before the start of the 1873 season, on 15 April, at which a compromise was agreed and the first steps were taken towards the founding of a properly-organised county championship competition.

It should be emphasised at this point that the counties did not see themselves as setting up a championship, otherwise some formula for the deciding of such a competition would also have been agreed upon in that spring. The pressure for an official recognition of merit came from the media. All through the 1860s newspapers had been publishing unofficial tables, based upon results, and this practice was to continue for another twenty-two years until MCC, again apparently reluctant arbiters, stepped in and decreed: 'After the close of each season the Committee of MCC shall decide the County Championship.'

Well, it wasn't quite as autocratic as it sounds. From 1873, the generally recognised year for the start of the Championship, the 'unofficial' table was determined by the number of defeats. From 1887 for two years, each win brought one point, a half-point being awarded for a draw; from 1890 for four years, defeats were deducted from victories and draws were ignored.

MCC then decided that one point should be awarded for each victory, one point deducted for each defeat, the total to be modified by the number of matches played (the regulation specified a minimum of eight matches but no maximum). This meant that a team playing ten matches, winning six and losing four, would finish with 2 points which, when turned into a percentage ($2 \times 100 \div 10$) would be represented in the Championship table by a percentage of 20. Thus was set the pattern for the complicated system of deciding England's premier county.

Over almost 120 years of Championship history, no form of calculation has been proof against some anomaly. The 'least defeats' principle fell in 1886 when Nottinghamshire, having won seven and drawn seven, won the Championship before a Surrey record of twelve won and three lost. The emphasis had to be switched to 'most wins' to maintain a reasonable balance and, in fairness to MCC, their method was successful enough to see the Championship launched successfully.

Yorkshire began their Championship career with what must have been a certain amount of optimism, fielding as they did a team of considerable skill and experience. Freeman had retired, but Emmett and Hill were as formidable a pair of fast bowlers as any, Ephraim Lockwood was regarded as the best professional batsman, Rowbotham and Thewlis were hardened veterans, Andrew Greenwood was entering his third season in third place in the averages; Pinder was supreme as wicket-keeper, while Luke Greenwood, even in his fortieth year, remained a powerful all-rounder. Waiting in the Colts were some as yet unfamiliar names such as Alf Smith, Louis Hall and George Ulyett; the Yorkshire fielding won praise everywhere.

Sadly, the expectations were rarely realised. The succession of professional captains was not a success, and the mercurial performances, from the brilliant to the pathetic, suggested that dressing-room discipline hardly existed. The line of captains – Iddison, Rowbotham, Luke Greenwood, Ephraim Lockwood and Emmett – never managed to take the side beyond third place and by 1877 Yorkshire had dropped to eighth (of nine). 'It may have been a fact,' wrote the Reverend Holmes, 'that some of the playing members were lacking in that self-control which is indispensable to conspicuous success.' A blunter reference to Yorkshire's team of this era was the description 'a team of ale-cans'.

London Life noted in 1863:

'A short life and a merry one' is all the professional can hope as regards his cricketing existence – younger and more brilliant men tread upon his heels. Popular applause is proverbially capricious and the smoking, drinking and good living during the summer, contrasted with greens and bacon – and not too much of the latter – all through the winter; all this is unfavourable to the preservation of high cricketing condition . . . for now five and thirty is old for an All-England man whereas Pilch and Lillywhite and their friends were deemed quite young at five and forty . . . we may add that in those days celebrated players had more of a monopoly. . . . Few of the professionals have a shilling left when winter has drained their store . . . these are the ups and downs of a professional that should make us one and all regard them with interest and kindly sympathy.

Keith Sandiford, in his paper 'Amateurs and Professionals in Victorian County Cricket', was able to illustrate further the professional cricketer's almost nihilistic approach to life by contrasting the income that could be expected by the working classes with that of the 'gentlemen' at a time when there was no social security net for the handicapped, unhealthy or unemployed:

The best [professional cricketers] could hope for was to be hired on the MCC ground staff at Lord's for £2–3 per week. Most first-class counties also paid a professional £5 for each county game at home and £6 for a match of the road (when he paid for his own travel and accommodation). The social significance of these statistics can perhaps best be understood when compared to Home Gordon's fees as a cricket reporter in the Golden Age. As a writer for the *Daily Express* he received £20 for covering a first-class match in London and £30 when he had to leave the capital. He also boasted that he seldom earned less than ten guineas for any of the articles he submitted to cricket journals.

Sandiford adds:

An equally vital role was played by basic economic realism. The fact is throughout the century the job market for professional cricketers was gutted. In the wake of the great cotton slump of the 1860s (a by-product of the American Civil War) and the prolonged agricultural depression after 1873 there were literally hundreds of competent cricketers, especially in the Northern counties, who were seeking to escape from an abject poverty.

Tom Emmett   *Sostenutor*

Emmett was the best-loved cricketer of his day and, after W.G., the most famous. He was a splendid left-arm fast bowler, a punishing left-hand batsman, a tireless fielder, a player alert to every nuance of the game, and a spontaneous wit who remained cheerful to the last ball of the longest, hottest day.

Many of cricket's hoariest old jokes originated with Emmett. It was Tom who first said 'There's an epidemic here today and it ain't catching.' A bad sailor, he observed on crossing the Bay of Biscay that they had forgotten the heavy roller. Emmett was so natural a fulcrum of the team that once, when bowling from the start till lunch, he completely forgot who was in charge, muttering 'Why doesn't the old fool take me off?' He himself was that 'old fool'.

On one occasion, after suffering all day at the hands of W.G., who served up 318 – a not uncommon occurrence for Yorkshire – Emmett summed it up by saying: 'It was Grace before meat, after meat and all day.' Another time he growled that Grace should be made to play with 'a littler bat'.

Emmett was born in Crib Lane, Halifax in September 1841, learning his cricket at the entrance to the driveway leading to the house of a local luminary, Henry Ambler. The stone gateposts served as stumps and it was here that young Emmett first learned to hit the post, round-arm. 'I have never been so big since as I used to be then.'

Between dodging the constabulary, Mr Ambler frowning upon such goings-on in his drive, and local residents fearing for their windows, young Emmett learned to be quick. He began, as a boy, bowling for the Illingworth club, learned to break back the ball and was eventually invited to play for Halifax – 'for five shillings, or two and six, I don't know which. My cricket bag, I do know, consisted of the *Halifax Courier* or the *Halifax Guardian* and I invariably went in clogs.'

For three years he played professionally for Keighley, being lured away by the promise of a winter job, and by 1866 was on the road followed by so many of his contemporaries, hired by local twenty-twos to take on All England, winning attention in a match for Keighley against Todmorden in which he scored 119 not out and 'took six or seven wickets'. In August of that year Yorkshire met his terms – £5 to play at Nottingham (this fee included travel and keep).

The following year Emmett had little opportunity to progress until, against Surrey at Bramall Lane in late June, after Freeman and Luke Greenwood had been frustrated by a stand between Stephenson and Tom Humphrey, he was called upon to bowl, with sensational results: six wickets for 7 runs in 12 overs. Emmett, when forty and close to retirement, was leading Yorkshire at The Oval when, in similar circumstances, he put himself on to take eight for 22, including a spell of five wickets for no runs in 3 overs.

Emmett was called the 'Wicket and Wide Man', and was probably the first top-class bowler to appreciate the advantage to be gained by the full use of the bowling crease in altering the angle of attack. He would also alter his length by delivering the ball from behind the crease, and was also perhaps the first to bowl deliberately wide of the off stump in the hope of inducing an edge. There seems little doubt that at least some of his many wayward balls were despatched quite deliberately to affect the batsman's concentration; one ball in any over was liable to be quick and dead on middle stump.

Then there was his 'sostenutor' ('What else would you call it?' he asked) that was acknowledged as being one of the marvels of the age. Said W. G.: 'I have had occasional balls from him that would have beaten any batsman; his best was one pitching between the legs and wicket with sufficient break and rise to hit the off bail.' Richard Daft described him as 'all wire and whipcord; one of the very best bits of stuff a cricketer was ever made of'.

Emmett's 1216 wickets for Yorkshire were taken at an average of 12.71. He also scored 6315 runs at an average of 15.10, his solitary first-class century coming against the premier power, Gloucestershire. Tom Emmett was also the fifth and last of Yorkshire's professional captains until the election of Vic Wilson in 1960. Tom was not, according to his contemporaries, an ideal leader, being over modest with his own bowling and taking a liberal view of Yorkshire's fielding, which was regarded as something of a joke among the counties, it being said that Emmett's team was too polite to run out an opponent.

County committees in the 1880s were veering strongly towards the view that professionals were ill suited to leadership. The Reverend Holmes wrote in 1904:

> Without the smallest grain of snobbishness all men like to be commanded by their social superior. One can with confidence point to Yorkshire cricket for confirmation during the last decade. That the County Committee were of the same opinion the following minute in 1878 shows: 'That T. Emmett be made captain in the absence of a gentleman'.

The Reverend adds: 'Perhaps the word "amateur" is less open to criticism.'

If Emmett was aware of this attitude within the Committee he never allowed such thoughts to spoil his delightful attitude to the game. After a stirring victory over Nottinghamshire the Yorkshire captain was recorded as having turned a somersault in the middle of the pitch by way of celebration. Hawke called him 'the greatest character that ever stepped on a cricket field, a merry wag who could never lose heart or temper'. Another peer, Lord Harris of Kent: 'I have never known a keener or merrier [cricketer] than dear old Tom. He was as hard as a board and as active as a cat.'

Emmett's ability to laugh at himself endeared him to the dressing rooms. His huge nose was described by Hawke as 'if not so obtrusive as that of Cyrano de Bergerac yet it was as highly coloured'. He must have laughed as much as anyone after the famous pitch invasion at Sydney when a crowd of 2000 in ugly mood swept up Lord Harris, A. N. Hornby and George Ulyett. A 'larrikin' struck at Harris, Ulyett prepared to hit back with a stump, but 'Monkey' seized the lad and used him as a battering ram to clear a path to a policeman. 'Where was Tom?' Ulyett was asked. Emmett had, in fact, returned to the pavilion to change his socks, but according to his fellow Yorkshiremen 'the crowd gave him such a fright he was seen running like a madman towards the harbour'.

Emmett was forty-seven when he retired, and even then many Yorkshiremen felt he should have been retained a little longer, although the parting was not entirely happy: 'When I finished a remark was made to the effect that they didn't want to see me any more. It may have been meant as a joke but it was not well put; indeed, after my long service on the county it seemed in bad taste and I felt it.'

His benefit match raised £620 and he played briefly as a professional with both Bradford and Leicester clubs, but his later days were remembered by pupils at Rugby where he became coach in March 1889 and sought to have the church bells silenced during practice and for some elms to be cut down to improve the ground. Sir Pelham Warner wrote: 'Every Rugby boy knew him and loved him. I can see him . . . striding across the Close with his grey and well-shaped head crowned by a Yorkshire cap held high and his body as straight as the most ramrod sergeant.'

His closing days, according to *Wisden*, were 'unhappily clouded', but he lived to sixty-three to see in the new century and the Golden Age.

George Pinder   *Prince of Keepers*

Pinder not only followed Ned Stephenson as Yorkshire's wicket-keeper, he also lived in the same street in Eccleshill, Sheffield. A tall, lean man with curly hair and deep moustache, Pinder had a tremendous reach and fiercely disputed Blackham's claim to be the first keeper to dispense with a long-stop.

According to Pinder it was in a match between North and South at Lord's in 1878 when A.N. Hornby, captaining The North, asked if he could do without a long-stop. The bowlers were Morley and Emmett, and Pinder replied truthfully: 'You know, sir, if one passes it means a four.' Hornby took the risk and The North won comfortably. Later, at The Oval, after Ephraim Lockwood had been fielding long-stop he came up to Pinder and said: 'I've been behind thee for twenty-three overs and have not had to stop a ball. I think I can find a better place.'

So who was the first to keep without a long-stop? G.D. Martineau in *The Valiant Stumper* is unable to give a verdict, although he points out that Australia's Jack Blackham was in England at that time. Blackham made his Test debut two years earlier, so he should have the stronger case in an argument that in no way detracts from Pinder's status as a pioneer of the craft.

Pinder has good claim to being the first to stand up to all his county bowlers, and as these included George Freeman, the fastest of his time, Allen Hill, almost as fast and deadly accurate, and the eccentric and erratic Tom Emmett, he must have been a sight. His leg-side work was legendary. He once managed to stump Tom Hearne of Middlesex off a shooter down the leg side.

Pinder, aged ten, was apprenticed to a pen and pocket-blade grinder in Sheffield and was almost eighteen before he got the chance to play for the St Mary's Club, as a bowler. For a match against the powerful Hallam Club St Mary's were without a keeper and pressed the young Pinder into the job, and so successful was he that his career was made.

He was twenty-four, still bent over the grindstone, when Sheffield Shrewsbury, a club he described as a 'gentlemen's organisation', asked him to keep for their twenty-two against All England. Pinder caught three and stumped two of the all-stars,

was invited by Ossett and Worksop to play against them, and finally played with them at Whitehaven.

Then a professional, he took over from Ned Stephenson and three years later, on Harry Sampson's recommendation and on condition that All England's fixtures took priority, replaced Stephenson as Yorkshire's keeper. Of keeping to Freeman, Hill and Emmett, he told 'Old Ebor':

> It was no joke, especially to Tom Emmett, who used to sling in the ball at times in a way that made the stumper keep his eyes wide open and his wits about him. There was a certain ball which appeared to be going to leg but which would whip in on the middle and off stumps. As soon as I saw that ball I gave the batsman up.

To the end of his days Pinder firmly believed he had stumped Arthur Shrewsbury before the great man completed his first century (for Nottinghamshire against All England), but the umpire had favoured the batsman. On W.G. Grace Pinder commented: 'I got his wicket oftener than anybody and more often than the umpires would give it to me. I think the umpires in those days either favoured or were a bit frightened at W.G. who of course had a tremendous reputation – and not more than he deserved.'

Pinder collected 246 victims in his 124 matches for Yorkshire, 100 of them stumped, and it is sad that his career with the county should have ended in controversy. In 1880, in a needle match with Nottinghamshire, he missed two catches and was dropped for the next match, although paid as an umpire. Yorkshire also wanted him to umpire in the next match, against Middlesex at Bramall Lane, but Pinder claims he was not told of this – 'It was scarcely likely that I would throw a £5 note away.'

He completed the season, and a benefit match that September raised £300. Pinder then turned down, on the advice of 'one or two Yorkshire committeemen', an invitation to join the staff at Lord's. The following spring, having heard nothing from Yorkshire, he attended the first match, at Bramall Lane, and was prevented from entering the pavilion by an official

who told him: 'You are not a player.' Pinder admits: 'I let my tongue slip more freely than was wise, though I think my provocation was great.' Thereafter the great Pinder had to pay to watch Yorkshire, becoming an innkeeper in Sheffield and in Worksop where 'Country Vicar' remembered him as 'a big man with grey, curly hair and a genial red face'.

Pinder was big enough to praise his successor Joe Hunter as 'a very good man', and in his last days, as groundsman at Hickleton Main Colliery, he felt compelled to compare, in a letter, the lot of professionals at the turn of the century, by which time they received £2 a week winter pay, with his own remuneration.

We only got £5 [a match] wherever we went, and the largest number of matches I played in one season was twenty-four. That was £120. Out of that I had to pay my hotel bills, my railway travelling and maintain my home, my wife and four children. We started in May and gave up in September and then seven months to get over.

Ephraim Lockwood *Old Mary Ann*

Eph Lockwood was the first Yorkshire cricketer to enter the county's folklore, a phlegmatic but easy-going character who became Yorkshire's fourth captain and their first major batsman whose cutting, off middle stump, was regarded as one of the wonders of the age.

He learned the game at Lascelles Hall and then became a 'Saturday man', a professional, for Kirkburton and, in turn, Meltham Mills, Lockwood and Cheetham Hill, Manchester, by then aged twenty-three. His first-class debut is a tale woven into the fabric of the game.

George Freeman and Luke Greenwood were injured in a bus accident at Derby, and Yorkshire arrived in London on the Saturday night knowing they were a man short for the match against Surrey starting on the Monday. The captain, Roger Iddison, wished to send for protégé Milner Gibson but John Thewlis, hearing substitutes being discussed, modestly put forward the name of his nephew. Iddison was unconvinced until Tom Emmett chimed in to say 'Eph's a good 'un.' A wire was sent to Cheetham Hill, but Lockwood had already left to play for Lascelles Hall at Yeadon and it says something for the telegraphic service of 1868 that the message reached him in time for him to present himself in London on Sunday evening.

Surrey made 195 after young Lockwood, his gear wrapped in a paper parcel under his arm, had apparently had some difficulty in winning admission to The Oval. Iddison, perhaps anxious to get over any embarrassment quickly, sent in the young man to open with his uncle, Thewlis, saying as they walked out: 'Eph, lad, play thi usual game and tha'll be all reet.' The crowd hooted at the sight of what appeared to be a boy in a green, black and red check shirt, too-tight trousers and borrowed boots that were too big for him. But he and Uncle John batted all through a hot afternoon and evening, Emmett appearing at one point with some drinks from what must have been a jubilant dressing room to tell Lockwood, with a straight face: 'Think on, tha's on thi merits.'

By the close Thewlis was 51, Lockwood 57, and the stand reached 176, a first-wicket record that stood for eighteen years, Lockwood making 91 on debut (Thewlis 108). Ned Stephenson, first wicket down, wore his pads through three sessions and got a duck.

Lockwood from that day was considered Yorkshire's premier batsman, the predecessor of a great line that led on to Tunnicliffe, Brown, Holmes, Sutcliffe, Hutton and Boycott. So important was he to the side that when he was out George Pinder would say to the number *eleven*: 'Get thi pads on, Mary Ann's out.' Observers spoke of his broad shoulders and, always, of the power of his cutting. One fast bowler is reported to have posted six slips to him and still they were pierced. He scored regularly with a half-cock shot over mid-off that appeared to be a mis-drive; he would also move out as if to drive on the leg side and then, at the last minute, play a late cut. This shot was known as 'Lockwood's Folly'.

Those were his major strengths, but he could play all round the wicket and in 1878 the Australians regarded Lockwood as second only to Grace for variety of strokes. In 1883 he hit 208 against Kent, an innings probably worth double on today's pitches. Twice invited to tour Australia he turned down a third invitation in order to marry Fuller Pilch's niece, of whom it was said that she was the one lady who knew as much about the game as her husband.

He did, however, tour America in 1879, the scene of the second classic Lockwood story. Taken with George Pinder to Niagara Falls he is supposed to have observed: 'Ah reckon nowt to it. Ah'd sooner be in Lascelles Hall.' A.A. Thomson thought that this somewhat dour reaction to one of the world's wonders might have been explained by Ephraim's punishment by mosquitoes, which made his face swell 'like a pudding'.

As Yorkshire's captain for two years (1876–7), he was by all contemporary accounts considered far too easy-going, causing even the jovial Emmett to flare up on one occasion when he failed to persuade Allen Hill to bowl again at the 'big 'un', W.G.: 'Why don't you make him, you're the captain?'

He was known to be careful with his money, once allegedly falling conveniently asleep when the collection plate came round, and when he retired in 1884 he eventually opened a sports shop in Huddersfield. He died as late as December 1921, and thus would have been able to tell a grand tale to modern generations.

He then remarks on the comparative affluence of the professional cricketer: 'an annual income of £100 in 1875 to about £250 by 1900'. The labourer's wage had risen from £80 to £100 per year over the same period. 'As late as 1904 E.J. Smith ["Tiger" of Warwickshire fame] was glad to escape from a factory job which had brought him only 16 shillings [80p] for 60 hours of hard labour.'

Sandiford also found an illustrative example of the vast gulf that existed between the Victorian notions of gentleman and player. In 1898 Henry Perkins retired after twenty-two years as Secretary to MCC, during which time he had received £500 a year; he was given life membership and a pension of £400 a year. On the very same day Tom Hearne, who had served the Club as head bowler and chief groundsman and who was forced to retire through ill health, was awarded a pension of £30 a year. There was intense pressure, too, on the professional to keep his place in the side; there were no contracts and a queue of eager and willing young cricketers at the county gate. It is hardly surprising then that many a professional made the very most of his good times and convivial evenings, knowing that a dark winter lay ahead.

Jeremy Lonsdale has been a diligent researcher into the environment of Yorkshire's early professionals and points out that a surfeit of parochial indulgence was sometimes a factor in shortening the careers of local favourites. Morley was happy to fete Bobby Peel (in a banquet at the Brunswick Arms in September 1877, attended by fifty including the mayor and council). Billy Bates was presented with a solid silver tankard in 1884, presumably in Huddersfield. When Louis Hall topped Yorkshire's averages in 1883, hundreds waited for him at Batley Station on his return home from the Surrey match; he was escorted by the Temperance Brass Band to the town hall where a 'vast crowd' heard him congratulated by the mayor. The crowd then massed outside Hall's home, demanding that he appear so that they could be guaranteed that the 'Batley Giant' was not the worse for drink. A lesser man might have succumbed.

That Yorkshire's players did weaken more than occasionally is confirmed by two notices in a Sheffield newspaper, the first a letter from 'An Old Cricketer':

At Dewsbury last year [1880] they stayed up so late on the Friday night that they lost the match against the Australians next day. We regret that occasionally the XI may have erred in not taking sufficient sleep or, owing to the generosity of their friends, they have taken a glass too much. *Lillywhite's Guide* says that Yorkshire lost the match at Dewsbury by their 'bad fielding' and it is no wonder when I am told that they went to bed at 4 or 5 o'clock.

Even ten years later the *East Riding Chronicle* reported:

> The Chairman said that the ill-fortune which had attended the county team during last season was largely due to people who called themselves supporters of cricket who could not see a professional on the ground without wanting to give him a glass of drink.

Jeremy Lonsdale found another reason for the professional need to take sustenance in copious quantities when offered: the time and tedium spent in travelling. The *Leeds Mercury* in 1883 mentioned one itinerary: from Leeds to The Oval, back to Bradford, two days at York and then on to Sheffield – and all this before the age

Allen Hill *Devastator*

Hill, fast right-arm, had the ultimate pedigree for a Yorkshire cricketer: born in Kirkheaton, birthplace of Hirst and Rhodes, he learned his cricket as a hand-loom weaver in Lascelles Hall, and it is the latter village which, quite rightly, claims him. Indeed, according to A.A. Thomson it was a Kirkheaton man who wished, in the 1890s, that Hirst would be as good a player as Hill.

The youngster's bowling prowess soon attracted attention, and at seventeen he became another 'Saturday man', playing for Dewsbury Savile and then Mirfield Old for five shillings a match (including all expenses). He then became coach and groundsman at Stonyhurst, on Luke Greenwood's recommendation, subsequently joined the Lancashire ground staff, and was actually Burnley's professional when he made one of the most sensational starts in cricketing history.

George Freeman had broken down, and Roger Iddison invited the almost unknown Hill to take his place against Surrey at The Oval on 21 August 1871. He was then twenty-six and unusual in that he stuck with a round-arm action even when over-arm bowling was legalised. He took a short run, relying mostly on accuracy, length and sheer pace, bringing the occasional ball back, and his action was described by a contemporary as 'a beautiful delivery'.

Surrey batted first, and Hill opened with Emmett taking six for 33 in 27 overs. When Yorkshire batted, raiding 100 to Surrey's 111, Hill was top scorer with 28 before taking the ball again to improve on his first-innings figures – six for 23 in 23 overs.

Hill had some difficulty in getting his release from Burnley for the rest of that season, but from 1872 he played regularly with Yorkshire for twelve seasons, taking over from Freeman who played only another five matches after that year.

Hill's accuracy and pace can be assessed by his three hat-tricks and by a performance against twenty-two of Cambridgeshire when, bowling on Parker's Piece, he thrice broke a middle stump in half. Among his hat-trick victims were 'Monkey' Hornby and W.G. Grace.

Emmett rated Hill Yorkshire's best fielder of that era but it may be that old Tom was biased. At Bramall Lane in July 1876, Lancashire needed only 89 to win and looked like completing an easy victory with Hornby and Barlow at the wicket. 'Never mind about Barlow,' said Emmett. 'We can get him out if he tries to get runs. But we must get rid of the other.' Emmett promptly bowled Hornby with what is remembered as one of the worst ever deliveries seen in a Roses match, a slow half-volley outside the off stump which Hornby leapt upon and hammered, only for Hill, at point, to take a most astonishing point-blank catch. Emmett promptly put Hill on to bowl at the other end where he took five wickets for 3 runs, all bowled, and Lancashire were all out for 70.

Hill was one of five Yorkshiremen, with Ulyett, Emmett, Armitage and Andrew Greenwood, who toured with Lillywhite's team in 1876–7, taking ten for 9 against sixteen of Adelaide ('we had to leave the match to catch our steamer'). Touring then presented hazards unfamiliar to today's players. Crossing a gorge in New Zealand in two coaches, the party found themselves caught in a sudden flood and had to wade to safety up to their waists: 'We expected to be drowned any moment.'

Hill's benefit match, appropriately against Lancashire, raised £376 in 1884, and when his career ended after he broke his collar bone, he returned to the Red Rose as a coach. Yet although Allen Hill spent five years as a young professional in Lancashire before Yorkshire's call, he was never approached to qualify for them.

of the motor car. Four years later the team were playing Gloucestershire at Dewsbury until 6 p.m. and had to start a game in Hastings the following day at 1 p.m. All-night journeys were expected and commonplace, but none the less tedious for that.

Any imposition, however, was to be preferred to not being a county cricketer, yet there is no doubt that the constant stress brought some careers, and even some lives, to an early close. Ikey Hodgson, for instance, was already broken in health in 1866 when, at the age of thirty-eight, he travelled to Glasgow and back for three games in seven days, and by August he was clearly exhausted but dare not refuse an engagement. On 30–31 July he played at Keighley, 2–3 August at Trent Bridge, 9, 10 and 11 at Stoke (where he bowled 20 consecutive overs for one run), 13, 14 and 15 at Mansfield and 16, 17 and 18 at Shrewsbury. He was back home in Bradford on 18 August and was due to play in Tynemouth on 20 August, but Tom Emmett had to deputise.

Hodgson never played cricket again; deteriorating health had forced him to give up a public house several years earlier, and by the summer of 1867 he knew he could not resume playing. One of the most famous cricketers in England, he nevertheless found himself unable even to support his wife. Fortunately for Ikey, his fellow Bradfordians and Yorkshiremen rallied around him, and although he died of consumption in November 1867, a fund of £230 was passed on to his wife. The Bradford club, which 120 years later had to leave Park Avenue because they could no longer afford the ground, gave his widow an annuity and paid the funeral expenses and doctors' fees. Hodgson's tragic end would have served as a lesson to every young Yorkshire cricketer.

As a team, Yorkshire's practice was to begin superbly but tail away disastrously. They were probably a popular side, and for all that they were professionals while most southern counties were amateurs, they did not lack sportsmanship. In the very first match in Championship history, which began at Prince's on 22 May 1873, Middlesex defeated Yorkshire by ten wickets – but only after the scorers had declared a Middlesex victory when in fact the

contest was tied. Yorkshire could have insisted on leaving the match a tie, but took the field again for Middlesex to score the one run needed.

If Iddison or Emmett had been giving evidence on the performance of the team over its first four years, they would no doubt have pointed out some extenuating circumstances. Pinder often had to stand down because of damaged hands, the result of his standing up to the fast bowlers on uneven pitches. And Hill had an unfortunate career in the number of injuries he sustained; as a cricketer he seemed accident prone.

In 1874, however, one good authority – W.G. himself – nominated Yorkshire as the true champions. They did win eight of their twelve matches, but Derbyshire won three of their four and were named the 'official' champions, as Yorkshire had also lost three while Derbyshire remained unbeaten.

The Committee took some criticism for a traditional reluctance to replace seasoned performers by untried Colts. The sober, studious Hall, for instance, was allowed to drift back into league cricket in 1873 and was not to reappear for five seasons, while many felt that Ulyett's undoubted promise should have been given greater encouragement.

If the playing results in this first era of professional captaincy were not all that was hoped, the county club was laying a firm foundation. With perhaps no more than 300 members the accounts showed a regular annual profit, enabling grants for £1250 to be made to Bramall Lane in the years 1874–83. In 1877 the first travelling expenses were paid, £1 each to those players engaged against Gloucestershire at Clifton; in 1884 came the first regular talent money, for the hat-trick. In 1892 it was minuted that '£1 be awarded for 50 runs, 30 shillings for 75, £2 for 100', but that, let it be noted, 'the question of talent money for bowling be postponed'.

In 1878 Yorkshire tried to broaden their programme by playing a first match at Wakefield, against Sussex, while York became the venue for Surrey's visit the following year. Those were the days of the patrons, for in 1874 the Earl of Londesborough financed both

Yorkshire, 1875.
Back row (from left): G. Martin (umpire), John Thewlis.
Middle row: George Pinder, George Ulyett, Tom Armitage, Joe Rowbotham, Allen Hill, Andrew Greenwood.
Front row: Tom Emmett, John Hicks, Ephraim Lockwood, Charlie Ullathorne.

matches against Middlesex, at Prince's and Scarborough.

There must have been a considerable celebration in 1875 when Gloucestershire were beaten for the first time despite scores of 111 and 43 from W.G. In that same summer Lancashire won the Old Trafford Roses match by ten wickets, those favourites of Francis Thompson, Hornby and Barlow, raising 148 in the second innings against Emmett, Hill, Tom Armitage and Ulyett.

There was a row at Sheffield, involving those perennial rivals Nottinghamshire, that would have caused a sensation today. Billy Oscroft of Nottinghamshire was given run out; he disputed the decision on the grounds that when the ball reached Pinder it was dead. Yorkshire

argued that Pinder had signalled Hill to throw him the ball in order to run out Oscroft. After *half an hour's* delay, the batsman gave way.

Two highly commendable bowlers emerged in these early years: Armitage and Robert Clayton. Armitage was a huge Sheffielder, described by Peter Thomas as a 'Falstaffian figure', who bowled cunning lobs that broke 'twice the width of the wicket' according to a Middlesex captain. Armitage was also a sound batsman. He first appeared in 1872 but was not given a regular place until three summers later when he routed Nottinghamshire, taking five for 8 in 4 overs, improving upon that the following season with a match return of thirteen for 46 against Surrey at Sheffield. That particular feat won him a place in the Lillywhite

George Ulyett *Happy Jack*

Wisden said at Ulyett's death in June 1898: 'A finer cricketer the county has never produced. He was for years the best bat in the team and if he had not been able to get a run he would have been worth his place for his bowling and his fielding.'

Ulyett was born in Pitsmoor, Sheffield, and learned to play with a team of boys in Crabtree Village who would challenge local teams to play for money, matches not always being decided by the 'Laws'. Ulyett remembered one such match in which he had one eye closed by contact with the ball and the other as a result of a difference with an opposing player. The Secretary of the Pitsmoor Club kept a benevolent eye on proceedings, and so impressed was he by the young Ulyett that he persuaded his committee to bend the rules to admit a sixteen-year-old two years before his eligibility for membership. Mr Pickersgill must soon have won a vote of confidence for his enterprise, for the new member took twelve wickets in his first match, a Whitsuntide two-day fixture against great rivals Staveley.

Young Ulyett was actually working in a rolling mill at this time, and although an enraged employer would frequently sack him for taking time off to play, the man must have been enough of a Yorkshireman to give the lad back his job. In time he became a professional at Bradford and it was there, on the old Horton Road ground, that he bowled for the club against a United South XI and dismissed W.G., Yorkshire showing an interest for the first time.

As a batsman Ulyett, for all he opened the innings, was renowned as a hitter, so it made sense for Yorkshire to install Louis Hall as his partner. A fierce driver, he was credited with clearing the players' seats at Lord's in 1878, dropping the ball into the gravel behind the pavilion, a hit of 109 yards. Said Grace: 'He threw all his gigantic strength into his strokes.' In America, challenged on his opinion that baseball was a child's sport, he hit a famous pitcher for 162 not out.

Ulyett bowled fast-medium with a break-back, could make the ball lift and was regarded as a very unpleasant prospect to face on some of the suspect pitches of those days. Tall, he weighed fourteen stone and his back was as broad and robust as his humour. He became Hawke's sergeant major, and when Hirst arrived they were known in the team as Old and Young George, Ulyett always referring to Hirst as 'young 'un'.

The first Englishman to score two fifties in a Test match, Ulyett also had some fine bowling perform-

ances against Australia, including a seven for 36 at Lord's in 1884 – a Test in which he made a catch that is still regarded as one of the most remarkable ever seen to put out George Bonnor, the 6 foot 6 inch Australian who was judged to be close to Jessop in hitting power. Bonnor hit back a half-volley with all his force and power. Ulyett put out a hand and the ball stuck. Grace and Harris both told Ulyett he was foolish for even attempting the catch, asserting that if the ball had hit arm or wrist bones would have been broken. Ulyett said the ball came back to him as if on an elastic string, and it was such a talking point that MCC's oldest member gave him a sovereign (probably worth about £30 today) and said it was the finest catch he had seen in his long life. *Punch* commented that more like Ulyett were needed to go to war, as they would be useful in catching cannonballs.

At his peak 'Happy Jack', a dressing-room nickname bestowed by Charlie Ullathorne, was described as tall, broad-shouldered, with a high colour and heavy dark moustache which, in almost every portrait, hides the beginning of a mischievous smile, often betrayed by his eyes. His jokes and humour have remained a legend.

He and Ted Peate once managed to get into a reception held by Mr Gladstone in 10 Downing Street, Ulyett evading queries by pretending to be stone deaf, Peate feigning ignorance as Ulyett's 'keeper'. All went well until one of the guests, a Lancashire amateur, recognised the pair and, recalled Peate, 'you should have seen the look of astonishment on his face'. Pressed for an explanation, Ulyett came up with: 'We thought it was a place of entertainment.'

An innings by Ulyett was recalled by 'Country Vicar', writing in 1930.

> He was good to watch; he played the game with such a light heart. No poking about for him. No allowing the ball to hit the bat. He did the hitting and with right good will from the first moment he reached the wicket. And his powerful strokes travelled in every direction; there was no paucity of strokes. Cuts, drives, leg-hits, he kept every shot in his locker . . . a little reckless perhaps at times and had he played a little more steadily he might have made even more runs. But to play steadily was not Ulyett's game; it was all fire and force but graceful withal. He was the greatest

professional batsman of his time and there is no professional batsman now, to my mind, who plays the dashing, dazzling game he did.

Ulyett's benefit match in 1887 lasted only two days, but a subscription list was opened and, in the end, the fun topped £1000, a very handsome sum for those days and a measure of Yorkshire's regard for 'Happy Jack'. He became landlord of the Vine Hotel in Sheffield, many reporting on the happy times to be had and laughter to be heard 'at the sign of the wicket'.

A golden autumn was sadly cut short in his forty-seventh year. Despite carrying a cold he insisted on attending Bramall Lane on a chill, damp day in June 1898. According to A.A. Thomson he met George Hirst on the pavilion steps and said, simply: 'I'm finished, young 'un.' Hirst, alarmed, replied: 'Nay, niver in this world.' But Ulyett's premonition was correct, for he died of pneumonia a few days later.

There was also a Jack Ulyett, George's older brother, who was groundsman at Bramall Lane for many years. George Ulyett also maintained the links between cricket and soccer in Sheffield in that era, keeping goal for the Wednesday for a spell up until 1883.

Louis Hall *The Batley Giant*

A strict tee-totaller, non-smoker and lay preacher in Methodist chapels, Louis Hall was the Roundhead to George Ulyett's Cavalier in Yorkshire's first regular opening partnership. They became the first pair to make a century stand in each innings, against Sussex at Hove in 1885, and raised a hundred together for the first wicket 12 times.

Hall was renowned for both his defence and slow scoring (12 in 165 minutes against Kent, 29 in 210 minutes against Kent, 40 in 265 minutes against Nottinghamshire). He carried his bat for Yorkshire on fourteen occasions, but there were times when he could hit, particularly to leg, once lifting W.G. Grace out of the Batley ground.

Hall made his debut in 1873 against Middlesex but his 37 in 100 minutes made little impression, for he was allowed to return to local cricket with Batley. In 1878, playing for a Hunslet eighteen, he scored 79 against the Australians, including Spofforth, an innings that brought him a hurried recall to Yorkshire, holding his place until 1894 and often captaining the side.

Apart from his stalwart batting over nine seasons and useful slow round-arm or lob bowling, Hall's

value to the side was his setting of a professional example to younger players who were so easily led down the primrose path. He led, too, in other ways, accepting deferment of his own benefit so that Billy Bates, who had damaged an eye in Melbourne, could have the first call on public sympathy. He was also able to help retiring cricketers, particularly those who had made no provision for old age, through his chairmanship of the Cricketers' Benevolent Fund.

His nickname, the 'Batley Giant', was probably due to his lean stature as much as his height, for he was barely six feet but was clearly always a commanding, if stooping figure to bowlers. In Heavy Woollen League circles he was known, of course, as 'Lewis', and after he had hit Lancashire for 160 at Bradford, in 1887, Yorkshire totalling 590, a song beginning 'Here's health and wealth to Lewis Hall', written earlier, became popular in his area.

'Country Vicar', writing in 1930, described what might be said to be the definitive Louis Hall scene:

The smoke of Sheffield drifting slowly across the ground, hanging over the field of play like a filmy curtain through which the flannelled figures of the Surrey players glimmered white. I can see Louis Hall, long and lean, dull to watch, dogged and dour.

A.G. Steel, of Lancashire and England, added: 'Nothing in cricket can be more dull and dismal than bowling to this batsman on a sodden wicket at Bramall Lane in a real "Sheffield fog".'

On retirement Hall himself was apologetic: 'I cannot tell how I acquired a slow style but I found afterwards that it was of more value to my side than to myself and I don't think I should adopt the same principle again.'

Hall became coach to Uppingham School in 1895, umpiring first-class during the holidays and opening a sports shop in the town. When the giant Australian Bonnor was ribbing that prodigious hitter C.I. Thornton, he joked: 'I've got a sister back home who can hit as well as you.' 'Right,' replied 'Buns'. 'Bring her over and we'll marry her to Louis Hall.'

Billy Bates *The Duke*

One of the country's great players who is almost forgotten today, Billy Bates won his nickname as much for his style of play as for his sartorial elegance at a time when professional cricketers were not expected to be well dressed. Lord Hawke thought him the finest professional batsman up until Jack Hobbs; W.G. Grace thought he would have been considered the 'greatest all-round player of his time' had his fielding matched his batting and bowling.

William Bates was another product of Lascelles Hall. His father loved the game, two brothers played for the club, and Billy was regarded as a prodigy as a boy. He was such a promising batsman that the village lads were reluctant to give him an innings, knowing that they might not get him out. It was while waiting for them to relent that he took to bowling slow to medium off-breaks, a skill that was curiously to bring him more fame than his batting.

He stood a slender 5 feet 10 inches and his bowling performances for Yorkshire, often at the other end to the great Peate, suggest that he was a bowler of great accuracy and flight: five for 1 in four overs against Surrey at The Oval in 1878; eight for 21, again at The Oval, the following year; six for 11 against Middlesex, eight for 45 against Lancashire, five for 15 against Derbyshire. As a batsman he was known in those days as a 'dasher'. He was especially prolific on fast pitches, hence his successes in Australia, and his on-drive was regarded as one of the great strokes of his era. On tour in 1886 he scored the first 46 runs on the board against New South Wales, and in 1884, for Yorkshire against Nottinghamshire, he hit 116 out of 137 scored in 165 minutes.

The pinnacle of his career came when, at the age of twenty-seven, he won a Test match virtually on his own, the second of Ivo Bligh's tour, at Melbourne in January 1883. England had been forced to follow on and lost the First Test, also in Melbourne, but in the Second England won the toss, scored 294, Bates 55, and then bowled out Australia for 114, Bates taking seven for 28 in 26.2 overs, including the first hat-trick.

Australia had reached 78 for 3 when Percy McDonnell was bowled and George Giffen gave a return catch of the next ball. Next man in was the giant George Bonnor, renowned as hitter and scourge of slow bowlers. After consultation it was agreed that even Bonnor, anxious to avert a hat-trick, would play forward to the first ball. Walter Read agreed to stand in the suicidal position of silly mid-on to Bonnor, and to creep forward if Bates could promise a quickish delivery on the leg stump.

The roar of welcome given Bonnor by the 'larrikins' was stilled as the ploy worked to perfection. Bonnor, astonished at Read's audacity, played slowly forward and guided the ball directly into Read's hands, six feet away. In those days a hat-trick meant exactly that, and Billy won what A.G. Steel described as a 'very smart, tall, silver hat for his pains'.

He was, it seems, generous and charming to a fault, although it needed both courage and tenacity in those days to tour Australia five times and America once. 'O dashing one', as a lady described him, so impressed the king of the Sandwich Isles with his rendering of 'The Bonny Yorkshire Lass' at a ship's concert that the king insisted on returning to the ship every day of the visit to hear Bates sing the song again.

Billy's midsummer marriage prompted a famous remark from Ted Peate: 'That Baates is a foo-il. He shoulda got married in t'middle o' winter so as to give his undivided attention to it.' Then again, perhaps Peate was deadly serious.

Billy Bates was in his high summer, at the the age of thirty-three, when in Melbourne in 1887 he was struck in the eye while at net practice. His sight was so impaired that an acute depression followed, and he tried to commit suicide on the voyage home. He recovered sufficiently to be able to coach and to return to league cricket with Leek, full circle to his first professional engagement, as a seventeen-year-old, at Rochdale.

Although a sick man, and living upon the generosity of friends, Billy insisted upon attending the funeral of John Thewlis on what was described as a bitterly cold day in January 1900. He suffered a severe chill and within ten days was dead himself and buried beside Thewlis in that same graveyard. He was forty-one.

tour of Australasia (1876–7) where, in the famous flood incident near Christchurch, New Zealand, jolly Tom distinguished himself. The two coaches could not cross a flooded gorge, so a horse was unharnessed and a rider put upon his back, with another man taking hold of his coat-tails. In this way a human chain was forged, the line of passengers being taken to safety, and Armitage carrying a young lady upon his back.

Bob Clayton might have been a famous name. A bowler from a village near Otley, he was for nine years among the fastest in England, serving for many years on the Lord's ground staff when not required by Yorkshire. In 1871, playing for Yorkshire against MCC, he had match figures of ten for 94, including the wicket of W.G., and when The North required a replacement for the great Freeman, it was Clayton who was called upon.

His county career did not begin until he was twenty-six and he took 154 wickets for Yorkshire at an average of 16, yet played only once for the county after 1877. When he and Andrew Greenwood were both dropped at the end of that same year there was considerable criticism

without any justification being offered. Only in comparatively recent times have county committees felt it necessary to vindicate their decisions, and it was left to Emmett, later, to hint at why Clayton was discarded: 'He was no judge of the game. He never studied the batsman's weak points.' In other words, in a team of professionals Clayton, for all his speed, wasn't considered professional enough.

By 1877, of course, another shooting star had arrived in the form of Billy Bates, spoken of, as a young man, as 'another Alfred Shaw'. Bates took 94 wickets in his second season. Ulyett, too, was developing into a superb batsman who could bowl. It may be that had Clayton been with another county, then more attention might have been paid to his prospects.

The overall results remained disappointing, only two county matches of twelve being won in 1877 and five (of fourteen) in 1880. Some highly significant happenings passed almost unnoticed. In 1879 Edmund Peate made his first appearance for the county; in 1881 a twenty-one-year-old Old Etonian, Martin Hawke; in 1882 Robert Peel. The team was gathering strength; the captain had arrived.

2

Lord Hawke and the Golden Age
1880–1914

The Golden Age of cricket is usually regarded as stretching from 1890 until the outbreak of the Great War in 1914, during which years the game was just one manifestation of a seemingly endless Edwardian summer when the world was at peace, the sun never set, wealthy benefactors abounded, civilisation advanced and all humanity knew that things could only get better. It was the time of Sherlock Holmes and Winnie the Pooh, of *The Wind in the Willows* and Jerome K. Jerome, of the striped blazer, the boater, the parasol, an era of good manners and genteel courtesy, when others really believed that an Englishman's word was his bond and nearly all small boys aspired to be gentlemen.

Nothing happens by chance. Britain was at the zenith of its empire-building, a nation of unbounded confidence drawing upon the planet's resources and bursting with talent. Similarly, cricket had come through its formative period, had climbed the hill and reached that plateau where bat and ball were achieving a

Yorkshire, 1884:
Back row (from left): Ted Peate, Tom Emmett, the scorer, William Harris, Joe Hunter.
Middle row: John Rawlin, Frederick Lee, Louis Hall, Bobby Peel, George Ulyett.
Front row: Billy Bates, Irwin Grimshaw.

graceful balance; both batting and bowling were becoming recognisably modern, and an all-white uniform had evolved. It had not been until 1788 that the rolling, watering, covering and mowing of a pitch had been permitted 'by mutual consent', and not until 1849 could a pitch be swept and rolled before each innings. By 1883, rolling was permitted before the start on each day.

Pads were first advertised in *Wisden* in 1880, thirty years after wicket-keepers had worn the first gauntlets. In 1816 the bowler had had to keep the hand below the elbow, in 1835 below the shoulder, over-arm bowling being legalised only in 1864. It was not until 1889 that a declaration was permitted, and then only on the third day (not until 1957 was a declaration at any time allowed). Boundaries are first mentioned in the 'Laws' in 1884, and in 1910 the six was changed from a hit out of the ground to a hit over the boundary.

Yorkshire entered this halcyon period with no presentiment of the great times ahead. Eight amateurs, including Hawke, appeared in 1882, and Pinder gave way to Joe Hunter behind the stumps. In 1883 Yorkshire had good cause to claim the Championship by virtue of their nine victories to two defeats, one of which was inflicted by Sussex, by 3 runs. Consolation was drawn from two defeats of Lancashire. Yet it was Nottinghamshire, the team of the decade, who headed the table with four wins to one loss.

Louis Hall was now Yorkshire's leading bat, although Eph Lockwood was still a batsman to be wondered at, as Kent did at Gravesend that year when 'Old Mary Ann' made 208 out of 297 scored while he was at the wicket. He contributed all but 40 to a partnership of 182 with Edward Lumb, another who is remembered as a batsman of potential greatness. Lumb, an amateur from Dalton, played for Yorkshire Colts at the age of fifteen and captained Dalton when he was twenty.

On his debut in 1883, Lumb carried his bat against Leicestershire for 82, and then went on to make 70 and 24 not out against Middlesex at Huddersfield. He was patient but stylish, the Reverend Holmes describing him as 'a beautiful batsman', such promise being sadly cut short by illness. He was forced to retire at the age of thirty-three, and he died in 1891. The Lumb Cup, in Huddersfield cricket, commemorated a player who was recalled with great affection.

Yorkshire's recruitment of amateurs was small but distinguished and despite the flush of 1882, when eight appeared, there were complaints that the Committee preferred professionals, a strange notion in those days. Jeremy Lonsdale uncovered some evidence of a minor but intriguing controversy on this subject. In March 1882 a delegation to the Committee raised this point and were told that the county often lost games in which amateurs were called upon and, secondly, that they often did not or could not turn up at the last minute.

There was, too, an underlying hint of animosity between the club and Yorkshire Gentlemen, who provided most of the amateurs, for at that same meeting the Secretary (Ellison) opposed the inclusion of a representative of the Gentlemen among the new members of the Committee: 'There was no reason to include Yorkshire Gentlemen; they wanted to have all games at York, at the expense of everywhere.'

There is little doubt that some of the amateurs whose names were put forward were simply not first-class players. Lonsdale cites Charles Landon who, despite the misfortune of his being born in Kent, came into the county side with a fine record for Yorkshire Gentlemen, but made five noughts in nine innings. Dr George Thornton, from Skipton, who went on to play for Middlesex and Transvaal, also appeared for Yorkshire in 1891 when he was described as being 'well out of his depth'.

There were gifted amateurs eligible, but the North–South divide of affluence has existed for much longer than a century and few northerners could afford to play county cricket and neglect careers or business, as could many landed and aristocratic southerners. The *Hull Daily Mail*, in 1904, mentioned two: Charles Gifkins (born in Surrey) and Lamplough Wallgate of Malton. Amateurs were, as we have seen, considered to be unreliable although, Lonsdale suggests, that might merely have meant that the Committee found them less easy to manage. The very brave *Dewsbury Reporter* commented in 1884: 'Hawke and Lumb will

Ted Peate   *The Immaculate*

The reference is, of course, to the length of his slow-left-arm bowling, the wonder of all his contemporaries, and not to his disorderly private life that, under Hawke's rule, caused a magnificent career to come to a premature close. He was, in the opinion of some of those who saw all three, including Yorkshire wicket-keeper David Hunter, superior to Peel and Rhodes, a judgement that never ceased to amaze those who saw the latter pair but not Peate himself.

Born in Holbeck, he began his career as a quick bowler in Yeadon, joining in 1875 a troupe called Treloar's Cricket Clowns which included acrobats. Yorkshire, and Sheffield in particular, took none too kindly to having the game held up to ridicule, and the Clowns were 'mobbed and sodded' by cricket-lovers. Peate then spent a winter practising in the Yeadon shed where he worked as a warp-twister, realising that by reducing the speed of his round-arm delivery he had much greater control of length and direction.

He was spotted at Scarborough by the Reverend E.S. Carter who, after several recommendations, persuaded Yorkshire to give him a trial with the Colts in 1879. Peate took seventeen wickets for 33 runs in the match and scored 25 not out, and Yorkshire had found their first slow left-arm bowler since Hodgson. He was promoted to the first team, his first two matches being all but washed out, but in his third, against Kent at Sheffield, he achieved match figures of twelve for 77.

From contemporary accounts it seems that Peate was no great spinner of the ball, relying on a teasing length, flight and variations of pace, the amount of turn depending upon conditions. He was blessed, wrote Hawke, 'with the most perfect action of any man I have seen deliver the ball'. He had, it was said, a 'natural break' and there could be no doubt he could be deadly when the pitch offered purchase. Not that he was purely a 'bad-wicket' bowler, as he demonstrated on the 1881–2 tour of Australia with returns of six for 100 against New South Wales, six for 30 against Victoria and eight for 57 against Murdoch's eleven. When the Australians visited England the following summer Peate was irresistible, taking 63 Australian wickets in all matches at an average of 12.9, twice as many as any other English bowler.

Peate's part in the Oval Test match that year, the contest won by Australia by 7 runs that originated the legend of the Ashes, has often been remarked

upon. England needed 9 runs to win and Peate, despite being a useful batsman (95 against Surrey in 1884), was last man, joining Charles Studd, the Cambridge all-rounder who that year was to follow W.G. as the second man ever to complete the 'double'. Peate scored 2 and then, in trying to force, was bowled. The recriminations have never ceased, and Peate is regularly chosen in mock elevens assembled for supposed incompetence and stupidity. The true story is rather different.

Studd, for all his ability, was twenty-two years old, an undergraduate playing in his first Test match. Peate was a hardened professional four years his senior, who had doubtless been through similar fires successfully. His error was to utter, when taxed afterwards, the famous phrase 'I couldn't trust Mr Studd.'

According to C.I. Thornton, who spoke about the incident as though he had been in the England dressing room at the time: 'Charlie was walking around with a blanket around him; Steel's teeth were all in a chatter and Barnes' teeth would have been chattering if he had not left them at home.' Peate, renowned for his impassivity, must have concluded that he had to take the responsibility. In that final half-hour, wrote a reporter, one spectator dropped dead and another gnawed through the handle of his umbrella.

Peate's only recorded comment afterwards was to say that he had not been nervous and that if three or four other England batsmen had scored as many runs as he there would have been a victory (Barlow, Steel and Read were all dismissed for nought).

The following year Peate gave his home town figures that astonished the world: eight wickets for 5 runs against Surrey (all out 31). Peate commented: 'Someone suggested to a Holbeck man that a collection should be made in recognition of my bowling. What do you think was the reply? "Oh, be — , he has

ruined the game. I shall object to the hat going round." '

In his eight seasons Peate took 1033 wickets at 13 runs apiece, his best being nine for 21 against Sussex in 1886, the year before Hawke ended his career. At least two contemporary observers used the phrase 'rapid decline' in reference to the years 1886–7. Failing eyesight was one reason, but he may also have fallen foul of his Lordship for his personal habits, for *Wisden* spoke in its obituary of 'his death, ostensibly through pneumonia, but for some time as a result of his way of life he had been in a poor condition'.

Hawke recorded afterwards: 'One of my saddest tasks was to dismiss him from the Yorkshire eleven. But he bore no grudge and . . . invariably . . . greeted me with the same, slow, spontaneous "Good morning, my lord, I hope you are as well as I am."'

Peate was able to play league cricket for several more years, still able to return figures worthy of red ink in the scorebooks. David Hunter remembered him as 'the finest left-arm slow bowler I ever saw. He had a beautiful action and was extraordinarily accurate, seldom if ever losing his length.'

Peate died at the age of forty-five, having spent five of his last seven years playing for Skipton. His memory would have been held all the greater but for his succession by two slow left-arm bowlers who were to become even more famous: Peel and Rhodes.

play when in humour but they cannot be replied upon.' Tadcaster, Lord Hawke's home, was presumably beyond the *Reporter's* circulation area.

One of 1892's flock, Robert Sidgwick of Embsay, was expected to play against the Australians at Dewsbury but did not appear 'because of business'. In 1893 the match against Essex would have caused a furore today: Hawke was unavailable, Arthur Sellers, the nominated deputy, withdrew over the weekend before the Monday start, and the next in line, F.S. Jackson, failed to appear. There had been rumbles three years earlier when Jackson, like many of his peers, wanted to have a choice of the games in which he played for Yorkshire; after considerable argument, during which Hawke threatened resignation, Jackson agreed

to make himself available for 1891 without conditions.

A proper gentleman's social obligations were, of course, many and varied, and it was most certainly not the done thing to evade them, not even in the cause of cricket. Robert Frank, of Pickering, objected to being called upon as a late choice (the Committee selected on Tuesday for a Thursday start), which is why he captained the Colts with distinction in the years 1900–14 but was not again invited into the first eleven. But Yorkshire's difficulties were no doubt minimal compared with those county clubs who relied much more heavily on the amateur and had few professional resources, such as Essex or Somerset.

If the years 1879 and 1880 were lean ones for Emmett – 76 wickets in two summers – York-

George Harrison   *Shoey*

A shoemaker in his native Scarborough, hence his nickname, George Puckrin Harrison was a bowler of genuine pace who had the distinction of appearing for the Players in his first season (1883), the equivalent then of playing for England in a first summer.

He made a sensational start for the Colts of the North against Colts of the South, not appearing to bowl until the second innings when he took nine for 14, taking four wickets with successive balls, then six in seven balls in all, hitting the stumps every time.

Such was the impact of this performance that he was chosen for the Players against the Gentlemen taking place a few days later. W.G. announced that he would open the innings to get a good look at this Colt, and in fifteen minutes all but destroyed the twenty-one-year-old. The other Gentlemen followed W.G.'s example, yet Harrison bowled 52 overs in the day (almost as many as some entire teams manage today) for 108 runs and three wickets, those of Lucas, Studd and Lord Harris. The boy only just a man admitted afterwards: 'When I got back to the hotel I couldn't eat me dinner. I took off me boots and let me feet cool on the oilcloth. Then I got into bed and cried like a babby.'

Harrison still managed to take 88 wickets, 72 of his victims being bowled, in his first season at 11.92, recovering some of his glory before 10,000 at Bramall Lane when he sent back three Lancastrians, including Steel and Royle, for 1 run. Alas, the following year he put out his arm when fielding substitute for a Gloucestershire player, and was never able to recapture that great pace for long.

He did return to form in the seasons of 1890–1, taking 123 wickets over the two summers although bowling at reduced speed. His action was thought by some to be doubtful but he was never called, and after leaving Yorkshire he became a highly successful professional with Bowling Old Lane and Idle, and then a first-class umpire of whom Jessop wrote, '"Shoey", whose smile when he dismissed one to the pavilion made one extremely loath to leave'. He lived until he was seventy-eight and for many years was a happy and regular spectator at the Scarborough Festival.

But for those two strokes of fate – meeting W.G. on a flat pitch and dislocating his arm – 'Shoey' might have had a great career, for he came into cricket when English fast bowlers were extremely rare.

shire's left-arm attack had been immeasurably sharpened by the advent of the slow left-arm Peate who, in his first four summers, 1879–83, collected 75, 139, 139 and 165 wickets respectively, his average cost never exceeding 13 runs. In 1883 he produced a staggering performance at Holbeck, taking eight for 5 against Surrey, a performance that was to stand for 67 years until displaced by that of Jim Laker, another Yorkshireman who unfortunately happened to be engaged by Surrey at that time.

George 'Shoey' Harrison also burst upon English cricket in that season of 1883, taking 88 wickets for under 12 runs each. But there is no doubt, in retrospect, what was to be the most important event of that summer, overshadowed as it may have been by Ulyett's hat-trick against Lancashire at Sheffield. The captaincy was offered to the twenty-three-year-old Cambridge undergraduate, Hawke.

The team continued under Emmett until the end of the University term, whereupon the greatest reign in county cricket history began, a captaincy that was to last twenty-seven years and was to establish Yorkshire supremacy for another half-century. Hawke was shrewd enough to learn slowly, thoroughly and carefully. He noted: 'The senior professional in the Yorkshire team always fielded at point. He was never told to go there but went as a matter of course. It was his right.'

Not that there was an immediate surge to greatness, for 1884 was another disappointment, the high promise of the previous summer fragmenting. In the spring Harrison, the fast-bowling sensation who had appeared for the Players (today's equivalent would be a Test selection) in his first season, dislocated his arm while fielding substitute for a Gloucestershire player in Moreton-in-Marsh, and was never able to bowl really fast again. John 'Tur-

Martin Bladen Hawke *Warlord*

Nearly a century-and-a-half ago one Edward Hawke, Rear-Admiral of the White, achieved so splendid a victory over the French that he presently got command of an expedition fitted out to act against the French coast; and having hoisted his flag aboard the *Royal George*, he led his fleet in pursuit of the enemy, whom he signally defeated off Bellisle, thereby making himself very memorable in our naval annals, and still more so in those of the French. He was the worthy beginning of the Barony to which Martin Bladen Hawke, seventh Baron, succeeded nearly five years ago. He was born two-and-thirty years ago, and in due course went to Eton, where he began to justify himself of his motto – (which is 'Strike') – better and more wholesomely than ever did labour-monger; hitting up runs at cricket with increasing vigour. He went on to Magdalene College, Cambridge, and continued to hit them up. He is now Captain of the 3rd Battalion of the Princess of Wales's Own Yorkshire Regiment, as well as Captain of the Yorkshire County Cricket Eleven; for which he has done great things, being the only amateur player who has regularly captained the County Eleven; and this he has done for ten years. And though, owing to an injury to his hand, he did not accomplish much for his county last year, he yet most creditably managed a team in America in the autumn; sparing no trouble to make his own men comfortable nor to teach the Americans cricket. And he is now about to take another team to India; for he is always full of keen love for the game, and though not so sure a run-getter as are some of his fellows, yet his zeal for, and his knowledge of, it make him an excellent and popular captain.

He is a member of the Carlton and of the Bachelors', and a good-looking, pleasant, modest fellow; and though he is not as yet a great statesman he is a good Conservative.

He is a light-hearted bachelor.

Vanity Fair, 24 September 1892

The greatest figure in Yorkshire's cricket history was a contradictory man. Made famous by one remark rejecting a professional captain of England, he advanced the cause of the professional cricketer as no man has before or since. The quintessential Yorkshireman, devising the players' white rose badge, he was actually born in Lincolnshire. A natural autocrat, he was respected and followed by Yorkshire's cricketers and public for almost seventy years, commanding such confidence and authority that he was also regarded as an obvious leader by MCC and the selectors.

A batsman of middling ambitions and ability, he played for England in five Test matches, captaining them in four. He took more teams abroad than any other tourist before or since – Australia, India, Ceylon, Canada, United States, South Africa and West Indies were all visited one or more times when travelling was an undoubted hardship. Yet when in England nothing would stop him attempting to get home on a Sunday in order to go to church with his mother. He passed on to Pelham Warner what he regarded as the 'two essentials' in choosing an eleven: 'good temper and good manners'.

At the close of his playing career, in 1911, Warner described him thus:

It is no secret that when he took over the leadeship of that famous county things were not as they should have been. There was litle discipline and practicaly no *esprit de corps*, but by wise and tactful management he soon altered that and under his guidance the Yorkshire eleven were looked on as the model of what a county side should be, well disciplined, well drilled and efficient.

Of course he had cricketers under his command but in the first instance he created the spirit and organisation out of which that splendid team arose. He has been a good friend to the professional.

Hawke was born in 1860 in the Lincolnshire rectory of the old Yorkshire family of the famous Admiral (whence the motto 'Strike'), and the family soon moved up to Tadcaster. His father could recite the whole of 'The Deserted Village' without error, and loved gladioli and hollyhocks. His grandmother danced at the famous ball in Brussels on the eve of Waterloo and the following day rode out to Quatre Bras 'to see what was going on'. While a schoolboy at Eton he began to play for Yorkshire Gentlemen (the successor to Vale of Derwent), with whom he caught the eye of the Reverend E.S. Carter, the founder, with Lord Londesborough, of the Scarborough Carnival (later Festival). Carter had already 'found' Ted Peate for Yorkshire, and his next discovery was invited to Scarborough. Carter it was who always denied that he was the cricketing cleric who announced, one Sunday morning from the pulpit: 'Here endeth the first innings.'

Hawke appeared twice for Yorkshire in 1881, scoring 46 runs in four innings, but won his blue at Cambridge the following year, returning to the county at the end of term to extend his career aggregate by another 353 runs in twenty-four innings. Hawke won further blues in 1883 and 1885, missing the intervening year 'for military duties', captaining the University in the final year when he led Cambridge to a seven-wicket victory over Oxford.

There seems little doubt that Yorkshire would have named him captain as early as 1882, as a twenty-two-year-old, but he preferred to find his way among a band of hard-bitten, some hard-drinking, professionals under Emmett's relaxed leadership until the official appointment came the following year, Hawke assuming office as soon as he came down. As no one expected immediate improvements, they were not disappointed. Hawke was only nominal captain in 1884–5, playing only seven matches in the late summer, and the professional aegis continued.

There is an excellent photograph, by E. Hawkins and Co. of Brighton, of Yorkshire in dour mood in 1884, not an amateur in sight, although the Greaseboro left-hander Billy Harris sports a suspiciously ringed cap of some brilliance. In the centre, wearing

Lord's, 1914. George V is talking to Hawke (President of MCC), C.B. Fry and J.W.H.T. Douglas.

what appears to be a paisley tie under his Yorkshire cap, is the sternly-moustachioed 'Batley Giant', the caption reading 'Hall (Captain)'.

There seems little doubt that Hawke used his sporadic appearances in his first three summers to assess his men thoroughly. By 1886 he was in full charge and the Yorkshire renaissance had begun. He was shrewd enough to listen carefully to his senior professionals and, unlike many amateurs of his time, willing to ask their advice publicly and to follow it. Hawke's success – eight Championships in his twenty-seven seasons – was founded upon the assessments of Hall, Emmett, John Tunnicliffe, George Hirst and David Hunter, but it was the captain who made the decisions, and once his mind was made up he acted swiftly and decisively.

One of his first targets was the club's financial structure, particularly the professionals' pay. He abolished the fixed talent payments of £1 for fifty runs or six wickets, preferring to award merit marks for performances according to the conditions, the state of the game, the condition of the pitch, the light and the weather, all being recorded in his notebook. Good fielding, enthusiasm and courage were also noted.

At the end of the season the team were invited to the Hawke seat at Wighill Park, the captain distributing the merit money in packets. The highest amount won in one year was £52.50 by George Hirst, possibly in his golden year of two thousand runs and two hundred wickets in 1906; this sum would be worth about £1250 today.

His generosity was balanced by his single-minded devotion to the cause, as exemplified by his attitude towards those players that he felt were letting down the side. He dismissed two of the greatest spin bowlers in history, Ted Peate and Bobby Peel, before their time. Three highly promising Colts, all of whom might have reached England status, were despatched. He introduced the Yorkshire cap, borrowing the idea from Lancashire, who wore a red rose on a navy-blue cap, designing his own white rose of petals, 'to be worn only by capped players'. The Hawke colours, Cambridge blue, Oxford blue and gold, became Yorkshire's.

As a right-hand middle-order batsman and deep field, Hawke probably underrated himself, often batting at nine or ten when he would have been five or six in lesser sides. He scored more than 700 runs in 1886–7, and a thousand in 1895, a figure he came close to equalling three times more in his career.

Warner described his play:

He was an uncertain starter as a batsman but he could drive very hard and late cut well, and when he got runs he got them in such good style that one wondered why he was not more often successful. More than once he pulled Yorkshire out of a tight place.

In 1898 he was directly resonsible for a long-needed national reform, publicly criticising the established system of selection of England's teams by the appropriate ground authority. Hawke spoke in May, and by July the selection of England's team was passed to the Committee of MCC.

As Yorkshire's captain he was astonishingly successful. In addition to the eight Championships his reign included the two unbeaten years of 1900 and 1908, a spell of nine years in which only eighteen matches were lost. While still captain, he succeeded Michael Ellison as Yorkshire's President in 1898. He delayed his retirement until his fifty-first year in the hope that T.L. Taylor would become available as captain. He became, in turn, Treasurer and then President of MCC and chairman of England's selectors.

In 1925 when Cec Parkin, in a newspaper, attacked Gilligan's captaincy of England in Australia, Hawke told Yorkshire's AGM: 'Pray God, no professional shall ever captain England. I love and admire them all but we have always had an amateur skipper and when the day comes when we shall have no more amateurs captaining England it will be a thousand pities.' It is perhaps easier to understand, if not agree with, such sentiments now than it was then. Professional captaincy has now ruled long enough for fair comparisons to be made with a system that, while growing rapidly obsolete, was not without its virtues. Hawke knew his Gentlemen and his Players; he also knew his players and his gentlemen.

keycock' Rawlin won distinction with Middlesex, and George Baker blossomed with Lancashire.

Time overtook the veteran Lockwood, Ulyett appeared to reserve his best performances for the Players, and Bates, apart from a

116 against Nottinghamshire, had a thin season. Over this period younger players – Fred Lee, Irwin Grimshaw and Joe Preston – appeared from the Colts without making the impact of a Harrison or a Lockwood.

Occasionally Yorkshire would flash into

form again, as when Gloucestershire were routed for 43 at Moreton-in-Marsh in 1884, Peate taking six for 13. At Brighton in 1885 Ulyett and Hall established a new record by scoring century stands in both innings against Sussex, while the arrival of a new talent from Sheffield, the all-rounder Edward Wainwright, promised stability in the future. The county's income had been increased handsomely by the raising of the subscription, in 1881, from a half-guinea to a full guinea, but while the team's form remained inconsistent the club depended more upon the loyalty of the members than on the response from the general public. On Whit Monday 1886 there was, reported Hawke, a 'nasty row' at Sheffield when the match against Kent was not resumed after lunch because of the wet conditions: 'The big holiday crowd trampled on the pitch, tearing up the stumps.'

It was also in 1886 that Hawke's old comrade

C.I. 'Buns' Thornton, who always batted without gloves and pads, played his famous innings at Scarborough in which he scored 107 in just over an hour, his hits from the pavilion end including one on a chimney pot on one of the tall houses opposite, another through a window in the same houses and a third through the air into Trafalgar Square. According to Hawke it was at Harrogate, later that summer, that a lady approached Thornton to check whether it was true that he had hit a ball into Trafalgar Square. Thornton nodded, whereupon the lady enquired: 'And were you batting at Lord's or The Oval?'

Four years later Thornton, together with Lord Londesborough, launched the famous Festival, 'Buns' going off to Lord's to ask for an MCC side. 'Certainly,' replied the then Secretary R. A. Fitzgerald, 'do as you like. Take any four professors and invite who you like.' Londesborough, too, gave generous support to

Joe Preston

From all contemporary accounts Joseph Merritt Preston might have been one of Yorkshire's great cricketers. As a bowler, fast to fast-medium and accurate, he was compared in pace and hostility, by 'Old Ebor', to Freeman, Hill and 'Shoey' Harrison. 'He could also bowl off-crease, all with an easy and attractive action, was a batsman who could hit fiercely if rashly but who could also defend, and a fielder of the highest class. Yorkshire fully expected him to become as accomplished an all-rounder as Billy Bates.'

'Country Vicar' (the Reverend R. Hodgson), to whom we owe thanks for his many engaging memories of Cambridge University and Yorkshire cricket in the final decade of the last century, has two memories of Preston. He saw him at Bramall Lane – 'a most promising player but he lost his form suddenly and died quite young'. And on another occasion on the same ground: 'They had a companion, a young man who wore a dark blue cap bearing a white rose, a dark blue blazer with a similar badge on the pocket and his flannels were quite beautiful – white as driven snow!'

The young Hodgson was introduced to Preston as 'a cricketer', whereupon Preston replied: 'That's good; now we're four cricketers together.'

Remarked 'Country Vicar': 'The gracefulness of that speech – J.M. Preston, most promising of the young Yorkshiremen, placed us in the same rank with himself.'

Preston was born in Yeadon, and played for that club and Rawdon before joining a touring band of cricket clowns. Professional engagements in Swinton and Farnworth followed and he first appeared for Yorkshire at the age of nineteen, his promise being confirmed by selection for the Colts of the North at Lord's. He had three splendid years, 1886–8, appearing for the Players, the equivalent today of Test-match selection, in the last-named year, a summer when he took 102 wickets at 13.05 apiece. His highest score was 93 against Derbyshire in 1887, and in the previous season he raised six scores of more than fifty.

Yet by 1889 his career was over, and he had died, at the age of twenty-six, by the following November. Hawke's comment pointed to a contributory factor to the shockingly early death of a personable and talented young man: 'Preston was an irresponsible individual who, had he possessed the least restraint, might have become one of the finest cricketers Yorkshire ever produced; he had too many friends.'

Ted Wainwright *Masterly*

Wainwright, like George Ulyett, was a Sheffield man from Tinsley, and he followed 'Happy Jack' into the eleven whereupon the mould must have been broken, for Wainright was the last great all-rounder to have been produced by the capital city of the county's cricket. In 1913, when Wainwright was forty-eight, he became coach to Shrewsbury when the assistant professional was the young Neville Cardus, who left us an affectionate sketch.

> He was a tall man with a shrewd, lean face who walked as though he didn't care a damn for anybody. There was something sinister about him. Every night he got drunk as a matter of course, quietly and masterfully.

One wet afternoon the coach and assistant were sitting in the dressing room overlooking 'misty green fields'.

> Suddenly the Headmaster rode straight across the sacred turf on a bicycle, Wainwright leapt to his feet, flung open the window, stuck out his head, put two fingers into his mouth, emitted a piercing whistle then shouted: 'What the 'ell dost tha think tha's doin'? Get off t'grass, tha bloody lookin' foo-il.'
>
> He waved the Headmaster of Shrewsbury to a by-path and the Reverend Cyril Alington abruptly and docilely veered to it and disappeared round a corner, most humbled. I was horrified.
>
> 'Ah doan't give a bugger who he was. Oought to 'ave more sense. Ridin' 'is bloody bicycle over t'turf on a day like this! T'ell wuth 'im.'
>
> The Reverend Alington admitted the following morning that he was at fault – 'my mind was pre-occupied. I had just come from a Governors' meeting. Wainwright was quite right. But I do think he might have admonished me in language a little, er, less drastic.'

In his autobiography published in 1947, Cardus described the changing times.

> He belonged to a period that marked a transition in the development of the social life of the English professional cricketer; he was a bridge from the simple and dignified fore-lock touching William [Attewell] to the Hammonds and the Sutcliffes who burnish their hair and go to Savile Row for their clothes.

He was also a masterly cricketer, ranked by Peter Thomas 'among the ten best professionals of his

day'. He played his first trial for the Colts at twenty-nine, reached the first eleven against MCC at Lord's in May 1888, and in June of that year, in misty weather at Park Avenue, he made his name.

The Australians scored 367, to which the giant George Bonnor contributed 115 of which 100 were boundaries. Yorkshire replied with 228 of which Wainwright, batting at number nine, made 20 not out. Following on, Yorkshire sent Wainwright in first and he scored 105 not out, the first of his twenty-one centuries for Yorkshire.

He went on to score 12,768 runs in the next fourteen seasons and to take 1173 wickets with his right-arm off-spin. He credited Ulyett with teaching him a grip for the off-break, fitting the ball between thumb and first finger with the finger along the seam. His turn, on a sticky pitch, was described by 'Old Ebor' as 'prodigious', but he often rubbed the finger raw and would finish an innings with it bleeding. Early in his career he often had to stand down because he was waiting for his hand to heal up; sometimes he would play with the finger bandaged, accepting a loss of purchase on the ball.

At Dewsbury in June 1894, after finishing with match figures of thirteen for 38 against Sussex, he was presented with a ball that bore this inscription: 'With this ball E. Wainwright clean bowled three men in three consecutive balls and took the last five wickets in seven balls for no runs.'

Wainwright was also the first Yorkshire bowler to take all ten wickets, for 31,against Staffordshire at Sheffield in August 1890. Four years later, also in his own city, he captured nine Middlesex wickets, Jackson depriving him of the tenth.

With Tunnicliffe he formed a deadly slip partnership, 'Long John' at first or 'short', Wainwright at second. He played in five Test matches and hit one double-century, against Surrey at The Oval. Six years after Cardus knew him he died, back in Sheffield, after a long illness, at the age of fifty-four.

Saul Wade *One Famous Over*

Wade has a place in history for one famous over bowled to the 1886 Australians. Born in Farsley, he came to Yorkshire's attention while playing as a professional opening batsman and occasional bowler with Saddleworth. However, it was his bowling, slow but formidable off-breaks, that brought him success. His best, among many successes in the four seasons he played with Yorkshire, was seven for 10 against Leicestershire, the team against whom he scored his highest innings, 103 not out.

At Sheffield in 1886, the Australians needed 19 off the last over (four balls) with six wickets standing, and Wade was summoned to bowl to the touring captain, Dr H.J.H. 'Tup' Scott, a batsman, according to Ray Robinson, whose 'batting was noted more for solidity than style, for grit rather than gaiety'. However, the doctor could hit, having on that same tour put a ball from A.G. Steel on to the roof of the Oval pavilion. Hawke knew that Yorkshire could not win the match, but clearly hoped to embarrass the tourists with Wade's unusual bowling, while the grinders, noting that Wade had puzzled earlier batsmen, saluted the move with cheers.

Scott leaned back and hoisted the first ball over square leg for six (which, in those days, had to be out of the ground); the second ball went in the same direction for four; the third was again pulled out of the ground. Such hitting had not been seen before, and in all the excitement the umpire miscounted and called 'Over'. Somehow, above all the hubbub, the scorers managed to signal a ball short, the umpires called the fielders back to their places, up rolled Wade again and BANG, the ball flew out of the ground again. Twenty-two runs off a four-ball over was a sensation.

Like several of his contemporaries, Wade's county career was short, the Reverend Holmes commenting that 'he had only himself to blame'. He went off to play for Church in the Lancashire League, and lived to be seventy-three.

cricket's cause; when the county played at Lord's he always arranged for boys from the Yorkshire Orphans' School to be given seats in the Grandstand and to be treated afterwards to a 'blow-out' tea. So taken was Louis Hall with the Londesborough family that he named his son and daughter after the Earl and Countess.

The following year, 1887, saw Peel replace Peate and stride immediately into the Players' team at Lord's and The Oval, the equivalent of instant Test selection. Yet despite Peel's achievements it was the only summer, said Hawke, 'in my recollection when Yorkshire's batting proved distinctly superior to its bowling' – a remark that may fall uncomfortably upon contemporary ears.

Yorkshire touched bottom in 1889, or at least, near enough to cause considerable alarm, losing twelve matches to eight won and finishing last but one in the table. One obvious factor in the decline was the loss, for various reasons, of Emmett, Bates and Peate, while Preston was dropped through loss of form. Less understandable, or forgivable, was the standard of fielding, which the Reverend Holmes dismissed as 'execrable'. It was alleged that no less than twelve catches were missed off Peel at Brighton alone.

Peel, in fact, would have been tempted by some of today's newspapers to tell an astonishing story. Personally he had a marvellous season, topping the batting and bowling averages, taking three times as many wickets as any other player and scoring the only century

David Hunter *Old Ironside*

Indisputably the greatest wicket-keeper never to play for England, David Hunter wore Yorkshire's gauntlets for twenty-one years. Tall for a keeper, a little over six feet, he refused to wear rubber tips in his gloves yet on his retirement his hands were unmarked. For Yorkshire he caught 952 batsmen and stumped 352, and in other matches his totals were 64 and 45. During his years Yorkshire won eight Championships, one of which, that of 1908, Hunter could claim as his own for he led the side in all but the eleven matches when Hawke was present.

A man who loved his seaside Scarborough home, as a boy playing cricket in the beach summer and winter until the tide washed away the stumps, and more than once in a snowstorm, Hunter was a man of many parts: clog dancer, follower on foot of the hunt, weight-lifter, skilled bell-ringer, concertina player and breeder of canaries.

His soft voice kept a gentle commentary of events from behind the stumps, as Pelham Warner recorded. Warner was facing Rhodes at Bradford: 'Ah, Mr Warner, you play Wilfred better than any of the others.' Before Warner could reply there was a sharp 'Howzat?', the bails were whipped off and Hunter continued: 'Good afternoon, Mr Warner. What a pity, when you were playing Wilfred so well.' Then, as the batsman trailed back to the pavilion, Warner heard that same soft voice up the wicket: 'Well bowled, Wilfred, well bowled.'

Hunter followed his brother Joe as Yorkshire's keeper, Joe ironically playing five times for England yet generally regarded as an inferior player to David who, incidentally, thought the younger William, who never played first-class cricket, the one with the most natural ability.

David Hunter at first insisted on standing up to the bowling, yet he kept to the most formidable and versatile trio, Hirst, Haigh and Rhodes, ever to play county cricket. Hirst's swing and break-back were lethal and legendary, Rhodes' fractional variations in length would have tested Job, Haigh was unfathomable, even to himself, yet summer by summer Hunter was always there, poised, the batsman knowing he would rarely be allowed even one slight error.

He wore what was known in those days as a cavalry moustache, described by A. A. Thomson as 'rich and hanging'. In his first match, as a Colt, he did not get a chance to keep wicket and in his second, at Bradford, he had to keep to Joe Preston. He told 'Old Ebor':

Preston bowled very fast – and by the way I thought I had never seen a better all-round cricketer than Merritt Preston – and I didn't know whether I was on my head or my heels, but after an over or two I took him quite easily. I always stood up to fast bowling until the late '90s and was then prevailed upon to stand back, though I did not like to do so.

Twice he took six wickets in an innings, and four times stumped five men in a match; against Surrey at Bradford in 1898 he stumped six and caught two. Such prowess should have made his selection for England mandatory, but his omission can be explained on two counts. He had some formidable rivals, among them Dick Lilley and Gregor McGregor, and, as C.B. Fry put it: 'He is second to none in catching and stumping . . . the only possible reason for the selectors to have ignored him so often can have been that the others were better batsmen; they were certainly not his superior behind the stumps.' At one point in 1891, when 3500 runs had been scored at the crease, Hunter had conceded 25 byes.

Hawke thought highly of Hunter's determination and 'grit' as a batsman and it was with his captain that Hunter put up a last-wicket stand for the county of 148, which stood for eighty-four years.

When his golden career ended in 1909, Hunter would coach young players on Scarborough afternoons, and Kilburn remembered him at sixty: 'His charm was irresistible, he never showed the slightest signs of impatience or disparagement. In ability we juniors were at widely different levels but the best and worst of us received exactly the same courteous attention.'

David Hunter died in January 1927 at the age of sixty-seven.

by a Yorkshireman in county matches. But the season's general disappointment was reflected in the financial figures, the club recording a profit of only £79 that was accompanied by a loss of £203 in Colts matches.

Not surprisingly there was a fairly ruthless reappraisal of the team at the end of that 1889 summer. Fred Lee, the Baildon batsman who had flared and faded for eight summers, Irwin Grimshaw, a Farsley batsman who had had three brilliant summers 1884–86, Saul Wade, also from Farsley, a batsman who could bowl huge off-breaks, and fast bowler Joe Preston, all ended their first-class careers. The decision was almost certainly made by Hawke as captain, and the only clue as to the reason for the dismissals came in a comment by President Ellison to the Committee: 'The great difficulty with which they had to contend arose from what I might term the "demon drink". They had to put out of the team one upon whom they relied as a tower of strength for a great many years and at a critical time they had to suspend another.'

That the Committee, no doubt prodded by Hawke, was aware of a crisis in the making is proved by their preparation for that turbulent summer: several matches were arranged before the competitive programme began, and six games were played between the Seniors and the Colts.

From this thorough investigation into playing resources, three new players appeared for the first time: David Hunter, Bobby Moorhouse and J.T. Brown. In the following season, 1890, Cambridge University made the giant contributions of F.S. Jackson and Ernest Smith.

It would be wrong to leave 1889 without mention of a curious contest at The Oval, renowned at the time as the 'Gaslight Match'. After a succession of low scores it was agreed that, in order to get a finish on the second day, play would be prolonged for half an hour. At a quarter to seven on 27 August Surrey needed another 8 runs to win, but the light was so poor that it was said that neither stumps nor ball could be seen beyond a few yards. Surrey's batsmen not surprisingly decided to play on, gas lights were lit in surrounding streets and the pavilion and spectators left their seats to crowd the boundary edge, to see the winning hit made on the stroke of seven.

So to 1890 when Ulyett alone managed a century, Hawke was the most consistent batsman, Hall was his stalwart self, and Peel was magnificent again, taking 91 wickets to Wainwright's 37. Various and many representative matches removed Ulyett, Peel, Hawke and Hunter from time to time and form remained unpredictable, the powerful Surrey being thrashed but both Warwickshire and Derbyshire beating Yorkshire twice.

Yet 1890, when compared with the following season, was deemed a success. In 1891 twice as many competitive matches were lost as were won, and Yorkshire again finished next to bottom of the table. Peel was probably wearying, Ulyett and Hall had passed forty and the amateurs were rarely available before midsummer, while 'Shoey' Harrison, who had made a welcome and promising return in 1890 (51 wickets), reached 72 wickets in this summer only to fade again and finish. Worse, such players as Jackson, Smith, Moorhouse and Brown were proving to be, according to the

George Hirst   *Lionheart*

Although he is only two-and-thirty-, it is not too much to say that he is the best all-round cricketer of this English generation. Born at Kirkheaton, near Huddersfield, he is a Yorkshireman to the backbone; and for Yorks he has played cricket since 1889, having scored a thousand runs or more and having taken a hundred wickets in four separate seasons. Though he is not so good a sailor as he is cricketer, he is willing to risk the voyages to Australia whenever he is wanted there; for he is full of grit. If he is not a great linguist, he is at least a complete master of the West Riding dialect, who has played for England no fewer than ten times. He bowls with a noted 'swerve', he bats with a daring 'pull', he fields with all the virtues, and he will ever be remembered as the hero of the England *v* Australia match at The Oval last year. His coming 'Benefit' should be a well deserved reward; and he may be summed up as a really fine fellow with the heart of a lion.

He has a good appetite and quite a nice smile.
Vanity Fair, 8 August 1903.

As Emmett's magnificent career ended in 1888 there was room in Yorkshire's ranks for another quick left-arm bowler to complement Peel, and the village of Kirkheaton, near Huddersfield and across the valley from Lascelles Hall, duly obliged, providing Hirst (always George Herbert, never just George), who was almost certainly the greatest county cricketer ever and an all-rounder who, in English conditions, would always be a contender for an all-time England eleven.

Six years older than Wilfred Rhodes, he gave his villagers that immortal, boasting question: who is the world's greatest all-rounder? Answer: he bowls left-handed, bats right and comes from Kirkheaton. Hirst, at 5 feet 6 inches, was the smaller of the two Titans, a more open and outgoing man than Wilfred, cheerful, good-humoured and with a smile, said Lord Hawke, that reached round to the back of his neck.

Born in the Brown Cow, a village pub since demolished by the entry of a new road, young Hirst was playing for Kirkheaton at the age of fifteen and was winning prizes, offered by a Sunday newspaper, for both batting and bowling. Pancake Tuesday was the recognised starting day for the practice to begin and so seriously was this undertaken on the ground, opened in 1883 when Hirst was twelve, that the side nets were taken away to ensure that the fielding was authentic.

By the age of ten Hirst had already left school, working first for a hand-loom weaver in a corner cottage, then in a dye works, and such were his prowess and reputation that he was taking professional engagements as the 'Saturday man' for the clubs of Elland, Mirfield and then Huddersfield. He was also remembered as a more than useful rugby union full-back.

Yorkshire could hardly overlook such a prodigy and he was called upon at the age of eighteen, proudly attending Bramall Lane with his gear in a canvas bag, although he admitted later that he had worn a sweater over his blue shirt. He bought a white shirt with his first pay.

His introduction to county cricket was gentle, playing in only one match in each of his first three seasons. *Wisden* confused him with one of the Huddersfield brothers, both amateurs, and referred to him as 'E. Hirst'. In those days Hirst bowled a brisk left-arm over attack, and batted at number ten. Lord Hawke thought him a bowler with 'a nice action, straight and quick', while the Reverend Holmes was already warning W.G. Grace that the young man, who could also hit straight and lustily, would develop into a powerful batsman.

The decline of Joe Preston left a gap in the team that Yorkshire had to fill, and 'Young George' as he was known, in contrast to 'Old George' Ulyett, was an obvious candidate. By 1893 Hirst had begun to develop, his striking rate improving as the season ended to finish third behind Peel and Wainwright with 69 wickets at an average of 16.

There was no confusion about his identity the following year, for Hirst strode to the forefront of the all-rounders, taking 125 wickets at 14 apiece and scoring 419 runs, playing a major part, along with Peel and Rhodes, in Yorkshire's first undisputed Championship.

Grace had no further doubts about Hirst in the next season when the Yorkshireman scored 115 against Gloucestershire, including seventeen fours, and also took 95 wickets at an average of 15, establishing himself as one of Yorkshire's opening partnership of Hirst (fast left-arm) and Peel (slow left-arm). Hirst also laid the foundation of his reputation as a one-man fire brigade, repeatedly rescuing Yorkshire from a hot spot with bat, ball or some consummate piece of fielding.

By the last decade of the nineteenth century Hirst was one of the pillars of Lord Hawke's team, a small but powerful man of tireless energy, his face and arms bronzed, a fund of good nature and humour, loved by both Yorkshiremen and the opposition. His bowling, which began with a little hop, step and jump, developed into one of the most potent weapons in cricket history, a prodigious swerve that had Somerset captain Sammy Woods complaining: 'I don't really see how one can be expected to play a ball which when it leaves the bowler's arm appears to be coming straight but when it reaches the wicket is like a very good throw from cover point.'

Hirst's ability to make the ball move in the air made him a terror to batsmen in all conditions, wet or dry. If they managed to keep a delivery out of their stumps they were liable, by a defensive reflex, to steer it into the ranks of leg-side fielders. Hawke said of him in 1901: 'It may be questioned if any other bowler ever swerved in the air, match after match, as Georgie did that summer – of course, it did not last through a long spell but in conjunction with his great pace it should be memorable as long as cricket is played.' Hirst hit, added Hawke, like a 'kicking horse'.

In 1896 he performed the first of his fourteen 'doubles', and a second in the Golden Jubilee summer of 1897 (in all matches) won him a place in A.E. Stoddart's team for Australia, where his bowling proved to be nothing like as forceful as in English conditions although he was hampered by a pulled muscle, an injury that followed him into the following summer when he began his historic partnership with Wilfred Rhodes.

By 1899 Hirst was as formidable a batsman as he was a bowler, topping 1500 runs and scoring centuries in succession against Surrey, Hampshire and Nottinghamshire. When he played for England against Australia at Trent Bridge he saw W.G.'s last appearance for England, although Hirst's own contribution to an historic occasion was unimpressive.

The new century brought new and powerful masters to English cricket, Yorkshire winning three successive Championships with Hirst, Rhodes and Schofield Haigh forming a triumvirate that ruled the kingdom and were unchallenged in their supremacy for a half-century until Surrey produced Bedser, Laker and Lock.

However, Hirst's fielding at mid-off was outstanding and it was suggested he was worth his place in the England side for that alone. A contemporary wrote of him: 'You might as well try to drive through a brick wall as try to pass those iron hands.'

By 1901, as Hawke noted, Hirst had fully developed his deadly swerve, a phenomenon that was to reduce the greatest batsmen to outraged exasperation. 'Sometimes it works, sometimes it doesn't' seems to be as near as George ever came to explaining a delivery that was ranked in its time alongside Bosanquet's googly. Hirst needed, for full effectiveness, not a crosswind but a headwind, and the vagaries of the English climate explain in part why he was more successful on some days than others. In 1901 he had a match return of twelve for 29 against Essex at Leyton on a pitch that would have brought TV crews hurtling down today, for Yorkshire, raising only 104 themselves, won by an innings and 33. Congratulated on that performance, Hirst would recall wryly his figures against Somerset: one for 89.

In that year of 1901 Yorkshire won twenty of their twenty-seven matches and lost only to Somerset at Headingley in a game that has excited comment ever since. The following year, 1902, Hirst took his place at Edgbaston in what is still regarded by many historians as England's finest team, to take three Australian wickets for 15 while Wilfred, from the other end, bowled one of the most devastating spells in Test-match history: 11–3–17–7. Australia were all out for 36, Victor Trumper making 19 in poor light.

C.B. Fry, as close and clear a witness as might be found, said afterwards that well as Rhodes had bowled it was Hirst who 'caused the débacle'.

A. A. Thomson, visiting Kirkheaton, mentioned this remarkable double performance, only to be told that the pair had once dismissed rivals Slaithwaite for 9, Hirst taking five for 2, Rhodes five for 3. There were 4 byes because, said Thomson's informant, 'ower stumper were reight freetened o' George Herbert'.

Although England could not force a victory because of the weather, Australia's escape was only temporary for from Edgbaston they travelled to Headingley to be put on the rack again, this time by Yorkshire, Hirst taking five for 9 and F. S. Jackson five for 12. Trumper again threatened to hold off an English victory until Hirst bowled him with what he afterwards described as 'the best ball of my life'. Yet Hirst admitted to Hawke that he felt he could not do himself justice in Test matches; he never liked them and never wanted to play in them.

A calf muscle injury reduced Hirst's power in 1903, Yorkshire slipping to third, yet any casual reader of the records would wonder at such judgement on a player that still managed to perform the 'double' and top both the batting and bowling averages for his county. Two years later his batting bloomed once again, averaging 61, his scores including a 341 against Leicestershire, still the highest by a Yorkshireman in county games, and one record that did elude Boycott.

That innings was characteristic of Hirst, for his seven hours at the wicket were not a mere orgy of scoring. The pitch must have been good, Leicestershire scoring 419, but Yorkshire were 74 for 5 when Hirst took charge, his hits (indicative that he was playing for the team) being a six and fifty-three fours. All this was merely the prologue to 1906, truly an *annus mirabilis* for Hirst managed the unmatched and unparalleled feat of scoring 2385 runs and taking 208 wickets in a declining team.

In a career of thirty-two years Hirst scored sixty centuries, fifty-six for Yorkshire, took 2569 wickets for Yorkshire, scored a thousand runs in nineteen summers, took a hundred or more wickets in seventeen, and of his fourteen 'doubles', eleven were performed in succession. He also took 551 catches.

He never once managed all ten wickets, but he did take nine four times. At Leeds, after dismissing nine Lancashire batsmen, bowling eight of them, he asked for the ball as a memento. 'Nay,' countered Schofield Haigh, who had taken the other wicket. 'We mun cut t'ball in half. We took 'em between us, George.'

Hirst's good nature, kindliness, patience and deep knowledge made him a great natural coach, a post he fulfilled for Eton, Scarborough and Yorkshire with enormous distinction. He did much towards making George Macaulay into a fine bowler, and Bill Bowes, another of his pupils, left a memorable epitaph: 'I never met a finer cricketer nor a finer man.' Such was Hirst's popularity that his benefit match, against Lancashire at Headingley in 1904, was attended by 78,792 spectators.

In these days when so much apparent cheating is almost officially sanctioned as 'professionalism', it is warming to hear Hirst's contemporaries, to a man, praise his absolute honesty. The England wicket-keeper Lilley, for instance, commented: 'Scrupulously fair – there has been more than one occasion when he would have been justified in appealing for lbw but he did not do so.'

Small wonder then that Hirst is one of the very few cricketers who have earned poems in their honour, Wiliam Kerr describing him thus:

> But here in common sunshine I have seen George Hirst,
> Not yet a ghost, substantial, his off-drives mellow as brown ale,
> And crisp Merry cuts and brave Chaucerian pulls.

When war broke out in 1914 Hirst was almost forty-four but continued playing league cricket, often, it was said, claiming only his expenses when he knew the club that had engaged him was short of funds. He resumed his cricket with Yorkshire in 1919 as though the Great War had been no more than a troubled weekend, hitting MCC for 180 not out in the opening match. He retired at fifty, was talked into playing a Festival match at the age of fifty-eight and, when bowled by Bowes for 1, told the bowler: 'That were a grand ball, lad. I couldn't have played that one when I were good.'

Reverend Holmes, 'cricketers of moderate class only'.

Readers of recent Yorkshire history will not be surprised by the reaction at that time of both members and public: 'Sack the Committee' was the prevailing cry. The Committee was alleged to have lost touch with popular feeling; it needed to be selected on a broader basis, it needed greater knowlege of grass-roots cricket. The members were not accused of being 'elitist' probably only because the word had yet to be invented.

As the club and Committee were still Sheffield based the southern city took much of the blame for the lack of success, just as the supposed 'gin and tonic brigade' were to be castigated almost a century later. The irony, not to be lost on succeeding generations, was that Yorkshire were upon the brink of their first great flowering of the White Rose, a bloom generated by the emergence and development of many truly great cricketers.

As to a broader representation of government, the club had been moving in that direction since 1883 when Bradford, Dewsbury, Halifax, Huddersfield, Hull, Leeds and York were each invited to nominate a committee member to join the fourteen that represented Sheffield. Although the Heavy Woollen Cup

Council was refused in 1887 and Wakefield in 1889, Barnsley (1888), Wakefield (1890) and Scarborough (1891) were admitted in turn, Sheffield's representation being reduced to thirteen although all the officers remained south Yorkshiremen.

The Committee undoubtedly heeded the agitation of 1890–1, for two years later a complete reorganisation was voted in that produced a body on recognisably modern lines: Sheffield members were reduced to seven, Bradford and Leeds were given three seats each, and eight other districts were awarded one seat each. Two new Vice-Presidents, Lord Hawke (York) and Major W.H. Shepherd (Bradford), were elected and after the death of Michael Ellison in 1898 Hawke became the club's first and only captain and President.

When, upon the death of Joseph Wostinholm

Bobby Peel *An Idol*

So great was the fame of Peate's successor that the illustrious Edwardian actor-director Henry Ainley always regarded the highlight of his life the time he was allowed to carry Peel's bag from station to ground. If Peate had fallen through too much hospitality, then Peel's fall also came about because the little man from Churwell, Morley, was too often the toast of the town.

Peel's career overlapped Peate's by five years, but while the latter was senior bowler Peel seemed content to play the lesser part, not fully blossoming until Peate's departure in 1887, this despite Peel's debut performance taking nine for 29 in the match against Surrey at Sheffield in 1882, Peate having sprained his ankle appearing for the Players. Hawke later recalled: 'Even Wilfred Rhodes did not make a more promising appearance.'

While a contemporary of Peate, Peel took 163 wickets in five seasons but his batting and fielding were such that Yorkshire could afford to play both, with the junior slow left-arm bowler in the role of all-rounder. From 1888 to his own departure in 1897 Peel took a further 1273 wickets. He completed the 'double' in 1887, making a thousand runs in five of his fifteen seasons, and toured Australia no less than four times, an extraordinary accomplishment at that time. He played twenty times for England, worth more than a hundred Tests today.

Peel's mastery of length matched Peate's, batsmen testifying to his ability to hold back the ball in flight;

he used a quicker arm ball and seems to have turned the ball more on a helpful pitch when, all agree, he was virtually unplayable. A.C. MacLaren called Peel 'the cleverest bowler of my time', a handsome tribute from a Lancashire captain who commanded

Johnny Briggs. MacLaren added:

> No one ever had a better knowledge of the game and he was the quickest I have ever played with or against at spotting the weak point of the batsman against whom he was bowling. I place Peel first on my list of great left-handed bowlers on account of his wonderful judgement, his diabolical cleverness and his great natural ability.

Peel's performance, season after season, brought him fame throughout the Empire. A cheerful, gregarious man, he took to hospitality and entertaining with alacrity and moved in such society, particularly in London, that when one of the foremost journalists of the day asked to see him he was fobbed off by a man who announced himself as 'Peel's secretary', adding: 'He does not like interviews and has little to say. He sent me to take his place.' It is not impossible, of course, that Bobby was either shy or 'indisposed' at that particular moment,

His departure from cricket is one of the saddest on record. The unpleasant story is that Peel arrived drunk on the pitch one morning, urinated publicly and was sacked on the spot. I have never been convinced of this account because it has always seemed to be so much out of character for a cricketer of that time when so much stress was placed upon behaving 'like a gentleman', even in one's cups.

When A.A. Thomson asked George Hirst for his account, a different tale emerges. According to Hirst he was preparing to leave the team's small Chesterfield hotel one morning when Peel appeared in what Hirst described as 'a proper condition'. A horrified Hirst persuaded Peel to return to his bedroom, got him undressed and into bed and then set off for the ground, explaining to Hawke: 'Peel was taken queer in the night, m'lord. He apologises but won't be able to turn out this morning.'

Hawke probably guessed that a cover-up was taking place but accepted the explanation, told the twelfth man he would be playing and, on losing the toss, led his men on to the field. A shaken Hirst then realised that Yorkshire had twelve men on the field, for out in the middle, red-faced and grinning, cap and ball in hand, was Bobby Peel, according to Hirst in 'a properer condition than before'. Hirst added that he dared not even glance at Hawke, but heard him say: 'Leave the field at once, Peel.' To which the the euphoric Peel replied: 'Not at all, m'lord. I'm in fine form this morning.' Then, as if to demonstrate the fact, he turned and wheeled his arm over to deliver a cunning ball in the direction of the sight-screen.

Later Hawke reported how he took Peel gently by the arm and led him back to the pavilion. When Hirst returned to the hotel that evening Peel was sleeping it off and then awoke, probably with a hangover, certainly truculent. 'You must write an apology to his lordship, at once,' said Hirst. Replied Peel: 'That I never will.'

'Then you're finished.'

'Niver in this world,' said Peel. 'They can't do wi-art me.'

Peel was, of course, sacked. 'Nothing ever gave me greater pain,' Hawke wrote later. A month earlier Peel had taken eight for 53 against Kent, and although aged forty was at his peak as a player.

For many years afterwards Peel played league cricket, notably for the Lancashire League club Accrington, and was later a hotelier in Leeds. He must have been a tough little man for he did not die until his eighty-fourth year, in 1941.

As with Peate, Lord Hawke soon made up with his departed cricketer and Peel never lost contact with Yorkshire. In 1922 he was helping Hirst with scouting and coaching, once asking a tall lad named Hedley Verity, who bowled swingers at the nets, 'Cannot you bowl faster than that?' In his seventy-fifth year he and 5000 other enthusiasts were at Leeds station to see Yorkshire's Australian tourists Sutcliffe, Leyland, Bowes and Verity depart, Bobby presenting each of them with a white rose.

in 1902 after thirty-eight years as Secretary, the offices were moved from Sheffield to the centre of Leeds (not Headingley), for the simple reason of geographical accessibility, it could be said that Yorkshire had become a proper county club. Reforms had clearly been necessary: in 1891 subscriptions had yielded only £90 and in 1893 the issue of the first *Yearbook* had revealed a membership list of only 175 names. The success of the team from 1893, and the wider appeal of club membership, brought startling increases, the membership reaching just under 1000 by 1897 and more than 3000 in 1903.

Contemporary historians were gratified by such progress and, indeed, most date the foundation of the club proper from this period. Only in one respect was the Committee found to be too pessimistic and doubtful of the loyalty of Yorkshire's members, for the Reverend Holmes was moved to predict: 'One dreads to anticipate the effect on the county membership of a decade of disasters to Yorkshire in the cricket field.' In fact, although Yorkshire lost their overall lead in the number of county members to Lancashire in the years of turmoil from 1970 onwards, the total never dipped below 9000, a testimony to the tradition built by Hawke and his committee members at the turn of the century. Indeed, by the mid 1920s Yorkshire boasted a larger membership than MCC.

So, despite the alarms and criticisms, the club was shaping up for the twentieth century by 1893, although no one could have possibly foreseen the golden era about to unfold. Surrey were the giants of that time, as grand and powerful as they were to become again in the 1950s, and as is the way with sporting teams, subtle shifts in strength can exert enormous influence on the balance of power. Surrey then lost that magnificent bowler George Lohmann through ill health, while Yorkshire were all but bursting with burgeoning talent.

Louis Hall had retired in 1892 but in the previous summer a lanky young man from Pudsey, John Tunnicliffe, had made his first appearance, reaching a thousand runs for the season for the first time in 1893. A Keighley amateur, Arthur Sellers, contributed two of the three centuries scored in that year and while Jackson and J.T. Brown were slow starters, Cambridge University found another substantial Yorkshireman in 1894, Frank Mitchell, while from Wakefield another batsman appeared, David Denton.

Yorkshire's early burst in 1892, unbeaten until the middle of June, had hinted of things to come, but Surrey, with Lohmann in form, won on the new Headingley ground while at Taunton the Somerset array of amateurs helped to build up the astonishing total of 592.

Perhaps the Championship of 1893 was the first confirmation of Hawke's striving for teamwork and discipline. By modern reckoning this was Yorkshire's first undisputed Championship and all contemporary reporters agreed that it was achieved by cumulative effort. Only four batsmen averaged more than 20, the wickets were shared by Wainwright

(overtaking Peel) and the fast-emerging Hirst, the last-named also making significant contributions with the bat. This was also the year of what many regard as the greatest Roses match. A.A. Thomson wrote of his Uncle Walter, who was present at Manchester that Bank Holiday, that 'the excitement of that game remained with him, warmly glowing, for the rest of his life'. Asked what was his chief impression, Uncle Walter replied: 'Funny umpiring'.

There were a record 25,000 present on the first day to see Lancashire make an horrendous start. MacLaren was caught by Hirst at mid-off from a drive the crowd thought was going for four; Sugg became the first of Tunnicliffe's six victims at slip; Briggs was lbw to Hirst, Peel and Ernest Smith then finishing off the innings for only 64.

Three Yorkshire wickets then went down for 7 to the enormous delight of an incredulous crowd, the innings being stabilised by Tunnicliffe and Brown (in the days before they became a famous opening partnership). Uncle Walter, suffering as any good Yorkshireman would, remembered Briggs bowling with a 'jiggly, bouncing deceptiveness', while Mold hurled them down from the other end. Only Peel made any real resistance and Yorkshire were put out for 58. Lancashire, MacLaren and Ward, then made 7 without further loss before close of play at 6.30 when the triumphant crowd headed back towards the city or out into Cheshire.

Overnight came the rain but in that summer, as in Camelot, the sun shone each morning and the pitch was steaming before another packed ground when Lancashire resumed play, the opening stand raising 22 before MacLaren was given out, caught Hunter, bowled Peel. MacLaren was reported to stand still for a moment, astonished, and then to say, 'Never within an ensanguined mile of it'. That story is almost certainly totally untrue but, as the editors of small-town newspapers in Arizona were wont to say around that time, 'Never let the facts spoil the legend.'

Sugg and Briggs went to the eight-armed Tunnicliffe at slip. Peel, the other England slow left-arm bowler in this match, was as devastat-

David Denton *Lucky*

Denton was, as Peter Thomas pointed out perceptively, the answer to all those who believed that to be a Yorkshire batsman was to be dull. *Wisden* thought his batting 'a calculated risk', but Denton always resented the nickname 'Lucky', once saying: 'I think a man who has made over 30,000 runs for Yorkshire must have something more than luck at the back of him.'

In another sense Denton was distinctly unlucky, for there is no doubt that had he not been a contemporary of Lancashire's Johnny Tyldesley he would have represented England far more often and won much greater fame for his audacious and entertaining play and brlliant deep fielding.

A glimpse of Denton in his prime came from 'Country Vicar' in 1912:

> He was a positive delight to anyone who likes to see the figures on the scoreboard to move rapidly. There was no waiting to play himself in; he thumped the first ball, if he could. And he hit right merrily as long as he was at the wicket. He had all the strokes, cuts, drives, pulls, leg-hits, but I think his off-side play was his main distinction. A glorious fieldsman too – magnificent in the deep. Very fast on his feet, a fine thrower and a sure catch. It was said on a melancholy occasion, when by some mischance he missed a 'ballooner' one of his colleagues burst into tears. Such an accident was entirely unexpected.

It was while our 'Country Vicar' was musing upon Denton on a sunny day at Southampton that his wife Angela went in search of Yorkshire autographs and came back with, upon one page, 'S. Haigh, W. Rhodes, G.H. Hirst, A. Drake', a page that would cause a few misty eyes among the Cricket Memorabilia Society today.

Another view of Denton in his prime came from Pelham Warner:

> … the hardest hitter of his size and weight I have ever seen and no one timed the ball better. He possessed very supple wrists. He was always going at the bowling and being possessed of plenty of strokes generally got his runs at a great pace. He had a lovely stroke over extra cover's head, pushed the good length ball between point and cover and on a slow wicket was a fine puller and hooker. His fielding in the long field and at third man has never been surpassed.

GEORGE H. HIRST
Played 1889–1921

JOHN TUNNICLIFFE
Played 1891–1907

DAVID HUNTER
Played 1888–1909

THE LATE SCHOFIELD HAIGH
Played 1895–1913

DAVID DENTON
Played 1894–1920

'Five Old Cricketers of the Period' – a contemporary card.

Denton won his place in 1895 behind Tunnicliffe and Brown, and when he retired in 1920 he came in at number three behind Holmes and Sutcliffe; with Hirst and Rhodes he saw the transition from the Golden Age to the Jazz Age. Three times he topped 200 in his sixty-nine centuries, and three times scored two centuries in one match. He played eleven times for England and scored one century, in comparison with Tyldesley's thirty-one Tests, and it was generally accepted that while there was little between the two, the Lancastrian was the better player of spin on a turning pitch.

Denton came from Thornes, near Wakefield, was originally recommended to the county as a bowler (he once had W.G. Grace lbw), and would no doubt have continued playing after the age of forty-six but for ill health. He was reckoned to be a shrewd man and when he died, aged seventy-four, he left more than £10,000.

Frank Mitchell   *Springbok*

Frank Mitchell, from Market Weighton, took an almost classical route into Yorkshire's team: St Peter's, York to Cambridge University (blues at cricket and rugby) and then the Gentlemen. After a distinguished ten years with the county, he broadened his career beyond any other wearer of the white rose, playing for London County, Transvaal, England and finally becoming captain of South Africa.

Mitchell bowled right-arm medium-fast but was renowned for the weight of his driving on the off side: 'There are not many batsmen against whom it is a heavier task to field mid-off,' was *Wisden*'s comment in 1902.

Hawke had already spotted him before, as an undergraduate, he made 75 and 92 against Yorkshire; the following year (1895) he hit two centuries. He became Cambridge captain in 1896 and changed the course of cricket history in the Varsity match of that year. There was a compulsory follow-on at that time for teams more than 120 runs in arrears, but as Mitchell wanted Oxford to bat last, Oxford needing 10 runs to clear the deficit, he ordered the bowler to concede extras, the next over costing 12.

Such was the uproar at Lord's, with booing and demonstrations – one irate Oxford supporter in the pavilion actually threw a pair of binoculars at the Cambridge captain – that the young Cambridge team made a nervous show of their second innings, scoring 212 and leaving Oxford to march to a triumphant 330 for 6 and victory.

The debate raged on for three more years before the regulations were altered, the follow-on becoming optional and the margin being raised to 150. Mitchell became a regular in the Yorkshire side after touring South Africa under Hawke in 1899, joining Wainwright in a partnership of 329 against Leicestershire and making two other centuries; in one spell of twelve days that summer he hit seven scores of more than fifty.

His love for South Africa was increased by his Boer War service after which, in 1901, he returned to Yorkshire to score seven centuries, hitting, in another purple patch, a sequence of 100, 100 and 4 not out, 106 not out and 12, 162 and 52. He opened the innings for England in Johannesburg and Cape Town in 1899, became Sir Abe Bailey's secretary and then led South Africa in the Triangular Tournament of 1912. He returned to England to fight as a Lt-Colonel in a West Riding regiment.

Mitchell also played for England at rugby, kept goal for Sussex FA, and wrote the Badminton book on rugby football. Pictured at the crease in David Frith's *The Golden Age of Cricket*, Mitchell is casually leaning his left hand on his pad, the impression being that the next ball will be hit no matter what the bowler contrives. Slim, dark, determined, he has the air of a man who might have flown a Sopwith Pup or a Spitfire.

John Tunnicliffe   *Long John, loyal of the loyal*

John Tunnicliffe stands among the first of Yorkshire's cricketers for several reasons. He was a man of iron discipline, an opening batsman who scored more than 20,000 runs in his seventeen seasons, and an outstanding lieutenant to Hawke, who nominated him the 'loyal of the loyal' for his service both to his captain and his team but above all for his astonishing dexterity as a slip catcher.

Tunnicliffe was a long-armed man of 6 feet 2 inches who was said to know instinctively where to stand for each bowler in whatever condition. He took 691 catches in his career, a total surpassed only by Wilfred Rhodes (704) who, of course, played for thirty-four years. It was Tunnicliffe's catching off Rhodes' bowling that made him world-renowned; many a batsman is said to have descended the pavilion steps, sniffed the damp, eyed the sunshine

and said to himself, 'Ullo, caught Tunnicliffe, bowled Rhodes' – and hundreds were, in both innings.

As a batsman he was, in his long and famous partnership with J.T. Brown, regarded as the long and dour half of the partnership, the Ironside to Brown's Cavalier, but that was because Tunnicliffe deliberately sublimated himself and his own instincts to the requirements of his career and the team. As a youth in Pudsey he was famous as a hitter – so famous in fact that the Britannia Club called a special general meeting to alter a rule that prevented playing membership until the age of eighteen. Young John was admitted as a sixteen-year-old, and two years later was playing for Yorkshire Colts.

His spectacular style of play, however, cannot have endeared him to the county coaches, for another seven years passed before he made his first-class debut. In that year of 1891 he was remembered for a colossal drive off a Nottinghamshire bowler that cleared the old Bramall Lane pavilion, crossed the road and landed in a brewer's yard.

He soon realised that he would have to modify his play and tighten his defence if he were to survive in the professional game, and it took him until 1895, at the age of twenty-nine, to pass a thousand runs for the first time and to score a maiden century. That was the first of twenty-two, his highest coming three years later – 243 of the world record of 554 with J.T. Brown at Chesterfield.

Only briefly did Tunnicliffe shed his cloak of care and austerity: A.A. Thomson mentions a 'screaming drive' in Ranji's direction at Fenner's; in 1893 he again drove a ball out of the ground at Bramall Lane, and another at Bradford. The Reverend Holmes, writing of him around this time, described his strokes as 'few but mighty'. His limitations may have precluded his playing for England, but he did appear for the players and was one of *Wisden*'s Five Cricketers of the Year in 1901.

Of his fielding it might have been thought, because of his height and the necessity to stoop at slip, that he would have difficulty in moving to either side, but this he overcame by the speed of his reflexes and the distance of his leap, rather like the modern goalkeeper. C.B. Fry saw him thus: 'yards of him wrapped up in the slips – alert to unfold – to shoot out an unerringly prehensile hand followed by an unerring eye'. So safe a catcher was Tunnicliffe that when one of the mighty hitters of his time, say Jessop, appeared, 'Long John' was despatched to the most likely spot in the deep.

He was regarded as being still in his prime at forty-one when, in 1907, having scored 1195 runs that summer, he accepted the post of coach at Clifton and also took care of the young Gloucestershire professionals, among them Hammond. A Methodist lay preacher, Tunnicliffe went on to become a member of the Gloucestershire Committee while his son became the county Secretary in 1921. He was eighty-two when he died in July 1948.

ing as Briggs, and the upshot was that Yorkshire needed 57 to win, the 25,000 crowd by then reeling with the intoxication of it all – when they were not booing the umpires.

Three innings of the match had then raised a total of 172 runs. Yorkshire sent in two of their amateurs, Jackson and Sellers, who after scoring 20 without great difficulty, appeared to have the match won. But at 24 Briggs hit Jackson on the pad, the ball scurried off down the leg side and the batsmen ran, Jackson pulling up in middle wicket thinking he had been given out leg before. The crowd howled, the umpire frantically signalled again to demonstrate a leg, by which time the ball was in the keeper's hands. 'Howzat?' he shouted at square-leg umpire. The umpire asked what the appeal was for, then refused to give a stumping; but when the keeper appealed for a run-out he raised his finger.

So Jackson went, and Yorkshire descended into a near lunacy. Brown, Tunnicliffe and Wainwright all followed quickly, and Ernest Smith was given out to a low, diving catch off a fierce drive, the amateur clearly believing the catch had not been made cleanly. So indignant

was Smith, a schoolmaster, that he had to be ordered to go by the umpire.

At 46 for 7, from 24 for 0, Yorkshire should have been beaten but their last four were Moorhouse, the young Hirst, Ulyett in his last season, and Hunter. It was a simple enough 'get 'em in singles' situation. But cool and sensible thinking had long since deserted this particular match. Moorhouse leapt at Briggs and was stumped; Hirst, then twenty-three and played for his bowling, went for one of his soon to be famous pulls, to be caught in the deep.

When Hunter joined Ulyett, 6 were still needed. Ulyett said afterwards that he feared for Hunter against Briggs – one explanation for his attempt to hit Briggs' next, tossed-up delivery, so that the match would be over with one blow. Alas, as Yorkshiremen in the crowd were on their feet and cheering, the ball failed to carry over the boundary and dropped, as if aimed, into the safe hands of Ward on the long-off boundary. That contest is still known as the 'mad' Roses match.

By 1895 the Championship was assuming modern proportions with the admission of five more county clubs, and Yorkshire never

F.S. Jackson *Jacker*

He is a nice young fellow of two-and-thirty, who may not be obnoxious even to Rudyard Kipling, since he was patriotic enough to give up cricket to serve his country in South Africa: whence he is returned safe and sound and Captain of the 3rd Royal Lancasters, as well as of the Yorkshire Eleven. He is also a director of W.L. Jackson and Sons, Limited; and the son of that Statesman who is just improved by his King into a Peer. Himself was sent to Harrow, where he played cricket; and thence to Trinity, Cambridge, where he played more cricket until he was made Captain of the Light Blue Eleven. Since then he has pretty constantly played for the Gentlemen and for England. He is good at most games, being an excellent shot, a keen man to hounds, and a devoted fisher; but, of course, it is as a cricketer that he has done most for his country. He was first chosen to play for England against Australia in 1893, and he has played in each home match against them since: being, indeed, so capable a player of the game that most people were grieved (and some aggrieved) when, on W.G. Grace's retirement from big matches, he was not called upon to captain the English Eleven. But he still played the game, despite the commiseration of his friends; for, as they say of him, a 'better chap never walked'. He is now about to plunge into matrimony, so that the other day a fellow-cricketer asked him if he had congratulated the young lady to whom he was to be sacrificed! Yet is he not at all conceited, for he can tell such a story against himself; and another: as when he overheard one of his brother Officers telling others that they had 'at last succeeded in making a good chap of him'! He has a jaunty step, a lordly manner, and exceeding confidence in himself: which is a very necessary quality at cricket. He has indeed shown himself the man for a big match, and he is probably the finest all-round cricketer of the day.

He is said to be full of childish simplicity, and he is quite well known as 'Jacker'.

Vanity Fair, 28 August 1902

The illustrious magazine was wrong on one point: Jackson was never elected captain of Yorkshire, often though he led the side, a circumstance that led the witty J.L. Carr to comment: 'Despairing of ambition's chiefest prize, the Yorkshire captaincy, he took to politics and was consoled with the Governorship

of Burma [sic]. There he escaped an assassin's sword by "the quickest duck I ever made".'

Mr Carr, too, was wrong for Jackson became Governor of Bengal in a career so dazzling that only Fry's can compare, at least inasmuch as Fry was offered the kingdom of Albania. Francis Stanley Jackson was an Englishman of Renaissance proportions: businessman, soldier, politician: MP for Howdenshire, Financial Secretary to the War Office, Chairman of the Conservative Party.

Born in Chapel Allerton, the son of Lord Allerton, the boy's prep schoolmaster in Hemel Hempstead predicted: 'That boy will play for England.' At Harrow his father promised him, in 1888, a shilling for every run he made and a sovereign for every wicket he took against Eton: he scored 80 runs and took eleven wickets. After that, not surprisingly, he went on to win a blue in all four summers at Cambridge, captaining the University for two years and appearing for England while an undergraduate, scoring 91 and 103 against Australia in the first innings of each of his first two Test matches. As captain of England, in 1905, he won the toss five times, won the series and topped the batting and bowling averages. He went on to become President of Yorkshire and President of MCC. F.S. Jackson, wrote 'Old Ebor', 'will always appear on the front page'.

Of his thirty-one centuries, twenty-one were scored for Yorkshire and no less than five against Australia in England; he played in eighteen successive home Tests between 1896 and 1905. Warner described his batting.

> [He] had a beautiful style and, though thoroughly orthodox, possessed all the strokes. He was a fine cutter and on-driver, excelled especially on soft wickets and his supreme confidence was an enormous asset both to himself and to his side. The reputation he gained as 'the man for the big occasion' was indeed throughly deserved.

He was a fast-medium right-hand bowler of deadly accuracy and puzzling length who could usually do enough off the pitch to worry the best. When Yorkshire played Australia at Leeds in 1902 the tourists collapsed in their second innings, losing six wickets for 23, five of them to Hirst, one to Jackson. Dissatisfied with his county's rate of progress, a voice in the crowd beseeched Hawke to take off

Jackson: 'Put Schof [Haigh] on!' Jackson promptly took four wickets in the next over and as he was leaving the field a small man in a bowler hat approached him: 'F.S., it were me who shouted to tak thee off.' Jackson, a little embarrassed, stroked his moustache and said: 'Well, I don't think you are a very good judge,' to which the little man replied: 'P'raps, but by gum, they batted bad.'

He played intermittently for Yorkshire over seventeen seasons, business or military commitments frequently taking him away, but he still managed more than ten thousand runs and five hundred wickets. His golf, too, was remarkable, for he played off one and many felt he could have taken the British amateur title had he put his mind to it.

When President of MCC he found a sub-committee in deep discussion about the exact wording to be placed on the Grace Gates. 'Why not "The Great Cricketer?"' he suggested.

In 1900 he was home on leave from the Boer War and was invited to play in the Scarborough Festival. Newspaper placards in the resort announced: 'F.S. JACKSON WILL DEFINITELY PLAY.' He did, and scored 134. Robertson-Glasgow wrote of him: 'He had dignity, not pomp; diplomacy with simplicity. He is a chapter in cricket history.'

Ernest Smith

Smith, of Morley, deserves to be better known, for he was a formidable all-rounder who, had he been a professional, would have been at the forefront of the game at the turn of the century. He was a quick bowler who used his head, a fierce hitter who could defend, and a fast and safe fielder anywhere. In 1890–1, years when he played against Cambridge, he was regarded as one of the best cricketers to appear at Oxford. Each summer from 1889 to 1907 he would leave his prep school in Eastbourne to ginger up Yorkshire's efforts in the crucial weeks of the summer.

Hawke was later to admit: 'I let him fall out of the side all too soon for he has retained his skill to an age when others had long lost it, nor has his excellence at golf – he has been captain at Rye – abated his enthusiasm for cricket.'

Smith was a schoolboy prodigy at Clifton: he scored 185 against East Gloucestershire and then 117 for Oxford against the Gentlemen, an innings that won him a blue and a place against the Players in 1891. Against MCC, for Yorkshire, he shared a stand of 66 in 18 minutes with Jackson, Smith

Left to right: Arthur Sellers, Ernest Smith, Lord Hawke, F.S. Jackson.

contributing 40: the same pair made 94 in an hour against Middlesex, and for The North against The South, also in 1891, he contributed 154 to a stand of 254 in 105 minutes.

Smith took 284 wickets for Yorkshire at an average of 23, and still holds a place in Yorkshire affections for a massive act of defiance. In 1905 at Leyton Yorkshire needed 408 to win on the final day with nine wickets gone; in a brilliant spell, Douglas had taken five wickets in eight balls, all bowled, and

Smith, with an hour to go, had to bat out time to save the game. This he did, finishing on nought not out.

He died at the age of seventy-six after amputations necessitated by a poisoning of the legs.

Bobby Moorhouse   *The Man of Bruises*

Moorhouse, from Berry Brow, Huddersfield, earned his nickname for his batting on the bumpy pitches in the last decade of the nineteenth century. The faster the bowling and the more spiteful the pitch, the more rock-like was Moorhouse, bringing to the Yorkshire team a courage and application that were to be handed down to Brian Close in a later era.

Bobby came to Yorkshire's attention when playing with Armitage Bridge, a club that also fostered his brother Fred (Warwickshire), John Beaumont (Surrey), another Warwickshire player in Crowther Charlesworth and, most famous of all, Schofield Haigh. Bobby played for the Colts in 1888 and was drafted straight into the first eleven for the match against Cambridge University at Fenner's in late May. His ability to shore up an innings made him a fairly regular member of the team for the next eleven years, his value being appreciated more in the dressing room than outside.

Moorhouse himself told 'Old Ebor' in 1904 that his finest performance came at Bramall Lane in June 1893 when Surrey, spearheaded by that magnificent pair of fast bowlers Richardson and Lockwood, dismissed Yorkshire for 98 and 91: 'The wicket was the roughest I have ever played on – I was badly knocked about and finished black and blue all over. I can still feel the blows to this day.' Moorhouse contributed 39 and 38 to Yorkshire's combined total and, due to the bowling of the Middlesbrough all-rounder Tom Wardall, a purveyor of 'donkey drops', Yorkshire won the match, Wardall claiming his

moment of fame with a match return of nine for 19.

The following year at Huddersfield, against the man reckoned the fastest of his time, Kortright of Essex, Moorhouse made 68 when Yorkshire, needing 299 to win in the fourth innings on a broken pitch, lost by 1 run. Kortright's bowling that day aroused the ire of the Huddersfield spectators and when Frank Milligan was struck the crowd roared 'Tak 'im off!' However, when Milligan, perhaps in desperation, struck Kortright for four fours in one over, they delightedly advised Hugh Owen, the Essex captain: 'Keep Kortright on!'

Moorhouse, a compact right-hander, was also a useful off-spinner and a renowned outfielder, C.B. Fry writing of him: '... he might be called quite a sprinter and had a very safe pair of hands for a steepling catch or a hard-hit skimmer'. It was sad, then, that a missed catch should have led to his departure.

Yorkshire were playing Middlesex at Lord's when, according to Frank Mitchell, Albert Trott, from the Nursery End, lifted a ball as high as the pavilion. Moorhouse, the man in line, let the ball drop about five yards in front of him and then had to explain himself to a very angry Lord Hawke: 'Ah didn't think it were coming that far. And when Ah seed it up there Ah says "Oh, damn it!"' Hawke wasted no more time: 'If you won't try, you'll have to go.' Moorhouse was then thirty-three; he played one more match, for MCC, in 1900, and died at the age of fifty-six, in Berry Brow.

Lees Whitehead   *Twelfth Man*

Whitehead, a useful all-rounder from Delph, won his county cap for his cheerful loyalty over fifteen summers when he was almost permanent twelfth man in Hawke's powerful sides. Hawke paid him the highest compliment: 'incomparable in that position, always sympathetic, ready to turn out at a moment's notice after being a jolly good practice bowler in the nets and useful in all departments, especially the most important, fielding, when called upon'.

A right-arm fast-medium bowler and sound batsman, Whitehead joined Yorkshire from the Lord's

ground staff. He scored his runs in half-centuries but in 1900 actually topped the averages, 321 runs at 53, while in 1889 he took 52 wickets at 16 apiece. In 1904 Yorkshire granted him £250 which was topped up to £400 with which he bought a business in West Hartlepool, having won a professional engagement for the local club in previous years.

In a team photograph of Hawke's twelve of 1901, which includes eight Test players, Whitehead is on the left of the back row, alongside Rhodes and behind Tunnicliffe, wearing his white rose cap and blazer proudly, looking very much a member of one of the great cricketing sides – which, no doubt, was always his chief ambition.

He caught a chill at a football match in 1913 and

died at the age of forty-nine. Long after he had finished playing, 'Old Ebor' wrote that 'no one could follow the fortunes of his colleagues with greater keenness and enthusiasm'.

recovered from a poor start, losing three of the first eight matches, although winning seven of the next ten was good enough to take them into third place. Brown, after an Australian tour, was less successful but Denton continued to thrive. Jackson burst to the front as an international all-rounder, while Peel and Hirst both topped 130 wickets. For the first time both Yorkshire openers, Tunnicliffe and Brown, the first famous pairing, each passed a thousand runs.

It was in that summer, too, that the first hint of discord between Yorkshire and Middlesex appeared, for when the 'Metropolitans' appeared at Bradford in August they were disconcerted to find Wainwright was present to play against them, Yorkshire having refused to release him to play for England, and Middlesex having forgone Stoddart.

Although the useful Sellers retired into business in 1894, Denton's arrival brought a new dimension to the batting, for here was a player who made his runs quickly – too quickly according to some watchers. But the season overall was a disappointment, Yorkshire finishing second as Surrey bounced back to the top. The weather was influential, Yorkshire being denied one, perhaps two victories; but there were compensations. Somerset, making a first visit to Huddersfield, were beaten in a day, and there were times in a damp summer when the combination of off-spin and leg-spin purveyed by Wainwright and Peel was almost unplayable.

Hirst, too, was making his presence the more powerful as the months passed, with 56 wickets at 13 and a century at Bristol. What caught the eye that summer, however, was Yorkshire's fielding, drawing praise wherever they played. The advent of younger, fitter, more disciplined cricketers had produced a class of specialists – Denton in the deep, J.T. Brown (succeeding Ulyett) at point, Hirst at mid-off, Wainwright and Tunnicliffe at slip.

Hunter, too, was in virile form, catching 54 and stumping 18, and 1895 was also the year of one of Jessop's hurricanes against Yorkshire, 63 out of 65 in thirty minutes at Cheltenham. The Committee, perhaps sensitive to comments about Wainwright in 1893, agreed to release any player chosen for the Gentlemen or Players at Lord's.

The Sun in Splendour, the badge of the Plantagenet House of York, might have symbolised Yorkshire's cricket in 1896. The Reverend Holmes rightly described it as 'prodigious': no less than seventeen centuries were scored, twelve players topped 20 in the averages, five innings topped 400 runs and four more than 300, and in five matches more than a thousand runs were scored. Yorkshire's batsmen broke records everywhere: an innings of 887 against Warwickshire, 660 against Leicestershire, 543 against Sussex.

Four Yorkshiremen (Jackson 117, Wainwright 126, Peel 210 and Hawke 166) made centuries in the Birmingham monster, Moorhouse (72) and Hirst (85) being among the failures in an innings of ten hours fifty minutes! It was perhaps from these three days in May 1896 that Edgbaston first won its reputation as a batsman's pitch. A declaration was not permitted, at that time, until the third day, so not surprisingly Warwickshire managed to draw after being bowled out for 203 (Hirst eight for 59).

In such a summer Wainwright, Peel and Hirst all paid a little more for their wickets, but the club found an immense compensation, just when Wainwright's career was past its peak, in the arrival from Huddersfield of Schofield Haigh, another professor of in-swing and off-spin. He won his county cap by taking fourteen Durham wickets, and then demonstrated that Hawke had not been impetuous in the award by finishing the season with 71 wickets. Not surprisingly, the advent of a fifth top-class bowler (with Wainwright, Peel, Hirst and Jackson),

J.T. Brown *Steathdy John*

Brown, from Driffield, was one of those Victorian cricketers, like Grace and later Fry, who were better known by their initials. His famous partner might be John Tunnicliffe, but to the public John Thomas Brown was 'J.T.' – 'Jack' to his intimates. His tendency to lisp made his cry of 'Steathdy, John' a feature of one of the most renowned partnerships in county cricket.

Jack Brown was a short, thick-set right-hander who excelled at the cut or 'chop', was a prolific scorer just wide of point, rarely drove straight or through mid-off and was a formidable hooker. At nineteen he was recommended to Perthshire by Louis Hall who had seen him play for Driffield, and it was the youth's disregard of Scotland's damp summers, so 'Old Ebor' believed, that caused so much later illness.

The following year, 1889, he made his debut for Yorkshire, against Leicestershire at Bradford. Ill health, notably a chronic rheumatism, delayed his progress but by 1893 he was established, passing a thousand runs for the first time, and the following season, after Bobby Abel had withdrawn, Brown was chosen for Stoddart's tour of Australia, winning national fame with his performance in the final Test.

The rubber stood at 2–2 and England, at Melbourne in March 1895, needed 297 to win in the last innings and lost their first two wickets for 28. Brown then joined Albert Ward (a Yorkshireman who played for Lancashire) in a stand of 210 of which Brown's share was 140, his first fifty coming in only 28 minutes, the fastest in Test history, as was his hundred (95 minutes). England won by six wickets to win the series and Brown returned a hero, four centuries to his name and top of the averages.

With Tunnicliffe, Brown now formed the first great Yorkshire opening partnership: against Sussex in 1897 they raised 378 (Brown 311); against Derbyshire the following year they broke all records with 554, Brown breaking his wicket when he reached 300. Tunnicliffe was the long, lean and patient one, Brown the compact dasher. He was also a fine off-side fielder at point or cover, and bowled what are described as 'innocent' leg-breaks which were, however, evil enough to take a hat-trick against Derbyshire in 1896. In his fourteen-year career he took 194 wickets for Yorkshire.

While he was generally a popular player he did, after his Australian success, needle Hawke sufficiently for the captain to say that he had 'more of an

eye to his figures than the rest of us'. Another eminent amateur said of Brown that he 'always appeared to have a grouse against life'.

Possibly Brown sensed that his career (and his life) would be a short one; he always wanted to score many runs and to score them quickly. He had a good sense of humour, liked to play a joke and could take one against himself – as, for instance, when the English umpire who travelled with Stoddart's team persuaded the local umpire at Newcastle, NSW that Brown was 'throwing' his leg-breaks. As soon as the local man went to square leg to view Brown's bowling he called 'no ball' and had the mystified Brown bowling from a good yard behind the crease before he realised, from the suppressed merriment of his colleagues, that he had been set up.

Brown scored twenty-five centuries for Yorkshire, played eight times for England and attracted 40,000 to his benefit match at Leeds in 1901 for a then record sum of £2282. Although he turned against alcohol, emptying all the beer in his house down the kitchen sink, he was a heavy smoker, another factor in his increasing asthma.

On the third day of the match against Leicestershire at Bradford in May 1904, he arrived at Leeds station to catch the train with David Hunter but found himself so unwell, through difficulty with his breathing, that he had to return home. The following 19 July he formally resigned from Yorkshire's team, and he died on 4 November, aged thirty-five.

Frank Milligan

Milligan loved to hit the ball hard and high, describing it as 'skyscraping', and was for many years the archetypal amateur of the Golden Age. An Etonian, he was actually born near Aldershot and may have owed his Yorkshire elevation to a friendship with Hawke and Jackson, playing first for the county in 1894 at the age of twenty-four.

He bowled fast, hit like a whirlwind, fielded superbly and was as impetuous in business as he was in his cricket. Milligan appeared four times for the Gentlemen, and toured South Africa in 1898–9 with Hawke's team, playing in both Test matches with limited success, although he did put out Sinclair, the noted South African hitter, with a well-remembered catch, nonchalantly leaning over the boundary to take the ball one-handed.

In his four summers he scored 2151 runs and took 136 wickets at 23.12, but his career was too short, as Peter Thomas wrote, for a full assessment. He was certainly a much-loved character, devoted to children, who volunteered, along with Frank Mitchell and F.S. Jackson, for service in the Boer War.

He was killed in action in the relief of Mafeking on 31 March 1900, and when Lord Hawke unveiled a memorial to him in Bradford in 1902 all Yorkshire's professionals attended. The memorial read: 'To the memory of Lieutenant Frank Milligan of Royds Hall, a member of the Yorkshire County Eleven. He fell bravely defending the position assigned to him under Colonel Plumer with the Rhodesian Frontier Forces in the attempted relief of Mafeking.' He was twenty-nine years old.

Schofield Haigh   *Sunshine*

'For eighteen years the sunshine of the Yorkshire eleven' was 'Old Ebor's' famous summary of Haigh who, from Berry Brow, Huddersfield, joined those two Kirkheaton men Hirst and Rhodes to form the mighty triumvirate of all-rounders that gave Yorkshire cricket so much supremacy in the Golden Age. If Haigh's achievements brought him only third ranking they were impressive enough by the measurements of any other county: a hundred wickets in a season nine times (2014 wickets at an average of 15.94), ten times top of Yorkshire's averages, three times top of the national averages; a thousand runs in 1904, four centuries for Yorkshire, and five hat-tricks! In all his career he scored 11,711 runs, and it was said that 'Scof's' off-drive was the finest in the county.

These are the bare bones of a career that is remembered with enormous affection even seventy years after his death. 'There is no nicer professional cricketer,' said Pelham Warner.

Haigh began as a quick bowler and as such won a professional engagement in Perth (Scotland) where he first began experimenting in shortening his run, slowing his pace and developing spin. Warner described him 'in his prime as difficult a bowler on a sticky wicket as any left-hander'. He possessed an enormous and very quick off-break and a capital fast yorker, and his flight was very deceptive for he used to 'pull the ball back' in the air without any apparent change of action.

His run-up to the wicket was very peculiar, for in his final stride his body was very near the ground,

his left leg being shot out in front of him with a very long reach. He dragged his right foot along the ground as his arm came up and for this reason wore an armour plate of brass on the toe of his right boot.

C.B. Fry described him as 'a bowler of temperament; one day the subtle spirit is alive within him; another strive he ever so hard and it is dead; but the lively day is often a long one'.

The off-break was perhaps a misnomer, for there was nothing gentle about it – 'like the kick of a horse' according to A.A. Thomson. His yorker was a scorcher. Often the break was such that he had to bowl round the wicket; his yorker, produced so sparingly that Hawke had to prod him to use it, was a fast and deadly accurate delivery, while the slow ball was also of a disconcertingly full length, described by one victim in the words: 'You think it's coming right on to you, then it hangs, and you have finished your stroke before the ball is on the floor and then you hear a nasty rattle of timber behind you.'

David Hunter, who kept to Haigh for so many years, described him as 'the worst bowler on earth for the batsman and the keeper. His break-backs were tremendous and at all times he could disguise what he was going to do. In Hawke's judgement, 'no bowler of his day could take more advantage of a wicket affected by rain and sun'.

Haigh was not an opening bowler, although England once believed him to be, and against Test-match batsmen on flat surfaces he was far less successful, although under Hawke in South Africa in

1905–6 he took 102 wickets at an average of 10.83. He helped Trott to dismiss the South Africans for 35 in 1898–9, taking six for 11.

A modest man, he was always happy to stand a little behind Hirst, his hero, and Rhodes, and whatever his personal feelings, in success or failure he always managed to greet the world with a smile, if not a joke – 'the stranger to despair, the enemy of long-faced misanthropy' according to 'Old Ebor'. Strangely, hardly ever did Haigh and Hirst enjoy a successful bowling season together; either one or the other was 'pretty expensive' according to Hawke.

Haigh left Yorkshire to coach at Winchester in 1913, and he had been acting as an umpire in the Scarborough Festival of 1920 when he told 'Old Ebor' that he had an 'athletic heart'. He wore such a broad grin that Mr Pullin thought some joking play on heart strain was intended and thought no more of it until he heard, the following February, that Haigh was dead, at fifty. 'The news stunned.'

added to the mighty weight of the batting, secured Yorkshire's second Championship.

Hawke celebrated his thirteenth year of captaincy, the Committee voting a hundred guineas towards a public testimonial which was later translated into a presentation of a portrait in oils and 'a handsome service of plate'. This was also the year in which winter pay for professionals was instituted, £2 a week from 7 September to the start of the following season. This was later amended, the club keeping half the winter pay, to which 4 per cent per annum was added, the whole being presented to the player on his retirement. A bonus fund, collected from an additional £2 awarded to each player for every county appearance, was also set up, and in the wondrous seasons of 1900–3 extra monies were added to the bonus fund. Thus did Yorkshire, much of it at Hawke's suggestion, lead the way in caring for the club's servants.

Yorkshire have also generously supported the grounds upon which the county have played first-class cricket. By 1902 as much as 35 per cent of the gross takings at the gate were passed on to the local club. Nor was the support confined to Yorkshire grounds: £25 was sent to Leicestershire in 1899 to help develop a headquarters.

After 1896 the following summer was certain to be something of an anticlimax, although a fall to fourth place was hardly expected. For various reasons the captain missed several matches, players suffered injury and neither the bowling nor the batting carried the penetration and confidence of the previous campaign. By mid July Yorkshire had been beaten only once, but in high August they were unable to force victory often enough to sustain the expected challenge.

At Sheffield another huge total, 681, was raised against Sussex, Tunnicliffe and Brown setting a new first-wicket record of 378. Schofield Haigh performed the hat-trick against Derbyshire, Essex won by one run at Huddersfield, while Jessop took on Yorkshire again, this time at Harrogate: 101 runs in forty minutes.

This summer held a particular sadness in that it saw the end of Bobby Peel's first-class career. He finished with 64 wickets at an average of 19, and his sudden departure must have worried many Yorkshire followers accustomed to the enormous contributions made by the all-rounder to the success of the county. History then records a succession that has to be described, in the words of any era, as sensational, but it was not, in fact, altogether as straightforward as it is sometimes remembered.

When Peel departed there were two candidates for this vacancy: Wilfred Rhodes of Kirkheaton, who had been playing as a professional for Galashiels and in whom Warwickshire were interested, and Albert Cordingley of Eccleshill. Cordingley was in fact given the first trial and played in one match, took none for 35, was never given another chance and went off to play briefly for Sussex and then Lytham. Yorkshire almost certainly planned to give Cordingley a longer trial, one match being a patently unfair test of a young player, and there is one story that selection for the following match, Cordingley or Rhodes, was decided by the toss of a coin between Hawke and Jackson.

What is certain is that Rhodes appeared for Yorkshire against MCC, twenty years old and,

Wilfred Rhodes *Legend*

It cannot have been entirely by chance that in his 1929 essay on Rhodes, Cardus described him as 'The Legendary', an apposite reference to one of the seven wonders of the ancient world. Born, like Hirst, in Kirkheaton, whose ground can be seen across the dale from Lascelles Hall, Rhodes was a unique cricketer whose career could, in one sense, be summed up by its longevity: he played for Yorkshire for thirty-two years, from 1898 to 1930; he first played for England in 1899, and played the last of his 58 Tests in 1926 at the age of forty-nine! Cardus could have replaced 'legendary' with 'phenomenal' and been equally accurate.

Rhodes opened both bowling and batting for England, and not as a makeshift; his defensive technique was such that he was regarded as the best man for the job. He began as a Test-match bowler, became a Test-match batsman and then, when the Great War had taken its toll, became a Test-match bowler again. As Peter Thomas wrote, Rhodes was 'having Peel, Sutcliffe and Tunnicliffe in one player'.

Sixteen times he did the 'double' of a hundred wickets and a thousand runs in one summer; in twenty-nine consecutive seasons he was missing from the top twenty in the bowling averages only four times; in his first five seasons he was twice first and three times second in the national bowling averages. Returning to bowling after the Great War he was four times first and once second in the years 1919–24; five times he reached scores of more than 190, and he twice scored a century in each innings of a match. Rhodes bowled 184,289 overs and took 4184 wickets at 16 apiece, scored 39,772 runs at 30 and took 708 catches; in his first three seasons he took, respectively, 154, 179 and 261 wickets.

He was a dour, some might say grim man, the introvert to George Hirst's expansive, open fellowship; they both played for Kirkheaton, for Yorkshire and for England, but (remembering that Rhodes was six years the junior, a long time in a cricketing career) he admitted:

> We were never buddies. Perhaps it might have started as professional jealousy. In my early days I had a ball which used to suddenly duck in towards the end of its flight much as Georgie's swerver, but much slower, of course. It was always George that had to have the wind right for his swerver; but I don't think jealousy was the real reason; more likely it was the things he said.

Hirst enjoyed a joke and is often pictured smiling; photographs of a Rhodes smile are very rare,

although Harry East was able to persuade Norman Hazell to publish a picture of a beaming Wilfred, with Hawke, in 1908. Perhaps Rhodes was always too conscious that he owed his start to not a little luck and was always wary that that good luck might just as easily desert him – although if there has been any cricketer in the game's whole existence who left less to chance then it can only be Geoffrey Boycott.

While Peel was the idol of Yorkshire and other parts of England, the young Rhodes was merely a promising trier from Hirst's home village. Rhodes went off to play with Galashiels, a club that to this day claims to have taught him all he knew, and it was while he was waiting to be called up for a trial with Warwickshire that Peel was sacked. Even then Rhodes' path into the first team was far from assured, for he had a rival whose claims, to the Committee, were as valid: Albert Cordingley. The Bradford man came highly recommended from Lytham and in an end-of-season trial he took eight for 33 against the Colts and three for 62 against the seniors. Rhodes, then nineteen, could manage only two for 99.

Both were included in the party for Lord's for the opening match against MCC in April 1898. There is one tale that Hawke and Jackson could not agree upon which left-hander to play and Rhodes was selected on the toss of a coin. Hawke later denied this: 'I never had any doubts as to choosing Rhodes. I asked Jackson to look at both bowlers in the nets at Lord's and he came back and said Rhodes.' After match figures of six for 33 Rhodes was naturally retained for the next match against Somerset, Cordingley travelling to Bath where, on the first day, he received a telegram informing him of his mother's death. Returning home he would read of Rhodes' match figures of thirteen for 45 and accept that he was unlikely ever to play for Yorkshire on a regular basis.

Cordingley never seemed able to recover from that early but deadly comparison with Rhodes. According to Michael Pulford's profile (*The White Rose*, May 1985), young Albert was well supported in his native Bradford, the *Daily Argus* noting: '...a pleasant, modest young man... a nice overhand action... varies his pace considerably'. After Rhodes had marched ahead into the Yorkshire team it seems that the Committee still had hopes of Cordingley whom, being nearer medium pace than slow, they might have seen as providing sufficient contrast to Rhodes.

Cordingley, however, felt that Yorkshire's interest was more in seeking a deputy for Rhodes and turned down the offer of an engagement in 1899 to become a professional with Wiseton Hall, Nottinghamshire. A year later he joined the Sussex of Fry and Ranji and spent 1901–2 qualifying in Brighton club cricket, where he bowled sufficiently well for the *Evening Argus* to claim, at the end of the 1901 season: 'We may be champions next year should Cordingley turn out to be a second Rhodes.'

However, Cordingley managed only two worthwhile performances, a five for 22 against Nottinghamshire and a 24 not out in a ninth-wicket stand of 115, with Ranji against Surrey; by 1903, although retained, he was second choice to George Cox. He

kept his Sussex connections, becoming player, coach and groundsman to Pease Pottage, near Crawley, and won praise from the *Sussex and Surrey Courier* in 1913 for 'doing his utmost to spread cricket among his neighbours'. He died in Crawley, aged seventy-two, in 1945, a few years before Rhodes was to follow him south, to neighbouring Hampshire.

Meanwhile the twenty-year-old Rhodes was one of *Wisden*'s 'Five' after taking 141 wickets for Yorkshire and playing for England, in his second year ousting Johnny Briggs from his place. His runs, too, began to increase – 561 in 1900, 841 in 1901 – and in 1902, by then a pillar of the England team, he and Hirst made history at The Oval in the Fifth Test. Needing 263 to beat Australia, England were reduced to 48 for 5 on a turning pitch, but Jessop hit 104 out of 139 in 75 minutes, and when last man Rhodes joined Hirst, 15 were still needed. 'We'll get 'em in singles,' Hirst is supposed to have told his Kirkheaton junior, but both afterwards denied that any words were spoken: who needed words? They scored the runs in singles.

Rhodes first toured Australia in 1903–4 as a bowler and improving batsman and returned in 1911–12 as Hobbs' opening partner. Hobbs averaged 82 in that series, Rhodes was second with 57 and bowled only 18 overs in the entire series without taking a wicket. Back in England the highly successful opening partnership continued and for Yorkshire, in 1914, he scored 1325 runs and took 117 wickets: 'He has never enjoyed bowling half so much as batting,' commented Hawke.

It was in 1903, at Sydney, that Rhodes produced what is remembered, by Englishman and Australian alike, as one of the great bowling performances in history. On a pitch described as 'hard and polished', with no possibility of turn, Australia scored almost 500 runs, Trumper making 185, yet Rhodes, with only variations of flight and pace to help him, had figures of five for 94 off 48 overs. Trumper, it was said of that innings, had three strokes for every ball, but it is also said that after playing yet another maiden from Rhodes he called down the wicket: 'Please, Wilfred, give me a little peace.'

Rhodes learned to bowl on a patch of grass cut by his father near their cottage. Practice went on summer and winter, in a woodshed, and to measure his power of spin he would coat one side of the ball with chalk. On the lightly prepared uncovered pitches of his youth he could turn the ball wickedly; as pitches improved and covering began, he turned to flight and length with spin, a subordinate weapon to use when conditions permitted and as a trap for the unwary batsman. 'If they think it's spinning,' he said more than once, 'then it's spinning.'

For a short spell he worked in the engine sheds at nearby Mirfield, finishing at two o'clock on a Saturday afternoon, which meant that he had virtually to run the three miles to Kirkheaton to begin play at 2.30. His railway service is said to have ended when one Saturday he rang the knocking-off bell at 1.30. A spell of labouring ended when Galashiels made him an offer to become a professional and, as A. A. Thomson pointed out, cricket in the Borders was not greatly different from that in the Pennines. Indeed, added Thomson, a kindly natured Borderer is likely to agree that a Yorkshireman is, after all, a second-class Scot.

As the Galashiels 'pro' he had to open the batting and bowling, at medium-fast pace, hence the legend that he learned to bowl slow in Scotland. After two years on the Borders he was advised to try Yorkshire; by then, as we know, the Peel reign had come to a sad and abrupt end.

It was in the nature of the man that he should have had the most economical of runs, bowling in his cap, a classical wheel of the arm – none of which in itself would have made him exceptional. The secret, say those who watched him bowl regularly, was in the flight. 'Is there anything in cricket, or in any game, more lovely to see?' asked Cardus. 'But the beauty is a skill; the monotonous rhythm of it, as ball after ball comes dropping, dropping on the same spot at the same pace – take heed, batsman, your senses are being numbed.' To the end of his life, at ninety-five, Rhodes would say: 'Ah were never hooked and ah were never cut.'

As a batsman he was no stylist – 'two or three effective strokes but a sound technique' according to Pelham Warner – and in later years was criticised for his square-on stance, perhaps the first indication of deteriorating eyesight. He brought to his batting a keen cricketing brain and as a runner between wickets he was superb; he and Hobbs were reckoned to have a perfect understanding. He made much use of his pads and rarely allowed anything loose on the off side to escape. One of his most famous remarks is supposed to have been addressed to a young batsman making his debut, who hit his first two balls for four. At the end of the over, we are told that Wilfred walked down the pitch: 'Hey, lad, what's tha doing? We doan't play cricket in Yorkshire for foon.'

According to A. A. Thomson, when MCC first elected a number of old professionals to life membership, all except Rhodes gave the expected reactions – 'pleased, proud or delighted'. Wilfred said: 'Ah doan't rightly knaw what it means yet.'

As he grew older (Yorkshire's benefit match was awarded before he was half-way through his career) his eyesight deserted him and he lived with his daughter in Bournemouth in his last years, occasionally appearing at Lord's where one or more of his contemporaries would report the happenings. Cardus met him again in 1950, when he was seventy-three, and was surprised to find that the terse, taciturn player had turned into an old man whose fast-failing sight had been balanced by an apparently inexhaustible flow of conversation – 'history comes from his mouth in rivers'. He had much to tell.

In the period between Hawke's departure and his own retirement (nineteen years) he, in tandem with Hirst and then, from 1919, Emmott Robinson and Sutcliffe, effectively captained Yorkshire in tactical terms, hence another famous story. Yorkshire had removed three eminent batsmen very cheaply, but their bowling was then set upon by two unknown youngsters who, with luck and bravado, began laying about them with abandon. As the ball flew past, or dropped short of fielders, or was edged to the boundary, Yorkshire's frustration, with the fiery Macaulay to the fore, was expressed in ripe and violent terms, bringing an outraged protest from one of the umpires who said it was like trying to 'keep order in a parrot house'. Why didn't the captain stop it? 'Ah,' was the reply, 'Wilfred had sent him into t'deep to save him from the language.'

One of the reasons, it was said, why Sutcliffe rejected the captaincy when it was offered to him in 1929 was because he sensed how much offence and embarrassment this might cause Rhodes who, although in his final two years, was still a very important member of the team. Characteristically there is no record of Rhodes making any comment on a matter that must have been very close to his heart. He went on to coach at Harrow but was not remembered as a success as was Hirst at Eton where, again, the difference in nature between the two men probably provides the explanation.

according to the Reverend Hodgson ('Country Vicar'), 'pleasant, ruddy faced with eyes of wonderful blue . . . with a high easy action'. Rhodes took two for 39 and four for 24, and

one of cricket's greatest careers had been launched.

Rhodes' second match was at Bath, where he achieved figures of thirteen for 45, and in a season of mixed weather when batsmen were often caught on drying pitches, the devastation continued until he finished his first season with 142 wickets for Yorkshire, at an average of 13.95 (and scored 515 runs).

Rhodes was not the only extraordinary performer in 1898. Tunnicliffe hit four centuries in an aggregate of 1713, Jackson five towards 1442, also taking 91 wickets at an average of 15; perhaps fortunately for the other counties Hirst was less effective, but Haigh also managed 107 wickets and 500 runs. Twenty matches were won and Yorkshire were handsome champions.

This was also the year of the great Tunnicliffe–Brown opening partnership of 554 against Derbyshire at Chesterfield. Tunnicliffe contributed 243 and Brown 300 on this famous occasion, the long man from Pudsey batting virtually without nourishment. He and David Hunter had spent the previous night in a Leeds hotel, and in dashing to catch the train Tunnicliffe had been able to seize no more than a biscuit. At lunch-time, such was the size of the crowd, the caterers were unable to satisfy the hungry multitude, and the Yorkshire professionals had to be satisfied with just a sandwich each. At five o'clock he managed a cup of tea in the interval and then, at the close, with Yorkshire 480 for 0, he walked back to the team's hotel and before dinner was served fell asleep, not to wake up until breakfast the following morning.

By then Hawke's orders to Tunnicliffe and Brown were to hit out – which they did, 63 coming in the first fifteen minutes, Tunnicliffe being caught when the total had reached 554. Hirst, ironically, was out for a duck in the match.

'A Country Vicar', trawling his memories in 1946, was unequivocal about the deep disappointment of the following season:

Which brings me back to the misfortunes of my own county in 1899. They had, I think, more than their share of bad luck but they also showed, at times, some very indifferent form. And the reason for this was at least partly due to a want of self-control on the part of the players – particularly to a desire to quench their thirst with little regard for the after effects of attempting to do so.

The Championship seemed likely to be retained in 1899 until a late defeat by Kent at Tonbridge enabled Surrey to take the lead. Jackson's bowling was severely limited by a damaged shoulder, Brown missed the August fixtures, Tunnicliffe's average dropped by 20, while Hirst, although batting better than ever, suffered a decline as a bowler. Cambridge University supplied another cricketer in T.L. Taylor, a future President, while Frank Mitchell recorded the highest aggregate. Rhodes, in his second season and in a batsman's summer, was even more impressive, taking 150 wickets for 16 runs each.

Another J.T. Brown appeared, this one from Darfield as opposed to Driffield, a fast bowler of a pace not seen since Shoey Harrison's days. He had played twice in 1898 but it was in the following season, against Worcestershire, that he recovered from a foot injury sustained the previous evening to wreck the second innings by taking six wickets for 19 in 9 overs; he was so fast, according to A.W. Pullin ('Old Ebor'), that 'the Worcestershire batsman could not or dare not look at him'. Yorkshire thus won a match they had appeared to have lost, by 11 runs.

On another occasion young Brown bowled a Gloucester batsman at Huddersfield with such fury that a bail flew 48 yards. Australia's Joe Darling, bowled first ball by Brown, commented afterwards: 'All I saw was a big fist high in the air, then I heard a thud and found the wicket down. I never saw the ball, it was so fast.'

In more modern times Yorkshire would either have had to give such a talent as Brown's a chance to expand or accept his transfer to another county. Despite his 57 wickets for the county that summer, Brown was never able to establish a place in the side and, like Harrison, his career ended abruptly, at the age of twenty-nine, when he dislocated a shoulder at Taunton in 1903.

Over the next three seasons Yorkshire came to full prosperity, days of sunshine and glory. Only two matches were lost of the eighty played in seasons 1900–2, and the Championship was not so much won as surrendered by a dazed opposition. Yorkshire's pre-eminence was rarely challenged, and the question in both

T.L. Taylor *Crown Prince*

Thomas Launcelot Taylor was the man designated by Hawke to be his successor as Yorkshire's captain, a position in fact denied him by business claims. He did, however, in time succeed Hawke and Jackson as the club's President, and also presided for many years at the Scarborough Festival so that Hawke's wish that Taylor's considerable capabilities be harnessed for the club were in one way fulfilled.

Born in Headingley, Taylor died in Chapel Allerton. He attended Uppingham, where rugby was his sport, but an early injury turned his attention to cricket and hockey and on arrival at Cambridge he won a blue at both sports, captaining the hockey team in his third year. He played three times for England at hockey and in 1902 was chosen to play for England against Australia at Lord's, but had to stand down.

According to Hawke he was ' . . . a lion-hearted bat; his style was essentially that of a strong defence but he possessed great punishing powers'. He batted so well in 1901–2 that in addition to being selected for England he was named, in 1902, as one of *Wisden*'s Cricketers of the Year (along with Haigh, Tunnicliffe and Hirst!) and there seems little doubt that he would have had a distinguished Test career had time allowed.

Taylor was also a high-class wicket-keeper but was given few opportunities to prove himself. When he arrived in the Yorkshire team David Hunter had worn the gauntlets for eleven years and was clearly irremoveable, although the view of one contemporary critic (E.H.D. Sewell) was that Taylor might have been even better than Hunter 'had he played regularly – Taylor was lighter and nimbler on his pins'.

Amateurs were always under the cosh at Sheffield

– Frank Mitchell once had a ginger-beer bottle thrown at him after missing a catch – and it was there that Taylor, letting slip a ball that went for four, was execrated as 'tha ugly little black devil, tha'll hev to do better'n that'.

the later years was simply who would be second. This was achieved despite the absence of Jackson, serving his country in South Africa, for two of those years, and the death of that brilliant but erratic all-rounder Frank Milligan, who was killed in the column that relieved Mafeking.

The year 1900 was garlanded in England by the bowling of Rhodes (206 wickets at 12 apiece) and Haigh (145 at 14), so it was not altogether surprising that Yorkshire's batting was less predominant than usual and Hirst's bowling a superfluous luxury. Hirst did average 40, Tunnicliffe was as reliable as ever and another of the Cantabs, T.L. Taylor, made regular contributions with the bat, while David Hunter, in his twelfth season, was unmatched.

Only Nottinghamshire and Surrey managed to top 300 against Yorkshire that season, and such was the prowess of the team that the Reverend Holmes called for a restoration of matches against England:

Let us have such a trial of strength as Surrey, Sussex and Kent did in olden times, in the height of the season and before the Players are getting stale through excess of cricket. Such a team as Yorkshire possessed in those years – a team in which every man could make and save runs and which had in Rhodes and Hirst a couple of bowlers superior perhaps to those in any other county – would certainly have made a great fight with the most carefully picked England eleven.

The strength and resilience of the sides seemed, to the opposition, beyond measure. In 1901, for example, Haigh had knee trouble so Hirst picked up the ball again to reveal that his swerve was deadlier than ever. The batting was led by Frank Mitchell, whose aggregate of 1674 was a new Yorkshire record, and of the sixteen players who appeared that season, three played in only one match each. J.T. Brown's benefit figure was a new record amount, too, of £2300.

But in a year of glory the rest of England's counties marked that summer for Somerset's visit to Leeds for what became one of the greatest Championship matches. As Cardus put in *West Country Lads* (1929):

> In one gaudy week in July 1901 piping hot history was written by these West Country gallants. At that time Yorkshire, as ever, were champions. And they were invincible. Leeds, Sheffield and Bradford had watched Yorkshire man and boy for a summer and a half and not once had they seen their darlings beaten.

Somerset batted first on a warm sunny morning at Leeds and were dismissed for 87 (who else but Hirst and Rhodes?), to which Yorkshire replied with 325 (Haigh 96), Somerset making plans to cancel their second night's accommodation. Near tea-time on the second afternoon, Cardus, a schoolboy in Manchester,

Yorkshire, 1901.
Back row (from left): Ted Wainwright, Lees Whitehead, Wilfred Rhodes, David Hunter.
Middle row: George Hirst, Ernest Smith, Lord Hawke, Frank Mitchell, John Tunnicliffe.
Front row: David Denton, T.L. Taylor, J.T. Brown.

recalled: 'During a change of lessons I was told Somerset was making a fight, that at long last Yorkshire's attack had been tied into strange complicated knots.'

Some fight! Braund and Palairet, opening Somerset's seemingly doomed second innings, hit Yorkshire for 222 in 140 minutes; the innings reached 630, and on a crumbling wicket on the third afternoon Yorkshire were dismissed for 111 and Somerset had won by 279. Again according to Cardus, Yorkshire believed that Braund had been caught at slip by Tunnicliffe when at 55. The umpire had his view impeded by the bowler, the square-leg umpire gave Braund the benefit, and the incident so wounded the chivalrous and scrupulously fair George Hirst that when Somerset passed 500 even he was moved to dissent, saying to umpire Wright: 'Eeh, Walter, tha knaws, thou'rt a reight foo-il.'

The whole point of the story, and of a glorious match, was of course the cracking of Yorkshire's apparent invincibility. A month earlier at Trent Bridge they had dealt the powerful Nottinghamshire team a deadly blow. Yorkshire had scored 204 (Denton 73) and then, to the astonishment of a cricket world accustomed to extraordinary performances from Lord Hawke's team, they had dismissed Nottinghamshire for 13 in 15.5 overs, Rhodes taking six for 4, Haigh four for 8; A.O. Jones was the Nottingham top scorer with 4. A second innings of 173 failed to save Nottinghamshire from an innings defeat.

Somerset were the only team to defeat Yorkshire that summer, as they were again in 1902 when F.S. Jackson returned to serve both Yorkshire and England. This year, too, saw the emergence of Irving Washington, the first left-hander to be played purely for his batting, 'who promises to be very brillliant' said *Wisden*. It was Washington, with the batsman of the year T.L. Taylor, who saved Yorkshire from the possibility of a rare defeat with a stand of 43 at The Oval.

That those summers were mostly good is confirmed by the fact that the abandonment of a match (in 1901 at The Oval, in 1902 at Chesterfield) was considered worthy of note. Tunnicliffe became the first Yorkshireman to take five hundred catches, while the incredible Rhodes passed a thousand wickets in his fifth season. Mitchell's emigration to South Africa, which would have been a shattering blow to most teams, was hardly noticed in the results, much though his personality was missed. So devastating were Rhodes and Haigh that Hirst was able to have one of his less strenuous years (by his measure). Particular satisfaction would have been gained by the dismissal of Lancashire for 72 and 54 (an innings defeat), from the fact that Middlesex failed to score 100 in four

Irving Washington *Wombwell Beauty*

William Arthur Irving Washington, from Wombwell, was a left-handed batsman of near genius and rare beauty who, although his county career was contained within the years 1900–2 and he died at the age of forty-eight, is still remembered with almost misty-eyed affection in South Yorkshire.

He was unable to force his way into Hawke's team until 1902 when *Wisden* declared him to be one 'who promises to be very brilliant'. A contemporary publication predicted that 'he bids fair to develop into the finest left-handed batsman in England', all this following a superb display against the Australians at Leeds where, with Yorkshire needing 48 to win on a treacherous pitch, the county had lost Brown, Tunnicliffe, Denton, T.L. Taylor and Jackson, the ball jumping around like a firecracker. Wainwright then joined Hirst who, remarkably, played the passive role while the twenty-three-year-old in his first full season hit off the runs, finishing 9 not out to give Yorkshire a famous victory.

By 1903 illness had overtaken Washington and although he went to South Africa (Griqualand West) in the hope of effecting a cure, his Yorkshire career was limited to just forty-three matches. He did have the consolation of seeing his nephews Roy and Norman Kilner rise to prominence, and it says much for his personality and play that his memory is kept shining bright by the Wombwell Cricket Lovers' Society.

completed innings, and that in seven successive matches in May and June the various opposition sides failed to reach 130 in an innings.

Apart from lacking a great fast bowler such as Freeman or Trueman (although in English conditions Hirst more than sufficed), Lord Hawke's team of those years could perhaps have been matched only by Yorkshire in 1939, Surrey in the 1950s and Yorkshire again in the 1960s. Most pundits would probably put their money on Hawke. To a string of gifted amateurs – Jackson, Mitchell, Taylor, Sellers, Ernest Smith – Hawke could add the best first three of any county at the time: Tunnicliffe, Brown and Denton, together with the astonishing all-round power of Hirst.

It was with reference to this era that J.M. Kilburn created what might be called the 'Yorkshire syndrome' in county cricket – the feeling in the other shires that Yorkshire's success had bred an arrogance and an insularity that left the team rather less than popular. This was not, of course, always the fault of the players. As we have noted, Middlesex were upset in 1893 when they discovered, after they had released Stoddart to England, that Yorkshire had kept Wainwright back to play against them. In 1901 Yorkshire, at Hawke's instigation, refused to allow Hirst and Rhodes to join A.C. MacLaren's team to tour Australia, at first glance another example of bloody-mindedness. In fact Hawke was making a point of principle, refusing to release players until Test matches were arranged by a properly constituted authority – as they soon were, by a Board of Control at home and MCC abroad.

Kilburn best defined this 'Yorkshireness':

> It was recognisable by more than a cap with a white rose. It came to be regarded as the cricket of a close community, cricket expressed in terms of high self-confidence, cricket of technical excellence moulded and devoted to a team purpose. Cricketers from Yorkshire underwent a subtle metamorphosis into Yorkshire cricketers.

It was Hawke, early in his captaincy, who gave Yorkshire their most famous identification, the White Rose badge, borrowing the idea from Lancashire who had already adopted the Red Rose. But while Lancashire's was an easily identifiable floribunda, the Yorkshire rose has never been seen on any tree, nor in any garden. Hawke devised his own version of the hedge rose, bearing eleven petals to denote the first eleven, and decreed that only capped players could wear the device.

His Lordship's wishes, even fifty years after his death, are rarely ignored within the club, and it took a radical and revolutionary Committee to give consent to the badge's use as a marketing device. Even now traditionalists within the club would still reserve the badge for players, and it is perhaps significant that the marketeers have not so far dared to sell ties or caps bearing only the Hawke's Rose.

Yorkshire's first golden age came to an end in 1903 when Middlesex and Sussex preceded Yorkshire in the table. The reason for the decline was glaringly obvious. One excellent amateur had been lost in Mitchell, while another, Taylor, went into business to re-emerge later as President. Illness deprived Washington of a season and Hawke a part of the summer, Jackson was rarely available, young fast bowler Brown's career ended at Taunton, and even the mighty Hirst was suddenly struck down with a leg injury that put him out for three weeks. On the positive side, two Colts, fast bowler Billy Ringrose and batsman Jim Rothery, made a promising start.

With such variations in strength it is hardly surprising that Yorkshire's results were inconsistent. By the end of June the once invincibles had been beaten four times, before eight of the next eleven matches were won and of the three that were drawn the opposition were happy to escape. Yorkshire's hopes of retaining the Championship were finally dashed at Brighton where Sussex completed their second victory of the summer, Fry having earlier scored 234 at Bradford.

The number of centuries scored declined to seven (as opposed to thirteen, seventeen and fourteen in the three previous years). Rhodes, after a poor start, was as penetrative as ever, taking eight for 12 against Worcestershire and thirteen for 152 against Lancashire. With so many former regulars missing at one stage or another of the season, it is to be expected that the fielding suffered. In match after match vital catches were missed, not by Hunter, who was as alert and safe as ever, but by the close field. A Middlesex opener at Leeds put three consecutive balls from Hirst into short-leg's hands, and all three were dropped. Hirst, despite his injury, had a phenomenal summer, hitting four centuries, averaging 44 and taking 118 wickets at 12 apiece. Fully fit he might have achieved his *annus mirabilis* three years earlier.

Among Yorkshire's defeats in 1903 was one by those perennial intractables Somerset, at Taunton in May, their first defeat outside the county since Tonbridge in August 1899. This was the same Taunton match in which Brown of Darfield ended his career, and Hirst took the leg injury that put him out for three weeks while Tunnicliffe injured a finger, so that Yorkshire batted two men short in their second innings.

Yorkshire suffered another severe loss the following season with the departure through ill health of their famous opening batsman J.T. Brown, thus breaking up the renowned record-breaking partnership with Tunnicliffe. His characteristically courteous and modest letter of resignation was, as a mark of respect, written into the club's minutes.

A more joyful occasion was a benefit for Hirst. Lancashire, on request, switched the Whitsun game from Headingley to Old Trafford so that the beneficiary could have the advantage of the August Bank Holiday, and Yorkshiremen showed their appreciation of the great man when, in idyllic weather, crowds of 31,826, 31,579 and 15,387 were recorded over the three days. The final figures brought in a new record of £3703, 'which in all probability will never be excelled' wrote 'Old Ebor'.

Lancashire arrived in Leeds unbeaten but their bowling was set about merrily, Yorkshire hitting 403 before dismissing MacLaren, Spooner and Johnny Tyldesley for 9. Two more Lancastrians were despatched before the score had reached 50, and although Hornby defended stoutly for 59 Lancashire had to follow on 230 behind. A splendid century by Tyldesley enabled Lancashire to hang on for the draw, still 67 behind at the close with seven wickets standing. They remained undefeated,

too, winning the Championship with Yorkshire second.

It was a placing that was perhaps better than expected, for the losses of the two previous summers had not been made up. Washington had been sent to South Africa in the hope of effecting a cure, and in all twenty-five players were tried including Grimshaw, Rudston, Rothery and Wilkinson, Rudston and Rothery winning further engagements. Yet Jackson, who had appeared in only seven games in 1903, was present on twelve occasions, averaging 43, while Hirst passed yet another record: the first Yorkshireman to get two thousand runs and a hundred wickets in a season. Inexhaustible, inextinguishable.

Denton and Tunnicliffe still contributed their quotas, the massive strength of the all-rounders compensated for any faltering of the middle order, and the bowling remained in such hands as those of Hirst, Haigh and Rhodes, with Jackson and Ringrose awaiting an opportunity. The player who did take his chance splendidly that season was Hubert Myers from Yeadon, an all-rounder who had appeared fleetingly in 1901 and 1903 and who owed his prolonged examination that following summer to the intervention of Frank Mitchell.

By then Mitchell was captain of the South African team touring England, but in the free and easy manner of those times he had arranged leave to play for Yorkshire at Oxford where, after a net, he expressed the opinion that Myers was underrated as a bowler and capable of swerving the ball almost as much as Hirst. Given Hawke's blessing, the twenty-six-year-old bowled with zest and confidence and by mid season was accepted as Hirst's partner on faster pitches. At Dewsbury in July, he shattered Gloucestershire with the best return of the season by a Yorkshireman – eight for 81 – following this with five for 68 against Warwickshire and five for 77 against Sussex. Myers finished second only to Haigh in the averages, with 78 wickets at 20 apiece, and Yorkshire felt that Brown of Darfield's place had been filled.

Lees Whitehead, the almost regular twelfth man for more than a decade, retired in 1904 after a summer of many draws (sixteen in twenty-seven matches) and of the 'Harrogate

Wicket Incident'. The match with Kent at St George's Road on 7, 8 and 9 July was abandoned on the second day as the pitch was judged to have been worked upon overnight, some spots being filled in with every indication that someone had rolled and watered it. Kent, their captain admitted, were happy to escape, for Yorkshire had batted first and the pitch had showed every sign of breaking up on the evening of the first day.

As a big crowd was waiting expectantly, the two teams played until five o'clock, Haigh performing the hat-trick with some experimental leg-breaks. The news was considered sensational in cricket: the Harrogate club called for an MCC inquiry, but Lord's sensibly backed the judgement of the umpires and the decision of the captains to abandon the match. Yorkshire concurred, but the controversy raged on in the press, locally and nationally, for some time, the General Committee member for Harrogate receiving a postcard referring him to Genesis: 'But there went up a mist from the earth that watered the whole face of the ground.' No culprit was ever discovered, and it is perhaps surprising that a telegram was not despatched to 221B Baker Street, for Holmes was then at the height of his fame, 1904 being the year of *The Missing Three-Quarter*.

In that year, too, Yorkshire and Nottinghamshire experimented with a time-limit match, a forerunner of limited overs. Each innings was to be of no more than four and a quarter hours, boundaries were not to exceed 60 yards and the result would be decided by the number of runs scored. Yorkshire won by lunch-time on the third day, all four innings having been played out thus making the time limit meaningless. MCC ruled firmly and decisively that matches under such conditions were not played according to the 'Laws' and therefore could not be included in the records. Some may feel it to be a tragedy that MCC were unable to make a similar ruling when one-day cricket was first proposed.

Jackson captained England against Australia in 1905 in the first bid to regain the Ashes, and Hawke proclaimed Yorkshire's unflagging loyalty to the cause by declaring it was to be 'England first and the rest nowhere'. This

meant a considerable sacrifice on Yorkshire's part for they lost Jackson for five Tests, Rhodes for four, Hirst for three and Denton and Haigh for one each. In three Championship matches they were without all five senior players, yet they still managed to improve upon their third place in 1903 and second in 1904 to win their seventh Championship. It had perhaps been the thought of their handicaps that had precipitated such a poor start, Lancashire, Derbyshire and Kent all recording victories by the end of June. But from July onwards they lost not another match, and they crowned a brilliant summer with a victory over the Rest of England at The Oval.

Lancashire's early win was at Old Trafford, Spooner and Johnny Tyldesley raising 223 for the second wicket in a first innings of 399 in excellent weather. The Lancashire pair had their moments, a ball from Jackson hitting Spooner's off stump, failing to dislodge the bail but nevertheless reaching the boundary for four. The partnership had then reached 33 and Tyldesley, when at 14, was dropped at slip. These escapes failed to inhibit the Lancashire pair, even 'Old Ebor' commenting on their 'delightful' stroke-play.

Rain followed and Yorkshire, batting on what was described as a 'bumpy pitch', were dismissed for 133 and 214 and beaten by an innings. A second defeat, by nine wickets, followed in the same week, Derbyshire recording their first victory over Yorkshire for ten years but this was one of the matches for which Jackson, Hirst, Haigh and Rhodes were absent on duty for England. Kent, on their first visit to Hull, then won through the bowling of Colin Blythe, whose match return of twelve for 89 won him a first appearance for England after Rhodes, who could bowl only three overs in the Kent second innings because of a sore finger, had to drop out.

Hirst, almost by habit, broke yet another record in 1905 – a figure that has still not been overtaken more than eighty years later. Leicestershire, batting first on their old Aylestone Road ground, raised 419 and then took Yorkshire's first five wickets, including Tunnicliffe, Denton and Rhodes, for 74. Hirst, entering this battered innings at number four, survived an lbw appeal before he had scored and then remained for seven hours, scoring 341 (a six and fifty-three fours), the highest individual score by a Yorkshireman in county cricket and one that Sutcliffe, Hutton and Boycott were unable to surpass.

Prime place in the county calendar had by this time been taken by Lancashire, and it was the August Bank Holiday fixture at Sheffield that decided the Championship in 1905, a Roses match that had the North agog for three days. On the first day it seemed that Lancashire would repeat their Whitsuntide success. Yorkshire's first innings raised only 76 runs, a total that MacLaren and Spooner passed, the first Lancashire wicket not falling until the score had reached 90, but the lead by the end of the second day must have disappointed MacLaren. From a position of 152 for 5 Jackson forced a collapse, taking four for 15 in fifty-six deliveries, the last five Lancastrians being dismissed for 25.

Again Lancashire made inroads, Tunnicliffe and Rothery falling for 11 before Denton and Jackson raised 143. Rhodes added another 74, he and Denton driving Walter Brearley so fiercely that his first-innings figures of seven for 35 were followed by six for 122 in the second. Lancashire thus needed 185 to win in the fourth innings, a difficult target at a time when pitches rarely lasted beyond two days. Lancashire started the third day needing another 135 with MacLaren and Spooner dismissed, and on a helpful surface Rhodes and Haigh were their demonic selves, the last eight wickets falling for 90 runs.

This victory set up Yorkshire for a final run-in to the Championship; Surrey were beaten at Leeds (Rhodes ten for 115), Essex at Huddersfield and rain saved Middlesex at Bradford when Yorkshire needed 33 runs with all second-innings wickets in hand. After the softer turf of the North the return match with Essex, on a hard Leyton pitch, proved a shock, Essex running up 521 and the famous Yorkshire bowlers having some embarrassing figures – Rhodes two for 107, Hirst none for 111, Haigh one for 53. Yorkshire needed to avoid defeat to clinch the Championship, but it was a task that seemed well beyond them after the disaster of their first innings.

Rothery was bowled for a duck before 'Johnny' Douglas struck with five wickets in eighteen balls for 3 runs, including a hat-trick: coming on as first change he knocked out Tunnicliffe's leg stump with his fifth ball, at which point lunch was taken. Resuming, Douglas bowled Hirst with the sixth ball of the uncompleted over, and two overs later he bowled Rhodes, Haigh and Myers with successive deliveries, genuine fast bowling on a pitch yards quicker than the Yorkshiremen had seen for weeks. Denton, who always enjoyed fast bowling, stood firm for 40, Hawke dug in for another 36, and the innings recovered from 42 for 7 to 98.

Rothery, sadly, failed again on the follow-on and Yorkshire began the third day 408 behind with nine wickets standing and a good Leyton crowd scenting Yorkshire blood. Unable to win, Yorkshire could aim for no more than a draw. Tunnicliffe and Hirst stayed together for 195 minutes and 136 runs for the second wicket, Hirst in all batting for 290 minutes for his 90 runs, but with an hour's play left Yorkshire had lost their sixth wicket. Ernest Smith then batted out time, assisted by Hawke, playing out the final sixty minutes without scoring a run. It was a performance not to the amusement or appreciation of the crowd, but it secured the Championship.

Both Hirst and Denton exceeded two thousand runs, Denton hitting eight centuries, seven in the Championship and 153 against the Australians at Bradford. Haigh, Hirst, Rhodes, Myers and Ringrose shared 433 wickets, with the last named being the most expensive – 60 wickets at 20 apiece.

By any reckoning 1906 had to be Hirst's year and yet, perhaps not seeing the wood for the trees, 'Old Ebor' remembered the summer mainly for the fact that Yorkshire could be said to have missed retaining the Championship by one run. That they came within this tiny margin was due almost entirely to George Hirst for what must still be regarded as the greatest individual performance in the history of county cricket. Asked if he thought anyone would ever match his feat of taking 2385 runs and over two hundred wickets in 1906, he replied in a now much-copied phrase: 'If he does, he'll be tired.'

Hirst's prodigious talents were needed, for the team was not in good shape, the school of younger players – Rothery, Grimshaw, Wilkinson, Rudston and Myers – being unable to mount a sustained challenge to the great veterans they were hoping to succeed. Jackson was available for only two matches, but Taylor, having been absent on family business for three summers, was free for a few fixtures. In all twenty-seven players were called upon, and in a summer of experiment two newcomers emerged, the Bradford amateur all-rounder Charles Midgley and a fast bowler professional from Littleborough, Herbert Sedgwick.

Midgley, brought into the side as a bowler, distinguished himself with a 59 not out at a critical moment against Derbyshire, while Sedgwick appeared to be a genuine discovery when, in his first match at Hull, he took five for 8 against Worcestershire and did the hat-trick in the second innings. *Wisden* reported a 'startling performance' and, once again, as with Brown of Darfield, Ringrose and Myers, Yorkshire thought they had discovered a partner for Hirst. Alas, the promise faded once more and neither Midgley nor Sedgwick played for Yorkshire again after 1906.

With all these handicaps Yorkshire must have surprised themselves by arriving at their last two matches, away to Gloucestershire and Somerset, needing only draws to retain the Championship. Gloucestershire were dismissed for 164 at Bristol. Rhodes, filling yet another gap as an opening batsman, was dismissed at 11 and five wickets went for 73 before Ernest Smith, captain in Hawke's absence, hit 34 and Haigh was left on 26 not out. Nevertheless Gloucester had won a lead of 5, which increased to 233 in their second innings.

Yorkshire thus needed 234 to win and at 185 for 6 seemed to be in a comfortable position. Rudston, who had hit an encouraging 40, then played on to Jessop and with two wickets remaining Yorkshire needed 27. Myers and Hunter had reduced the deficit to 11 when last man Ringrose joined Myers, and the all-rounder had knocked off 9 of those runs when Ringrose faced the bowling. Jessop, Gloucestershire's captain, put himself back on to bowl

and his first delivery was a near wide down the leg side that would have given Yorkshire victory had not John Board, the wicket-keeper, dived, got the tip of his glove to the ball and turned it back to hold it. Two balls later the left-handed Ringrose was leg before, Gloucester had won by one and Yorkshire's Championship chance had gone.

Yorkshire remained the premier attraction on the county circuit, bringing 80,000 to The Oval in three days to watch the benefit of Surrey's Yorkshire-born Walter Lees. This was also the year of the curious but well-remembered appearance of Cecil Parkin, later to become so famous with Lancashire and England.

Parkin was one of the younger players called up in the diligent search for new talent, and he appeared against Gloucestershire at Headingley in the first week in July, taking two for 23 in the first innings. He did not score and bowled only two overs in the second innings, whereupon it was discovered that he had been born on the wrong (Durham) side of the Tees and was therefore not qualified by birth. An obviously shocked 'Old Ebor' intoned: 'The Yorkshire Committee and Lord Hawke did not require to be told their duty in the matter.'

Parkin, not surprisingly, had a different version of events, as he recorded in his memoirs.

I was born at Eaglescliffe, near Yarm, 20 yards over the Yorkshire border. That season [1906] I played for Yorkshire II in several matches, taking 13 wickets at an average of 14.30 so you can guess that I was delighted when I received the invitation to play with the Yorkshire County Eleven. And my two wickets for a score or so runs delighted me still more.

Imagine my disappointment when, after one match with the White Rose the news reached me that I had been disqualified from playing for Yorkshire because my birthplace was not actually in Yorkshire. But let me say here that Lord Hawke was fully aware, when I first played for Yorkshire, that I was born in Durham. I did not get into the Yorkshire Eleven under false pretences. And it was not, as the story goes, Yorkshire County that got me disqualified. The MCC did the disqualification from information received from some evidently kind friend of mine.

Parkin, a stormy petrel in his career with

Lancashire, retained one memory of his Yorkshire match:

> I had a severe attack of nerves as I was going on to bowl. As I was rolling up my sleeves, I was only a nipper, with my fingers trembling on the ball, I got a pat on the back. It was George Hirst who, with a kindly glance, said 'Don't worry, just stick at it.' He is a human being in a thousand.

The season of 1907 was that seeming rarity, a damp summer. The loss of a whole day's play was thought worthy of mention, and May of that year was fairly dreadful even by the standards of the 1980s, not a match being completed for four weeks.

Fry's 85 at Sheffield led to a Sussex victory, but from 13 July to 21 August Yorkshire were unbeaten, Worcestershire then completing a rare double. They had won at Worcester on a fast pitch, and then won again at Bradford when Yorkshire did have an excuse, being without Hirst, Hawke, Rhodes and Rothery for various reasons. Nottinghamshire were the eventual champions and it was to Yorkshire's abiding regret that the weather prevented the two teams from getting to grips; play was abandoned at Trent Bridge with Yorkshire on 47 for 1, while not a ball was bowled in the return fixture at Huddersfield.

By calling on another twenty-four players Yorkshire signalled they were not happy with the composition of the team. Even those stalwarts Tunnicliffe and Hirst were showing signs of the wear and tear of many years of professional cricket, although it was in this summer that both passed 20,000 runs for the county.

Indeed, it turned out to be Tunnicliffe's last season – his seventeenth – his retirement being hastened by an excellent offer of the position of cricket coach to Clifton College. His departure must have saddened a few, for it was probably difficult to imagine Yorkshire without his long lean figure emerging to open the innings or taking his customary position at first slip.

That the old order was changing was never more evident. Jackson and Ernest Smith each appeared only once; Rothery was ill from June until August and played only one more innings, for 2 runs, before being injured; Grimshaw, Myers and Rudston all faded, although the left-handed Wilkinson remained an interesting prospect. W.E., the son of the great Billy Bates, made a first appearance and seemed to be a great outfielder in the making. In all the circumstances Yorkshire's finishing joint second with Worcestershire was a minor miracle; perhaps it was that the team was simply carried on to some victories by the sheer momentum gained in the great years.

Hawke celebrated his twenty-fifth year as captain in 1908, an extraordinary service in any era, and with a team sadly lacking in great names nevertheless managed to win an eighth Championship – an achievement, opined 'Old Ebor', 'that created as much surprise in Yorkshire as it did throughout the country'. The team picture of that year, taken at Headingley in July under some blessed foliage, shows six very familiar faces along the front row: Haigh, Hirst, Hawke, Hunter, Denton and Rhodes. Otherwise we are faced with relative 'unknowns'.

Completing the front row is Billy Wilkinson, the left-hander from Thorpe Hesley whose form that year – 1232 runs at 24 – brought him a county cap. This was his one sound year, however, and he was never able to sustain that form, departing in 1910 after having spent seven years trying to establish himself.

Uncapped players on the back row are Billy (William Edric) Bates junior, mentioned above. Like his famous father he was an elegant dresser, so it was not unnatural that, his father having been nicknamed 'The Duke', Junior should be known in the dressing room as 'The Marquis'. He was always a brilliant fielder but his batting suffered, inevitably, by comparison with his father's and after six seasons he moved on to Glamorgan where he enjoyed much more success, founding a famous opening partnership with another Yorkshireman, Arnold Dyson.

Another contributor to the Championship was Charlie Hardisty from Leeds who played so well in the match against the Rest of England that year (66 and 59) that *Wisden* seriously suggested that Yorkshire had found a successor to J.T. Brown. The following year Hardisty could hardly put an innings together, and dropped out of the side.

Rothery and Myers had both won their caps without achieving a consistency of form, but the tall remaining figure is of considerable interest: Jack Newstead, from Middlesbrough. He stands proudly in what appears to be a new Yorkshire cap, but glowering as if he knew what to expect from a tantalising fate: tried as a batsman in two matches in 1903, he went on to the ground staff at Lord's where Yorkshire refused his request to qualify for Middlesex.

Four years later he was recalled by Yorkshire as a right-arm medium to fast bowler whose repertoire included what was described as a 'fast off-break'. He had an extraordinary spell against Kent of 17–14–3–2 and followed that, at Bradford, by taking seven Worcestershire wickets for 10. His impact on the 1908 season was enormous and there is no doubt that his contribution, supporting the veterans, propelled Yorkshire to the Championship, for Newstead took 131 wickets at 15 and scored 885 runs at 25. 'Had there been a Test match that season,' wrote 'Old Ebor', 'Newstead would have been chosen as leader of the England attack.' His consolation was to be one of *Wisden*'s Five Cricketers of the Year.

Newstead owed his advance partly to a damaging injury to Haigh, who suffered a broken finger when batting against Brearley of Lancashire in the Whitsuntide Roses match. Haigh was unable to bowl for several weeks and struggled to regain his former grip and power of spin, but he nevertheless managed 97 wickets to supplement Rhodes' 100 while the almighty Hirst, at the age of thirty-seven, scored 1513 runs and took 164 wickets.

As for Newstead, his decline after that one glorious summer was sad and inexplicable: 89 wickets in 1909, 36 the following year, and only 19 in 1911. The harder he tried, thought 'Old Ebor', the more difficult he found it to regain that perfect length and 'fizz' that had made him such a prodigy in1908. His batting, too, declined almost as quickly and it was Hawke, an admirer of his play, who summed up: 'Who would have believed that he was to be virtually a one-season man, being also a careful, capable bat into the bargain?'

More than Newstead had their moments in Yorkshire's summer without defeat: Wilkinson

hit 1200 runs, Hardisty 733, Rothery 735, the latter pair sharing the job of opening the innings with Rhodes (a sight that must have brought many a sigh for Tunnicliffe and Brown from the Bramall Lane grinders). Rothery's 161 against Kent at Dover was described as an innings of considerable force and artistry.

'Old Ebor' described 1908's success as the 'clean sheet Championship', and such was the all-round level of bowling and fielding that only twice did the opposition reach more than 300 in an innings – Leicestershire and the Rest of England. Yorkshire–Middlesex rivalry was again keen, Yorkshire winning at Lord's by three wickets after being required to score 127 in the last innings. At Bradford Yorkshire felt confident enough to declare at 153 for 1 in the second innings and were a little shaken when Middlesex finished only 36 short of victory with eight wickets standing. In contrast, Northamptonshire were dismissed for 27 and 15 at Northampton.

But many Yorkshiremen will have noted the year for the celebration of Hawke's twenty-five years of captaincy. The club raised a fund of £1000 and the *Yorkshire Evening Post* another £824 through their 'Tyke Fund', the 'Tyke' being a creation of that newspaper's cartoonist, J.A. Dodgson. Hawke, in selecting his gifts, chose six heirlooms. The crowd watched and applauded the presentation, at Headingley in July, and went off in high good humour, Nottinghamshire having been beaten by 140 runs.

The following summer the expected decline in the team's performance occurred, a year later than expected, perhaps, but none the less disappointing. Hardisty, Bates and Newstead slipped backwards, Rothery stood still, Wilkinson was less successful (but a thumb injury removed him from several matches and must have affected his form). More trials were needed and two more promising newcomers were found: a stubborn and useful batsman in Benny Wilson, who actually reached a thousand runs in his first full season, and a player whose actual entry was that of a left-handed batsman, the piratically named Alonzo Drake.

An invaluable account of cricket at all levels in this period comes from the memoirs of E.J.,

Alonzo Drake *Lonza*

Although Hawke believed that Drake's temperament would prevent his becoming a player 'of the highest rank', his sudden death in 1919, from heart disease, at the age of thirty-five, was a major blow to Yorkshire for he and Major Booth, who had been killed in the Great War, were the bowling partnership expected to carry the county into the middle of the 1920s.

Like many families in the mid-nineteenth century the Drakes moved from the land, near Huddersfield, towards the great new industrial cities and Alonzo was born at Parkgate, near Rotherham, his father seeking a better living in the coal and steel industries of South Yorkshire. The boy had an obvious leaning to sport and his early promise at soccer took him from Rotherham Town Reserves to Doncaster Rovers, then in the Second Division, scoring as a seventeen-year-old debutant. He went on to play for Sheffield United (24 goals in the First Division), Birmingham City, Queen's Park Rangers and Huddersfield Town before his cricketing form with Honley, in the Huddersfield League, attracted Yorkshire's attention.

He played for the Colts, a left-arm medium-pace bowler and punishing left-handed batsman, in 1908, and Yorkshire felt there was sufficient promise to move him to Harrogate for the following summer; his record there persuaded the Committee, that August, that he should be tried in the first team as deputy to Hirst, who needed a rest. Drake took four for 34 against Derbyshire and was returned for the following match, against Middlesex, in which he took six for 34 in 9 overs, four wickets falling in one over.

Like many players he failed to justify himself in his second season, but by 1911 he swept into the side, scoring 1500 runs and taking 84 wickets at 21 each; in 1913 he did the 'double', topping the Yorkshire bowling averages with 115 wickets (seven for 7 against Somerset at Bath) and in that sad summer of 1914 rode the fields of England like another Hirst, finishing with 158 wickets.

Against Derbyshire he took five for 6, their innings collapsing from 67 for 4 to 68 all out; he and Booth bowled unchanged in an innings victory at Bristol and then, at Weston-super-Mare, Somerset were dismissed by the pair for 44 and in the second innings Drake entered history with an analysis of 8.5–0–35–10.

He twice volunteered for war service and was

rejected as unfit, continuing his cricket for Honley and playing the occasional charity game, but even then it was clear his health was failing. Snooker was another love and in February 1919, after having been advised by his doctor to stay indoors, he insisted on attending the local Liberal Club to play a match. Three mornings later he suffered a heart attack and died.

He was remembered affectionately by the team as a man of droll humour and for his spells of what Peter Thomas described as 'swift destruction'. On damaged pitches his swing and break either way made him a deadly proposition, but he was known to become downcast on his less successful days, hence Hawke's view of his temperament. 'Lonza' deserves to be better remembered, for he was, as Mick Pope pointed out in his excellent essay, the bowler who beat Verity to all ten.

later Sir Everard, Radcliffe who occasionally deputised for Hawke as captain and eventually succeeded to that position, once half-humorously described by J.L. Carr as 'the greatest honour an Englishman can aspire to'. He arrived at Downside in May 1894.

There was one ground on the site of the present one, but only about half of its present size. Except on 1st XI match days, when the whole ground was reserved for the XI, the 1st and 3rd games played there, the 2nd on a pitch between the school buildings and big chestnut tree, and the 4th between the Old house and the new swimming baths. It was to the 4th game I was allocated, and I gradually crept up until in 1898 I played twice for the 1st XI. In 1896 a match was played between Mr Roper's school, then at Bournemouth, and an under-14 XI of Downside, in which I distinguished myself by taking 7 wickets for 7 runs. I daresay I was perhaps unusually promising as a slow leg break bowler as the ball turned sharply without any great effort on my behalf. Unfortunately in November 1897 I had to have an operation for hernia, and the surgeon forbad me to bowl the following season, with the result that I found I had entirely lost my natural leg break, indeed I have never been able to bowl from the same finger since then.

Except for Bruno Hicks, Charlie Nevile, and perhaps Thaedie Ryan, there were few cricketers of any note amongst the boys during my time, but Sebastian Cave, an outstanding athlete in every department, Joe McEvoy and one or two others were good players amongst the Masters, though how they managed to play any game with efficiency is difficult to fathom, as the Monks always had to be attired in black trousers and unsuitable kit all round.

There was little coaching in my time, in the first place few knew sufficient about the game, and the few professionals were poor coaches. If only I had been taught the real rudiments of the game I might have been a fifty per cent better player than I was. I captained the XI in 1900 and 1901, anyhow for the first time, because there was really no one else! We opposed few teams of any note, or indeed few players of eminence either, though I remember Paish, then about the second best slow bowler in England, being hit all over the place by Charlie Nevile, and several visits by Board, the Gloucestershire wicket keeper, and Jimmy Cranston, a well known left-hand bat for that county. The latter was fond of a little jump-

ing powder before going in to bat, and used to regale himself heartily from the contents of a silver flask!

George Nicholls, a Somerset player, coached for a period in 1900, and in 1901; being left without a coach, my father enlisted the services of Lord Hawke, who prevailed on the celebrated Tom Emmett to come. Tom had been one of the stalwarts of the Yorkshire XI in previous years, but was really beyond his job in 1901. He was, as he had always been, a great and really amusing wit, but having been afflicted to his detriment with an ever present thirst he was more intent on warning the young against the evils of alcohol than on teaching cricket. Constantly did he say 'Mr Radcliffe beware o' drink for it was fair ruin o' me!' Poor old Emmett became a great responsibility of mine, and one day it was reported to me he had not been seen for twenty-four hours. In due course he was found wandering on a railway line and taken to Leicester Asylum where he died.

During the summer holidays I spent the whole time either playing or watching cricket and I recollect the Australians at Cheltenham in, I think, 1895 and 1896, Blackham, who wore a beard, keeping wicket, Ferris with his curious semi-circular run up to the wicket when bowling, Murdoch, Trumble, George Giffen, the incomparable 'W.G.' and others. When at Rudding I was frequently at Bradford or Headingley with my Uncle Henry, who rarely missed a Yorkshire match, and usually Canon Wood. I have recollections of seeing Bobby Peel, who was the best left-hand bowler in England, Wainwright, John Tunnicliffe and others of the then Yorkshire side, and of Stoddart, and McGregor of Middlesex and Lionel Palairet and Hewett of Somerset. I think Palairet and Spooner were the two most graceful batsmen, with perhaps Stan Jackson and Frank Woolley very close seconds, whom I ever saw.

Fred Corballis, a great friend of the family, invited me to stay with him at Manchester for a Roses Match, and there I watched the great ones of the day, Monkey Hornby, Albert Ward, Mold, etc. competing against the Tykes. Mold was a very fast right-arm bowler, but he and Tyler were 'warned off' around 1900 owing to suspected deliveries.

It was in 1900 I think that I was lucky enough to see a hundred made in the then record time of forty minutes for a first class match. It was at Harrogate where Yorkshire was playing Gloucestershire and the century, 101 to be exact, was made of course by the incomparable G.L. Jessop, with whom W.G. Grace was in for a time and Frank Bateman-Champain for the remainder. I think Champain later entered the Established Church and eventually became Bishop of Knaresborough.

In 1902 I played little cricket until the end of July, and then only a few village matches. The following two years I played for Christ Church and intermittently in 1905, but I had no time for anything except work until after the end of term in 1906. It is sad to recollect that out of three teams some 70 per cent were killed in the 1914 War.

I was very gratified, owing to the kindness of C.E. de Trafford, at being made a member of I Zingari in 1903. Ned de Trafford was Captain of Leicestershire, a very hard hitting batsman, a splendid man to hounds and a connoisseur of port! He rarely spoke at all and enjoyed the name of 'Noisy' amongst his intimates! I think he and Tim O'Brien, both Uncles of Charles Moore, were the only Catholic members of I Zingari in those days.

In 1907 I played for Yorkshire 2nd XI at The Oval, scoring I think either 19 or 29, and it was through taking part in this Match I became associated, as related elsewhere, with Galloway.

At Skaife, by Blubberhouses, Galloway had a little cricket ground whence he gathered many of the elite, Stan Jackson, Bosanquet, Hewett, Gilbert, Joe Hornsby, Charles Wright with his glass eye which, not pleasant to relate, he used to pop in and out! and others of past England & Gents v Players fame taking part. I have vivid recollections of a Match in which one Moss was an opponent. This Moss played for one of the Yorkshire Council teams as a professional, and very fast bowler. He took but two or three steps to the wicket and hurled the ball down at a terrific speed to break back sharply, and he completely defeated Jacker and most of the Internationals. Of course he undoubtedly threw, as did one Knutton who used to play for Bradford. This Knutton was never no-balled in Council cricket, neither I think was Moss, and I believe it was mutually agreed that he should not be no-balled when playing against the Australians around 1900, with the result that he captured nine wickets.

It was in 1908 – or perhaps 1907, that I was fortunate to see Jessop play one of the 'immortal' innings against the South Africans at Lord's. Daisy was with me, and she being a great friend of Ben Lacey's [Sir Francis Lacey, Secretary of Lord's], he let us sit in his private box in the new stand then just opened. I shall never forget Jessop's treatment of Kotze the South African fast bowler, and the way he almost knelt down on his right knee and hit balls of great pace to square leg. When Jessop really got going it must indeed have been a problem for the opposing Captain to set his field. Together with us in the box were the future Kings, Edward and George, and one couldn't but be sorry for their tutor, Mr Hansell, who was bombarded with questions 'non-stop'.

I shall always feel I was far too rash to have embarked on first class cricket in 1909, especially such an onerous position as Captain of renowned Yorkshire. In the first place the Yorkshire team were on the downgrade, several leading players having lately given up, several others passing their zenith, and the prestige of Lord Hawke in addition! Hawke was not a great cricketer, but he was certainly in the first class, though what was far more important he had undoubtedly 'made' the Yorkshire CC XI. When he originally took over, although there were some good players, they were on the whole a rough uneducated lot, and there was much drinking. Peate, Ulyett, Emmett and Freeman were some of the best players. It is related that Freeman on receiving a telegram from the Secretary, Mr Perkins, of MCC asking him to play in a representative Match at Lord's, replied: 'Right, meet me at Station, Freeman.'

In the second place, being invited to Captain Yorkshire at a moment's notice did not give me the necessary time to think out the implications, that I was certainly not a good enough player, but that over all other considerations I had most assuredly, owing to ever increasing bouts of ear trouble and consequent giddiness, neither the fitness nor the health for the task. However I accepted and really completely failed, and I cannot say I enjoyed the experience! Though looking back it is something to have known fairly intimately such immortals of the game as dear old George Hirst and Schofield Haigh, the latter one of the cheeriest nicest souls ever, Wilfred Rhodes and David Denton, one of the greatest 'out' fielders ever, and to have been associated in a lesser way with Archie MacLaren, Walter Brearley, Plum Warner, A.O. Jones, a great athlete, K.L. Hutchings, a magnificent batsman and fielder, Blythe and Woolley, the latter a charming modest man, a great left-hand batsman and wonderful left-hand slow bowler on a sticky wicket who would or should probably attain a place in a world XI.

Of the matches in which I took part the few outstanding in my memory are the third Match in which I played on the lovely Worcester ground on which I had played as a boy. We were beaten by 12 runs, but I played a good innings of 30 not out, as I did against Lancaster on a nasty soft turning wicket the following year, making around 25 not out, out of a total of I think, under 100. In another Roses Match we were in a very bad way and had I think 8 down for about 40 at 1.10 p.m., but I managed to remain with George Hirst till 2.0 o'clock lunch, and after in spite of the crowd roaring every time I received a ball. I remember being hit all over on a beastly sort of wicket.

My efforts were brought to a close at Sheffield in 1911, Johnny Douglas hitting a ball very hard to me at mid off and splitting my hand twixt thumb and finger. Georgie Hirst said it was entirely my fault as I snapped at the ball! The Professionals were kindness itself to me and no one could have given greater and more loyal help than Hirst who was a man of real commonsense with a deep knowledge of cricket. He kept all the young Professionals in order, taught them how to 'turn out', how to behave on and off the field.

Two Professionals of great ability made the debut under me, either or both of whom would probably have been internationals. Booth and Drake were the two, and entirely unlike in every way. Booth, a charming well educated quiet man, a fine bowler and very useful batsman. Drake, very good natured, but rough and no brain, a splendid left-hand bat and bowler. It is related of him that on making his first big score his wife sent him a telegram of congratulation. Alonzo Drake, being none too sure of his ability to read, turned to Denton, saying 'Open and read it to me' which Denton did saying it was from his (Drake's) wife congratulating him. Whereupon Drake replied 'Give it to me' and when he'd had a good look remarked, 'Garn, you're kidding me, this ain't me wife's writin''!

I believe Drake died shortly after the 1914 War, and poor Booth was killed in the same action on the Somme in France, in which Dolphin, our wicket-keeper, was wounded.

The Booth mentioned was Major Booth who, with Drake, might have become one of the great names. The 1909 season was a summer of poor weather, an Australian visit helping county finances, and Yorkshire's share of runs and wickets was maintained, as ever, by those imperishables Hirst, Haigh, Rhodes and Den-

ton and, in his last season, the great David Hunter.

This season also brought the death, at the age of seventy-three, of a man whose service to Yorkshire cricket outspanned even Lord Hawke's: that of Joseph Wostinholm, Honorary Secretary from 1864 to 1902. For forty years Wostinholm was also Secretary of Sheffield United and is given the credit for that club's advance to the First Division of the Football League. 'Shrewd' and 'autocratic' are two regular descriptions of a man who, with Hawke, ruled Yorkshire cricket through the formative years. He was, according to Peter Thomas, 'less a servant of the members, more of a dictator', but the members nevertheless felt sufficiently of his service to vote him a testimonial of £200 and several 'silver articles' on his retirement in 1902. In fact, so highly were his services regarded that the club had to advertise the post at a salary of £350.

Wostinholm was succeeded by F.C., later Sir Frederick, Toone, who had been Secretary of Leicestershire from 1897 to 1902. A short-list of three from 140 applicants had been drawn up: Toone, E.H.D. Sewell and the Sheffield journalist J.H. Stainton. The final interviews were conducted at the Station Hotel on, according to Sewell:

> . . . a bleak morning. Directly I saw the third [Toone] I knew my number was up but was determined to die as game as possible.
>
> So when Lord Hawke who did the questioning of the victims before surely the mightiest committee in the world (those who've only seen the United Nations ought to have taken a dekko at the full committee of YCCC when the war drums are throbbing) put the vital question 'Do you go in for betting' I replied at once: 'Well, sir, I had a bet yesterday that I shouldn't get this job.'

Toone saw his first task as that of bringing county cricket's most successful club into the twentieth century. He revised the club's rules, put the organisation of benefits on a more professional basis, and marketed the club so successfully that he doubled the membership of 3000. He and Hawke ensured the advance and progress of Yorkshire's professionals: up to the outbreak of the Great War the players were paid £5 per home match, £6 for an away match with

Major Booth   *A light gone out*

Major William were his Christian names; he died a 2nd Lieutenant in the West Yorkshire Regiment in the Somme battles of 1916 in the same action in which Roy Kilner was injured. He was thirty years old and but for the Great War might be remembered as one of the game's great all-rounders.

Sutcliffe described him as "a great batsman and a great bowler". Hawke said: "England lost one of the most promising and charming young cricketers it was ever my lot to meet. Having gained a commission he was killed 'going over the top' gallantly leading his men." Another captain, Archibald White, added "A magnificent cricketer and a splendid fellow in every way".

Booth was a powerful right-hand batsman – he scored 210 at 50 an hour at Worcester in 1911, mostly off drives and square-cuts – and a right arm medium-fast bowler with a very high action. *Wisden* described his bowling: "he makes the ball swerve away at the very last moment. There is, too, something puzzling about his flight and if the wicket is doing anything he can make the ball pop up nastily." A comparison was made with S.F. Barnes.

Booth was not a strong man and was used mostly in short spells, but he could be devastating: two hat-tricks, bowling unchanged with Drake in 1914 in two matches, taking more than a hundred wickets in 1912–13–14; three wickets in four balls three times; against Middlesex in 1912 he had match figures of eight for 136 and scored 107 not out. His Test appearances (2) were limited only by the conflict.

His was an unusual if brief career: in 1913 he was one of *Wisden*'s Five and by the following year the only right-handed member of Yorkshire's attack. In the intervening winter, on the Sunday of the First Test, Booth, along with Hobbs and Strudwick, was thrown out of a car as it hit a bank approaching a level crossing in Umbito, South Africa. Booth and the driver lay below the overturned car, the cricketer escaping with a minor back strain although he did need, according to Cliver Porter, a runner when batting in the Test.

Just over three years later he was killed near La Cigny and buried in Serre Military Cemetery Number 1. His death brought sad poems to his local newspaper in Pudsey. His sister, unable to accept that he had been killed, always kept a light burning in the window of their cottage in the hope that he would return. Nor was his room disturbed until after his sister's death in 1950 when, Paul Dyson reported, the cottage, close by the Pudsey Britannia ground, was sold.

His surname is commemorated in a Pudsey side-street, Booth's Yard. In September 1920 a memorial service was held in St Lawrence's Church, Pudsey and a tablet unveiled. He was also remembered by Roy Kilner, who named his younger son Major.

a £1 winning bonus, plus talent money of five shillings each for special performances, awarded by the captain and distributed at the end of each season. Capped players had to join the Cricketers' Friendly Society and were given winter pay (32 weeks) of £2 per week. The whole or part of the winter pay was retained by the club and invested on the players' behalf at a rate of 4 per cent, for their retirement from cricket.

The 1914–18 War accelerated life enormously, and in 1921 the club announced new pay scales: £11 per home match, £15 per away match, £1 winning bonus and £150 set aside for talent money. When injured a player received half pay, when out of the team through loss of form, £8 a week up to 31 August. The Committee could, and did, increase bonuses, as for instance when they doubled the talent money available in 1922 and raised it to £450 in 1923.

The club was also concerned about the effect of adverse weather upon benefit matches, and set aside a sum of £200 a year to augment those benefits that the Committee felt failed to raise the sum expected. This system applied from 1905 to 1921 when the Committee decided to guarantee all capped players of ten years' service a benefit of at least £1000. Capped players of five years' service were guaranteed £250 with an increment of £50 per year up to ten.

The summer of 1909 was Haigh's benefit year and was remembered for two mighty Roses matches, the second being Haigh's choice. At Old Trafford on Whit Monday, in poor light and with the threat of rain, Brearley came bounding in for 35 overs to take nine Yorkshire wickets for 80 in a paltry first-innings score of 133. The sun broke through on Tuesday for Lancashire to bat on a drying surface, Haigh first taking two wickets with successive balls and then surpassing himself with a hat-trick: Lancashire 89 all out, Haigh seven for 25.

Yorkshire, batting again, then lost their first four wickets for 44 and began the last day 88 ahead, Huddlestone then carving through the remainder of the innings and finishing with eight for 24. So Lancashire needed 123 to win, but Hirst's valiant left arm shook the Red Rose to such an extent that five batsmen were dismissed for 6 runs; 'Monkey' Hornby added 31 with Heap, but three brilliant catches helped to send Lancashire crashing to 57 all out (Hirst six for 23).

The weather was poor again for the return at Bradford on August Bank Holiday, Yorkshire hitting out in the hour's play allowed on the first day to reach 111 for 4. Next morning, in fourteen deliveries, Heap took four wickets for 5 runs and Yorkshire were out for 159. Then it was Rhodes' turn: his seven for 68 meant that Lancashire fell 39 behind. Heap got at York-

shire again (seven for 49), and with Lancashire needing 186 to win Rhodes applied the *coup de grâce* for Yorkshire to win by 100, leaving spectators in need of stiff refreshment.

The shadows lengthened in 1910. The latter part of the summer was spoiled by poor weather, and an age ended with the demise of Edward the Peacemaker, who died as the season began. Cricket had lost a friend, for this was a monarch who had played the game, who had an eye for a good stroke as well as a pretty shape. Cambridge University had owed money on their sadly now demolished pavilion at Fenner's; the King contributed to the building fund and offered to make up the balance required at the end of the term. He was the largest contributor when MCC were struggling to buy the freehold at Lord's; as Prince of Wales (and Duke of Cornwall) it was said he was a very good friend to Surrey.

Blériot had flown the Channel, the Liberal Party was in office, the Old Age Pension and the Labour Exchange had arrived, and such was the onrush of change that Yorkshire fell to eighth place, Lord Hawke formally ending his long reign as captain in that November.

The Committee publicly expressed regret at the disappointment of a summer in which ten matches were won and seven lost. There were high moments, notably against Lancashire at Leeds where Hirst took nine for 23, hitting the stumps eight times. At Lord's against the other regular rivals Middlesex, Yorkshire needed 331 to win and accomplished victory by two wickets, the winning run coming from the penultimate delivery, Hirst scoring 137.

Rhodes had a superb match against Surrey on a difficult pitch at Bradford. With the ball he captured eleven wickets for 72, and when Yorkshire needed 157 to win on a surface described as treacherous, Rhodes, in his regular role as opener, hit a fierce 88 not out to bring victory. Another exciting win, by 6 runs over Hampshire at Portsmouth, featured two of the new players: Booth, and the wicket-keeper on trial to succeed David Hunter, Arthur Dolphin.

Hampshire needed another 32 runs to win when last man John Newman joined Horace Bowell who, coolly and carefully, led his county towards the summit. Hirst, Booth,

Arthur Dolphin *Quickhands*

Dolphin began with the almost impossible task of replacing David Hunter in the esteem of the team and the affection of the Yorkshire public, and that he was able to lay the ghost of 'Old Ironsides' is tribute enough to his ability and courage.

He spent twenty-two years as Yorkshire's first choice wicket-keeper, and played just once for England. His contemporary was Surrey's Strudwick, still regarded by some as the finest of all keepers, and Strudwick's view of Dolphin gives some indication of the Yorkshireman's reputation: 'He stood with his right leg a little further back. This helped him take the ball that is going away from the leg to the off which Rhodes and Kilner served up on sticky wickets, so giving him a quicker sweep to the wicket. In my opinion Dolphin moves the bails more quickly than any other keeper.'

John Callaghan, in *Yorkshire's Pride*, points out the high proportion of stumpings in Dolphin's victims: 231 to 488 catches. But, of course, he did keep to an unparalleled variety of bowlers: the left-arm seam, swing and cut of Hirst, Drake and Waddington, the medium-pace off-breaks of Haigh and Macaulay, the left-arm spin of Rhodes and Kilner, the late swing of Booth and Robinson. Sutcliffe wrote of him: 'His quick brain and exceptionally keen eyesight were responsible for disposing of large numbers of batsmen from chances which many keepers would have missed without even affecting their reputations.'

Dolphin was also a tenacious batsman, a renowned last-ditcher who once scored 93 against Middlesex. A quiet man who deplored ostentation, he once, according to Callaghan, silenced a raucous and ugly crowd in a public house by merely putting his scarred and bruised hands before him on a table. The ruffians assumed him to be a professional bare-knuckle fighter.

In later years Dolphin became a respected umpire, renowned for never wearing a hat at a time when everyone covered their heads.

Rhodes, Haigh, Myers and the Etonian Alfred Legard had all bowled and bowled, and the Portsmouth crowd sensed they were all bowled out. Richard Binns tells the rest of the story:

> Schofield Haigh, a comfortable looking man of medium height, not of little more than corresponding build, and of a most likeable smiling countenance, might have been seen plucking at his thick short moustache and thoughtfully bending his head as he was put on once more to bowl. Some scheme as dark as his skin was simmering in his brain, surely.
>
> Bowell played him very gingerly. His extreme caution was manifest in the way he increasingly stepped back to deal with balls well pitched up to him.
>
> Six short of a tie, seven wanted for victory. How the crowd cheered. Haigh started his next over . . . the ball was noticeably well pitched up and Bowell once more went back to it. The bails were seen to fall, Bowell was out, the match was over.

Haigh explained afterwards that he had noted how Bowell had gone back to full-length balls and played on that caution, inch by inch forcing the batsman back until he played on.

Against these successes had to be recorded some dismal batting performances, particularly against Kent's Blythe and Woolley. At Sheffield in June, Northamptonshire achieved an historic victory, their first against Yorkshire; Essex won by ten wickets at Leyton, Leicestershire by 259 runs at Headingley, while at Old Trafford, shame of shame, Yorkshire went down by an innings and 111. Brearley took nine wickets in the match, while the elegant Spooner recorded a 200 not out, being missed twice in his first 14 runs.

A wrenched ankle put the doughty Denton out for a month from 15 July, Wilson again scored three centuries but his aggregate dropped to 757, while of the younger players the major hopes were now Drake and Booth. After a trial of skill between Haworth Watson, from Skipton, and Dolphin, the latter finally won the wicket-keeping place vacated by 'Old Ironsides', David Hunter, and was to keep it for the next twenty-two years.

At Wighill Park that summer, Hawke arranged a farewell photograph seating himself, cross-legged and flat-capped in the middle of the front row, on the carpet between a downcast Watson and a straw-hatted Wilkinson. Behind him Hirst, between two ladies, exudes good cheer, while Rhodes, standing on a chair at the back alongside Booth, might have been assessing the cameraman's stance. Everard Radcliffe, Hawke's successor, is a tall, fair-haired young man at outside right, obviously of the family but not the inner circle.

Hawke's career epitomised the zenith of the Edwardian amateur cricketer. He scored 16,794 runs in his twenty-nine years of first-class cricket, at an average of 20.15, captained his county and England, toured the then cricketing world, and was respected and admired everywhere. Modern comparisons, or accusations of paternalism, are pointless for he simply would not have understood contemporary attitudes – although he would certainly have been pleased to see the county cricketer well cared for in a respected niche in society.

In 1914 Hawke was elected President of MCC, adding to his life presidency of Yorkshire, and MCC had the good sense to retain him in that position all through the Great War. One imagines that even if Ludendorff's armies had reached London, the Kaiser would have received short shrift at Lord's!

It followed that 1911, a year of glorious summer – 'how the sun shone' wrote 'Country Vicar' – had to be a season of considerable change. Radcliffe took the captaincy, although he had deputised for Hawke so often in the two preceding summers that the Committee was in effect officially sanctioning a change that had already evolved gradually. But Hawke's influence was undiminished, even if emanating only from the Committee room.

Rothery and Myers were each granted £250 and left the county, Booth and Drake were given regular places, and another left-hander of promise, Roy Kilner, was unearthed. For £600 a winter shed was built at Headingley, enabling coaching and practice to continue throughout the year. However, there was little immediate improvement on the field, the final Championship placing being a gain of one, from eighth to seventh. Eight matches were lost, bringing the number of defeats over two summers to fifteen, as many as in the previous six years together, but there were indications that the team was

recovering strength and in Booth and Drake the club had two cricketers of the highest promise.

Yorkshire began by beating MCC at Lord's before being caught on a drying pitch at Leyton, but after that, apart from a surprising defeat by Cambridge University, the team recorded eight consecutive victories. Worcester provided a memorable match on a beautiful pitch. Hirst, at forty, was bowling as fast as at any time in his career, taking nine for 41 in 15.2 overs, again hitting the stumps eight times. Hirst's performance can be judged by the fact that the next three innings of the match raised 994 runs, Yorkshire winning by ten wickets after Booth, in his second season, scored 210 in four hours, his off-driving and square-cutting being long remembered. Hirst, not to be outdone, then added a furious hundred.

Middlesex ended Yorkshire's triumphal progress at Lord's in June, where the team's catching was so sloppy that a written rebuke was received from Hawke. Not that matters improved the following week at Dewsbury, where three more batsmen were given lives as Northamptonshire reached 401, a record that was even excelled in the return match at Northampton in July in which four batsmen were missed and, despite Rhodes' fourteen wickets, the match was lost.

Drake hinted of emerging power by taking six Lancashire wickets for 57 at Old Trafford, following Hirst's 156, performances that ensured a substantial Yorkshire win. The 1911 season was also that of Warwickshire's advance to the front rank in which Frank Foster was so prominent: in Yorkshire's visit to Edgbaston he scored his maiden hundred and then took twelve wickets, but even that wasn't enough to overthrow the old aristos, Yorkshire still winning by four wickets.

However, by late July, when Warwickshire played the return fixture at Harrogate, the balance had swung. Foster continued in tremendous form, scoring 60 in the first innings and 101 in the second (in a total time of only 135 minutes for both innings), and Yorkshire were left eventually to score 247 on a worn pitch. It was a difficult task, but there could have been few excuses for the debacle that followed: Yorkshire dismissed for 58, Benny

Roy Kilner   *A delight*

Roy Kilner, from Wombwell, could claim to be the most popular Yorkshire cricketer. He never lacked friends at home or abroad at a time when Yorkshire, in their grim, winning mood of the 1920s, were less than welcome on many grounds.

He was a nephew of Irving Washington and inherited some of his uncle's stylish left-handed batting; as a left-arm slow-medium bowler he was skilful enough to play in nine Tests and to undertake two MCC tours; he was also considered by Yorkshire good enough, and of sufficient contrast, to bowl at the other end to Wilfred Rhodes.

Like Rhodes, too, he was adaptable. He first won his place, before the Great War, as a batsman and his play was highly regarded, if considered a little eccentric by orthodox Yorkshiremen. After the war he developed his bowling, just as Rhodes returned to it, to help cover the loss of Booth and Drake. He scored fifteen centuries, including a 206 against Derbyshire in 1920, and between 1922 and 1925 his bowling, especially on drying pitches, was feared. He passed a hundred wickets in each of those four summers and his career aggregate of 858 wickets was taken at an average of 17.33.

The 1930 Australians attend Roy Kilner's grave at Wombwell.

Yet it is as a personality that he is best remembered and he was a great favourite of Cardus who, fortunately, passed on a little of this delightful man's philosophy. It was Kilner who summed up the dour Roses matches of those days with two remarks: 'What we want is no umpires and fair cheating all round,' and 'We say good morning and after that all we say is "Howzat?"'

Cricket, then as now, was under self-analysis and when Cardus asked Kilner the essential question,

'What is wrong with the game?' he replied: 'Nowt. Game's all reight, it's t'crowd that wants educating up to it.'

In the winter of 1927–8 he took a coaching engagement in India, hit 283 in a local match (including six sixes and forty fours) but contracted enteric fever and died in Barnsley on his return. It was reported that 100,000 lined the funeral route to Wombwell Parish Church. Roy was the brother of Norman Kilner of Warwickshire.

Wilson being top scorer with 11, Field taking seven for 20 and the new champions deservedly taking the crown.

An even worse collapse followed at Aylestone Road where Leicestershire, in their only victory in a programme of twenty-two matches, dismissed Yorkshire's second innings for 47 (from 27 for 2), King finishing with eight for 17. Radcliffe's team concluded a sorry season with a southern tour that did nothing for their reputation. They were saved from defeat at The Oval, where Surrey had run up 540 in their first innings, by a heavy storm on the third day; they lost by six wickets at Southampton on a pitch of which they had first use; Blythe and Woolley, again, dismissed them for 75 at Canterbury, Kent winning by ten wickets. So the spirit of the side must have been sagging by the time the team reached Hastings, especially after Sussex raised 522 for 7 declared.

But here was a good, fast pitch and Yorkshire for once took full advantage, Hirst's 218 being followed by Drake's 115, the pair putting on 259 for the fourth wicket in 150 minutes. A second victory that season over Sussex was accomplished by an innings and 32 on the third afternoon. Nottinghamshire, too, had gone down twice, at Trent Bridge and Hull.

Wilfred Rhodes took the Lancashire match at Sheffield as his benefit, a disappointment in that Yorkshire appeared to have the game won comfortably by the evening of the second day, the public contributing only £83 at the turnstiles on the third. But the Red Rose, only 45 ahead with half their second-innings wickets gone, managed a remarkable recovery through McLeod (121), Makepeace and Hornby, leaving Yorkshire to score 251 in three hours.

Three wickets went for 45 before Denton, 101 not out, forced an honourable draw.

It was, in fact, Denton's year, hitting six centuries and scoring 2223 runs in Yorkshire's matches. Rhodes, Hirst, Wilson, Drake and Booth also passed a thousand, while the untouchable trio of Hirst, Rhodes and Haigh all passed a hundred wickets and were well supported by Drake (84) and Booth (79). Worth noting, too, is the fact that All India, as India and Pakistan were then known in cricket, were routed by an innings and 43 at Hull.

On paper Yorkshire had the strength to reassert their old supremacy, even if short of at least one more batsman of the highest class, but the 1911 results were below expectations and at the end of the season Radcliffe resigned to be succeeded by Sir Archibald White, who led the side up until the outbreak of the Great War in 1914.

Radcliffe, although nominally captain for only one summer, had in effect led the side for almost three, so often had he been deputy for Hawke in 1909–10, and he had been in charge of a major reconstruction as Drake, Booth and Dolphin came into the team, a process that was to continue into 1912 when Roy Kilner and Edgar Oldroyd made their presence felt. Indeed, the team photograph of 1912 had a settled, assured, commanding look about it, showing ten capped players and the Colts Kilner and Oldroyd cross-legged on the grass at the front.

White had been in the Wellington School XI in 1894–6 and had played once for Yorkshire, in 1908, before his appointment. He led Yorkshire to the Championship in his first season (a feat emulated by Geoffrey Wilson, Barber, Burton,

Edgar Oldroyd *Little Ack*

Oldroyd came from Louis Hall's home town of Batley, and much of the Giant's durability and steadfastness ran in his genes. His record, as Peter Thomas pointed out, puts him among the best number-three batsmen in county cricket, scoring 38 centuries for Yorkshire and sharing in ten partnerships of 200 or more, including a 333 with Percy Holmes against Warwickshire in 1922.

He forced his way into the Yorkshire side before the Great War through his tenacious defensive batting, and he developed, in the 1920s, into a hardhitting middle-order player who could always hold one end in whatever circumstances. In 1931, when he went to play for Pudsey St Lawrence, he won this admiring memory from the boy Hutton: 'One of the best I ever saw on a turning pitch'.

He was one of the characters of the Yorkshire side of his era who won admiring tributes from Cardus and Robertson-Glasgow, the latter addressing him with style and affection in one of his 'Cricket Prints':

> His name might have been Jess Oakroyd. He was one of those small, tough, humorous militant

men who make the comedy and greatness of a country. They are to be found answering back something or someone which may or may not have existence: fate, a tax collector, Monday morning, a bus conductor, thirst or a Hyde Park orator. They bounce and argue down time's corridors. And they generally win the battle.

> Oldroyd could not be one of those who, when bowled by an amateur, accept the unwelcome visitation with a resigned calm; he was very angry indeed; he looked it and he said it. For you had not only wrecked Oldroyd for some hours, you had ended an integral section of Yorkshire. You had wrecked a parish and interfered with the workings of the only county that mattered. There lies the secret of the Yorkshire cricketer. He comes second in his own estimation.

According to John Callaghan, Oldroyd was not too happy when Yorkshire released him in 1931, but he became a professional with Pudsey St Lawrence and he died in Truro, just before New Year of 1965, at the age of seventy-six.

Vic Wilson and Close) but was able to attain no better than second in 1913 and fourth the following summer.

White's years were also those of Yorkshire's unwanted but growing reputation for stolid, dour batting, a criticism that seems a little unfair of a side that included Denton, Hirst and Booth. Much of the disapproval was directed at Benny Wilson who, after displaying his strokes and hitting well, would inexplicably relapse into implacable defence, patting back halfvolleys. Oldroyd, too, soon developed a reputation as a sticker, and the whole team was often accused of 'sitting on the splice'. White admitted to 'Old Ebor':

> Benny Wilson and Edgar Oldroyd were apt on occasions to be a little deliberate in their methods. I will say, however, that in nearly every case in which this happened we had made a bad start and their caution was justified, although it may not have been to the liking of the spectators . . . .

> At times I own I have had to issue the order to 'sit on the splice'. This I only did when I realised it

was impossible to win a match but that it might be saved. 'If you can't win a match, why should you be beaten?' was Lord Hawke's great question. I think that a good deal of the criticism of slow play on Yorkshire's part was due to the ignorance of the plan of campaign that the team were endeavouring to carry out.

The other point that should be made about the White era, before a detailed consideration of the last three summers of the Golden Age, was that both Hirst and Kilner were absent for much of the 1914 summer, two players who would always contribute much to the enterprise of any cricket team. Another factor in Yorkshire's inability to continue their domination of the Hawke years was a general levelling up among the other counties, as exemplified by the rise of one of the 'newcomers', Warwickshire.

By 1914, before shrapnel and the machine gun mowed down the flower of a European generation, cricket had become a great and much-loved national institution, and for boys in all grades of society it represented a wonderful portal to achievement and glory, if not exactly riches – a magic door. For this was a time of the craftsman, when 'hand-made' was a tautology, when the tradesmen, carpenters, joiners and blacksmiths took great pride in their skills and the rigorous training, from early boyhood, that was needed. And that sense of genuine professionalism, very hard but scrupulously fair, at a time of rigorous religious instruction, overflowed into cricket, to the game of English willow against English leather.

White's Championship victory of 1912 was Yorkshire's ninth in twenty seasons, and with Rhodes missing six and Haigh one of the matches, called up for the Triangular Test series against Australia and South Africa, to finish first again with a debutant captain was an achievement regarded with both relief and surprise. No wonder then that the eleven contributed to buy their new captain a silver salver.

That same year also shattered the legend that the sun never ceased to shine during the summers of the Golden Age. It was miserable, only one of Yorkshire's nineteen home matches escaping with no interruption. In June at Sheffield and Huddersfield, rain washed out play for four successive days, as it was to do again in successive fixtures at Bradford and Hull.

Nevertheless Yorkshire lost only one match all summer, that against Middlesex at Lord's. White won the toss and had no wish to bat first on a pitch made soft by preceding rain, but in those days of deteriorating surfaces to send in the opposition was regarded as reckless if not foolhardy. Accordingly Yorkshire went in and lost the first seven wickets for 76, Booth, Haigh and White rallying the tail to take the innings to 157. Middlesex won a lead of 28 and needed only 139 in the fourth innings; at the close on the second day they needed only 15 with five wickets standing, but elected to wait until the morrow and were lucky that the rain stayed away until later in the day, winning by four wickets.

Difficult pitches meant, of course, that Yorkshire's extraordinarily versatile attack could operate in favourable conditions match after match. Lancashire were routed by ten wickets at Bradford, Hirst, Drake and Haigh doing the damage. In these circumstances it is the side

that possesses the batsman who can master the turn and lift that usually wins; on this occasion it was Yorkshire and Rhodes, who made a masterly 107.

At Nottingham in June, Hirst was nursing an injured knee and with Rhodes out for 8, Yorkshire needed 248 to win. Wilson shored up one end, 150 minutes for 48, while Kilner, who had taken four wickets, added 84 not out aided by another young man, amateur James Tasker, whose promising batting career was cut short by the demands of business.

Northamptonshire had a narrow escape at Bradford, at 24 for 8 in their second innings and needing 143 to escape an innings defeat when time ran out. The sun did shine, brilliantly, at Tunbridge Wells in mid July where Yorkshire won some revenge for several earlier humiliations. Batting first they scored 543 (Denton 221), Kent eventually going down by an innings and 45, two of their batsmen being run out, according to 'Old Ebor', 'chiefly through the impetuosity of Woolley'. The great left-hander did, however, raise 42 and 75 in his two innings.

At Southampton in that same month Fry contributed 186 to a Hampshire first-innings total of 378 for 4, Yorkshire replying with 429, Denton's 191 reportedly outshining even Fry's grand display. On the second night the Solent saw heavy rain and Hampshire were caught on another drying surface, Hirst and Haigh gleefully inflicting the usual damage to dismiss them for 95, the preliminary to another Yorkshire victory by nine wickets.

In a wet summer Denton totalled 2127 in all matches, only Hobbs approaching him with an aggregate of 2042. If England's selectors regarded him, at thirty-eight, as too old, opposing bowlers recognised a master, a batsman who added to the prolific stroke-making of his youth the steadiness and additional defensive technique of maturity and experience. Haigh, at forty-one, took 125 wickets, Booth and Hirst both following him to the hundred, Drake failing by 13.

Haigh brought red ruin to the Australians at Bradford, returning match figures of eleven for 36. 'I wish we could take him back with us to Australia,' wrote the touring manager. Hawke was sufficiently confident to tell the annual general meeting: 'Yorkshire will have a very excellent team for many years to come.'

Yorkshire won sixteen matches in 1913, to thirteen in the previous Championship season, yet finished second to Kent and could not complain, for strong as Yorkshire were and excellent as was the effort and teamwork, Kent were accepted everywhere as outstanding and deserving champions.

The pressing questions of the time were Home Rule for Ireland and the intentions of Imperial Germany, both sides of the North Sea frantically building dreadnoughts. Conrad, Lawrence, Yeats and Joyce will be remembered as great writers of the time, while Yorkshire was more concerned by the infernal motor car that had had the effrontery to strike Schofield Haigh on the foot and put him out for most of July. As Hirst was also missing, injured, in that month there remained a suspicion that, good as Kent were, without these interventions Yorkshire might have held on to the crown.

The weather bucked up to bring a fine summer and, because George V was visiting Merseyside and a special holiday had been proclaimed, three Roses matches were played that summer, Yorkshire visiting Aigburth for the first time. Lancashire got away to a good start, shooting out Yorkshire for 74 and 53 in the season's opening match at Old Trafford, Heap taking eleven for 39, Lancashire winning by an innings and 39. Lancashire also won at Liverpool, on another drying pitch, Dean taking seventeen for 91.

By August Bank Holiday, however, Yorkshire were well into their stride and were left to get 217, on a fast, good pitch, in 150 minutes. After half an hour the score was 32 for 2 with Rhodes and Kilner gone, but after 82 minutes the score had reached 141, Haigh and Benny Wilson driving furiously. With five wickets down, Yorkshire needed 71 in 45 minutes, then 26 in 18. White made a spirited 27 not out and brought the scores level for Drake, who had been kept back, as a left-hander, to avoid the loss of time on changing the field, to drive Dean for four with six minutes to spare.

After the opening defeat in Manchester, Yorkshire won ten matches and could have

won three more had time and the weather allowed. Haigh was absent when Gloucestershire won at Sheffield by 2 runs, and at Leeds when Northamptonshire won by 20. Hirst missed Surrey's victory at Hull but a valuable recruit, Rockley Wilson, reappeared in August, scoring 104 not out against Essex at Bradford, and re-established the link between Cambridge University and the county. A master at Winchester, Wilson also had a qualification for Hampshire, by residence, and 'Old Ebor' avers that the Committee did not recall the all-rounder who had first appeared in the county team in 1899 until they feared losing him.

Seven members of the 1913 team scored more than a thousand runs and eight of the side scored centuries – a formidable demonstration of the team's batting power. Booth, 167 wickets at 18 apiece, had confirmed himself as the pace bowler needed and he, Drake and Hirst all managed the 'double'. Indeed, a fourth 'double' was missed by only fourteen wickets, and that by the team's number one batsman and former premier left-arm spinner, Rhodes. After nineteen years Schofield Haigh retired honourably to the position of coach at Winchester.

Hawke was MCC President for the celebration of the centenary of the opening of Lord's Ground, the other significant event of 1914. Yorkshire in that year, as they were to be in 1939, were experienced, confident, puissant and capable of dominating the Championship for several years. They began with three successive victories by an innings, against Northamptonshire, MCC and Essex.

Mead, with an innings of 213 at Southampton, put a stop to this rampage. Denton (168 not out) and Hirst (146) made the now customary response, raising 312 for the fourth wicket, but as might be expected the match was drawn. The first match at home, against Surrey at Bradford, was a surprise to the faithful, for Hobbs and Hayes both made centuries in the Surrey first innings, Hobbs adding 74 for good measure in the second. Hirst was leading the charge to victory in Yorkshire's second innings when he played on to Fender and Surrey were winners by 28 runs.

Tom Birtles, who had made his debut the previous summer, seemed to be a batsman of

Rockley Wilson *Humorist*

Evelyn Rockley Wilson had an extraordinary career even by the standards of the Golden Age, into which he was born in 1879, near Sheffield. Only Rhodes' career spanned a greater number of years, for Wilson first appeared for Yorkshire in 1899 and said his final farewell in 1923.

He was the brother of two excellent cricketers, C.E.M. Wilson, who captained Cambridge and, an all-rounder, appeared intermittently for Yorkshire during 1896–9 before becoming vicar of Sand Hutton, and C.R. Wilson who, while never playing first-class, served the Committee for thirty-two years. Rockley was described as a 'joyous' batsman of sound defence who appalled the professors with his delight in the hook; he was also an extremely skilful and accurate right-arm spin bowler of low action who moved the ball a little both ways, accompanying all this with a delightful sense of humour: 'My best ball is the one which broke from the off when I meant to break from the leg.'

At Cambridge, on his first-class debut, he appeared as a last-minute substitute for A.J. Webbe's eleven and scored 117 not out and 70; he made 108 against Oxford in 1901 and was thus able to claim a century against both Universities 'whilst in residence'. He played only nine games for Yorkshire between 1899 and 1902, partly because of the strength of the side and partly, as noted elsewhere, because the Committee was reluctant to leave out top-class professionals who would do as they were told in favour of amateurs who came and went as they pleased. He began teaching French and coaching cricket at Winchester in 1903, and was then available only in the holidays, not reappearing until 1913.

After the Great War Yorkshire had need of him. Drake and Booth had been lost, the team had to be rebuilt and the forty-year-old schoolmaster was a valuable reinforcement from July. In 1919 Rockley Wilson finished seventh in the national averages and second the following year, being chosen as vice-captain to J.W.H.T. Douglas for the 1920–1 tour of Australia. Although England had a desperate time,

losing all five Tests, Wilson finished with 51 wickets at 11.19 each.

Described by R.L. Arrowsmith as 'a brilliant scholar as a boy', he had an astonishing memory for facts and figures and became renowned as a coach, a raconteur and a character. It was ironical, noted Arrowsmith, that articles written by Wilson while on tour in Australia, and published in the *Daily Express*, led to players being banned from writing for the press while on tour.

Such a character appealed, of course, to R.C. Robertson-Glasgow, and it was he who told the most famous 'Rockley' story: 'a noble lord, whose awful majesty hid a kindly heart', according to 'Crusoe', was holding court in the pavilion and, seeing Wilson, shook his hand in passing. 'Lucky to get a touch,' whispered Wilson to his companion.

some promise, following his 40 against Surrey with a much-praised 104 against Lancashire at Sheffield. These performances encouraged the Committee to play him regularly, and but for the war years he might have won a place. Birtle did play again in 1919, but was never able to realise his early potential.

Lancashire, too, had to settle for a draw, but Rhodes was in masterly form on a soft pitch at Leeds, and Derbyshire went down by an innings. But Yorkshire then struck a lean spell, losing twice to Kent while Hirst was injured and Kilner, still recovering from a winter illness, was clearly not fully fit. Modern cricketers will recognise some of the factors in the Tonbridge defeat: play against Warwickshire at Dewsbury had not finished until 5.40 and that meant, in those days, an all-night journey. The same discomfort and privations, of course, applied to teams facing long journeys to play Yorkshire.

Blythe, eight for 55, was the principal reason for Kent's win at Sheffield, but after that Yorkshire, from the first week in July, won eleven of their remaining twelve matches, Lancashire going down by an innings at Old Trafford. But the June wobble was enough to prevent another Championship victory, Yorkshire finishing fourth after winning exactly half their twenty-eight games and drawing ten.

War against Germany was declared on 4 August and the latter part of the summer was confused. Surrey, declared champions by MCC, cancelled their last two matches but had done enough, as second-placed Middlesex admitted by raising no objection. Middlesex's visit to Sheffield was at first declared off at Lord's, then reconsidered. By the time Surrey were to be visited in mid August, the army had taken over The Oval and the match was switched to Lord's, where Hobbs reached 202, he and Hayward raising 290 for the first wicket and the Surrey first innings reaching 549 for 6. 'Old Ebor' felt that the situation was so unreal that the players had great difficulty in concentrating on their play.

Back home Benny Wilson made 208 against Sussex at Bradford before the two final home fixtures – against an England eleven at Harrogate and in the Scarborough Festival – were cancelled. Yorkshire then set off on their final tour in the last sunset of the Golden Age, winning at Bristol by an innings and at Weston by 227 runs, and achieving a draw in the very last match with Sussex at Brighton. Two exceptional all-rounders, Major Booth and Alonzo Drake, played in their last match for the county.

Booth and Roy Kilner told 'Old Ebor' at Brighton that both were planning to enlist as soon as they returned home: 'It's our duty, Mr Pullin.' Both joined the Leeds 'Pals' Battalion, along with Dolphin. Booth, commissioned a second lieutenant, was killed on the Western Front on 1 July 1916 in the same attack in which Kilner was wounded in the right wrist, an offensive that brought heavy losses and much grief to the whole of the West Riding. That sorrow stayed with many families right up until the outbreak of the Second World War, and it was a common experience on visiting a house in what is now metropolitan West Yorkshire to see, on the wall, the photograph of father, brother or son, in uniform, and empty shell cases, chromium plated, on the mantelpiece.

Drake was rejected for military service on health grounds and died three months after the end of the war, in February 1919. How great was Yorkshire's loss can be seen from some of their last performances. Booth and Drake bowled unchanged against Gloucestershire, Booth taking twelve wickets and Drake eight, the first time this feat had been accomplished since Hirst and Haigh in 1910. Drake then went on to take all ten wickets in Somerset's second innings, finishing with match figures of fifteen for 51, Booth and Drake again bowling unchanged and Booth, on five for 27, deliberately allowing Drake the ball when he saw he had a chance of all ten.

In that fateful year of 1914 Drake took 158 wickets and Booth 155, and each scored more than 800 runs. Even seventy-five years later it is hard to accept that two such splendid all-round cricketers were never to be seen wearing the White Rose again.

3

Rhodes to Hutton 1919–1939

The Great War was not over by Christmas 1914, as had been the initial optimistic hope, and as the conflict widened and deepened the county cricket clubs had to consider their financial stability and resources. Yorkshire's members, asked to continue their support despite the absence of cricket, responded so well that the club was able to collect £5560 in subscriptions, a sum that enabled the structure to remain and donations to continue towards the upkeep of playing grounds. Allowances were also given to the professionals who, when duties permitted, were able to appear in charity matches.

The club office, then in Leeds centre, became the headquarters of the West Riding Volunteers, the County Adjutant being Major the Lord Hawke, a distinguished militiaman of the previous century. When the Major was promoted to Colonel he was followed in the post by Captain Frederick Toone, and should any reader suspect that these jobs were sinecures it should be remembered that the Volunteers comprised twenty battalions of infantry, five motor sections and two ambulance corps.

Yorkshire despatched almost five hundred parcels of cricketing materials to military camps at home and abroad, and it was estimated that more than £20,000 was raised for war charities by the playing of matches. Yorkshire cricket's contributions were worthy of her.

After the cessation of hostilities, 1919 brought a colder, harder world. The day of the great amateur had passed and although amateurs would continue to make substantial efforts in first-class cricket for another thirty years, much of the wealth and blood of their families had been spent on the Western Front. Rich patrons were to linger on for another twenty years or so, the Duke of Devonshire's family still supporting Derbyshire to this day, but they became fewer as the West rolled on into the Jazz Age, the hedonism of living for the moment, engendered by the war, continuing into the 1920s.

Cash was much tighter. Clubs had to double admission charges partly to provide for the new Amusement Tax, and MCC, as if fearful that leisure hours and a love of cricket were also in shorter supply, agreed to a programme of two-day Championship matches in 1919, the hours of play being 11.30 to 7.30. The experiment was regarded as a disaster all round, not least the late closures, there being few spectators left by that hour of the evening – an experience that was to be visited upon the Test and County Cricket Board almost seventy years later when they attempted to continue play until 8 p.m. or later in order to complete a mandatory number of overs in the day. Essex, never afraid of innovation, did try to keep their public at the ground in 1919 by advertising that 'supper will be provided at the close of play', but by 7.30 of an evening, no matter how fine, even the most ardent cricket-lover is anxious for dinner, the odd glass of refreshment and convivial company.

This same year also brought a 'new' method of deciding the Championship. From 1895 to 1909 it had been decided on the basis of one point per win, one point deducted for each defeat, the order being determined by the proportion of points won to games played. An increasing number of drawn games had brought about the next change, in 1910, when the order became dependent upon the percentage of wins to games played. The following year brought the introduction of first-innings points in drawn matches – a system that stayed, despite the anomalies, until 1919 when, with truncated two-day games, it was felt that the 1910 method was best suited to the circumstances.

Roy Webber, who made as detailed a study of the Championship as a professional cricket historian, always insisted that dividing the number of games played by the number of victories promoted the most aggressive county cricket up until the time when all counties played the same number of Championship matches. 'Old Ebor' was one who would not have agreed with Mr Webber, even though Yorkshire won the first post-war Championship at a time when they were not expected to make a serious challenge. He pointed out that 'every unfinished match meant a lowering of the clubs concerned'.

Yorkshire, in fact, learned of the winning of their tenth Championship at Victoria Station, London at nine o'clock in the evening of their last day of the season, on their return from Brighton. Rain had washed out the first day, Yorkshire had declared on the second with a lead of 87, and Sussex were 38 for 2 in their second innings when, with an hour's play left, the rain returned. Kent needed to defeat Middlesex at Lord's over the same two days to retain the Championship, and it was only after 'Old Ebor' had telephoned the *Yorkshire Post* office that the news spread that Middlesex had forced a draw.

Yorkshire, as well as 'Old Ebor', would have had good reason to complain about the scoring method had Kent succeeded, for they had

Champions, 1919:
Back row (from left): Arthur Dolphin, Roy Kilner, Abe Waddington, 'Bill' Williams, Herbert Sutcliffe.
Middle row: George Hirst, Wilfred Rhodes, David Burton, Rockley Wilson, David Denton.
Front row: Percy Holmes, Emmott Robinson.

played only fourteen matches to Yorkshire's twenty-six, of which eleven were drawn, an increasingly probable result in two-day matches. Yorkshire felt that but for time and weather they would have defeated Lancashire, Middlesex, Kent, Hampshire and Sussex, but they would also, by the same reckoning, have lost to Surrey at The Oval.

For Yorkshire to have succeeded, after a break of four summers and with a much-changed team, was a pleasant surprise in the Ridings. Booth, Drake, Benny Wilson and Sir Archibald White had gone, Hirst was forty-eight, Rhodes forty-two, and Kilner had been wounded. The new captain was D.C.F. (David) Burton, who had first batted for Yorkshire while a Cambridge undergraduate in 1907. An excellent sprinter at Rugby School, he had won his blue at Rugby for three successive years and was, not surprisingly, regarded as a brilliant cover-point. He served with the Northumberland Fusiliers before succeeding White, and he developed, always listening to Hirst and Rhodes, into a shrewd captain and useful middle-order batsman. He must also be given much of the credit for rebuilding the side in a difficult period.

With hindsight, Yorkshire might have retained Wilson for another season or so for, at thirty-nine, he had a record of fifteen centuries. The Committee may have felt that his ultra-cautious batting was unsuitable for two-day matches and taken the decision to draft in new blood – and who can say now, as the names appeared one by one, that they were wrong?

Percy Holmes and Tommy Birtles had appeared in 1913 to be followed the next year by Ernest Smith of Ossett who was thought, all too briefly, to be a possible successor to Wilfred Rhodes or Roy Kilner as the slow left-arm bowler. The season of 1919 was a fruitful one, for among the ten debutants were Herbert Sutcliffe, Norman Kilner, Emmott Robinson, Abe Waddington and a future captain, Geoffrey Wilson.

Burton has since revealed how he began the season with Rhodes and Holmes as his opening batsman with that young man from Pudsey, Sutcliffe, at number seven, and it was only after several discussions with Hirst that, later in the season, he moved Sutcliffe up to number two to create one of the great partnerships. Burton could take less credit for Waddington's introduction, having been hit under the eye by Jack Gregory during a match at Sheffield against the Australian Imperial Forces, and missing several matches. While Hirst stepped in as captain Waddington entered the side in June, and almost immediately Yorkshire sensed they had the bowler they needed to turn them into a team of traditional prowess.

Burton also worked hard on polishing up the fielding, winning praise from Charlie Macartney: 'You have the best fielding side in England.' Emmott Robinson, patrolling the off side with Burton, was one reason for the improvement, soon joining Waddington in opening the attack with his swing bowling before turning to spin.

The opening weeks of the season were hardly propitious, Yorkshire being dismissed by MCC for 120 before being cracked around Lord's for a massive 488. The reply at least demonstrated that Yorkshire remained obdurate: Hirst 180 not out, Roy Kilner 120, Holmes 99, Burton declaring at 528 for 8.

A thumb injury to David Denton, which put him out of the team for a fortnight, was a factor in a heavy defeat at Old Trafford, where Makepeace and Parkin helped to contrive a Lancashire victory by 140 runs. Parkin's match figures of fourteen for 140 must have made felicitous reading for him over breakfast.

Nottinghamshire then won at Sheffield by six wickets, Yorkshire making a poor showing against slow bowling in their first innings, but after that the only defeat came, rather surprisingly, from Sussex at Harrogate. The return Roses match was to be remembered particularly, with a fanfare of trumpets announcing to the world the arrival of Holmes and Sutcliffe, for their opening stand of 253.

Parkin had a somewhat painful Bank Holiday, finishing with none for 97. At Dewsbury against Hampshire came one of those meteoric performances that occasionally flash across the skies, when a fast right-arm bowler known to the records only as A.C. Williams shattered Hampshire with a return of nine for 29 in 77 deliveries, hitting the stumps eight times. He

Percy Holmes *A gloss*

It was his great misfortune to be born a contemporary of Sutcliffe and Hobbs: had neither existed it is likely that Holmes, from Oakes near Huddersfield, would have been remembered as an outstanding, possibly great Test-match batsman. He had all the attributes, including a gloss to his batting that meant many of his innings were more enjoyable than those of his partner Sutcliffe. As a pair they were worthy openers to follow Ulyett and Hall and then Tunnicliffe and Brown, and for figures they were unapproachable.

They raised sixty-nine century opening partnerships for Yorkshire, seventy-four in all matches, and in 1932 they surpassed the 554 of Tunnicliffe and Brown against Derbyshire by one run to set a new world record, the occasion being the match at Leyton against Essex. Sutcliffe played on when 313; thereupon Sellers declared, only to see the scoreboard move back to 554!

The scorers, on checking, could find only 554 runs and while arguments raged in the scorebox, press box and pavilion, 'a reverend gentleman in the crowd', according to Holmes, suggested that a no-ball might have been missed. This apparently convenient solution was met with considerable scepticism, not least by *Wisden*, which commented: 'Some of the circumstances surrounding this Leyton achievement were not quite desirable owing to the scorers being unable to see what was exhibited on the board.' At least one contemporary county captain felt that the Essex captain in that match should have protested at the later alteration.

However, Leslie Duckworth tracked down the two umpires, Frank Field and 'Tiger' Smith, and the latter insisted that a no-ball had been missed, the first ball of the opening over of the day which Holmes played to mid-on, not taking a run. 'Tiger' insisted that he had had a signal from the Yorkshire scorer Billy Ringrose who, at that moment, was attending to both scorebooks, the Essex scorer answering a call of nature (according to Ringrose).

If the umpire's call was acknowledged the no-ball was not debited until later in the day, after Ringrose had been convinced that he had failed to record it. An unsatisfactory means of breaking a record, perhaps, but as *Wisden* added a little more gracefully, 'Had they [the batsmen] not felt assured they had beaten the record, they could have put on heaps more runs.'

Since 1932 Holmes has been remembered as much for that one day at Leyton as for any of his long list of honours. Yet in his day he was accepted, by all but

Portsmouth, 1920. Percy Holmes after his 302.

the selectors, as one of the shining stars in the firmament. A right-hander, he was compared by Peter Thomas to Denton for his attacking approach to the opening bowling, although 'Denton had the conscience to bat further down the list than number one.'

Holmes reached Yorkshire in 1913 via Lindley Zion Sunday School, Golcar Paddock and then Spen Victoria, batting as low as number ten, but a 61 scored against Middlesex in the following year confirmed the promise his admirers had been reporting to the county club. He first met Sutcliffe when both boys were travelling on the top deck of a Leeds tram between City Square and the Headingley nets. A famous partnership was formed which was to flower in 1919, at Sheffield against Nottinghamshire, after Holmes had made 99 in the opening fixture against MCC at Lord's.

Holmes' aggregate that season was 1877 and included a partnership with Sutcliffe of 253 against Lancashire. A year later he had moved from seventeenth to fourth in the national averages with an aggregate of 2254 at 50.08. Astonishingly he was not selected for Douglas's team for Australia that following winter (in which, of course, England lost all five Tests) but in the following years he was past 2000 runs on another six occasions and included a 315 not out against Middlesex at Lord's in 1925.

He played only seven times for England, including against Australia, Gregory and McDonald, at Trent Bridge in 1921, but was not selected again in that series as one of the selectors decided that he was unsettled by pace. As Holmes was England's top scorer, with 38, it was a harsh judgement. He then toured South Africa under Stanyforth, four times topping fifty in the five Tests, and after his Leyton effort opened with Sutcliffe against All India in 1932, but his great days were past and he retired the following year. He was often taxed as to why he thought he had been given so few opportunities by England, but would turn away such queries with a smile; he once told Norman Kilner: 'I'm not saying, lad. I'm happy playing with my own team.'

He was a very cheerful and popular cricketer, a master, according to Pelham Warner, of the square-cut and hook and his expertise with the latter stroke hardly suggests he lacked courage; indeed, that same expertise is supposed to have been developed, as a boy, by a school coach who ensured that his charges stayed in line by tethering the back foot to the leg stump.

It is a fact that through much of his 224 not out at Leyton, an innings that lasted 7 hours 25 minutes, he was troubled by lumbago.

Holmes' fame may shed a lesser light than that of his formidable partner but it is always a pleasant glow, affectionately remembered. He died in 1971, aged eighty-four, a few miles from where he was born.

Herbert Sutcliffe *Man of Style*

Sutcliffe is now remembered as the junior partner to Hobbs in the greatest English opening partnership; a right-hand batsman of iron resolve who could seemingly play any bowler on any surface and one who batted the better as the odds against him increased, no matter what the condition. On figures alone he stands among the immortals (50,135 runs at an average of 52, a thousand runs or more in twenty-one summers), but there was much more to the man than that.

Sutcliffe could have become, had he chosen, the first great professional to turn amateur for he cloaked his hard professionalism in an amateur's lifestyle. When in 1939 half the Yorkshire team joined HM Forces, the amateurs became officers as a matter of course while the professionals, Sutcliffe, Verity and later Smailes excepted, were among the ranks. Even the War Office must have accepted that Herbert Sutcliffe would be a disconcerting subordinate for any young subaltern. Sutcliffe played his lifetime's innings with the aplomb of a brigadier.

Sutcliffe was born at Summerbridge, near Harrogate. His father was a medium-pace bowler of such accuracy that he was called for Yorkshire trials at the same time as George Hirst. While Herbert was a baby the family moved to Pudsey where his father played for St Lawrence while the son played for the other Pudsey club, Britannia, making his first-team debut at fourteen. He lost both his parents while a small child and was brought up by his three aunts who must have accepted early on that they were nurturing a cricketer.

As a boy he was remembered for his assiduous practice, particularly at the nets, where even as a child he would continue as long as someone would

partner him. At sixteen, on the first day he wore long trousers, he played his first match for Yorkshire Colts, finishing his first season with an average of 35.

He later recalled how, as a Colt facing George Hirst, a mighty in-swinger came at him 'like a cow's horn' to bowl him. He broke a Bradford League batting record in 1914, when twenty, with an aggregate of 715 at an average of 47. In the Great War he served with the Ordnance Corps and then the Sher-

The quiet confidence of champion cricketers:
Frank Smailes and Herbert Sutcliffe, 1936, veterans of conquering campaigns.

wood Foresters. While stationed at York he would take French leave to cycle to Pudsey to play for St Lawrence under an assumed name, a common practice at the time that the officers commanding must have winked at.

Before the war ended, Sutcliffe was commissioned into the Green Howards and was playing for West of Scotland. In May 1919 he scored 51 for the Colts against Yorkshire at Headingley, a signal that he was ready for a greater arena.

The Great War, of course, took four years from all cricket careers and when Holmes and Sutcliffe came together to form their mighty partnership, Percy was already thirty-two, Herbert twenty-four, the pairing first being made by Burton, against Kent, at Leeds at the end of June. Both went on to score five centuries that season: they raised five century partnerships, each scored more than 1800 runs, both averaged over 44 and both were named among *Wisden's* Five Cricketers of the Year, Sutcliffe's first summer being described as 'without parallel. This being so, the highest honours of the cricket field should fall to him in the near future. By reason of his fine driving he is perhaps a more attractive bat to watch than Holmes but he may not be so strong in defence.'

As Leslie Duckworth observed, 'in the light of their subsequent development these assessments read a little strangely for in later years Holmes seemed the more impatient of the two – and it was Sutcliffe who developed a defence without parallel among modern batsmen.'

Sutcliffe was always a fierce driver on the off side and developed a splendid, dismissive hook. 'Herbert', the veteran Bradford journalist Dick Williamson would assert on rainy afternoons at Park Avenue, 'could hook 'em off his eyebrows.' Contemporary critics asserted that the hook was Sutcliffe's weakness, a notion possibly based on the fact that this was one stroke with which he lived a little dangerously. He profited from it often enough to ensure that opposing bowlers were most careful in their use of bouncers.

That he could hit is confirmed by his position as the leading six-hitter in Yorkshire's history, including ten in an innings against Northamptonshire in 1933 and eight against Gloucestershire in 1932. When this power was added to his vast patience and enormous defensive technique his scoring feats are understandable: between 1922 and 1935 he never failed to score less than two thousand runs; in 1931 and '32 he topped three thousand. He scored 112 centuries for Yorkshire and 149 in his career; on the 1924–5 tour of Australia he raised a Test aggregate of 734 runs at an average of 81.55 against Gregory and Mailey.

He was shrewd enough to turn down, tactfully, Yorkshire's offer of the captaincy knowing that an acceptance could only upset players senior to himself, notably Rhodes. He was probably the first professional to use, on hot days, what would now be called a deodorant – Cardus referred to it as 'eau de cologne' and there seems little doubt that some fellow professionals regarded his sleek, black hair and crisp, spotless white shirts and general air of superiority as a bit 'uppity'. But if crowds, particu-

Pride: the young off-spinner Ellis Robinson strides out to resume an innings with maestro Sutcliffe.

larly at Old Trafford, barracked him, Sutcliffe ignored them utterly and his general good nature, good manners and total competence brought him many friends and admirers and few, if any, enemies.

Cardus, who saw more of him than possibly any other cricket writer except Kilburn, wrote: 'He made a strong contrast to the grim conquering Yorkshire XI of his heyday. He was almost decorative among a company out to kill. No "foony" stuff. Yet beneath the outward show of the debonair Sutcliffe was the true toughness. In his bones' marrow Sutcliffe was Yorkshire enough.' Wrote Kilburn: 'He gave to professional cricketers the same sort of credit-card status that Henry Cotton gave to professional golfers.'

Kilburn also recorded how Sutcliffe used every spare minute to attend to whatever professional or social engagement was occupying him: 'Benefits accruing from personal distinction were interpreted by Sutcliffe (when senior professional) as applying to Yorkshire cricket teams. "Thank you for your invitation to (golf or the theatre). There will be (eight or fifteen) in the party."'

Herbert Sutcliffe played fifty-four times for England and died at the age of eighty-four in Keighley, living long enough to see both Hutton and Boycott join him as scorers of more than a hundred centuries.

Emmott Robinson *Tactician*

Emmott was the first of Yorkshire's Robinsons from Keighley, an all-rounder called up, at the age of thirty-six, to patch up the side in 1919, who stayed to become one of the great characters in the post-Great War side. It was Cardus who spotted that Emmott was the epitome of the ultra-professionalism of Yorkshire of the 1920s, where the environment and upbringing of thrift and hard graft permeated their cricket.

He was a useful right-arm swing bowler (nine for 36 against Lancashire in 1920) but managed a hundred wickets in a season only once and reached a thousand runs only twice. He was a bits and pieces contributor, lean, wiry, an excellent fielder whose service was not to be measured by the figures in the scorebook but by the time and circumstance of his efforts. Emmott had a keen tactical brain and was given credit second only to Rhodes for the running and supervision of the supremely efficient team.

Cardus was so taken by the man that he wrote of him countless times – to such an extent that Emmott,

when a veteran, is once supposed to have protested to the writer that he had in fact been re-invented. If some of Cardus's Emmott stories were tarted up a little they did no one harm, least of all Emmott who, after the Second World War, was engaged to write a newspaper column mostly on the strength of the fame he had accrued through Cardus's writings.

His passion, and uncompromising pursuit of Yorkshire's victories, earned him a place in the affection and memory of his contemporaries. In the season after he retired (in 1931, when forty-eight) he had to be called upon to field as substitute in a Roses match and almost instantly appealed for lbw, from short leg. The umpire, Arthur Morton, upbraided him, adding: 'Anyroad, Emmott, it's got nowt to do wi' thee. Tha's not really playing.'

Robinson went on to become an umpire himself, and coached Yorkshire (1944–6) and Leicestershire the following year. He died in Hinckley in 1969 but his spirit lives on, not least around the ringside at Headingley and Abbeydale.

Abraham Waddington   *Man of Temper*

Waddington appeared in July 1919 from Wakefield cricket, although born in Clayton, Bradford, and had an immediate impact, appearing as he did to many followers as another George Hirst. Both bowled left-arm medium to fast but in very different styles: Hirst was powerful, vigorous, Waddington rhythmical, running in on a curve with a classical delivery. There was much difference in temperament, too, for Waddington was a volatile personality, quick tempered and quick tongued.

In that first half-season of two-day Championship matches, Waddington's line of attack and versatility brought him 100 wickets at 18.74. In 1920 his return was 140 wickets and as the discovery of the first post-war period he went on Douglas's disastrous 1920–1 tour of Australia in which all five Tests were lost. Waddington, used as a stock bowler, was written off as a failure but he returned to England where Yorkshire used him much more profitably and in the following two summers he added another 237 wickets.

Running up to bowl on a wet outfield at Huddersfield in 1923, Waddington fell and damaged his arm ligaments and was unable to play again until the following summer when, after a bad-tempered match against Middlesex at Sheffield, the umpires reported him, writing, 'Waddington's attitude towards decisions incited barracking.' Middlesex cancelled the following season's fixtures against Yorkshire but after MCC, at Yorkshire's invitation, had investigated the matter and Waddington had made a written apology, no break in meetings between the two counties occurred. In August of that same summer there was one report of bad blood between Yorkshire and Surrey, although no formal protests were made.

Waddington came back for one more fiery summer, in 1925, when he took 105 wickets, but two years later, his powers seemingly in decline at thirty-four and troubled by the old shoulder injury, he refused Yorkshire's terms, a disappointing end to a comet-like career.

He was a more than useful batsman, although given to an occasional impetuosity that was the despair of Robinson and Rhodes, and he also played soccer for Bradford City and Halifax Town. In his sixties he joined Hutton and other cricketers to visit Verity's grave at the Military Cemetery at Caserta and left his white rose cap on the gravestone. Abe Waddington died in Scarborough at the age of

sixty-six and Peter Thomas suggested that a phrase of Leslie Duckworth's might have been inscribed on his tombstone: 'Yes, a man of temper, Waddington, but a fine cricketer.'

also took five for 67 against Lancashire at Sheffield, but then failed to get a single wicket against Middlesex before drifting off into league cricket.

Yet Bradford had provided Waddington and Emmott Robinson for Burton's new Yorkshire team, and Rhodes had taken up his spinners again, still fiendishly accurate if not turning the ball quite so much (155 wickets). Waddington had an extraordinary start. Entering first-class cricket at the beginning of July he ended with a hundred wickets at a cost of 18.74 each. Rockley Wilson, too, made some invaluable contributions to the bowling, not least against Middlesex at Leeds when, after an opening stand of 100 in seventy minutes, he dismissed Jack Hearne and Bosanquet in successive overs.

The batting, meanwhile, had taken on a new sheen with the establishment of the county's best opening partnership since Tunnicliffe and Brown. There were seven years between Holmes and Sutcliffe when they came together, the latter having made his debut for the Yorkshire second eleven on the day, he recalled, he went into 'long trousers'. They first came together against Kent at Headingley on 30 June, Holmes collecting a duck, but by the summer's end they had raised five century opening stands and each had scored five hundreds. The first major partnership was 279 against Northamptonshire at Northampton, Sutcliffe reaching his century with a straight six.

Hirst, Denton, Rhodes and Roy Kilner also passed a thousand runs, seven players in all scoring centuries. The club had completed a long and arduous climb, and the 1920s, a sunlit upland, lay before them. Frederick Delius, who had fond memories of watching cricket at Scarborough and who was about to be asked to write the incidental music for *Hassan*, would have caught the mood.

The public greatly welcomed the return of three-day 'proper' Championship cricket in 1920, gate receipts increasing by £5000 and attendances rising by almost 90,000, but the strains told upon the team, which finished fourth. Burton maintained 'we were every bit as good a side as in 1919', yet the records suggest that by the second half of the summer the bowling was simply not good enough.

Rhodes and Waddington, sharing 296 wickets, all but carried the attack: Hirst, now coach at Eton, was available, along with Rockley Wilson, in the school holidays; Roy Kilner, absent through illness, took only 27 wickets, Robinson only 53.

No criticism could be applied to Rockley Wilson, who bowled, at the age of forty-one, his right-arm slow-medium spinners so accurately throughout August that he was chosen as vice-captain for the winter tour of Australia, jokingly describing himself as 'the discovery of the season'.

A great deal of cricket was played in 1920. Kent, for instance, increased their programme from fourteen two-day matches to twenty-six three-day games. Yorkshire's Championship cricket was increased from 52 days to 84. This was 'Lucky' Denton's last season (1229 runs with a top score of 209 not out – some farewell!), and Hirst was playing his penultimate summer in the ranks.

Middlesex were 1920's eventual champions, but only after two extraordinary escapes against Yorkshire. At Bradford, where Rockley Wilson had match figures of six for 62 (from 44 overs!), Yorkshire, due to a splendid Middlesex second-innings revival, had to score 198 and lost eight wickets for 140 which meant that, with Roy Kilner ill, Waddington and Wilson represented the last hope. With 4 runs needed Waddington drove Stevens straight back, and with no one in the outfield Yorkshire would have won the match and, as it happened, the Championship. The ball hit the opposite wicket, and in the same over Waddington was bowled.

At Lord's earlier in the summer, after Holmes and Sutcliffe had raised 191, Middlesex had forced a draw after escaping a follow-on by 1 run.

Headingley's growing reputation as a fine batting pitch was glorified on a sunny weekend in June when Hampshire began by scoring 456 for 2 on the Saturday (Brown 232), a day's play in which Dolphin conceded byes. Sunday evening brought heavy rain and Yorkshire, batting in returning sunshine on Monday morning, were caught on a 'sticky', being bowled out for 159 and 228.

Two months later, in similar conditions at Portsmouth, Yorkshire batted first. Holmes and Sutcliffe started with 347, Denton then joining Holmes to take the score to 456 for 2, with Holmes reaching 302 before Burton declared at 585 for 3. Holmes' innings occupied seven and a half hours, and he was mildly reprimanded for offering two faint chances between 200 and 271. Faced with the enormity of this total, Hampshire collapsed twice to Rhodes (eleven for 129) and Rockley Wilson (five for 20 in 25.1 overs in the first innings). Rhodes also scored 63 not out and completed the 'double' for the eleventh time, his only characteristic comment being: 'Fancy scratching for it until this time of the year.'

There are various references to the frequency of wearing and dusty pitches during this summer, a nostalgic thought for cricketers in the damp 1980s. At Leicester Yorkshire brought criticism upon themselves by refusing to gamble on winning a first-innings lead in a match curtailed by the weather. In a Championship decided by percentages of matches played, a 'no result' was a more profitable option than a draw on first innings. Yorkshire claimed that they had sought a first-innings lead right up until their last partnership (Dolphin and Wilson) and could have played for a 'no result' an hour earlier, but Burton declined when Leicestershire proposed taking the extra half-hour in order to ensure a decision.

Holmes had a magnificent summer, averaging 54.97 and scoring seven centuries, including two in the Roses match at Manchester, the first time this feat had been accomplished in a Roses match.

The following year, 1921, a much wetter summer, saw the post-war reorganisation of the team completed, enabling David Burton to stand down from the captaincy that September conscious of a job well done and with the gratitude of the club and the Yorkshire public. Burton recalled that through his three years he had received regular messages (as did his predecessor White) from an elderly clergyman who, clearly, was as partisan and hawk-eyed as that modern observer Tommy Naylor of Mixenden.

I remember he always finished his letters 'Be strong and play a forward game, your fielding crisp and clean and no mistake in catching clean.' Very often too I would receive a telegram from him before a big game which ran 'Yorkshire expects every man this day to do his duty – Watchman.'

Changing customs are recorded:

It is rather curious that in all his great career Wilfred Rhodes did not perform the hat trick until we played Derbyshire at Derby [1920] . . . the following game at Northampton produced the hat trick for Waddington in his first season. I had the ball in each case mounted and presented to the performer instead of giving them new hats.

Burton also regretted the loss, that season, of Humphrey Ward, the son of a Malton vicar who emerged at Shrewsbury as an outstanding soccer player (an England amateur cap) and cricketer who won his cricket blue at Oxford in 1919–20 but played only once for Yorkshire before joining the Indian Civil Service.

Burton was obviously a popular and successful captain. He even thanked the press on his retirement from first-class cricket.

The team still lacked a high-class fast bowler, but the arrival of George Macaulay, who was advised by Hirst to reduce his pace to medium and to concentrate on medium pace and off-spin, gave the attack versatility and range in English conditions: Waddington and Robinson with the new ball, swing, seam and cut, Rhodes' classical left-arm spin, Kilner a little quicker than Rhodes and often bowling over the wicket, when in tandem, to provide a different line, and now the always belligerent Macaulay, seeking a wicket with every ball.

Hirst and Denton had gone, but Edgar Oldroyd appeared as the supporting cast drop-anchor at number three for the next twenty years, the confidence born of a regular place enabling him to expand a game based upon stubborn defence into an instrument of punishment for Yorkshire's enemies. No less a judge than Leonard Hutton thought Oldroyd the best 'bad wicket' batsman he ever saw play.

The season of 1921 was one of great frustration for Yorkshire, Middlesex keeping the

George Macaulay *Mac*

George Gibson Macaulay was related to the fast round-arm bowler Charles Macaulay, also from Thirsk, and uncle to Joe Lister. He, too, wished to be a fast bowler when he first appeared at the Headingley nets, a late starter at twenty-three, part of the new wave in 1919–20, and it was Hirst who spotted that the 'Country Boy's' talents were elsewhere than in speed. He had served in the Royal Field Artillery in 1914–18 and was to join the RAF in the Second World War at the age of forty-three. Between the two wars, up until 1935, he served Yorkshire with zest and unremitting spirit.

Hirst converted him into a medium-pacer of high delivery who could swing the new ball and spin the old from the off; Yorkshire has never possessed another bowler of such sustained hostility. Macaulay, in Yorkshire's cause, was never satisfied: Leyland recorded that in 1933, after Yorkshire had won by an innings at Old Trafford and Macaulay had match figures of twelve for 49 including the hat-trick and four wickets in five balls, he was lamenting: 'If only they had to go in again.'

In that same year Macaulay took seven for 9 against Northamptonshire; four times he did the hat-trick, he shattered Derbyshire in his second season with six for 3 and his 1773 wickets for the county cost an average of only 17.08. He took a long but short-stepped, aggressive run that made his shoulders sway, often bowling round the wicket to use his huge off-break; almost as much feared was his tongue, and that was among his own team-mates. Madame Tussaud's, it was said, needed new waxworks to replace some destroyed by fire: 'They can have my three slips,' snapped George.

A nimble fielder, especially to his own bowling, and good close catcher (six against Leicestershire in 1933), he, along with Emmott Robinson and Waddington formed a dangerous squad on Yorkshire's lower batting order, often turning an innings when more illustrious names had failed – Macaulay has, in fact, three centuries to his name. His most famous batting performance was for England against Australia at Leeds in 1926 when he scored 76 in a ninth-wicket partnership of 108 to save the match.

Macaulay played for England eight times in all, including the 1922–3 tour of South Africa, but it was on English pitches he was most remembered and feared. 'Antagonism personified' according to Kilburn; 'the passion in his bowling supplied fuel for his most dramatic performances and gave him a strength

to endure when a rather frail physique was obviously hard-pressed.'

Bowes saw Macaulay on entering the side in 1929:

Fiery, hostile, yes, sometimes even wicked, Macaulay was renowned as one of the most magnificent fielders to his own bowling there has ever been. He knew all the dodges. He glared at batsmen, thought nothing of bowling a fast 'un straight at the head and, pouncing on the ball, as lithe as a panther, could hurl it back at the wicket, fast and true.

Sutcliffe claimed that Macaulay was a charming companion off the field but admitted his wit could be sharp.

He was, nevertheless, a much admired figure at his Barnard Castle school, where he took a side every year after his retirement which was hastened by rheumatic attacks. He died while in the RAF, at Lerwick in 1940, aged only forty-three.

Championship after Yorkshire had been deprived of victory by bad weather in four matches that they firmly believed they would have won. Yet in the match that mattered, against Middlesex at Lord's, Middlesex won by an innings and 72, Sutcliffe having to retire with a pulled muscle after two balls in the second innings. 'Old Ebor' insisted that the injury was no excuse for a deserved defeat.

Another blow occurred immediately at the end of the match when the indomitable Dolphin, standing on a chair in the dressing room to reach his locker, fell to the floor and fractured his wrist as the chair collapsed under him. Yorkshire without Dolphin, keeper since 1905, seemed inconceivable, especially as, at the age of thirty-five, his return was uncertain. His deputy, the twenty-seven-year-old Reg Allen, was highly capable (taking six wickets in an innings that summer), and Dolphin was in fact to return, as vigorous as ever, the following spring.

Lancashire, with three second-innings wickets down, needed 192 to avoid an innings defeat at Headingley, with little play being possible on the third day. Leicestershire, with four wickets standing, needed 260 to avoid an innings defeat at Leicester, where there was no play at all on the third day. Middlesex were dismissed for 82 at Sheffield – there was no play on the second and third days. Surrey were 210 for 8, needing 49 to escape an innings defeat on the third day at The Oval where it rained continuously from 3.30 onwards.

Yet Yorkshire could make little of 'Tich' Freeman at Bradford, Kent winning by nine wickets. The arrival of Rockley Wilson, after term, gave them an additional match-winning bowler (and occasional batsman) for the last two months, but during this time they did not win a game. There was, however, a highly satisfying reprisal against Kent at Tunbridge Wells: the latter needed 265 to win and had reached 216 for 5 when Waddington and Macaulay swept out the last five men for 17 runs.

Rhodes, at forty-four, had another astonishing year: 1329 runs (including 267 not out against Leicestershire at Leeds) and 128 wickets. Macaulay and Waddington also passed a hun-

dred wickets, followed by Roy Kilner (61), Robinson (55) and a late burst by Rockley Wilson (51 at 11.19). Oldroyd, Holmes, Sutcliffe, Robinson and Roy Kilner also passed a thousand runs, and although Yorkshire could not celebrate F.S. Jackson's election to the presidency of MCC with the Championship, the team was sound and the future looked bright.

Geoffrey Wilson followed White and Burton in winning the Championship in his first season of 1922, although an operation for the removal of his appendix meant that he missed the closing weeks and the final triumph during an August of variable weather. This was a year when social and environmental changes, precipitated and accelerated partly by the Great War, began to invade the national consciousness. Radio broadcasts ('the wireless') began, girls had begun attending Oxford University, the United States had introduced prohibition of the sale of alcohol, Ireland was free (although the 'Irish Free State' was engulfed in civil war). The writers of the year were T.S. Eliot (*The Waste Land*) and James Joyce (*Ulysses*), while in Italy members of a new political creed, costumed in black shirts, were proclaiming fascism.

Although Yorkshire's eleventh Championship win became, in the end, a cliff-hanger, the start was propitious with six successive victories, including two over Northamptonshire. But by the end of May they were meeting stronger resistance, Leicestershire, for instance, defending for seven hours and 298 runs. As Yorkshire finished 15 behind on the first innings, this was equivalent, under the scoring method, to a defeat and therefore a serious matter. Lancashire and Warwickshire were then added to the victories before Surrey inflicted another first-innings defeat at Bradford, a match Yorkshire would probably have lost completely but for rain on the third day.

Macaulay (five for 31) and Roy Kilner helped Yorkshire to an impressive victory over Middlesex at Lord's, by an innings and 21. But delight was soon dispelled by an inexplicable crash against Nottinghamshire at Sheffield where first Richmond (three wickets in four balls) and then Staples (four wickets in 3 overs for 2 runs) caused two batting collapses, the margin of defeat being an innings and 75. Yorkshire did, however, beat Nottinghamshire, their great rivals that summer, at Trent Bridge, recorded two victories over Kent for the first time in twenty years, and for the first time in about forty years demonstrated, almost publicly, the player power in the team.

Against Essex, at Harrogate, an arrangement had been made for the team to catch an evening train to Maidstone for the following fixture against Kent. At the agreed closure time Essex, with their last pair at the wicket, needed 60 to avoid an innings defeat. The Yorkshire professionals, no doubt conscious of the winning bonus, thought the extra half-hour should have been taken and made no attempt to catch the early train, thus necessitating an all-night journey that got the team to their Maidstone hotel just before breakfast.

'Old Ebor' refers to the players' 'momentary petulance'. The difference in the attitude of the professional and amateur is neatly if unconsciously summed up by Geoffrey Wilson: 'I feel personally that any match, however serious it might be, and however much may depend upon the result, should be played in the most friendly spirit. The result should be second in importance.'

Wilson also agreed that Yorkshire had come under increasing criticism in the South for slow batting, 'and I feel bound to agree that at times such criticisms have been merited. A score of 450 or so against the weaker counties may have no more practical value than 250 or 300 yet some batsmen are content to plod along at a slow rate of scoring until they pile up huge individual scores.'

The Sussex match at Hull in 1922 brought an electrifying bowling performance from Waddington of seven wickets for 6 runs in 42 balls; he took his first four wickets without conceding a run. Sussex were dismissed in their second innings for 20, and although they had some revenge in the return fixture at Brighton, dismissing Yorkshire for 42, Wilson's team was able to achieve victory both home and away.

The power of Yorkshire's bowling can be assessed by the record of having had only two centuries scored against them that summer.

The first came from Ernest Tyldesley of Lancashire, whose 178 enabled his side to take a first-innings lead, but in their second innings they lost their last six wickets to Rhodes and Roy Kilner for only 35, Yorkshire making the 146 needed for the loss of four wickets.

The return match, at Bank Holiday in Manchester, had a finish so memorable that the contest entered the list of great Roses matches. A crowd of 20,000 saw the first day's play when Lancashire made 118 and Yorkshire 108 for 6. Cardus described the action thus: 'Yorkshire batted moderately well against a capital attack, as Lancashire batted with weakness against an attack of not uncommon quality.' Lancashire toiled over their innings but were forgiven by Manchester when Yorkshire sank to 13 for 3 (Holmes, Oldroyd, Kilner). Rhodes, carpeted by Cardus for his 'ugly two-eyed stance', had two narrow escapes but stayed with Sutcliffe to add 60, but with the score at 79 Yorkshire had lost Sutcliffe, Rhodes and the captain, leaving Robinson and Macaulay to defy an avid Red Rose attack, adding 29 runs until the close.

Why, Cardus demanded to know, was not Sutcliffe an England batsman? The crowd had opportunity to argue the point at length on Monday, for after morning rain play was abandoned. The third day began with Yorkshire scraping that all-important first-innings lead (by 4 runs) and then taking five Lancashire wickets, in fragile sunshine and heavy atmosphere, for 42, before a mid-innings rally left Yorkshire needing 132 to win in about 160 minutes on a pitch that was damp and slow but which had sowed suspicion in every batsman's mind.

Sutcliffe was caught on the boundary from Parkin's first ball. Oldroyd was run out brilliantly by Makepeace at 30, and before tea Kilner had gone, hitting wildly at 36. In the third over after the interval Holmes was caught behind, and at 52 Robinson went leg before. Rhodes and Macaulay then added 20 and at six o'clock, after Rhodes had taken two boundaries off Parkin in one over, Yorkshire needed another 44 in the remaining hour (including the extra half-hour) with five wickets standing, and Mancunians were thinking of early buses.

Perhaps Yorkshire were too eager to crush their old rivals. At 89 Macaulay tried to clear long on and was caught, Dolphin was caught at 106 and with Geoffrey Wilson off to hospital (with appendicitis) what had appeared to be a Yorkshire victory was being stood upon its head.

Rhodes, 'a Gibraltar of certitude' in Cardus's words, was firm at one end, and with Waddington and Rockley Wilson to come the odds must still have favoured Yorkshire, but at 6.30, with 25 needed, Makepeace swooped again. Waddington was run out and was so overcome that he stood unbelieving at the wicket for some seconds before running back to the pavilion. Lancashire thus had 25 minutes, or just under, to break the last pair, while Yorkshire had to get as many runs. Rockley Wilson decided that while he might lose the match, Rhodes was the only one capable of winning it, and he stonewalled through seven overs for 2 runs while Rhodes inched Yorkshire nearer the target.

So came the last over, Yorkshire needing 5, Parkin to bowl at Rhodes. 'The crowd,' wrote Cardus, 'sat in dumb futility, all aching eyes but helpless. The tension seemed to have a low throbbing sound.' Four balls Parkin bowled, and four were patted back to him; the fifth delivery was called 'no ball', and Rhodes said afterwards that had he heard the call earlier he would have driven a four through the off side to at least tie the game. But the chance was missed, the fifth ball had been blocked, and Rhodes scored only a single off the last ball. Death or glory? Perhaps only a Roses match could have ended in such a fashion but, with a first-innings lead in their possession, Yorkshire knew that not losing was more important than victory.

So Yorkshire came to the finale. Nottinghamshire needed to beat Hampshire to have a chance of taking the Championship, while Yorkshire failed to win on first innings against Essex. Nottinghamshire did win, and Yorkshire were frustrated by the weather at Leyton. No play, in fact, was possible until the third afternoon when Essex, batting for fifteen minutes, lost a wicket for 5 runs. The match was recorded as 'no result' which meant that

Yorkshire were champions, and although Trent Bridge no doubt felt aggrieved, Yorkshire had won nineteen matches (of thirty) and lost two, while Nottinghamshire had won seventeen (of twenty-eight) and lost five.

Five batsmen scored more than a thousand runs, four bowlers took more than a hundred wickets, and Rhodes and Kilner did the 'double', a quality of individual performance that made invalid any suggestion that Yorkshire were unworthy champions. This they confirmed in the most striking manner in 1923 when such was the weight of their talents and the confidence and authority of their play that they won twenty-five of their thirty-two Championship matches.

Yorkshire had won twenty matches in 1901, a figure equalled by Kent in 1913; to win twenty-five in one season meant virtual annihilation of the opposition. Ten counties were beaten both home and away. They led on first innings against Lancashire, Kent, Nottinghamshire and Sussex and were hopeful of victory at the close. Thirteen matches were won by an innings, and the Yorkshire innings topped 300 twelve times and failed to reach 100 only once (against Glamorgan). The opposition were dismissed for less than 100 on twenty-two occasions.

Yorkshire averaged a fraction under 30 runs per wicket, the opposition a fraction under 15. Only one match was lost, to Nottinghamshire at Leeds in early June, and that defeat still needs explanation for with five wickets standing only 36 were needed for victory. Staples, returning over the wicket, then produced a startling upset, and Yorkshire lost by 25.

That one blemish apart, Yorkshire enjoyed triumph after triumph. At Bradford, for the return Roses match, 26,000 saw play on Bank Holiday Monday. The gates were closed hours before the start and it was estimated that another 50,000 were turned away. Pictures of Park Avenue on that day show the multitude, mostly middle-aged men and woman all wearing hats, and what could be one policeman.

Rhodes, Kilner and Macaulay each passed a hundred wickets, Robinson (96) and Waddington (65) following, and what was regarded as a poor season for Waddington is explained

Park Avenue, Bradford, August 1923. Part of the 26,000 crowd for the Roses match. An estimated 50,000 were locked out.

by an injury in July, when he slipped on wet grass at Huddersfield and pulled ligaments in his left shoulder. Waddington's virtual absence for the rest of the season meant increased opportunities for Kilner, Macaulay and, returning, Robinson.

Rhodes completed yet another 'double' and his hundred wickets for he fourteenth time brought him level with Hirst's achievement. Kilner and Oldroyd joined Holmes and Sutcliffe in passing a thousand runs, and this was the first full season for a left-hand batsman of high promise, Maurice Leyland of Harrogate. Leyland, according to that assiduous journalist and statistician C.R. 'Dick' Williamson of Bradford, was registered as 'Morris' on his birth certificate, but cricket has preferred to remember him by the more princely spelling of his first name, for no one would argue that Leyland did not rank among the nobility of batsmen.

The presence of two high-class left-handers (with Kilner) in the Yorkshire order was

another example of burgeoning strength. Kilner, too, in Waddington's absence, spent many an hour in tandem with Rhodes. As 'Old Ebor' recorded:

It was nothing uncommon for Rhodes and Kilner to bowl 40 overs or so in the course of an innings and how securely they could keep batsmen 'pegged down' is shown in their proportion of maiden overs.

On the whole season more than a third of the overs bowled by each of these two left-handers were scoreless while not infrequently half was the registered number . . . though left arm they are bowlers of distinct characteristics.

Rhodes has less of the finger spin than formerly, nor can he get the same bodywork into his deliveries that he could in his younger days but besides being a master of length he has an almost uncanny method of blocking a batsman's scoring avenues.

Kilner spins the ball probably better than any slow bowler in England and it must have been noted that he bowls over the wicket with a frequency very unusual in the case of left-arm bowlers. The effect is to make a contrast with Rhodes which unsettles the batsman, also it enables Kilner occasionally to slip in his fast 'going away' ball by which many batsmen have been taken unawares, or get them leg before with an illusive straight one.

'Old Ebor' pointed out that Yorkshire had perhaps been slow to assess Kilner's possibilities as a bowler, explaining that when he first appeared in the side there were three left-arm bowlers ahead in Hirst, Rhodes and Drake and that he had to wait for a retirement and a death to be given the chance of fulfilment.

The fielding in 1923 was said to compare with that of any previous Yorkshire eleven, with Macaulay, Kilner, Rhodes and Robinson close in and Holmes, Sutcliffe, Oldroyd and Leyland in the deep. Geoffrey Wilson was an outstanding cover-point, while Dolphin recovered from his wrist injury of the previous year to return better than ever.

The shadow over Yorkshire's cricket – a growing conviction among some spectators and some players that success was an inherent right and failure a blasphemy against God and nature – grew longer in 1924, culminating in a stormy return match against Middlesex that all but brought about a suspension of fixtures between the two county clubs.

The team's first tour was another easy conquest, Glamorgan, Gloucestershire and Cambridge University all succumbing, the match at Cardiff ending by 3.30 on the second day, with Kilner and Macaulay sharing sixteen wickets. Yorkshire were now, to use the modern term, the superstars of county cricket, and Headingley attracted 25,000 spectators for the first day of the first home match, against Surrey. Rain prevented a finish, after Oldroyd's century, but the triumphal procession continued with wins against Northamptonshire and Nottinghamshire, the first indication that all was not well with the temper of a highly successful team coming with the visit to Lord's to play Middlesex. A Test trial claimed Holmes, Sutcliffe, Kilner, Macaulay, Hearne and Hendren.

Middlesex stiffened their side with amateurs who proved to be more consistent than Yorkshire's young professionals. Yorkshire were dismissed for 192, to which Middlesex replied with 456 for 8, Frank Mann hitting Rhodes for four sixes in his 79, two of them successive hits on to the pavilion roof. The shock to the nervous system was such that Yorkshire's second innings collapsed, the margin of defeat being an innings and 152.

Clearly Yorkshire were seeking revenge when Middlesex visited Bramall Lane in July, but the pitch played more easily than expected and Middlesex, sent in, raised 358, a foundation that ensured a drawn match. A highly unpleasant first day led to the umpires reporting to MCC that Waddington's attitude had incited barracking. Yorkshire asked MCC to set up an enquiry, but this was pre-empted by a letter from Middlesex cancelling fixtures for 1925. They must have been mollified by MCC's report, which substantiated both their complaints and the umpires' report; Waddington's conduct was criticised and the inference was that Yorkshire's general behaviour, and the captaincy of Geoffrey Wilson, were not beyond reproach.

Communications between the two county clubs were not published, but Waddington did write a letter of apology to MCC and fixtures were not interrupted. However, while letters were flying between Leeds and Lord's Yorkshire came under attack again, in a London newspaper, for alleged incidents in a match against Surrey at The Oval. Whatever the basis for the story there were no complaints from Surrey to Yorkshire, but in a stormy season Yorkshire were left in no doubt about their unpopularity, especially in London. They were in danger, wrote J.M. Kilburn, of becoming 'social outcasts'.

The Oval match brought Yorkshire's third defeat of the season. Left to score 300 on the final afternoon on a wearing pitch Yorkshire, without Holmes, set out to avoid defeat and were roundly accused of wasting time. The loss of four wickets quickly, to Sadler, encouraged Surrey to take the extra half-hour, in which they completed a win by 109.

Earlier in that 1924 season Yorkshire engaged in a Roses match at Headingley that fully deserves the description 'sensational'. The Whitsun weather was uncertain and Lancashire, batting first, spent four hours in compiling 113.

Maurice Leyland

Registered as Morris (a fact winkled out by Dick Williamson) after his birth in Harrogate, Leyland rightly aspired to the more noble spelling for he is properly remembered as a prince of left-handers. Whether batting first or at number six, bowling his left-arm 'foony stuff' or fielding, Leyland was always a principal contributor to Yorkshire and England (forty-one Tests). He was born to the game for his father had once been a groundsman at Headingley and the boy was appearing in Moorside's team at twelve, batting in the Lancashire League at fourteen and was Harrogate's professional from his eighteenth to twentieth years.

It was then that Yorkshire, rebuilding after the Great War, called upon him but his progress was slow, averaging 19 in 1921 and only 13 the following season. But the club felt there was potential and he gradually blossomed into one of the peers of what Kilburn called the Silver Age, the 1930s. Leyland possessed a magnificent temperament – he scored 137 on his debut against Australia in Melbourne in 1929 – and a hawk's eye, becoming a devastating player against the great right-hand spinners of his day, particularly O'Reilly and Grimmett.

Of medium height, broad-shouldered and thick-chested, he was admirably balanced, always suiting his innings to the needs of the team. Leyland was a superb cutter at a time when many of Yorkshire's old professionals thought the shot too risky. He made a thousand runs a season from 1923 to 1939, scored, in all, eighty centuries including three in the 1934 series against Australia and, as a final reminder to Australia, also scored 187 on his final appearance against them, at The Oval in 1938, for a second-wicket partnership of 382 with Hutton.

Had Yorkshire needed his bowling more often he would have been remembered as an accomplished all-rounder. Even as an occasional performer he took 411 wickets at 26 each, including a hat-trick against Surrey and a seven for 52 against Lancashire.

A courageous, modest, good-natured man, he distilled his experience for the good of cricket and of Yorkshire, for whom he briefly served as a coach on retirement in 1946. He once corrected Cardus: 'Wickets can't be too good: they can be too slow.' On another occasion when the acerbic Arthur Mitchell told Cardus bluntly that his writing was 'too flowery' Leyland interjected: 'Well nobody can say that about thy batting, Arthur.'

Robertson-Glasgow, as usual, captured much of the flavour of this well-loved cricketer:

When runs come easily on a perfect pitch in the sun and life flows gaily as the sparkling Thames, you might not particularly notice him. His element was foul weather. He would disappear into the haze of Bramall Lane, where a sterner sort of game was being played under the name of cricket and entrench himself among the sawdust and the smoke and off breaks and appeals and do his raw, tough work in silence.

Leyland's attitude to bowlers, suggested Robertson-Glasgow, could, with slight change, be taken from a letter by Dr Johnson: 'Any violence offered me I shall do my best to repel. I shall not be deterred by the menaces of a ruffian. Your rages I defy. Your abilities are not so formidable. I pay regard not to what you say but to what you shall prove.'

For most of two decades Leyland represented all that was best in the cricket of Yorkshire and England and it was his pride to wear Yorkshire's cap when he batted for his country. He died in Knaresborough, aged sixty-six, and his career is commemorated by a set of gates at the Harrogate ground.

On the Monday Yorkshire reached 130 before Kilner and Macaulay routed Lancashire for 74, leaving Yorkshire the formality of scoring 57 to win on the Tuesday morning, a vast 30,000 crowd catching their trams or trudging off in some jubilation at such an exhibition of Yorkshire's prowess.

According to Cardus, a good and affable crowd turned up under blue sky on that final morning as Holmes and Sutcliffe, with twenty-five opening partnerships of a hundred or more behind them, walked out to knock off the runs, a small dog raising laughter as he trotted at their heels.

The pitch was still not to be trusted but was, if anything, a little slower than on the previous day, and Lancashire began with their slower bowlers Parkin and Richard Tyldesley. Sutcliffe had scored 3 of the 57 when he was leg before to the third ball of Parkin's second over, bowled round the wicket and breaking back. Tyldesley, in the next over, gave Holmes four orthodox leg-breaks and then hit his pads with the top-spinner – two for 3. In Tyldesley's next over he caught and bowled Leyland: three for 3. The crowd was silenced, Lancashire suddenly inspired, and Yorkshire aware that a simple stroll had turned into a hard climb.

The score remained at 3 when Oldroyd was surprised by a vicious off-break from Parkin that he turned into the leg-trap where the diving Iddon missed the catch. Rhodes, at the other end, tried to break the bowler's grip by hitting out and 10 were added before Rhodes was hopelessly confounded by another leg-break: four for 13. Before another run could be added Oldroyd was bowled utterly by Parkin; a spasm of rain threatened to end the agony for both teams, Kilner continuing where Rhodes had left off, while Robinson played with caution. Another 3 runs and Robinson was run out: five for 16. The left-handed Kilner seemed to have the measure of Tyldesley, actually reaching the boundary, so Lancashire countered his pugnacity by trying to keep him from the bowling.

Turner was bowled by Tyldesley – seven for 23 – which brought Macaulay, a batsman given to quick solutions, to join Kilner, and the eighth-wicket pair actually added 9 before he,

too, was bowled by Parkin: eight for 32. Tyldesley then bowled Waddington and had Dolphin stumped, both for nought, and Yorkshire, amazingly, were all out for 33. 'Old Trafford will talk about this famous day till the end of cricket's history,' wrote Cardus.

Again according to Cardus, the conductor of the Leeds tram that was carrying him back to the city station was so overcome by the news that he completely forgot to signal any stops all the way from Headingley to City Square, standing on his platform and shaking his head, saying 'Who'd a tho't it? Who'd a tho't it?'

The Leeds crowd did have the manners to give Lancashire's surprised and happy players, almost dancing for joy in the sunshine, a proper reception as they returned to the pavilion after bowling out Yorkshire for their lowest score in the series. It was a fitting way to crown Lancashire's jubilee year.

All the above suggests that Yorkshire had an unhappy and unsuccessful season, when in fact they celebrated a third successive Championship, winning sixteen of their thirty matches in a damp summer in which five fixtures involving other counties were lost without a ball being bowled. Middlesex had good reason to claim that they were the strongest county and finished second, winning eleven of their twenty-two games, while Surrey, third, were beaten only once in twenty-four matches. Middlesex slipped up twice, against Kent, where they failed to take a first-innings lead, and against Gloucestershire at Bristol, while Yorkshire rarely gave opponents a second chance.

Five batsmen passed a thousand runs, Macaulay and Kilner headed the national averages and while Rhodes, Robinson and Waddington were all perhaps a little behind their form of previous years, the five together were unmatched in county cricket.

Geoffrey Wilson resigned in the autumn of 1924, at the age of twenty-nine, after winning three Championships in his three years of office. He never revealed his reasons publicly, but probably felt he had to assume responsibility for the clouded summer and that his departure might help to heal the breach with Middlesex. The Committee, in turn, felt that a firmer hand was needed with some of the more temperamental professionals, and while Hawke used his influence at Lord's to keep the peace he may also have engineered a change of captain. At the same time Hawke, as ever, was defending his 'boys': 'You never meet a "rotter" in these post-war days. They are men, good straight fellows, some of the very flower of the land.'

Wilson took with him the gratitude of the membership and public, for Yorkshire's following was rarely greater than in his years. The players certainly admired him, especially for his fielding, and his farewell gesture to the team was to arrange a coaching appointment at his old school, Harrow, for the man who had been at his right hand through those three summers, Wilfred Rhodes.

The new man, Arthur William Lupton, was a soldier, an army major who took over the captaincy at the age of forty-six although he had made his debut as early as 1908. Born in Bradford, he had attended Sedbergh and was a hard-hitting left-hander and fast-medium bowler who was never quite a first-class player although very successful at club level, notably for Yorkshire Gentlemen. His task was to restore discipline and dignity to the Yorkshire team and this he did admirably, leaving the cricket to a joint dictatorship of Rhodes and Emmott Robinson. In effect the structure was virtually unchanged, but a new and respectable facade was added.

Lupton led the side into 1925, the last English summer free of Test matches, when the County Championship was the sole competition. Much as many cricket-lovers see 1925 as the end of halcyon days – 'we must not make a fetish of Test matches' was Hawke's warning – the fact is that without the income generated by international cricket it is very doubtful whether there would still be seventeen counties extant today. Glamorgan, for instance, were given an interest-free loan of £1000 in 1922 but were not able to repay it for twelve years and then only by a handsome share-out of Test receipts.

Without Test-match calls, Yorkshire could field their full handsome power to go through the summer of 1925 undefeated in thirty-two matches and winning twenty-one. Holmes had

a magnificent summer, scoring six centuries and 2543 runs; Sutcliffe also passed two thousand while Rhodes, Leyland, Oldroyd and Kilner all passed a thousand, no mean achievement for the middle-order men who, in a side of such dominance, were rarely given the chance to bat twice in one match. Twelve victories were won by an innings.

Macaulay passed two hundred wickets and was at his peak – antagonistic, hostile, demanding a victim with every delivery. Yorkshire's five principal bowlers shared 546 wickets, and as all could use the bat one can imagine Lupton's team, so well equipped were they for all conditions, performing the 'Grand Slam' today – the Championship, the two knock-out competitions and the Sunday League. True, their fielding might have been shown up at first, but there was enough tactical intuition and invention in the team to match speed and throwing with intelligence and placing.

The 1925 team photograph exudes confidence: of the twelve players pictured only John Bell, the Batley-born opening batsman who was later to play for Glamorgan, lacks his county cap. Major Lupton looks every inch a man who expects to be addressed as 'sir'. Waddington wears a slight scowl, Rhodes clasps hands that have wrought miracles in Yorkshire's service, Robinson looks quizzical. There could have been no doubt in the photographer's mind that he was recording champions for posterity.

The matches against Middlesex were, for once, regarded as of even more concern and importance than the Roses encounters. At Lord's Yorkshire recorded a major triumph, winning by an innings and 149 runs; Middlesex were dismissed for 118, Holmes and Sutcliffe replied with a stand of 140, and the declaration came at 538 for 6 (Holmes 315 in 410 minutes, thirty-eight fours) before Middlesex, despite some resistance from Stevens and Hearne, were bowled out again.

Sussex gave Yorkshire a fright at Bradford in August when, by lunch on the third day, they needed 40 to win with six wickets in hand. The legend is that Macaulay drank champagne for lunch, but this cannot be true for if it were Yorkshire would surely have bought the vineyard and stocked every cellar in the county with the conquering vintage of such penetration and accuracy. Macaulay returned from lunch to bowl 33 balls for five wickets and 8 runs, while Kilner, at the other end, took one for 8. It was such an astonishing performance that the crowd, ever ready to cheer a Yorkshire success, were all but struck dumb by such a wonder.

Such was the crowd for Middlesex's visit to Headingley (Roy Kilner's benefit) that Holmes was unable to get to the ground for the start and Yorkshire had to open their innings with Sutcliffe and Leyland who, no doubt to Percy's outrage, opened with a stand of 218, the declaration this time coming at 528 for 6 (Sutcliffe 235). Middlesex were then dismissed for 184, but a gallant rearguard led by Stevens batted out time in the follow-on.

Yorkshire's visit to The Oval in 1925 brought in a crowd of 25,000 on the first day, but the contest, ruined by rain, was left drawn.

The next year, 1926, was that of the General Strike, itself an indication of the strong current for social change in the country. An important rising young novelist was Aldous Huxley, 'Rhapsody in Blue' by Gershwin and Respighi's 'Pines of Rome' could be heard on the wireless, Duke Ellington had formed his first orchestra, and one of the most beautiful sounds in popular music was the golden cornet of Bix Beiderbecke. Of far greater moment in the broad acres, however, was the fact that, after four successive Championships, the title was stolen away, and by Lancashire!

Yorkshire lost on a fraction of a percentage – 75.71 to 74.28 – after leading the table for most of the summer, the difference coming in August when Lancashire won their last three matches while Yorkshire won two but lost on first innings to Surrey at The Oval. As Yorkshire did not lose a match and inflicted upon the new champions one of their two defeats, there was some criticism of the system; in fact Lancashire won seventeen of thirty-two matches played, to Yorkshire's fourteen of thirty-one.

As the summer lengthened, Yorkshire's power waned while Lancashire grew in strength. Yorkshire won ten of their first fourteen matches and drew nine of the last thirteen when the weather deteriorated, no less than eleven days of home cricket being washed out. Another influencing factor was the return of a full Test-match programme, Sutcliffe, Kilner, Macaulay and Rhodes all being called upon by the selectors.

The batting remained a bristling fortress to opposing bowlers. Six players passed a thousand runs and twenty-two individual centuries were scored despite the loss of Oldroyd after the August Bank Holiday, when he had been struck on the head by the Australian fast bowler McDonald, who had joined Lancashire. The bowling lost a little from August and only Rhodes and Macaulay passed a hundred wickets, although Kilner, in all matches, bowled 1200 overs and of the 890 he bowled in the Championship 340 were maidens – figures a modern bowler may have to read twice to assure himself of their not being misprints.

At Bradford Lancashire were routed at Whitsun by an innings and 94, their last seven wickets going down in 75 minutes after play had been delayed, on the third day, until three o'clock. Rhodes did not get to bowl. Hendren saved Middlesex at Lord's in the first of the blood matches of that era, but Yorkshire were comprehensive winners at Park Avenue, Kilner taking six for 15 in an hour's bowling on the third afternoon. Glamorgan were beaten by tea-time on the second day at Hull, Robinson and Macaulay bowling unchanged in Glamorgan's first innings of 52.

Both Yorkshire and Surrey were sadly under strength at Bramall Lane where Yorkshire's makeshift openers, Leyland and Arthur Mitchell, made a first-wicket stand of 192. Surrey had to follow on and the Hull fast bowler George Crawford took five for 59. Crawford had first appeared for Yorkshire in 1914 and it is a tribute to his professionalism that he should have returned to have his best, if fleeting, summer at the age of thirty-six.

The return match at The Oval was the moment when Lancashire overtook Yorkshire in the Championship table, a momentous event in the mid twenties. Yorkshire struggled to 274, Surrey batted dourly (Hobbs spent almost five hours over 102) but took first-innings lead at 355 for 9, and although Holmes and Sutcliffe relieved some Yorkist frustrations by hitting

Arthur Mitchell *Ticker*

The nickname should be more properly spelt 'Ticka', it being applied first by Yorkshiremen returning from a coaching engagement in India and, as Mitchell put it, 'It stuck.' A Baildon man, dour, hard and patient, he batted right-handed and served Yorkshire mostly at number three in succession to Oldroyd, although he was often pressed as an opener and this after waiting six years in the Colts for an opening to appear.

He was a wonderful catcher at slip and more notably at gully, especially to Verity, whose ability to make the ball bounce and whip away needed specialist close attention in the field which Mitchell always provided. His batting, he admitted, was based on a solid defence and his obduracy was known to incite opposing crowds, especially Lancashire's, whom he delighted in riling. But he could also score quickly when necessary and was as powerful a driver as any in Sellers' team although it was a stroke he would normally use sparingly.

In 1933, the one season when he passed two thousand runs, he and Sutcliffe scored 105 in 55 minutes against Surrey at Bradford, after Hutton had been dismissed when Yorkshire needed 199 to win against the clock. He passed a thousand runs ten times in his seventeen seasons, scored thirty-nine centuries for Yorkshire (forty-four in all) and played six times for England.

His call-up is a legend. England were playing South Africa at Leeds and Leyland had to withdraw, through illness, on the morning of the match. Yorkshire were not playing and Sellers was deputed to drive to Baildon, ten miles away, to pick up Mitchell, who was in his garden. 'Let me tidy me-sen up a bit,' he told Sellers, who then drove him at such speed back to Headingley that forever afterwards

Mitchell gave the impression that playing in his first Test match came as a relief. He scored 72 of an opening partnership of 128 made in 110 minutes, but although he toured India under Jardine in 1933–4 he could not consolidate a place in the face of the stern competition at that time.

Mitchell was a dry, straight man who was much respected as the county coach after the Second World War and yet it will be for his close fielding that he will be best remembered, making slips to gully as much his kingdom as it had been Long John Tunnicliffe's. 'What's tha doing here?' he queried of the young Hutton when he was first moved into the slips; but the remark 'Ticker' Mitchell's memory will be treasured for came when he was joined in that department by another brilliant young fielder, Ellis Robinson. Ellis made a diving catch followed by a somersault, throwing the ball in the air and catching it again as it dropped. The Headingley crowd were on their feet cheering a magnificent piece of athleticism and co-ordination. 'Gerrup,' growled Mitchell, standing alongside. 'Tha's makkin' an exhibition o' thisen.'

Mitchell was Yorkshire's coach from 1945 to 1970 and he died, aged seventy-four, in a Bradford hospital on Christmas Day 1976. He was, said *Wisden*, 'a wonderful man in a crisis. No match was ever lost until the opposition had got him out.'

Mitchell's austerity, according to Gerald Howat, lay in his total reluctance to award praise or encouragement (he relented a little in his coaching days): 'After one particular burst of sarcasm, Hutton "gave him a wide berth. He was too hard for me." Sutcliffe described him as "grim as a piece of stone from Baildon Moor".'

256 in 150 minutes, the match was drawn and, had Yorkshire known it, the Championship gone.

Cardus, the previous season, had echoed national irritation at continuing White Rose supremacy by suggesting, in the *Manchester Guardian*, that Yorkshire be awarded the permanent title of Honorary Champions 'so that the rest of us can get on with enjoying the game'.

He would have been in a better humour at

the Bank Holiday Roses encounter, for Lancashire batted through the Saturday for 297 for 2 and went on for nine hours, finally to declare at 509 for 9. Rhodes, then aged forty-eight, bowled 42 overs to take seven for 116. Yorkshire replied with 352 despite Oldroyd's departure for hospital and the match was a stalemate as was, in the end, Yorkshire's summer. Not since August 1924 had the team been beaten and the preservation of that record had begun to affect the team's cricket, an avoidance of defeat taking priority. When other teams playing Yorkshire adopted a similar attitude, the game became moribund.

At Hull in May 1927, the great run ended with a victory that brought Warwickshire headlines for a week. Yorkshire began with a competent 272, Oldroyd returning with a 67. Warwickshire then built a lead of 121 by the third morning and a draw seemed inevitable after Yorkshire had cleared the arrears without too much trouble. But Yorkshire's last four wickets raised only 22 and Warwickshire, by claiming the extra half-hour, knocked off the 42 needed for a reverberating victory with the loss of just two wickets to Waddington.

There had been no hint of impending disaster. Holmes and Sutcliffe had been as prolific as usual, Macaulay was proving himself a first-class all-rounder and the bowlers were rampant. After Hull Yorkshire did not run into further trouble until they visited Lancashire at Old Trafford at Whitsun, the champions being unbeaten. Lancashire also had the most feared fast bowler of his time, Ted McDonald, and he gave Leyland and Sutcliffe a fearful opening barrage, bowling bouncers at batsmen who, in those days, wore protection only on the lower half of the body.

Holmes had been injured in the previous match. Sutcliffe was lbw for a duck, to a ball that did not lift, and Leyland was caught at slip in the first fifteen minutes: 10 for 2. Oldroyd, said to have been never truly happy against real fast bowling since his previous meeting with McDonald, and Mitchell took the score to 38 before the latter was also taken at slip. Oldroyd, relieved to be at the other end, swung at Sibbles and was well caught at square leg, and the first five wickets had gone for 57. George Kennie, a twenty-three-year-old Bradford batsman, brought into this furnace in the absence of Holmes and Lupton, was lbw to Tyldesley in this his only first-class match, for nought, and at ten minutes to one o'clock Rhodes, by then forty-nine, marched out to join Kilner with Yorkshire deep in crisis.

Doggedly they pushed Yorkshire along to 93 before Kilner was taken at slip; Rhodes, top scorer with 44, was caught behind off the returning McDonald, but the total of 166 repre-

sented a formidable recovery. Lancashire then built upon McDonald's five for 68 by spending 390 minutes in raising 234 before McDonald struck again: six for 67. Lancashire knocked off the 86 runs in two hours for the loss of two wickets.

Middlesex retrieved prestige at Lord's where Haig, seven for 33, helped to dismiss Yorkshire for 81. Kilner (53) rallied Yorkshire's second innings but Middlesex managed to win, dashing through the third-day showers. The return match at Sheffield was drawn and distinguished by Leyland's 204 not out.

Eight successive matches in August were interrupted by rain but Yorkshire were able to finish happily, defeating Sussex at Hove by nine wickets, Kilner scoring 91 not out and taking eight wickets. MCC were then beaten by eight wickets at Scarborough in what was in effect a finale to one of the most successful Yorkshire teams and a match that could be considered, certainly within the context of county cricket, as one of the great ones.

The autumn and winter of 1927–8 brought great changes to Yorkshire. Major Lupton, his task well completed, retired to the club cricket he loved so much at the age of forty-nine; Arthur Dolphin, after twenty-two years of magnificent service as wicket-keeper, retired at the age of forty-one. Abe Waddington, volatile, temperamental and occasionally brilliant, refused terms. He was thirty-four and still troubled by the left shoulder ligament he had strained in 1923, taking only 45 wickets at 30.62 in his final summer, but his departure was a sad loss.

Rhodes was then fifty and Emmott Robinson thirty-five; and an even greater blow was to befall the team. Kilner, then the leading all-rounder, contracted typhoid fever while coaching in India that winter and was taken from the ship to Barnsley Fever Hospital, but he died on a spring day, 5 April, a date when Yorkshire and England had been looking forward to seeing him play again. Of the five bowlers who had done so much for Yorkshire in the decade, only one, George Macaulay, could be said to remain at his peak.

Tom Jacques, a fast right-hander from York, had done well enough in his first season to win selection as an amateur for The Rest in the Test trial, taking four England wickets for 53, but while he showed promise he was clearly not ready to fill one of several huge gaps in the side.

Dolphin's successor was to hand – Arthur Wood from Eccleshill, Bradford, who, at twenty-nine, was experienced both behind the stumps and with the bat, hardened by his long apprenticeship. Wood fitted the gauntlets as comfortably as when Dolphin had replaced David Hunter. That succession, at least, was secure.

But what of the captaincy? Word soon spread that Yorkshire were thinking of reverting to a professional, the first since Tom Emmett the previous century. Neither Hawke nor Toone would comment, but on 2 November 1927 a letter was despatched to Sutcliffe, then touring South Africa with MCC, appointing him captain 'without your status being altered'. Sutcliffe, according to Leslie Duckworth, knew what was in the wind before he left for the tour. Being a shrewd man he may also have guessed that Lord Hawke, despite protestations of loyalty to the Committee's decision, was not entirely in favour.

Arthur Wood *Rhubarb*

'A rare and vigorous character' was G.D. Martineau's summary of Wood, a short, stocky man from Bradford who succeeded Arthur Dolphin as Yorkshire's wicket-keeper and went on to create two records, since overtaken: he kept wicket in 225 consecutive matches (J.G. Binks) and was the first keeper to pass a thousand runs in a season (D.L. Bairstow). A witty, cheerful humorist, 'Rhubarb' or 'Sawdust' joined the Bradford club from Eccleshill Parish Church team and was given his chance when Dolphin became an umpire. His ability to take Macaulay, Bowes and Verity, all difficult bowlers, won him his place immediately.

He was especially capable down the leg side and throughout his career, 1927–46, he averaged 60 victims and 700 runs a season, a consistency that might have won him more than four Test appearances. His most famous call came in 1938 for the Oval Test against Australia when he arrived from Scarborough: 'It's my first Test; I'll do it in style.' He was then forty and the oldest player to make his debut for England; he went in to bat with the score at 770 for 6, made 53 in a stand of 100 in 90 minutes, was caught and bowled off a full toss and returned to the dressing room to throw his bat across in mock disgust: 'Just like me to lose my head in a crisis.'

It was Wood who first coined one of cricket's most famous remarks. Verity was being given some fearful hammer by the South African Cameron at Bradford when Wood remarked: 'You've got him in two minds, Hedley. He doesn't know whether to hit you for four or six.'

His companions, wrote Kilburn, 'appreciated him as a competent technician who filled a difficult part in a bowling scheme that relied so much on catches

Hutton and Wood pictured at Scarborough.

from the edge of the bat and they also gave him licence to wear cap and bells in the light relief desirable to balance the intense concentration applied to business on the field'. Asked to stand down for the Cambridge blue Paul Gibb, towards the end of his career, he did so without complaint.

He died at Ilkley, aged seventy-five, in 1973.

Sutcliffe would also have known that a majority of members, sounded unofficially, was in favour of Rhodes if there were to be a professional captain. According to Kilburn, Sutcliffe replied to Lord Hawke by cable, saying: 'Official invitation received yesterday. Many thanks you and committee great honour. Question carefully considered. Regret to decline. Willing to play under any captain elected.'

According to Duckworth, this cable had been preceded by another to Sutcliffe from the Committee, following their letter of invitation, asking him if he would withdraw his letter of acceptance. Sutcliffe was a wise man, and much as he may have been attracted by the thought of becoming Yorkshire's first professional captain for forty-four years he must also have realised the rifts that might have opened within the club between those who insisted upon amateur leadership (a section of the Committee would have preferred Sutcliffe to turn amateur) and those who favoured a professional, the majority of whom wanted the fifty-year-old Rhodes as captain. Sutcliffe put the club first.

Duckworth, no doubt recalling many conversations with Sutcliffe, was to write later (1970): 'I believe he now regrets that he withdrew his acceptance and thinks he should have stuck to his original decision.' That was written forty-two years later when professional captains were common if not universal and the amateur had disappeared from first-class cricket; in the climate of the late 1920s his decision was the right one, saving him, one suspects, from a great deal of heartbreak and the club from strife.

The Committee, casting around, lit upon Captain William Worsley of Hovingham Hall, a right-hand batsman of good club standard who liked to crack the ball. His family's links with Yorkshire cricket went back at least to 1858 when 'Sir William Worsley and the Earl of Carlisle were both in attendance during the All England match at Hovingham'. Captain Worsley's father was a renowned patron of the game, entertaining many famous players at the Hall, as did the new Sir William when he succeeded to the title. His daughter Katherine grew up within sight and sound of Yorkshire cricket, and on becoming Duchess of Kent gave the club a gracious and royal patronage.

Worsley, an Old Etonian, the third captain in five years, led the side for two years when the loss of Kilner and Waddington might have undermined the whole structure. Much weight was thrown upon Macaulay and the fifty-year-old Rhodes, supported by Robinson and occasionally Leyland, slow left arm. Jacques remained the most promising of the new fast bowlers but soon realised that his legs would not stand up to bowling every day, and he eventually retired into league cricket and farming.

Other fast bowlers to be tried were Frank Dennis, from Leeds, Charles (Henry) Hall, a tall quick bowler from York, and Arthur Rhodes, a fast-medium all-rounder from Headingley who Yorkshire hoped would prove to be the natural successor to Robinson. An unusual trialist was Harry Bedford, a leg-break bowler from Morley, whose eight wickets did, at least, take him to second in the averages in 1928.

Wilfred, who never ceased to astonish, finished top once again, taking 112 wickets at an average of 19.21, with Macaulay, who missed much of May with a foot injury, taking 117 at 23.75. Rhodes, Macaulay and Robinson delivered 3660 overs. With the new wicket-keeper, Wood, settling in, all under a new captain, Yorkshire could be more than satisfied with their fourth place, won mostly through the enormous power of their batting; five players passed a thousand runs to average more than 50, and the team recorded thirty-two centuries.

Sutcliffe averaged 83.38 for his 2400 runs and shared with Holmes eleven century opening partnerships. Leyland emerged as a Test-match batsman and tourist, while Mitchell, having faithfully served a long apprenticeship as twelfth man, established himself at number three. Another batsman of promise, Wilfred Barber, appeared when England required the senior batsmen.

Robinson took eight for 13 when Cambridge University were dismissed for 30, but Yorkshire had to wait until June for their first victory, despite passing 500 against Worcestershire (Leyland 247), and Essex (Holmes and Sutcliffe 268). By 1928 the object of a Roses

Wilf Barber   *Old Tiddley-push*

Barber, from Cleckheaton, was in Gerald Howat's words the 'fourth pillar' (after Sutcliffe, Leyland and Mitchell) of Yorkshire's batting in the mid 1930s. A right-hand bat and fast-medium bowler, an excellent fielder, he, like his contemporary Cyril Turner, was an invaluable member of the side who took what few opportunities came his way.

His true value to Yorkshire was to be seen when England demanded three or four players from the side; it was then that players such as Barber and Turner were able to demonstrate their own right to wear the White Rose.

Again like Turner, he had to wait for his place, making his debut in 1926 after joining the Warwickshire ground staff. He went to Scarborough in 1929 and rejoined Yorkshire in 1932, missing a thousand runs only once in the next nine seasons and, with Hutton, managing a thousand again in 1946. Barber twice scored double hundreds, scored twenty-seven centuries for Yorkshire and compiled 346 with Leyland for the second wicket against Middlesex at Sheffield in 1932. He played well enough in 1935 to win a place in two Tests against South Africa.

Kilburn described Barber as 'a handsome batsman, small in stature but upright in style with a liking for the off-drive. He was happier in the routine situation than crisis and he preferred the trustworthy pitch to the turning ball but in his own inassertive way he

Wilf Barber, pictured with Len Hutton.

fitted neatly into Yorkshire's pattern.'

He played on for one match in 1947 and died in Bradford, aged sixty-seven, in 1968.

match, with both counties potential champions, was to prevent the other team from taking points; at Bramall Lane Lancashire spent 450 minutes in scoring 385, to which Yorkshire replied with 473 (Sutcliffe 140). Victory at last arrived at Lord's where Yorkshire scored 479 (centuries by Holmes, Oldroyd and Mitchell) and Middlesex were forced to follow on despite five missed catches in Hendren's 67, to be beaten by an innings and 88.

The weather prevented play on the first two days of the match against Glamorgan at Huddersfield, Sutcliffe (147) and Leyland (189) using the third day to break the county's third-wicket record.

Yorkshire ran into a fearsome force in cricket in the Nottinghamshire match at Sheffield. Nottinghamshire were dismissed for 134 and when Leyland and Oldroyd appeared to be on

their way to establishing a lead, Larwood shattered Yorkshire with what Kilburn described as one of the 'finest spells of fast bowling in history'. In four overs Larwood bowled Mitchell, Robinson, Wood and Worsley and had Rhodes lbw, all for 7 runs. The batting of both teams recovered in the second innings to ensure a draw.

Yorkshire had to follow on in Holmes' benefit match at Leeds after Middlesex had raised 488, Holmes and Sutcliffe replying in the second innings with a partnership of 290 in 180 minutes. Holmes followed his 179 not out in this match with a score of 275 against Warwickshire at Bradford, scored in 310 minutes and containing forty-nine fours. Macaulay, bowling on a rain-affected surface at Headingley, took six for 30 against the touring West Indies.

Cyril Turner

Cyril Turner, from Wombwell, batted left-handed, bowled medium pace right, fielded superbly any-where yet was a modest man who, in Kilburn's eyes, was 'self-effacing and made of modesty'. Neverthe-less Turner served Yorkshire over a span of thirty-one years and was the first to spot, while coaching at Sheffield United, the enormous potential of Freddie Trueman.

His patience can be assessed by his record: he first played in 1925 but did not break into the side until eight years later and did not win his cap until 1934. If substantial contributions from him were rarely needed, he could perform when necessary: 51 out of 101 on a drying pitch against Warwickshire, who raised 45; seven for 54 on a bitterly cold day against Gloucestershire; in 1937, against a then strong Derbyshire side, he scored 81 not out and then took five for 45 and three for 63.

Cyril Turner was an ideal reserve, a player who could do a little of everything and accepted his role with good grace and gave it great endeavour. As a fielder he was ranked with Mitchell and Sellers. 'They stopped the breath with their catching,' wrote Kilburn. It was Turner's task, when the boy prodigy Hutton came into the dressing room, to look after him.

He played one season after the war and then became senior professional and coach to the Colts before continuing his service as scorer. He died, still talking and watching cricket, aged sixty-six in Wath on Dearne in November 1968.

Worsley's second year of captaincy, 1929, brought Yorkshire to a shared second place in the Championship with Lancashire, but it will be remembered chiefly as the threshold for another great era in the county's history. After only one summer of an under-strength attack the first reinforcement arrived in the form of the tall, bespectacled, shock-haired Bill Bowes from the Lord's ground staff, but born in Elland. Although he was allowed sufficient leave from the MCC to bowl in only thirteen innings, he took 40 wickets at 17.77 apiece and finished second to Rhodes.

With Dennis, too, having a better season, Yorkshire were sharper in their seam bowling than for some seasons, and although the num-ber of centuries scored dropped from thirty-two to twenty-three, it was a damp summer, almost every home match being affected. Yorkshire's first win, over Essex at Leyton, owed much to Leyland (134) but more espec-ially to Rhodes who, in the second innings, took the first seven wickets for 14 and finished with nine for 39.

Rhodes and Dennis helped to defeat Kent at Sheffield but the return match, at Tonbridge in June, brought the first defeat for two years. Sutcliffe and Leyland were absent and Kent started by scoring 421 for 4 on the first day, Hardinge and Woolley raising 239 in 180 minutes for the second wicket. The weather intervened and on the Monday morning, after

Bill Bowes *Lofty*

His nickname was obvious for a man of well over six feet and more than a little apposite since William Eric Bowes, from Elland, saw the game from a more distant and objective viewpoint than most of his contemporary professionals, a critical detachment that served him well when he later became a much-respected cricket correspondent of the *Yorkshire Evening News* and then the *Evening Post*.

As a fast bowler he was one of the great performers of the 1930s, the spearhead of Sellers' attack, capable of genuine pace, an ability to swing the ball both ways and, not least, to use his height (6 feet 5 inches) to win an awkward bounce. So effective were Bowes and his great friend and partner Verity that Sellers, supported by electric fielding, was usually able to disguise, to a generally apprehensive opposition, that the supporting cast of bowlers were not quite as deadly as they appeared. Bowes and Verity, managed by Sellers, dominated English county cricket so forcibly in the years up to the Second World War that it seemed that their lingering presence could still win matches for Yorkshire even when they were away playing for England.

Bowes was the son of a goods superintendent on the Lancashire and Yorkshire Railway who, no player himself, had the countryman's love of the game and took his small son, on summer evenings, to watch the local club, Armley, in play: 'My earliest memories are of warm summer evenings – the sun sinking slowly into a red smoke haze beyond the trees, my father, glass in hand, sitting on the form behind me, enjoying the peace of it all.'

The young Bowes performed the hat-trick for West Leeds High School but his mother wanted him to become a teacher, a career for which he was ideally suited. However when he left school he started in an estate agent's office and became joint secretary and bowler for the Armley Wesleyan Sunday School Club. One Easter Monday he was invited to play in an impromptu match in a Leeds park and his performance led to a further invitation to play for Kirkstall Educational Second XI against Leeds City Gas Works.

By the age of eighteen he had learned to type, use shorthand and had a smattering of legal knowledge, all useful skills that would help him later in life. He had to work on Saturdays until 1.15 and on that day managed only a bar of chocolate for lunch but once took six wickets for 5 runs, including the hat-trick, and won enough from the only collection of his career to buy a pie and treat the team to some 'pop'

and to take a proud 'shilling or so' home to show his mother. A career was launched.

Bowes was offered up to £5 a week to turn professional in league cricket (his wages were then £1.22 a week) but friends persuaded him to write to Warwickshire for a trial. A neighbour pointed out that MCC, planning fixtures against all the first-class counties, were also seeking to enlarge their ground staff; he was invited for a trial at Lord's in January 1928, spending the previous autumn bowling in Armley Park until it was too dark and working in the basement of the estate agent's. He bowled stones at telegraph poles, snowballs at lamp-posts.

At Lord's he bowled for an hour, full out, against, among others, Pelham Warner and the then Assistant Secretary Ronnie Aird and was offered a season's trial at £5 a week; by this time Yorkshire had been alerted and the Secretary Frederick Toone steered Bowes towards Lord's rather than Edgbaston – 'Yorkshire will be able to play you if you turn out right.' He went immediately to Hirst at the Headingley nets and, characteristically, won another £1 a week on his MCC agreement.

In his first season he performed another hat-trick, against Cambridge University at Lord's – the right time, the right team, the right place – won another year's engagement and a rise and on his return to Leeds in September was summoned by Lord Hawke who then concluded a formal agreement with MCC that the twenty-year-old should be made available to the county when not required by that club.

In the next two years Bowes, who hitherto had relied on his pace, bounce and a big in-swing, learned diligently, listening to his peers, especially to the then Yorkshire scorer Billy Ringrose, a renowned out-swinger of his day. But it was not until he read an instructional booklet by Sutcliffe, advising a close study of the placing of the feet in delivery stride, that the penny dropped. Once he had included the away swinger in his armoury, Bowes moved from county to Test-class fast bowler.

He took a hundred wickets or more in eight of the next nine seasons in an era of batsman's pitches; under a burning sun at Scarborough in 1932 he bowled 40 overs in three and a half hours and took nine for 120 against Essex. When pitches did help him he was deadly: in four successive matches in 1935 he took 40 wickets for 321 runs and in August of that same season took 34 wickets in four succes-

sive games. His 1351 wickets for Yorkshire cost 15.16 runs apiece and it always amused him that his career record also listed 1251 runs. As a batsman and a fielder he rarely won the approbation of Macaulay and Mitchell.

Bowes was a late selection, behind Larwood, Allen and Tate, for Jardine's Bodyline tour of 1932–3 and although he played in only one Test and took only one wicket, that wicket was Bradman's. In English conditions he made the Australians remember: in 1934 at Lord's he and Verity shared nineteen wickets, the pair taking 43 wickets in that series. Bowes did not play until the last two Tests of the 1938 series but finished top of the averages with 10 wickets at 18.

Bowes spent two and a half years in prisoner of war camps and returned to England four and a half stone lighter than in 1939; he was never again able to bowl more than medium pace but served Yorkshire for two more years, helping them to a Championship in 1946. He suffered pulled muscles when playing, ironically, in Verity's testimonial match and although the club hoped he would continue into 1948 even bowling off-spinners, he retired at the end of that golden summer: 'Much of the pleasure had gone out of bowling. I had accuracy without pace, there was no nip in my deliveries, the fast yorker was a memory; cricket had become a toil.'

Bowes enjoyed mathematics and conjuring tricks, becoming a member of the Magic Circle, and was a highly respected member of the press box from his entry. To many a young reporter he was a friend and genial guide on technical matters, brushing aside thanks by saying, 'I'm only returning a little of the help I received when I first came into the box.' In his retirement years he liked walking his dog on the moors near his Menston home and usually turned up at Headingley for a chat at least once a season.

He died in September 1987. J.M. Kilburn penned an affectionate obituary to his old friend in *The Cricketer* that included the sentence: 'The outswinger had a magnetic quality and Bowes must have bruised more edges than any bowler of his time – in both his careers Billy Bowes was a proud professional and the best of companions.' Asked by *The Observer* to compare Bowes with bowlers a half-century later, Hutton replied: 'He had a little of Willis and a lot of Hadlee.'

Rhodes had taken another four wickets, Kent declared at 471 for 9.

Yorkshire were dismissed for 108 (Freeman six for 53), and although they resisted more firmly in the second innings the match was over by tea-time. With Nottinghamshire, eventual champions, equally determined to give Yorkshire no points, the match at Trent Bridge became a grim affair: Holmes batted for more than nine hours, first in last out, to score 289 in a total of 498, to which Nottinghamshire replied with 190 for 4 in seven and a quarter hours, George Gunn batting for 320 minutes, Carr 150 minutes for 23. The normally diplomatic Kilburn was moved to write: 'The fantastic and deplorable performances in this match left an unhappy legacy; there have been many occasions since when Yorkshire v Nottinghamshire at Trent Bridge has been neither worth playing in nor worth watching.'

The Roses matches attracted great crowds but little happiness. Both teams by then firmly believed that in order to win the Championship the other side had to be prevented, at all costs, even from taking first-innings points. Lancashire's excellent attack, spearheaded by the great McDonald, was supported by solid but far from adventurous batting; Yorkshire had batsmen to spare but their bowlers, without assistance from the conditions, were rarely capable of enforcing their will on good pitches. Neither team had the confidence born of strength and success to seek out victory, nor could they afford defeat.

So bored was Cardus, on the Saturday of the Whitsuntide Roses match at Old Trafford, with Lancashire's batting, that he found more enjoyment from watching another match on the adjoining field where the umpire, he remembered, 'wore a bowler hat'. He did enjoy Leyland's experiments with left-arm spinners, telling *Manchester Guardian* readers that the late Roy Kilner had once predicted that the next development in cricket would be the advent of a left-arm googly bowler. Sixteen years later, Johnny Wardle would appear.

Lancashire took eight hours over their 305 in that match, McDonald soon shooting out Holmes and Mitchell, whereupon Sutcliffe and Leyland, proper to the occasion, set their sights

firmly on a first-innings lead. This was achieved, Rhodes bringing his usual stability to the mid innings, after seven hours, past three o'clock on the third day.

The Bradford return, too, was drawn, although little criticism could be addressed to the players, play being delayed on the first two days and the match being abandoned before two o'clock on the Tuesday.

The 1929 summer, rainy weeks before the Wall Street crash in November, did provide an open Championship. Gloucestershire won the most matches but could only finish fourth (and in fact unsuccessfully sought, in the autumn, to have the points for wins increased and the first-innings award reduced), while Nottinghamshire ended ten points ahead of both Lancashire and Yorkshire – although any one of the three might have been successful up to the end.

William Worsley ended a not unsuccessful captaincy that September and in 1930 was succeeded by Alan Barber who, at twenty-five, had captained Oxford University the previous summer, winning a blue in each of his three years. Born in Eccleshall, Sheffield, he attended Shrewsbury where he also won a soccer and a golf blue, and his leadership of Yorkshire in that one summer left an excellent impression and an accolade from the recently disappointed Sutcliffe: 'a great captain'.

Appointing a young man with little first-class experience was a gamble, but a highly successful one for Barber was able to give the side inspired leadership in a momentous summer, the last for Wilfred Rhodes. In his fifty-third year the grand old man took 73 wickets and scored 478 runs before taking his legendary prowess and unparalleled knowledge into the service of Harrow. Kilburn's valedictory read: 'He had bowled at Grace and he bowled at Bradman. At twenty, at thirty, at forty and at fifty he had shown himself master of his world, and his kingdom was never usurped.'

Yorkshire without Rhodes was as unthinkable as Yorkshire without Peel, or Peate. Horace Fisher, from Pontefract, who was to make his mark in cricket in an unexpected fashion, had deputised for Rhodes occasionally in the two previous summers, bowling economically without taking wickets. It was to be the great good fortune of both Yorkshire and their new captain that Rhodes' successor appeared, by that same magic that produced Peel for Peate and Rhodes for Peel, in the shape of Hedley Verity.

Bowes had been an imposing newcomer in 1929, but Verity was sensational. Tall, he bowled at nearer medium pace than slow and was enough of a contrast to Rhodes for them to bowl occasionally in tandem for that one summer. By August it was clear that an old king had been succeeded by a young prince: Verity took 64 wickets, from 406 overs, to top the national averages in his very first season, collecting 26 wickets in the final fortnight.

Yorkshire were fortunate in that Verity, from Headingley, was devoted to the cause. At twenty-one he had gone into league cricket in Lancashire, leaving Accrington when he discovered that they had once refused to release their professional to Old Trafford and insisting, on his move to Central Lancashire League Middleton, that his contract should include a release clause, in case the call ever came from Yorkshire.

Arthur Booth, a shrewd little bowler from Featherstone whose time would come, and Stanley Douglas, from Bradford, were, with Fisher, also competing for Rhodes' place, but of all the young bowlers who had been through George Hirst's nets it was Verity who had the old man's confidence and, after he had appeared in a friendly match with Sussex, seemingly also that of Rhodes. Any Yorkshire Colt who received the approbation of both the old titans could be fairly confident of playing for England.

Bowes was able to play in twice as many matches as in 1929, and the arrival of two bowlers of such performance transformed Yorkshire. However, although they won two more matches than the eventual champions Lancashire, they could rise no further than third. The inequity of the system (eight points for a win, five points for first-innings lead) told against frustrated Gloucestershire, who won no less than five more matches than the champions.

Macauley began the season superbly, taking seven for 22 in MCC's second innings at Lord's (twelve for 95 in the match), but a nagging foot injury reduced his effectiveness for much of the season. Robinson remained a fine bowler in support (80 wickets at 23.93) but could not be considered a regular match-winner, and the bowling, overall, offered much more promise for the future than it delivered in present fulfilment, neither Dennis nor Hall showing the consistency expected of a county opening bowler.

William Harbord, an Old Etonian who had played for Oxford without gaining a blue, referred to as an amateur batsman from Tadcaster, was actually born in Rutland but somehow managed to play sixteen matches over six seasons for Yorkshire without being found out. He made a century at Oxford and later served the club with distinction as committee member for York and Vice-President.

Both Yorkshire's defeats occurred at home, Kent, mainly through Woolley, winning at Headingley while Surrey must have upset Robinson, in his benefit match, by winning at Bramall Lane. In a wet summer, with Rhodes almost retired and Macaulay handicapped, the

Hedley Verity

Verity died from wounds after leading a company of the Green Howards in night action across a blazing Sicilian cornfield under machine-gun fire from the Herman Goering Division in July 1943. A few years earlier an unthinking Yorkshireman had observed to Bowes and Verity, unaware that they had already volunteered: 'I would have thought anyone good enough to play for England would be good enough to fight for England.' Bowes wrote, fifteen years

later: 'As it happened Hedley was good enough to die for England.'

Verity's manner of dying epitomised his career; he brought style and dignity to professional cricket, to his regiment, to Yorkshire and England. One of the great left-arm bowlers, perhaps nearer medium pace than slow, he had to wait until he was twenty-five before Yorkshire called him from the Central Lancashire League club Middleton to succeed Rhodes, although they had known of his ability from his days at Yeadon Secondary School and his debut in the Yorkshire Council at fifteen. Playing as a professional in the Lancashire leagues meant that he reached Yorkshire, for one more summer under the guidance of Rhodes and Hirst, a hardened and experienced performer, yet Verity was always keen to listen and learn.

When he did succeed Rhodes in his first full season, 1932, he made such an impact that only Rhodes stood as a comparison; Verity took 188 wickets at 13.13 apiece and became the third bowler in Yorkshire's history to take all ten against Warwickshire, including four in one over, all on his twenty-sixth birthday. The second season is always crucial for the high-flier but Verity did it again in 1933, 162 wickets at 13.88.

What is more he repeated his feat of taking all ten, this time creating a world record: against Nottinghamshire at Headingley his analysis read 19.4–16–10–10. Larwood and Voce had shattered the Yorkshire first innings, a thunderstorm intervened and Sellers declared at 71 behind; play did not start until 12.30 and by lunch Nottinghamshire had extended their lead by another 35 runs without loss. Verity's first two overs after lunch were maidens and only another 29 were added as Verity did the hat-trick and twice took two wickets in two balls. He bowled 113 balls without conceding a run and seven wickets came in fifteen deliveries for 3 runs.

All but one of the Nottinghamshire batsmen had made a first-class century, and bowling at the other end was Macaulay who, characteristically, gave not an inch: 'If he's good enough to get nine let him earn the tenth,' he said. 'I'll get it if I can.'

Verity's biographer Alan Hill noted that in neither of his ten-wicket performances did the bowler hit the stumps. In both of these famous performances eight batsmen were caught, one was stumped and one was leg before. His method was the same, pitching on leg stump or middle and spinning the ball away from the right-hander on a varying bounce and speed; he used his height, length, flight and pace in an irresistible number of variations.

The postscript to this remarkable performance came from Holmes and Sutcliffe. Yorkshire needed 139 to win on a pitch that had left Nottinghamshire paralysed and the opening pair knocked them off in 90 minutes. Souvenir scorecards were printed on the ground and hundreds queued afterwards for Verity's signature upon them; he signed until darkness fell and pleaded then to be let off until another day.

Verity had been capped in June the previous (first) season and first played for England a month later; all the bold predictions that 'another Rhodes' had appeared were borne out and after another summer of sensational success he had to be taken, with Bowes, on Jardine's tour of Australia, the Bodyline episode of 1932–3. Comparisons with Rhodes were, as Home Gordon wrote, 'illogical – their respective methods are entirely different'. When, years later, A.A. Thomson asked Rhodes if Verity had bowled any delivery not used by the old master, he got a reply of mordant wit: 'Yes. The one they cut for four.'

Although Verity had only one good Test in Australia, the Fifth, when he returned match figures of nine for 95, he, like Bowes, returned to England and took ample revenge on Woodfull's and Bradman's teams of 1934 and 1938. Verity's batting – he was a quick learner – also showed signs of development in Australia; his style was to be described by Robertson-Glasgow as 'like Sutcliffe gone stale; that is, pretty good'.

At Lord's in 1934, on a drying pitch, Verity took seven for 61 and eight for 43 against Australia, fourteen of those wickets falling to him in one day, a record until Laker's nineteen wickets at Old Trafford in 1953. In 1935, '36 and '37 Verity topped two hundred wickets per summer so that 1938, the year of England's crushing of Australia at The Oval, was a setback for Verity, only 158 wickets. He also toured Australia in 1936–7 where, although less successful as a bowler, he did emulate Rhodes once again; after batting number ten for England he opened the innings, with Charlie Barnett, in the Fourth Test in Adelaide.

In his last season, 1939, Verity took 191 wickets. The final fixture was against Sussex at Hove and on the last morning Sellers received a telegram from Leeds advising him to complete the fixture as quickly as possible as war was imminent; Verity took seven for 9 in six overs and Sussex were dismissed for 33.

After training Verity was commissioned in the Green Howards, which was also Yardley's regiment, passed some time in further training in Northern Ireland and spent his last days before embarkation with his wife Kathleen in London. His sister Grace Verity told Alan Hill: 'Kathleen knew it wouldn't be long. He had been issued with his tropical kit but he didn't say anything about his impending departure. One night he said, "Kathleen, I'm going now." He put his arms around her and repeated, "This is it. I'm going. I must go tonight." It was a frosty night and she could hear his footsteps right away down the garden path until they died away in the distance.'

newcomer Verity found pitch after pitch to his liking, much to the frustration of Bowes, who was to become his closest friend. Bowes once burst out at him, while they were sheltering under a tree: 'Ever since you came into the side it's done nothing but rain.'

Verity had some hard taskmasters. After he had taken nine for 60 against Glamorgan he was told, firmly, by Emmot Robinson: 'You should have 'ad 'em for 20. You are pitching about the same place' – Emmott making the point that Verity had to learn to vary his length with his speed without losing direction.

Robinson and Rhodes remained the supreme court, and Bowes recorded how the two veterans would wait until he and Verity returned to the team's hotel whereupon they would be taken up to a bedroom, toilet articles would be arrayed on the bed to represent fielding positions, and the lectures would begin. Verity, having taken seven for 26, was on one evening severely castigated by Robinson for conceding a four.

By September 1930, however, Rhodes had already told a disappointed Arthur Booth that Verity had the job, and he is supposed to have

Frank Greenwood

Frank Greenwood, born in Huddersfield and educated at Oundle, was a right-hand bat and medium-pace bowler who succeeded Alan Barber as captain in 1931 after making his debut two years earlier. From Barber he inherited the nucleus of the team that was to dominate the Championship for the next decade, a team that greeted the new leadership by losing only one match in taking the title that summer. That one defeat brought about a change of regulations.

There had been growing concern at the number of drawn matches, bringing an outcry in 1930 when Gloucestershire, who won fifteen matches, finished second to Lancashire, who won only ten but who profited from the complicated points system on drawn matches. From 1931 fifteen points were awarded for victory instead of eight (and five for first-innings lead in a draw), an incitement for freak declarations.

When Yorkshire met Gloucestershire at Sheffield, the first two days were lost to rain whereupon Beverly Lyon won the agreement of Greenwood for each team to bowl four wides in the first innings before declaring, the match becoming, in essence, a one-innings contest. Yorkshire lost by 47 runs but Greenwood learned from the experience and proved himself a keen tactician afterwards; he was also a useful batsman, scoring one century and missing another by 3 runs.

He was also the official captain for the 1932 season but managed only seven matches, his deputy being his successor in 1932, Brian Sellers.

A postscript to the Gloucestershire match, worth recording, is that after Emmott Robinson had bowled the one ball in the Gloucestershire first innings the players trooped off and the Press Asso-

ciation reporter, according to Kilburn, exasperated after the long wait, declared, wrongly, that it was raining yet again.

told Hawke, as the pair watched the twenty-five-year-old man bowl: 'He'll do.'

Alan Barber handed over a team of Championship potential in 1931 to Frank Greenwood, a twenty-six-year-old former Oundle pupil whose cricket had been learned in the Huddersfield League. A useful batsman, he was an innovative captain, receptive to ideas, a seeker of victories, and in his first summer he took Yorkshire to an impressive Championship in which they lost only one match and finished, under the latest system, almost 70 points ahead of their nearest rivals, Gloucestershire. The pursuit of victory had been made more attractive by the award of 15 points for a win, and that season is now remembered as one of freak declarations, made with the object of averting a draw at all costs, earning the disapproval of many in high places, including Hawke.

Yorkshire's home match against Gloucestershire, a crucial contest, aroused a world-wide controversy. Yorkshire had been cooped up by the rain in Bradford for two days, and on arrival at Bramall Lane on 3 June spent two more days in shelter. Both teams were eager to play and even more eager to get a result, the two captains, Greenwood and Beverley Lyon, coming to an agreement.

Greenwood won the toss and sent in Gloucestershire; Robinson's first ball went for four, whereupon Gloucester declared. The local press agency man, according to Kilburn, believed that the rain had resumed. When Yorkshire batted, Hammond's first ball also went for four byes, there came another declaration and the match proper started, Gloucestershire winning by 47. In the course of that summer similar methods were used in four other matches, the authorities being rightly concerned at what was happening to the first-class game.

All counties suffered much frustration through May and early June when, because of the weather, Yorkshire had to accept a draw in seven of the first twelve matches. But the tremendous potential strength of the side was apparent, with Macaulay and Verity always among the wickets. After the first home match, against Warwickshire, Verity had become an international figure; Warwickshire had struggled to 201 in their first innings at Headingley,

Yorkshire won a lead of 97 by tea on the Monday, and at 3.45, the sun just starting to break through on a cold, dull day, Verity had begun a spell of 18.4 overs, six of which were maidens, to take all ten wickets for 36.

It was Verity's twenty-sixth birthday, his fourteenth first-class match, and he was still uncapped. Verity, wrote Alan Hill, saw the whole event in his usual modest fashion, praising Macaulay's effort (18 overs for 20 runs) at the other end, saying: 'It was one of those rare days when everything was set right for the bowler at one end.' That chill evening of 18 May 1931 left a small crowd of less than 4000 in raptures, forgetting their means of getting home. One Yorkshireman, according to Hill, declared: 'I've now got two hours to wait for my train, but it's worth it to have seen this.'

Warwickshire felt the weight of Yorkshire's batting in the return match, Holmes and Sutcliffe rattling on 309 runs in 220 minutes, Holmes continuing to score to 250. At Bradford, in another abbreviated encounter, that regular scourge Woolley hit 188 of Kent's 296 for 4 at a run a minute, the innings including seven sixes, five of them off Verity!

Once the weather broke Yorkshire got into their stride, winning five successive matches by an innings (Bowes, batting eleven, played in twenty-five matches that summer, being still under contract to MCC, and managed to get to the wicket only eleven times). The big man was in especial form at Lord's, with match figures of eleven for 99 against Middlesex.

There would have been some muttering at Folkestone during the return fixture with Kent, for Sutcliffe, who had declared himself unfit for a Test match, scored 230 while Woolley was playing for England at Lord's, scoring 80 against New Zealand.

Only Lancashire escaped defeat in that triumphant summer, Yorkshire taking some fearful stick from Cardus in the *Manchester Guardian* for, after failing to make Lancashire follow on at Old Trafford, they batted out time on the third afternoon. After Sutcliffe had spent 75 minutes over 11 runs, Cardus mused indignantly: 'If cricket were under the jurisdiction of a body similar to the Football Assocation I wonder what would happen.'

Cricket's greatest writer also gave his first considered view of Verity:

[He] has a beautiful action – supple, upright and economic. He brings the ball from a height and is quicker through the air than Rhodes (with whom he ought not to be compared; his style is different and his own). He can spin the ball well enough and he has something of that 'extra' pace which made the incomparable Blythe more difficult to 'get at' than most slow bowlers.

At Bramall Lane in August, on a flat pitch, Yorkshire retaliated vigorously to Cardus's criticism, Holmes and Sutcliffe assembling 323 for the first wicket, a stand that was broken only by a masterly diving catch by Paynter on the long-on boundary, after 265 minutes. 'A scalding day' was Cardus's verdict, Yorkshire eventually declaring 70 minutes into the second day at 484 for 7. They did force a follow-on, but were unable to break Lancashire again, Paynter defying them for 87.

Yorkshire had the Championship won by mid August, a task made easier by a car accident that robbed Nottinghamshire of Larwood, Staples and G. V. Gunn for several weeks.

The individual figures made glorious reading: Sutcliffe scored more than three thousand runs in all matches at an average of just under 100; Verity took 169 wickets at an average of 12.76, Bowes 117 at 15.08. Macaulay took 97 wickets, Robinson 51, while both Leyland and Holmes passed a thousand runs. Three other batsmen, including Greenwood, passed 700.

In the winter of 1931 Leicestershire proposed a further change in the Championship system, points to be awarded only for victories, but then withdrew the motion. Northern counties who, by and large, suffer more from the weather than those in the South-East, are always liable to be suspicious of proposals to remove points from matches that, curtailed by the elements, are doomed to be drawn. Under the Leicestershire system, as Roy Webber pointed out, Kent would have lost one Championship between 1896 and 1950 but would have gained six!

The summer of 1932 also began badly, Yorkshire winning only one of their first five Championship fixtures, but play was wiped out entirely in two games and confined to one day

in a third. Indeed, in May Yorkshire had dropped to sixteenth in the table, tremor enough to shake the Ridings. What's more, Lancashire had been to Bradford and won by an innings and 50, the first time in five years the Roses fixture had brought a result.

The match was Eddie Paynter's. The great left-hander held the Lancashire first innings together for 210 minutes on a far from easy surface, scoring 152 (including five sixes off Verity) in a total of 263. More rain over the weekend prevented a restart until after lunch on Whit Monday, when Yorkshire were dismissed for 46 ('a dear old lady threatened hysterics' according to Cardus), and although Sutcliffe (61) and Leyland (43) batted defiantly in the follow-on, they could only delay the inevitable.

The team was changing, but losing very little of its power, as the latter half of the 1932 summer was to prove. Macaulay was now a specialist off-break bowler, Bowes sharing the new ball mostly with Arthur Rhodes, the hoped-for successor to Robinson. Horace Fisher, then left-arm medium, deputised for Verity and won a measure of immortality by taking the first lbw hat-trick, against Somerset, at Bramall Lane. Fisher, the subject of many a legend in league cricket, had figures of five for 12 in that match, and Kilburn reported that when the umpire, Billy Reeves, put up his finger for the hat-trick lbw ball he felt obliged to explain, to no one in particular but the world at large: 'As God is my witness, he's out.'

The most significant difference was in the leadership where, because of Greenwood's increasing unavailability, Brian Sellers, son of Arthur Sellers, a distinguished amateur of the previous generation and long-serving committee member, took the major responsibility. Sellers, by his own example as much as anything, brought to an already successful and confident team, brimming with ability, an extra aggression. Under Sellers it was accepted that Yorkshire fielders (without any protection other than a box) always posted themselves a yard nearer the bat than other county players. This extra intimidation of the batsmen, struggling to overcome bowlers of the class of Bowes and Verity (who shared 352 wickets that summer), explains the great surge that occurred

Brian Sellers *Crackerjack*

Arthur Brian Sellers won the Championship six times in his nine years of captaincy, from 1933 to 1948, a record challenged only by Hawke and Stuart Surridge. Keighley-born and the son of Arthur Sellers, he led a formidable team with dash and what Peter Thomas described as 'a lust for victory'. When suddenly on the scent of half-expected success, Hutton was reminded of 'a house set on fire, set alight by the sudden flaring truth of the old maxim – a game is never lost until it is won'.

A tall, strong, right-hand batsman he compensated for limited ability with outstanding courage when facing the fast bowlers and sustained, punishing hitting against the spinners. A brilliant fielder in suicidal positions, Sellers intimidated dozens of batsmen by his presence and field settings; playing against Yorkshire under Sellers was as much a test of temperament and character as it was of technique.

He scored the first of his four centuries in 1934, against the Australians, and two years later raised the record score by a Yorkshire amateur, 204 at Fenner's. In 1937 his two centuries were hit against two of the strongest county attacks, those of Kent and Nottinghamshire. The following year he passed a thousand runs.

He may have owed his original election to the captaincy to the advocacy of his father, chairman of the cricket sub-committee at that time, but never has nepotism been more justified. While all contemporaries speak of Yorkshire in that period as a team of dedicated professionals inhabiting a happy dressing room, there was always the possibility, under less inspired leadership, of a fall into disarray through lack of success for half the side were regular candidates for England selection. No matter how the team might be weakened by Test calls, Sellers was usually able to whip Yorkshire into a match-winning combination, as his record proves.

Sellers read the opposition thoroughly, always used the conditions to advantage, was alert to every tactical nuance and was an extraordinary motivator. He never allowed personal failures – he once began a season with four successive ducks – to affect his leadership as, for example, in 1935 when he lost the toss thirteen times, lost Leyland, Sutcliffe, Verity, Bowes, Mitchell and Barber to England at various stages of the five-match series against South Africa and yet still won the Championship. Only one defeat was suffered and six consecutive matches were won in July and another six in August, during which months four Tests were played.

He must have won the heart of that craggy

character Alec Coxon when he awarded him his county cap in mid-wicket. Sellers took off his own cap and asked Coxon to try it on. 'It fits OK,' said Sellers. 'You keep it. You've earned it.'

Bowes believed that Sellers was at his greatest in 1946: 'For a side weakened by the war years he set a magnificent example, finishing third in the averages with 33.24. Frequently during the post-war period he would say, "We must keep at it Bill, until Yorkshire have a side again."'

In 1948 he shared the captaincy with Yardley and then retired to the committee room until 1972, the most powerful influence in the county's cricket. To the new recruits of 1946–7 he was often referred to, out of hearing, as the 'sergeant-major', in itself an indication of changing attitudes towards authority. Wardle remembers a pre-match lecture by Sellers: 'You've got to concentrate on every single ball in the match and still have enough concentration left to keep an eye on me.'

Sellers' retirement from playing, at forty, was, it can now be seen, a mistake. The team's newcomers, as Wardle admitted, would have greatly benefited from another two or three seasons of Sellers' leadership and inculcation into the ethos and traditions of Yorkshire cricket.

Not only was his successor, Yardley, an officer and a gentleman, he was also captain of England which meant he missed up to twelve Championship matches a summer at a time when it was imperative that his dressing-room presence was regular and commanding. The seeds of Yorkshire's discontent may have been sown in the years 1948–50 through Yardley's circumstances and Sellers' good intentions in making way for a younger and, in playing ability, better captain.

Sellers then diverted his tremendous energy and zest for the cause into the committee room, becoming cricket chairman in 1959 and directing, from his chair, Close and his team of the Silver Sixties, but in 1968 came the first confrontation between a disciplinarian chairman and a very independently minded player.

Illingworth, then thirty-seven, was under challenge from a younger off-spinner, Cope. Anxious to prolong his career he asked John Nash, the then Secretary, if the Committee would either release him or give him a contract – 'Please don't mess me about for a year and then sack me when I've missed the chance of getting a three- or four-year contract somewhere else.' Nash, in Illingworth's account, replied that the club's policy (unlike the other sixteen county clubs) was not to give contracts but that he

(Nash) had no reason to think that Illingworth would be sacked.

Illingworth was not convinced and decided to seek a contract elsewhere, writing a letter of resignation. According to Illingworth he was then approached by Bill Bowes in the Park Avenue dressing room, in his role as cricket correspondent of the *Yorkshire Evening Post*. Illingworth, upset at learning that the contents of his letter had been already leaked to the press, wanted to know how Bowes had been told. The reply was: 'Mr Nash has rung Sellers and Sellers says that you can go and any bugger else that wants to can go with you.'

There seems little doubt that, in retrospect, there would have been a breach between Illingworth and Sellers at some point for Sellers probably saw the astute all-rounder in the guise of a barrack-room lawyer while the player viewed Sellers as an outdated autocrat. The pair had rowed violently on at least one occasion.

The Committee's statement contained the phrase 'a pistol at the head', which in itself suggests a vast distance between the committee room and the dressing room, for other senior players (Close, Trueman, Boycott) also believed that it was time that Yorkshire got into step and offered the security of contracts instead of an annual verbal agreement. Contracts were available the following year but a legacy of mistrust, an atmosphere of 'them and us', remained in the dressing room.

Sellers was again at the centre of the uproar that

Yorkshire, under Sellers, at Scarborough: Arthur Wood, Bill Bowes, Hedley Verity, Wilf Barber, Brian Sellers, Herbert Sutcliffe, George Macaulay, Frank Smailes, Maurice Leyland, Cyril Turner, Arthur Mitchell.

followed the dismissal of Brian Close from the captaincy in 1970. Close had won four Championships and two Gillette Cups in his seven years as captain, a record compatible with that of Sellers, but in November of that year he was called to Headingley to be confronted by Sellers and John Nash and told that he had the choice of resignation or the sack. He was thirty-nine.

According to Close, Sellers gave him ten minutes to make up his mind. Badly shaken, Close resigned and was told that a statement to that effect would be issued at two o'clock. Close wrote: 'I drove away with my mind in a whirl. I wanted to cry – my vision misted up so much I had to stop and there, by the side of the road [Kirkstall Road], I was sick.'

His wife Vivienne persuaded him he should not resign and at noon he rang back to say that he had changed his mind, only to find that the resignation announcement had already been published. Close was asked to appear on television; the Reform Group was formed in his defence. This was the first time members had organised themselves as a body in opposition to the elected Committee.

Close later elicited three reasons for his ruthless dismissal: he did not encourage the youngsters; he was not fit; he was too critical of one-day cricket. If all three accusations had been proved beyond all doubt, he deserved better treatment. His departure could be likened only to the treatment of a professional captain by an amateur Committee of the previous century and as such marked the end of an era both in the government of the club and in its success on the field.

Sellers must therefore be remembered with both gratitude and regret for just as he as a captain enlarged and stabilised the empire founded by Hawke, he was also at least partly responsible for its dismantling. There is no doubt that Yorkshire's history would have been very different if Close had relinquished the captaincy to Illingworth in 1972 and Illingworth to Boycott in 1975.

Sellers served as a major in the Royal Artillery during the Second World War, winning the MBE, and died in Bingley, aged seventy-three. Among his other distinctions were the chairmanship of England's selectors and a tour of Australia as a newspaper correspondent. He never wavered in his belief that what he did was best for Yorkshire.

from June – five wins in nine matches and another five wins in July. From August, Yorkshire were supreme.

What became Sellers' team were renowned for their unremitting belligerence, whether expressed in the tilt of Mitchell's cap, the fast, sudden bounce or zip-away of Bowes, the hostility of Macaulay, Verity's turn and lift, all whips and scorpions above the shining batting edifice of Sutcliffe, Holmes and Leyland.

But all this was to come after the gloom and disappointments of May, for after Lancashire's salutary lesson, Hampshire won by 49 runs at Headingley – although that was the last taste of defeat. The first southern tour of the summer brought victories at Bristol, Tonbridge, Leyton and Lord's.

The Essex match, at Leyton, was an historic landmark. Holmes and Sutcliffe broke the thirty-four-year-old record by Brown and Tunnicliffe for an opening stand, 554 at Chesterfield. At 555 Sutcliffe gave his wicket away, not realising that there was confusion over the actual score, an hour passing, so the official version went, before a missing no-ball was discovered. Later Percy Fender, the Surrey captain of that era, was to blame the Essex Captain Charlie Bray for 'allowing' that no-ball to be discovered.

Not that anyone could really jib at the performance, Sutcliffe scoring 313 (one six and thirty-three fours) and Holmes 224 (nineteen fours). The match was over early on the third morning, Yorkshire winning by an innings and 313.

Sutcliffe followed this triumph with a 270 against Sussex, his aggregate in three consecutive matches reaching 789. At Bradford Sutcliffe reached his hundredth hundred, 132 in under two hours (eight sixes and eight fours) against Gloucestershire in a match of furious scoring: Yorkshire 472 for 7, Gloucester 404 (Hammond 147 out of 190 in 130 minutes), Yorkshire 240 for 6. Bowes won the match as Gloucester, led by Hammond, raced for victory, by bowling last man Tom Goddard with the first ball of the final over.

More history was recorded in the following match, against Nottinghamshire at Headingley. When a thunderstorm intervened on the second afternoon, Yorkshire were 163 for 9 in reply to a Nottinghamshire total of 234. Play was delayed on the Tuesday morning before Yorkshire declared, Nottinghamshire being 38 for 0 at lunch. Verity bowled nine overs without conceding a run and then, as the pitch began drying, the ball started to bite; he did the hat-trick, twice taking two wickets in two balls, and finished with figures of 19.4–16–10–10. Twice in his career, twice in two summers he had taken all ten wickets. Again Macaulay was the bowler at the other end, declaring this time that he continued to bowl at the stumps: 'I'll do my best to get one.' In one spell of 15 deliveries Verity took seven wickets for 3 runs. In both his ten-wicket feats the manner and number of dismissals were the same: eight batsmen caught, one stumped, one leg before.

The team had an equal satisfaction at Old Trafford, after the humiliation of Whitsuntide, where Lancashire were beaten by an innings and 5 runs, Cardus complaining that the 'hordes from Laisterdyke and Kirkheaton and other barbarous habitations' revealed themselves only when Yorkshire was winning. The climax to a glorious summer came in blazing weather at Scarborough where Essex made 325, Bowes bowling 40 overs for his nine for 120 and suffering dropped catches, before Yorkshire's reply was made in a thunder of guns: Sutcliffe reached 100 in 120 minutes and then added 94 in the next 40 minutes; with Leyland he added 102 in 6 overs, the stand being worth in all 149 in 55 minutes. Hardly surprisingly, a somewhat shattered Essex succumbed by the early afternoon of the third day, the margin an innings and 9 runs.

Sutcliffe had another magnificent summer, 2883 runs at an average of 80, and Leyland, Holmes, Mitchell and Barber all passed a thousand. Macaulay was third behind the two titans with 84 wickets, the averages actually being topped by a useful all-rounder from Ripley, twenty-three-year-old Frank Smailes, a cricketer of sufficient versatility to be thought of as a successor to Macaulay.

The world turned a little faster in 1933. In Germany a somewhat comical demagogue named Adolf Hitler became Chancellor of that country, and the British Empire, whose status then was analogous to that of the United States today, recognised another dictator alongside Stalin and Mussolini. George Orwell wrote *Down and Out in Paris and London*, and with the US economy in deep recession, unemployment stalked the Western world; the search for quick, sharp solutions was more apparent then even than it is now.

In what might have been regarded in Bradford as an attempt to rob Yorkshire of a third successive Championship, the scoring system was changed again, back to percentages, each county having to play a minimum of twenty-four matches to qualify. If such a plot existed then it failed miserably, for Yorkshire won their first seven matches then had a run of twelve successive victories in June, winning nineteen games overall. By 18 August the Championship was won again, after which there came a perhaps unsurprising relaxation, their last six matches bringing three draws and three defeats.

This was partially explained by an injury to Bowes, and it was as well for Yorkshire that Macaulay, at thirty-six and two years from retirement, had an Indian summer. Bowling off-breaks around the wicket Macaulay collected 141 wickets at an average of 15, bowling more overs even than Verity. Kilburn makes the point that, as well as Macaulay bowled – he was recalled by England – both he and Verity owed much to the close fielding of Arthur Wood and Mitchell, the latter 'among the leading fieldsmen in the world'.

There were strains showing elsewhere. The great opening partnership of Holmes and Sutcliffe, as famous in their day as Marks and Spencer, managed only one century opening stand. When Percy Holmes took until 17 August to reach his first fifty, it was accepted, reluctantly, that an illustrious career was ending.

One of the great victories occurred at Old Trafford at Whitsun when loudspeakers were used for the first time in a Roses match. What next, demanded Cardus, 'side shows for dancing and a bearded lady?' The batsmen were less amused by a pitch that was soon broken and dusty. Sutcliffe went for 7, Holmes for 22, Leyland for 3, and when Percy reached the

Frank Smailes

Thomas Frank Smailes was a high-class all-rounder who lost his best years to the Second World War. Born in Ripley, he first appeared in 1932 as a left-handed bat who could adapt his game to circumstances and as a dual-purpose bowler; it was with the ball that he advanced his career.

In the middle to late 1930s Frank Smailes became a vital member of Sellers' Championship teams, being able to use the new ball at fast-medium pace, taking full advantage of English conditions, and then switching to off-spin when the pitch offered turn. He was thus able to fill the gap in the side when Macaulay departed and to cover for Ellis Robinson as the specialist off-spinner. His batting was good enough to qualify him as Yorkshire's principal all-rounder in the years just before and immediately after the war. If Yorkshire had specifically asked for a strong, reliable, capable all-rounder who could maintain momentum in the regular absences of Hutton, Leyland, Bowes and Verity then they could not have been granted a better one than Smailes.

Even when the selectors looked at Smailes, fortune favoured his retention by Yorkshire; his form in 1938 was such that he was in the twelve for the Old Trafford Test against Australia when rain prevented a final selection. He did play for England once, after the war, against India but at thirty-four, after an arduous war in the Mediterranean, he was past his best.

He scored almost 6000 runs, including three centuries, passing a thousand once (1938), and took 823 wickets at 20.77 apiece. At Bramall Lane in 1938 he took six for 29 and four for 45 against the Australians and the following year reached his zenith, against Derbyshire, also at Bramall Lane, when he followed Verity, Wainwright and Drake in taking all ten wickets (and four for 11 in the second innings). In 1938 Smailes also completed the first 'double' by a

Yorkshireman since 1926, the ultimate qualification to be an all-rounder.

A Pocklington School pupil, Smailes was commissioned into the infantry during the war and was the first to erect a monument on Verity's grave at Caserta.

dressing room he predicted the match would not last a day. Mitchell, in a dour, grinding innings of 360 minutes, proved it was possible to stay, and his century enabled Yorkshire to reach 341, an extraordinary achievement in all the circumstances but 'the worst day's cricket I've ever seen' according to the *Manchester Guardian* correspondent.

On the Monday before a crowd of 25,000,

the loudspeakers playing Lehar, a fresh sunny morning alive with anticipation of excitement, Yorkshire's last five wickets went down for 54 runs in 75 minutes. Bowes was given only three overs, despite winning movement and bounce before Verity appeared. Macaulay immediately set a leg-trap of four and Lancashire were dismissed for 92 and 93 (Macaulay twelve for 49), Cardus concluding (on 5 June) with a resigned 'they [Yorkshire] are so obviously the champions of this season'.

At Edgbaston Yorkshire were defied by Norman Kilner, younger brother of Roy and nephew of Irving Washington, who had left Yorkshire ten years earlier to forge a new career with Warwickshire. In a gritty six hours worthy of his native Wombwell, Kilner scored 197 when no other batsman in his side could exceed 30, all done with a split finger injured while fielding on the first day.

At Kettering Northamptonshire were beaten before lunch on the second day, Macaulay taking eleven for 34. When England called on Sutcliffe, Verity, Leyland and Macaulay, two defeats followed at Trent Bridge and Hull, Sussex being the one side to complete a double over Yorkshire that year, finishing second in successive years. At Brighton, with the crown already locked away again in Headingley, Sussex dismissed Yorkshire for 114 and 115. Leyland scored 210 not out at Dover, but Yorkshire, dismissed for 88 in their second innings, were beaten by Kent.

Sussex, not unexpectedly, made a bold assault in 1934 and by late July were favourites to win their first Championship, but only one win in their last ten matches (one more would have been enough) let in Lancashire. Yorkshire dropped to sixth but, in an Australian year, they had more than adequate explanation. Leyland and Verity played in five Tests, Sutcliffe in four, Bowes in three; no county could have withstood such a diminution of strength. Yorkshire had to treat that summer as one of experiment, an opportunity to test younger players at first-class level.

Holmes had retired (30,000 runs at an average of 42) and Macaulay, increasingly bothered by rheumatism, injured a finger in 1934 which hastened his retirement. In that summer he took only 55 wickets, but Yorkshire's consolation, if there could be one at the impending loss of one of the elite, was that Smailes was eager and ready for the first team. Even the magnificent Sutcliffe had to accept that he was on the far and downward slope, although Herbert was already satisfied and content that his successor, a sixteen-year-old right-hander from Pudsey, was waiting in the wings.

Sutcliffe nevertheless topped two thousand runs in 1934 while Leyland, six years younger, had his best year. Wilf Barber, from Cleckheaton, who could bat anywhere in the order and field expertly, was now established and made invaluable contributions when the team was weakened by Test calls. Cyril Turner, a patient left-hander from Wombwell, a superb fielder and occasional right-arm bowler, was another who might have achieved far greater fame elsewhere but who was content in the company of greatness. The jewel, of course, was the boy from Pudsey, Leonard Hutton, for whom Sutcliffe had predicted an England place almost on first sight.

So advanced was the boy in his technique, and so sound in his application and concentration, that when he first appeared at the winter shed Bowes and Verity, no less, were there to greet him and to bowl to him. Bill Bowes, Sir Leonard recalled in 1987, wanted to know how he had come by his bat (a gift that was an old and trusted favourite) and then advised him, in the kindliest manner, that he needed an instrument of better quality. Had the boy played the violin, Yorkshire would have found him a Stradivarius.

It was firmly impressed upon the seventeen-year-old that his sole duty in 1934 was the gathering of experience, that runs were far less important than priceless minutes at the crease. He began his first-class career with a duck, the professors pointing out to him that he had begun, as was proper, at the bottom and could not get any worse. In his second match he spent 180 minutes over 57 against Oxford University, but before July was out he had scored 196 against Worcestershire.

The new opening partnership of Sutcliffe and Mitchell began with a promising start of 143 against Lancashire on a cold Saturday at Bramall Lane. By Monday the pitch had turned awkward and Verity was soon plucking the Red Rose, with match figures of eight for 53 as Lancashire followed on to defeat.

Yorkshire then managed to subdue the new power in county cricket, Derbyshire, at Chesterfield, winning by 102 after losing on the first innings, with Ken Davidson, a stylish right-hander from Calverley, scoring 61. Davidson

Sir Len Hutton

Technically and aesthetically the best batsman to play for Yorkshire, Leonard Hutton was born in Fulneck near Pudsey, of Scottish descent, and his promise was such that even in his early teens he was spoken of as a future England batsman. In a town that had already given Tunnicliffe, Major Booth and Sutcliffe to Yorkshire, the environment was conducive to cricketers and the young Hutton was appearing for Pudsey St Lawrence's second eleven when twelve years old.

Sutcliffe spoke of him as a future England opener and such was his reputation among the Yorkshire cognoscenti that when he first appeared at the Headingley nets he had an audience that included Bowes and Verity, forewarned by George Hirst. At sixteen Hutton was opening for the St Lawrence first team, in the Bradford League, with Oldroyd, of whose technique on turning pitches he always spoke highly. He was also opening the innings for Yorkshire II and began his county career with a duck against Cheshire followed by another against Lancashire II, for whom one C. Washbrook made 202 not out.

The Denbighshire bowlers proved to be more to his liking and scores of 86 not out and 128 reassured his admirers; a 69 not out against a Staffordshire that included the veteran S.F. Barnes convinced the club that he was not being advanced too rapidly and he interspersed his Colts outings with twelfth-man duties for the first team.

Speaking at the pre-season lunch, before the 1934 season, Brian Sellers indicated that Test-match calls upon Yorkshire would provide more opportunities than usual for young players, names mentioned being Hutton, Yardley, Kenneth Davidson, an audacious batsman from Bingley who promised a fine career but became a professional badminton player, Cyril Turner and William Harbord.

Hirst, who knew he had a good young batsman in Hutton, was also impressed with the young man's leg-break bowling and his inclusion in the Yorkshire side for the opening Southern tour was greeted with acclaim, although he followed a similar course to that in the Colts: playing against Cambridge University, batting at number five, he was run out for a duck. Hutton was nevertheless pushed up the order to open with Sutcliffe against the other University where he made an impressive half-century – 'three hours without a mistake', reported Wisden.

His Championship debut, against Warwickshire at Edgbaston, brought another half-century and the wickets of both openers, the first with his second ball

in Championship cricket, the *Birmingham Post* hailing him as an all-rounder. He was also reproached, in *The Times*, for being over-cautious.

Hutton was placed under Turner's wing in the dressing room, was seen as Sutcliffe's protégé and was befriended by Bowes and Verity, an introduction that reads in considerable contrast to the greeting given young players entering that same room twenty years later. In July Hutton made his maiden century, almost a double hundred (196) against Worcestershire, the youngest Yorkshireman to score a century, three sixes and twenty-one fours, and carried his bat.

An operation on his nose, damaged in a Colts match two years earlier, delayed his start to the 1935 season and in June of that year he was ordered to rest. Returning towards the end of July he made three consecutive noughts, but a century against Middlesex and 92 against MCC at Scarborough revived his confidence and before the 1936 season he toured Jamaica with Yorkshire, scoring one century at Montego Bay. However, it was not until July of 1936 that Hutton emerged from under the cloud to score 163 against Surrey at Headingley and the Committee, perhaps anxious to confirm their faith in his future, made him, at twenty, the youngest capped player. Ironically his bowling, four for 49 against Lancashire and eight for 77 against MCC at Scarborough, won almost as much attention as his batting that season and he was chided for a 'negative attitude'.

By 1937 all doubts were resolved. He began with 161 against MCC, following with a century for North against South (part of MCC's 150th birthday celebrations) and centuries against Worcestershire and Kent, and celebrated his selection to play for England against New Zealand with a massive 271 not out aginst Derbyshire, then the reigning champions, at Bramall Lane. A third successive century (153) followed against Leicestershire at Hull on his twenty-first birthday, only for this glut of runs to end abysmally with a duck in his first Test match, at Lord's, bowled by John Cowie.

Hutton soon exacted retribution, taking a century off the New Zealanders for Yorkshire and then scoring his first century for England in the Second Test at Old Trafford, and he finished the season in a blaze, becoming the seventh Yorkshireman to score more than two thousand runs for the club in one season. The apprenticeship, at twenty-one, was over and his aggregate, in all matches, was 2880.

The following summer, 1938, was historical both for Hutton and for English cricket. The seemingly invincible Bradman brought his Australians to tour and the young Hutton was second only to Hammond in public attention with all England anticipating that the twenty-two-year-old Yorkshireman would challenge the most prolific batsman in Test-match history. He did not fail.

Hutton scored 100 in the First Test, disappointed in the Second, sat in the pavilion through the washed-out Third and missed the Fourth because of a finger injury (Australia won at Headingley), but returned for the Fifth at The Oval for the greatest

The Centurions: This photograph celebrates Yorkshire's three scorers of 100 first-class centuries, Boycott, Sutcliffe and Sir Leonard Hutton.

individual triumph by an English player, batting for 13 hours and 20 minutes to score 364 not out to overtake Bradman's world record 334. Hutton's name rang round the world.

Five Yorkshire players (Hutton, Bowes, Verity, Leyland and Wood) shared in England's greatest victory over Australia (an innings and 579); with Leyland, Hutton added 382 for England's second wicket. That winter he toured South Africa, forming another all-Yorkshire opening partnership with the emerging Paul Gibb and in the penultimate season before the Second World War hit twelve centuries including 196 and 165 not out against West Indies and a 280 not out against Hampshire.

Hutton, at twenty-three, was at a dazzling peak when the war took five years from his career. He also suffered a severe injury to his left elbow that threatened his future and he made a quiet return, burdened by a giant reputation in Yorkshire's patched-up Championship side of 1946.

The following year, when the sun shone, he confirmed that he was still a great batsman, scoring eleven centuries and passing two thousand runs, including a 270 not out against Hampshire and a century against South Africa.

Abroad he first saw Australia in Hammond's team of 1946–7, facing Bradman's potent new fast attack of Lindwall and Miller and, after a poor start, scoring 94, 76 and 122 in the Fourth and Fifth Tests and establishing a famous partnership with Cyril Washbrook. He was hurriedly called out, as a late reinforcement, to Gubby Allen's team in the West Indies in 1947–8 and the following summer, with the Australians touring England again, he recovered his pre-war majesty.

He and Compton gave England hope through a tense, dramatic Test series in which Bradman commanded the best all-purpose bowling ever seen, while in county cricket Hutton scored ten centuries and passed 2500 runs. June 1949 was a glorious month, for sunshine and for Hutton. In seven county matches and two Tests he amassed 1294 runs at an average of 92; sixteen innings, highest score 201, seven centuries and amazingly, continuing what Tom Naylor called Hutton's 'affinity for ducks', three successive noughts. In all matches that season Hutton achieved the fourth-highest aggregate in history, 3429 runs at 68, a total surpassed only by Compton, Edrich and Hayward.

Hutton's highest score in that phenomenal summer was 269 not out against Northamptonshire; his 201 was made against Lancashire (91 not out in the second innings and a match return of five for 75!), he hit 165 and 100 against Sussex at Hove and 206 for England against New Zealand.

In 1950, the year of Ramadhin and Valentine, Hutton carried his bat for 202 not out at The Oval and in Brisbane the following winter he managed to score 62 in an England total of 122, 156 in Adelaide and 79 and 60 not out in Melbourne in a series won 4–1 by Australia.

In 1952 Hutton became England's first professional captain, an inevitable step by the selectors although the appointment did not win universal approval, with Lord Hawke's famous dictum being much quoted. He scored two centuries in his first series, against India, and with the rampant young Trueman to call upon, had a highly successful start, winning three of the four Tests.

The following year, to great acclamation, Hutton led England to victory, after four draws, at The Oval to regain the Ashes, held by Australia for almost nineteen years (Hutton lost the toss five times). In the West Indies he squared the rubber, after West Indies had taken a 2–0 lead, contributing 205 in a total of 414 at Sabina Park during a controversial tour when off-the-field stories began appearing in the media and when the Georgetown Test erupted

into a bottle-throwing riot. According to Gerald Howat, Hutton's biographer, the governor of British Guiana offered the England captain a battalion of the Argylls.

At a time when amateurs were still prominent in English cricket (May, Sheppard, Bailey), the rumbles from the West Indies brought a fresh wave of criticism directed at professional leadership. There was speculation before the next home series against Pakistan that Hutton might be replaced by David Sheppard who, indeed, led in two of the drawn series when Hutton, then thirty-eight, rested on medical advice.

In the end the selectors made the right decision and appointed Hutton to defend the Ashes in Australia where, with Tyson and Statham as his spearhead (he wanted Trueman too, but was overruled by his fellow selectors), England won 3–1 after losing the First Test by an innings and 154.

That tour was, in effect, Hutton's last hurrah. After such a triumph the selectors, despite a grumble about time-wasting, had no option but to appoint Hutton for the 1955 home series against South Africa but continuing lumbar pains caused him to withdraw before the selection process began. He struggled on until the start of July, after taking 194 off Nottinghamshire at Trent Bridge, an innings of more than five hours that seemed to have left him finally burned out. After seeing specialists the following winter Hutton formally retired in the January of 1956; in the birthday honours of that year he received a knighthood, the first Yorkshire cricketer to be so honoured for his playing achievements.

Radio broadcasting, then television followed. In 1957, at a dinner in Manchester Town Hall to commemorate the centenary of Old Trafford, one sad fact of Hutton's career was pointed out: that Hutton was still only forty and that the world had been granted only a dozen years of his play since his apotheosis at The Oval in 1938.

Hutton played the odd game for MCC and an offer of employment by the *Evening News*, London, brought the reluctant but inevitable decision to leave Pudsey for Kingston-on-Thames. Sidney Hainsworth, a Yorkshire Vice-president, Pudsey-born, who became managing director of a Hull firm of transmission engineers, Fenner Ltd, and a generous benefactor of Yorkshire cricket, found a role for him that lasted twenty-five years until he retired in 1984. He served briefly as an England selector in 1974–5 but found the office clashed with his business commitment and withdrew. In later years he has contributed fairly regularly to *The Observer*, pieces of great wisdom and no little wit, that are always perceptive.

A man who never enjoyed controversy, he was

critical of Boycott's supporters during Yorkshire's traumas of the 1975–85 decade while showing some sympathy for Boycott himself.

The esteem in which he is held nationally was very evident in 1988, the 50th anniversary of his 364, one of the most treasured tributes coming from his fellow batting knight, Sir Donald Bradman.

From a purely selfish point of view Yorkshiremen could have regretted his success with England for the loss of the dressing room's two senior members, Yardley and Hutton. Their absence for so much of those summers between 1946 and 1954 must have been a handicap in the successful rebuilding of the post-war team. Continuity of leadership is essential for a successful team and neither of these excellent captains was able to give his total attention to Yorkshire's cause at times when experienced direction was a priority.

That Hutton never captained Yorkshire as more than senior professional was simply a quirk of history. He was a contemporary of Yardley's and the pair retired together in 1955. If Hutton's health had been better he might have been tempted to become Yorkshire's first professional captain this century, but the situation never arose. He was tired, too. As his close friend Kilburn observed, 'The playing routine was losing its attraction; he had completed an exhausting journey.' Moreover the Yorkshire dressing room at that time no longer had the appeal for him that it had for some of the fresh-faced young men who were entering the doorway for the first time.

A right-hand batsman of peerless skill on difficult pitches, Hutton was as good a player against all opposition in all conditions as cricket has ever seen: his off-drive is remembered as one of the great glories of the game.

scored 1034 runs for Yorkshire that summer and turned professional, but was later to desert cricket for professional badminton.

Middlesex took advantage of the Test-match absentees at Lord's, winning by two wickets, as did Sussex at Sheffield, Gloucester at Bristol, Warwickshire at Scarborough and Essex at Southend, but there could be no such excuses for the stirring victory by Leicestershire at Leicester, their first over Yorkshire for twenty-three years.

Leicestershire were dismissed for 94 in the first innings, Sellers then declaring, perhaps over-confidently, at 196 for 5. But Leicester refused to collapse again and when Yorkshire were left to score 149 on a wearing pitch they were, to their own surprise, bundled out for 93. Leyland's benefit, against Nottinghamshire, brought receipts of almost £2500, and once a draw was seen to be inevitable, Larwood enlivened a final hour by bowling, at the beneficiary's request, controversial leg theory at Leyland.

It was ironical that Macaulay's last season, 1935, should have seen the introduction of the off-side lbw law, making a batsman liable to dismissal to a ball pitched outside his off stump. The value of every bowler who brought the ball in from the off was enhanced, and some authorities to this day claim that the restrictions thus placed on batsmen reduced much of the handsome stroke-play of the Golden Age.

If Sutcliffe had been displaced in the England side, playing in only two Tests that year, he brought all his class and resolution back to the Yorkshire innings, scoring eight centuries, and his achievements cast such a gloss upon all Yorkshire's batsmen that both Mitchell and Barber won England caps, while Wood, whose batting had advanced steadily, became the first Yorkshire wicket-keeper to pass a thousand runs.

With the bowling heavily reliant upon Verity and Bowes it was surprising that Yorkshire should win the Championship with such authority – 'by this time their successes were beginning to appear rather monotonous' wrote Roy Webber. Certainly no one could argue with a team that could win six successive victories in July and another six in succession in August.

Macaulay's health was such that he bowled in only fourteen innings, and although Smailes, now a recognised opening bowler, Bowes and Fisher, still bowling left-arm medium, played their part, there was no obvious successor to the off-spinner. Turner's in-swing brought him seven for 45 at Gloucester.

May was a desperate month, a full fortnight swept by bitter winds, the match at Chesterfield being abandoned in a snowstorm. June was not a great deal better, but Yorkshire's stumbling start turned into a steady gallop in July, interrupted only by a sensational fall at Huddersfield.

Essex had been thrashed at Colchester and no one anticipated the electrifying news of the first hour's play in the return match: Yorkshire all out in less than a hour for 31, Read six for 11, Nicholls four for 17. By the close of play that day Essex were 303 ahead, Nicholls having scored 146. The match was all over before lunch on the second day, Yorkshire going down a second time for 99, Nicholls seven for 37. The Fartown crowd were so stunned that one member even turned on that perennial favourite Leyland, telling him as he returned in the second innings: 'Tha's brok thi bat, tha's brok thi wicket [he had been bowled] and tha's brok thi reputation.' Maurice's reply, if there was one, went unrecorded; he probably returned a sad smile. Kilburn's verdict on one of the most unexpected reverses in Yorkshire's history was simple: 'Everything went right for Essex and wrong for Yorkshire.'

Lancashire, in the next match, caught the full force of Yorkshire's anger and wounded pride. Bowes took six for 16 in a Lancashire first innings of 53 and another six in the follow-on, Yorkshire winning by seven wickets. As England did not think highly enough of Bowes' services, he was also able to play for Yorkshire in the following match at Kettering where Northamptonshire provided him with match figures of sixteen for 35, 18 of his 29.3 overs being maidens.

As a final flourish of prowess Yorkshire ended the 1935 summer with a handsome beating of the Rest of England by 149 runs, the first victory by the champions over The Rest for thirty years (the previous winners having been Yorkshire), although Wyatt was unable to bat in either innings for The Rest.

Two new names appeared in the Yorkshire averages for the first time: Paul Gibb, batsman wicket-keeper from Brandsby, who had won a blue at Cambridge in the years 1935–9, and Ellis Robinson, from Denaby, a right-arm slow bowler who had originally appeared at the winter shed bowling leg-breaks but was persuaded by George Hirst to convert, with Macaulay's retirement impending, to off-spin.

Gibb, in fact, captained Yorkshire on their first overseas tour, to Jamaica in the winter of 1935–6. An invitation also went to another Cambridge undergradaute, Norman Yardley, but he was unable to get leave, and with Barber in New Zealand with MCC, thirteen players were chosen, including the second-team captain J. Raper, Sutcliffe and Hirst acting as joint managers. The ship, from Avonmouth, took a week to reach the Caribbean, Hirst writing home to say he dreaded the return trip (which was, in fact, much smoother).

Yorkshire won the first match against Jamaica by five wickets, Verity ten for 96, Robinson becoming an instant success by big hitting that brought him scores of 68 and 63. Two more five-day matches against Jamaica were drawn, the batsmen enjoying themselves far more than the bowlers. Fisher, renowned for his tight bowling, delivered 46 overs for 33 runs (and 33 maidens), while Verity bowled 59 overs for his two for 91 but did have the satisfaction, in the last match, of scoring 101.

The season of 1936, the year of the Abdication and the beginning of the Spanish Civil War, and of Prokofiev's 'Peter and the Wolf', was also Derbyshire's Championship, won by the fiery pace of Copson and the artful leg-spin of Mitchell. Eighteen of Yorkshire's matches were affected by the weather, a partial explanation of their fall to third place, but they were also over-reliant upon the bowling of Bowes and Verity, and although Smailes took 130 wickets there was no Macaulay. Yorkshire's ability to contrive victory from impossible situations was no longer assured.

Sutcliffe, by his own measures, had a poor season with 1500 runs. Bowes was not in the best of health and is thought to have played when he would have been better resting muscle strains. Verity took 216 wickets in his thousand overs, and Smailes proved he was able to fill part of the gap left by Macaulay by turning to off-spin once the shine had gone. Most welcome was the advance of Hutton, now Sutcliffe's partner, to his first thousand runs, and Yardley who, on vacation, averaged 30 in his ten innings.

The two matches against the eventual cham-

Paul Gibb *Non-conformist*

Gibb's career was a unique one, ranging from success with Yorkshire and England, Cambridge University and the Gentlemen to a professional with Essex and finally to first-class umpire. His decision to leave Yorkshire and become a professional with Essex was historic: no other Cambridge blue (Gibb played from 1935–8) had ever turned professional; nor had one ever become a professional umpire. But Gibb had a penchant for historic 'firsts'.

In his first match for Yorkshire he scored a century – 157 not out against Nottinghamshire at Sheffield (he had, however, scored a century earlier for Cambridge).

In his first Test – at Johannesburg against South Africa during the 1938–9 tour – he scored 93 and 106, a record Test debut. Twice in the match he shared century partnerships – with Eddie Paynter of Lancashire – 184 and 168. He scored 58 in his third Test innings of the same tour, a start in representative cricket equalled only by Yorkshire's Herbert Sutcliffe (64, 122, 83). And in the tedious, timeless final Test at Durban his 120 took 451 minutes, the slowest century on record for England in any Test match until P.E. Richardson's 100 in 490 minutes at Johannesburg in 1956–7.

During Gibb's innings at Durban he added 280 for the second wicket with W.J. Edrich, a record for the Anglo-Saxon African series.

Gibb's touring experience was wide. He toured Canada, America and Bermuda with Sir Julian Cahn's team in 1933; he captained a Yorkshire team that toured Jamaica; in 1937–8 he went to India under Lord Tennyson; he toured South Africa under Walter Hammond in 1938–9 and after a distinguished war record with the RAF, he toured Australia in 1946–7. He went on this tour as first-choice wicket-keeper, but after only one Test he was replaced by Godfrey Evans.

In 1953–4 Gibb again visited India, this time with a Commonwealth side. Gibb also played two Tests against the Nawab of Pataudi's Indian side in 1946 and at Lord's set up a fifth record for the series of 182 with Joe Hardstaff.

His complete Test figures are impressive: in eight Tests he scored 581 runs averaging 44.69 and he scored two centuries. His University career was a distinguished one. His wicket-keeping ability was so highly thought of that he kept out, in 1935, S.C. Griffith, a future Test keeper.

As well as scoring 122 against Oxford in 1938 he carried his bat through Cambridge's innings of 163 (Gibb 83 not out) against the 1938 Australians under

Bradman and his patient batsmanship won him an invitation to meet Bradman's men in the Leeds and Old Trafford Tests. But Gibb, always prone to injury early in his career, missed both. The Old Trafford match was washed out without a ball being bowled, and Gibb was unfit for Leeds.

Gibb's greatest performances were reserved for Essex in the field of county cricket. He scored only two centuries for Yorkshire, his 157 not out against Nottinghamshire and 104 against Warwickshire in 1946. The war must take the blame for his slight returns for the county (1545 runs at 32.87). He was a dour batsman with the perfect nerveless temperament for the big occasion.

Though he wore spectacles he was a fearless wicket-keeper, taking knocks with typical nonchalance and always ready to come back for more. He was a dependable keeper with moments of brilliance. In a Minor Counties against Cambridge University match he dismissed seven batsmen, three being stumped in the course of seven balls bowled by H.R.W. Butterworth; he claimed six victims in an innings against an Indian eleven at Bombay in 1937–8.

Blessed with an enormous capacity for food in general and ice-cream in particular, Gibb stamped his character on the game and as an umpire he was as imperturbable and as drily humorous as he was when a player. He died in 1977 in Guildford Bus Station, where he was employed as a driver. **P.T.**

- The above profile was written by the late Peter Thomas for inclusion in a projected but never published second edition of his *Yorkshire Cricketers* and is reproduced by permission of Mrs Margaret Thomas.

Ellis Robinson

Ellis Pembroke Robinson, from Denaby Main, became Macaulay's successor as the team's off-spinner but did not confirm his place in the side until 1937, when he took 78 wickets. He arrived as a leg-break bowler, blessed with long, strong fingers and was advised by Hirst that he had a better chance of reaching the first team by spinning the ball the other way and thus competing for a forthcoming vacancy. He developed such a power of spin that he was often forced to bowl around the wicket and could not always command the length and direction demanded of one of Sellers' spinners.

Robinson was nevertheless a key member, as a lusty, left-handed batsman, of the Championship teams immediately pre-war. He formed, with Mitchell, Turner, Yardley and Sellers, the brilliant close-wicket cordon that captured so many wickets in those years by catching of anticipation and audacity.

Robinson continued for four more seasons after the Second World War but in 1949, at the age of thirty-eight, he was allowed to move on to Somerset where he managed one last splendid summer, 1951, when he bowled 200 more overs, at the age of forty-one, than any other bowler in the team and took 107 wickets.

In retirement Ellis Robinson never lost his enthusiasm for cricket and was elected an honorary life member of the club.

pions Derbyshire were both drawn, as were the two Roses matches, both holiday fixtures suffering from the weather. Leyland scored seven centuries this summer, overtaking Sutcliffe as the team's premier batsman, including a 263 against Essex at Hull, some retribution for the 'broken bat' jibe.

Yorkshire lost to Worcestershire for the first time since 1909, while at Sheffield, after Barber had scored an excellent 158, Kent were dismissed for 39, Verity having another of his omnipotent days, finishing with nine for 12 in 39 deliveries.

The next year, 1937, saw a resumption of the old Yorkshire–Middlesex rivalry that led, in mid-summer, to a challenge from London to an extra match, no matter who were champions, to be played over four days. Hawke was reluctant but the Committee sanctioned the match, the players were enthusiastic and it was eventually agreed that all proceeds should go to charity.

Yorkshire lost their opening fixture, MCC beating them for the first time in thirty-three years by 25 runs with twenty minutes remaining. Yorkshire were set to make 406 to win, MCC being without Bowes in the second innings because of a knee strain; Hutton stayed five hours for 161, Leyland made a forceful 69, and Smailes was left at 57 not out.

Yorkshire also lost on their second visit to Lord's, to Middlesex by an innings and 22, Jim Smith taking six for 75 in the first innings, Sims taking five for 36 in the second. After such a result the Middlesex confidence mounted, hence the challenge. The two counties competed fiercely through a summer in which the twenty-year-old Hutton blossomed, scoring ten centuries and reaching three thousand runs, but if Middlesex could have won their last two matches they would have been champions. They beat Kent, but were then held by their local rivals Surrey.

Yorkshire, despite their bowling limitations, ensured their pre-eminence by winning their last two fixtures against Sussex and Hampshire. Robinson won a regular place, showing his ability to spin the ball without always being in control of his length and direction, while Yardley, again on vacation, hit 600 runs and increased his average to 44. Lancashire won back a little self-esteem when, for once, Verity was outshone by another left-arm bowler, Iddon, Yorkshire taking five wickets before Lancashire scored the 91 they needed.

So to the Challenge Match, scheduled for The Oval from 11 to 15 September. Sellers, who had an outstanding season, being invited to captain the Gentlemen, virtually put Yorkshire beyond danger when he won the toss and batted first, leaving Middlesex to struggle on a damp pitch. Hutton, Sutcliffe and Mitchell, raising 256, gave the champions a grip they never relaxed. Monday's skies were even darker and when Middlesex batted, replying to Yorkshire's 401, they were in immediate trouble before Bowes and Smailes, sinking to 46 for 6 and then 63 for 6 before a storm ended play for the day.

Play could not restart until 2.30 on the third day, when Yorkshire allowed Middlesex to recover to 185 but were still able to enforce a follow-on. By then the pitch was drying and Verity was in his element, taking eight for 43, and by six o'clock, in warm sunshine, Yorkshire were winners by an innings and 115, and the crowd had contributed £1329, giving Patsy Hendren an affectionate farewell to the first-class game.

There was one might-have-been about 1937: Sutcliffe and Hutton had raised 315 in 280 minutes against Leicestershire at Hull when the junior partner was bowled. Sutcliffe was said to have been disappointed, having a target of 556 in mind, but on Hutton's twenty-first birthday, he never mentioned his ambition.

Yorkshire had every reason to feel delighted about the Championship of 1938, for not since 1912 had the feat been accomplished in an Australian summer. England's demands were heavy, five players being called upon for the Oval Test, and of the two Championship matches lost, to Middlesex at Lord's and to Surrey at The Oval, the latter occurred while Tests were being played. Of the other nine matches that clashed with Tests, five were won.

Faced with such a drain on strength York-

shire had to rely on the lesser-known players to bring results, especially in bowling. Ellis Robinson did well enough to win his cap, 104 wickets at 21 apiece. Leyland contributed 61 wickets at 18, while Frank Wilkinson, an in-swing bowler from Hull, added 24 wickets at 20. In addition to the batting stars, Gibb, Barber and Sellers all made more than a thousand runs, while Smailes became the first Yorkshireman since Rhodes and Kilner to complete the 'double'.

The team took its share of knocks, too, with Turner, Mitchell, Smailes and Bowes all having to drop out at some point with injury. There was, not surprisingly, some feeling after the defeat by Middlesex at Lord's when, on a very lively first day's pitch, Hutton suffered a broken finger, Leyland a broken thumb and Gibb a split head when he ducked into an expected bouncer that didn't. Middlesex's frustrations can be partially explained by the fact that they finished second in each of the years from 1936 to 1939.

Lancashire were beaten twice, an experience they had not suffered for twenty-eight years. Cardus pleaded with the selectors to pick the entire Yorkshire team, 'with or without Hammond or Paynter', for the last Test. They all but took him at his word.

Middlesex were beaten at Headingley in another important match (England claiming Edrich, Compton, Hutton and Verity) in which Leyland's left-arm spin brought him four for 15.

The Championship apart, the other two great events of the year were Hutton's world record 364 for England against Australia at The Oval and Yorkshire's match with Bradman's Australians at Bramall Lane, the first day's play drawing a crowd of 35,000. To a modern generation, accustomed to watching overseas visitors on television to the point of ennui, it is difficult to convey the excitement spread by the touring team of whom one could only read, glimpse briefly on the cinema newsreels, or watch live.

The whole nation hunched around their radios, waiting for Hutton to break the record; a small boy was brought in expressly from an Ampthill garden, in Bedfordshire, and ordered

Sutcliffe and Barber coming out to bat before lunch at Old Trafford. July, 1936.

to stand silently by the loudspeaker until the magic moment passed, whereupon grandparents, parents and assorted relatives stood up, clapped and cheered and delightedly opened bottles.

Ten years later that same boy queued at Lord's to see Bradman, a long wait from early morning, only to be near heartbroken when the gates were closed with only 20 more yards to go. Today's small boys, fed pictures of the world on television, cannot know either the exaltation or the anguish, and they are the poorer for it.

That is why such a huge crowd gathered in Sheffield, for Bradman's Australians were as fiercely proud of their record as Yorkshiremen, and aimed not merely to stay unbeaten on tour but for annihilation of the opposition. Bradman's 1938 team may not have had the firepower of the side he brought in 1948, but they were not one whit less resolute.

Overnight rain meant play had to start fifteen minutes late, and the crowd buzzed when it was learnt that Sellers had won the toss and sent in the Australians. In alien conditions the tourists

struggled to 222, Bradman 59, the chief contributor being Hassett who, on his first tour of England, demonstrated both an excellent defensive technique and attacking stroke-play when, with the tail in support, he added 44 in 25 minutes.

Yorkshire in turn had their difficulties and finished 20 behind. Monday's pitch was as awkward to negotiate and Bowes, it was said, produced his finest ever spell of 18 overs for only two for 28, although both Badcock and Bradman were missed off him in the slips. However, the last six Australian wickets were swept aside for 32 and Yorkshire needed 150 to win, rain intervening before the second innings could start.

The following morning Yorkshire soon lost their night watchmen Wood and Verity, for 18, but by lunch Yorkshire needed another 67 for an historic victory with seven wickets standing, Sutcliffe's among them. Sadly, rain showers through the afternoon prevented a restart, and at four o'clock a disappointed Sellers out on the pitch signalled the abandonment.

The last season before the Second World War, 1939, saw Yorkshire as champions again but also brought, in Kilburn's words 'the last triumph of one of the greatest county teams of all time'. Again Yorkshire and Middlesex dominated the table through the summer when cricket competed with ever more glaring and ominous headlines. Everyone accepted that war was coming; the only question was when.

Yorkshire was actually beaten four times that summer, but as they also won twenty of their twenty-eight matches there was no argument as to their supremacy. Two world-class bowlers, one world-class batsman and two, Sutcliffe and Leyland, who still had claims; most of the rest of the team were Test class, they were led by a shrewd and fearless captain, and they contained a close-field cordon that has never been surpassed. Six batsmen, in all matches, passed a thousand runs, Verity took 191 wickets, Bowes 122, and although four players were taken for Test matches such was the supporting cast that Yorkshire lost only one match while weakened.

Gloucestershire defeated the champions twice, once by virtue of a fierce attacking innings by Barnett at Bradford, 90 in an hour,

Norman Yardley

Norman Walter Dransfield Yardley, born in Barnsley, was Yorkshire's unluckiest captain. He succeeded Brian Sellers, supervised the rebuilding of the side after the Second World War, presided over some special talents in the 1950s, was popular and able, and yet passed into retirement without winning the Championship; a mystery.

He was a player of distinction at cricket (a blue in all four years at Cambridge), hockey (a blue) and squash (six times North of England champion). Of all Yorkshire's captains perhaps only Close surpassed him in all-round ability. He led England in fourteen Test matches, took huge delight in dismissing Bradman with his thoughtful seam bowling, was a good tactician and excellent close field. Peter Thomas compared him with Lord Peter Wimsey, another cultured man of many parts with a patrician disdain for the ordinary.

Yardley succeeded Sellers as captain at St Peter's, York, won his blue as a freshman and then inherited the Cambridge captaincy. He first appeared for Yorkshire in 1936, already the unspoken heir-apparent to Sellers, was twice in the England twelve against Australia in 1938 and was Hammond's vice-captain in Australia in 1946–7.

Yardley scored seventeen centuries in his 11,632 runs for Yorkshire and was always a reliable change bowler or fielder. He was in the county's great tradition of being able to turn his hand, successfully, to any part of the game. The single exception was winning the one prize that eluded him in a highly distinguished career which concluded with the chairmanship of England's selectors and the presidency of Yorkshire.

Kilburn, who saw all of Yardley's reign and who might be described as a friendly critic, gave this verdict:

> Yardley could do no more than weave a logical, orthodox pattern from the material at his disposal. When the material was inadequate he could not devise success and he did not expect it to fall to him through a disproportionate share of good fortune. Yardley recognised merit as the groundwork of achievement and all his character, all his training, led him to accept failure or success with equal grace and equanimity.

Don Mosey's explanation:

> Yardley had been introduced to Yorkshire cricket in the mid-thirties when the side, individually and collectively, would have died for the cause. He

had picked up the pieces after the war and it must have come as a total shock to someone with his background to find players in his side who rocked the boat. He had been schooled in that one-for-all and all-for-one tradition and any attitude in the side that showed itself as less than that was alien to him – I cannot see that it diminishes him as a human being that this was so; rather, one feels, it diminishes those who rocked the boat.

Illingworth, who entered the Yorkshire side towards the end of Yardley's era, was openly critical in print of Yardley's captaincy and his failure to control two of the big temperaments in the team, Wardle and Appleyard. That Yorkshire team had a captain and senior professional (Hutton) both of whom were relaxed and detached individuals, when it seems that what Yardley needed was a top-class sergeant-major.

It should be emphasised that for most of the summer both Yardley and Hutton were concerned as much with England's problems as Yorkshire's and it must have been difficult to switch, in hours, from consideration of the difficulties of facing Lindwall and Miller at Lord's to a decision upon whether Appleyard or Wardle or young Illy should have which end at Bath. Neither captain nor senior professional had a regular occupancy of the dressing room in those years, losing an essential continuity that is always vital to a successful team.

Yorkshire tempers, too, were strained by the frustrations, year after year, of chasing home Surrey when, man for man, Yorkshire believed they were the superior cricketers but were never able to prove it. Just one breakthrough, one Championship amid

Surrey's magnificent seven, would surely have totally changed the ambience of Yardley's captaincy. Nevertheless Yardley is remembered with great respect and affection by all those who played and worked with him.

after Sellers had made an ultra sporting declaration: 189 in 100 minutes, time for Gloucestershire to win but not long enough for Yorkshire to bowl them out. At Bristol, Goddard's subtle spin was decisive.

Against these defeats could be balanced the successive victories against Hampshire, Leicestershire and Middlesex, achieved with the loss of only thirteen wickets in all. The Derbyshire match at Bramall Lane is still remembered: Yorkshire were bowled out by the Popes for 83, Derbyshire replied with 20, Smailes four for 11, and Jim Smurthwaite, a twenty-two-year-old fast-medium bowler from North Ormsby, who was deputising for Bowes, taking five for 7. Yorkshire batted again, Barber scoring 100 in a total of 310 before Derbyshire were shattered again, Smailes joining Verity, Drake and Wainwright in taking all ten wickets, his analysis reading 17.1–5–47–10.

Much criticism was attracted by a 'batting out' at Bramall Lane against Nottinghamshire, although the points system at the time must take most of the blame. With no chance of a result Yorkshire's average would have suffered by a decision on the first innings, so the object of ensuring a 'no decision' was attained.

The final southern tour, bringing victories at Dover, Bournemouth and Brighton, was accomplished in the feverish atmosphere of

impending war. At Dover, Kilburn reported, telegraph boys came to the ground in a constant stream calling up reservists, while communications were so interrupted and delayed that the evening newspaper correspondents found it almost impossible to file their reports.

The Scarborough Festival, Yorkshire heard, had been cancelled. Sutcliffe was the first player to hear from the War Office and did not travel on to Brighton. On 1 September, with only one match remaining on the fixture list, Verity (seven for 9) bowled out Sussex for 33 as German troops invaded Poland.

Rail traffic to the North was dislocated; neither seats on trains, nor the trains themselves, could be guaranteed, so Yorkshire set off one sunny mid-afternoon to return by coach. A blackout had been ordered, roads out of London were crowded, and Yorkshire's coach stayed overnight in Leicester where improvised sleeping arrangements were made. By dawn the journey was resumed, players being dropped off one by one until this bizarre return ended in City Square, Leeds. The goodbyes, reported Kilburn, were perfunctory, because no one could anticipate the next meeting: 'It was a sad and silent party . . . and thence departed their several ways one of the finest county teams in the whole history of cricket. It never assembled again.'

4

Yardley to Close 1945–1970

The World War again dealt Yorkshire some hard blows: Verity killed leading Green Howards across a Sicilian cornfield; Bowes debilitated by years as a prisoner of war; an operation on Hutton's left elbow that shortened his arm; of course, six years from the careers of the other champions of 1939. Sellers, Leyland, Smailes, Bowes, Verity, Hutton, Turner, Robinson, Gibb and Yardley all served in H.M. Forces as did the club Secretary John Nash, a proud record that, with the service of the Great War, will surely be commemorated somewhere when the club eventually finds a permanent home.

Sellers, Leyland and Smailes went into the Royal Artillery. Sellers eventually took charge of a stretch of coastal defence in Sussex and Kent, while Smailes served in North Africa, Italy and Greece. Bowes returned after three years, lighter by 63 pounds; Yardley was commissioned into the Green Howards and saw Northern Ireland, India, Iran, Egypt and Sicily and was wounded by a mortar bomb in Italy. Nash served the Signals in the Middle East. Gibb was an RAF flying-boat pilot over the Bay of Biscay, the North Atlantic, ferried aircraft from Scotland and Northern Ireland to East and South Africa, and as the war ended in Europe he flew in Ceylon and Burma. Turner and Robinson were also in the RAF; Sutcliffe was commissioned in the Royal Ordnance Corps, while Hutton damaged his arm on a Commando course while an instructor in the Physical Training Corps. So serious was Hutton's injury that his career was threatened, but so successful was the subsequent operation on his arm that a grateful Yorkshire elected the surgeon, Reginald Broomhead of Leeds, to honorary life membership.

The club was prudent enough to point out to members that heavy expenditure would be needed as soon as the war was over, and many members continued to pay their subscriptions while the authorities used the cricket grounds. One ground, dear old dirty Bramall Lane, was smashed by German bombs in December 1940.

By the summer of 1945 it was clear that the European conflict, at least, was drawing to a close and although no competitive cricket could be organised the game stirred again, spurred by the deeds of the Royal Australian Air Force's superb young team, a warning of what Bradman had in store for England. Yorkshire organised two-day matches against Derbyshire and the Australian Services and played a third, against Lancashire at Bradford, for Verity's family. Although Sutcliffe had announced his retirement he did make a final appearance, captaining a Yorkshire eleven against the RAF at Scarborough.

Comparisons between the two post-war eras when on each occasion the team had to be rebuilt are interesting. Yorkshire had given ten players a debut in 1919, which does smack slightly of panic although Sutcliffe, Waddington and Emmott Robinson were among them. In the seasons 1945–6–7 Yorkshire blooded fourteen, which suggests the later team had fewer vacancies – although another explanation might be that in the intervening twenty-five years professional cricketers had begun to learn to take better care of themselves, preserving their health and fitness.

There were, nevertheless, some awkward gaps. Sutcliffe had gone, as had Verity, while Sellers, Wood, Bowes, Leyland, Barber and Turner were in their final years. Mitchell and become county coach. Gibb, a batsman/wicket-keeper of high class, filled in for Wood successfully enough to be chosen to tour Aus-

Alec Coxon

Alexander Coxon, a wiry, fast-medium right-arm bowler from Huddersfield, took his opportunity well in Yorkshire's rebuilding after the Second World War. Persistent and hostile, he lacked the pace to reach the highest level but served Yorkshire well for five years up to 1950, taking 483 wickets at an average of 20.91.

He was also a man of temperament and there was for years a rumour of a clash with Compton in the Lord's dressing room during Coxon's only Test appearance, against Australia at Lord's in 1948 when he was one of several seam bowlers to appear as aspiring partners to Alec Bedser. Certainly when he left Yorkshire, at the age of thirty-four, he had many years of cricket left which he took with him to Durham.

John Arlott, in his biography of Trueman, quotes an unnamed Yorkshire player as saying that Coxon's 'face didn't fit'. Close, in his biography, referred to Coxon's 'harsh and grating manner'.

tralia in 1946–7. Bowes was not much more than medium pace but was able, by husbanding his strength and using all his abilities except speed and bounce, to remain highly effective; Smailes turned more and more to off-spin and a new-ball bowler was discovered in Alec Coxon of Huddersfield, an old-fashioned English seamer whose volatile personality fuelled great endurance and endeavour.

The batting revolved almost entirely around Hutton, a dependency upon one man that Yorkshire had perhaps not undergone since the days of Ephraim Lockwood. Only Hutton and Barber passed a thousand runs in Yorkshire matches and of the seven centuries scored Hutton took four, the others coming from Barber, Gibb and Yardley. Yet the middle and tail failed only rarely and no less than eight players passed five hundred runs and, surprisingly, Yorkshire won the Championship yet again. It was, perhaps, a psychological triumph, for with other counties in a similar state of reorganisation it was, wrote one cricket writer, 'quite enough to see the white rose on the caps to put the thought of a follow-on into the opposition'.

It was also a wet summer and on uncovered pitches Yorkshire found two practitioners of the old skills, slow left-arm and right-hand off-spin, to run through most sides. Ellis Robinson emerged as the senior off-spinner, being selected for a Test trial and appearing for the Players, taking 129 wickets at 14 apiece, including such returns as seven for 22 against Glamorgan and seven for 24 against Hampshire.

The surprise, mystery and romance of the season all came from the forty-three-year-old, almost creaking figure of Arthur Booth whose slow left-arm bowling headed the national averages at 111 wickets for 11 each, an astonishing performance from a player hardly heard of outside his county. Booth, from Featherstone, had first played for Yorkshire in 1931 but, like Horace Fisher among others, had had little opportunity in Verity's time. Almost fifteen years of professional service in the leagues meant, however, that Booth had little to learn in first-class cricket, and if the weather got into his bones occasionally (rheumatism forced him to retire early in 1947) this little man bowled with a superb consistency. It was as if Sellers had walked into a dusty little room marked 'SLA', opened a locker, taken Booth off a hook, dusted him down and sent him out to confound Yorkshire's foes.

Much of the summer was cold and wet, poor weather for bowlers approaching middle age, yet fuelled by some distant warmth – perhaps the legacy of those glorious wartime summers. Yorkshire swept past Cambridge University, Glamorgan, Kent and Oxford University, this run being brought to a draw by who else but Lancashire in a rain-affected clash at Bramall Lane. Only Somerset hindered progress in June and July, the Yorkshire bowling taking a hammering at Taunton. Booth and Leyland bowled Warwickshire out twice for less than a hundred each innings at Edgbaston, Leyland also contributing 52 runs, and Lord's provided another turning pitch for an absorbing struggle against

Arthur Booth *Latecomer*

A left-arm slow bowler of small stature but great guile, Arthur Booth, born in Featherstone, gave one magnificent summer to Yorkshire. At the age of forty-three he headed the first-class averages, taking 111 wickets at 11.61, and was thus highly instrumental in the winning of the 1946 Championship.

Booth first appeared for Yorkshire in 1931 when he was among several candidates for the place to be vacated by Wilfred Rhodes, and it was Wilfred who broke the news to him that Hedley Verity had won the race. The little man went off into league cricket and Northumberland, as did another rival Horace Fisher, not to appear again until 1945 when Yorkshire were casting around for a successor to Verity and Booth. It was clear that he was a long way ahead of the younger school of Wardle, Mason and Wood.

Booth fought off rheumatic attacks in a damp summer to help bowl Yorkshire to another title before retiring. He once bowled in tandem with Wardle so that the Committee could assess the merits of the younger man and Wardle gave Booth much credit for his own advance. He was respected as a coach and earned another distinction in that he became the only former Yorkshire professional to become a member of the Lancashire Committee.

Booth played his cricket at a time when a place in the Yorkshire side could be won only by either genius or professionalism of the highest order. He would tell the tale of a Colts match in which he bowled a no-ball and was told, by the captain, to take his sweater at the end of the over. Yorkshire slow left-arm bowlers, he was reminded, were not permitted to bowl no-balls.

Middlesex. Yardley scored 53 of Yorkshire's 140; Jack Robertson replied with 38 of Middlesex's 74. Jack Young then took eight for 31 in a Yorkshire second innings of 108, far too many for the Metropolitans, victory coming by 73 before lunch on the third day.

Despite contributing Hutton, Gibb, Smailes and Bowes to England, Yorkshire defeated Nottinghamshire by an innings at Bradford (Turner 68 and five for 39 in the follow-on). Glamorgan put out Yorkshire for 83 at Sheffield but were still beaten by six wickets, Smailes and Coxon sharing ten wickets; Hutton gave a magnificent demonstration of playing the turning ball in a tense second innings, victory coming when the maestro was on 99.

Hutton was hawk-eyed, too, at Chesterfield, Derbyshire batting for two overs on a pitch that was later confirmed as being 24 yards long before Hutton spotted the discrepancy. The match had to be re-started, Sellers conceding the runs already scored. Yorkshire seemed likely to be beaten, for the first time, by Worcestershire at Headingley; although only 89 runs were needed neither Hutton nor Sellers was playing, but Willie Watson held one end while Robinson and then Smailes steered Yorkshire to a victory attained only with the last pair at the wicket.

Lancashire made a determined attempt to crack Yorkshire's record at Old Trafford, Leyland and Sellers playing out time. Hampshire were beaten at Scarborough in a festival for off-spinners, only the first of four innings passing a hundred. The Championship was finally won at Eastbourne: Sussex were all out for 91, Yorkshire for 82. John Langridge was stumped at 34 as Sussex rallied to 105 while Yorkshire, needing 105, lost four wickets for 26 before Leyland defended while Smailes attacked, and Yorkshire had won the match and the title before tea on the second day.

The return to cricket had been a happy one. The veterans had reasserted their supremacy, Hutton was the world's premier batsman on a difficult surface and several young players had been introduced who would play a major part in the future: Vic Wilson, a left-hander, built like a rock with a temperament to match; Ted Lester, like Wilson from the North Riding but an unorthodox right-hander with a vast appetite for runs; Gerald Smithson, a left-hander from Spofforth who was to be the first of Yorkshire's post-war players to attract the selectors; two potential left-arm successors to Arthur Booth, Ron Wood from Ossett and Johnny Wardle from Ardsley; a fast bowler from Uppermill who promised genuine speed,

Vic Wilson

John Victor Wilson, born near Malton, was a huge, strong left-hander of intense courage and application who anchored the Yorkshire innings at number three from 1948 to 1962, took 521 catches, mostly around short leg, in his 477 matches, scored twenty-nine centuries, passed a thousand runs fourteen times and two thousand once, hit two double-centuries and in all reached almost 22,000 runs at an average of 31.33.

A farmer, Wilson could bat according to the needs of the side and was a formidable driver when on the attack; as a fielder he was so respected he was chosen for all five Tests against Australia in 1954–5 as twelfth man without actually appearing for England.

Yet Wilson is honoured and remembered mostly for his three years as Yorkshire's captain, 1960–62, in which he twice led the side to the Championship and to a second place in 1961 when it could so easily have been a hat-trick before retirement. After the furore of Wardle's departure in 1958, with Watson moving on to Leicestershire, Wilson suddenly found himself as senior professional to the thirty-nine-year-old Ronnie Burnet, an amateur appointed to the captaincy in highly controversial circumstances. Wilson's steadfast insistence of standing aloof from all factions and in putting the welfare of the team first, made him a loyal and ideal lieutenant to Burnet at a difficult time.

It was natural, then, that he should succeed Burnet as captain, becoming the first professional to be elected since Tom Emmett seventy years earlier. Wilson revealed a natural ability to lead and to motivate a talented team without too often upsetting some of the strong temperaments it contained. He could be firm, too, as when he sent home Trueman, for being late, from Taunton in 1962. A phlegmatic

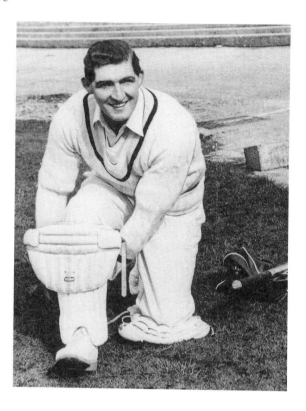

man of great strength, Wilson's authority was rarely challenged; he ruled firmly, fairly and very successfully, laying the foundation for Close and the Silver Sixties.

John Whitehead; and another left-hand batsman, a gritty character from Holmfirth, Freddie Jakeman, whose fielding made an immediate impact. But there would be a gap, obviously, between the retirement of Sellers' generation and the growing to full maturity of these young players, and in 1946 Yorkshire were resigned to a spell of more accomplishments away from the glare of the Championship.

Perhaps 1947 was more truly the first postwar summer. The South Africans toured and, seemingly, always in those days brought sunshine with them. It was the summer of Compton and Edrich when Middlesex not so much won but stormed the Championship; no score was beyond them. India became independent, the school-leaving age was raised to fifteen, England's March floods were the worst on record and in November the Princess Elizabeth married. Yorkshire knew that Leyland, Barber and Turner had retired, with Booth shortly to follow them, and that Sellers and Bowes were in their last season, while Gibb, on turning

Ted Lester *Hawkeye*

Edward Ibson Lester, from Scarborough, was among the most unorthodox batsmen ever to play for Yorkshire. A powerful, forcing right-hander, he forced himself to the Committee's attention by his prolific scoring on the excellent batting pitches of North Marine Road and, when the side was being revitalised after the Second World War, whatever doubts Yorkshire may have had about his methods were dispelled by his scoring rate and he became the established number four in what was one of Yorkshire's most powerful orders: Hutton, Lowson, J.V. Wilson, Lester, Watson, Yardley.

The young Lester, along with the young Wardle, was photographed with George Hirst at the Headingley nets in 1939; he played in a Colts trial at York later that summer. His achievements for Scarborough kept him in the public eye and in 1945 he played in several two-day friendly matches for Yorkshire under the captaincy of Leyland.

In the hot summer of 1947 Lester grew to full power, hitting three centuries in succession, two of them against Northamptonshire, and finishing even ahead of Hutton in the averages with an extraordinary figure of 73. If he was less prolific in 1948, a wet summer, he still achieved a century in each innings of a Roses match. John Callaghan recorded an instance of Sellers' attention to detail after the Northampton episode. In a hurry to board the team coach after the match, Lester forgot to put on a tie. Sellers spotted his omission and Lester was obliged to open a suitcase and dress according to the captain's instructions before the coach was allowed to move off.

Lester's highest aggregate came in 1959 (1801) but he passed a thousand runs six times in his eleven seasons and 228 matches. Especially strong on the leg side, Lester's fast scoring, based on an extremely quick eye and fine co-ordination, could turn a three-day match inside a couple of hours and he was always a dangerous batsman once set.

His last good season was in 1954 (four centuries) when he was having increasing difficulty, because of a foot problem, in playing three-day cricket. Lester then became the Colts' senior professional and captain before launching into a second career as Yorkshire's scorer, a position he held for more than twenty-five years when he was also guide, counsellor and friend to a line of captains all of whom rarely made a major decision without consulting him.

Despite the travelling involved, Lester always refused to leave his beloved Scarborough and not until 1988, at the age of sixty-five, did he cease to attend all Yorkshire's away matches. Ted Lester was a qualified MCC coach for more than thirty years.

professional, had migrated to Essex. The gaps were many and it is hardly surprising that in such a time of experiment twenty-five names were listed in the averages. Nor could there be much surprise at the team's fall to eighth place in the table, the lowest position for thirty-seven years.

Hard pitches suited Lester, for one, and his aggregate of 657, from eleven innings, brought him an average of 73 and a professional contract. Smithson won much praise; Watson progressed. Bowes led the averages for the last time, his benefit year bringing a new record for the county of £8000, while a new fast-medium

Gerald Smithson   *Bevin Boy*

Gerald Arthur Smithson, born in Spofforth, was an attractive left-hander of high promise who will be chiefly remembered as the only Yorkshire cricketer to have served as a 'Bevin Boy', a National Serviceman who worked as a coal miner rather than as a member of HM Forces.

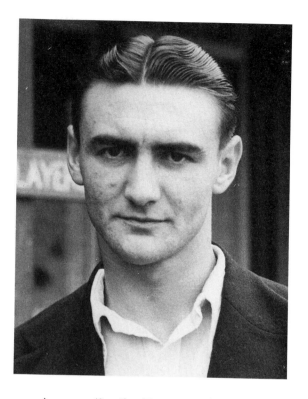

He played in thirty-nine matches for Yorkshire between 1946 and 1950 and a 98 against Lancashire brought him to the attention of the selectors. Along with Wardle he was chosen for the 1947–8 tour of the West Indies, a selection that brought a debate in the House of Commons and the special government dispensation that was needed before he could be released from the mines to tour the Caribbean.

Norman Yardley (1950) described Smithson's 98 as 'one of the most polished displays of batting I have seen given by so young a player. He began with extreme confidence, making some delightful shots and he was soon cover driving, hooking and cutting with great skill, reminiscent of some of the young Australians.'

Sadly Smithson suffered an arm injury on that tour and missed the whole of the 1948 season. On his return he could not establish a place in the side and played for Leicestershire in 154 matches between 1951 and 1956. If his career was brief, he did play twice for England and scored eight centuries for his two counties.

Along with Wardle and Brennan he was one of three players capped by Yorkshire in 1947, the first time there had been such a wholesale distribution of caps since 1934 (Smailes, Turner, Davidson). Smithson played for Hertfordshire from 1957 to 1962 and died in Abingdon at the early age of forty-three.

bowler was uncovered – Ron Aspinall from Almondbury, strong and eager. Wardle won the race for Booth's place perhaps a summer too soon, yet took enough wickets to win a place, along with Smithson, on the winter tour of the West Indies. Robinson and Coxon bore the brunt of the bowling and in conditions more helpful to batsmen spent many a hot and weary day in the field. A new wicket-keeper from Downside and born in Eccleshill, Don Brennan, became Yorkshire's second amateur in succession.

So many changes inevitably meant that the settling-in process had to be repeated match after match, with the consequent decline in Yorkshire's expected and intended fielding standards. MCC, in the opening match, were allowed to recover to 343 for 9 in their second innings, sufficient margin to impose a defeat by 164 runs despite Wilson's defiant 74.

Centuries by Hutton at Oxford and Swansea (197 against Glamorgan) brought the more usual victories, Smailes flourishing that strong right arm. Hutton made another century at Cambridge but not until after the University had for once enjoyed the county's bowling, Guy Willatt and Trevor Bailey scoring hundreds in a total of 402. Sussex, aided by some fierce hitting by Hugh Bartlett, won by three wickets at Bradford, although Hutton managed

Ron Aspinall

Between 1946 and 1950 Ron Aspinall, from Almondbury, was a candidate to open the bowling for England. Coming into the Yorkshire side upon Bowes' retirement he had two excellent seasons in 1947 and 1949 and was expected, by the England captain of that period, Norman Yardley, to reach Test-match status. Yardley first saw him playing in Service teams in the Middle East during the war.

A strongly built, right-arm fast-medium bowler, he formed a good partnership with Coxon that might have carried Yorkshire through to the advent of Trueman had not a strained Achilles tendon, in 1950, limited Aspinall's career to thirty-six matches. He was also a hard-hitting lower-order batsman.

He played seven seasons for Durham before becoming a first-class umpire.

Don Brennan

Donald Vincent Brennan, born in Eccleshill, Bradford and educated at Downside, was a wicket-keeper of sufficient class to displace Godfrey Evans for two Tests against South Africa in 1951. He was another product of the Bradford League whose career was delayed by the Second World War and who owed his opportunity, after the retirement of Arthur Wood, to Gibb's turning professional and removing to Essex.

Tall, slim, Brennan was commissioned during the war and continued to play for Yorkshire, as an amateur, from the age of twenty-seven, often acting as vice-captain to Yardley. After his brief Test appearances he toured India and Ceylon the following winter but thereafter the genius of Evans prevented a permanent claim to an England place.

Brennan was nevertheless highly regarded by the professionals, especially for his work standing up, keeping as he did to such 'difficult' bowlers as Appleyard, Wardle and Leadbeater. He was especially remembered for his leg-side work, regularly described by contemporaries as 'brilliant'.

In his 204 matches for Yorkshire he caught 280 batsmen and stumped 100, his white gloves and dark-blue cap making him a distinguished figure in Yorkshire's team from 1947 to 1953. As a right-hand batsman he was remembered for his defiance rather than his strokes, although he did once add 106 with Brian Sellers for the tenth wicket against Worcestershire.

His retirement was brought about by a need to attend to the family textile business but he repre-

Billy Sutcliffe (left) and Don Brennan.

sented Bradford on the General Committee from 1971 until illness prevented his standing for re-election in 1984. Brennan was a fierce and outspoken critic of the Boycott group. He died in Ilkley in January 1985, aged sixty-four.

Johnny Wardle *Chinaman*

John Henry Wardle, from Ardsley, was a unique slow left-arm bowler, a genius who could deliver the orthodox ball, turning away from the bat, the chinaman, turning into the bat, and the googly from the back of the hand, apparently an off-break, in fact a leg-break often turning prodigiously. Many left-hand bowlers have been able to produce all three deliveries but none but Wardle was able to bowl them consistently and successfully at the highest level. It is a modern cricket tragedy that Wardle is not acknowledged and remembered as one of the greatest spin bowlers.

That he is only now being given full recognition for his abilities is due partly to his own nature and a conspiracy of circumstances; even in his autumn, reconciled with Yorkshire and appointed bowling consultant, he was frustrated in an attempt to tell his side of the story, in an autobiography to be written with the author of this history, by his early death, aged sixty-two, in July 1985.

He did have time to tell me, in preliminary discussions about the book, that his famous chinaman in fact appeared before he became a slow left-arm bowler: 'As a kid I tried to bowl quick but soon realised that I was never going to be big enough or fast enough to trouble good batsmen so I started giving the ball a flip as I delivered and had learned to bowl that delivery before I ever took up slow left-arm.'

Wardle was built like a welterweight, a pugnacious, quick-tempered man, a fierce competitor determined to win his way out of a mining area in the depression years of the 1930s. He shared this environment with another Yorkshire player of intense determination, the comparison being first made by Wardle's friend in the dressing room, Ted Lester: 'In his dedication to the game, his attitude and discipline he most resembled Geoff Boycott.' Boycott, for all his rumbles with authority, achieved most of his ambitions, while Wardle carried that sense of frustration, of touching but not capturing the prizes, almost to his grave.

Alan Hill brought a posthumous compensation to Wardle in his 1988 biography *Cricket Conjurer*, a scrupulous balancing of the facts for and against someone who, even as a boy, was known to be moody. Wardle first demonstrated oustanding ability at Wath Grammar School (a scholarship boy) when he took eight wickets for 4 runs.

It was at this school, according to Hill, that Wardle suffered the first of a long series of setbacks that were to dog his career: he topped the batting and bowling

averages for the school first eleven yet was not awarded his school cap. 'He was halfway out of his seat when he realised that the . . . cap was to be presented to someone else.' It was not until 1956 that Old Wathonians remedied the injustice.

Perhaps this led him to scorn further education and to take a job as an apprentice fitter at Hickleton Main where he could fit his sporting engagements into a colliery life. He had manifold skills as a rugby full-back and an outside-left footballer, in which role he joined Wolves' nursery team Wath Wanderers. Playing for Wanderers (he had trials with Wolves) he responded to a heavy foul by a defender by getting up, punching the aggressor and being sent off.

In four of five wartime seasons Wardle won the Yorkshire Council junior bowling prize, sometimes opening the bowling with what Charlie Lee recalled as 'little in-duckers'; he took all ten wickets for Brampton against Rockingham (for 36 runs) in 1940.

George Hirst called him to a net in Barnsley in 1942 and reported good progress by 'Wardle, the Brampton all-rounder'. By 1944 he had taken 113 wickets at 7.85 for Denaby and when county cricket resumed he was clearly a candidate, along with Arthur Booth and Alan Mason from Addingham. Booth, at forty-three, headed the national averages in 1946 but had to retire with a rheumatic affliction, leaving the race to Mason and Wardle in 1947, a dry summer.

Both spinners were given a six-match trial. Mason

bowled intelligently but on the good batting pitches of early summer he managed only two wickets in 77 overs. When Wardle took over he had the advantage of a few damper, drying pitches and took his chances. He finished with 70 wickets in the Championship at an average of 23, and in August, along with Smithson and Brennan, was given his cap. The question of Verity's successor, a tormenting one for all Yorkshiremen in those early post-war seasons, had been settled. Or had it?

The retirement, in quick succession, of Bowes, Booth and Smailes and the decline of Robinson meant that more and more work fell on Wardle who, his new captain in 1948, Yardley, admitted, 'was first change in any conditions'. Wardle even had to use the new ball on occasions and in those circumstances, experiment, even variation from the stock slow left-hander's ball, was frowned upon. Lester recalled: 'Johnny was crucified by the Yorkshire press who couldn't accept that he was different from his predecessors. Rhodes and Verity didn't need to bowl chinamen so why should he? Did he think he was a cut above them? And when things went wrong, as they will with any spinner, and he got some tap, they were twice as hard on him.'

In addition, waiting in the wings were Mason and two more slow left-arm challengers, Johnny Ashman and Ronnie Wood. Wardle, as he would reveal privately from time to time, never felt sure despite his county cap and prodigious service to the club (1247 overs in 1948). Bradman, who batted against Wardle that season, commented: 'There was the usual immaculate length, direction perhaps astray at times, good spin and a deceptiveness of flight more reminiscent of Rhodes than Verity.'

Despite Bradman's approbation, Wardle was chopped in 1949 while his rivals were given a trial. Yorkshire wanted Wardle to remodel his action, to present a more classic, cartwheel, sideways-on pose when delivering the ball. Wardle tried to adapt, failed, was dropped and reverted to his old approach which, according to Trevor Bailey, was good for his wrist spin. No further attempts were made to turn Wardle into another Rhodes.

Bowling orthodox, Wardle swept back into favour in 1950, the peak performance being an eight for 26 against Middlesex, and in 1953 Bowes, who was also the club's bowling coach, wrote, in commenting on *Wisden*'s choice of Cricketers of the Year: 'There is no doubt . . . that Wardle has been over-bowled. With much truth the players named him "perpetual motion Wardle". Originality and experiment in his bowling had, of necessity, to be replaced by negative attack.'

In 1952 Wardle bowled 1847 overs for 177 wickets at an average of 19.54, an almost single-handed attempt to win better than second place for Yorkshire. By then a new generation of bowlers had appeared to offer assistance – Close, Appleyard and Trueman. By 1955 Wardle was able to use his irregular attack more often, taking 195 wickets at 16.14, but by then his place as England's premier slow left-arm bowler had been usurped by Tony Lock who was to admit, years afterwards, that his faster ball was illegal, a fact that Wardle and many other bowlers knew but to which the umpires made almost no objection.

Lock's preference by England's selectors was a thorn in Wardle's side for a decade. According to Hill, 'he could not dismiss the iniquity of his exclusion'. Hill quoted a contemporary Yorkshire player: 'If Johnny had an Achilles heel it was Lock. He shouldn't have shown it. "Come on lads," he would call out. "Just watch that bastard throwing it out there."'

Wardle was not the only Yorkshireman to feel needled by the Lock affair and memories of that controversy were revived twenty years later when Surrey were one of the counties to complain about Cope's action at a time when authority was much quicker to clamp down on any suspicion of throwing. Cope, of course, was eventually forced into minor counties cricket.

Wardle had been dumbfounded when Bob Berry of Lancashire had been preferred to himself on the 1950–1 tour of Australia – 'an appalling decision' according to one dissenting selector – and then found his pre-eminence challenged by a 'chucker'. The bitterness ran deep. One England player believes that Surrey's other spinner of that era, the Yorkshireman Jim Laker, would not have achieved his historic nineteen wickets against Australia at Old Trafford in 1956 if Wardle and not Lock had been at the other end: 'Johnny would have had five or six wickets.'

In fairness to Lock, after watching himself on film he tried, at the age of thirty, to remodel his action and won high praise from his captain, Dexter, on the 1961–2 tour of India. Many good judges, including Peter May, believe England should have played both Lock and Wardle, but there is no doubt that had Lock not emerged, Wardle would have been as much an England fixture as had been Verity.

Perhaps the greatest humiliation the selectors heaped upon Wardle came in 1953 when, after he had taken four Australian wickets for 7 runs in five overs, the selectors replaced him with Lock for the two remaining Tests, a choice vindicated by the recapture of the Ashes but no balm to Wardle's wounded temperament.

He was to have great days for England, on Hutton's tour of Australia and more especially in South Africa where, in 1956–7, he took twenty-six Test wickets at an average of 13 and headed the tour averages with ninety at 12. His twelve for 89 at Cape Town in the Second Test was regarded by Hammond, an onlooker, and Insole, a playing colleague, as the best spin bowling they had ever seen.

From the full glory of that tour Wardle returned home to Yorkshire as the newly installed senior professional to a newly elected captain, Ronnie Burnet, called up from the Bradford League to impose some discipline and leadership on the dressing room. Wardle, at the height of his fame and in peak form, was expected to take orders from a thirty-nine-year-old with no experience of first-class cricket and a confrontation was inevitable. Sadly for the club it meant Wardle's departure into Lancashire League cricket and to Cambridgeshire. The circumstances of the rift are dealt with in Burnet's details.

Hill records that Wardle, speaking to a meeting of miners in South Elmsall after leaving Yorkshire, was asked pointedly: 'Doesn't tha think tha's been a foo-il, Johnny?' Wardle looked at the questioner and replied: 'Aye, I have.'

The loss of such a talented bowler, hard-hitting batsman, consummate entertainer and humorist, the man who, as Appleyard said, knew 'more about bowling than the rest of us put together', was as great a blow as the county has ever suffered. Peel replaced Peate, Rhodes replaced Peel, Verity replaced Rhodes and Wardle replaced Verity, but there the line ended.

Wardle was a devoted family man, a hundred per cent professional, who kept himself fit and always ensured he had a good night's sleep; a joker with a keen sense of humour on or off the field. In short he would have made, in his later years, the ideal senior professional and it is not too much of an exaggeration to say that much of Yorkshire's post-war troubles stemmed initially from the decision to sack Wardle. His loss was a grievous self-inflicted wound to the club.

As to his prowess, Hill quotes E.W. Swanton, who saw all of the careers of both Verity and Wardle:

> You would want Hedley on your side because you could always be sure of a minimum performance from him. If he had anything to help him he could be very dangerous. In all circumstances he would be steady. Johnny, on a bad day could be expensive. But if matters went well for him – if he had wickets that took wrist spin – he could be a good deal the more dangerous of the two bowlers. He also spun it more as an orthodox slow left-hander than Hedley.

yet another century before missing the next match with a throat ailment.

The other senior batsman, Yardley, filled the gap with 137, Yorkshire beating Glamorgan by nine wickets at Sheffield, and although Lancashire managed to stop Hutton's extraordinary sequence at Old Trafford (they confined him to 95 and 86) Yorkshire had by far the better of the draw. Bowes and Coxon, bowling unchanged, saw off Warwickshire at Edgbaston before Gloucestershire managed to reduce Charlie Barnett's benefit match by defeating Yorkshire in two days, Sam Cook taking nine wickets for 42 runs and winning an England cap.

Going home Yorkshire were able to beat Somerset at Headingley, but the next two matches were drawn and their new humbler circumstances brought to national attention by four successive defeats in mid-summer. Without Sellers, Yardley and Hutton, Yorkshire lost to Nottinghamshire at Sheffield before engaging Middlesex at Leeds for Bowes's benefit, 41,000 attending over two days. Middlesex were sent in and out for 124 (Edrich 70), Yorkshire were then dismissed for 85 (Yardley 41), and by the close of an eventful day Middlesex extended their lead to 119 with seven wickets standing. Edrich went on to make 102 out of 165, a magnificent innings on a difficult pitch that included two sixes and eleven fours, before Yorkshire fell on the second afternoon for 186, some desperate late hitting atoning for a miserable start of 52 for 6.

Yorkshire again failed in the fourth innings at Tunbridge Wells; Surrey were the next comfortable victors, despite a 107 from Smithson, in four and a half hours; and Gloucestershire achieved a double with a win at Bradford by 8 runs. This was a defeat that would have enraged the old professors. With 10 runs wanted, Wardle, Brennan and Robinson allowed themselves to be caught off Goddard. Warwickshire, at long last, provided some relief at Headingley, just failing to score the 261 needed for victory, Yorkshire winning by 6 with less than two minutes' play remaining.

The final tour lifted hearts, for two of the younger players emerged: Lester scored a century in each innings at Northampton (126 and 142), while Aspinall had match figures of fourteen for 65. Hutton made 197 and 104 against Essex at Southend and then capped his season with 270 not out at Bournemouth. Bowes bowed out in majestic manner: 30 overs, five for 52. Hutton topped two thousand runs in all Yorkshire matches, but only two others, Yardley and Watson, passed a thousand and only Robinson took a hundred wickets. There was undoubted promise among the many younger players – but how much of it was flawed?

If 1947 emphasised how much Hutton and Yardley meant to Yorkshire's experimental teams, then the damper following year proved the point more painfully. Yardley inherited the captaincy, as expected, but was also chosen to lead England against Bradman's Australians in all five Tests. He also missed several early matches and, later, in his position as England's captain, was called to other events.

Nor was Hutton in the best of health that summer yet, despite facing Lindwall and Miller and emerging, with Compton, in glory, he still managed to score nine of Yorkshire's twenty-two centuries and his batting average was more than double that of the second-placed Watson, 92 to 44. Halliday, Lester and Wilson also passed a thousand runs, suggesting that the batting was gaining depth and assurance, yet the order was still prone to almost inexplicable collapses, especially so when Hutton and/or Yardley were absent. As Kilburn put it: 'In the great years, with the toss won at Brighton, numbers ten and eleven could safely spend a morning on the beach; nobody dare go far from the dressing room in 1948.'

However, it was in Yorkshire's bowling and fielding that the fall from grace was more often apparent. Coxon bowled steadily enough to be chosen to play in the Second Test, while Wardle averaged 18 for his 148 wickets, a formidable record scarred only by occasional lapses in concentration and accuracy that mystified elder

members of the side. Aspinall was less forceful in his second season, Smailes was in his last summer, while Robinson was dropped for a spell, recovering his more usual form in August. Bill Foord, a schoolmaster from Scarborough, was a useful reinforcement for the team attack, while Ken Smales, an off-spinner from Horsforth who was later to gain greater distinction as secretary of Nottingham Forest, was promoted to fill the gap left by Robinson.

By the standards of forty years later 1948 was a successful year, for Yorkshire won eleven of their twenty-six Championship matches and lost only four, another indication of the strength of the batting. A fourth place in the Championship persuaded many supporters and members that, in fact, the corner had been turned and that the county were about to reclaim their pre-war supremacy. More knowledgeable persons inside the Committee were not happy with the long-term trends, and what was less obvious to all was that, in the post-war world, attitudes and ambitions were fast changing: the whole concept of gentleman and player was being put into question and all authority was coming under challenge.

MCC again won the opening match at Lord's, Yorkshire falling twice to the left-arm spin of Jack Young – the biter bit. The Australians made a memorable visit to Bradford, Sellers leading the county as Yardley was indisposed, while Hassett captained the tourists. Yorkshire batted first on a surface that soon turned, and Miller, as always supremely confident, bowled experimental slow off-spin to dismiss a disappointing Yorkshire for 71. Bill Johnston, too, reduced his pace, demonstrating the enormous cricketing versatility of a team that is still regarded as the greatest ever to tour England.

However, the Australians, too, would have been in trouble had not the irresistible Miller appeared at 38 for 4 to hit 34, including two sixes, the tourists eventually leading by 30, Smailes six for 51. Yorkshire's second innings was a disaster, Sellers being top scorer with 21, Johnston taking six for 18 in 15 overs. That left the Australians to score 60 for victory but they, too, were 20 for 5 and 31 for 6, with Sam Loxton unable to bat; Yorkshire then allowed the fresh-faced young Harvey to escape at short leg, their bowling fell away and Harvey finished the match with a straight six. It was an enthralling match, but one that sharply exposed all Yorkshire's then current frailties. Coxon and Aspinall both had their moment in Yorkshire's later drawn match against the Australians at Sheffield.

In the domestic programme Oxford had the better of a drawn match despite Lester's sparkling 149, and May brought more disappointments, defeats coming at Bristol and Birmingham and Lancashire romping away with first-innings points at Headingley; only a ten-wicket defeat of Northamptonshire at Huddersfield lifted the gloom.

Gloucestershire's victory was another sharp lesson to Yorkshire's bowlers, for the batting, reaching 312 for 7 on the Saturday, had put the side in a commanding position when weekend rain brought the declaration on Monday morning. The spinners bowled so inaccurately that Gloucestershire were able to save the follow-on, and although Lester added another fine century Gloucestershire were left to score 389 to win in 270 minutes. Emmett and Barnett raised 226 in 120 minutes, the latter scattering the bowling to the winds, hitting eighteen fours and a six in his 141. Gloucestershire romped home by four wickets, with 45 minutes to spare!

Hutton's 176 not out laid the basis for a defeat of Sussex on another turning pitch at Sheffield. Hutton followed this with 133 against Middlesex at Lord's, and this time Wardle and Robinson were so in command that Middlesex followed on to bring another innings victory. Even a break-in of Hutton's car in London, another indication of changing times, in which he lost his cricket bag and even the petrol from the tank, hardly affected his continuing golden seam.

Another win, against Kent at Bradford, raised hopes that a genuine challenge was developing, until George Pope, at Chesterfield, put matters into perspective: Yorkshire were dismissed for 44. Derbyshire made 277 before rain wiped out play on the Monday and permitted only 90 minutes on the last day, Yorkshire thus escaping certain defeat at 37 for 6.

Pope had match figures of ten for 25 and he also scored 73.

Surrey's visit to Sheffield was played for Smailes's benefit and Yorkshire won in two days, Coxon taking six for 17 in Surrey's first innings of 42, following on to Yorkshire's 355 for 5. When Northamptonshire and Surrey (again) were defeated in July, Yorkshire's return to premier place seemed more than a possibility, but another dip in form brought the final disappointment. Lancashire again took first-innings points, this time at Old Trafford, although Lester had the personal distinction of scoring centuries in each innings of a Roses match.

Dropped catches enabled Leicestershire to reach 300 on the first day at Sheffield and a match that had begun in high expectation ended in defeat by 66 runs. Yorkshire making a hash of trying to score 267 in 180 minutes. Yorkshire rallied to defeat Worcestershire at Bradford, but then lost on first innings at Worcester.

Victory was vital at Taunton if the challenge was to be sustained in the closing weeks, but the leg-spin of Johnny Lawrence brought another collapse, Yorkshire following on and being saved, in all probability, only by a back injury that prevented Lawrence from bowling again. The bowlers found better form at Bournemouth where Hutton and a new partner, Geoffrey Keighley, born in Nice of a Yorkshire family and educated at Eton and Oxford, hit off the 113 runs needed in the second innings.

Hutton raised 155 against Sussex in the final match; Yorkshire declared at 315 for 9 and after Foord had taken the first four wickets with the score at 75, another success seemed imminent. Sussex, however, managed to reach 192, and the Yorkshire second innings, with Hutton batting down the order because of lumbago, was undervalued and Sussex, set to score 243 in the fourth innings, managed their task for the loss of only five wickets as once again Yorkshire in the field failed to reach even moderate standards.

Not for the first time in their history Yorkshire surprised themselves and their critics in 1949 by sharing the Championship with Middlesex, an extraordinary performance in many ways, for the team, still being rebuilt, was not considered either settled or able enough for such distinction.

Surrey and Middlesex, who had finished second and third in 1948, were, as expected, the chief contenders, and with a little more consistency earlier in the summer might each have taken the title. Middlesex, however, did win their last five matches, which meant Yorkshire had to win their last match against the reigning champions Glamorgan at Newport, a task they accomplished in two days. Nor could Yorkshire be accused of inconsistency in the run-in, for they themselves reeled off six victories in succession, a brief return to the heady days of Hirst, Haigh and Rhodes.

It was a fine summer, week upon week of sunshine, captains feeling that their best hope of winning on so many splendid batting surfaces was to send in the opposition in the hope that the pitch on the first morning might be faintly green and damp. At Fenner's the undergraduates Hubert Doggart and John Dewes piled up massive scores, while Hutton had another glittering summer, scoring 2640 runs for Yorkshire at an average of 69. Wilson, Lester, Yardley and the newcomer from Bradford, Frank Lowson, all passed a thousand runs and an eighteen-year-old all-rounder from Rawdon, Brian Close, who batted left and bowled right, completed an astonishing 'double' of a thousand runs and a hundred wickets in all matches. Also appearing for the first time that season were the seam bowlers Eric Barraclough (Bradford), Frank McHugh (Leeds) and Freddie Trueman (Maltby), wicket-keeper Jack Firth (Cottingley) and a leg-spinner from Huddersfield, Eddie Leadbeater.

The writer was serving at RAF Hospital, Ely in 1949 when the station adjutant, a very kindly man and cricket-lover, offered seats on a coach to those interested in seeing someone the flight lieutenant described as 'the new Lindwall from Yorkshire. His name is Truman, like the President's.'

Fenner's was at its best that day, shafts of sunlight through the trees (were there really so many more in those days?) mellowing the old pavilion, now sadly demolished and replaced by a building that looks rather like a slightly superior supermarket. To be honest neither Trueman nor Close, both of whom bowled, made much impression on this observer; nor did Hutton's new partner Lowson, a pale, thin lad who was dismissed very perfunctorily in the first innings. But in fact neither Lowson nor Close looked back again that summer, while Trueman, hostility and raw speed contained by a magnificent action, was shrewdly and carefully nursed by Yardley.

In that dusty summer Wardle bowled more than a thousand overs for his hundred wickets, despite being dropped to allow the Committee to assess another left-arm spinner, Alan Mason from Addingham, who took 37 wickets at 28. Coxon also bowled 920 overs for his 101 wickets, while the prodigy, Close, bowled 1089 overs for 105 wickets at 25, an extraordinary performance for a bowler of eighteen, for he also batted 42 times to score 958 runs for the county at an average of 28. Robinson, sadly, slipped down the order and was to move on to Somerset at the end of the season.

Fourteen of the twenty-six matches were won and only two lost, Surrey hinting of the power to come in their win at The Oval and Worcestershire, leaders for much of the season, winning at Sheffield, another leg-spinner, Roly Jenkins, taking five for 39. The major clashes were with Middlesex, both matches being drawn but attracting huge crowds for what had become the premier fixture in the competition. A good pitch at Lord's meant that both teams reached 300 plus in the first innings, Yorkshire taking first-innings points after Robertson and Brown had raised 198 for the first Middlesex wicket.

In the return fixture at Bramall Lane a crowd of 27,000 sat enthralled through hot sunshine after Yorkshire, sent in, assembled 296 for 6, Lowson scoring his first century and Yardley 81 as the total reached 336 on the Monday, attended by a mere 18,000. Five Middlesex wickets went for 143 but Denis Compton's was among those remaining and he went on to score a century, with brother Leslie contributing 44, and although Compton played on at 287 the Middlesex tail, finding the pitch and the wearying bowling much to their liking, took the total to 400 on the third afternoon, Warr and Young

Brian Close

Dennis Brian Close came from a cricketing family embedded into the Bradford League. That he should appear as an accomplished all-rounder was not surprising in itself but to accomplish the 'double' in his first season and to win an England cap in that same season, at the age of eighteen, was the stuff of boyhood comic papers. Close went on to enlarge the fantasy by becoming the third most successful captain in the club's history, a captain of England and of Somerset, a close fielder of superhuman courage, a batsman of massive power and a bowler of unquenchable optimism. Nor is that sufficient summary of a career that included controversial spells as the club's chairman of cricket, an England selector and an insurance executive. He had an ability to drive motor cars in such a fashion as to reduce steel-nerved opening batsmen to jelly. He was also a prodigious player of golf, snooker and squash, and good enough at soccer to play professionally for Arsenal.

Close was playing for Rawdon's first team at eleven, developed both his cricket and soccer at Aireborough Grammar, Verity's old school, went on to play for Guiseley and Yeadon and on his appearance at the Yorkshire nets, pre-season 1949, Bowes described him as a natural successor to Frank Smailes. Close himself was impressed, but never overawed, by the names in that year's call-up: Smales (Yorkshire and Nottinghamshire), Foord, Lowson, Trueman, Leadbeater, Illingworth, McHugh (Gloucestershire), Horner (Warwickshire), Firth (Leicestershire) and Booth (Worcestershire). Even by Yorkshire's pre-war standards it was a vintage crop.

Close's school results were impressive enough to win him a university place, which he delayed until after National Service. He had signed professional forms (a striker) with Leeds United and cricket was possibly more of a pastime than a career when he was invited into Yorkshire's squad for the first Southern tour of 1949; a six-footer, he was shy compared with the other debutants Lowson, who was five years older, and the even then extrovert Trueman.

Close scored 28 runs and had match figures of four for 102, opening the bowling with Trueman in the opening victory against Cambridge University at Fenner's. By mid-season the young prodigy had scored 579 runs and taken 67 wickets. Selected for the Test trial, then for the Players against the Gentlemen (top scoring with 65), Close was finally selected for the Third Test against New Zealand at Old Trafford.

He was 18 years and 149 days old when he first played Test cricket in a somewhat dampening debut, match figures of one for 85 and a duck, but Close was under orders to chase runs and he was caught on the long-on boundary. In September Close began the Scarborough Festival with a hundred wickets and needing 63 more runs for the 'double', duly accomplished with 44 and 46 not out against MCC. He and Lowson were capped in their first season and Close then went off to serve in the Royal Signals.

He had played only one first-class match for Yorkshire when he was chosen, the following summer, for Freddie Brown's tour, the actual selection being announced while he was confined to barracks for seven days, the result of a misunderstanding over leave granted to play cricket!

He had a miserable first tour, being injured twice and finding little sympathy from the senior members of Brown's party. Transferred to Arsenal he found that cricket and soccer were becoming almost incompatible, and although he completed a second 'double' in his second full season (1952) another football injury, this time playing for Bradford City, put him out of all sport for eighteen months. He began the 1954 summer purely as a batsman but when Appleyard dropped out, tested his knee, found he was able to bowl again and finished with 66 wickets. By 1955 he was fully restored to all-round glory and, six years after his extraordinary start, his career was fully under way.

Close became one of the most forbidding figures, to the opposition, in the English game, whether bowling right-arm seam or off-breaks, batting left-handed stubbornly or spectacularly, or fielding at suicidal short positions. In all his first-class career with Yorkshire, Somerset and England he scored almost 35,000 runs at an average of 33, including 52 centuries and took 1171 wickets at 26 apiece. He also made 814 dismissals, including one stumping!

Witnesses will affirm they have seen catches taken at second slip off Close's forehead, at short leg; he once stood at silly point, with blood pouring over his boot from a gashed shin, blasting the bowler for the delay in getting back to his mark, with amazed team-mates waiting for him to keel over. Against Hall and Griffith at Lord's in 1963 he saved and almost won a Test match by taking hostile fast bowling on his body. The next day, before he appeared for Yorkshire against Glamorgan at Bramall Lane, a famous picture showed his body to be a mass of ugle purple bruises. Against Glamorgan he bowled 25 overs and took six for 55, then scored 61, then bowled another 16 overs to take four for 19, Yorkshire winning by ten wickets.

Iron player though he was, Close was of most value to the club for his captaincy; for in his seven years he won four Championships and two Gillette Cups, a record that must have impressed Hawke although not, or so it seemed, Sellers. Mosey described his leadership:

'His side of the sixties, though occasionally exasperated when he went off on one of his mental walkabouts, sometimes moved to laughter at his fixations, nevertheless regarded him in affectionate wonderment and professional respect. As a captain in the field he had, above all, flair. He would bring about a bowling change or switch a fielding position where there was absolutely no reason in the world for doing so and nine times out of ten it came off. He was an implicit believer in his ability to make something happen in the field when nothing seemed likely.'

This intuition was a gift he passed on to another great captain, and son of a Yorkshireman, Mike Brearley, of whom David Gower once wrote, 'As a player under JMB I always felt confident that the right thing was being done at the right time and that if Australia were 150 for two then it was probably their fault and not his.'

Brearley, in his book on captaincy, had high praise for Close's charisma and embellished the story of the catch at second slip:

'He of all the captains I have known led from the front. His courage was notorious. Fielding incredibly close in at short square leg, the great dome of his head thrust belligerently forward, he was regularly struck by the ball. The story goes that it once rebounded from his forehead to second slip. "Catch it," Close shouted . . . he assured [the Yorkshire players] he was all right. "But what if it had hit you an inch lower?" one asked. "He'd have been caught in t'gully."'

Close himself had much praise for Yardley's warmth and understanding of his players and was not too sympathetic to those who saw kindness to young players as weakness, although in later years Close himself took some criticism for his reluctance to blood youngsters. Close, typically, would have seen it merely as a defence of his old tried and trusted servants.

Close was always an inspiration to his bowlers and it was he, as leader and tactician, who transformed Don Wilson from the somewhat hesitant successor to Johnny Wardle into an international bowler.

Close was an enormous influence upon his bowlers, particularly the spinners and especially Don Wilson. When Wilson was injured and Keith Gillhouley, from Huddersfield, deputised, the latter took 73 wickets at 21 each and Wilson, for that season, could not regain his place. But once Gillhouley moved on to Trent Bridge he was a disappointment to both Nottinghamshire and himself; without Close's inspiration and Yorkshire's aggressive close fielding and catching, Gillhouley became an ordinary bowler.

Close's translation to the England captaincy was inevitable. West Indies, under Sobers were leading England 3–0 with one draw when Close replaced Cowdrey for the last Test at The Oval in August 1966. He immediately insisted upon Illingworth's inclusion and won the Test by an innings and 34, a performance that won him charge against India and Pakistan the following summer. He led in all three victories against India and although the Pakistanis managed a draw at Lord's, England won at Trent Bridge and The Oval.

Whatever misgivings the selectors might have had about Close's diplomatic skills as captain of England's winter tour to the increasingly touchy Caribbean, they could not have displaced him after a record of six wins and a draw. But once again, Close was to be disappointed.

Close wrote in his memoirs that he had been warned that summer that, 'they are just waiting at Lord's for a chance to prevent you leading the side in West Indies. Keep your nose clean.' Yorkshire went to Edgbaston needing to beat Warwickshire to displace Kent as leaders but Yorkshire trailed by 4 runs on the first innings and were bowled out for 145 on the third morning, leaving Warwickshire to score 142 to win in 102 minutes.

The innings began in a light drizzle and was interrupted by rain at the beginning of the last hour when Warwickshire needed another 72 runs. Trueman, Nicholson and Hutton needed to dry the ball and Close claimed that in the hubbub from the crowd his instructions on field placings were not always heard and had to be repeated. Yorkshire bowled 16 overs in the first 42 minutes but only 24 in the last 105, 6 in the final 30, and there is no doubt that the Edgbaston crowd was convinced that Yorkshire were deliberately wasting time. Trueman was reported to have been struck by an umbrella, and Yorkshire cars were damaged.

Close was called to appear before a panel of county captains at Lord's and formally censured for 'delaying tactics', an incident that brought about a change in the law and the introduction of the mandatory 20 overs at the start of the last hour's play. Close then found himself criticised in a Sunday newspaper for an alleged attack on a man in the crowd. Close's version was that the incident happened at lunch-time on the second day when he heard an unpleasant remark addressed to him as he came off the field.

He walked into the members' enclosure, put his hand on the shoulder of a spectator and asked the man if he had made that remark. The man said no, Close apologised and also apologised to the Warwickshire club. This version of events was confirmed by the Warwickshire member involved, but the ensuing publicity did Close's cause no good and he knew his chances of leading in the West Indies were fading, even when he won the Oval Test match of that year. More than a decade later another England captain, David Gower, was verbally assailed in that same area at Edgbaston.

Close returned to lead Yorkshire as successfully as before and began the process of rebuilding a team that had lost Trueman, Illingworth and Taylor by 1968–9, to win the Gillette Cup in 1969. The relationship between the Committee and the dressing room was not perfect: Close had one or two clashes and claimed that the resignation of Binks, at the end of the 1969 summer, stemmed directly from a critical conversation that brilliant wicket-keeper had with two members of the Committee during an early Gillette Cup tie.

1970 saw Yorkshire recover to fourth in the Championship and Close considered that the side was taking shape again when, in late November, he was invited to 'resign or be sacked'. He fired a parting shot at two committee members at a dinner later that winter: 'In the next ten years you will realise your mistake.'

He went off to play for both Somerset and England, retiring in 1977 when he was awarded a CBE for his services to cricket. Returning to Yorkshire he joined the General Committee as a member for Bradford, was cricket chairman when the pro-Boycott committee took over but resigned the chair in protest over Boycott's dual role as player and committee man, resuming office during the next series of elections. He was always a strong supporter of retaining first-class cricket at Park Avenue, and was one of the prime movers behind the planned establishment of the Cricket Academy on that site.

adding 98 for the last wicket and Young being last out for 62.

Nothing, however, could diminish the last six matches of the campaign when, on each occasion, the victory had to be won to maintain a viable challenge. Hampshire were beaten by 106 at Hull, and Derbyshire by six wickets at Bradford (Hutton was away scoring 200 for England at The Oval), Yorkshire having to make 185 in 90 minutes in the fourth innings. Warwickshire went down by an innings and 68 at Scarborough, Kent by 122 at Dover, and Gloucestershire, after an awkward struggle, by eight wickets at Huddersfield.

Middlesex had then completed their programme and Yorkshire had to extract the maximum 12 points from Glamorgan at Newport. Hutton and Lowson began with 78 before Hever's five wickets in the afternoon brought the innings to a disappointing 224. Nevertheless Glamorgan were left on 32 for 4 on Saturday evening and although the follow-on was saved Yorkshire were batting again on Monday afternoon with a lead of 108, the declaration coming at 5.30 with Glamorgan needing 347.

The pitch was wearing, the light deteriorating and Coxon's first ball, 'one of the finest he ever bowled' according to Kilburn, beat Emrys Davies, Glamorgan collapsing for 69.

Lester had another fine season, averaging 38, Brennan won himself a Test trial, and the advent of so many promising young players meant that Wilson, Watson and Wardle were all dropped at some time during the summer. The

Frank Lowson *Shadow*

Frank Anderson Lowson's career was summed up in one sentence by J.M. Kilburn: 'He had all the attributes of a Test cricketer except perhaps the driving force of ambition.' A slim, dark right-hander from Bradford he made his debut, with Close and Trueman, at Fenner's in 1949 at a time when Yorkshire were searching everywhere for a regular opening partner for Hutton. Lowson scored 78 in the second innings against Cambridge University and never looked back.

He scored 15,000 runs in his nine years and spent so much time at the other end from Hutton that his cutting and driving could be seen to be based upon the maestro's. Fortunately, said the Yorkshire Yearbook of 1985, the selectors saw in him more than just a shadow of Hutton and he was selected for seven Tests, scoring 245 runs, a record, almost all his contemporaries stressed, that would have been much more impressive had he sustained better health.

Alan Ross, describing Lowson's batting against South Africa at Lord's, referred to 'an air of waifish, Sinatra-like melancholy', a fair description of Lowson's play as seen from the ring, and yet he was a highly effective batsman of sound defensive technique, well organised in his stroke play, who never failed to pass a thousand runs (1700 in 1949, 2100 in 1950) and Yorkshire were sorry to see him go, at the age of thirty-three, when county cricket became too much of a burden for a limited physique.

He died at the age of fifty-nine and for a quiet, unassuming cricketer, won some handsome tributes: 'After Hutton he was, at the time, the most effective batsman in the country and he should have played for England many more times,' said Brian Close. Trueman made the point that when a Hutton-Lowson partnership was in full flow it sometimes was difficult, from a distance, to distinguish them apart. 'A good companion, a fine batsman and a good friend' was Hutton's comment.

His health may not have been the only reason for his retirement. The Yorkshire dressing room was not a happy one in the 1950s and when Lowson was approached by Michael Stevenson about a particular cricket project, he said: 'I'd like to help but honestly I just don't want to think about those days.'

Fred Trueman *Fiery*

If Frederick Sewards Trueman was not, in his own words 't'finest bloody fast bowler that ever drew breath', he does have an excellent claim to the title. He was undoubtedly Yorkshire's greatest fast bowler – only Freeman, from all accounts, could be compared in pace – and most critics would put him among England's first ten, if not first five. He had all the attributes: strength, speed, stamina, determination, hostility, a hatred of defeat, and all the fast bowler's weapons – yorker, bouncer, in-swing and a lethal out-swinger. In his later years he could bowl a highly respectable off-break, and he was a punishing lower-order batsman with a reputable defensive technique and dazzling catcher, especially at short leg.

He was born near Stainton, the fourth child of a miner who encouraged all his children to play cricket, being a useful all-rounder himself. When the boy was twelve the family moved to Maltby where, at the local modern school, young Trueman was richly encouraged in his ambition to become a fast bowler. He advanced sufficiently to be included in the Schools' Federation team's Southern tour (along with Close) and at seventeen he was taken by his father to Bramall Lane.

Charlie Lee, a Yorkshire Colt who was later to captain Derbyshire, tells the story in Keith Farnsworth's *Before and After Bramall Lane*:

'We were ready to shut up shop when Cyril [Turner] asked me to put my pads on again. We had two long batting sessions but Cyril explained, "There's a bloke here brought his lad from Maltby. Reckons he's a bit quick. Let's have a look at him." Having been at it all day and facing a journey home to Wath, Cyril could have been forgiven for telling them to come back again. But that wasn't Cyril's way and this was one occasion when his patience paid a dividend.

'Old "Dick" Trueman was a typical miner of the period – dark suit, cloth cap, heavy boots; Fred was in ordinary clothes – he had no whites – and a pair of plimsolls. You couldn't imagine the scene was set for a significant moment in cricket history.

'There wasn't room for much of a run-up in the nets at the Lane but nevertheless Fred got some pace into his first ball which pitched and shot right over the top of the net and wall behind me and just missed a tram going down Shoreham Street! Those first few deliveries were all over the place.

'Then Fred suddenly got one on line. I played at it, was a bit surprised not to connect and when I turned round there were two stumps sticking out of the net like herrings on a Grimsby trawler.

'Lee sat on a tramcar with Turner that evening: "We sat quiet for some time and then suddenly Cyril began to chuckle and I knew what he was going to say: 'He'll play for Yorkshire, this lad, tha' knows. He just needs to find a bit of control. There's nowt needs doing to that action.'"'

Trueman made his debut for Sheffield United's third team and by late July had reached the first team, taking four for 47 against Wakefield on his debut although, Lee recalled, when the young man was wayward he would take 'some awful hammer'.

In five matches for United in the late summer of 1948, Trueman took fifteen wickets and his pace brought a recommendation that he should attend the winter school at Headingley for scrutiny by Mitchell and Bowes, the latter later reporting him to be 'an ideal pupil'. The first report was 'superb action, fairly fast'.

Control, and an impulse to hurl in the bouncer whenever the batsman proved aggressive, were where the young bowler needed attention, but he had made sufficient impression to be chosen to play at Cambridge University the following May without an appearance for the Colts and he accordingly made his debut, along with Close and Lowson. It was a trial, as Trueman was a long way down the pecking order for seam bowlers, led by Coxon, Aspinall, Yardley, Foord and Whitehead.

Trueman took three wickets on the usual placid Fenner's pitch, including that of the University's then outstanding batsman, Hubert Doggart (bowled), and then, on a friendlier surface in the Parks, he had match figures of six for 72, his victims this time including Clive van Ryneveld (bowled).

Trueman was then due to stand down to allow the regulars to return for the more testing Championship matches but an injury to Aspinall late in May, when neither Foord nor Whitehead was available as a replacement, brought him opportunities that were unexpected and unplanned. He made little impact until, playing against the Minor Counties at Lord's, he produced the first spell of his career that brought him attention, and not just in Yorkshire. In a nine-over morning spell he took five wickets for 30; Yardley kept him on after lunch for him to return final figures of eight for 70, and a great career was launched.

Foord, a schoolmaster, and Whitehead, an undergraduate, were both available later in the summer and Trueman, accordingly, went off to make his debut for Yorkshire II, already known as a fast but somewhat wild young bowler. Trueman returned for the match against the New Zealanders at Bramall Lane, a happy family occasion, and in trying to prove himself wrenched a thigh muscle that effectively ended the 1949 summer for him.

According to his biographer John Arlott, Trueman was among several young players who found the Yorkshire dressing room of the 1950s a far from comfortable place, and Arlott traces much of Trueman's mistrust of authority to his early experiences

there. But Trueman was never critical, unlike others, of his captain, Yardley, and always spoke of him in the highest terms. It was Yardley who first nicknamed the young man 'Fiery', a description so apt that it became synonymous with Trueman.

Trueman was still working at Maltby Main, often taking night shifts in order to play cricket. It was to some surprise that he was chosen for a Test trial at Bradford in 1950, the prevailing theory being that the selectors wanted their chosen batsmen, soon to face Lindwall and Miller, to be given practice against pace, however wayward. This, of course, was Laker's match (eight for 2) and Trueman had little opportunity, although he did recall with great pride the fact that he had bowled his hero, Hutton.

Coxon's departure might have given Trueman an opportunity in 1951, but that was Appleyard's year and the young man had to compete with Whitehead and Foord until a return of eleven for 94 against Nottinghamshire at Bramall Lane pushed him to the head of the queue, and in the return match at Trent Bridge he performed the first Yorkshire hat-trick for five years, an indication of fast-improving control, in an analysis of eight for 53. Another good performance, at Harrogate on a flat pitch, convinced the Committee he was the real thing and in August, at Park Avenue, he and Appleyard were presented with their county caps by Yardley.

He was summoned by the RAF for National Service at the end of 1951 and the air marshals proved to be liberal employers as far as their cricketing prodigy was concerned. For this the club was very grateful as Trueman, twenty at the start of 1951, a year later became virtually the senior pace bowler: Coxon gone, Aspinall retired through injury, Appleyard ill and Foord and Whitehead discarded. Unknowingly, Yorkshire began a near twenty-year quest to find an opening partner for Trueman.

Trueman responded magnificently to his opportunity and told Arlott later that in the summer of 1952 he was probably at his fastest. He was twenty-one, stood 5 feet 10 inches, had a 46-inch chest and weighed 13½ stone when fully fit. He took thirty-two wickets at 14 apiece in four Championship matches, and there was no question that England had to select him for the first of his 67 Test matches. The public, depressed by years of aggression from Australian fast bowlers, were demanding an Englishman of genuine pace.

Hutton was his first (and England's first professional) captain and Trueman began with that now famous spell from the Kirkstall Lane End, before 30,000 at Headingley, which reduced India's second innings to 0 for 4, three wickets to Trueman, in the first fourteen deliveries. He finished that series with a record 29 wickets, and the legend was made.

He became the first bowler to reach 300 Test wickets (307 at 21.57), he took ten or more wickets three times in a Test match, and his twenty-year first-class career brought him 2304 wickets at an average of 18.29, figures that qualify for immortality. He was a rumbustious character, falling foul of several captains (including Hutton and Vic Wilson), a raconteur good enough to speak professionally, a journalist, broadcaster and commentator, and it is a scandal that no Prime Minister, not even Harold Wilson who described Trueman as 'the greatest living Yorkshireman', thought fit to propose him for an honour until his OBE in 1989.

He served the Yorkshire Committee until swept away in the Boycott tide and thereafter refused to stand again, disclaiming all connections with the club although he remained an honorary life member. His severance from Yorkshire and the team was never such that he could not be induced to talk, at great length and with little encouragement, about the team. His place in cricket, and in the heart of Yorkshire, will remain unchallenged for ever.

1949 season was the high summer of Yardley's captaincy, Hutton had remained at the summit, the White Rose bloomed again and not a Yorkshireman alive would have believed that another nine years would pass before the Championship was to be won again.

As joint champions Yorkshire were confidently expected in 1950 to improve sufficiently to resume their traditional place at the head of affairs. Instead, a poor start, three matches being lost before the Championship began, brought hesitation. Yet the team settled well and after two small defeats went twenty-three matches without another reverse, the Committee being able to congratulate Norman Yardley 'upon the spirit of adventure which permeated his captaincy and gave so much pleasure to the spectators'.

Hutton was absent, through injury and representative calls, for half of the matches, but Lowson passed two thousand runs, Wilson improved and Watson, entering the side in August after soccer duties, had a magnificent spell, scoring 600 runs, including three centuries, in eight matches. Lester in a damper summer was 700 runs less successful, but with Halliday, who also passed a thousand runs, Yardley, Keighley, Sutcliffe and Smithson all available, the batting was rarely inadequate.

Too much of the bowling was borne by Coxon and Wardle, who sent down 2300 overs between them, Wardle taking 144 wickets and Coxon 113, yet Yorkshire's attack that year may be best remembered for the presence of Leadbeater, the leg-break bowler who was given 700 overs to take 73 wickets. Yorkshire needed an extra seam bowler to support Coxon, and a regular off-spinner; there were some interesting names in the Colts, including Trueman, Whitehead, Foord, Barraclough and Bob Appleyard, a tall twenty-five-year-old from Wibsey. Hutton's benefit raised £9000 and he and 1949's prodigy Brian Close were selected for England's winter tour of Australasia.

The 1951 Championship could have been Yorkshire's but for their contribution to England. They finished 28 points behind Warwickshire and although the eventual champions beat Yorkshire twice, the defeat at Edgbaston was against a team lacking Hutton, Lowson, Watson, Yardley and Brennan.

Hutton and Watson played in all five Test matches, Lowson, Brennan and Wardle in two, while Yardley's duties as chairman of the Test selectors kept him from some county matches; even the Gentlemen v Players reduced Yorkshire's strength. Nevertheless, Hutton and Wilson still had time to score five Championship centuries each; Lowson scored two and Yardley, Lester, Watson, Keighley and Halliday contributed one each. But there remained an unevenness in the batting, made more apparent in Hutton's frequent absences, and only three batsmen, Hutton, Wilson and Lowson, passed a thousand runs in the Championship.

The season will be best remembered for Appleyard's astonishing performance: two hundred wickets in all, 169 in the Championship, a seasonal debut that seems unlikely ever to be surpassed. Wardle, with 99 wickets, was his chief supporter. The young Trueman,

Bob Appleyard

Robert Appleyard, born in Wibsey, near Bradford, was probably the best bowler ever to play for Yorkshire; he was certainly the best this writer saw in an experience of first-class cricket that goes back to 1947 in a comparison that includes such candidates as Lindwall and Lillee.

Appleyard was so good because he possessed, in addition to the basic requirements of line and length, such a formidable armoury of deliveries and a keen intelligence that ensured the weapon to hand matched the conditions. Batsmen facing him, even on good pitches, were in a constant state of indecision and it is not surprising that Bowes placed Appleyard in the class of S.F. Barnes and O'Reilly.

His bowling was perhaps made all the more lethal by the apparently innocuous approach. There was nothing especially threatening about his sixteen-yard run-up and the delivery, while smooth and controlled, contained none of Trueman's sometimes demonic fury or Wardle's mischievous cunning. To many batsmen, facing Appleyard for the first time, he must have seemed ingenuous.

When Appleyard first appeared, from the Bradford League, in the Headingley nets, Bowes, as bowling coach, reported to Arthur Mitchell: 'I can't teach this lad anything. His action and control are good and he spins the ball.' The 'lad' in fact was a late developer, passed over, in Trevor Bailey's opinion, because he did look ordinary in his approach and because he did not fit into any one category of bowler.

After Bowes' report, however, Appleyard played regularly for the Colts and, in 1950, at the age of twenty-six, he was given three first-team matches and managed one impressive spell against Surrey; but, wondered Bailey, would he have been given even that opportunity had not Coxon gone into the leagues and Close been required for National Service?

In 1951, after MCC's batsmen had hammered the Yorkshire bowling at Lord's in the opening match, Appleyard was recalled to the first team and in an astonishing first summer he took 200 wickets at 14 apiece, a debut that in all history can be compared only with that of Rhodes. In that first season he was basically a fast-medium in-swing bowler, using his near 6 feet 2 inches to win bounce, a method of attack supplemented by a deadly yorker and, always, extraordinary accuracy.

Later he worked on his bowling. He had quickly sensed, in the 1950 match at The Oval, when his victims included Peter May, that he had a limited future as a medium-pace in-swinger. In that game he had experimented with a slow off-spinner and was delighted to see the batsman swing at what appeared to be an easy picking only to have his middle stump knocked out.

Appleyard worked for hours, often on his own, perfecting an out-swinger. Yardley encouraged him to develop the off-break through the winter of 1950–1 and Appleyard soon found that bowling off his first finger, in the orthodox manner, removed the skin and made work painful. He tried bowling off the middle finger and discovered, to his delight, that he could bowl an off-break at almost full pace with no lack of power or control. By mid-summer of 1951, as Wardle commented, Appleyard was bowling 'sometimes like Alec Bedser, sometimes like Jim Laker'. No wonder batsmen fell like ninepins.

But the tremendous effort of that summer bit deeply into Appleyard's health. He contracted tuberculosis and missed the next two seasons, the club sending him to a Swiss sanatorium, and he did not appear again until 1954. But he had, apparently, lost none of the magic, for he took another 127 wickets at 14 each and emerged as an England bowler with seven wickets against Pakistan in his first Test.

He was a natural choice, before Laker, for Hutton's tour of Australia where he proved that his style and success could be extended beyond England's damp climate, Bailey mentioning that his late dip in flight was just as disconcerting. The following summer a shoulder injury reduced his appearances to three matches from June, although he still ended with 73 wickets at 11.54. Thereafter, from the age of thirty-one, the wear and tear of professional cricket took an increasing toll of a far from robust frame and he eventually retired in 1958 when it was clear his extraordinary power had been reduced by physical decline.

Twenty years later, Appleyard reappeared in Yorkshire cricket as a committee representative for Bradford and a vociferous opponent of Boycott's group. He worked hard for the establishment of a cricket school and the encouragement of young players and was one of the principals behind the setting up of the Cricket Academy at Park Avenue, the first step, he hoped, towards a full restoration of the historic Bradford ground.

Willie Watson

Willie (the name on his birth certificate) Watson was so called to differentiate him from his father, the famous Billy Watson of Huddersfield Town. None the less, his dressing-room name was Billy, even though he remained Willie to the world and left a memory of grace, ease and style of movement, whether playing wing-half for Huddersfield and England, batting left-handed for Yorkshire and England or fielding at the boundary. Willie Watson, tall, fair-haired, brought lustre to any playing field.

He first appeared in 1939, a batsman of fluent style and calm temperament who was even then considered as the possible eventual replacement for Leyland, and played fifteen innings in the Championship side of 1946; after Leyland's retirement he confirmed his promise by scoring 1331 runs in the golden summer of 1947, an aggregate he exceeded in the much damper climate of 1948. By the following year the Committee's impatience with seemingly inexplicable inconsistencies in the form of younger players brought relegation to Watson, along with Vic Wilson and Wardle, to the Colts.

By then Watson had also advanced in his other chosen career and had reached international status as a footballer, missing most of the 1950 summer to play football for England in the World Cup, but on his return in August he showed great zest for cricket, hitting three centuries and finishing with an average of more than 70. He went on to score twenty-six centuries for Yorkshire and to pass a thousand runs eight times between 1947 and 1955.

By 1951 he had become that rarity, a double international, starting a career of twenty-three Test matches including two tours, and he reached the zenith of his career at Lord's in 1953 when, making his debut against Australia and with England facing defeat, he batted five and three-quarter hours for 109, adding 163 with Trevor Bailey for the fifth wicket to save the match. The *Daily Sketch* led the front page with the story, hailing 'Wonderful Willie Watson', and Watson achieved that rare accolade for a cricketer, a mention in *Time* magazine. Much of England spent that tense day within hearing of the radio commentary.

After that epic Watson might have been expected to occupy one of the highest places in English cricket history, yet he played throughout a distinguished career as if suspicious of fame and publicity, reluctant to take the final step towards being described as a 'great' cricketer.

He left Yorkshire for Leicestershire in 1957 where his form implied that this had effected a release, for he was an outstanding success, heading his adopted county's averages each year, passing two thousand runs in 1959 at an average of 55. He became Assistant Secretary and captain of his new county before emigrating to South Africa in 1968 to become coach to the Wanderers club in Johannesburg. His full first-class career brought him 25,670 runs at an average of 39, including 55 centuries.

He was elected an honorary life member of Yorkshire.

---

chided by *Wisden* for sacrificing accuracy and direction by not bowling within himself, managed 75 and in a summer of generally soft turf Leadbeater had 66 victims with his leg-breaks.

Members and supporters were optimistic. In 1951 the bowling was equipped for any type of wicket: pace from Trueman and Whitehead, swing and off-spin from Appleyard, slow left-arm from Wardle, leg-breaks from Leadbeater, and such useful performers as Yardley, Close and Halliday in reserve. Waiting in the Colts were Billy Sutcliffe (son of Herbert), Keighley, Charlie Lee (Rotherham), Doug Padgett (Bradford), Ken Taylor (Huddersfield), Bryan Stott (Yeadon), Ray Illingworth (Pudsey) and Roy Booth (Marsden).

Domestically the year saw the retirement of masseur Bright Heyhirst, after twenty years' service. Maurice Leyland joined Arthur Mitchell as a club coach and John Nash was presented with £2000 of savings bonds to mark his twenty-one years' service as Secretary. The club was left a legacy of £1000 by Mrs William Wilson of Horsley Gate, near Sheffield, to set up a fund to benefit young cricketers. But damper weather and, perhaps, failed expectations in 1951 caused a drop of £8000 in gate receipts.

The following year, 1952, brought a glorious failure: Yorkshire excelled themselves in the Championship by finishing second to Surrey, a disappointment remembering the hopes of 1951 yet a splendid performance considering all the handicaps. Trueman's call-up for National Service meant, in the end, that he was available for only four Championship matches. His growing power was clear in his record in those four games – 32 wickets at 14.21 apiece. The grievous loss was Appleyard. After his *annus mirabilis* of 1951 all Yorkshire expected another brilliant year from this wonderful bowler, but a breakdown in health meant that he played in only one match.

Yorkshire still managed to win seventeen of their twenty-eight Championship matches despite again contributing Hutton, Watson and Trueman to England and Yardley to his duties as a selector. Hutton, with all the cares of captaining England, scored seven Championship centuries. Watson, Lowson, Lester, Wilson and Halliday also passed a thousand runs, while Sutcliffe and Close reached 950, Close doing the 'double' in all matches.

Wardle bore a tremendous burden, as the leading bowler, with magnificent panache. He sent down 1500 overs for his 158 wickets (at 17.13). Close filled one of the bowling positions (98 Championship wickets), with Halliday (44) and Ron Wood, slow left-arm from Ossett (18), giving good support. Seam bowling was the weakness. Coxon had gone into league cricket, Whitehead had moved on to Worcestershire, Trueman's leave was spent in England service devastating the Indians, and of the six Colts tried only Eric Burgin, from Sheffield United, showed promise with 24 wickets. The fielding and catching, *Wisden* was pleased to note, approached the high standard of pre-war years.

Attendances improved with the weather, the loss of £2900 in 1951 turning into a profit of £690, and after mentioning improvements at Park Avenue, Bradford, the Committee cheerfully claimed: 'The Park Avenue ground will be one of the finest equipped cricket grounds in the country.' But the Committee report of 1953 made no bones about the cricket: 'from the playing point of view the worst since 1892, the team finishing 13th in the Championship table compared with second position in 1952', adding (no doubt after swallowing hard), 'Congratulations are extended to Surrey on

winning the County Championship for the second year in succession.'

Yorkshire were not, in fact, quite as poor a team as their record suggests. In any normal decade they would have won several Championships, but in the 1950s they were a good side, sometimes even a very good side, yet destined to meet, for another five galling years, a great side in Surrey.

There were significant contributory factors to Yorkshire's decline in 1953. Hutton, Watson, Wardle and Trueman were all required by England and Yardley missed some matches through his selector's duties. Trueman, in the RAF, played in only ten matches. Close, having a cartilage removed, in only two. Appleyard was still recuperating, Lowson missed all of May because of injury, and in a generally damp summer the free-scoring Lester was curtailed.

Watson, making his famous stand with T.E. Bailey against the Australians at Lord's, and Wardle, who took 146 wickets, were deservedly named among *Wisden's* Five Cricketers of the Year. The young player of the year was Raymond Illingworth, who took 69 wickets with his off-breaks and scored 747 runs, while the left-arm quick bowler from Leeds, Michael Cowan, contributed 31 wickets at 23.9 each.

Yet all the facts proclaimed that Yorkshire were an indifferent and inconsistent team that summer, drawing sixteen Championship matches and causing *Wisden* to censure: 'A general depression seemed to overtake the side, for besides their disappointing bowling, the fielding fell a long way below the high standard which used to make them such a powerful force, and even the batting was unreliable.' Brennan, Yorkshire's wicket-keeper for seven seasons, announced his retirement.

Yorkshire were strong again in 1954, but not strong enough, second yet again to all-conquering Surrey. In yet another damp summer Surrey's all-round bowling strength was decisive, mightily as Yorkshire tried to close the gap. While Surrey had four Test bowlers Yorkshire had three, and though Trueman, Appleyard and Wardle shared 392 wickets, the absence of one or more of the three meant a gap that could not be closed. Close was called up for National Service in mid-season and none of the Colts was yet ready for sustained front-line service.

The batting, with Hutton missing matches on England duty, always appeared strong enough for the task in prospect yet there were often the unaccountable failures. Again Lowson, Close, Wilson, Lester and Watson all passed a thousand runs and all played splendidly on occasion, their difficulty being, it seemed, finding form together.

There was a rare tied match with Leicestershire at Huddersfield and a crushing victory,

by 96 runs, by Middlesex at Leeds, a defeat which signalled that the way was open for Surrey to take their third successive Championship.

The next year, 1955, saw a fine summer in which Yorkshire began with every reason to believe they would break Surrey's monopoly. Yardley's team was in full flower; the captain contributed astute and experienced leadership and was still a useful performer with bat and ball. He had a galaxy of batsmen – Hutton, Lowson, Wilson and Watson – three Test-class bowlers in Appleyard, Wardle and Trueman, and a highly consistent and sometimes brilliant

Jimmy Binks

James Graham Binks, born in Hull, was another wicket-keeper of the highest class who won little recognition from the selectors, appearing in only two Test matches. He has fair claim to be regarded alongside David Hunter, who kept to Hirst, Haigh and Rhodes, and Brennan (Trueman, Appleyard and Wardle), among the county's best in terms of the variety and difficulty posed by the bowlers of their time. Other candidates such as Dolphin, Wood and Bairstow have a claim to be contenders on their records but had, through most of their careers, more predictable bowling to judge.

Binks won a battle with Roy Booth of Marsden, who was later to serve Worcestershire on and off the field, to succeed Brennan, although the capabilities of the 'lad from Hull' had been known of and extolled for some time previously. He made his reputation in the last two seasons of Wardle and Appleyard and then developed into a vital performer in Close's Championship sides of the sixties, missing not a single Championship fixture between his debut, against Nottinghamshire in June 1955, to his retirement in 1969, 412 consecutive appearances.

This is, of course, a county record, as is his haul of 107 victims in 1960, including 96 catches, another record. Taller than the norm for a keeper he was a quiet and undramatic performer who won the admiration of the cognoscenti for his ability to stand up to Yorkshire's string of in-swing bowlers of that period such as Platt and Nicholson, the ball coming in to the right-handed batsman being always the most difficult for the keeper to measure.

He also became a useful batsman, scoring almost 7000 runs in his fourteen-year career, including a 95

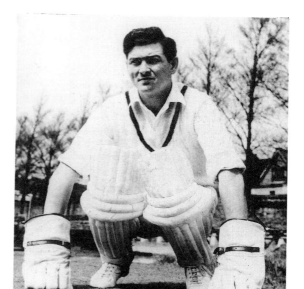

against Middlesex at Lord's. Binks was so quick of movement and adept in his timing that he suffered only one injury, a broken finger in 1966, which was not allowed to interfere with his play. Unlike almost all wicket-keepers, his hands were unmarked when he retired from the game to take up a business appointment at the age of thirty-four. As Ted Lester once said of him: 'He could have come straight off the field and played the piano.'

wicket-keeper in Binks. Behind these nine were a dozen young players striving hard for a place: Close, Illingworth, Taylor, Cowan, Ryan, Padgett, Platt, van Geloven, Bird, Stott, Oates and Roy Booth. Even when Yardley stepped down at the end of the season, he had an automatic successor in W.H.H. Sutcliffe, an assured and popular young batsman. Helping the second team, and in reserve, was the free-scoring Lester.

The first six matches were won at a canter. Northamptonshire fell by tea-time on the second day at Bradford, with Appleyard and Wardle sharing eighteen wickets in a match in which Yorkshire, in their second innings, reached 104, the highest total. Gloucestershire went down by an innings at Bristol, Yardley scoring a century and Appleyard striking again (ten for 110), and it was Appleyard once more, with Wardle contributing seven for 60, who caused Somerset's downfall at Headingley. This triumphal procession continued right through May, with Lancashire being beaten by five wickets at Old Trafford. It was the merriest of months for Bob Appleyard who reigned supreme throughout England, taking 49 wickets at 8 runs apiece.

After such a start Yorkshire were entitled to feel they had the measure of their deadly rivals from The Oval, but Surrey were still level with them and showed no signs of strain. It was Yorkshire who stumbled. A low-scoring match dominated by the spinners was lost by 21 runs at Hove, the last five Yorkshire wickets falling for only 31 runs on the third afternoon. Defeat by Surrey, by only 41, in the next match at The Oval, was no disgrace although more must have been expected after the champions had been put out for 85 in their first innings (Appleyard seven for 29).

What was totally unexpected was a third successive defeat, this time at Bradford, by Hampshire and by an innings. The Hampshire tail retrieved a mediocre start of 93 for 5 to total 224. Hutton, not a hundred per cent, batted down the order and Yorkshire were routed twice by the spinners in one of their own fortresses, Sainsbury returning match figures of nine for 62. Wardle and Appleyard, with England, would almost certainly have reversed

the result, although Surrey could have argued that they had to surrender May and Barrington to Test matches and, later in the season, Bedser, Lock, Laker and Loader in turn.

Although those three defeats were soon forgotten in a glorious run of victories interrupted only by the inevitable Roses draw and a defeat by Middlesex, Yorkshire, leading at the end of July, were always conscious of Surrey's two games in hand, and despite a prodigious effort – twenty-one Championship victories including one against Surrey at Leeds, won in appalling light – the Championship remained at The Oval.

Kilburn, in the 1956 *Wisden*, reflected upon the Yardley era.

> Yorkshire made mistakes in selectorial judgement as well as in playing technique and they had therefore to extend the period of experiment beyond the term expected (from 1946). Yardley found himself with as difficult a task as any county captain for he had played long enough to appreciate needs and desires but could find no illustrations of intentions for the newcomers.
>
> Young Yorkshiremen did not know what was expected of them and were short of a yardstick for comparison. Social circumstances were a handicap to every county and a particular trial to Yorkshire who have long expected their young players to fit into a given pattern, of proven worth. Yardley's success in captaincy has been limited by the lack of understanding and ambition in some of his players but he has done invaluable work in keeping the good name of Yorkshire cricket at the highest level.

Indeed, in retrospect it can be seen that Yardley was an outstanding captain, his record in Championship placings reading: 4, joint 1, 3, 2, 2, 12, 2, 2. There is much evidence that his players expected a firmer hand but, as we have seen, for many of his years of office Yorkshire were in a peculiar position in that either the captain or senior professional, or both, were as much concerned with England's fortunes as with Yorkshire's.

Had the club been less successful in Yardley's time it is possible that more time and thought would have been expended upon the spirit and morale of the dressing room. But as each spring rolled around the hope was there that the following summer would be Yorkshire's and that Surrey would be overtaken; yet by each autumn it could be seen clearly that Surrey always had that one extra top-class player, usually a bowler, to tip the balance in their favour. If Yardley was too much of a gentleman, the most common charge levelled at him, then he was also unlucky to have captained the club at a time when another county could field a side that, certainly at The Oval, was as powerful and ruthless as any team led by Hawke or Sellers.

Surrey won the Championship for a fifth successive year in 1956 – a record – while Yorkshire, in a wet summer and under a new captain, Billy Sutcliffe, dropped five places to seventh. Equally alarming was a drop in attendances by 92,000, a reflection on both the wet weather and what the Yorkshire public clearly regarded as declining standards.

Seven matches were lost against eight won, and the Committee considered that 'more matches would have been won had the players played in a more determined manner'. In retrospect that may seem a hard judgement, for Yorkshire did have to contend with injuries and a wet spell that contributed to eight of the last twelve matches being drawn, the team being in third position in mid July.

Hutton became Sir Leonard but was, alas, no longer opening the Yorkshire innings, and although the county had two excellent young

---

Billy Sutcliffe

William Herbert Hobbs Sutcliffe, son of Herbert, born in Pudsey, was destined to be elected to the office his father had declined in 1928, the captaincy of Yorkshire, in 1956. He succeeded Yardley at the age of twenty-nine, with ten seasons of senior cricket and six centuries behind him, and was, at a time when amateurs still took preference, the logical successor. He was both capable and popular.

He did, however, take over at a difficult time. Hutton had retired along with Yardley; Watson and Lester were soon to depart, while the careers of Lowson and Appleyard were in their closing stages. That feature of the dressing room so often mentioned at that time, factionalism, was at its most rampant and it was to Sutcliffe's disadvantage, as Kilburn has pointed out, that he was so well known and so much a part of that talented but unruly team.

After Sutcliffe's first season the Committee report was unequivocal: 'More matches would have been won had the players played in a more determined manner on all occasions.' Sutcliffe had little luck; Trueman had one of his lean years in 1956, while his most promising partner, the left-arm Cowan, broke down. Yorkshire finished seventh and although Sutcliffe was able to take them back to respectability and third place in 1957, he had already informed the Committee, in August, that he would be resigning 'very definitely for business reasons'.

Sutcliffe's experience over two seasons almost certainly led the Committee into seeking a captain who was both detached and a disciplinarian, a path

that was to lead them eventually to the choice of Ronnie Burnet.

Sutcliffe later served the club on the General Committee until losing his seat when opposing the Boycott group.

batting prospects in Taylor and Padgett neither could yet give an innings of Hutton's confidence and assurance, nor match his appeal at the gate. Only three batsmen passed a thousand runs, only Watson averaged more than forty and he, Taylor and Lowson were the only batsmen to contribute centuries.

Pitches were rarely suitable for fast bowling, Trueman taking only 33 wickets this season. Cowan had been sent home from Pakistan with back trouble, throwing more weight on the less experienced seam bowlers Ryan, Platt, Peter Broughton and Close. The successes were the spinners: Wardle took 105 wickets, Appleyard 94 and Illingworth 85, the last-named passing the hundred in all matches for the first time.

Binks was acclaimed by *Wisden* for his wicket-keeping, but 1956 was remembered mainly for the rain: eleven full playing days were lost from the home programme and play was restricted on many others. The county's experiment in taking a Championship match to Middlesbrough for the first time was reported a success: 'The gate money of £1467 on a cloudy day showed there is a demand for First-Class cricket in the area.' Ted Lester, who had been unable to play first-team cricket because of foot trouble, was retained as senior professional with the Colts.

Yorkshire were in better heart in the slightly warmer weather of 1957, although the rain was again blamed for its effect on finances and the team fortunes. The side did finish third, a return to respectability, but the summer ended in an atmosphere of uncertainty. Sutcliffe, after two seasons, announced he would not be available to captain the team in 1958. Close, a rising influence in the dressing room, saw Sutcliffe in the light of a friend rather than a captain.

> . . . a super lad. He made himself into a county cricketer because it was expected of him and because he believed in Yorkshire cricket and its divine right to pre-eminence. He was happier having a pint and a natter when a day's work was over than he was cracking the whip on the field. His problem as a captain was that he had fixed, preconceived ideas about the way a day's play would go. You cannot be rigid in ideas as Billy was and lead successfully because circumstances can change completely with one ball in a long

cricketing day . . . . Billy did not have as much knowledge as his players but he had a good, pleasant personality. His trouble was really in handling the bowling and the field placing.

Watson, the senior professional, left to join Leicestershire. Lowson, the regular opening batsman, was so afflicted by leg trouble that he did not play after mid June. In compensation the Colts won the Minor Counties Championship under J.R. Burnet, and the changes in the first team did afford some of those Colts early promotion. Bryan Stott, a left-handed batsman from Yeadon, made his debut against Scotland in the last match in May and by the end of the season had scored 1248 runs, hit three centuries and, in late July, established a new opening partnership with Taylor. In the second innings against Nottinghamshire at Trent Bridge their stand of 230 was the best for any Yorkshire wicket for five years.

Finding Trueman a partner was the perennial problem, with Cowan still handicapped. In the early part of the season Appleyard was often called upon to use the new ball, while later in the year David Pickles, a tall right-arm bowler from Halifax, made an extremely promising beginning, taking 31 wickets at 19.06 in twelve games. Trueman took 76 wickets, while the invaluable Illingworth did the 'double' for the first time.

For perhaps a decade 1958 was remembered as the most unhappy year in Yorkshire's history, a time of dissension and upset on and off the field. The Committee's report concentrated on the weather ('appalling') and the playing record ('disappointing'). Of the real drama of the season, the sacking of three Test players, the reference is remarkable for its omissions:

> After very careful consideration your Committee decided that the services of F.A. Lowson, R. Appleyard and J.H. Wardle would not be called upon after the 1958 season. Your Committee places on record its appreciation of the loyal services of Lowson and Appleyard and has awarded them a joint testimonial in 1959.

Wardle had received a benefit of £8000 in 1957, but the real bitterness arose from the circumstances surrounding, and the sequel to, his sacking. The new captain, Ronnie Burnet, a

Ray Illingworth *Illy*

'Raymond', as he is usually addressed, was not a great off-spinner, nor a great batsman, nor a great fielder, but he was sufficiently expert, in his employment of experience, knowledge, tactical insight and psychology as a captain, to be remembered without qualification as a great cricketer. Gower, who served under him at Leicester, accords him the highest praise.

He was, it should be added quickly, of sufficient class as a spinner to be often named as first choice for England and, in fact, played in sixty-one Test matches. But it was Illingworth's ancillary talents that usually gave him the edge over worthy competitors; he was almost always involved in the game, at whatever level, and if by some chance the ball ignored him, he would be scheming to seek it out.

'Illy' was the thinking man's cricketer. When he arrived at Grace Road in 1969 to assume the captaincy of Leicestershire he took a look at the ground and ordered the boundary to be increased, the outfield shaved so that the ball did not keep its shine for long, and the pitches made harder. Pace bowlers had to work hard to get wickets, the spinners thrived, the batsmen enjoyed the ball coming on to the bat and the bowling rate went up to 20 overs an hour.

Yorkshire were hoping for similar results when, ten years later, he was recalled as cricket manager and, eventually, captain, but politics prevented his aims being accomplished and he retired at fifty-one years of age, after his bowling had played a major part in the winning of the John Player Sunday League. He is now a highly respected commentator in the media and Yorkshire lost the services of one of the keenest brains in the game's history.

He was born in Pudsey, the son of a cabinet-maker and joiner from whom he no doubt inherited his delight in seeing a task completed properly and well. At the age of three he and his family moved to nearby Farsley where, at school, the eight-year-old Illingworth began demonstrating an obvious aptitude for cricket. The school played on the Farsley club ground and the story is familiar of that generation: every spare moment given to practice and nets.

At fifteen he was playing for Farsley's first team in the Bradford League and an innings of 148 not out, spread over several evenings and attracting a record attendance, brought him more than local attention. He joined the Yorkshire Federation team's annual tour, along with Close and Trueman, and still recalls, according to his biographer Michael Stevenson, a slender Trueman bowling slow left-arm

before the match and very fast right-arm during it, to the great discomfiture of the Sussex schoolboys.

Illingworth spent his National Service at RAF Dishforth where a sympathetic CO ensured that he was given time to further his cricket for Farsley, Yorkshire Colts, and RAF and Combined Services. He made his debut for Yorkshire in August 1951, against Hampshire at Headingley, scoring 56 in a stand with Yardley after Yorkshire had lost four wickets cheaply. By then he had all but forsaken the medium-pace seamers of his boyhood for off-spin and the occasional delivery that 'went with the arm', which 'Illy' was always a master at concealing.

He had yet another year of RAF duty to complete

so his appearances in 1952 were restricted to four Championship matches, but the following year, with Appleyard ill, Trueman on National Service and Close injured, he was suddenly a valuable member of the team bearing, with Wardle, the brunt of the bowling. At Hull Yorkshire were 104 for five against Essex when Illingworth joined Yardley to add 146, another 115 being added with Brennan, the twenty-one-year-old Illingworth scoring 146 not out.

Illingworth, according to his biographer, was far from happy in the dressing room of the 1950s, the junior spinner to Appleyard and Wardle and therefore usually bowling when conditions were most inimical to his type of bowling. Even so, the lessons he learned in restricting batsmen when all was in their favour were invaluable later.

He particularly resented, after being put on to bowl by Yardley, being told to 'bugger off' by either Appleyard or Wardle. When 'Illy' did get on to bowl it was always at the wrong end. Neither Wardle nor Appleyard was lenient with dropped catches and Cowan, Roy Booth and Illingworth all testified to being humiliated on the field to such an extent that they felt their confidence was being eroded. It was a very hard upbringing for a young cricketer but it must be said that those that did survive also prospered to an extraordinary degree – Close, Trueman and Illingworth in particular.

Illingworth discovered, after a shouting match with Wardle, that relations improved to such an extent that he became the favourite out-fielder, taking 33 catches in the deep off Wardle in one summer. It was not however, until the arrival of Burnet and the departure of the two great spinners that Illingworth came into his own as the fulcrum of the Yorkshire attack, able to deliver with nagging accuracy or, in helpful conditions, a sharper spin than almost all his contemporaries. When Yorkshire found a slow left-arm replacement for Wardle in Don Wilson, it was Illingworth's consistency that provided the needed foil for the likeable Wilson's excesses and experiments. Together, supported by Close's field settings and Yorkshire's tight fielding, they became a formidable combination in the Silver Sixties.

Illingworth's Test career was initially delayed for the same reason he had had to wait for full establishment in the Yorkshire side: the ability of those in competition for places. England was awash with good off-spinners in the 1950s, including two of the immortals, Laker and Appleyard, and it was not until 1958 that the twenty-six-year-old Yorkshire all-rounder was selected for the Fourth Test match against New Zealand, at Old Trafford.

He bowled 45 overs, 18 of which were maidens, to return with match figures of three for 59, but won congratulations from his captain Peter May. It was during May's term as captain that Illingworth's Test career flourished for there was an obvious empathy between the pair. Once May had gone, and although Illingworth had a valid claim to be England's best off-spinner after Laker's retirement, he was less favoured by England, possibly the result of making his views known on certain aspects of the Duke of Norfolk's management of Illingworth's Australian tour and Dexter's captaincy.

Close's first move, on being appointed England captain in 1966, was to recall Illingworth and he had emerged as Close's second-in-command and heir-apparent to the Yorkshire captaincy, without challenge, when in 1968 came the argument over a contract, a situation exacerbated by Sellers' undoubtedly autocratic attitude, that led to the resignation of the thirty-seven-year-old Illingworth and his move to Leicestershire.

At Grace Road he takes second place only to the architect of the modern county administration, Mike Turner, in the lustre brought to the Running Fox over the past twenty years: in Illingworth's time as captain of Leicestershire they won their first Championship (1975), the Benson and Hedges Cup twice and the Sunday League twice. Such success restored Illingworth to the England captaincy and when that international career ended he had much to look back upon: regaining the Ashes and leading England in thirty-six Tests.

A man of such distinction would have been attractive to any county seeking leadership; to Yorkshire, Ray Illingworth represented perhaps the only way out of their maze of troubles, beset by factions seeking the deposition of Boycott as captain on one side and the Boycott loyalists on the other. Accordingly he was invited back in 1979 as manager and recorded, at the end of that summer: 'Shirley and I wished we had not made the move back.'

Illingworth did take Yorkshire to a Benson and Hedges semi-final against Essex, a match marred by a public dispute between manager and senior professional over Boycott's fitness; without Boycott, Yorkshire lost the match and with it the chance of a Final at Lord's that Illingworth believed, in restropect, would have re-established him in Yorkshire.

In 1980 Yorkshire finished sixth in the Championship when, with a little luck with the weather in the last match, the final placing would have been fourth, but Illingworth's hopes of rebuilding the side were set back when Hampshire resigned from the captaincy and moved to Derbyshire. The following year, under Old, the team suffered eight separate fractures and slipped from sixth to tenth with the agitation against Illingworth reflected almost daily in the Yorkshire press. The summer ended with Illingworth's controversial preference of the uncapped Neil Hartley as captain in Old's absence and the suspension of Boycott.

Fifteen days after Illingworth's fiftieth birthday, in 1982, the club dismissed Old from the captaincy and handed it to Illingworth to become the first manager-captain in the club's history. He himself would have preferred Neil Hartley to take over but no doubt sensed that the Committee, under intense pressure from the Boycott group, would have been unwilling to re-open the war on another front.

Illingworth's last eighteen months in cricket brought a stabilisation to the team and the winning of a trophy for the first time in fourteen years, the John Player Sunday League Championship, an honour that might have been disregarded a quarter-century before, but in the context of the civil war represented as heartfelt and warming a prize as any won by Hawke or Sellers. This triumph did not save Illingworth when the new Committee took office after the annual general meeting, but it did restore some spirit to the dressing room as Bairstow succeeded to the captaincy.

Illingworth then departed to become a radio and TV commentator and newspaper correspondent and was offered the job of England team manager in 1986, rejecting it when it became clear to him that he would have at best only partial control of team matters. 'Illy' would accept himself that he could be a difficult character, but it was Yorkshire's misfortune that England and Leicestershire managed to harness his considerable talents so much more successfully.

Doug Padgett

Next to Hutton, Douglas Ernest Vernon Padgett was the most technically correct batsman to appear for Yorkshire in the years after the Second World War, a credential that led to his appointment as Yorkshire's chief coach in succession to Arthur Mitchell.

A right-hander of medium height, neat and stylish, always a pleasure to watch whatever the batting circumstances, Padgett was born in Bradford and developed through the Bradford League and was such an outstanding prospect as a boy that he made his first-class debut in 1951, when Hutton and Watson were playing for England. At the age of sixteen years and 321 days, he was the youngest to appear for Yorkshire until Jarvis.

In his twenty seasons Padgett scored 21,124 polished runs at an average of 28.58, exceeding a thousand runs twelve times and twice playing for England; in addition he toured New Zealand. Padgett scored twenty-nine centuries and all judges agree that he had the ability to have been a regular member of the England team, lacking perhaps, like fellow Bradfordian Lowson, the final spur of ambition.

Padgett was a genial character, a stalwart of Close's team in the 1960s, a splendid and safe deep field and always a popular figure on Yorkshire grounds. He also gave lifelong devotion to Bradford City Football Club.

His style was summed up by Kilburn when Yorkshire defeated Sussex at Hove in 1959 to win the Championship. The final target was 215 in 105

minutes and Stott and Padgett got the runs, in a stand of 141, with seven minutes to spare – 'Padgett plundered 79 with the serenity of A.J. Raffles abstracting diamonds from a duchess.'

Bryan Stott

William Bryan Stott, from Yeadon, was a stocky left-hander who, with Ken Taylor, formed what was perhaps the most fleet-footed of Yorkshire opening partnerships between 1957 and 1963. In those seven seasons Stott passed a thousand runs five times (2034 in 1959) and the pair raised three double-century opening partnerships, often giving Close's team that near essential basis to a Championship win, a large first-innings total raised in quick time.

Stott scored 9000 runs at an average of 31 in a career curtailed by business commitments. The running between wickets of himself and Taylor was an exhibition of anticipation and understanding; the pair once astonished a Roses match audience by taking five singles off the first over.

Stott and Taylor, with Padgett at three, were almost always capable of a fast and successful start to the innings and had not Stott been obliged to attend to the family business at twenty-nine, his playing career might have been distinguished; a longer career would certainly have delayed the establishment of Boycott.

When time became available to him, Stott was able to return to the club as a member of the General Committee, serving on the cricket sub-committee and paying special attention to the county's schooling and coaching facilities.

Ken Taylor   *Fleetfoot*

Ken Taylor was a superb athlete from Huddersfield, following Willie Watson as both a gifted cricketer and footballer (Huddersfield Town and Bradford Park Avenue). A right-handed opener who could play with dash, he scored sixteen centuries in his twelve seasons (four in 1961, including a 203 not out against Warwickshire) and passed a thousand runs six times; he was also one of the great cover-points in the club's history.

With Stott he formed a fast-scoring opening partnership for Yorkshire that was able to give Close's team the kind of start enjoyed by Middlesex in the days of Robertson and Brown or by Hampshire with Greenidge and Richards. The pair were famous for their understanding between the wickets and Taylor was considered good enough technically to play for England three times, against India and Australia.

He had a fair claim, too, to be considered an all-rounder for he could also bowl medium, naggingly accurate seamers that brought him 131 wickets at an average of 28.

Taylor was also an artist who had studied at the Slade, and after his playing career had taken him on to Auckland and Norfolk, he taught at Gresham's School. His son Nick showed promise as a fast bowler with Yorkshire, Surrey and Somerset.

thirty-nine-year-old amateur, had been appointed on the strength of his leadership and rebuilding of the Colts' team. The notion, true or false depending on one's view of the Yorkshire dressing room, had got abroad that the senior members of the team, after the departure of Yardley and Hutton, had not given Sutcliffe their full backing and support. Burnet was reportedly briefed to 'sort things out', and whether or not he was responsible the fact is that by 1959 only Vic Wilson remained of what might be regarded as Norman Yardley's regulars – Hutton, Lowson, Sutcliffe, Lester, Watson and Wardle.

Lowson and Appleyard had not been in the best of health and although their departure (Lowson was thirty-two, Appleyard thirty-three) was surprising it could have been argued that Yorkshire did have younger opening batsmen and a first-class off-spinner in Illingworth. But the shock came at Bramall Lane on 30 July during Yorkshire's match against Somerset when the club's Secretary, J.H. Nash, anounced that the Committee would not be calling on Wardle's services after that season. Wardle, thirty-five, was at his peak: the best slow left-arm bowler of his type in the world, a hard-hitting batsman and an immensely popular figure with the crowd.

He was chosen for the next match, against

Lancashire at Old Trafford, but stood down after announcing that he intended to contribute some articles to the *Daily Mail*. Following the publication of those articles the MCC withdrew their invitation to him to tour Australia. The Yorkshire Committee then stated, on 11 August:

> The Committee regret the unpleasant publicity given to their decision to dispense with the services of J.H. Wardle after the present season. In past years Wardle has been warned on several occasions that his general behaviour on the field and in the dressing rooms left much to be desired.
>
> As no improvement was shown this year the decision to dispense with his services was made as it was unanimously considered that it was essential to have discipline and a happy and loyal team before any lasting improvement could be expected in the play of the Yorkshire XI.

It is felt that recent articles published in the *Daily Mail* fully justify the Committee's decision. Wardle broke his contract when he wrote those articles without first obtaining permission and the Committee are therefore terminating his contract forthwith.

Wardle then said he would join Nottinghamshire, a move upon which *Wisden* commented: 'Consent of Yorkshire and MCC would have been necessary.' He did, in fact, entertain Lancashire League audiences for several seasons.

Yorkshire had scarcely a happier time on the field. In all, twenty-four playing days were lost to rain, seventeen in Yorkshire, receipts dropped by £5000 and not one bowler passed the hundred wickets, Wardle, with 76, being the most successful. The three seam bowlers vying to be Trueman's partner – Cowan, Pickles and

Ronnie Burnet

John Ronald Burnet, from Saltaire, entered county cricket from the Bradford League at the age of thirty-nine, won the Championship in his second and last season, thus ending seven years of Surrey supremacy, and won the eternal gratitude of the club for restoring spirit and harmony to the dressing room. Burnet was also the captain responsible for the sacking of Wardle, in Burnet's first season, 1958.

Burnet had been a useful middle-order batsman for Baildon, then the Bradford League's most successful club, and, more important, a popular captain of the Yorkshire Second team, developing through the ranks such players as Stott, Taylor, Birkenshaw, Cowan, Ryan, Platt and Don Wilson, the bulk of the team for the next decade. The Committee, wishing to end the factionalism that had arisen in the first-team dressing room, decided to go to the leagues for an amateur captain who would be distant from old feuds and arguments, rather than for a professional, already immersed.

In the winter of 1957, according to Close, Burnet met Wardle at a league dinner and told him that he had been offered the captaincy, adding that if he did not take the offer another amateur, Derek Blackburn of Bradford, was next in line. Wardle, said Close, was deeply disappointed but consoled himself with the thought that, with Watson departed for Leicestershire, he would be the new senior professional, an appointment greeted with delight by Close: 'I had

learned more about cricket from Johnny than from all the other senior players put together.'

According to Burnet, however, he had to fight for Wardle's seniority as the Committee wanted to leapfrog Wardle and name Vic Wilson. Burnet told Alan Hill: 'I told the Committee that Wardle had to be given his chance and if he performed his duties correctly we should have no trouble.'

That there would be a clash was so obvious that the suspicion remains that it was deliberately engineered. For six weeks all was peaceful for Burnet was injured and Wardle led the side, but then he no doubt found life even more galling when the captain, a tyrant in his eyes, returned.

The first clash, according to Burnet, came during a match against Derbyshire at Chesterfield when Wardle reacted with violent language to a suggestion from the captain that he might bowl a fuller length. Burnet then switched him to the less responsive end of a drying pitch, whereupon Wardle bowled 'an over of long hops' and was promptly ordered to take his sweater.

Close may have dismissed this as one of 'several brushes' between the pair, and he pinpoints the Sussex match at Worthing as the first real flare-up. Overnight rain had got under the covers at one end and Wardle, much the senior bowler in a very inexperienced attack, expected to bowl to the drying end. But Burnet insisted that Wardle should bowl to the other end and gave the advantage to the young off-spinners, Birkenshaw and Close himself (Trueman and Illingworth were with England). 'We gave away too many runs,' reported Close, and Sussex won a low-scoring match that had been Yorkshire's for the taking.

The climax came against Somerset at Sheffield. Burnet was already angry at having to read in the newspapers of the imminent departure of Lowson and Appleyard and complained to the then cricket chairman Clifford Hesketh: 'My opinion should have been sought. Had I been consulted I would have included a third party – Johnny Wardle. As long as we have him in the side we shall never have any team spirit.'

Hereabouts accounts differ. Alan Hill, from Burnet, reports that a lunchtime meeting took place after which Burnet handed Wardle a note in the dressing room informing him that he had been sacked. Close wrote that there had been a further row between the pair that morning when Wardle, taken off after a fruitless spell on a good batting pitch, had been recalled, taken wickets but had been accused by the captain of 'not trying'. Burnet went off, according to Close, to attend a committee meeting called, it was thought, to pick a side for the next match, against Lancashire at Old Trafford. Wardle, in charge on the field, was resting on figures of six for 46 at tea when Burnet returned to tell Wardle that the Committee wanted to see him. Wardle put on his blazer, to return later with all the colour gone from his usually ruddy cheeks. He had been told he had been sacked.

There is little dispute about what happened afterwards. As soon as the news broke, the *Daily Mail* signed Wardle for an exclusive series of articles (for

£400 according to the man who wrote them, Alex Bannister) in which the player attacked the club, the captain and the conduct of some younger players. Wardle warned Yorkshire of the impending publication and stood down voluntarily from the match at Old Trafford. Yorkshire announced a breach of contract and in effect instant dismissal, and the MCC, after getting confirmation from Wardle personally that he had seen the articles before publication, withdrew their invitation to him to tour Australia in 1958–9, to the intense chagrin of their captain, Peter May.

Could it all have been avoided? Yardley believed that the then Yorkshire engagement system, which meant players had to be notified of an offer for the following year by the end of July, was partly responsible. Had the present contract method been operating, there would have been time for reconsideration.

Billy Sutcliffe thought the decision both unwise and unnecessary. Wardle, we know from many accounts, regretted his *Daily Mail* adventure almost immediately; without that public attack on his captain and club he would have gone on tour and probably have joined Nottinghamshire, who were prepared to make him a handsome offer, the following summer.

The younger players were split on his presence in the dressing room but agreed on his value to the side. Long afterwards, Burnet told Alan Hill:

I had the highest possible regard for Johnny as a cricketer. What happened was an absolute tragedy. He should have been in the side for another ten years. I would have loved to have captained him when he was a younger cricketer. He would not have become a sour man. But in 1958 his character, and the way he approached the game were, as far as Yorkshire were concerned, luxuries we could not afford.

Burnet then took over a team that had lost four Test players – Watson, Lowson, Appleyard and Wardle – in a little over a year and promptly won the Championship. He did it, too, with the young Colts he had brought up himself, in a blaze of batsmanship from such as Stott, Taylor and Padgett, even leading Yorkshire to a memorable victory over the Rest of England, scoring 425 after a follow-on to win by 66 runs!

Burnet then returned to his Bradford League, served Yorkshire as a committee man for many years and, as might be expected, was a very firm and outspoken opponent of Boycott's admirers some quarter-century after his own great battle.

Ryan – managed only 57 wickets between them. However, Stott hit two more centuries, Close passed a thousand runs and Philip Sharpe, from Worksop College, made an auspicious start, scoring 141 against Somerset in his third match and finishing with 433 runs in nineteen innings.

Before the 1959 season started Brian Sellars, newly appointed Cricket Committee chairman, believed that Yorkshire would need another three years to become Championship contenders. In 1958 they had finished eleventh and after a season of turmoil it was expected that a comparatively young team would need time to settle. But to the surprise of English cricket, to the astonishment of members and to the amazement of the Committee, Ronnie Burnet's team won the Championship.

It was won in style, too, on the afternoon of 1 September at Hove where Sussex set Yorkshire the apparently impossible target of scoring 215 runs in 105 minutes. Stott scored 13 of the 15 hit off the first over; the 50 came up in 20 minutes, 77 in half an hour and the first 100 in 43 minutes. In three minutes over the first hour the score had reached 150, the 200 was reached in 85 minutes and Bolus hit the winning boundary, a deflection to fine leg, at 4.23 – victory by five wickets with just seven minutes to spare. Stott scored his 96 in 86 minutes and he and Padgett added 141 in just over an hour for the third wicket. The *Daily Express* exclaimed: 'The White Hot Rose'.

So Yorkshire returned to Scarborough as Champions, and when challenged by MCC to display their scoring prowess did just that by hitting 260 in 150 minutes to win by seven wickets with no less than 25 minutes to spare.

But Yorkshire's cricket had not been so assured and dominant for the entire season. In mid June they had been only half-way up the table, but a sudden surge of three victories took them to the top and having gained that impetus they thereafter were never out of the first three and always played like contenders. Their only setback came on the western tour with defeats by Somerset and Gloucestershire, being dismissed for 35 at Bristol, their lowest total for twenty-four years.

Burnet's team had great spirit and once suc-

cess had given them confidence their talents flowed, and this despite a pervading feeling that their luck was out. Burnet lost the toss on twenty occasions and only once was there a three-figure opening stand. Yet Yorkshire in 1959 did have great faith in their own individual ability and more often than not someone succeeded.

Illingworth did the 'double' and became one of *Wisden's* Famous Five. Padgett added 1787 runs thanks to his highly polished technique, while Stott, starting indifferently, finished gloriously. Close may have been inconsistent but he was also explosive and Bolus and Bird finished with strong challenges to the places held by Sharpe and Taylor. Platt, with 82 wickets, gave splendid support to the indefatigable Trueman, while Ryan, Taylor and Close could all contribute useful spells of seam bowling. Wardle's departure was partly compensated for by Don Wilson's advance and a varied off-spin attack of Illingworth, Close and Birkenshaw.

A fine summer also brought a farewell to the captain, Burnet, who at forty decided to make way for a younger man. Having been given the onerous task, in 1958, of restoring authority to the dressing room, and having seen the departure of the nucleus of the fine side of the early 1950s, he cannot have imagined so great a reward as Yorkshire's first outright Championship since 1946.

Ironically Burnet departed knowing that several of his senior players, delighted as they were to be champions again, still believed that Wardle should have been retained. Close went further:

> My own choice for the captaincy, being a professional myself, would have been Wardle . . . . He knew his cricket inside out; he knew the opposition; he knew about field placing and he knew about bowling; he had a shrewd calculating cricketing brain and he was interested in winning matches. He hated losing and most of all he hated losing games which could be won.

Significantly when Vic Wilson, the senior professional, was dropped for a short spell in 1959 and Close won a temporary promotion, he lost no time in telling his captain: 'I don't want the same thing to happen to me as Johnny. If I offer you advice it will be something that has been reasoned out as the best thing for the side. If you disregard my advice I shall stop offering it.'

Nevertheless, according to Close, Burnet had a spell during which he paid little attention to his professionals when three matches were lost and one drawn. So Close tried a different tack and told the senior bowlers, especially Trueman and Illingworth, to insist on their field placings. Close, too, maintains that it was he who persuaded Burnet to restore Vic Wilson to the team for The Champions against The Rest match at The Oval, and that rumours that Wilson was not to be offered a new contract were confounded when the batsman who had twice been dropped in a Championship season was appointed the captain for 1960.

Vic Wilson, who had lost his place in the team in 1959, accepted the leadership after Burnet's resignation, thus becoming Yorkshire's first professional captain this century. Wilson did not have the good weather of 1959 and there were times when Yorkshire's play slipped below the standard expected of champions, yet by the end of the season Wilson had led the team to a second successive Championship.

Returning to Hove, scene of that great triumph the previous September, Yorkshire lost to Sussex by 32 runs, but the next six matches were won. By 24 May Yorkshire were on top again, and although they were deposed by Lancashire in July their final margin over the oldest rivals was 32 points, a highly satisfactory conclusion after two defeats by the Red Rose.

Trueman, with 132 Championship wickets, had a great season. Platt and Ryan were both handicapped by injuries but the left-arm Cowan returned in hostile fashion, taking 66 wickets, and with Trueman in such sharp form the seam attack was rarely quelled. Illingworth did the 'double' again but the spin attack overall was less impressive, the covering of wickets a handicap. The batting, as in 1959, was rarely reliable yet rarely failed. Stott loss his place for a while but returned in tremendous form, while Bolus replaced Taylor, who moved down the order, as Stott's opening partner. Padgett, who hit five centuries, played for England without looking the player all Yorkshire knew him to be.

Binks had a splendid season, becoming the first Yorkshire wicket-keeper to record a hundred victims in a summer. Bolus, Cowan, Sharpe and Don Wilson were all awarded their caps and such was the strength of the side that Bird and the fast-medium bowler Peter Broughton were allowed to leave for Leicestershire. Birkenshaw, too, restive at being denied a place, applied for his release, but the Committee felt he was too valuable a player to lose, a judgement that was to be vindicated in later years.

After successive Championships Yorkshire began the following season as unchallenged favourites, and had 1961's weather been a little kinder Wilson's ambitions may have been realised. The captain deserved some sympathy, for it was hard to understand a team that could play so well, and then so badly, in a matter of days. Yorkshire's batting in 1961 defied explanation. The batsmen had hit thirteen centuries in 1959, a good summer. The following season, in much damper weather, they had raised the total to fifteen, a promising advance. In 1961, a year similar in climate to its predecessor, eighteen centuries were scored yet five matches were lost (two to Middlesex), and as those defeats came towards the end rather than the beginning of the summer, Hampshire became the new champions.

The start was auspicious enough, Yorkshire winning seven of the first eight games. Four games without a win from the middle of June was the first hint of fallibility, and although the side rallied with something of its old style in late July, they fell away again in August. Six batsmen scored a thousand runs but only Bolus averaged over 35, and a Yorkshire innings left a hit-and-miss impression far too often. Yorkshire's attack did all that was asked of them. Trueman and Illingworth both took more than a hundred wickets and although Cowan missed much of the season through injury, Platt and Ryan shared 109 victims. An injury to Don Wilson might have been critical had not his replacement, Keith Gillhouley from Huddersfield, bowled well enough to take 73 wickets in his first season.

Don Wilson

Don Wilson was an unusual Yorkshire cricketer. He was born in Settle, not a natural nursery, and as a left-arm spinner he was the opposite of almost all his great predecessors in that Peate, Peel, Rhodes, Verity and Wardle all considered their basic task to be that of restricting the batsman's strokes and attacking when conditions were totally in their favour, while Wilson was an adventurer who saw his priority as the early downfall of his opponent.

His career was greatly advanced by his arrival during Close's captaincy, for Close also believed in unlimited aggression and it was the field settings and brilliant close catching engineered by the captain that brought Wilson much of his success. When defensive bowling was required Close could normally call upon Illingworth, operating his seam bowlers from the other end.

Don Mosey records that it was Close, early in Wilson's career, who convinced the bowler that he needed a leg-slip on the grounds that although Wilson did not include the chinaman in his armoury, the presence of a fielder in that position would cast serious doubt in the batsman's mind.

Wilson had the serious disadvantage of having to follow into the team that public hero Wardle. Another misfortune was that Wilson's appearance, tall, lean, angular, almost gauche, suggested he was a beginner long after he had established his place and won England recognition. But eventually his terrific enthusiasm, his unquenchable optimism and belief in always thinking that something was about to hap-

pen, inspired no doubt by his captain, won over the suspicious Yorkshire crowds.

He passed a hundred wickets three times, in 1966, '68 and '69, and is one of only thirteen bowlers to have taken a thousand wickets for the club. In 1966 he twice performed the hat-trick, against Nottinghamshire and Kent, and six times in his career took seven wickets in an innings. Although not a fierce spinner of the ball, his height enabled him to win bounce and, with his tail up, Wilson became a valuable weapon for Close, not least because of his unpredictability.

Wilson was also a useful tail-ender, able to swing the bat in a late chase for runs, camouflaging a less than perfect defence with his aggressive attitude. He was a superb fielder anywhere.

He played in six Tests encompassing tours to Australia, New Zealand, India and Sri Lanka, and expanded his communication skills while coaching in Soweto. According to Boycott he was favoured for the captaincy after Close's dismissal and was eventually named vice-captain to Boycott, always an unlikely partnership.

After leaving Yorkshire, Wilson became coach to the Indoor School at Lord's where, in a second career, he won even more approval from cricket generally. In his fifties he claimed he was bowling better than ever, illustrating his oft-repeated belief that 'There's always something new to learn in this game.'

Yorkshire's President, Sir William Worsley, was elected President of MCC, while in another important position Ted Lester became Yorkshire's scorer in succession to Cyril Turner. In the Colts a young right-handed batsman from Thurnscoe, John Hampshire, continued to make an excellent impression on good judges. Vic Wilson, like Ronnie Burnet before him, was able to complete his career with a Championship, Yorkshire's twenty-fifth, a happy event upon which Maurice Leyland retired as coach after forty-two years of service to the county's cricket.

The 1962 season was dry but cold and Sharpe, for one, relished the change. His

talents, as batsman and fielder, blossomed in the keen winds for he scored 1800 runs and, just as important, held 71 catches, beating the 1901 record (70) of the renowned Long John Tunnicliffe. Sharpe's batting was crucial in the first half of the season. After a good start (three victories) had won them the leadership, they had a rocky spell of three defeats in six matches without a win.

The fighting spirit which had seemed to fade in 1961 was all too evident this season as Yorkshire regained their competitive edge and re-established themselves, clearly, as the team the others had to beat. There were disappointments. The opening partnership of Bolus and

Stott failed so signally that Stott was dropped and Bolus released and a new pair, the experienced Taylor and the Colt Hampshire, made the eighth partnership tried that season.

Wilson scored two centuries in his last year and was always a solid and heartening figure in a crisis. In his three years of leadership Yorkshire had finished 1–2–1 so that any criticisms of his captaincy – too orthodox, too cautious – were really academic.

Trueman (106 wickets) retained his fire admirably, Illingworth did the 'double' again (including almost 1500 runs) and while Platt faded somewhat, Ryan advanced to 74 wickets. Wilson returned triumphantly to claim the slow left-arm place, 83 wickets at 22, and new, interesting names were those of the right-arm medium-pace seam bowler Tony Nicholson, the Cambridge blue and all-rounder Richard Hutton, son of Sir Leonard, and Geoffrey

Boycott, a bespectacled middle-order right-handed batsman from Fitzwilliam.

A win over Lancashire at Leeds, the first Lancastrian defeat in Yorkshire since 1939, was rightly regarded as a good omen, and from the end of June Yorkshire were unbeaten, winning nine and drawing eleven of their last twenty games. However, the season ended in some tension for, with a match to go, Worcestershire edged in front, leaving Yorkshire having to beat Glamorgan at Harrogate for the Championship.

This deciding match was a thriller. Glamorgan, sent in on a drying wicket, were routed by Wilson for 65, his analysis of six for 24 including two magnificent return catches. Only Taylor, apparently, could deal with the Glamorgan bowlers when Yorkshire batted. First in and eighth out at 100, Taylor batted 140 minutes for 67 in his most vital innings for the county.

Yorkshire, 1962.
Back row (from left): Jackie Hampshire, Bryan Stott, Ken Taylor, Don Wilson, Mel Ryan, Doug Padgett, Phil Sharpe.
Front row: Ray Illingworth, Brian Close, Vic Wilson, Fred Trueman, Jimmy Binks.

Philip Sharpe

Next to Tunnicliffe, Philip Sharpe will be remembered as the finest slip catcher in Yorkshire's history, a short, stocky figure who won such confidence from his captains and bowlers that his prowess won him selection for England. He was also a capable right-hand batsman who scored 22,530 runs in his career at 30.73, including twenty-nine centuries; his Test record, 786 runs at 46.23, suggests he was happier in higher company.

He made his reputation by scoring a thousand runs for Worksop School, and he was capped by Yorkshire in 1960 before joining Derbyshire for two seasons in 1975. A man who enjoyed his cricket, along with music (Gilbert and Sullivan, the Black and White Minstrels), cards and hockey, he and Don Wilson brought much fun and laughter into the often fractious dressing room of Close's champions.

Sharpe was an excellent player of fast bowling and might have had a much more prosperous career, in terms of runs, had he played twenty years later, by which time he had become an England selector faced with the task of finding young Englishmen who were as capable of dealing with West Indian pace as he had been in 1963 and 1969.

But it is for his 616 catches that Sharpe will be best remembered; such were his skill and co-ordination that bowlers and fielders would claim, after another dazzler, that the ball had actually passed him before the catch was completed. The truth was probably that the ball seemed to have passed, and would have passed any other fielder of his time. In his own position Sharpe was as much a vital contributor to the Championships of the 1960s as any specialist batsman or bowler.

After retirement he became the General Committee member for York and was popular and capable enough to keep his seat, despite his known opposition to the Boycott group, in the upheaval of 1983. It may have been the recognition, by dour and aggrieved Yorkshiremen of both persuasions, that in Sharpe they saw a man who always kept his sense of humour.

Brian Bolus

Bolus was a right-hand batsman of various talents ranging from his most sedate style with Yorkshire to a sudden, and effective, aggression with Nottinghamshire which earned him the highest honours in the game. He played one match for the club in 1956, and his progress was steady rather than spectacular. The true measure of his style and dependability was shown in 1959 in two innings which do not rank among his highest, but in quality were certainly among his best.

Yorkshire were destroyed by Smith and Brown of Gloucestershire at Bristol and only Bolus, with 12, reached double figures in an innings score of 35, the last six batsmen all making ducks. In the follow-on Bolus was promoted to opening batsman and he defied the Gloucester attack for almost four hours, scoring 91 of his county's total of 182. In 1960 Bolus hit two centuries, his 146 not out against Hampshire being the highest of his Yorkshire career, and he was awarded his county cap. He scored four more in 1961, another in 1962, and then, inexplicably, controversy crossed his career for the first, but certainly not the last time.

He was not retained by the county, and joined

Nottinghamshire – as captain! Here he adopted a swashbuckling style for a time, and it earned him a Test place in two of the matches against the West Indies of 1963 and a tour of India in 1963–4 where he appeared as opener in all five Tests.

He scored 2190 runs in 1963 and made his highest score of his career, 202 not out against Glamorgan. After serving under Sobers as vice-captain, and then again as captain in 1972, Bolus suddenly left Trent Bridge and joined Derbyshire, as captain, in 1973.

Bolus was introduced, doubtless, to spark a fire in a Derbyshire side losing credibility with its supporters. Confrontation is the price a captain often pays when he attempts to impress a new style and discipline on a side, and in June of that first year he felt compelled to use a measure employed only twice previously in the history of the game. Alan Ward, the Test fast bowler, was dismissed from the field by Bolus at Chesterfield for refusing to bowl a second spell – ironically against Yorkshire. Only Lord Hawke, of Yorkshire, and Lord Tennyson, of Hampshire, had previously taken such an autocratic step. Ward announced his retirement from the game,

but in 1974 was back in the side and playing under Bolus. That all was not well is reflected in *Wisden*'s review of the 1974 season. Michael Carey wrote: ' . . . team spirit sagged as the season went on. Bolus's leadership, so inspiring in difficult days the previous year, became questionable.'

In the early part of 1975 Bolus stood down from the captaincy and, relieved of the tension and responsibility, showed support for his successor, Bob Taylor, by topping the county's averages with 968 runs at 33.47.

Bolus's undoubted versatility as a batsman and his willingness to accept responsibility perhaps called for too much diversification of a talent that was high but yet not quite of the highest. He graduated in a Yorkshire side that had produced such captains as Watson (Leicestershire), Illingworth (Leicestershire), Close (Yorkshire and Somerset) and Vic Wilson (Yorkshire). That Bolus achieved less than his contemporaries may well be due to the player himself; it is also true that the counties who employed him often expected instant miracles, and when they did not materialise, insisted on instant sacrifices. **P.T.**

Harold Bird *Dickie*

Bird, a right-handed batsman from Barnsley, had three years with Yorkshire before joining Leicestershire in 1960. His best score was 181 not out against Glamorgan at Bradford in 1959. Another good performance was his top score of 62 for Yorkshire against MCC at Scarborough. Bird was appointed a first-class umpire in 1970 and it is in this capacity that 'Dickie' Bird has gained public notice.

His approach to the job was affected by modern influences that liberate showmanship – an approach that would have found little favour in the eyes of earlier and legendary umpires such as Syd Buller, himself an ex-Yorkshire player, and Frank Chester. They favoured judicial dignity and authority in isolation; this, indeed, was the accepted norm in their profession. Times changed sharply, and Bird's approach suddenly moved pace for pace with those times. His flamboyance and extravagance of gesture provoked conflicting reactions. It was a dramatic technique that sometimes teetered and often fell into the melodramatic, but it was also, in many ways, an unconscious display.

The natural wit and integrity that enriched Bird, while endearing off the field was not easily communicated from the square to the circle. Few umpires have excited (or even invited) such attention in an age when the pressures facing officials are more strenuous and opinions more openly asserted.

Television added to the stress and increased the exposure, thus encouraging the indulgences of the eccentric and the assertive. The cameras doggedly tracked Bird at his best and his most excessive. He was the umpire who, during an unhappy and tense bomb scare at Lord's, preferred to sit on the covers and protect the wicket while the alarm was on.

Bird it was who strictly enforced the controversial 'front foot law' in 1974, on one occasion no-balling Peter Lever, of Lancashire, nine times in his first six overs, and it was Bird who crusaded strongly and bravely on the inflammatory question of intimidation, becoming the first umpire to act against the bowling of persistent short-pitched deliveries in 1975.

Bird was, with veteran Tom Spencer, umpire in the dramatic, historic Prudential World Cup Final of 1975 between Australia and West Indies at Lord's. The match started at 11 a.m. and ended, in chaos, at 8.43 p.m. on a burning hot day. The ground was invaded by excited West Indian enthusiasts who thought Australia had lost – and had not heard a no-ball called. During the fracas Bird was knocked unconscious as he tried to repel invaders who were rushing the square. The conditions for umpiring could not have been more exacting, for not only was it the longest day of the year and one of the hottest, it was also one of the longest days in cricket history, played throughout to a tin-can cacophony that made conversation impossible, decisions inaudible.

Bird's performance was, from a cricketing point of view, impeccable, and full of understanding; he hastened to excuse his 'knockout' – 'I just think a few were over-excited.'

Both captains, Clive Lloyd and Ian Chappell, congratulated the umpires. But Bird's sense of the dramatic did not please many, including Jack Fingleton, that eminently sensible commentator and former Australian cricketer. Indeed, there could have been a flashpoint to the match when Bird was uncertain about an appeal from Marsh, the Australian wicket-keeper, for a catch off Lloyd. Bird walked slowly to consult with Tom Spencer, the square-leg umpire, debated the question at length, then walked equally dramatically to the wicket, and flourished his forefinger to denote Lloyd's dismissal.

Many feel it was fortunate that Lloyd was on 102 at the time and not 99, for such hesitation and slow deliberation – although justifiable within the law – were so ponderous and theatrical that it could well have sparked anger in what was an otherwise happy, if over-ebullient, West Indian section of the crowd. Against the unhappy Australians of 1977 it seemed that there was no detail too small to occupy Bird's personal attention; the merest trifles occasioned excessive gesticulations, and no opportunity of walking to boundaries to ascertain facts or still spectators was neglected.

Certain sections of the crowd, both knowledgeable and unruly, and sections of the media expressed warm criticism and disapproval. But such individual eccentricities could not conceal the warmth and integrity of Harold Bird. Not since Buller had there been a more balanced and discriminating judge of fair play, for Bird's creed was one of instinctive justice and understanding and he ranks high in the opinion of many players and judges of the game.

Denis Compton said of him: 'Harold Bird is one of those level-headed, strictly no-nonsense types so valuable in cricket. Having played as a batsman for Yorkshire and Leicestershire he knows what it is all about. Now he talks to players firmly, but in a friendly manner, and he obtains results. Most players respect him for it.'

There were mixed problems with the 1976 West Indians. Bird and Spencer, in the First Test, showed early patience and understanding with Wayne Daniel, a raw young fast bowler, obviously striving for length and direction and struggling with his run-up. It was Bird who finally warned him for running on to the pitch in his follow-through. As early as June 1976 Bird warned Daniel for this offence, and also for intimidation after he had sent down several short-pitched balls to Arnold Long, the Sussex wicket-keeper and number eight batsman.

The Second Test – in which Bird stood – passed without comment, but the wisdom of his reaction in the First Test bore witness to the steps that were necessary when, at Old Trafford in a match that produced bowling described as 'unsavoury as well as being bad cricket', umpire Bill Alley publicly warned Holding for intimidation.

An unprejudiced verdict on Bird is difficult; it is not what he did, which was always within the law – more the way he did it. As one writer reminded him: 'The owl is considered a wise bird, but it carries out its duties in secret and silence; the peacock is flamboyant and spectacular, but it has no real purpose in life; it is only fine to look upon.'

Bird was approached by Kerry Packer to join his 'World Series', which showed how little the Australian entrepreneur understood about Bird the man, rather than Bird the umpire. Bird wanted no role as ringmaster to Packer's circus. The puzzling thing is that perhaps Bird did not know why he was ever approached in the first place.   **P.T.**

Yorkshire's slender lead of 31 was reduced to 18 without loss by Glamorgan when rain washed out play on the second day with 5000 spectators waiting patiently. The weather relented on the last day, and the ground was filled to a capacity 10,000 as Illingworth and Wilson got to work on the Glamorgan second innings. They managed just 101, leaving Yorkshire needing 66 to win. Jones completed a hat-trick by bowling Taylor with the first ball

of the innings, but that was Yorkshire's last setback. Hampshire, with a mature 24, put the Championship in safe keeping with the loss of only two more wickets.

The summer of 1963 was one of which Yorkshire could be proud. Despite injuries, heavy Test calls and the advent of a new captain, the county still managed to retain the Championship. At various times Illingworth, Padgett, Stott and Taylor all missed several

Tony Nicholson *Teapot*

The nickname came from a famous Nicholson pose, standing hands on hips and glaring at some hapless batsman who, in the considered Nicholson judgement, was palpably leg before. In any poll conducted among Yorkshire players and members over the last forty years, Tony Nicholson would be very close to being elected the most popular cricketer.

Anthony George Nicholson, from Dewsbury, appeared late in Trueman's career after a roundabout route into professional cricket that included a spell as a policeman in what is now Zimbabwe. But he was that great man's best partner; had the pair been of the same generation (Trueman was seven years older, a long span for a pace bowler) they might have formed one of the great pairings.

Nicholson, a man totally without malice and with a joyous humour, was a strong right-arm fast-medium bowler who learned how to extract the maximum help from all English conditions and his intelligent mixture of speed, seam and cut brought him an impressive total of victims, many of whom were off guard and relaxing at the thought of escaping Trueman at the other end.

He twice reached a hundred wickets and took 879 wickets in his 282 matches at 19.76 apiece. He was selected for the tour of South Africa in 1964–5 but had to withdraw through injury, and he did much to encourage the career of the next generation of seam bowlers, including Old and Sidebottom. He retired, in declining health, at the age of thirty-seven and was much mourned when he died in Harrogate ten years later.

A fit and forceful Nicholson, loyal to the club's cause, could have been a greatly beneficial influence in the dressing room of the late 1970s.

matches through injury; England made regular calls on Trueman and Close, and Sharpe, too, was needed by his country.

The weather was far from kind, a definite result being impossible in twelve Championship matches, but when Yorkshire could play they played to some purpose: thirteen of the other sixteen matches were won, and of their three defeats only one, by an innings and 57 runs to Worcestershire, could be described as overwhelming. Even without Trueman for twelve matches, the attack was powerful. With Platt playing in only one match and retiring, seam support was needed for Ryan and Tony Nicholson emerged to take 65 wickets at 16.24

apiece. Wilson was the leading wicket-taker with 82, and Trueman, despite his absences, recorded the impressive figures of 76 wickets at 12.84 each.

Close assumed the captaincy in succession to Vic Wilson, an appointment that was as natural as it was successful. Close's leadership, tactical appreciation and accurate knowledge of each individual's capabilities were soon reflected in the team performances. He averaged 35 with the bat, was a fearless near fielder and won back his place in the England team. He also had much to do with the startling advances made by the promoted Colts. Of these Boycott had an impressive first season as a regular player,

Geoffrey Boycott

Geoffrey Boycott, from Fitzwilliam, the son of a miner who died early from industrial disease, has been the most controversial figure in the club's history, the most prolifically scoring batsman in the records and the captain for eight turbulent summers. As a right-handed opening batsman he was without peer in the world as a defensive player for a span of almost twenty years, and he was usually the premier target for opposing bowlers in the great majority of his 108 Test matches.

He was also a capable in-swing bowler of considerable accuracy who became a valuable member, for two or three years, of the Sunday League attack. A poor fielder when he first arrived, he turned himself into an excellent deep field, a safe catcher with a good, accurate throw, and he also served his county and country occasionally at slip. A keen student of the game, his deep knowledge and assessments of players, pitches and conditions were respected around the world. In short, he was qualified as few of his predecessors had been to lead both his county and his country with distinction for many years.

That he failed to do so was due to the many contradictions within his own character. Lester's comparison of Boycott and Wardle is justified: both were South Yorkshiremen from mining backgrounds, ambitious, fiercely competitive, ultra-careful in offering friendship, disdainful if not derisive of enemies and with an in-born mistrust of all authority. As all Yorkshiremen know, Robin Hood was born in Locksley, near Sheffield, probably spent more time in Barnsdale Forest than Sherwood and almost certainly had a Boycott and a Wardle in his band – although not necessarily among the Merry Men.

Both were rebels but emerged at different times into vastly dissimilar circumstances. Wardle was one of several great players in the Yorkshire team of his time; Boycott, from his election to the captaincy, was the only truly great cricketer in the side. Wardle was a member of a team that may have had only limited success but could never have been described as unsuccessful; in Boycott's time as captain, Yorkshire had the most disastrous Championship record in their history.

Wardle also made the tactical error of attacking Yorkshire in public print; Boycott was shrewd enough to reserve his criticisms to specific areas on specific points, and although there is evidence to suggest he might have moved to another county had the proper terms been offered, he always professed to his supporters his devotion to Yorkshire.

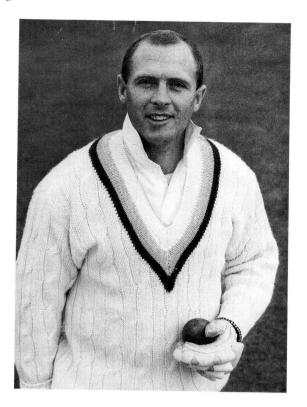

His early interest in the game persuaded his family to send the ten-year-old Geoffrey to Johnny Lawrence's Cricket School at Rothwell, fourteen miles away, a journey that the youngster dutifully undertook, with three changes of buses, through the winter sleet, snow and rain. He joined Ackworth Cricket Club at about the same time (1950) and was in the first team (Yorkshire Council) at thirteen. Upset at being told he had to wear spectacles, he treasured a letter from Mike (M.J.K.) Smith, captain of Warwickshire and England who, of course, had a highly successful batting career wearing glasses.

At fifteen the young Boycott started to play for Barnsley in the Yorkshire League, deepening and extending his roots in the South Yorkshire area. Don Mosey quotes a local cricketer, Alan Kilvington, who saw Boycott grow up: 'He's very open when he's with people he knows and trusts, almost the opposite of the public view of him.' Another view of the fifteen-year-old batsman: 'He was inclined to be a bit abusive as a lad. He were a slow starter, never a prolific scorer – at fifteen or sixteen I'd think that

Martyn Moxon looked a far better player than Geoff.'

At twenty Boycott had moved to Leeds, then captained by Billy Sutcliffe, where his defensive play was admired and his scoring rate, in league cricket, heavily criticised. Robin Feather, later to become captain of the Yorkshire second team, recalled a Colts match at Durham when Yorkshire needed 46 to win in 45 minutes with Boycott spending eight overs in scoring 5 runs.

By 1962 Boycott appeared for Yorkshire's first team in a season of transition, Vic Wilson having retired for Close to assume the captaincy. His 688 runs for the Colts had forced attention upon him although he was very much at the back of the field in intense competition for places, with such as Hampshire, Sharpe and Richard Hutton much more highly regarded. Boycott was dismissed for 4, opening against the Pakistanis at Bradford, in each innings, scored 6 and 17 in his first Championship match, at Northampton, and was considered to have run out Ken Taylor in his third, at Chesterfield.

He spent the rest of the 1962 season in the Colts, with little success, and returned to his applied practice through the following winter, showing remarkable confidence in surrendering a secure if dull job with the Ministry of Pensions in Barnsley.

He was returned to Yorkshire's first team at Northampton early in May, batting at six and scoring 8. Dropped for four matches, he played only a small part, batting at seven, in a win over Kent, but then, with Yorkshire 56 for 3 against Lancashire at Bramall Lane on an awkward pitch, Boycott helped Stott to raise 249 for the fourth wicket, completing his own maiden century, 145, a major achievement by the twenty-two-year-old who could no longer be disregarded.

He had, however, not convinced Close that he was an opening batsman and had to wait his turn for injuries and Test calls to move up the order. Boycott hit another Roses century at Old Trafford, scored 90 out of 144 on a difficult surface at Lord's and had three fine innings against Leicestershire; at the end of the season the Committee realised that he had raised 1628 runs at an average of 45.22, and in October he was presented with his cap.

Boycott began 1964 with three centuries and a 77 in the opening six matches; Test selection was inescapable and a great career was under way. His place at the top of Yorkshire's averages, and near the top of the national averages, became a routine; he became as much a fixture at number one for Yorkshire and England as Hutton had been before him. His 146 in the 1965 Gillette Cup Final, including three sixes and fifteen fours, is remembered as one of the finest of all one-day innings and yet, inevitably, was accompanied by controversy.

According to Close the opening pair of Taylor and Boycott had become so bogged down by the Surrey seam attack that he, the captain, went in at three to move things along and told Boycott first to start looking for singles, then to put some force into his shots and finally to 'hit everything'. According to Boycott, his mid-wicket conversation with Close, on the captain's arrival, concerned details as to who was bowling well and who was to be attacked. The extreme version of the story, unconfirmed but part of the legend, is that Close threatened to run out Boycott unless he accelerated.

With Illingworth departed to Leicester, Close had already decided that Boycott was his long-term replacement as captain but had, of course, no say in the decision in 1970 when he was given his 'resign or be sacked' ultimatum. It was certainly too soon for Boycott at that time, in Close's opinion, but the die was cast and at twenty-nine, the man from Fitzwilliam, his spectacles having given way to contact lenses, his turn-out immaculate on or off the field, became Yorkshire's twenty-second captain in 107 years.

A score of 246 not out against India at Headingley in 1967 brought censure from the selectors and he was dropped for slow scoring. To many of his growing band of admirers this was merely proof of the establishment's attitude towards 'Our Geoff', and few captains entered into their kingdom with as much prestige and general public goodwill.

Close's attitude to captaincy was that it was an act of giving, the total subordination of the individual's ambitions and desires to the welfare and success of the team, and under that philosophy Yorkshire had flourished, achieving their most resplendent spell since Sellers' time. Boycott assumed charge of a team accustomed to this style of leadership, although it was changing fast with the departure, in recent times, of Trueman, Illingworth, Taylor and Binks.

As might have been expected, Boycott began his reign with a blaze of runs, 2503 in the season at the astonishing average of 102; equally astonishingly, considering the sheer weight of the captain's contribution, Yorkshire finished in their lowest ever position in the table – thirteenth, the fourth time (all since the Second World War) they had finished outside the leading ten. An indication of a change in public perceptions, even in Yorkshire, came with the sense that such a disaster made no impact on the captain's personal reputation; his light shone all the brighter.

One reason for this failure, according to memoirs since published, was a divided dressing room and although the Committee has been criticised in some quarters for allowing Sharpe, Wilson and Hutton to disappear while still capable of considerable contribution to the cause, it must also have been argued that one decision had to be made: either the captain had to go or the captain had to be confirmed in charge.

In the next three years of captaincy by Boycott, Yorkshire finished tenth, fourteenth and eleventh; Andrew Dalton, a very talented but independently minded young batsman from Leeds, refused to play after 1972; Peter Squires, another promising player and brilliant fielder (a rugby union international), was rarely happy, both players preceding an even bigger loss in Bill Athey in 1983.

In 1972, the captain missing half the season with a hand injury, Yorkshire faded and lost the first Benson and Hedges Cup Final to Leicestershire (Illingworth's revenge!), which Boycott missed.

In 1974 Yorkshire did not win a Championship match until mid July and in the ensuing discontent over the leadership, five capped players (a sixth, Sharpe, refused) intended to send the Committee a signed motion of no confidence in the captain. The Committee was well aware of the anger in the dressing room, but that motion never reached them because the rebels were led to believe that Boycott, who had already stood down from Test cricket, intended to retire.

When, at the end of the season, it was discovered that Boycott was carrying on, the rebels went into exile and by the end of 1975 only Hampshire was left of the team Boycott had taken over in 1971. The first

impressions were favourable, for the influx of younger players under Boycott's unchallenged command brought a vast improvement to second place in the table, the title going to Illingworth's Leicestershire, their first.

When it became clear that the advance was no return to full prosperity, the team sliding to eighth in 1976 and twelfth the following year, when Boycott returned to Test-match cricket, all the old wounds were re-opened, culminating in the return of Illingworth as team manager in 1979 with Hampshire displacing Boycott as captain.

The 'Battles and Leaders of the Civil War' (to quote a famous history of greater conflict in America) are dealt with in the general narrative. Even when forced to choose between a new contract and a place on the General Committee, Boycott proved to be an ambivalent committee man, highly respected and supported by a majority of his Wakefield constituents and yet to be seen only sporadically at Yorkshire matches or Annual General Meetings. His erratic attendances at General Committee and sub-committee meetings kept him under fire, but rarely was he criticised from his own heartland. Despite sporadic attacks on his personal life from the tabloid newspapers, his popularity with the masses diminished little. His ability to talk fluently and wisely about the game took him inevitably into the media where he flourished again as a people's champion. Reluctant to be officially engaged in coaching he nevertheless helped many players, very quietly. From first to last, Geoffrey Boycott was an enigma.

scoring almost 1500 runs at an average of 46. He began as a middle-order batsman and moved to opener at the captain's suggestion, a position in which he was clearly born to play. Boycott's advance was such that he overshadowed the progress of Hampshire, who finished his first regular season only five short of a thousand runs.

Hampshire travelled Boycott's path in reverse; beginning as an opening batsman he was to become the county's regular number four. With Stott joining Platt in retirement at the end of the season, Yorkshire were able to give all three deserving Colts – Nicholson, Hampshire and Boycott – their county caps. Yorkshire went into the lead in the Championship table early in June, faltered towards the end of that month, but from 26 July onwards they

stayed ahead, finishing 20 points clear of Glamorgan.

Rebuilding meant that Yorkshire had to vacate their head office in Leeds, and a Centenary Fund raised £15,610 towards the cost of new offices and dressing rooms at Headingley, estimated at £21,000. Sir Stuart Goodwin gave £5000, and another £2000 came from John Smith's Tadcaster Brewery. Lancashire marked the centenary by presenting Yorkshire with a clock for the new offices.

Yorkshire failed to take a third successive Championship in 1964, and the reason was not hard to find: after fifteen splendid seasons, some of them magnificent, Fred Trueman's career was approaching its end. He finished fourth in the county averages with 67 wickets at 20 each, other counties soon appreciating that

John Hampshire *Jake*

John Harry Hampshire, born in Thurnscoe, was a powerful right-hand batsman and occasional and underemployed leg-spinner. The son of a former Yorkshire Colt, he was always regarded as the pick of his class and yet could not establish himself beyond the ranks of the best county batsmen. Eight appearances for England, including a century on debut, against West Indies, is a poor reflection of his true ability.

As a boy he was outstanding and anticipated success as the elder son of a man who had bowled for Yorkshire in 1937 and played soccer for Manchester City. He emerged, like Trueman, from the Cyril Turner–Charlie Lee school at Bramall Lane, as a leg-spinner who could bat. He later recalled the time when, as a trialist, he gave 'Ticker' Mitchell an opportunity to display his black humour: Tony Clarkson, who was later to play for Somerset, hammered the young spinner, bringing from umpire Mitchell the remark: 'There's one thing about it, lad. Tha's giving it plenty of air.'

From Rotherham Town and School he graduated to the same Federation team that included Boycott, Jack Birkenshaw and Duncan Fearnley, later the Chairman of Worcestershire. At fifteen the young Hampshire was playing for Town's first team and a year later was receiving offers from Northamptonshire and Warwickshire; not until 1959 was he asked to play for Yorkshire Colts at Chesterfield and was then made twelfth man, while a batsman who had made 181 for the first team the day before, Dickie Bird, returned to his regular place with the Colts. At the end of that season H.D. Bird was released by Yorkshire to join Leicestershire and another unforeseen career. This, at least, left a Colts place for Hampshire, now less a spinner, much more a batsman.

Hampshire's future was assured next season when, for the Colts, he scored 120 in a stand of 256 with Stott against Northumberland and shared an opening partnership of 145 with Sharpe at Old Trafford against a Lancashire team including Tattersall, Malcolm Hilton, Pilling and Bond. By 1961 he was an occasional first-team member, scoring 129 and 54 for Minor Counties against the Australians, and admits to being surprised the following season, when the first senior batting vacancy occurred, that it should have gone to Boycott and not himself. The rivalry between the pair, seen much more acutely by the less

extrovert player, then began and dogged Hampshire for the rest of his career.

Hampshire, usually tolerant, went on to make his career in his own style, that of a fierce driver with a good defence when necessary, a safe catcher and a number four called by England in 1969. In his twenty-three years of first-class cricket, including two for Derbyshire after he had resigned the Yorkshire captaincy, he scored 28,059 runs at 34, including forty-three centuries, almost all of which were good to watch.

In 1978 he overtook Boycott in the county averages for the first time and was then appointed captain for two seasons before resigning after personal attacks on his wife and children from the more extreme Boycott supporters. He later became a first-class umpire and manager of a cricket school, qualifications that opened further career opportunities.

Richard Hutton *Archie*

Richard Anthony Hutton, eldest son of Sir Leonard, was a tall, strong, right-handed all-rounder capable enough to have played in five Test matches. His nickname derived from a sharp sense of humour and a radio programme of his youth, but his sometimes savage wit was not always appreciated in a Yorkshire dressing room that tended to look askance at public-school graduates.

His father sent him to Repton because of its reputation as a cricket school which Sir Leonard thought, shrewdly and correctly, would bring less pressure on the boy because of his name. In 1959 he scored more than 700 runs for the school, became captain in 1961 and had his father lbw for 3 when MCC visited Repton.

He scored more than a thousand runs that season, topping both the batting and bowling averages, fast-medium. He was turned down by an Oxford College but once installed at Christ's, Cambridge, he joined Tony Lewis and Mike Brearley in the 1962 University team.

Yorkshire gave him a debut in the Roses match at Old Trafford that year and he went on to become a highly capable all-rounder, scoring 5000 runs and taking almost 500 wickets at an average of 21. He was also a fine slip catcher and an eminent candidate as an alternative captain to Boycott, either in 1970, when Close was dismissed, or later when there were several meetings between groups of players and members of the Committee to discuss the captaincy.

Hutton, who later qualified as an accountant, married and moved to Kent, was never shy in making known his opposition to Boycott's style and methods and as a tall, well-spoken, well-educated person he was an obvious standard-bearer for the rebels. There is evidence, too, that several members of the Committee were in favour of a change of leadership in Hutton's favour.

Don Mosey, who as a reporter was close to Yorkshire in the 1960s, believes Hutton should have displaced Boycott:

As events turned out he certainly could not have brought about a more melancholy state of affairs than the regime of Boycott produced. He was certainly worth his place in the team simply as a player; he got on well with other members of the side and yet his background and own personality equipped him to stand, at times when it was necessary, aloof from personal friendships within the team and to take a long objective view at the progress of the game. Above all in his favour was his attitude to captaincy – 'An essential part is the ability to make other people play to the best of their ability and beyond it. I think all the successful captains of sides which have not been outstanding have had that ability.'

There is a good case for Hutton, but was such a change possible given all the circumstances of the time? Hutton would almost certainly have had the support of most senior members of the dressing room but there were some players who would have objected (Bairstow, Sidebottom, Stevenson). Could the Committee have carried out such a change, deposing the hero Boycott for a Cambridge blue and public-school product and the son of a very famous father?

One of the first lessons of democracy is the realisation and acceptance that the best man for the job is rarely the one who gets elected, and all the club's history from 1980 suggests that any attempt by the Committee to replace Boycott by Hutton would have brought the overthrow of the Committee that much sooner.

the great fire was fading. Yorkshire faltered to fifth place, the first time they had been out of the top two places since 1958.

Nicholson, with 70 wickets, finished well enough to be selected for the winter tour of South Africa, but had then to withdraw because of back trouble. Illingworth, with 104 wickets and 1055 runs, was clearly Yorkshire's player of the year. Boycott established himself as England's opening batsman and was joined in the Test side by Trueman, Sharpe and Taylor, a contribution that must have affected Yorkshire's domestic progress.

Close, as captain, attracted criticism on this point, for Yorkshire's champions had become a highly select band. To the regular eleven the only additions this season were the Huddersfield Colt Chris Balderstone and, when down from Cambridge, Richard Hutton. The captain's argument might have been that Barrie Leadbeater, Barry Wood and the sixteen-year-old Chris Old apart, there were no Colts playing well enough to command his attention.

Yorkshire lost only three matches in what became, after the cold winds of May and early June, an exceptionally fine summer. As the pitches improved Yorkshire's deficiencies in attack were revealed and the spell of seven matches without a definite result, in early summer, set the pattern for the remainder of the year. Binks improved his batting average from 14 to 31 without affecting his consistently high standard of keeping wicket.

The first eleven had a happy, unofficial tour of North America and Bermuda in September, and at home the Development Association was formed. The overall loss on matches in a fine and not totally unsuccessful season was £10,000. Yorkshire had another fleeting appearance in the Gillette Cup, losing to Middlesex in the second round at Lord's after having a bye in the first.

If the 1965 season was a sad one for traditionalists – Yorkshire were soon out of the running for the Championship – there was a great blaze of glory in September when Yorkshire won the Gillette Cup Final at Lord's for the first time and in brilliant fashion. The Championship record, a rise from fifth to fourth, would undoubtedly have been bettered but for the weather, Yorkshire being robbed of victory on several occasions. Batting, on difficult and varying pitches, was usually hazardous, Hampshire rightly winning praise for being the only batsman to pass a thousand runs in Championship matches. Boycott, absent from eleven matches through Test duty and injury, scored only one century (in the Gillette Final) and was the only batsman to average more than 30.

The bowling, too, was mostly inconsistent. Trueman had days of devastation and his 115 wickets at 11 runs each was a notable performance, yet he was less effective for England and was disciplined by the Committee for a breach of contract connected with newspaper contributions. Richard Hutton took 58 wickets, nine more than Nicholson, and with Ryan announcing his retirement it was clear that Yorkshire would again have to seek out a young seam bowler. Binks continued his astonishingly consistent form behind the stumps and his 308 consecutive matches was easily a Yorkshire record. Less happily remembered was the dismissal for 23 (another record) by Hampshire at Middlesbrough, Yorkshire being defeated by ten wickets before lunch on the second day.

So for once Yorkshire were happy to be involved in the instant euphoria of one-day cricket. Leicestershire were beaten comfortably by six wickets at Leicester, Boycott contributing 56. Somerset were dismissed for 63 at Taunton (Trueman six for 15) for a seven-wicket win, while Warwickshire were a much tougher proposition and five batsmen had to be run out for Yorkshire to get home by 20 runs.

Boycott's 146 against Surrey, in the Final, was possibly the finest innings of his career. Losing Taylor at 22, he and Close then added 192, of which Close contributed 79, for the second wicket, a foundation that enabled Yorkshire to total 317 for 4 in the 60 overs. Surrey, faced with such a massive total, were always struggling, their later batsmen paying the penalty for trying to hit Illingworth (five for 29). Yorkshire, it seemed, had at long last mastered the form of one-day cricket.

Mrs F. Frazer gave the club £10,000 in memory of her late husband Hector Frazer, the money to be used for an indoor shed at Headingley. Gate receipts dropped by £8000, so a contribution of £3000 from the Development Association was gratefully acknowledged.

Yorkshire's twenty-seventh Championship in 1966 was won with more than a few tremors. Early in August they dominated the table with a lead of 40 points before taking a slide that brought them only one victory in the next seven matches. At the start of the last match Worcestershire, also with one match to play, were only 6 points behind.

In a summer of indifferent weather and poor pitches the introduction of a 65-over rule for the first innings brought further distortion to the game and extra pressure on the batsmen seeking form. Although five Yorkshire players passed a thousand runs, only Boycott and Close averaged more than 30 and the team were often indebted to Trueman and Wilson for late, quick runs. Nicholson overtook Trueman in overs and wickets (105 to 101) despite having his action scrutinised – and passed; but neither Illingworth nor Wilson was as effective as expected. Binks was as immaculate as ever and Yorkshire's fielding remained almost beyond reproach, while Close crowned a Championship year with his appointment as England captain for the final Test against West Indies.

So to the last match: Worcestershire lost to Sussex, leaving Yorkshire as champions even without a 24-run victory over Kent at Harrogate when the young Underwood took eleven wickets in the match. It was in this match that Don Wilson recorded a second hat-trick of the season, his first coming against Nottinghamshire at Worksop. The Gillette Cup was held the minimal length of time for, after a bye in the first round, Yorkshire lost the first tie of the new season, falling by 40 runs to Somerset at Taunton.

Notable Colts that season were the Leeds pair Barrie Leadbeater and Geoffrey Cope, John Waring from Ripon, Balderstone from Huddersfield and Old from Middlesbrough.

Although 1967 was the year of Yorkshire's twenty-eighth Championship, the most potent memory of the summer dates from 16, 17 and 18 August at Edgbaston and a drawn game with Warwickshire. After gaining a lead of 4 runs on the first innings, Warwickshire were eventually set to score 142 to win in an hour

and 40 minutes. In the event Yorkshire bowled only 24 overs in that time, only two in the last 15 minutes, during which time, reported *Wisden*, they left the field to the umpires and batsmen during a shower. Warwickshire failed to win by 9 runs and the acrimony aroused had many repercussions. The Laws were changed, first-class matches ending in a mandatory 20 overs from the start of the last hour. Close, as captain, was censured publicly for his tactics, and a minor incident with a spectator during the game, which was heavily sensationalised, led eventually to his deposition as England's captain.

Curiously, the official Yorkshire report for the season makes no mention of this match or its aftermath, an indication, perhaps, of the Committee's feelings on the matter at that time. Considering that Close, as England's captain, missed eleven Championship matches and that Boycott played in five Tests and Illingworth in four, Yorkshire did well to retain the Championship.

May was cold and wet, only one of six Championship matches being finished. Yorkshire were defeated twice in June and not until mid-July did they reassert themselves, in much better weather, as contenders. By August the team, often with Trueman in command, were in full flight and a defeat of Kent at Canterbury was ominous for the opposition. With two matches remaining Yorkshire needed 14 points from a possible 24 to keep their title. At Middlesbrough Warwickshire were crushed by 229 runs, Wilson taking thirteen wickets, and the final fixture was against Gloucestershire on a ground of happy omen, Harrogate.

Yorkshire were sent in on a soft wicket but masterly batting by Boycott and Sharpe raised 127 for the first wicket in between showers. By the second day the drying had begun and Gloucestershire were dismissed twice for 134 and 99, twenty wickets falling in the day, fourteen of them to Illingworth, whose second-innings analysis read 13–9–6–7.

Such a triumphant ending to the season masked the difficulties ahead. Only Boycott averaged more than 40 among the batsmen and the all-conquering seam attack of Trueman and Nicholson was showing signs of wear and tear. Two younger quick bowlers, Old and Peter

Chris Old *Chilly*

In Mike Brearley's time-honoured phrase, Christopher Middleton Old was 'a displaced gene away from greatness'. A very high-class all-rounder he was unfortunate to spend the bulk of his career in the troubled 1970s and '80s; had he been able to play in a settled and successful side he could have emerged as one of the most successful players of the post-war period.

He was nevertheless a powerful presence in his sixteen years with Yorkshire, two with Warwickshire and forty-six Test matches, scoring almost eight thousand runs and taking more than a thousand wickets. Two outstanding performances stick in the mind: at Old Trafford where, taking over the captaincy from an injured Hampshire, he scored a century from number seven and bowled out Lancashire twice to win a Roses match almost single-handed; and another at Headingley where, returning as a Warwickshire player, he bowled his new county to an outstanding and emphatic victory.

The brother of the rugby international Alan Old, 'Chilly', a nickname dispensed by Hampshire that gave the opposite impression of Old's amiable, gregarious nature, appeared from Middlesbrough at an opportune moment to replace Trueman as Nicholson's opening partner – although as a boy his talents were such that it was difficult to predict whether he would become better known as a bowler or a batsman. His height, increasing pace and ability to use the seam and swing turned Old into a right-arm quick bowler who could bat left-handed.

Coming in to bat down the order meant that his natural hitting powers were developed, and with the growth of one-day cricket he adapted very successfully. His century in 37 minutes against Warwickshire in 1977, on a third afternoon when no result was possible, is the third fastest in history.

At his best Old was highly admired and respected by his captains. Hampshire wrote of him (1983):

> . . . as good a practitioner with the new ball as we saw in his time. When he was past his pomp, so to speak, he traded all-out speed for accuracy and guile and became a supreme player in that field. I was lucky enough to go into the 1977 Centenary Test in Melbourne and saw him bowl quite superbly there. I am told of his immensely long spell into the wind at Wellington the following year – 30-11-54-6 – into a real snorter of a gale coming down the Hutt Valley.

What Old lacked was that essential streak of ruthlessness in his character and toughness in his frame to reach the very front rank. He was remarkably fallible to injury, so much so that when a new bowling machine was installed at Headingley that broke down regularly it was immediately dubbed 'Chilly'.

So although he was the natural choice to succeed Hampshire as captain in 1982 he was unable, at thirty-four, greatly to affect the course of events upon the field and found leading a side containing a General Committee member and ex-England captain in Boycott, managed by another ex-England captain in Illingworth, altogether too much for his essentially good-natured personality.

After being replaced as captain by Illingworth in 1983 he moved on to Warwickshire and later played for Northumberland. He was then able to impart his experience to children when he became a cricket consultant to the Humberside Education Authority.

Stringer, showed promise but both broke down, and Richard Hutton's arrival from Cambridge had less impact than was hoped. Cope appeared as an off-spinner of definite potential, and in one department Yorkshire could claim unchallenged pre-eminence: fielding.

Yorkshire had an adventurous if unsuccessful time in the Gillette Cup. In the first round, in the last week of May, the weather prevented play on three successive days at Leeds. Play eventually began, in a match reduced to 10 overs a side, at Castleford where Cambridgeshire, who included Johnny Wardle, scored 43 for 8, their opening batsman, D. Fairey, hitting Trueman for six. The minor county then fielded in drenching rain while Yorkshire made 46 for 4, Wardle taking two wickets.

Old, the Middlesbrough Colt, took four for 32 at Old Trafford, but Lancashire totalled 194 and Yorkshire, despite a steady start, were dismissed for 190, 4 runs being needed from the last five deliveries.

For the first time both Yorkshire's first and second elevens won their respective Championships and the Australians were beaten at Sheffield; so 1968 was, on record, one of the great years. There were, however, many sad overtones to a jubilant summer. Trueman retired (and when would Yorkshire see his like again?) as did Ken Taylor, while Illingworth moved to Leicestershire after a contractual dispute with the county.

Illingworth's departure proved to be a total catastrophe, a move that cost Yorkshire more dearly than almost any other in the county club's history. *Wisden* touched on Illingworth's value, unaware of the storm to come.

[His] off-spin was the foundation of the Yorkshire bowling. He could be relied upon for economy and for decisive attack when conditions gave him opportunity, and as his batting and fielding reflected his long experience and high competence he was clearly the outstanding all-rounder. He was also a respected counsellor on the field to Close, the appointed captain, and to Trueman who acted during the period of Close's absence through injury.

Illingworth's skill and sagacity tilted the balance against Yorkshire for a whole decade. With him they would have struggled to maintain their high place in county cricket; without him they went into deep decline.

For a few short months Yorkshire basked, metaphorically at least, in an Indian summer, the weather itself being wretched. Boycott, fortunately, was in tremendous form until he injured his back in July; Sharpe, Padgett and Hampshire all made their contributions and Yorkshire's middle and tail, led by Illingworth, rarely had a cumulative failure. Nicholson enjoyed the latter part of the season when Richard Hutton also showed encouraging form as an all-rounder, and Old made further progress.

Bonus points, awarded for performances in a first innings limited to 85 overs, were happily embraced by Yorkshire, 160 of the 270 raised for the Championship coming this way. Kent, finishing second, won one more match but Yorkshire, defeating Surrey by 60 runs at Hull just before five o'clock on the third day, ensured that they could not be overtaken.

A fall from grace was expected after the departures of 1968, but a drop from first to thirteenth, then the lowest position in Yorkshire's history, surprised even the pessimists. The winning of the Gillette Cup, for the second time, was little consolation. Trueman and Taylor retired and Illingworth moved to Leicestershire; Close missed most of the latter half of the season through injury, Nicholson broke a finger and lost form, while Boycott, Sharpe and Hampshire were required for representative games.

Not surprisingly, Yorkshire played ten Colts during the season and while the team at full strength was still capable of doing honour to the title of champions, a weak and inexperienced side was rarely able to represent Yorkshire in the manner expected by supporters and public. The Championship season was made all the more depressing by the success of Yorkshire batsmen in other spheres. Boycott, Sharpe and Hampshire all scored centuries in Test matches, Close scored 146 against the New Zealanders and Sharpe hit another century against MCC. The only Championship century was Boycott's 105 not out against Somerset at Headingley.

In the first seven Championship matches Yorkshire managed six draws and one defeat, a start only mildly excused by the wet weather. Gloucestershire were beaten at Middlesbrough but only two more victories – and only 30 batting bonus points – were obtained all season. Hampshire scored a splendid maiden century for England at Lord's but his county form was unconvincing until August, while neither Boycott nor Padgett passed a thousand runs.

Among the Colts, Leadbeater played a determined innings of 76 in the Gillette Final and Woodford showed distinct promise. Old, who with Leadbeater was awarded a cap, took 55 wickets at 17, but Wilson was the mainstay of the attack, taking 85 wickets. Hutton, with five hundred runs and fifty wickets, made a useful contribution while Cope, the off-spinner, did not advance as well as expected. In short, the team lacked the presence and personality of Trueman, whose powers may have waned but who was still capable of intimidating the opposition; Taylor's experience and steadiness at the start of an innings; and, most of all, the all-round ability and tactical expertise of Illingworth.

That all was not well in the dressing room was confirmed during the winter when Jimmy Binks, the most consistent top-class wicket-keeper in cricket and Close's deputy as captain, announced his retirement. The Committee took cheer from the one-day competitions, the second of which, the John Player Sunday League, was launched in 1969. Yorkshire finished eighth in this new League without showing any great enthusiasm for the novelty. Indeed, senior players were openly hostile to the 40-over competition, compelling, as it did, the abandonment of much of the training and disciplines they had learnt as boys.

Yorkshire's happy days in 1969 were mostly in the Gillette Cup. The bowling and catching overwhelmed Norfolk at Lakenham and the batting, Boycott and Sharpe opening with 137, was too good for Lancashire at Old Trafford. Boycott (92) and Close (96) helped Yorkshire to raise 272 at The Oval, Surrey failing by 137, and the Final was reached before a packed Scarborough ground where Nottinghamshire, including Sobers, were beaten by 68.

With Boycott injured, Yorkshire opened with Leadbeater and Woodford against Derbyshire in the Final at Lord's, scoring 219 in the 60 overs and then dismissing Derbyshire for 150, Close and Wilson taking three wickets each.

The Yorkshire public had become accustomed to shocks in the seasons since the war, but few events startled them as much as the Committee's decision at the end of this season to dispense with Brian Close. Their statement read: 'After long and careful consideration your Committee decided not to re-appoint D.B. Close as first team captain for 1971 and in view of this decision it was also decided that he should no longer be a playing member of the team.' The Committee then went on to pay tribute to Close's twenty-two years' service that encompassed almost 23,000 runs and nearly a thousand wickets, while in his eight years as captain he had won the Championship four times and the Gillette Cup twice.

The uproar that followed was not confined to the public at large. Yorkshire's members, as loyal to their own cause as the Brigade of Guards, also revolted, forming an Action Group from within their own ranks that brought such pressure on the Committee that changes were forced.

Yet the furore did not reinstate Close, and the wave of sympathy for a great cricketer obviously broken-hearted by the decision was transferred in time to his successor, Geoffrey Boycott. Boycott heard the news while touring Australia with MCC, and as he was expected to continue as a regular member of the England team the club appointed a vice-captain, Don Wilson. That the Committee should take such a decision at the end of the 1970 season was even more surprising in that Close had apparently rebuilt the side after the upheavals of 1968–9.

Yorkshire climbed from thirteenth to fourth place in the Championship and at one time in mid-season were seriously considered as contenders again. Despite Close's return to form as batsman and fielder, and Boycott's superb form after an uncharacteristic lean start (353 runs in his first fifteen first-class innings), Yorkshire were too inconsistent to aspire to trophies. Of the regular batsmen only Hampshire advanced sufficiently to gain a tour place. Wilson and Leadbeater both missed several matches through injury. Cope increased his wickets from 37 to 75 despite the unsettling news of another investigation into his action.

Two interesting newcomers appeared! Yorkshire were expected to have difficulty in replacing the immaculate Jimmy Binks as wicket-keeper and their first choice, Neil Smith, was displaced in early July by another Bradfordian, eighteen-year-old David Bairstow. This young man's natural enthusiasm behind the stumps or when batting soon won him a regular place and high praise. Smith, meanwhile, proved that Yorkshire's original judgement had not been unfounded by depart-

ing for a distinguished career with Essex. The other new name was that of Phillip Carrick, a left-arm slow bowler from Leeds, who took six for 85 in the second innings of MCC's match in the Scarborough Festival.

A clue to the Committee's disquiet at the summer's end came in the financial report – 'the most disastrous in the history of the Club' – recording a loss of more than £8000. Half of this loss could be attributed almost directly to Yorkshire's elimination from the Gillette Cup, in wintry weather, in the first round, a stark contrast to the Final triumph of 1969. As the team won only five of the sixteen John Player League matches, Yorkshire's record in the lucrative one-day games was extremely disappointing and the captain's clearly expressed

David Bairstow *Bluey*

David Leslie Bairstow, a stocky, strong Bradfordian with red hair and blue eyes, an Australian characteristic that won him his nickname (another inspiration of Hampshire's), was one of the great wicket-keepers whose full ability was never measured for he played during a time of covered pitches and was thus rarely offered the opportunity to demonstrate what he could do while standing up to the stumps keeping to high-class spin bowling. Ted Lester, who saw all the great post-war wicket-keepers, rated Bairstow as good as Binks when standing back.

His record puts his ability beyond question: there are ten instances in the club's history of a wicket-keeper claiming six or more victims in an innings, Bairstow performing the feat five times, including a seven against Derbyshire at Scarborough in 1982. He is one of six wicket-keepers in the game to have made eleven or more dismissals in a match (eleven caught in that same match) and is the only Yorkshire wicket-keeper to have passed a thousand runs in a season three times (1981, 1983, 1985).

After Binks' unexpected retirement Neil Smith, from Ossett, who was later to play with distinction for Essex and Cheshire, was the original replacement but by 1970 it was clear that an early opportunity had to be given to the seventeen-year-old Hanson Grammar schoolboy Bairstow, who was showing promise of outstanding ability. He was, in fact, due to take his 'A' level examinations that day and actually sat them at 6 a.m. in order to make his debut against Gloucestershire at Park Avenue later.

Bairstow spent the rest of that season under Close

and in May 1971, under Boycott, he took six catches (equalling David Hunter's record) in the Whitsuntide Roses match and another three in the second innings. Yet it was 1973 before Bairstow was capped, a delay brought about not so much by any lack of faith in his future but more probably by a feeling that so much natural ebullience needed a little restraint.

Bairstow also faced competition to follow Alan Knott and Bob Taylor as England's wicket-keeper and although he played in four Test matches he only once began a tour, to West Indies in 1981, as senior keeper, the selectors seemingly preferring the more reliable defensive technique of Paul Downton at a time when every run was invaluable.

But he was recognised as the one player who could, as new Yorkshire captain, unite warring spectators and members in the aftermath of the 1983–4 Committee upheaval, and in three years he did. By leading from the front and by an exhibition of ferocious loyalty to the club, he settled a dressing room that could have been split again and again. In retrospect, from the club's view, it was a setback that he did not accept Close's suggestion that he should

captain the side as a batsman, thus allowing Steven Rhodes to stay with the county, but after the recent frequent departures of Yorkshire captains he did have good reason to be highly suspicious of the offer.

In the end his captaincy lived and died in the Benson and Hedges semi-final in June 1984 when they lost to Warwickshire by 3 runs, Bairstow being caught at full stretch on the boundary by the very tall Bob Willis when the former was going for a six. A Lord's final at that stage in his career would have sealed his term of office, as it did for his successor.

Although he lost his place briefly in 1988, at the age of thirty-seven, he returned in September to claim his thousandth first-class victim, and indicated then that he would not go gently, becoming second only to David Hunter in the aggregate number of victims.

dislike of some features of limited-overs cricket did not further his cause in the committee room.

As a player and personality Close had always found one hundred per cent acceptance rare. Kilburn noted of his appointment: '. . . he was 32 years old, saddled with a public reputation for irresponsibility, seen as a gifted batsman and a bowler of modest but uncrystallised talent and recognised within the Yorkshire team as a tactician whose views had sometimes received less than due appreciation in the period of Wilson's captaincy.'

For Mosey, his captaincy was: '. . .brilliant at getting the best out of others, at pointing out faults in technique, at ways of improvement. That is why he was an inspirational captain. He had an encyclopaedic knowledge of the strengths and weaknesses of opposition players and of his own team. Rarely, one is forced to

conclude, did he look at his own fallibility. If only he had been . . . able to adopt an attitude of do-as-you-would-be-done-by there is no telling what heights he might have achieved.'

As captain of Somerset Close won golden opinions from young players, who were none the less more than a little afraid of his reputation (there is a tale of one young batsman, dismissed through making an error for which he had been previously castigated by his captain, crawling back into the pavilion by a back window rather than face Close's wrath by returning up the steps). Ian Botham once said of him: 'He gave me the killer instinct.' Yet he was also a protective leader, and Richard Hutton's memory of him was that: '. . . he protected the players under his command . . . his approach earned him the support and loyalty of his team and made his verbal ear-bashings the more tolerable'.

5

Boycott to Bairstow 1970–1986

If the first rift between the government of the club and the members was the dismissal of Wardle in 1958, the sacking of Close twelve years later brought full dissent into the open in a manner unknown for almost a century; the following twelve years were to bring bitter controversy, unending argument and eventually a revolt that would topple the Committee. Only success on the field could have averted a tragedy that had the crashing inexorability that accompanies the downfall of a regime, be it in Petrograd or Teheran. No blood was shed in the Ridings – at least none is recorded as having been lost – but much bitterness ensued, legal fees abounded, the club won enormous media attention and the membership, whether for or against the Committee, flaunted their emotions so strongly and publicly that observers and reporters reacted first in sorrow, then in anger and, finally, in derision, a mood which matched that of much of the rest of the cricketing world.

If the catalyst was the captaincy and personality of Geoffrey Boycott, the cause was the deep dissatisfaction with the team's performances, finishing as they did thirteenth, tenth, fourteenth and eleventh in the seasons of 1971–75. Boycott, as captain, had to take a major share of the responsibility, but there were many other factors in the worst decade in the club's history: the invasion of the domestic game by world-class overseas players that almost overnight transformed Yorkshire from one of the stronger to one of the weaker teams; the covering of pitches, reducing the efficiency of the county's traditional cutting edge, spin bowling; the growing emphasis on one-day cricket, reducing the need for the traditional arts, especially wicket-taking; the swing to limited-overs cricket in the leagues, cutting the harvest of

potential Test-class, if not first-class cricketers, in a competition in which the accurate medium-pace all-rounder was the most valuable player.

To blame Boycott for all this is to contribute to that school of history that ascribes the fall of the Romanovs to Rasputin; yet just as a Richeleu might have at least delayed, if not averted revolution, so a captain of different temperament might have been able to bring to the club an adhesive rather than divisive influence.

That Close would so soon follow Illingworth meant that the club had lost its two major tactical influences inside two years. That Brian Sellers should step down from his perhaps too autocratic chairmanship of the cricket sub-committee, a direct result of members' criticism of the Close sacking, meant that the powerful voices that had dominated the field and the committee room through the Silver Sixties had all gone. And while it would be unfair to say that a vacuum of leadership existed, the new control, both on and off the field, was uncertain and lacked experience.

Even the decision to appoint Boycott before Phil Sharpe may be challenged in retrospect; Boycott was certainly the more forceful personality and on those grounds the Committee sought to recruit the driving force that had turned the shy boy from Fitzwilliam into a world-class batsman. However, they also overlooked Sharpe as vice-captain, to take charge while Boycott was playing for England, preferring Don Wilson and thus removing the experienced and amiable Sharpe from authority inside the dressing room. According to Boycott it was Wilson, not Sharpe, who almost became captain before Boycott.

Without Boycott, who had broken his arm in Australia, Yorkshire's poor start in 1971 turned into catastrophe. When Boycott did return to the side, his own form contrasted so strongly with that of his colleagues that the first argument began: was Boycott, who became the first Englishman to average a hundred in a season (a figure three times better than that of Sharpe), playing for himself or for Yorkshire? Years later Boycott was to maintain that Yorkshire did not win a match in which he did not make a big score. He also produced statistics to prove that almost all the batting and bowling bonus points were gained under his leadership. Back in 1971, the debate was under way.

One player who was successful enough that season to be called upon by England was the all-rounder Richard Hutton, elder son of Sir Leonard, whom Boycott was to blame for leading an ill-starred and flickering players' rebellion against him that same year. Boycott called a players' meeting at the house of a friend; the cricket sub-committee under the new chairman, John Temple from York, called another, and although both events passed almost unnoticed at the time, the civil war had begun. Of the senior players Hutton, Wilson and Sharpe made no bones about their opposition to Boycott's continuing captaincy, while Hampshire, Nicholson and Padgett seemed aghast that the Yorkshire dressing room should come to this.

Boycott himself recorded of that time: 'I wish I had given up the Yorkshire captaincy at the end of that year.' It is fascinating to consider what might have happened had he resigned, but in retrospect there seems to be not the slightest possibility that Yorkshire could have accepted his departure from office and, probably, thence to another county. Both then and for years to come, Boycott was almost the only star in the sky above the broad acres.

So the battle lines were drawn and the new Secretary, Joe Lister, the successor to John Nash who was a batsman good enough to play twice for the first team before joining Worcestershire, was soon to realise that he had a dressing room as factional as an Italian court of the Renaissance. An outsider would have seen that the bowling had deteriorated alarmingly in that Wilson had lost form and Cope, although promising, was not yet an Illingworth, while if

any of the three regular seamers Nicholson, Hutton or Old was unavailable for any reason, there was little reserve strength.

That winter brought the retirement of Padgett, who became coach in succession to Arthur Mitchell and second-team captain. Boycott would have preferred to keep the commonsensical Bradfordian, a wise and experienced judge in the first-team dressing room, for another season and Padgett offered to continue for a while as player-coach, but the club's decision was that he was needed with the Colts. In theory this was probably the correct decision, but in practice it meant that a voice of moderation had gone.

Despite the undercurrent of rumour and intrigue, the 1972 summer began so well that Yorkshire followers were temporarily deluded into thinking the storm had passed. Yorkshire's limited success in one-day cricket, particularly on Sundays, had given the impression that they found adaptation difficult, but they swept through the newly-created 55-over Benson and Hedges competition to reach the Final. Another indication of things to come was a match award, early in the zonal series, in which the adjudicator, Bill Voce, gave Barry Wood, then with Lancashire, the prize. In the same match Don Wilson had taken five for 26. When asked, Boycott naturally enough replied that he thought Wilson should have had the award; the subsequent headline, 'Boycott Lashes Voce', should have warned him of what he was up against.

By early June Yorkshire had actually climbed to the top of the Championship table when one blow after another fell upon the side: Wilson lost form alarmingly, Cope's action was questioned, and worst of all, Bob Willis broke a finger of Boycott's in a Gillette Cup tie, which meant that his batting for the rest of that summer was as much a gradual easing back into play of an injured hand as scoring runs. Spirits were low, and when Yorkshire lost the Benson and Hedges Final to Leicestershire, a victory engineered by Ray Illingworth and sealed by a former Yorkshire Colt, Chris Balderstone, acrimony flared again.

Hutton was continually being mentioned as an alternative captain, but as he had taken only

Boycott signs a new contract (April 1973) attended by a relieved County Secretary, Joe Lister.

a one-year contract and had hinted of business commitments his longer cricketing future must have been, to some of the Committee, in doubt. Certainly Hutton made it clear that any Yorkshire team under his leadership would not contain Boycott, so that once again the Committee was brought up against the harsh reality that while they might want to change the captain it was probable that a majority of the members, supported by an irate public and most of the popular press, would seek to sack them if they did. Their attitude can rightly be criticised as being head-in-the-sand, but it is difficult to see what alternative was open to them other than to temporise and hope that the dressing room would settle down of its own accord.

They had some reason for hope: the team had raised itself to tenth place in the Championship (a marginal improvement perhaps, but three places nevertheless), had reached the Benson and Hedges Final and finished joint third in the John Player Sunday League (40 overs). A new generation of bowlers was emerging in the two left-arm spinners, Phillip Carrick from Leeds and Mike Bore from Hull, who first appeared bowling slow-medium, Underwood-style, and three seamers all of whom were to serve Yorkshire well in differing and difficult circumstances, Christopher Old, Arthur Robinson (Northallerton), a strong left-armer who rejoiced in the nickname 'Rocker' and who compensated in heart for whatever he may have lacked in ability, and the steady Howard Cooper (Great Horton). In addition Hampshire had emerged to join Boycott as a Test batsman, Bairstow was developing into a top-flight wicket-keeper and punishing tail-ender, and a tall new opener with excellent defensive technique had emerged from Doncaster – Richard Lumb.

The winter of 1973 brought more controversy, for at a public forum the question 'What's wrong with Yorkshire cricket?' was put to a panel including Boycott. His reply embraced many suggestions, including a team manager (possibly Ted Lester, the then scorer), and a central ground owned by the club – which would have meant, of course, that several traditional grounds would lose their fixtures. By then the media were well aware that Boycott's sayings sold newspapers, and the Committee had to agree to another meeting in which, according to Boycott, the captain was 'icily ticked off' by the Chairman of the General Committee for pronouncing upon policy. Boycott wrote later that he did not know what club policy was, and it was this valid point that may have led to the inclusion of the club captain and coach in selection meetings. Hampshire recorded in his own memoirs that it was during this period that he went to see Boycott to put some points of dissension to him and 'hoped I had achieved something'.

That winter was a dramatic one for the Yorkshire club: the President, Sir William Worsley, father of the club's patron the Duchess of Kent, died, as did Wilfred Rhodes and Arthur Wood, and any hopes that followers

Richard Lumb

Richard Graham Lumb, from Doncaster, was the most successful of Boycott's opening partners, a tall right-hand batsman of courage, even temperament and good defensive technique. He scored twenty-two centuries in his thirteen seasons starting with 114 in difficult circumstances in a Roses match at Old Trafford, when twenty-three.

In all, Lumb scored 11,000 runs at an average of 30 and passed a thousand five times. With Boycott, Lumb shared five opening partnerships of more than 200 and their total number of opening century partnerships is surpassed only by Sutcliffe and Holmes, 29 to 69. Against Sussex at Leeds in 1974

Boycott and Lumb shared century opening stands in each innings, the eighth pair to do so.

Lumb, a gregarious and easy-going man, played twice in Test trials and was close to selection for England on a number of occasions. With his height and reach he might also have been a first-class slip, but he was not an ambitious man as he proved when he was offered the captaincy after Boycott.

Lumb married the sister of South Africa's then best wicket-keeper and emigrated to that country in 1984. He was a batsman who, in happier circumstances, might have made a much more substantial contribution.

Phillip Carrick *Fergie*

Carrick, a talented slow left-arm bowler who had to temper his skills to the demands of one-day cricket, and a useful right-hand batsman, was a thinking cricketer who derived great satisfaction in seeing the club through stormy water into a sunlit calm when he led the team to victory in the Benson and Hedges Cup competition at Lord's in July 1987.

By the standards of the club's great eras it was only a minor triumph, yet the satisfaction of actually winning a competition again, in the high-profile, televised circumstances of a Lord's final, did much to dissipate the anger, bitterness and frustrations of the previous decade. When Yorkshire were given a standing ovation, before the Sunday match at Scarborough the following day, a Middlesex cricketer, accustomed to playing in the echoing emptiness of Lord's on a Championship day, observed: 'It was very moving to see that the game meant so much to so many people.'

Carrick, born in Armley but a product of the Bradford League, came from a cricketing family and at fifteen was a member of the Farsley first team and playing for Yorkshire Schools. At seventeen he first played for the Colts and made his debut the following year when Wilson was injured. At twenty-one, as Wilson lost form, Carrick was moving towards seniority in 1973, taking eight for 33 against Cambridge. But his cap was delayed for another three years, being awarded, to his intense disappointment, when he was coaching and playing in South Africa.

In 1978, batting superbly on a bumpy Headingley pitch against a rampant Lancashire attack, he made a maiden century that qualified him to be termed an all-rounder. How good a bowler he might have been in the days of uncovered pitches is hard to assess but

he was shrewd enough to point out, on one occasion, that a spinner's figures, in the 1980s, might well depend upon the fixture list: 'If you happened to play both at Bradford and Swansea, where the ball would turn, you could double your wickets.'

Much of Carrick's career was spent bowling defensively at the leg stump without recourse to spin or flight because containment was the only task allotted to him. When conditions did favour him he could strike, as a twelve for 89 against Derbyshire in 1983 attests.

In 1985, at the age of thirty-two, when starting his benefit year (£73,020), he told Jane Harrison: 'All I ever wanted to do was to be a Yorkshire cricketer and now I just want to continue playing until they sack me.' He added: 'I'd like to see Yorkshire competing in a Lord's final again. We haven't been there since 1972.'

His election to the captaincy in 1987 was not a complete surprise for he had deputised successfully when Bairstow, with one of his rare injuries, was absent. Nevertheless his initial success surprised even friends for in the first half of the 1987 summer Yorkshire were almost invincible and, very briefly, younger followers of the club had a glimpse of county cricket as it had appeared to a Yorkshireman at the turn of the century.

The anti-climax, after the Cup win, demonstrated how difficult it is to sustain a Championship challenge without at least one Test-class bowler. Carrick was able to supervise the advance of Paul Jarvis who, had he not broken down half-way through 1988, might have given Carrick a second successful year as captain.

might have had of a new spring in 1973 were dashed. Wilson, dropped the previous summer, was dropped again and Carrick and Bore given a run; Cope, his action remodelled by Johnny Wardle, returned to the side but seemed reluctant to use his full power of spin and made little impression.

Despite an improvement in the batting, a splendid return after an operation by Tony Nicholson and an impressive advance by Old, the Championship position was fourteenth, another all-time low. Only three Championship matches were won and the nadir was a defeat in the Gillette Cup by Durham, the first victory by a minor over a first-class county. Yorkshire were bowled out for 135 at Harrogate and lost by five wickets, a result that rang round the world confirming, from Wellington to the Windwards, that there was trouble at t'mill.

For the first time the sense of disquiet in the club surfaced from within the Committee, the former captain Ronnie Burnet, one of Bradford's representatives, saying publicly that Hutton should be captain. The Boycott camp quickly pointed out that Hutton had been available for only ten first-class games in the summer of 1973, an absence that had brought forward the career of two young seamers from South Yorkshire, Arnie Sidebottom, also a Manchester United footballer, and Graham Stevenson.

Nevertheless a team was taking shape, the principal weakness being in the spin bowling for unless Cope or Wilson could recover their form, Yorkshire, for so long the academy of arts and sciences in spin bowling, would be without a seasoned spinner. Not that such mundane matters as team-building were allowed to interfere with the increasingly uncivil war.

To traditionalists the saddest moment of the summer of 1973, even more depressing than the defeat by Durham, was the closing of the famous old ground at Bramall Lane, the club's birthplace. Sheffield United, the host club, had been in effect taken over by the football section of the Committee who decreed that there was no place in this modern world for cricket at Bramall Lane. A grandstand was built across

the pitch and the old Victorian pavilion knocked down to provide a car park. J.M. Kilburn had no regrets, believing that cricket had run its course at the Lane, but the United Cricket Club, a famous local institution, was left homeless and there has been an element of doubt about the future of the first-class game in one of its founding cities ever since.

The dinner to mark the end of Bramall Lane fired fresh argument when Fred Trueman, later to become the committee member for Craven, attacked Boycott's captaincy; one by one, it seemed, the main protagonists were taking position and showing their colours. Another committee member from Bradford, Don Brennan, joined in the attack on Boycott's leadership in 1974, a year allotted to the captain's benefit which inadvertently proved to be a rallying point for the growing pro-Boycott, anti-Committee faction. To the outsider it seemed incongruous that the county captain, the only world-class player in the side, should come under constant criticism from names that belonged to previous generations. Those members of the Committee, including Joe Lister, trying to keep the club on course and on an even keel were not helped by waves from either side – for Boycott was never averse to expounding his own views as to how the club should be directed, once notably in an article in the *Sunday Mirror* co-written with Ted Dexter.

Yorkshire's Sheffield fixtures had by then moved to the home of the Collegiate Club at Abbeydale Park and it was there, amid the sponsors' tents, that the captain, already being assailed in the press for his alleged weakness against left-arm seamers, particularly the Indian Solkar, revealed that his benefit plans were in disarray after a disagreement with his organiser. Once again a Boycott story seized the headlines, the team's performance became an irrelevance and the club was made to appear merely a stage upon which one dramatic act after another was unfolded.

There was a row about the Roses match at Headingley, in which both the cricket chairman and the captain were made to look either absent-minded or foolish, or both. Boycott withdrew from selection for the Second Test against India and had another finger broken,

Graham Stevenson *Moonbeam*

Graham Barry Stevenson was one of the great unrealised talents of recent history. A right-arm batsman and bowler from Ackworth he had the ability to bowl fast at the highest level and as a batsman he was a hitter of prodigious power. His great lack was confidence in his own ability; in different circumstances and in a successful side, Stevenson might have matured into an all-rounder with the talent to match Botham at his own game.

His figures of 4000 runs and 450 wickets in thirteen seasons tell almost nothing about his career. Fair, strongly built, he could win bounce on a hard pitch and move the ball in more usual English conditions. His range of strokes was limited but his favourite, a lofted drive between long on and long off, was worth travelling to see. He could also take excellent catches anywhere and his throw-in, from the boundary, was bullet-like, catching many an unwary batsman, among them Brian Close when captain of Somerset.

Stevenson's most glorious moment came in a night match at Sydney when England, needing 35 to win with two wickets standing and 30 balls remaining, relied on the comparatively untried Bairstow and Stevenson to win the game. Stevenson, batting number ten, hit 28 not out against Dymock and Thomson in a fiery demonstration of hitting that left the Hill, normally so noisy and ebullient, strangely hushed.

Stevenson scored one of his two first-class centuries when batting at number eleven against Warwickshire and, partnered by the number one, Boycott, set a new last-wicket record for the county of 149. Stevenson also holds the record for the highest number of sixes in a Sunday League game (John Player/Refuge Assurance) – ten, when he smote Somerset for a tempestuous 81 off 29 balls at Middlesbrough on 4 June 1984.

His nickname was bestowed upon him by Don Wilson when Stevenson first appeared, as a round-faced, smiling eighteen-year-old in the dressing room.

Yorkshire then losing to Worcestershire by an innings at Hull. By this time all the popular newspapers had a man permanently stationed in the Yorkshire press box, less concerned with the cricket than with the next Boycott story, which was never long in coming.

Speculation that the Committee would sack Boycott at the end of that summer was freely aired in the press, and although officially denied by the club, the rumours continued. A petition, signed by Hutton (playing his last full season), Nicholson and Wilson and calling for Boycott's removal, was supposed to have been drawn up to be presented to the Committee, but the other two senior members of the team, Sharpe and Hampshire, were not, according to Boycott, in full support, so it was torn up.

No one could doubt that 1974 was a low point for the captain. A string of injuries, concern about his form for England, the club, dissent in the dressing room, a suspicion that he was being deliberately downgraded in the list of possible Test captains, all caused him to contemplate an early retirement. Fortunately for both him and the club, Yorkshire, with injured players returning, had a reasonably successful and happy August, winning four matches in the Championship and three in the Sunday League.

The team moved up three places in the Championship, to eleventh, Lumb won his county cap, and enough promising Colts in the clever seamer Steve Oldham (Sheffield) and the batsmen Colin Johnson (Pocklington) and Peter Squires (Ripon), the latter an England rugby union three-quarter who certainly enlivened the fielding, emerged to suggest that a new wave of talent might be forthcoming. What was essential, in the Committee's view, was that the bickering of 1974 had to cease, and in September of that year Boycott was re-elected captain (although by a margin of only one vote, according to Boycott) and Wilson, Sharpe and Hutton all ended their careers with the county.

Wilson was able to take his great gift of communication and love of the game into a greater career as head coach at MCC; Sharpe moved on temporarily to Derbyshire before returning to Yorkshire as a committee member for York, while Hutton went off to a career in the City and publishing. Not one of the three

'Percy' – Peter Squires, talented batsman, brilliant field and rugby international, unhappy in the 1970s dressing room. A talent lost in troubled times.

has happy memories of his later years with Yorkshire.

Thus 1975 began with, at the very least, the feeling that the air had been cleared. Boycott was unchallenged in the dressing room although he records that he had been asked, the previous autumn, by one committee member: 'What do you think of Hampshire as captain?' – an indication, perhaps, that the leadership issue was at best only in suspense.

Despite worries about his mother's declining health, his principal but unannounced reason for declining the England winter tour of Australia (a decision that rebounded upon him when he sought TCCB permission to make a short tour of South Africa in the February), Boycott did approach the Committee Chairman, Arthur Connell, and the new President, Sir Kenneth Parkinson, for a pre-season meeting in which he put several points to them upon the future of the club, finishing by saying that

he was contemplating giving up Test cricket to concentrate on Yorkshire. The fact that the cricket chairman, John Temple, was by-passed did not help his cause with the less sympathetic members of the Committee.

There was certainly a massive improvement in Yorkshire's summer: the team rose to second in the Championship, without ever looking likely to finish on top, were fifth in the Sunday League and enjoyed their Benson and Hedges campaign. A new team had taken shape, based on a sound opening partnership of Boycott and Lumb, averaging 64, that briefly hinted at former great combinations. Leadbeater and Hampshire, the latter named vice-captain, gave the middle a touch of class and an array of strokes; Bairstow was fast becoming an England contender, Old was a Test all-rounder, Nicholson, although in his last season, still a formidable force, especially in one-day matches, Sidebottom and Stevenson gave full support, while Cope seemed to have mastered his new action and Carrick was developing well. What was especially pleasing, in view of the increasing emphasis on one-day cricket, was that the new generation could all bat, and there would be many occasions in the next few years when Yorkshire would field a team all of whom had completed at least one first-class century.

The reserves, too, were strong, with such players as Andrew Dalton, John Woodford, Robinson, Cooper, Bore, Johnson and Squires all awaiting their chance, and for a short while many Yorkshiremen felt that the corner had been turned and the club could look forward to a rise to and a camp upon the summit. In that hot, old-fashioned summer Boycott passed two thousand runs, Lumb fifteen hundred and Hampshire a thousand, while the two spinners blossomed, Cope with 69 wickets and Carrick 79, both at an average of 21.

What Hampshire called the honeymoon period did not last too long. Boycott was re-elected captain unanimously but quickly spotted that two of his regular critics, Don Brennan and the former Colts captain Robin Feather, had missed the crucial meeting. Boycott, with first a broken finger and then a strained back, was missing from 16 May until

The Cope investigation. Padgett and Cope bring a film of the off-spinner's action to be viewed by the Yorkshire Committee.

14 July; Old also broke down and the team, without the leading batsman and bowler, inevitably suffered. Nicholson had retired, his vast experience, genial good humour and ability to remove the best of the opposition in his day was sorely missed, and the lack of success brought rumblings about the leadership of the vice-captain, Hampshire.

The team dropped to eighth in the Championship, third from bottom in the Player League and suffered a second-round exit in the Gillette Cup, but the greatest humiliation was a knock-out in the Benson and Hedges Cup at Barnsley by Oxford and Cambridge Universities. Yorkshire's seamers, particularly Old who strained his shoulder, bowled badly on a hard pitch with short boundaries, and so stunned was the dressing room afterwards that the door stayed locked until after a prolonged inquest. In retrospect it will be seen that the Universities had an exceptional side, for it contained Roe-

buck, Tavaré, Marks, Parker, Coverdale and Gurr, all of whom were to play first-class, three of them for England.

That fact, however, was lost upon the Yorkshire membership and public at the time, and although Boycott could not be blamed the dissatisfaction grew, as the hopes that had blossomed in 1975 withered away, to the point that Committee debates grew fierce again. Boycott later wrote that the cricket sub-committee wanted to sack five uncapped players and that the one who did leave, Squires, departed against the captain's recommendations. He sought caps for Robinson, Carrick and Cooper, and won two of those battles.

Unexpectedly, and probably against the wishes and hopes of all connected with Yorkshire cricket, 1977 was another turning point. With the injuries cleared, the team restored to strength and the younger players recognised in their approaching maturity, there was some expectation that the revival begun two years earlier might pick up steam again. This time, however, the disruption came from another source – the England selectors.

Approaches had been made to Boycott in 1976, seeking his assistance against the growing power of West Indies, but his broken finger and the possible bribe (according to Boycott) of the vice-captaincy under Greig of the winter tour of India, Sri Lanka and Australia were deterrents to his return. There is evidence from several quarters that he was genuinely reluctant to leave his young players and they, in turn, were anxious not to lose the one player in the side whose mere presence, very often, was a guarantee against defeat.

Despite the loss of Old through injury, Yorkshire were unbeaten in their first twelve matches, and when Old returned after missing twelve fixtures he thrashed Warwickshire's occasional bowlers for a century in 37 minutes, then the second-fastest in history. Warwickshire managed to bowl 42 overs in 90 minutes in a match that was an unavoidable draw, as Old hit six sixes and thirteen fours in 107 made in 41 minutes, his second fifty coming off only 21 deliveries.

Boycott was then lured back into the

England side against Australia at Trent Bridge, rewarding the selectors with a slow but invaluable century, adding an 80 not out in the second innings and then, to scenes of great euphoria, completing his hundredth century against Australia in the Fourth Test at Headingley. It was a highly charged occasion and all honour was due the man, returning to cricket at the highest level to demonstrate his then unmatched quality as an opening batsman. A lesser, but no less significant point was the amount of money and the number of runs Boycott had passed up by his self-imposed exile from Test cricket.

However, the captain's absence from the Yorkshire team was felt immediately. Five of the next nine matches were lost and it was clear, according to Hampshire, that Boycott's attention was now fixed firmly on his resuscitated international career and that Yorkshire's cause

was secondary. Boycott maintains that while Yorkshire officials publicly supported his returning to play for England they were privately insisting that his prime duty lay with Yorkshire; nor was he prepared to take the blame for the county's defeats while he was away with England.

The situation became political and commanded front-page attention when the news broke that the England captain, Tony Greig, had been an agent in organising a pirate tournament, Kerry Packer's 'World Series'. That meant a new captain for the winter tour of Pakistan and New Zealand, and although the primary position went to Mike Brearley of Middlesex the tour vice-captain was Boycott, the implication being that his long-term ambition to lead England might still be realised.

In a radio broadcast that winter Don Brennan

Yorkshire before the 1976 season.
Back row (from left): Bill Athey, Mike Bore, Graham Stevenson, Colin Johnson, Peter Squires.
Middle row: Colin Kaye (physiotherapist), David Bairstow, Phil Carrick, Steve Oldham, Arthur Robinson, Richard Lumb, Jim Love, Howard Cooper.
Front row: Barrie Leadbeater, Jack Hampshire, Geoff Boycott (captain), Chris Old, Geoff Cope.

made a case for a change of captain on the grounds that Boycott did not inspire his team-mates and that he would not, in the foreseeable future, be available often enough to retain the leadership. Whatever validity there was in Brennan's argument was drowned in an uproar from members and followers to whom Boycott had become, as England's and perhaps the world's number one batsman and a leading member of the Test hierarchy and the heir apparent, a knight errant trailing clouds of glory.

Brennan was rebuked by the club Chairman Arthur Connell, and the Reform Group, originally formed to protest against Close's dismissal, took on new life with a fast-expanding membership. Brennan's head was called for and although the Committee then had no power to expel a properly elected member, the former wicket-keeper did step down from the cricket sub-committee in an effort to calm the furore.

Then, for the first time, came the appearance of two distinct factions: the Reform Group, who gave unwavering support to Boycott whether he wanted it or not – and sometimes, it seemed, to his embarrassment – and the Committee and their supporters. War had broken out. The media were divided, the popular press and the mass of the public on the whole supporting the rebels and Boycott, the quality newspapers and a majority of the members, at that time, standing by the Committee. Local radio, by and large, was pro-Boycott, reflecting the views of their listeners, and BBC stations pro-Committee, while television, sensing a great story but often unsure of both facts and background, thrashed around like a huge safari party caught in dense jungle. Views were sought in voice and print, meetings called, letters written, lawyers consulted, jokes cracked, barbs exchanged; it was a tale altogether so rich in character, humour, intrigue and plot that perhaps only Dickens or Trollope could have done it full justice.

It was, of course, much less funny to the entangled principals, especially to those embattled on the Committee trying to see both sides of the argument and to the harassed Secretary Joe Lister, who was to bear the brunt of a tempestuous decade. Yorkshire's playing record since

1977 will preclude Lister from being named alongside such as Ellison, Toone and Nash, but he can take credit for being the executive officer who steered Yorkshire through even stormier waters than the great Sheffield controversies of a century before.

Amid all the shot and shell a new batsman had emerged in Boycott's absence: an accomplished right-hander from Middlesbrough, Bill Athey, who hinted from an early age that he had the ability to reach international level, and in whom the club had high hopes of his one day succeeding Boycott as Lumb's partner; some saw Athey as a possible county captain.

The Committee members, who had spent a winter under fire from the Reform Group, then loosed their own thunderbolt: from 1979, they announced, Ray Illingworth would be returning from Leicestershire to become Yorkshire's team manager on a three-year basis. The negotiations to bring in Illingworth, Leicestershire's highly successful captain, had been conducted mostly by telephone by no more than three or four members of the Committee, so careful was the club to ensure that there were no leaks. The reaction of one reporter at the press conference announcing Illingworth's appointment was this: 'It's very clever. They've sacked Boycott without sacking him.'

Two days later Illingworth told the *Yorkshire Post*: 'I will be in charge and I will have the final say on all cricket matters, including team selection.' This, of course, was a direct infringement of Boycott's authority as captain and the Reform Group, on one side, girded themselves for the vital battles of 1979. In the meantime Yorkshire had another season to play under the old regime and, obviously, much hinged upon their record.

Boycott, meanwhile, had returned from the winter tour less pleased with his international prospects. An injury to Brearley had left him in charge of England in New Zealand where, for the first time, a Test match was lost. Objective opinion on that defeat was that there was little Boycott could have done about it, signalling as it did the rise in New Zealand cricket and the advent of Richard Hadlee, but in all the circumstances, Boycott's personality being as it was, it did not enlarge his circle of friends.

Bill Athey *Bumpah*

The nickname was given to the schoolboy as praise for his skill in hooking attempted bumpers. Charles William Jeffery Athey, a neat, stylish right-hand batsman, fine close field and occasional medium-pace bowler, was the best batsman to emerge from Middlesbrough, from a cricketing family.

His talent and technique were outstanding enough to mark him from his first appearance, in 1976, as the long-term successor to Boycott as number one for Yorkshire and England. Even as a pale, shy young Colt his ability to play on a difficult pitch, as on one celebrated occasion at Northampton, marked him as a coming international. In his seven summers with Yorkshire he scored more than six thousand runs, including ten centuries, four in 1982, twice passing a thousand runs.

Although he never expressed discontent publicly, Athey was said to be unhappy with the atmosphere in the dressing room and in 1984, after marrying the sister of a Middlesex cricketer, he moved to Gloucestershire in whose service he regained his place in the England side and succeeded to the county captaincy in 1989. Athey's departure, along with that of Steven Rhodes, was a serious setback to the club.

That there was also considerable potential in the side was proved in 1978 when the Championship position improved to fourth from twelfth – and perhaps only in Yorkshire could this have been seized upon by both factions as ammunition. Boycott captained the side in twelve matches, Hampshire in ten, both winning five, so the argument flared over whether Hampshire might make the better captain and, with success, restore peace. As Hampshire displaced Boycott at the top of the county's batting averages (the first time Boycott had lost the premier position since 1963) there was the faintest hint, also, that he might be overtaken as the principal batsman.

The rivalry between Boycott and Hampshire was fuelled by an incident during the Yorkshire visit to Grace Road in June. Illingworth and Hampshire had dinner together, in the course of which, according to both separate accounts of the conversation, the new team manager told the vice-captain that Boycott did not trust

Hampshire. Wrote Hampshire: 'I went straight up the wall. For seven years I had refused to take sides against him . . . now I learned that he had obviously told other people he did not trust me for it to get back to Illy.'

Boycott, in his memoirs, flatly denied ever having made such a remark but added: 'I regarded Hampshire as something of a fence-sitter, a man who would rarely stand up and be counted. I regarded him as a basically weak individual but I certainly did not consider him untrustworthy.' Boycott goes on to say that he then wrote to the Committee supporting Hampshire's position as vice-captain.

Whatever the absolute truth (is there such a thing?) of the incident the division between the pair flared up a month later at Northampton. The facts are simple enough. On 17 July on a good pitch and against a standard county attack the Colt Athey scored 114 in 210 minutes with fifteen fours; Boycott, reported *Wisden*, took 367 minutes over 113 with ten boundaries, not one of which came in his half-century. When Hampshire joined Colin Johnson Yorkshire needed 33 off the last 10 overs to win a fourth batting bonus point, and the fourth-wicket pair added only 11. At the wicket Hampshire told Johnson he was taking full responsibility for the famous 'go-slow', writing later: 'Call it a brain-storm if you like but towards the end of that innings I decided I was going to play the way we had seen Boycott play so many times.'

Hampshire recorded that the Northants team soon sensed what was going on and began laughing. From the Northampton press box, one of the best views in county cricket, it was also clear to this observer and the then cricket correspondent of the *Yorkshire Post*, Terry Brindle, that something extraordinary was happening. Standing by the boundary boards was a member of the cricket sub-committee, former captain Billy Sutcliffe, who soon confirmed to a now very agitated media contingent that the incident had been noted and would be referred to the Committee. Boycott wrote that his innings took four and a half hours: ' . . . pretty grim stuff, I admit, but my thumb injury was still giving me a bit of bother and I wasn't playing well at the time'. Boycott needed 86 overs to reach his century, 90 to reach 113.

At this point the two accounts diverge. Hampshire says he returned to the inner Northampton dressing room, empty of all but Boycott who said nothing to him, sitting with his head in his hands. Boycott says that Hampshire was challenged on his return by a furious David Bairstow, who wrote: 'I was angry at what was happening and refused to pad up.'

By the following morning the media representation had all but doubled and the club was again under fire from all directions. The inquest took place at Bradford during the following match, a rain-affected Gillette Cup tie, both players being called before the selection committee (Temple, Sutcliffe, Burnet), the club then making the grave error of issuing a non-committal statement on the grounds that the whole affair was an internal matter. Hampshire left without comment, Boycott, as was his right as captain, staying behind to answer questions.

Hampshire was then further angered to read the following day that he had been repri-manded, and he warned: 'What they did say, which made sense, was that if I had wanted to make a protest I should have gone for the one remaining point available and made my view known afterwards, off the field.'

Boycott's recollection is of the sort of bland non-statement that was bound to excite the curiosity of the press. 'Reporters buttonholed me (they had been waiting around until 8 p.m.) and frankly I saw no reason to protect Hampshire or the Committee. The whole hear-ing was rigged to put me in unfavourable light and I wasn't having it.'

The captain made it clear to the enquiry that he had expected disciplinary action against Hampshire, citing suspensions imposed upon Trueman, by Brian Sellers, for minor infrac-tions. In retrospect a firm statement, if not action, was demanded and the only conclusion the historian can reach over this curious episode is that with major changes on the way, includ-ing the known arrival of a team manager and the (then unknown) displacement of Boycott as captain, the Committee must have felt its first duty was towards the team, and rocking the boat in mid-stream was at best unhelpful.

The rivalry between the Boycott and Hampshire camps grew more intense when the *Daily Express* revealed that Derbyshire would offer Hampshire the captaincy if Yorkshire were to release him. As Hampshire had already been sounded out about the Yorkshire cap-taincy, he was frank enough to tell Derbyshire that he would be happy to join them – but only if he was passed over.

The decision was taken at the end of Septem-ber to replace Boycott with Hampshire, the news reaching Boycott as he flew back from a short break in Bermuda, carrying in his pocket a telegram announcing that his mother had died of cancer. To lose a beloved parent and a prime position all within a few hours was a double blow enough to rock any man, and it is hardly surprising that Boycott left England, for the England tour of Australia under Brearley, in an emotional state. The club, inevitably, attracted some bitter criticism from the Reform Group's allies and no doubt wished heartily themselves that their timing had been a little better. Eight of the General Committee had, in fact, voted against the change.

Whatever the chronology, the deed had been done – in effect a declaration of war for by then the county was hopelessly divided between pro- and anti-Boycott factions and the man himself must have later flown out of Heathrow, with the England team, a little grateful to be putting it all behind him.

It would have been unlike Boycott not to react, and before departure he duly appeared, in his county blazer, on the *Michael Parkinson Show*, the prime British television chat show of that time, to make some characteristically trenchant comments about the Committee. Calls for him to be disciplined brought another appearance before the Committee, on 23 October, when he was accompanied by his solicitor, Duncan Mutch of Barnsley, who presented a dossier aimed at proving that Boycott had had poor support during his captaincy.

Arthur Connell, the General Committee Chairman who, with Michael Crawford, the Treasurer, had been generally regarded as a moderate and bridge-builder during the controversy, then poured fuel on the fire when, in answering questions afterwards on the Committee's statement, he replied: 'It is nothing to do with what Mr Boycott has done or has not done. It is to do with what he is.'

While the former captain and the new captain spent the winter in Australia (Hampshire playing for Tasmania), the pair having a frosty meeting in Hobart, the storms blew in full force in Yorkshire. The Reform Group, re-formed in Huddersfield in October 1977, collected sufficient signatures to call for a special general meeting that would be asked to reinstate Boycott as captain and express their lack of confidence in the cricket sub-committee. The Group opened a membership account, engaged lawyers and solicited all the club's members.

The Committee countered by challenging the Group's list of signatures, pointing out that some of the names listed belonged to members who were not up to date with their subscriptions and therefore technically unable to vote. The Committee also called for a special general meeting to seek a vote of confidence in themselves. The Group responded with a High Court hearing in Liverpool (13 November), the judge agreeing with the Group and calling on the Committee to 'pay heed to the requirements of the petitioning members'.

The meeting eventually took place in Harrogate on 9 December and the Committee won comfortably, the move to reinstate Boycott being defeated by 2224, the confidence vote by 1355, the cricket sub-committee vote by 870. However, many Reformers left that meeting angry at what they regarded as an intrusion by the incoming team manager Ray Illingworth. A letter from Illingworth to the Committee, written before the September sacking of Boycott, was read out to the special general meeting, the team manager affirming that the great majority of the players wanted a change of captain.

Boycott later claimed that the players' poll organised by Geoff Cope, upon which the finding was based, was fraudulent in that Old had refused to give an opinion and Bairstow and five of the junior players had not been asked. There is no doubt that Illingworth's letter rallied support for the Committee in the hall, but the consequence was that many of the Reformers felt they had been cheated and that Illingworth, in their eyes, was then firmly in the camp of Hampshire and the Committee.

This, then, was the background to the 1979 season, Hampshire's first as captain, with Boycott, despite rumours of his moving elsewhere (even Lancashire was mentioned), still a Yorkshire player with a new two-year contract. The Committee had avoided a direct clash of wills between Illingworth and Boycott, but in order to win their argument with many recalcitrant members and supporters, and with the public at large, a successful season was crucial.

A good run to the semi-final in the Benson and Hedges Cup was promising, but the overall Championship position declined to seventh and the conclusion was that Yorkshire were a fairly ordinary mid-table team. The younger players such as Stevenson, Sidebottom, Athey, Kevin Sharp and Jim Love were inconsistent and although two useful Colts appeared, the all-rounder Neil Hartley (Shipley) and the fast bowler Alan Ramage (Middlesbrough), the end

Kevin Sharp

Kevin Sharp, from Leeds, was a fair-haired, good-looking left-hander whose early career, like his appearance, resembled David Gower's. Indeed, in their school days he was thought to have the more potential.

He made his debut in 1976 as a seventeen-year-old but did not score his first century until four years later, although his opportunities, in an unsuccessful side, were irregular. Since then he has scored eight centuries, passing a thousand runs in 1984 and 1988, and in the four modern competitions has batted from one to six in the order. His potential was underlined in 1977 when he scored 260 not out for Young England against Young West Indies, and he was captain of the England Under-19 team the following season.

His occasional off-spin bowling brought the sobriquet 'Freddie Laker' and he has taken some notable catches both close to the wicket and in the field. He rested during part of the 1980 season on medical advice and often gave the impression that as a player he would have been much happier on the old three-day, one-competition schedule.

product was disappointing. Hampshire was criticised for being too defensive, Old struggled with injuries, Cope returned for a third time without being able to bowl, under scrutiny, with his old venom, while the new young off-spinner Peter Whiteley (Otley) obviously needed time.

Carrick advanced as an all-rounder but the need for him to bowl negatively at the leg stump in the one-day games affected his first-class form. The one player to shine, inevitably, was Boycott, averaging a hundred for the second time in his career (the only batsman ever to do so) and even topping the bowling averages, a feat not achieved since the glory of George Hirst in 1910. Hampshire later wrote that he felt sometimes as if 98 per cent of the crowd were against him, willing him to fail: 'A sort of anarchy was reigning throughout the county's cricket. The manager, the captain, the Committee were being reviled by people professing to have the club's best interests at heart and the players, especially the younger and less

mature ones, cannot have helped feeling that there was a lowering of standards all around them.'

If Hampshire's assessment of the mood of the dressing room was correct then it was not surprising that 1980 was yet another disappointment, only five Championship matches being won. Cope finally retired to bowl happily and unchallenged in minor county cricket for several years, a talent discouraged by officialdom. If there was a flaw in Cope's action it was all but indiscernible unless seen on a slowed film. He could never have done physical harm to a batsman and yet there were fast bowlers in the first-class game who were known by everyone to throw the odd delivery but who had been clever enough never to be caught on film.

Carrick, too, was less effective, while the seam attack had to be chosen from the fittest in a continuing list of casualties. Love, Athey and Sidebottom were all capped and it was clear that all had outstanding ability yet without the application to produce it consistently. Athey was a batsman of high promise and performed particularly well in the John Player League, but only after the first six matches had been lost and the team had been eliminated from the Benson and Hedges Cup. However, a late rally took the side to sixth place in the Championship and in Simon Dennis, from Scarborough, a nephew of Hutton, the club seemed to have discovered the most potentially hostile left-arm quick bowler since Cowan.

The fighting was by no means over, but for a spell the shooting was sporadic. In an effort to stall speculation the club offered new contracts to the three senior players, Boycott, Hampshire and Old, in mid July, a well-meaning effort that only brought further criticism, both factions seeing the gesture as appeasement. Hampshire, meanwhile, had had enough. His wife was insulted in a supermarket, his children at school, and, as he wrote, 'I could not for the life of me understand the personal bitterness with which they seemed to hold me responsible for the fact that their man was not captain.'

Illingworth's next choice was Richard Lumb, but he made it clear that he had no wish to lead a team containing two ex-captains, Boycott and Hampshire. So on 3 September, at Scarborough, Chris Old was offered the captaincy, and he went off the following January to tour West Indies with England (and Boycott) under

Ian Botham's captaincy. Always a cheerful, gregarious character, Old firmly believed he could improve the atmosphere in the dressing room and returned from that tour to tell the manager and Hampshire: 'Boycott is my senior professional and vice-captain and all the help I want I'll get from him.'

According to Illingworth the harmony lasted until 27 May in the 1981 season when, at Dartford, the team manager castigated Boycott and Bairstow for leaving the ground under the impression that there would be no play before lunch. Both returned in time to take the field for a start earlier than expected, but when Old, according to Illingworth's memoirs, later that day asked Boycott for some advice the reported reply was: 'It's nothing to do with me. You get on with it, you're the captain.'

Old had little luck. In a wet summer the side suffered eight fractures and nine players in all were injured at one point or another; only once in the entire season were all ten capped players available, and even then Old played when less than a hundred per cent. A drop to tenth, in all the circumstances, was a not unreasonable performance, but one decision by the manager and one incident sparked further controversies.

Looking ahead, too far in the view of many, Illingworth indicated his future Yorkshire captain by naming the twenty-five-year-old

Jim Love

James Derek Love, a tall, fair right-hander who could drive with immense power, was born in Headingley and made his debut in 1975, emerging as a highly influential player in one-day matches who was rarely able to translate his undoubted ability into the first-class game.

His ability to accelerate the scoring rate brought him England recognition in one-day matches and there were times in his career when the club hoped that he would prove to be the successor at number four to Hampshire. He passed a thousand runs twice and scored thirteen centuries, but it was as a forcing batsman in limited overs that his full value was to be seen and he was rightly declared the Gold Award winner for his outstanding batting in the Benson and Hedges victory at Lord's in 1987.

Northamptonshire, having scored 244 for 7 in their 55 overs, reduced Yorkshire to 103 for 3 in 29 overs when Love, supported in turn by Sharp, Bairstow and Carrick, led a furious counter-attack that resulted in Yorkshire's needing 4 runs off the last over with Sidebottom, at number eight, Love's new partner.

Three singles were scrambled off the first four balls; Sidebottom should have been run out off the fifth and although Love only blocked the final ball, with the scores level, Yorkshire were winners on the loss of one less wicket, Love finishing 75 not out and, for a man who rarely showed his emotions, punching the sky.

uncapped Neil Hartley to head the side against Warwickshire on 29 July. Amid all the injuries and in Old's absence both Hampshire and Bairstow had led the team, but Hartley's appointment was a major shock – not least to Bairstow, who felt very strongly as the professional next senior in line that he should be given an opportunity of leadership. A furious argument in a cocktail bar in the Royal Hotel in Scarborough, where the team were staying, between Illingworth and Bairstow spread, in many colourful versions, like wildfire around the county.

Hartley, according to gossip, had been favoured because he was then courting Illingworth's elder daughter Vicki. In fact the relationship had ended the previous year, but a good tale was not to be spoilt. Illingworth always maintained that Hartley would have made a highly successful captain, a claim that the club recognised partially in 1987 when he was appointed Colts captain. Impartial judges accept that with Old injured, Boycott on Test duty and both Hampshire and Lumb disinclined, Hartley did a good job with limited resources and little opportunity.

Illingworth believes that Hartley might have succeeded to the job in 1983 had not the Committee been overthrown by the Reformers; certainly Bairstow, whether he welcomed it or not, found himself the Reformers' alternative candidate for office and yet another fracas was under way. Illingworth had provided his opponents with further ammunition and they made good use of it, a further stock falling into their hands in September when Boycott, in an unexpected television interview in York, said he was seeking a 'clear-the-air' meeting with Illingworth, wanting an explanation for his omission from the team for the Fenner Trophy Festival matches.

Illingworth's stated intention was that Boycott should rest after the Test match and return for the final home Championship match against Northamptonshire, also at Scarborough. The following morning the manager, after consulting the captain (Old) and two members of the cricket sub-committee (Brennan and Trueman), formally suspended Boycott for the rest of the season for making unauthorised public

statements in breach of the disciplinary clause in his contract. What Illingworth did not know was that Boycott had excised the disciplinary clause before signing his last contract, a fact known only to himself, his solicitor, the club Secretary (Lister) and Arthur Connell's successor as Chairman, Michael Crawford.

There has possibly never been more uproar before the start of a county cricket match. Boycott changed but did not leave the ground as he had promised to sign some bats for Bairstow's forthcoming benefit. Mysteriously television crews appeared at the ground, and the Reform Group members were busy collecting signatures calling for another special general meeting – this time with the intention of dismissing Illingworth. The furore was such that members and supporters spilled into the outfield, through which the Northants fielders had to make their way, dodging arguing groups of Yorkshiremen.

The situation had its humorous moments. When Tim Lamb, later the TCCB's Assistant Secretary, offered a mild passing comment he was told to 'bugger off back to South Africa', the intended target, of course, being Allan Lamb, some yards away. A colleague of mine, Richard Streeton, left the press box for closer investigation and introduced himself to one angry dialogue by saying: 'Excuse me, I'm from *The Times* of London,' and then got no further. He was told, very firmly: 'Tha can sod off! It's nowt to do with thee.'

Illingworth believes to this day that he was deliberately ambushed; that he was set up to suspend Boycott and provoke an end-of-season crisis, the Reform Group being aware that he was overstepping his authority. Boycott insisted that he had been given permission by the club Secretary to make the television interview. With almost whoops of joy the media fell upon what they saw as the inevitable outcome: Boycott or Illingworth? One, they decided, would have to go.

Whatever the view from the press box, or the committee room, the dressing room saw the whole episode as especially depressing. Lumb and Martyn Moxon (Barnsley) walked out to bat to a little perfunctory clapping, as if the start of the match was a minor and inconsequential

Martyn Moxon

Martyn Douglas Moxon was another product of that prolific South Yorkshire nursery between Barnsley and Wakefield. His father, again, was an excellent league cricketer and coach to Wombwell Cricket Lovers, so the young Moxon was given an early love for the game.

A strong, forcing right-hander, Moxon captained Yorkshire Schools at Under-15 and Senior Schools, and captained the North of England Under-19 tour of Canada in 1979. On his debut in 1981 he became the first Yorkshireman to score centuries in his first two home Championship matches and his 116 was the highest score on debut until it was overtaken by Ashley Metcalfe.

Despite his early success he had to wait until 1984 for a regular place, after scoring 153 against Lancashire in his first Roses match the previous year, and would have made his debut for England, against West Indies at Lord's, but for a rib injury in that season.

On the following tour of India he missed a chance of establishing his place as England's regular opener by having to return to attend the funeral of his father, and he had to wait until 1986 to make his Test debut. A quiet, studious man with university qualifications and a business degree, he became an excellent first slip and occasionally useful medium-pace swing bowler. He was appointed the Club's vice-captain in 1989.

Paul Jarvis

Paul William Jarvis was the youngest player on debut for Yorkshire (sixteen years two months in the Player League, thirteen days later in the Championship), displacing Padgett, the only other player to start at sixteen. His father played for Marske for thirty years and a brother appeared for England Schools, and Paul was chosen for Marske Under-14s at the age of eight.

A right-arm fast-medium bowler and hard-hitting tail-ender, he was bowling second change for Marske first team at fifteen and would have played for the Colts that same year had he not been sitting school examinations. After five Colts matches in 1982 he made his debut in the John Player League against Lancashire, his first-team debut coming in the next match, against Barbados, to be followed by a Championship debut at Hove against Sussex, all in a fortnight.

Winter cricket in Australia, a shortened run, added

control and the ability to deliver the occasional genuinely fast ball brought him seven wickets in one innings in each of 1985, '86 and '87, including a hat-trick against Derbyshire in 1985. He was chosen as reserve seam bowler for the England Reliance Cup party in 1987–8 and was expected to be a firm challenger for an England place when he broke down at Hove in mid 1988 and spent the rest of the summer attempting to shed a back strain. He nevertheless finished fourth in the national averages with 37 wickets at an average of 17 and, fitness permitting, was on the verge of a successful career for Yorkshire and England at the age of twenty-three.

sub-plot; rarely can a Yorkshire opening pair have been greeted with so little enthusiasm on a home ground. One watching player, Hampshire, finally decided that morning to sever his links and join Derbyshire; similar thoughts must have crossed younger minds.

Moxon was a tall, powerful right-hander, and Paul Jarvis, from Redcar, a promising quick bowler who at sixteen was the youngest ever player to appear for Yorkshire, an indication of both his ability and the dire weakness of the attack. Moxon became the first Yorkshireman since Cecil Tyson to score a century on debut, with 116 off a strong Essex bowling; he then underlined his entry into the records by becoming the first Yorkshireman to score centuries in his first two home matches.

Alas, there was far too much happening off the field for either of these young men to receive more than fleeting attention. On 17 September the General Committee met for what the media saw as the shoot-out between Illingworth and Boycott, solicitors being present. In the event the hullabaloo at Scarborough was glossed over, much to Illingworth's indignation, although it was clear that Boycott could not be charged with breach of contract.

A Committee of Enquiry consisting of seven members of the General Committee was set up under an independent chairman; the Committee was instructed to look into all aspects of Yorkshire cricket and make recommendations. Thirty-two witnesses were called, beginning with Illingworth, but Boycott, to the anger of a body he already believed biased against him, had gone on holiday before joining England's tour of India and his evidence would not be heard for months.

Meanwhile the media, thwarted of a dénouement, kept the pot boiling by conducting a poll of the players, which provided a substantial majority for Illingworth and against Boycott. The Committee of Enquiry's report mentioned this, one member of the General Committee resigning in protest at its publication, and also came out strongly for the disbandment of the Reform Group: 'We believe that the presence of this body has done untold harm . . . it has addressed itself to many matters to which it was not fully informed; it has made statements . . . which have been detrimental to the club.' The team, the Enquiry concluded, would be better off without Boycott.

The Reformers argued that six of the eight members of the Committee of Enquiry had made up their minds before any depositions had been taken, and made it clear that they would not accept the findings. More significantly one of the Reform Group's leading members, Sidney Fielden, won the Doncaster vacancy on the General Committee, immeasurably strengthening the representation in the government of the club.

In order to move more quickly the General Committee set up a sub-committee of three (Burnet, Trueman and Sutcliffe) with the power to make quick decisions in cricketing matters, in effect to give Illingworth immediate support. The trio were soon named the 'Peacemakers' by the media, which must have given them an occasional chuckle in troubled times. Illingworth, desperate to reinforce the attack, recalled Oldham who had been allowed to move to Derbyshire, and publicly regretted the loss of prospects such as Tim Boon and Neal Mallender, who moved on to other counties. Hampshire had already gone, and there were rumours that Athey was unsettled.

Even the unthinkable, the holy writ of Yorkshire cricket, was publicly aired: should York-

Steve Oldham

shire abandon the birth qualification and sign an overseas professional? When the members were polled they gave a decisive rejection and Illingworth returned to team planning for 1982. Whatever he had in mind was swept aside in a desperately poor start, culminating in a disastrous weekend at Middlesbrough when, on successive days, Northamptonshire began the Championship match with an opening stand of 278 and followed with a Sunday League score of 282. Illingworth wrote: 'It was terrible, and something had to be done. And the next week, as soon as the county game was over, Chilly [Old] was relieved of the captaincy and the Committee asked me to take over at Ilford, fifteen days after my 50th birthday.'

Old had, in fact, been contemplating resignation and Illingworth's reappearance on the field did remove the dichotomy from the direction of the team. The new captain also managed to establish a kind of armed truce with Boycott

Neil Lloyd *Rosebud*

Neil Lloyd is the only cricketer to appear in this history who did not play for the club's first team. He is included because he made such an impression in his seventeen years of life before his death in September 1982 that a commemorative booklet was published and a trophy, to be awarded to young cricketers, named after him.

Born in Ackworth, and of a physique that had to be strengthened by winter training, known to his colleagues as 'torture sessions', he was a left-handed batsman whose stroke play and technique brought him a fast-growing reputation from the age of thirteen. The son of Doug Lloyd, a left-hand batsman and wicket-keeper good enough to attract offers from Nottinghamshire and Northamptonshire, the boy went to the same school, at Hemsworth, as Boycott. He first fielded for his club, Ackworth, as a nine-year-old, and played for the second eleven the following year. At thirteen he was playing for Yorkshire Schools, scoring a record aggregate of 1240 runs in the next three summers, including three centuries. At sixteen he joined the Yorkshire staff, the season after making his debut for the Colts.

At seventeen, in 1982, he was chosen to play for

the England Under-19 team against West Indies at Hove, after which he joined his father and several Ackworth members for a holiday at the Scarborough Festival. There he developed the first symptoms of a neurological disease and a week later he died in a Wakefield Hospital.

Keith Andrew, the National Cricket Association's chief executive and former England wicket-keeper, said of him, after watching him on an Under-13 course: 'Probably for the first and only time in my life I am forecasting that a twelve-year-old boy will play cricket for Yorkshire and England before he is twenty-one years old.'

Steven Coverdale, now Northamptonshire Secretary and once Yorkshire Colts' wicket-keeper, wrote of him:

> The loss the game suffered by his death can never be measured though surely he would have proved to be a magnificent cricketer. But life is more than cricket and in life Neil was a magnificent individual. When he died the game and the county lost a young man of immense talent. But we all lost a very dear friend.

and results did improve, particularly in the one-day competitions where Illingworth was best able to bring his experience and ability to bear. Sidebottom took 62 Championship wickets, with patched-up support as Old, Stevenson and Ramage were all again afflicted by injuries. A Nat-West semi-final against Warwickshire was lost at Edgbaston, Yorkshire having to bat first on a pitch that improved during the day, confirmation that the team had recovered a sense of purpose and were no longer a chopping block. Even the sniping off the field fell away, although any Yorkshireman attending a match would soon realise that he was in the presence of two heavily armed camps, highly suspicious of any movement.

A tenth position in the Championship represented an honourable recovery, and there was a slight swelling of optimism for 1983. Old departed for Warwickshire (and was to inflict a terrible hiding on Yorkshire, with bat and ball, at Headingley) and the actual play that summer could hardly have gone worse for a club celebrating its 150th anniversary: Yorkshire finished bottom of the Championship table (no reason to celebrate for the Reform Group, but plentiful opportunity to hammer the Committee and Illingworth). The side did, however, win the John Player Sunday League, their first trophy since 1969 (an achievement for Illingworth and the Committee). Yorkshire managed only one Championship victory, at Southampton, lost four successive matches in one spell and failed to win a home match for the first time. The Sunday League was won by the ability of Illingworth and Carrick, two spinners, to put the brake on the middle part of the opposing innings, and Yorkshire's ability, especially in the tail, to flail away at almost any target.

The euphoria of the winning of the League at Chelmsford, a delight to the younger element of the team who had never known success, was shadowed by growing storm clouds. On the previous 13 August, against Gloucestershire at Cheltenham, another incident had occurred involving Boycott that had received as much prominence as the Northampton 'go-slow'.

According to Illingworth the day began badly when he had to reprimand Boycott for his rudeness in dealing with several small boys seeking autographs (and apologise to some Gloucestershire members). On what all agree was a good pitch, with a short boundary, Boycott scored 140 not out in 375 minutes, facing 347 balls. Illingworth, seeing that a fourth batting bonus point might be missed, claims that he tried to signal to Boycott to speed up progress, even sending out a message with an incoming batsman, Sharp. Called for a quick run, Sharp was run out and when Stevenson was also dismissed quickly the bonus point was lost. With 35 minutes left Illingworth recorded that he sent out another message to Boycott and Love, by the twelfth man, asking for quick runs in the hope of a declaration; Boycott scored another 6 runs.

Boycott's version: ' . . . accepting that there may have been misunderstandings I totally reject that I wilfully refused any instructions from Illingworth.'

Bairstow's view of the incident: 'I do believe there was some kind of breakdown in communications and that Boycott was in some confusion – it also has to be said that with his [Boycott's] vast experience he should have had a good idea of what was needed without having to be told.'

David Warner, of the *Telegraph and Argus*, Bradford, asked Illingworth if he intended to report Boycott for slow scoring. The reply: 'I can't say. You had better draw your own conclusions', which Warner promptly did.

Boycott wrote that Illingworth said nothing to him on his return to the pavilion that evening. The press that weekend was full of speculation about another confrontation and the following week both captain and senior professional were called in to appear before the three Peacemakers at Headingley. The statement afterwards read: 'We are satisfied that in this instance his [Boycott's] batting was not in the best interests of the side and again he has been told that he must play the sort of innings the side needs irrespective of his own ambitions.'

It was, the Peacemakers hoped, an announcement carefully attuned to the mood of the moment, saying what had to be said in a moderate manner. 'Does this mean,' asked Don Mosey of the BBC, of Ronnie Burnet, 'that

Boycott had been reprimanded?' He had, said the sub-committee chairman. Boycott denied that he had been reprimanded as such, claiming he had a letter from Burnet saying just that. The Reform Group was up in arms and when Boycott, in the next match at Bradford, scored a century in each innings against Nottinghamshire, the old Park Avenue pavilion almost shook with the pent-up emotion inside. Both factions realised that there could now be no bridging of the issue this time: a definite decision had to be made.

At the tempest's very height, in August 1983, *The Guardian*, scarcely bothering to hide its Lancastrian connections, could not resist linking Yorkshire's difficulties with another current cricketing concern in a deliciously risible leader:

> Of the 38 paintings on show in the Lord's Memorial Gallery 16 are fakes according to a report. Fourteen of the suspect works come from the collection of the late Sir Jeremiah Colman, described as a 'mustard magnate', and could well be of a single hand. . . .
>
> Assuming that the *Mail on Sunday*'s report is correct there seems a reasonable chance that more such pictures will have found their way into other collections and that these two may see the light before long.
>
> There were, for instance, unconfirmed reports yesterday that a work said to be entitled 'Sir Geoffrey Accepts the Repentance of his Detractors' had been found in a disused fish store in east London. Attributed to Andrea Mantegna (1431–1506) it depicts a scene on Lord's Cricket Ground some time in the closing years of this century. Illuminated in a sublime shaft of sunlight, Geoffrey Boycott stands at the wicket, his bat raised above his head in modest acknowledgement of the ovation raging around him. By scoring 238 not out in 95 minutes he has just ensured that Yorkshire have at last regained the County Championship. In the foreground, a gnarled figure all in white, dimly recognisable as Mr Raymond Illingworth, lies full length in abject supplication.
>
> Beside him, on bended knee, one hand outstretched, the tears of penitence coursing freely down his face, is Mr Ronnie Burnet, chairman of the county's peace-keeping committee. In the top left-hand corner of the painting a host of cherubic figures, possibly angels, possibly members of the MCC ground staff, hymn the apotheosis of the hero. A flurry of activity at the pavilion gate announces the imminent arrival of Her Majesty the Queen, who has come hotfoot from the Palace on hearing the news to confer upon Mr Boycott that knighthood which has so long eluded him. The jovial bearded figure at the bottom right-hand corner of the canvas is Mr Bill Frindall, who has just calculated that this is the first occasion in the history of the game on which a batsman who has made 238 runs in 95 minutes has been knighted on the field of play in the presence of Signor Mantegna.
>
> The police last night were said to regard the painting, masterpiece though it unquestionably is, as yet another forgery. A statement by the chairman of the Art Treasures sub-committee of the Yorkshire County Cricket Club, however, said that this was not necessarily the case. It might equally well prove, Mr Trueman said, to be an authentic work of the great Paduan master, painted in a moment when he had been vouchsafed an uncannily prophetic vision of what the County eleven would achieve either next season or the season after that.

The Reformers began collecting signatures for the calling of another special general meeting, but before the procedural machinery clanked into action again Illingworth pre-empted one issue by announcing that he was resigning and retiring at the end of the season. He had become increasingly concerned about his wife and family, about the obscene phone calls and barrage of letters; on one occasion, he records, two players left the dressing room to ensure that his two daughters passed safely through the car park.

It was then Illingworth's turn to receive a flood of support, publicly and privately, from Yorkshire members and public alike. When, three weeks later, Yorkshire had won the Sunday League, he softened and said he would be happy to continue, but only on a part-time playing basis. He still had a year of his contract remaining.

Amidst all the rumbling of the Nottinghamshire match at Bradford a remarkable debut had taken place: Ashley Metcalfe, a slim, confident nineteen-year-old right-hander from Farsley, had opened with Boycott and emulated Moxon of two years before with a century on his first appearance, an impressive 122 contain-

Ashley Metcalfe *Panache*

Ashley Anthony Metcalfe had the most auspicious start of any Yorkshire batsman. A stylish, adventurous right-hand batsman from Horsforth, he had broken Bradford League records when he first appeared, as Boycott's partner, against Nottinghamshire at Bradford in 1983, scoring 122. He had been accepted by London University when he took up a professional contract, but could not command a first-team place until Boycott's retirement when, apart from a spell in 1988, he became Moxon's regular opening partner.

With Moxon he scored 282 for the first wicket against Lancashire at Old Trafford ifn 1986. Metcalfe had a poor start to 1988 but recovered splendidly to pass a thousand runs for a third time, including a 216 not out against Middlesex. He had a natural flair for attack, which prompted some judges to suggest he should bat at number three or four, but he made it clear that he liked to attack the new ball in the manner of the player he most admired, Barry Richards.

In April 1986 he marrie Diane, the younger daughter of Ray Illingworth.

ing some auspicious stroke-play from Yorkshire's youngest centurion on debut.

At the next meeting of the cricket sub-committee, on the morning of 3 October, it was decided by a unanimous vote to release Boycott, to appoint Bairstow as the new captain and to confirm Illingworth as team manager. At the General Committee meeting that afternoon those decisions were endorsed by a majority of two to one; it was as if beacons blazed from every high point in Yorkshire.

The following Sunday the Reform Group met at Ossett, 400 strong according to one report, and called for the cricket sub-committee to reconsider. They did this, on 17 October, and voted unanimously to reaffirm their decision. The same afternoon the General Committee again voted: 18–8 in support. This time the Chairman, Michael Crawford, issued a statement in which the reasons for the decision were reviewed: room had to be made, it was pointed out, for younger players such as Moxon and Metcalfe, and in order to help retain promising talents (Athey was joining Gloucestershire). The Committee felt that 'the necessity to build team spirit for the good of Yorkshire cricket must override the interests of any one individual'.

Crawford also appealed to the members to consider the cost to the club of another special general meeting (£10,000 was the estimate) – 'but if 2.5 per cent of its [the club's] members think that money spent convening a special general meeting is better spent on printing, postal and hire charges and professional fees then the General Committee, whilst strongly disagreeing, will have to incur such expenditure.'

What followed was an all-out propaganda war in which the Reform Group had the advantage of having their three members on the General Committee – Reg Kirk, Peter Charles and Sid Fielden – join their colleagues outside the club while the Committee, bound by procedure, was left in a position where it could usually react only through the one person empowered to pronounce upon policy, Chairman Michael Crawford. In this situation, with one tabloid newspaper (the *Daily Star*) actually issuing 'I back Boycott' stickers, and given the Yorkshireman's natural propensity to defy authority, the odds were soon mounting against the establishment.

One last attempt was made to be seen to be fair to both sides.

During the course of the year soundings were taken as to the possibility of Geoffrey Boycott's retiring at the end of next season for which he had already been granted a testimonial. Geoffrey indicated that it was at that time his wish to continue playing after next season and it had been his hope that he would regain his place as an opening batsman for England. The General Committee had taken its decision to award Geoffrey Boycott a testimonial independently of any decision in regard to his contract because it was felt that members of the club and the cricket-loving public should have the opportunity of showing their appreciation of Geoff Boycott's years of service to the county since his benefit in 1974.

The incongruity of sacking Boycott and simultaneously offering him a testimonial could not have occurred to the Committee in what was a laudable, if misconceived effort to treat the club's most famous player with absolute impartiality. The media soon left the Committee in

no doubt as to how the public would view that statement. The reference to a future Test career for Boycott was also puzzling to the cricket public at large: Boycott had returned early from the tour of India under a cloud after an argument with the management over his fitness, and had then played a leading part in an unauthorised tour of South Africa, for which he was to receive a three-year suspension from international cricket.

The special general meeting was called for 3

The 1983 crisis and an official publication from the club.

YORKSHIRE CCC SPECIAL BULLETIN

THE REASONS FOR IT ALL

NORMAN YARDLEY
20 England caps

MUCH has been made of Geoffrey Boycott's unwavering loyalty to Yorkshire. "He only ever wanted to play for Yorkshire" is the argument.

But it is known that he has approached other counties to establish the basis on which he might play for them.

However, the fact is that he has played continuously for Yorkshire in the ten years since his benefit was granted.

The Committee believed, in July, that the members and public would want a further opportunity to show their appreciation of his performances.

Hence the testimonial decision. The Committee wish him every success with it and are pledged to support it.

Successful testimonials take a lot of planning. Time is needed. So that decision was taken in July.

The contract decision was not pre-judged. The

Consider these factors before you vote

forward cricketing policy was not then crystallised. But imagine the outcry to be orchestrated by the dissident Committee men if the decision had been "a testimonial only on condition it's your last year"!

Contract decisions are taken for *all* players *after* the season. This accords with strong representations by the players to the Club's chairman, Michael Crawford, in 1980. He gave them his personal assurance for the future.

After July, soundings were taken on Boycott's future plans. He wished to continue playing beyond 1984. He hoped to regain his England place when the TCCB ban expires in 1985. One more year was not enough.

Before the October 3 decision, he had <u>not</u> suggested that he would be prepared to play for his testimonial season only.

Boycott has been the centre of factional controversy within the Club. That controversy increased in the later part of the season. The new cricket policy was launched against that background.

In this context, his contract was not renewed and interdependent decisions were taken. A new captain was appointed and the manager would play only in emergency.

A new spirit IS essential. The very promising young players have to be retained and must be given full opportunity.

Between October 3 and 18, Boycott indicated that he would be willing to retire at the end of the 1984 season. No other factor had changed except that the rancour and controversy had increased.

The Committees re-convened and confirmed their original decisions in the light of all the factors, and knowing that the other interdependent decisions had been made and announced. These included the appointment of the new captain and the changed emphasis of the manager's role.

Some argue that a man should not be released before his testimonial or benefit — but there are several examples in Yorkshire's post-war history.

They include Bob Appleyard, Frank Lowson and, most recently, Barrie Leadbeater in only 1980. There was no uproar then.

Statement

The Committee, in its first published statement after the original October 3 decision, said:

'We are entering a new era, and, if we wish to be successful, it is essential that all Yorkshire cricket lovers, be they members or supporters, give David Bairstow and his young team every support and encouragement, which until recently has always been a tradition of Yorkshire cricket, and has been a major contribution to past successes.'

Many have said this has been long overdue. We cannot risk losing any more young players.

They can't all be wrong . . .

Your eleven-man Cricket Committee comprises some of the most experienced and talented cricketers to represent the county. They have made a combined total of 162 Test appearances for England, and have played in more than 2,000 first-class matches for Yorkshire. No other team can boast a more experienced and balanced Cricket Committee. (Dates against names show when elected).

BILLY SUTCLIFFE

BRYAN STOTT

PHIL SHARPE

These are your decision - makers

RONNIE BURNET (1959-69, 1978-): Appointed Yorkshire captain in 1958, at the age of 39, without having previously played first-class cricket. But his leadership had moulded an outstanding second eleven, and Yorkshire won the County Championship under him for the captaincy in 1959. Was chairman and managing director of a chemical company for 23 years. Currently chairman of the Cricket Committee.
DON BRENNAN (1973-77, 1979-): A brilliant wicketkeeper who helped in the dismissal of nearly 500 batsmen. A compelling character and England tourist, who played two Tests for England against South Africa in 1951. Retired to concentrate on business after the 1953 season.
ERIC BURGIN (1982-): Medium-paced inswing bowler who played for Yorkshire in 1952 and 1953. Dedicated worker for junior cricket in South Yorkshire, and deeply involved in the work of the Yorkshire Cricket Association.
PHIL SHARPE (1980-): Scored more than 22,000 runs in a first-class career that extended from 1956 to 1976. Made 786 runs at 46.23 in his 12 Test matches for England — including an innings of 111 against New Zealand at Trent Bridge in 1969. Became an England selector in 1983. One of the finest slip fielders of all time, taking more than 600

catches in fewer than 500 matches.
BRYAN STOTT (1983-): Played for Yorkshire for 12 years between 1952 and 1963. Scored more than 9,000 runs in first-class cricket for Yorkshire at an average of more than 31. A true team performer, who retired early to concentrate on his family business.
BILLY SUTCLIFFE (1969-): Attacking right-handed batsman who played for Yorkshire between 1948 and 1957, and captained the county in 1956-1957. Scored more than 6,000 runs in first-class matches, before retiring to run the family business. Test selector for two years.
FRED TRUEMAN (1982-): Still the most successful England bowler of all time with 307 wickets in 67 Test matches. 'Fiery Fred' took a career total of 2,304 wickets — more than any other fast bowler — at 18.29 with a mixture of hostility and guile. Captain of the Yorkshire side which beat the Australians in 1968. Now he captains the Courage Old England team and is a respected writer and broadcaster.
RAYMOND ILLINGWORTH Captained England in 31 of his 61 Test matches. A superb tactician. Played for Yorkshire from 1951 until joining Leicestershire in 1969. Transformed that county's fortunes and led them to the County

Championship in 1975 and to the John Player League and Benson and Hedges Cup twice each. Returned to Yorkshire in 1979, took over the captaincy midway during the 1982 season, and has completed the career double of 20,000 runs and 2,000 wickets.
NORMAN YARDLEY: Club president. Captained England in 14 of his 20 Test matches, and twice dismissed Bradman in the same Test match. All-rounder who scored more than 18,000 first-class runs and was an accurate medium-pace bowler. Skippered Yorkshire from 1948 to 1955 — and the county shared the Championship with Middlesex in 1949. Test selector for seven years and chairman in 1952. A universally respected elder statesman of cricket.
MICHAEL CRAWFORD: Chairman of the Club since 1980, after previously being treasurer from 1963 to 1979. Played once for the county, captained the Second Eleven for two years and was an outstanding league cricketer. For 25 years a partner in a firm of chartered accountants.
DAVID WELCH: Treasurer of Yorkshire CCC since 1980, and a partner in a South Yorkshire firm of chartered accountants.

THE WAY AHEAD

Leading positions in the Second XI County Championship table 1983.

	P	W	L	D	Pts	Ave
Leicestershire	10	6	1	3	161	16.10
Yorkshire	11	5	1	5	148	13.45
Surrey	13	5	3	5	155	11.92

● At a lower level, the YCA Under-19 team won the Cambridge Festival.
● At representative level: Steven Rhodes, Paul Jarvis and Ashley Metcalfe all played for Young England against Young Australia this summer.

December 1983 at Harrogate, but an immediate complication arose as to the eligibility of those members who were in arrears with their subscriptions. The club tried to impose a date, 24 October, when all those who had not paid their subscriptions for 1983 would be ineligible. Two members, supported by the Reform Group (soon to change their name to Yorkshire Members 1984), took legal opinion and although it was clear that both the Committee and the dissident members were acting correctly, under two different rules, counsel warned the club that with up to 800 members in dispute over their rights, any decision from the

Part of the 'rebel' view in 1983. A leaflet urging pro-Boycott voting at the special general meeting, 3 December.

Before casting your votes on 3rd December 1983 we urge you to consider the following facts:

A Regarding Resolution No. 1: Boycott's contract

1. Contrary to rumours and insinuations Boycott has had no argument or differences with Illingworth or any member of the Committee for the last two seasons. Bairstow is on record as saying that Boycott is a firm friend and that he, Bairstow, knows of no rows.

2. As a member of the team Boycott performed admirably in the last season; he delivered runs prodigously as usual. On 12 July 1983 the Committee awarded him a testimonial.

3. On 3 October 1983 the Committee voted not to offer Boycott another contract. All that happened between the 12th July and the 3rd October involving Boycott was the Cheltenham incident when Illingworth criticized him for slow scoring, which Ronnie Burnet described as not a very serious matter, a storm in a teacup, and which resulted (again in the words of Burnet) in Boycott being rapped on the knuckles.

4. There was no reasonable justification for the sacking. There was no discord in the dressing room, nor any on the field of play; the team won the John Player League; Boycott made a valuable contribution to that; and he had his testimonial to look forward to. He never did nor said anything that justified the ending of his career with Yorkshire.

5. The Chairman has said publicly that the sacking was not due to anything done or said by Boycott but to the atmosphere created by some of Boycott's supporters. There is undoubtedly dissension within the General Committee but it is unfair for those who command the majority in the Committee to seek to put the critics in their place by penalising Boycott.

6. By awarding him a testimonial and at the same time refusing to re-engage him the Club is effectively preventing Boycott from playing first-class cricket next season. He could hardly participate in his testimonial in Yorkshire and play for another county even if he so wished.

7. It would cause embarrassment for all concerned to have Boycott attending matches in a lounge suit to receive his collections if the team should happen to be struggling for runs. The decision could have calamitous financial consequences to the Club in loss of membership, loss of gate money and possible loss of sponsorship.

8. In any case the decision is unnecessary since Boycott has been and is prepared to accept a contract for one more season only at the end of which he would retire as a Yorkshire player with dignity and on a happy note.

9. The decision was reached by way of an unnecessary package. There was not even a separate resolution not to offer Boycott a contract. Instead the members of the General Committee were presented with a composite resolution:-
   (i)   to appoint Bairstow captain, a most popular choice
   (ii) to change the status and function of Illingworth and
   (iii) not to renew Boycott's contract.
   The option before the members of the General Committee was to vote for the whole package or for none of the constituent parts. Boycott's long and distinguished service deserved better treatment.

meeting on 3 December could be ruled invalid in another court.

Bob Appleyard, not then a member of the General Committee, proposed a compromise whereby Yorkshire would give Boycott a new one-year contract on the undertaking that he would be prepared to bat down the order. By then attitudes had hardened and both sides needed confrontation if only to clear the air, although the then chairman of the public relations sub-committee of the club, Julian Vallance, warned that the costs of the SGM, including legal charges, had risen to £25,000.

The new date set was 21 January 1984, an unfortunate delay which saw what amounted to a general election campaign stretching over almost two months, during which considerable bitterness was engendered with both sides holding meetings and conducting publicity campaigns in an effort to win an argument that divided the Ridings as nothing had since perhaps the General Strike of 1926.

'Members '84' sought votes of no confidence in the General Committee and the cricket sub-committee, and the reinstatement of Boycott as a player. Before the meeting the cricket chairman Ronnie Burnet, expanding on a suggestion that the Committee was not bound by the SGM's decisions but only advised, added: 'If we find we are duty-bound to reinstate Boycott we might all resign and seek re-election on the Boycott issue.'

After a four-hour debate Members '84 were victorious on all three issues. The call for Boycott to be reinstated was won by 4115 votes to 3109; the votes of confidence in the General Committee (3609 to 3578) and the cricket sub-committee (3997 to 3209) were both lost, but the margin in all three contests was sufficiently narrow to give the General Committee the confidence to seek re-election en masse.

Doug Ibbotson reported in the *Daily Telegraph*:

On balance the '84 Group provided the more forceful and persuasive oratory and it became apparent from the enthusiastic response to the opening speech by Sid Fielden, a South Yorkshire detective sergeant, that a vast majority of the 1400 members present were on their side.

But if Fielden, who is also a methodist lay preacher, fired the converted with evangelical zeal then the masterly summing up of Brian Walsh, a Queen's Counsel, finally confirmed that the dissidents had carried the day in terms of preparation and delivery.

Despite the intensive lobbying almost 3000 members refused to vote for either side, a possible indication of confusion over the issues and an uneasy sense of an injustice having been done to Boycott – the General Committee's belief that in sacking Boycott and giving him a testimonial they were acting with total propriety and in absolute fairness being a very difficult case to present to members on the periphery of the argument, who were more than a little dismayed at the stark division within the club.

Accordingly the General Committee resigned en bloc and not all offered themselves for re-election, three of the principals, President Norman Yardley, Chairman Michael Crawford and Robin Feather intimating they would not be seeking office again. Most members agreed that the loss of the trio was a heavy price to pay on top of the new meeting cost estimate of £30,000. (This sum almost halved the profit for 1983, announced as £48,000 on 17 February.)

The club, and the county, then faced what amounted to a war of attrition between the beginning of February and 3 March, the date of the AGM, a contest into which added controversy was injected by the news that Boycott was to stand for election to the General Committee as district representative for Wakefield, a constituency represented by Dr John Turner who, it had been thought, was a supporter of Boycott and the general aims of Members '84. Brian Close and Bob Appleyard stood for seats in Bradford and an invitation to stand was even made to the new county captain, David Bairstow.

To ensure that the poll and the counting of votes were beyond criticism, the club engaged a firm of Leeds accountants to conduct the operation and the results were known the evening before the Harrogate AGM: Members '84 swept the board and some of the most famous names in Yorkshire cricket – Trueman, Burnet, Platt, Sutcliffe, Burgin – lost office. Of the old

Committee the only survivors were Raymond Clegg (Bradford), Bryan Stott (Wharfedale) and Phil Sharpe (York), although Close, of the newcomers, was expected to be very much in their camp. Burnet lost Harrogate by only 4 votes, Platt lost Huddersfield by 21 and Sharpe's majority was only 12. Boycott defeated Dr Turner by 56 and he and his supporters were expected to have a substantial majority on the new General Committee.

Peter Briggs, secretary of Members '84 but who was ineligible to stand because of his residence in Manchester, said the group would be disbanded but would 'keep the promises made to Members'. These included the reinstatement of Boycott, who would thus become the first committee member who was also a paid professional of the club, and a promise of more open government, such as the release of committee minutes to members on request. The first meeting of the new General Committee, on 8 March, elected Reg Kirk, a chartered secretary from Hull, as the new Chairman and, a little surprisingly, Close as cricket chairman.

The full impact of the redistribution of power was not felt until later that month when Illingworth's contract was paid up after the second meeting of the new General Commit-

tee. After a six-and-a-half-hour meeting there was obvious dissent, for the newly elected Treasurer, David Welch, resigned and the club dispensed with the tradition of exchanging committee members with the Headingley landlords, the Leeds club, which meant the departure of Norman Shuttleworth. Both Welch and Shuttleworth were regarded as supporters of the old establishment. Welch, who was later to return to the Committee as member for Rotherham, left saying: 'The club is being run by a caucus and I fear to forecast the future.' Close, too, was upset by Illingworth's departure and was reported as saying: 'It's a terrible waste of ability and money.'

Nor did Close receive the cricket sub-committee he was seeking, the only other ex-cricketer joining him being Sharpe, which meant that Close could always be outvoted by the three laymen on the sub-committee and by the Chairman, who had a casting vote, a point of procedure that became very important in the ensuing months. The new Committee's view was that the manager–captain relationship had not worked and that a partnership between Close and Bairstow was the best formula for success on the field.

6

Bairstow to Carrick 1987–1988

No Yorkshireman truly believed that all the troubles and disaffection of the two previous years had been put aside when the players reported for training, amid snow showers, on 25 April 1984, but almost everyone was prepared to give the new regime a trial, while the partnership of Close and Bairstow was granted almost honeymoon status. The difficulty that might arise from having a senior professional in the dressing room who was also the leader of the majority on the General Committee was not overlooked, merely shelved in a sense of common purpose.

Bairstow began his reign by winning from Close an assurance that the captain would pick the team, the cricket chairman having a supervisory role. Peter Townend, a chartered accountant from Halifax, was elected Honorary Treasurer to replace David Welch, while three Colts (Stuart Fletcher, nineteen, a seamer from Lascelles Hall, Ian Swallow, twenty-one, an off-spinning all-rounder from Sheffield United, and Paul Booth, twenty-one, a left-arm spinner and batsman from Huddersfield) were given second-eleven caps at the pre-season lunch, always an indication that they were on the fringe of first-team selection.

Boycott and Moxon were the new opening partnership, Lumb was nominated to fill the departed Athey's place at number three, and, on paper and provided the seam bowlers stayed fit, Yorkshire had good reason to expect a reasonably successful summer. The bowling did not look strong enough to win three-day matches but, as John Player League champions, the side had proved their capability in one-day cricket.

The first match, at Taunton, against Somerset led for the first time by Ian Botham, brought an unexpected victory by three wickets, after two declarations by Botham. Stevenson's bowling broke down but Yorkshire gave an ample declaration of their power in a run chase. It gave Bairstow a fine start, perked up the dressing room and sent the team back to Headingley for a handsome seven-wicket win in the opening Benson and Hedges match against a weakened Leicestershire. Even a defeat in the opening John Player fixture did not dampen spirits, although Bairstow recorded having words with Boycott. Two more victories (one Championship) followed before Sidebottom pulled a hamstring at Edgbaston which meant, half-way through May, that both of Bairstow's principal seam bowlers were injured.

Sidebottom was only just fit enough to return for the Whitsun Roses match, a draw, before Bairstow was selected for the three one-day internationals against West Indies and, to some surprise, Yorkshire settled down apparently amicably under Boycott's captaincy. Two Championship matches were drawn but an astonishing innings by Stevenson, hitting 81 off 29 balls, brought a delayed John Player victory against Somerset at Middlesbrough. In Bairstow's absence the Bradford wicket-keeper Steven Rhodes also won high praise.

Yorkshire entered the Benson and Hedges semi-finals after an encouraging victory at Hove where the young Fletcher, having to bowl the final spell, gave a highly encouraging performance. A draw at Basingstoke in mid June, a match Yorkshire should have won as Hampshire were without both Gordon Greenidge and Malcolm Marshall, dimmed Championship ambitions; but in the next Sunday match an encouraging debut came from a right-hander from Keighley, Phil Robinson, whose sheer weight of runs in the Colts had forced his selection. Metcalfe, too, was making it plain that he could not be contained in second-team cricket.

Bairstow's career as a Yorkshire captain hinged, in the end, on the Benson and Hedges semi-final against Warwickshire at Headingley – which he lost, by 3 runs. Had he taken Yorkshire to their first Lord's final since 1969 the one certain panacea for all Yorkshire's ills – success on the field – would have come in 1984 instead of 1987 and would have satisfied both dressing room and the membership.

Headingley was sold out; Bairstow won the toss and sent in Warwickshire, who scored 276 off the 55 overs. Stevenson, who may not have been a hundred per cent, conceded 70 runs in his 11 overs and the current common fault of all the Yorkshire bowlers, wides and no-balls, helped raise the extras to 19. Boycott fell to Old in Warwickshire's attack, Moxon raised 50 off 81 balls, Sharp rallied the middle and when Bairstow and Stevenson added 71 in 10 overs Yorkshire seemed likely to pull off an astonishing victory. But Stevenson was brilliantly caught on the boundary while Bairstow, aiming for a six, was also caught on the rope by Willis, the only man on either side tall enough to have taken the catch.

Good bowling by two left-hand spinners, Carrick and Booth, brought Yorkshire a Championship victory at Northampton where Moxon suffered a cracked rib that delayed his England debut. By the time Yorkshire met Essex at Leeds at the end of June, four senior players and the promising Fletcher were all absent through injury; by Monday the captain, who had been struggling with an Achilles tendon injury and cracked knuckles, had developed an alarming rash that took him out of the match for the day. Essex totalled 547, their highest against Yorkshire, winning by an innings and 153, the heaviest defeat at Headingley since the opening of the ground in 1891.

A patched-up Yorkshire went down to another ignominious defeat, by 37 runs to minor county Shropshire at Telford, and although weakness through injuries (Moxon, Hartley, Stevenson and Bairstow all played when below par) played a major part in Yorkshire's third humiliation in eleven years, there

was no excuse to be offered afterwards. Gloucestershire were beaten in a run chase at Bradford. To soothe the hurt (Athey scoring a century for Gloucestershire), Boycott passed 45,000 runs in completing his 142nd century (100 in 148 minutes). Yorkshire then had to apologise to Gloucestershire after the Sunday match at Scarborough for the loutish and probably drunken barracking of the English-born black fast bowler David Lawrence.

As the season fell away and success once more became a stranger, the inevitable reaction came off the field. The captain was called to a special meeting of the cricket sub-committee convened to discuss the team's apparent inability to field a fully fit side. Rumours also floated of a Boycott return to the captaincy, but the man himself killed those instantly by saying that eight years in that job was long enough. He was also honest enough to admit that he would not refuse the job of team manager, were it to be offered.

At the end of August the media seized upon what looked like another flare-up at The Oval when Yorkshire had to take the field without Boycott and Moxon, both declared unfit on the morning of the Championship match against Surrey, a match that Yorkshire went on to lose by an innings and 195. According to the tabloid newspapers the cricket chairman was hurrying south to investigate; according to the captain Close had a business appointment in London and his presence at The Oval was planned. Yorkshire's opening batsmen in that match were Metcalfe and opening bowler Sidebottom.

An innings victory over Derbyshire at Chesterfield lifted morale, Sharp, Robinson and Metcalfe all contributing useful performances, yet perhaps the true barometer of Yorkshire's fortunes lay in the fact that there were as many reporters at Barnsley, where Boycott was playing in the second team to prove his fitness, as at Queen's Park.

By then the so-called 'dual role' controversy had taken wings and Close, as cricket chairman, was known to be opposed to giving Boycott another contract as a player while he remained a member of the General Committee. On 12 September the General Committee met and later announced that all the first-team players would be given new two-year contracts and that Boycott and Colin Johnson, the latter becoming a successful Colts captain, would be awarded one-year contracts. A decision on reappointing Bairstow as captain was deferred.

It was obvious that Close was on a collision course with the majority of the General Committee, and the significant decisions came at the end of October when the cricket chairman's proposal, echoing a newspaper opinion of Illingworth's that if Boycott was to remain a Committee man he should also be captain, was dismissed.

A new President emerged, no one having been found to fill the vacancy since Yardley's resignation (although approaches were reportedly made to Lord Hanson and Sir Harold Wilson) in Viscount Mountgarret, Yorkshire-born and formerly of Eton and the Irish Guards. Lord Mountgarret was known to be a keen cricket-lover who managed his own estate near Ripon and who would have time for the club's affairs. Of much more immediate interest to Yorkshire at large was the appearance of a sudden rift in the dominant majority on the General Committee, with Sid Fielden and Brian Walsh, architects of the 1983 revolution, both publicly attacking Boycott's dual role.

On the vexed question of captaincy a proposal was passed, by 11 votes to 10, asking Bairstow to continue to lead the side as a batsman, thus making room for Steven Rhodes who, it was clear, would not be content to stay much longer in the Colts. The meeting was interrupted while Close consulted Bairstow and when the latter refused to give up the gauntlets the Committee voted 16–5 to reappoint him captain without qualification.

On 30 October Close resigned from the cricket sub-committee with England selector Phil Sharpe following suit a day later. On the same day another group of members, opposed to the General Committee and led by former committee members Desmond Bailey and Bob Platt, later to be known as 'Yorkshire Cricket Devotees', was launched; a year's uneasy peace was over. One of the newer committee men, allegedly a Boycott supporter, burst out: 'I'd

rather breed pigeons than speak to newspapers, to be truthful.'

By 9 November Close had also resigned his General Committee seat, using his freedom to attack Chairman Reg Kirk and the majority of the General Committee, saying he had been 'used by a Boycott-dominated committee'. He accused Bairstow of 'hitching his wagon to Boycott's star', but then softened the blow by telling the Yorkshire Post: 'I felt that David had had a rough ride for the simple reason that he did not know who his boss was. He owed his allegiance to Geoff because if he did not protect him his power could guarantee Bairstow's days as captain were numbered.' Kirk reacted by saying that 'we have never had the slightest difficulty in controlling Boycott. If Brian Close thinks he cannot control him then he should get off the Committee.'

The rise of 'Yorkshire Devotees' kept in being Yorkshire Members '84 and both sides were soon issuing statements to rally support. Sid Fielden's criticism of the dual role brought him a letter from Boycott's solicitor asking him to stay away from a meeting of Boycott's supporters in Ripon, while by the end of November Rhodes was given formal permission to join Worcestershire, a decision that was to be attacked bitterly and frequently over the next few years.

Close joined the Devotees, and Sharpe attacked the Members '84 for allegedly leaking Committee information. Another blow for the Committee was a TCCB decision, announced on 12 December, that Headingley would no longer occupy a permanent place on the Test-match rota, a sharp slap to Yorkshire pride which brought further criticism upon the head of Chairman Kirk, the club's chief delegate at the meeting. The year ended with the Devotees (at that time known, to the huge delight of the media, as the 'Lovers') proposing another vote of no confidence in the Committee for the AGM on 2 March, adding further resolutions designed to strengthen the central government of the club and making it more difficult to call special general meetings.

The season of goodwill was barely over in January 1985 when, in the first week, slates of candidates were announced for Committee elections and the first hint of a pendulum swing came in the news that five committee members generally regarded as either anti-Boycott or moderate had been returned unopposed.

The publication of a letter to Chairman Kirk, from an elderly lady member, alleging financial payments to Sidney Fielden, brought a further escalation of the war of words. Fielden, after an unhappy forty-eight hours, emerged with one of the memorable statements of the whole war: 'He [Boycott] is a very great cricketer. I wish I had never met him.'

Amid the threats of further legal action, with the piquant possibility of Brian Walsh QC acting on Fielden's behalf against Boycott's lawyers, the news that David Byas, a twenty-one-year-old strong left-hander with a prolific record for Scarborough, had been given a contract was almost unnoticed. By the end of January no fewer than 31 resolutions, mostly dealing with rule changes, had been tabled for the AGM and the Committee then set up a rules revision sub-committee charged with the task of sifting wheat from chaff and drawing up acceptable changes for the AGM, a move that was predictably denounced as an attempt by the Devotees to 'prolong Boycott's tenure on the Committee for another year'.

In fact the rules sub-committee, composed of the President, Chairman, the club's new solicitor Duncan Mutch and three members of the General Committee, was an attempt to balance the views of both factions. Lord Mountgarret was at that time very much an unknown quantity on the Boycott issue, although it was very plain to those of us who had interviewed him that he had absolutely no intention of being merely an ornamental figurehead. The Viscount had the military man's direct, even abrupt approach to problems and was not averse, as he confided, 'to knocking a few heads together if necessary'. It was obvious from the start that whatever power he gained, or was granted, would be used forcefully.

Boycott meanwhile went back to his constituency to receive the endorsement of the Wakefield members, reiterating that even if the Devotees did enforce a change of rule that prevented a player from serving on the Committee he would resign his seat, a stance that was loudly applauded in the hall.

Yorkshire Television tried to get Kirk and Close to debate the issue in a studio, Kirk declaring 'I'm determined to avoid any unnecessary contention,' Close refusing to meet the designated substitute Peter Briggs. In Northampton a group of touring Yorkshire rugby players were refused an extra round of drinks, the landlord's excuse being: 'Any more and you'll be fighting among yourselves.' The Committee, opening the election campaign, pointed out that the membership figure had risen; the *Daily Telegraph* suggested that recruits might not be joining for the cricket.

By that time the *Yorkshire Post* could have awarded the cricket letters from readers a half-page every day, so heavy was the flow and urge to contribute to the debate. Ten days before the AGM cricket recovered a little ground when the club announced that Johnny Wardle, then aged sixty-two, would be appointed a bowling coach from 1 March and would accompany the team on away matches as a guide and counsellor to the captain, an appointment that implied that the future of the senior professional might be in doubt. Blakey and Booth returned from a Young England tour of West Indies as considerably more experienced players, while former captain John Hampshire reappeared as the manager of a new indoor cricket school in Sheffield.

On 26 February the new President entered the lists for the first time with a typically forthright denunciation of committee members who criticised the club: 'What I deprecate is that certain members have resorted to actions that undermine the running of the club. Eventually it might be necessary to suspend members from the Committee.'

Another row flared up on the evening of the AGM after the Committee had refused to include an amendment from the Devotees on the agenda, but threats of legal action did not materialise. The election results, announced before the meeting, were pronounced a 2–2 draw: the Devotees won seats in Bradford (Close being re-elected) and in Sheffield but failed to win Hull (where Kirk was re-elected) or Craven (Trueman's former seat).

The 1985 AGM took up most of Saturday in

Leeds. The Committee survived the confidence vote (545 to 297) in the hall, more narrowly outside, but were attacked so fiercely over their proposal to refer all the rule changes to the sub-committee (three lawyers warning them of legal pitfalls) that they agreed to hold another special general meeting in Harrogate on 30 March purely to discuss rule changes and, in effect, the drawing up of a new constitution. The one clear winner was the new President who, swinging a bat, declared: 'This is not for hitting each other but for knocking other counties for six' – an act that might have come from Churchill, Montgomery or Hailsham but one that went down magnificently with the membership who, it was clear, saw in Mountgarret the long-sought unifying figure.

The Committee did take advantage of their restored power by re-appointing Kirk as Chairman, defeating Brian Walsh's challenge by 11 votes to 8, removing Fielden from the chair of the public relations sub-committee, Peter Quinn (North Riding) taking over and blocking Close's path back to the cricket sub-committee, Tony Vann (Leeds), a regular club cricketer but without first-class experience, replacing him. The Committee also changed solicitors after the débacle over the rules revision.

By then a majority of the General Committee were highly sensitive to attack on two points: the cost of yet another special general meeting, estimated between £5000 and £8000, and uncertainty over the propriety of the 'dual role'. Could an employer be also an employee without accepting the full responsibility and power of becoming managing director (if the constitution of the club were to provide such a position)?

At that point, towards the end of March 1985, Mountgarret intervened again, held talks with both camps and persuaded them both to cancel the SGM, to instruct the rules sub-committee to continue with their task and then, when a new constitution had been drawn up, submit it to legal opinion. The President warned that his compromise was vulnerable to a legal challenge from any member, but by then it seemed that both sides were seeking a way out of the impasse.

No attempt was made to force the SGM and a month later a referendum of members, in which only a third bothered to vote, gave a clear majority to a change of rule that would end the 'dual role' controversy. As Yorkshire returned for practice in April – Bairstow having taken the contracted players for a fitness training course with the army at Catterick – a change in the selection procedure was announced, the final word going to a selection sub-committee of cricket chairman Tony Vann, captain David Bairstow and senior professional Boycott.

A new rules revision sub-committee was set up under the President, consisting of the Chairman (Kirk), the Treasurer (Peter Charles) and General Committee members Peter Quinn, Brian Walsh QC, Tony Cawdry (Halifax) and Tim Reed (Sheffield), the last-named a solicitor – a reasonable representation of both sides. At the annual pre-season lunch Bairstow delivered a strong speech on behalf of the dressing room: 'We are not pawns in a chess game with the prize an end to our credibility. This club was formed to play cricket, not to become a debating society . . . there is no doubt that the differences of opinion off the field have, and will continue to have, an adverse effect on the players.' Cricket chairman Vann also struck a controversial note when he declared: 'We shall be more impressed with a rapid, match-winning 70 under pressure than with a five-hour century on a shirt-front.'

Bairstow began the 1985 summer with, once again on paper, a reasonably strong side: in fitness and in form he had six first-class seamers, Sidebottom, Stevenson (both of whom played for England), Dennis, Jarvis (who would play for England), Fletcher and Chris Shaw, a right-arm fast-medium bowler from Hemsworth who, at twenty, had made an impressive debut in 1984, his forte being accuracy. Those players represented the best all-English attack in county cricket, but Bairstow's difficulty was in keeping them fit and he was bedevilled by a succession of serious breakdowns during the summer. A sprained wrist caused Boycott to miss early matches, giving an unexpected opportunity to Richard Blakey, aged eighteen, from Elland, a right-handed

Richard Blakey

Richard John Blakey, born in Huddersfield and a graduate of the Elland Club, was a correct right-hand batsman of excellent temperament who first made his name for his ability to make big scores: at eighteen he scored a record 273 not out for the Colts and at age twenty scored 204 not out against Gloucestershire for the first team. In 1987, his first full season, he scored 1387 runs, including four centuries, a performance that evoked comparisons with the young Hutton and led to his being elected Young Cricketer of the Year.

Blakey was also a useful and improving wicket-keeper and in 1988 when he, and most Yorkshire batsmen, had a difficult time and lost form, was used more often as a keeper, at one point that summer displacing Bairstow.

batsman whose obvious class had already been demonstrated for Young England. Blakey was also rumoured to be a useful wicket-keeper, a valuable talent after Rhodes' departure for Worcestershire.

Boycott's testimonial, it was revealed in May, raised almost £150,000, a testimony of the esteem in which he was held by the public at large. Blakey shone in a drawn Roses match at Old Trafford; by the beginning of June the Yorkshire attack (against Viv Richards and Somerset) had been stricken again, the responsibility being carried by Fletcher, Jarvis, Booth and Carrick, only the last-named being capped. Shaw and a nineteen-year-old all-rounder from Cleckheaton, Chris Pickles, were drafted in to score a notable Sunday victory over Hampshire at Middlesbrough, Boycott returning and, in characteristic fashion, scoring centuries in successive Championship matches. A century against the touring Australians at Headingley was a gilt-edged certainty, but a reasonably serene if inconsistent summer flared into argument at Harrogate.

Asked to score 271 in what became 59 overs by Worcestershire, who dangled the carrot, Yorkshire meandered to 124 for 3, Boycott finishing on 64 not out. Bairstow made an attempt to score runs quickly but he was isolated and was reported to be 'shaking with

anger afterwards', but the Committee took no action and what could have become another Northampton, or Cheltenham, was this time filed away for possible use as ammunition. Cricket chairman Vann said that 'in the view of the senior players the target was high by 20 or 30 runs'.

Bairstow unleashed some of his frustrations with a century before lunch against Leicestershire at Bradford, his fourth first-class; Sidebottom went off to play for England and collected another injury, and three successive defeats in July sent Yorkshire to the bottom of the Championship table. The team's last hope of recognition in 1985, the Nat-West competition, ended with a contentious defeat by Somerset at Headingley after which the Somerset captain Ian Botham provoked a diplomatic incident by accusing a section of the Leeds crowd of making racist remarks about Viv Richards. Richards had affected to walk after an appeal for a catch behind, but had returned to end premature Yorkshire celebrations and effectively win the tie. The umpire said afterwards that he had neither seen nor heard a snick, which should have ended the matter, but Botham's radio statement and Yorkshire's reactions blew up another media storm.

By the end of July Yorkshire were settled into bottom place in the Championship, 105 points behind the leaders Middlesex but with, the optimists pointed out, two games in hand. Boycott, Moxon and Phil Robinson batted well enough at Worksop to avert what would have been four defeats in five Championship matches, while the captain hit his third undefeated century of the summer against Derbyshire at Bradford, the spinners Carrick and Swallow then completing a victory that lifted the team six places.

Early in August the *Daily Telegraph* reported that Derbyshire were proposing that each county be allowed to play two overseas professionals, a move that immediately brought rumours that Yorkshire were considering abandoning their 120-year tradition of fielding only native-born players. Bairstow, Boycott and most of the players were said to be in favour and although the last referendum of members had voted 90 per cent against, the notion that all other counties would be allowed two world-class players put pressure upon Yorkshire to compete by fielding, at the very least, one outsider. The suggestion floated in the Yorkshire media was that Yorkshire should insist on all players being born within the county with the one exception.

On the eve of the Headingley Roses match the first fruits of the rules revision sub-committee's work were revealed, to be decided upon at the next AGM in February 1986: the club would be governed on a daily basis by a Management Committee under the President, who would have a much more executive role; no player would be able to serve as a committee member once existing contracts expired (i.e. Boycott could continue in the dual role until 1987); and 400 members at least, not 2.5 per cent of the membership, would be required to sign a requisition for a special general meeting.

So serious was Yorkshire's casualty list that another seam bowler had to be drafted in from the leagues – Peter Hartley, a strong right-hander from Heighley who was twenty-five and who had served Warwickshire for a spell. The fact that Yorkshire, once the nursery for a quarter of English domestic cricketers, were having to take up players rejected by other counties did not pass without comment, but in fairness to Hartley he did learn quickly, made

excellent contributions with bat and ball and not undeservedly won a county cap. Hartley was a diligent cricketer even if lack of consistency was one of his hallmarks, bringing as it did the nickname 'Somedays', originating, according to his captain, in the phrase 'Some days he does, some days he don't.'

The pressure on Bairstow, knowing his position was under threat, caused him to respond with the best batting of his career; but he also kept wicket when, by his own later admission, he was far from fully fit. Due to the battle against injury, both personal and of the team, seeking to take the side up the table, and his own individual effort – the *Daily Telegraph* described Bairstow's three-year captaincy as 'a series of uphill cavalry charges' – he became short-tempered over moments of sheer bad luck, clashed with umpires and was officially reprimanded. The TCCB sub-committee followed this with a suspension from four John Player League matches, but Bairstow's bristling endeavour and unflagging effort in the end took Yorkshire to eleventh in the table, an improvement of three positions on 1984 and a far better finish than the public would have expected after the nadir of July. Hartley finished with five for 75 against Nottinghamshire at Scarborough, he and Fletcher carrying a burden in the closing weeks that was far beyond their experience.

The winter of 1985–6 was the quietest for years, possibly an indication of the President's success in keeping continuing arguments under cover. The first move towards setting up a new indoor cricket school was made with a brisk debate, which did reach the media, on the relative merits of siting the school at either Headingley or Park Avenue. If Leeds won the contest, it was predicted, Bradford might lose first-class cricket.

Bairstow's disciplinary appeal resulted in what amounted to a deferred sentence: his suspension from four John Player League games was to take effect only if he was involved in further disciplinary action before the end of 1987. Strains surfaced between President Mountgarret and Chairman Kirk, especially over the club's reaction to the Somerset Botham–Richards furore – Kirk wanted the matter referred to the TCCB – and the Chairman only just survived a confidence vote (11–11) in September, the President refusing to use a casting vote on what he considered to be a 'personal matter'.

Bairstow was relieved to be given another season as captain; Boycott was given another one-year contract; contracts were also awarded to Shaw, Hartley and Pickles while Oldham replaced Colin Johnson as second-team captain, and the club and the Committee reiterated their commitment to fielding only Yorkshire-born players.

November brought the sad news that Park Avenue, with the Bradford club £50,000 in debt and little hope of further aid from the local authorities, was in danger of closure. By 1 December a further twelve months' reprieve had been won, but only through the generosity of a hard-pressed Bradford City Council. The Yorkshire club was offered the ground but was chary of taking on such a huge commitment, especially when it was clear that all the support that was required for the new indoor school was available at a site across the road from the Headingley Ground in Leeds.

By late December the General Committee had agreed, by 14 to 3, to put the new constitution before the AGM, by then arranged for the following March, but one member, Peter Fretwell (Craven), resigned in some anger, saying: 'The club is in a ridiculous situation when meetings are dominated by personal abuse.'

Almost immediately it became clear that President Mountgarret and Chairman Kirk were on diametrically opposite paths. Kirk, referring to the new constitution, told the *Yorkshire Post*: 'The only reason the package of rules is being bludgeoned through is to get rid of a forty-five-year-old cricketer.' Mountgarret retorted on 20 December by saying that 'if Mr Kirk cannot accept majority decisions then he has no course but to resign'. Mountgarret also accepted that if the new constitution were rejected at the AGM then he, too, would have to leave office.

Two days into 1986 Kirk resigned the chairmanship of the General Committee (although keeping his Hull seat), saying: 'I have been disgusted with the personal attacks directed against me.' He added that he wanted freedom

to campaign against the new constitution. A day later the club announced that four committee members – Jack Sokell (Barnsley), Sid Fielden (Doncaster), Phillip Akroyd (Dewsbury) and David Drabble (Sheffield) – had been returned unopposed. In a critical situation when every vote was vital, what had once been parochial elections were scrutinised with almost Parliamentary attention.

At snow-covered Headingley on 9 January the President was confirmed as caretaker Chairman, but news was received that an alternative set of rules, put forward by Mr Kirk's group, would be proposed at the AGM, then set for 22 February, a move that had both sides consulting lawyers once more. At an emergency meeting on 19 February three of the dissidents, Peter Quinn, Peter Charles and Roy Ickringill, were effectively barred from a General Committee that voted 11 to 4 with two abstentions to turn itself into a sub-committee of those supporting the new constitution. There was an angry response from those barred, Ickringill complaining: 'We are faced with a naked dictatorship.'

Quinn resigned as public relations chairman, adding, 'We've seen nothing like this since Lord Hawke's time.' January ended on a knife-edge: the club was threatened by legal action both by those who wanted the alternative constitution on the AGM agenda and also by their opponents who intended to claim that they were being prevented from putting amendments to the alternative constitution. The *Daily Telegraph* commented, a little wearily: 'It is a case worthy of King Solomon whose adjudication might be, from precedent, the setting up of two Yorkshire clubs, Boycottshire and Othershire.' The Committee, with little option, elected to go ahead with their own agenda and risk court action.

The General Committee member for Huddersfield, Tony Ramsden, a popular and respected man who had defeated Bob Platt in 1983, died unexpectedly in the month of the AGM, while more distress calls were heard from Park Avenue where, it became clear, Bradford City Council's offer of £15,000 would not be enough to save the ground. News of the closure came on the eve of the AGM, acting perhaps as a sharp reminder to the 11,000 club members that civil war inevitably brings some form of devastation in its wake. A united club might have been able to devote more attention, and resources, to keeping Park Avenue alive, although heroic efforts were made by two of the Committee's Bradford representatives, Raymond Clegg and Appleyard.

Boycott was in Jamaica when the 1986 AGM took place in the City Hall, Sheffield – an absence that brought derisive comments from his opponents in the hall. The meeting was a landslide for Mountgarret, 92 per cent of the 35 per cent of members voting backing the President and the new constitution. By the following Tuesday Close was restored to the job of cricket chairman, Fielden to public relations, Tony Cawdry became the new finance chairman, while the new General Committee chairman was the Queen's Counsel Brian Walsh, whose witty and forceful speaking made him the outstanding candidate. Almost as an aside, Park Avenue's three Championship matches were transferred to Headingley.

Boycott then had a summer in which to decide whether to seek to continue his playing career, at forty-five, with another contract, or resign his seat on the General Committee. The new cricket chairman Close promised that captain Bairstow would be able to command the team in 1986 'without interference or favours – he will certainly be tested this year without someone more powerful than him in his own team'.

Almost the first move of the new government was to designate 1987 as a benefit year for the club, the immediate target being to raise £200,000 towards the £500,000 needed to build the new indoor school at Leeds. The City Council offered £115,000 in exchange for partial use during school hours, and the departing metropolitan West Yorkshire Council deserve to be fondly remembered for their gift of £100,000.

An indication of future planning, before the season began, came with the appointment of Phil Carrick as vice-captain to Bairstow. A studious player, Carrick was a skilful left-arm bowler whose career had been restrained by covered pitches and one-day matches but who

had developed into a very useful late-order batsman of excellent defensive technique. On the Committee two vacancies were filled by men who could be described as Mountgarret supporters, Bob Platt recovering his old seat in Huddersfield while Reg Kirk's unexpected resignation in Hull opened the way for Geoffrey Denton; for good or ill the club was being steered in one direction.

Despite Boycott's absence the Championship began, as it had in Bairstow's first year of captaincy, with an exciting victory at Taunton, Somerset just failing to score 324 in what became 75 overs, Peter Hartley's diving boundary catch bringing a win by 5 runs off the last delivery. One-day victories over Somerset (John Player League) and Lancashire (Benson and Hedges), the second by eight wickets (Moxon 106, Boycott 55), brought a stirring first ten days to the summer, the shadow of continual crisis fleeing in a sunburst of success that sent a sense of well-being flooding through the club, members and supporters.

By 10 May, after another nerve-tingling victory over Sussex by one wicket with five balls to spare, Yorkshire actually led the Championship table; a fifth successive victory was a John Player win at The Oval, the run coming to an end in a Benson and Hedges zonal defeat, by 8 runs, at Trent Bridge. The Nottinghamshire victory also cost Boycott a pulled hamstring and the end of what had been a valuable opening partnership with Moxon. Uncertainty was the root cause of a vital defeat by Worcestershire, four batsmen being run out, in another Benson and Hedges competition at Headingley, costing a place in the quarter-finals, and Yorkshire lost their Championship lead at Chelmsford in late May when Essex won another exciting contest by 26 runs with 38 balls remaining.

Headingley, for the Roses match, had a touch of old times about it, for Lancashire and Yorkshire were first and second in the table. Jarvis emphasised his growing power, at twenty, with a return of five for 60 (following his six for 78 against Essex), but the match became a ninth successive draw in the series, the final day being remembered for a 55 mph gale that took caps, bails and (according to the *Yorkshire Evening*

Post) even a chair, under grey cloud. Ireland were well chastised at Malahide, 'maintaining Yorkshire's unbeaten sequence in this fixture' the *Yorkshire Post* noted wryly.

Jarvis went on to record match figures of eleven for 92 against Middlesex at Lord's, the best performance by a bowler there since Wardle's twelve for 90 in 1950, and with Sharpe and Metcalfe, the latter blossoming even beyond his admirers' expectations, Yorkshire remained second throughout June.

Five successive draws were punctuated by Boycott's 150th century at Middlesbrough (passing Sutcliffe) and Sidebottom returning a career-best eight for 72, but injuries to Stevenson and Sidebottom again weakened the bowling and although both Metcalfe and Jarvis had excellent summers the momentum could not be maintained, the final position of tenth being a disappointment after so many high hopes in May.

In all ten successive matches were drawn, but the batting remained solid – never more so than when Moxon and Metcalfe raised 282, the second highest in Roses history, at Old Trafford. Metcalfe scored six centuries in his 1803 runs and he and Jarvis were both capped.

7

A Crown of Thorns: Looking to the Future

The autumn of 1986 was one of speculation. The club's new constitution meant that Boycott had to choose between remaining a member of the General Committee or continuing as a player and there was considerable interest in a notion that he would remain as the representative for Wakefield but appear for Derbyshire. In the event he retired from cricket and ended an era.

Would Bairstow remain as captain? There had been several disagreements over team selection between the captain and the cricket chairman, Brian Close, culminating in the chairman overruling the captain over the choice of team for a John Player League match against Warwickshire, in the event Bairstow was forced to surrender Chris Shaw to the Yorkshire XI for the Under-25 Final at Edgbaston, not a happy augury for a future season.

Who would succeed Bairstow if a change was made? Boycott was firmly favoured in one quarter, the next senior professional Carrick in another. A third view was that Bairstow should be given another year without Boycott in the dressing room. Not until 15 November was the decision made when the General Committee endorsed 12–7 a 5 to 1 decision by the cricket sub-committee that Carrick, at thirty-four should replace Bairstow, thirty-five. Close explained: 'We have no doubt that David's wicket-keeping suffered over the last season because of his extra responsibilities.'

Carrick was shrewd enough to realise that he was inheriting the crown of thorns at a more opportune moment than most of his immediate predecessors. Boycott, for good or ill, had departed and, wrote David Hopps in the *Yorkshire Post*, 'the county possesses the best crop of youngsters for a generation in terms of ability

but even more strikingly in attitude. They are all ready to learn.'

The year ended with Boycott's announcement that he had rejected the offer of a two-year contract with Derbyshire (a planned autobiography was due to be published which would have been subject to TCCB scrutiny had he remained a player), adding that he believed Lord Mountgarret and certain committee members were trying to 'hound me out of the club'. Carrick's captaincy thus began under critical eyes from the boundary.

In February the new Indoor School at Headingley, costing £500,000, 'a shiny green and white palace bigger than the Lord's school' according to *The Independent*, was opened, bringing Yorkshire's players into practice earlier than any previous year. Boycott was re-elected to the Committee and Carrick, the club's sixth captain in nine years, began with a personal point in his favour: the TCCB, by a narrow majority, agreed to uncover pitches for an experimental season. As the run-ups were left covered and the summer was mostly cold and dry the trial was inconclusive and the batting lobby reversed the decision for 1988.

By the second week in May Yorkshire had won four matches, including two in the Championship, and by the following week the sequence had been stretched to seven straight wins. Not until 23 May, with Somerset hanging on in their second innings at 61 for 7, was the gallop stopped in the Championship, although the Benson and Hedges surge continued, a nine-wicket victory over Hampshire (Metcalfe and Blakey hitting 100 in 22 overs) taking them into the semi-final.

Yorkshire were drawn against Surrey at what had become happy Headingley. Greig, the

Surrey captain, followed the accepted one-day pattern by asking Yorkshire to bat first, Moxon responding with a superb 97 from 160 deliveries while Love, foreshadowing his Final form, went to 40 in 19 balls, hitting three sixes. With firm support from Bairstow, Yorkshire raised 238. The Surrey innings, interrupted by the weather, stretched into Friday after the second day had been lost to rain, the Yorkshire seam bowlers dismissing them for 162 in the 49th over.

By early June, despite the intervention of rain and gloom, Yorkshire had joined Lancashire as joint Championship leaders but in the Roses match at Old Trafford there was a rare outburst from Jack Simmons after Yorkshire had held on to draw, the last pair, Blakey and Stuart Fletcher, staying for 18 overs. Simmons claimed that Fletcher had been caught at silly point off his bowling; umpire David Evans turned down the appeal but Lancashiremen continued to claim that Fletcher was out.

A nine-wicket victory in murky Headingley put Yorkshire on top of the Championship table at the end of June but the unfamiliar strain, for that team, of seeking two prizes simultaneously, became evident. Northamptonshire, the other Benson and Hedges finalists, gave the Yorkshire bowling a fearful thrashing at Northampton where, asked to score 283 to win in 45 overs, the target was achieved by seven wickets with nine balls to spare (Jarvis one for 85, Sidebottom one for 66). Worse followed at Trent Bridge, where Nottinghamshire won in two days, on this occasion the Yorkshire batting collapsing, but a comfortable nine-wicket victory over Glamorgan at Headingley did much to calm nerves before the fateful sunny morning at Lord's.

Northamptonshire were sent in to bat and lost Cook, Larkins, Bailey and Lamb for 92 runs to the opening burst of Jarvis, but Fletcher and Peter Hartley were punished in a stand of 120 by Capel and Williams and the eventual total of 244 meant Yorkshire's batsmen had to average more than 4 runs an over to win. An opening stand of 97 by Moxon and Metcalfe gave them the necessary foundation; there was a tremor in the middle when Williams took

three wickets while only 6 runs were scored, but Love's batting was reassuring and confident and although the scores were tied Yorkshire took the handsome Cup, amid great jubilation, by losing fewer wickets.

A senior Northamptonshire official, trailing despondently down the stairs in the Lord's pavilion at the conclusion, was not cheered by a greeting from an equally senior MCC official: 'Hard luck, old man, that you should lose by such a margin, but cricket needed a Yorkshire victory.'

Boycott's absence from the club's happiest day for almost twenty years was much remarked upon and Carrick clashed with reporters at the post-match press conference when he assumed they were trying to make him say that the team was improved because of Boycott's absence.

The team took a long and merry coach ride north to win a John Player League match against Middlesex before a cheering Scarborough crowd, but the following week they knew they were back with the steel and sawdust, Surrey bowling them out for 121 at The Oval as a prelude to what would have been a substantial victory but for rain. The next fixture, against Sussex at Hastings, a contest in which Yorkshire would have been hoping for victory, was washed out entirely and by the time the next Roses match was due, in the remaining days of July, Yorkshire were still the Championship leaders but by only one point from Northamptonshire, who had three games in hand.

The Headingley square, under fire for much of the summer for its alleged inconsistencies, had been treated to a heavy rolling by a machine of several tons' weight which must have persuaded any lurking devils to scamper off sharply for all bowlers had next to no help for the remaining month of the 1987 season and with Yorkshire also due on that other batting pitch, Scarborough, any real hope of the Championship faded rapidly; for them to have won their first Championship since 1968 they needed to sustain a higher performance level than was possible and, more important, for their challengers to falter. Nottinghamshire, with Rice and Hadlee in their ranks for a last summer, made certain of plucking the rose.

The season ended with Headingley being reassured that Test matches would continue to be played on its controversial surface, although the visit of the TCCB's Inspector of Pitches was an obvious warning.

That winter, 1987–8, brought the introduction of mixed three- and four-day matches in the Championship but restored the covering of pitches. The next summer was a deep disappointment for Carrick and all those who believed a genuine revival had taken place, a fall from eighth to thirteenth in the Championship table and meagre results in the one-day competitions combining to restore the clouds over the club and revive muted criticism of the Committee.

The weather was little help, the defence of the Benson and Hedges Cup starting with a match at Headingley, against smarting finalists Northamptonshire, that was washed out.

The start in the Championship was a painful one, three successive matches being lost in what became the worst start in the club's history. What had been regarded as the strongest department in the team, the batting, collapsed time and again on what were, unarguably, poor surfaces but in circumstances in which previous Yorkshire teams, penetrative in bowling and relishing such conditions, would have thrived at the expense of the opposition.

In an effort to restore confidence Carrick shook up the order, moving Metcalfe down and dropping Blakey altogether, trying various opening combinations including giving a long spell to the Sheffield United all-rounder Ian Swallow. Even when Yorkshire did play themselves into a winning position, as against Hampshire at Middlesbrough at the beginning of June, rain robbed them of both the points and a chance to restore confidence.

An interesting finish at Northampton, that could easily have brought Yorkshire another success, also ended in early rain, and a defeat by Warwickshire at Headingley, their first double over Yorkshire since 1951, took Carrick's team to the foot of the Championship table. At that point, in late June, Carrick had scored the second most runs (273) and topped the batting averages, Moxon the senior batsman was averaging 26, while Blakey, the wonder of 1987, was averaging just 13.

June did not pass, however, without relief and on the 29th, at Hove, the first win of the season was recorded only to be followed by another trouncing, from Middlesex at Lord's. An unexpected victory in a run chase against Leicestershire, third placed, at Headingley was made the more welcome by the fact that it was accomplished without the fast-improving Jarvis whose back, strained again at Hove, cost him both a possible place in the Third Test match and the rest of the summer for Yorkshire.

Yet from the nadir of Lord's the team, buttressed by the hard-working seam trio of Sidebottom, in his benefit year, Fletcher, who was to win his cap for his efforts, and Shaw, rallied well. The batting settled into recognisable form, Philip Robinson improved sufficiently to win his cap, the strong Scarborough left-hander David Byas, after years apparently beyond the fringe, forced his way into regular contention for a place, and especially pleasing to the traditionalists was the sight of Paul Booth, the Colts' left-arm spinner, winning a place by the strength of both his bowling and batting.

In late July Yorkshire narrowly failed to defeat the next champions, Worcestershire, losing by 21 runs in a last-afternoon chase through a drizzle. Even more satisfying and uplifting was a thorough thrashing of Lancashire, by ten wickets in two days at Headingley, a result that even Hawke would not have sniffed at; injuries had removed both Lancashire's opening bowlers but Yorkshire's win was achieved by some hard and sensible cricket, a re-affirmation of the principles of attacking play.

At Abbeydale the then current champions Nottinghamshire avoided a follow-on by 7 runs and a summer that had begun in abject gloom was brightened by the autumn when, in a welcome gesture, Bairstow was restored to the wicket-keeping and Blakey to his batting, enabling the keeper to take his one thousandth victim for Yorkshire. The gesture might have been sentimental but was justified, for few players had better expressed the character of Yorkshire cricket, during their careers, than Bairstow.

As 1988 ended there was a certain familiarity about events: there was an argument continuing over the use of one ground for first-class cricket (a ground staff and 'academy' were planned to help revive Park Avenue), discussion about strengthening the team (even a proposal to recruit Viv Richards was aired) and conversations about improving the government of the club. It was even suggested in one corner that the Duke of York should stand for election against Lord Mountgarret for the presidency, but the House of Windsor had the good sense and discretion not to become involved.

Yorkshire traditions die hard, as a brewery discovered when they tried to remove the portrait of Richard III from an inn sign and replace 'The King's Head' with that of Henry VIII. Such was the uproar in Malton that they soon backed down.

The key question facing the club in the last decade of the twentieth century was that of adaptation. The birthright qualification had served the club splendidly and remained a source of great pride to players, members and the Yorkshire public, but would a new and perhaps more cosmopolitan generation continue to accept the self-imposed handicap that prevented recruitment from outside the county?

When, in 1988, Hampshire fielded a cricketer who had been actually born inside the boundary the news was broadcast with some astonishment and delight; even Lancashire, with all the resources of a County Palatine, were progressing to the point where almost half their staff had been born elsewhere.

By judicious manipulation of the rules it was possible for a county club to engage as many as a half-dozen top-class players born overseas; London, with its highly energetic West Indian population, began supplying a steady stream of British-born or qualified cricketers, recruiting areas denied Yorkshire.

When a player lost form, or heart, became ill or simply too old, sixteen county clubs could immediately register another. Yorkshire had to wait until another youngster emerged from the Colts and while the waiting was not too long in the more leisured days of purely Championship cricket, when skills and experience could be accumulated steadily, in the more frenetic world of three one-day competitions, one of which began in April, a boy's confidence could be shattered in ten days. All counties found great difficulty in producing young English players of outstanding ability, but only Yorkshire could not help fill the gaps from outside.

English cricket needed Yorkshire to succeed, but when days in the sun were so few and far between, the chill of repeated failure began to gnaw at Yorkshire bones.

Elsewhere the game continued to act as both manual and mirror to the society it served. The South African schism was cricket's struggle for equality; Lancashire tried hard to persuade its male members to allow females into the pavilion while on Easter Sunday in Wombwell, one of the heartlands, Canon David Hawkins was reported to have surprised his parishioners by taking guard in front of the altar and hitting a number of soft-ball deliveries down the aisle. "I told a parable about cricket," he explained.

And in Manhattan, Brooklyn, Queen's and the Bronx, the four New York City boroughs in which the crack-cocaine epidemic was raging, a scheme was announced to encourage youngsters to take up cricket: "Organised cricket can instil discipline, encourage teamwork, and teach respect for law and authority better than any American sport like baseball or basketball," said the promoter, New Yorker Bert Smith. "One simply does not dispute the decision of the umpire in a cricket match."

Weather Fine, Wicket Good: Yorkshire Grounds

Before the start of each day's play in every first-class match played in England, the representative of the Exchange Telegraph Agency in the press box has to telephone to London the state of the weather and the pitch; he needs to be conservative in his assessments. The ExTel's copytakers and sub-editors do not take kindly to judgements outside the norm: ''Ere mate, wot's all this abaht then? Wicket dangerous? You can't say that. 'Ow abaht "Wicket wearing"? Will that do? Thanks mate. 'Ear from you at 11.30, then.'

Each partner having had a little joke, the day's business starts as it has done in Yorkshire from around the middle of the last century as the county side has turned out at Darnall, Hyde Park, Bramall Lane, Holbeck, Wakefield, Bradford, Dewsbury, Hunslet, Headingley, York, Halifax, Huddersfield, Hull, Harrogate, Scarborough, Barnsley, Middlesbrough and Abbeydale. We have read much of some of the exploits on those early grounds, and we owe the following account of the smartly-named Savile Town, Dewsbury, to Peter Snape.

Yorkshire played county cricket there, usually during Dewsbury Feast week, from 1867 to 1933 and of the first-class counties only Middlesex and Glamorgan were never visitors. In 1921 a crowd of 11,000 saw the first Saturday start to a Championship match, against Sussex, and a total of 29,000 watched Warwickshire four years later. Even the Roses match was scheduled at Savile Town in 1886 but Lancashire never got on the field, all three days being washed out.

According to Snape, Dewsbury was favoured because the club President, Ellison, enjoyed grouse shooting with Lord Savile's agent and once the President had satisfied himself that the ground was large enough (the playing area is bigger than Park Avenue's), county cricket continued there until 1933 when complaints about the lack of covered accommodation ended an era.

Grace, Jessop, Spofforth all appeared at Savile Town although there were grumbles late last century when it was said that the local hotel accommodation was 'hardly suitable for gentlemen cricketers'. Cambridgeshire were Yorkshire's first opponents there, Luke Greenwood and Tom Emmett sharing fourteen wickets in a four-wicket victory. Ted Wainwright performed the hat-trick, Hirst took three wickets in seven balls against Nottinghamshire, Oldroyd hit three centuries in five years, Sutcliffe topped 200 in successive seasons. Greenflies stopped play when Jessop was batting in 1904 and seven years later the Northamptonshire visit coincided with the coronation of George V. At the lunch interval a baritone led the singing of the national anthem, accompanied by the orchestra of the Dewsbury Empire. In 1899 Derbyshire took the field in their normal clothing, their kit being sodden after the dressing room had been flooded by a tap left on overnight, as Yorkshire scored the 32 needed to win. In 1890 a manufacturer living nearby offered to buy supper for the players if one could put a ball through his conservatory window, and giant Australian Bonnor duly obliged.

Yorkshire's headquarters are now at Headingley but that ground did not enter the schedule until 1890, Lord Hawke being Chairman of the Leeds Cricket, Football and Athletic Co. Ltd (now better known as Leeds Rugby League

Club). Nine years later Headingley joined Trent Bridge on the Test-match rota, giving the ground a premier position in the county, a status Bramall Lane did not relinquish without a struggle, promoting a Test match in Sheffield in 1902.

David Thornton, in his booklet *A Century at Headingley*, hints at Saxon origins – 'The Forest Clearing that belongs to Hedde' – and by early last century the land was owned by Lord Cardigan, presumably of the Balaclava family. A club named Leeds St John's played rugby there, in blue and amber, and when the new Leeds club set about erecting a stadium, at the then sensational expense of £20,000, there were only a few protestors.

A resident of Cardigan Road wrote to the *Yorkshire Post* in July 1890, complaining that 'great quantities of ash-pit refuse are being used for raising the level of the ground round the cricket field. The smell arising from this garbage is disgusting.' Critics of the Headingley pitches from other parts of the kingdom should note carefully that no part of this 'disgusting garbage' is reported as being on the cricket field.

On 27 May 1890, a crowd of 5000 attended the opening of the new ground to watch Leeds play Scarborough and a famous ground's history began. In 1893 it was favoured by rugby union, the Yorkshire Cup Final being played there as was a Scotland–England international, attracting a record 30,000. Eight years later came the split, with Leeds joining the newly formed Northern Union that became in time the Rugby League. In June 1891 Yorkshire played their first match, a friendly, at Headingley, and lost to Derbyshire by 45 runs. Two months later the first Championship game was played there, a draw against Kent.

Jackson scored Headingley's first first-class century, 145 against Nottinghamshire in July 1894, and in June 1902 Yorkshire bowled out the Australians there for 23 (Jackson five for 12, Hirst five for 9). Sutcliffe scored 270 there, Verity took all ten against Nottinghamshire in May 1931, but the ground will perhaps be best remembered for Bradman. The great Australian scored 334 there in 1930, 304 in 1934, 106 and 16 in 1938 and 33 and 173 in 1948. His 309 in a day in 1930 (105 before lunch, 115 between lunch and tea, 89 to the close) is an innings that appears unsurpassable.

Headingley has long held a reputation for

Headingley, 1897.

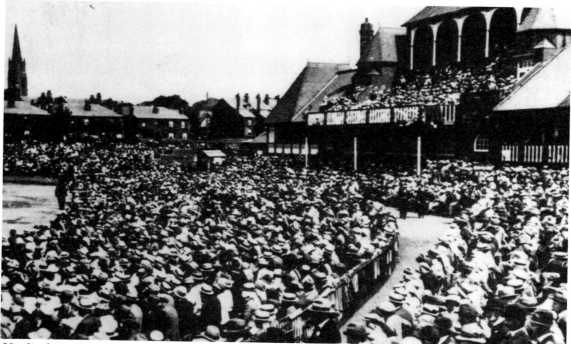

Headingley, 1921. England v Australia.

helping swing bowling when under cloud cover, so it is not surprising that Trueman, who could swing the ball in addition to using the seam, all at considerable pace, should find it a highly successful home. It has been a good ground for England, despite the many complaints of recent years; the defeat of Australia in 1956 was the start of six successive victories at Leeds.

Boycott scored his hundredth century at Leeds in August 1977, and in July 1981 Headingley laid claim to promoting the greatest ever Test match; England followed on to Australia in the Third Test and on the Monday morning resumed 92 behind with three wickets standing. With nothing to lose Dilley and then Botham began hitting out, Botham picking up the tempo to score a magnificent 149 not out. Australia needed only 130 to win with most of two days remaining, but an inspired Willis, shrewdly captained by Brearley, took eight for 43 and to the exhilaration of most of the United Kingdom, England won an astonishing victory by 18 runs.

Hawke's vision, and that of Sir Edwain Airey, Chairman for thirty-two years, was enlarged after the Second World War although, in the view of many, the ground was not improved by the building of a new, small pavilion, square to the pitch, to house Yorkshire's offices and the dressing rooms after the move from Park Row in the city centre. In early 1989 the two clubs, Yorkshire and Leeds CF and AC, unveiled a planned new development of the Grandstand and West Terrace costing £2.7 million.

Bramall Lane was part of the Duke of Norfolk's estate, not inappropriate because that most 'Yorkshire' of England's kings, Richard III, first created the dukedom. 'Lord's is upper class, Worcester New Road is middle class, Bramall Lane is working class and proud of it' is an old saying about this grimy but much-loved old stadium, focus of many of the hopes and dreams of the Sheffield grinders and cutlers, hosting as it did the Sheffield United Cricket and Football Club as well as Yorkshire. Near the city centre, it cost little to reach and until just after the Second World War the crowd was renowned for its appreciation of the finer points; an ovation for a performance at Sheffield, it was reckoned, was worth a gold watch elsewhere.

Such was the industrial haze surrounding the ground – although in 1855 it was chosen as a site because, said the Duke, 'it was free from smoke' – that it became a visitors' joke that when they went in to bat every chimney for miles around was immediately stoked up. Yet both Bradman and Sutcliffe held it in affection, Sutcliffe declaring it to be 'fitting Yorkshire cricket better than any other ground'.

Visitors were also regular targets for verbal volleys, sometimes witty, sometimes crude, usually caustic. Denis Compton, batting on yet another pitch drying after rain, spent much time battering at offending pieces of turf and was assailed by 'Dosta want roof t'cave in?', the implication being that there were miners beneath the square.

In 1968 Bramall Lane gave Trueman, on his home first-class ground, his greatest moment. Deputising for Close as captain, he allowed Yorkshire to pile up 355 for 9 and then helped dismiss the Australians for 148 and, following on, 138 (Trueman's match figures were six for 83, Illingworth's eight for 67).

In 1972 the Football Club foreclosed on cricket, Yorkshire and United's cricket section being exiled to find new homes. Yorkshire became guests of the Collegiate Cricket Club in leafy Abbeydale, as contrasting an environment to Bramall Lane as could have been found in Sheffield. The two clubs have now struck up a warm and profitable partnership and although the sloping playing area poses problems, especially in wet weather, the hospitality is warm and Abbeydale gives Yorkshire a home like no other in the county. Boycott certainly took to Abbeydale, scoring five centuries there since 1974, including two superbly defiant innings against Derbyshire on very difficult pitches. In 1983 Derbyshire recorded their first win over Yorkshire for 25 years.

Yorkshire first played at Park Avenue, Bradford in 1881 and continued for 104 years until the burden of ground maintenance and the improvement required by law proved to be too much for both the Bradford club and Yorkshire. Park Avenue's demise as a cricket ground was followed almost immediately by the formation of a society, 'The Friends of Park Avenue', dedicated to winning back first-class status. The establishment of the Cricket Academy there in 1989 was a pledge of help from the county club.

Park Avenue was thought by many members and supporters to be the most 'Yorkshire' of all the county grounds, dominated by a stylish old Victorian pavilion that always seemed on the point of collapse, with two sides of the ground white-walled and fronted by wooden benching. For most of its life the end opposite the pavilion was occupied by the rear of the Bradford Park Avenue Football Club's grandstand, surmounted by a clock, a recognised target for the big hitter. The small playing area, particularly straight, made it a hazardous ground for spinners and both Rhodes and Verity suffered for their art before Bradford's shrewd and perceptive crowd.

Scarborough is best known for the Festival, the traditional end of the English cricket season during the early days of September. Yorkshire first played there in 1896 and since then it has become renowned for its ability to combine good cricket with a vacationing air; indeed, Kilburn described the town as 'first-class cricket on holiday'. Sadly much of the Victorian elegance of the resort has disappeared under a multitude of slot-machines and fast-food take-aways and one cannot now imagine why Delius chose to spend time there at the end of the last century.

Yet North Marine Road retains its charm: the pavilion is unspoilt, despite the alterations, the marquees and the flags and the band bring an authentic touch to the Festival and the press box remains one of the cosiest and best-sited in the world. Scarborough's resplendent years were during the Edwardian Golden Age when all the great names expected to end their summer in that town in the great traditional fixtures Yorkshire *v* MCC, Gentlemen *v* Players and an invitation (Levenson-Gower's, Pearce's) against the touring team.

Lord Londesborough was the first great patron and it was his grandson, Osbert Sitwell, whose autobiography was quoted in George Plumptre's *Homes of Cricket*: 'there was feasting in the hot tents of the rich at the ground's edge. My grandfather, the founder and president, delighted to entertain . . . the tents blazed with the ties of the cricketing clubs and the port-wine coloured faces of the aficionados, and between the rounds of cold salmon and cold chicken we would have to sit and watch . . .'

C. I. 'Buns' Thornton first raised the invitation elevens and was also renowned for hitting the ball over the high Victorian lodging houses at the Town End and into adjoining Trafalgar Square. In more recent times the Australian Pepper reached the Square over the buildings.

The pitch has a reputation for helping free-scoring batsmen, Lester and Byas being graduates, but the early morning sea air, somewhere between a mist and a drizzle, known locally as a 'fret', can give considerable help to seam bowlers and there have been a few startling batting collapses in Scarborough's history. In the 1980s the Festival was given over almost entirely to one-day cricket, which attracted the holidaying public and swelled the club's funds but won little favour with the traditionalist Yorkshire members. England played New Zealand in a Prudential Trophy one-day international in 1978 and in 1989, for the first time, the Roses Championship match was allocated to North Marine Road.

Another Festival takes place at Harrogate in mid season, giving a welcome opportunity to cricket-lovers to visit that handsome town that seems to have captured much of the North Yorkshire charm once held by Scarborough. In the Silver Sixties Harrogate became Yorkshire's favourite ground, for four of the six Championships in that decade were won at St George's Road.

It was also at Harrogate, during the Tilcon Trophy one-day competition, that umpire Don Oslear first formulated the solution to finding a result when the weather had washed out a chance of a full match by devising a competition of skill that involved bowling at a single stump. The system ought to be known as the 'Harrogate Rule'.

Yorkshire played at Hull until superseded in the fixture list by Middlesbrough where the club Committee at Acklam Park always seemed the more aware of just what was required to attract and to keep a first-class fixture. The facilities at Hull had become so neglected that it was no real surprise when Anlaby Circle was first struck off the Championship list and then, temporarily, off the one-day schedule; the good news is that the Hull club has since been making strenuous efforts to restore the ground.

Acklam Park, meanwhile, developed into a splendid playing area, supplying other parts of England with chief groundsmen of impeccable credentials. First-class cricket arrived in 1956 and in the early years the pitch had a poor reputation with batsmen – Yorkshire were dismissed for 23 by Hampshire in 1965 – but since then all teams have enjoyed their visit to the most northerly ground where, given good weather, the crowds are large, enthusiastic and warm-hearted.

RECORDS OF

Yorkshire County Cricket Club

compiled by
ROY D. WILKINSON

(All records in the Appendix refer to first-class matches only, unless otherwise indicated.)

Officials

President	Treasurer	Captain	Secretary
1863 T.R. Barker	1863–1893 M.J. Ellison	1863–1872 R. Iddison	1863 Geo. Padley
1864–1897 M.J. Ellison	1894–1898 M. Ellison, Jnr	1873 J. Rowbotham	1864–1902 J.B. Wostinholm
1898–1938 Lord Hawke	1899–1912 Chas Stokes	1874 L. Greenwood	
		1875 J. Rowbotham	1903–1930 F.C. (Sir Fredk)
		1876–1877 E. Lockwood	Toone
1939–1947 Rt Hon. Sir F.S.	1913–1931 R.T. Heselton	1878–1882 T. Emmett	
Jackson		1883–1910 Hon. M.B. (Lord)	1934–1971 J.H. Nash
	1932–1962 A. Wyndham	Hawke	
1948–1960 T.L. Taylor	Heselton	1911 E.J. Radcliffe	1972– J. Lister
		1912–1918 Sir A.W. White	
1961–1973 Sir W.A. Worsley	1963–1979 M.G. Crawford	1919–1921 D.C.F. Burton	
Bart		1922–1924 Geoff Wilson	
	1980–19 March 1984	1925–1927 A.W. Lupton	
1974–1981 Sir K. Parkinson	J.D. Welch	1928–1929 W.A. Worsley	
		1930 A.T. Barber	
		1931–1932 F.E. Greenwood	
1981–23 Jan 1984 N.W.D.	24th April 1984	1933–1947 A.B. Sellers	
Yardley	P.W. Townend	1948–1955 N.W.D. Yardley	
		1956–1957 W.H.H. Sutcliffe	
22 Oct 1984 The Viscount	*Chairman of General Committee*	1958–1959 J.R. Burnet	
Mountgarret	1971–1979	1960–1962 J.V. Wilson	
	A.H. Connell D.L.	1963–1970 D.B. Close	
		1971–1978 G. Boycott	
	1980–23 Jan 1984	1979–1980 J.H. Hampshire	
	M.G. Crawford	1981–1982 C.M. Old	
		1982–1983 R. Illingworth	
	8 March 1984–31 Dec 1985	1981–1986 D.L. Bairstow	
	H.R. Kirk	1987– P. Carrick	
	1986 B. Walsh QC		

Benefit matches and grants since 1890

		Amount £			Amount £
Louis Hall	1891	570	C. Turner	★1946	2439
Robert Peel	1894	2000	W. E. Bowes	1947	8083
David Hunter	1897	1975	T. F. Smailes	1948	5104
Edward Wainwright	1898	1800	E. P. Robinson	★1949	1500
E. Peate	§1900	200	L. Hutton	1950	9712
Robert Moorhouse	§1900	500	H. Halliday	★1954	2500
John T. Brown, Snr	1901	2282	W. Watson	1956	5356
John Tunnicliffe	1903	1750	E. I. Lester	★1956	3000
George H. Hirst	1904	3703	J. H. Wardle	1957	8129
Lees Whitehead	§1905	250	J. V. Wilson	1958	5757
David Denton	1907	1915	F. A. Lowson	★1959	2500
Schofield Haigh	1909	2071	R. Appleyard	★1959	2000
Wilfred Rhodes	1911	2202	D. B. Close	1961	8154
Hubert Myers	§1911	250	F. S. Trueman	1962	9331
J. W. Rothery	§1911	250	R. Illingworth	1963	6604
Mrs A. Drake	§1919	250	J. G. Binks	1967	6093
B. B. Wilson	§1919	250	K. Taylor	1968	6301
George H. Hirst	★1921	700	D. E. V. Padgett	1969	7385
A. Dolphin	1922	1891	D. B. Close	★1970	6540
Roy Kilner	1925	4106	P. J. Sharpe	1971	6668
Wilfred Rhodes	★1927	1821	D. Wilson	1972	7621
E. Oldroyd	1927	1700	A. G. Nicholson	1973	13,214
A. Waddington	§1928	1000	G. Boycott	1974	20,639
P. Holmes	1928	2620	J. H. Hampshire	1976	28,425
H. Sutcliffe	1929	3056	D. E. V. Padgett	★1978	15,460
E. Robinson	1930	2205	C. M. Old	1979	32,916
G. G. Macaulay	1931	1633	G. A. Cope	1980 ⎫	
P. Holmes	§1933	250	B. Leadbeater	1980 ⎭	33,846
M. Leyland	1934	3648	D. L. Bairstow	1982	56,913
H. Sutcliffe	★1935	701	R. G. Lumb	1983	50,235
G. G. Macaulay	§1936	250	G. Boycott	★1984	147,954
A. Mitchell	1937	2227	P. Carrick	1985	73,020
A. Wood	1939	2563	C. Johnson	★★1986	46,200
H. Verity Memorial Fund	1945	8233	A. Sidebottom	1988	103,240
W. Barber	★1946	2958			

§Grant ★Testimonial ★★Appreciation Fund

Honours

County Champions (31) 1867, 1870, 1893, 1896, 1898, 1900, 1901, 1902, 1905, 1908, 1912, 1919, 1922, 1923, 1924, 1925, 1931, 1932, 1933, 1935, 1937, 1938, 1939, 1946, 1959, 1960, 1962, 1963, 1966, 1967, 1968.

Joint Champions (2) 1869, 1949

Gillette Cup Winners (2) 1965, 1969

Benson & Hedges Cup Winners (1) 1987

John Player Special League Winners (1) 1983

Fenner Trophy Winners (3) 1972, 1974, 1981

Asda Challenge Winners (1) 1987

Second Eleven Champions (2) 1977, 1984

Joint Champions (1) 1987

Minor Counties Champions (5) 1947, 1957, 1958, 1968, 1971

Under-25 Competition Winners (3) 1976, 1978, 1987

Bain Clarkson Trophy Winners (1) 1988

Champion Counties since 1873

Year	County	Yorkshire's Position	Year	County	Yorkshire's Position
1873	Gloucestershire / Nottinghamshire	7th	1929	Nottinghamshire	2nd
1874	Gloucestershire	4th	1930	Lancashire	3rd
1875	Nottinghamshire	4th	1931	Yorkshire	1st
1876	Gloucestershire	3rd	1932	Yorkshire	1st
1877	Gloucestershire	7th	1933	Yorkshire	1st
1878	Middlesex	6th	1934	Lancashire	5th
1879	Nottinghamshire / Lancashire	6th	1935	Yorkshire	1st
1880	Nottinghamshire	5th	1936	Derbyshire	3rd
1881	Lancashire	3rd	1937	Yorkshire	1st
1882	Nottinghamshire / Lancashire	3rd	1938	Yorkshire	1st
1883	Nottinghamshire	2nd	1939	Yorkshire	1st
1884	Nottinghamshire	3rd	1946	Yorkshire	1st
1885	Nottinghamshire	2nd	1947	Middlesex	7th
1886	Nottinghamshire	4th	1948	Glamorgan	4th
1887	Surrey	3rd	1949	Yorkshire / Middlesex	1st
1888	Surrey	2nd	1950	Lancashire / Surrey	3rd
1889	Surrey / Lancashire / Nottinghamshire	7th	1951	Warwickshire	2nd
1890	Surrey	3rd	1952	Surrey	2nd
1891	Surrey	8th	1953	Surrey	12th
1892	Surrey	6th	1954	Surrey	2nd
1893	Yorkshire	1st	1955	Surrey	2nd
1894	Surrey	2nd	1956	Surrey	7th
1895	Surrey	3rd	1957	Surrey	3rd
1896	Yorkshire	1st	1958	Surrey	11th
1897	Lancashire	4th	1959	Yorkshire	1st
1898	Yorkshire	1st	1960	Yorkshire	1st
1899	Surrey	3rd	1961	Hampshire	2nd
1900	Yorkshire	1st	1962	Yorkshire	1st
1901	Yorkshire	1st	1963	Yorkshire	1st
1902	Yorkshire	1st	1964	Worcestershire	5th
1903	Middlesex	3rd	1965	Worcestershire	4th
1904	Lancashire	2nd	1966	Yorkshire	1st
1905	Yorkshire	1st	1967	Yorkshire	1st
1906	Kent	2nd	1968	Yorkshire	1st
1907	Nottinghamshire	2nd	1969	Glamorgan	12th
1908	Yorkshire	1st	1970	Kent	4th
1909	Kent	3rd	1971	Surrey	13th
1910	Kent	8th	1972	Warwickshire	10th
1911	Warwickshire	7th	1973	Hampshire	14th
1912	Yorkshire	1st	1974	Worcestershire	11th
1913	Kent	2nd	1975	Leicestershire	2nd
1914	Surrey	4th	1976	Middlesex	8th
1919	Yorkshire	1st	1977	Kent / Middlesex	12th
1920	Middlesex	4th	1978	Kent	4th
1921	Middlesex	3rd	1979	Essex	7th
1922	Yorkshire	1st	1980	Middlesex	6th
1923	Yorkshire	1st	1981	Nottinghamshire	10th
1924	Yorkshire	1st	1982	Middlesex	10th
1925	Yorkshire	1st	1983	Essex	17th
1926	Lancashire	2nd	1984	Essex	17th
1927	Lancashire	3rd	1985	Middlesex	11th
1928	Lancashire	4th	1986	Essex	10th
			1987	Nottinghamshire	8th
			1988	Worcestershire	13th

Chart of Yorkshire matches

W – Won   L – Lost   D – Drawn   T – Tied   A – Abandoned
(home matches in **bold** type)

Opponent	1863	1864	1865	1866	1867	1868	1869	1870	1871	1872	1873	1874	1875	1876	1877	1878	1879	1880	1881	1882	1883	1884	1885	1886	1887	1888	1889	1890	1891	1892	1893	1894	1895	1896
West Indians																																		
South Africans																																		
Pakistanis																																		
New Zealanders																																		
Indians																																		
Australians															LW		**LD**		llll		**L**		LD		**LDD**			**WW**			**WDL**			LDL
Oxford Univ.																																	L	
Cambridge Univ.												L		**LW**		W		**D**	W	**WD**	LW	**D**	L	W	**L**	L	W	**L**	L	**D**	L		
MCC							W	L	L	L		**LD**	**DL**	L	**D**	LD	LW	LL	**LW**	WD	LW	**DD**	L	**LD**	LW	AL	**WD**	AA	LD	**WW**	LW	**WL**	D	
Worcestershire																																		
Warwickshire																														DD	**DD**	**WD**	**DW**	
Sussex						WW	WW			WW			WW		**WW**	LW	WL	**DD**	DD	**WD**	WW	**LW**	LW	WW	**WW**	WW	**WD**	WD	WD	**WW**			
Surrey	DW	DL	LL		WW	LW	WW	DW	LW	WW	WW	WW	LD	WW	WD	DW	WD	DW	DD	WV	LL	LL	LL	DW	LL	LL	WL	WL	LW	DL			
Somerset																								WL	LD	LD	WD	WL	DL	WW	**WD**			
Nottinghamshire	WL	WL	LL	DL		WL	LW	WD	LW	LLD	LDW	WW	WW	DL	LD	WL	DW	LW	WD	LW	DL	LL	DW	LD	DD	LD	LD	LL	DD	**DW**	WW	DL		
Northamptonshire																																		
Middlesex				WL			W	L	**WD**	DW	**WD**	WD	LL	**WW**	WL	**WW**	LW	**WV**	WD	**DD**	WL	DW	LD	**LL**	LD	**WD**	WL	**WL**	WW	**WW**	WD			
Leicestershire																												LW	**LW**	**WW**			
Lancashire				**WW**	**W**		WL	LL	WW	LW	WW	LL	LD	WD	DL	DL	WW	WL	DW	LD	DW	DL	LL	DL	LL	WW	WWD	LD	WW			
Kent		**W**	DL				WW								WL	DL	WW	WL	WW	WW	LD	DL	WD	DL	WD	LD	WD	LL	AW	DW	WW			
Hampshire																																WL	**DW**	
Gloucestershire									L	LL	LL	WL	LD	DL	WD	WD	LD	LD	WL	DW	WW	WD	DW	DW	WD	LW	WL	WW	DD	WW	WL	**WW**		
Glamorgan																																		
Essex																																WW	WL	WL
Derbyshire													WD	WL	LL	**WW**	WD	WW	DW	WW	WD	WW									WL	LW	**DW**	

253

Season	1897	1898	1899	1900	1901	1902	1903	1904	1905	1906	1907	1908	1909	1910	1911	1912	1913	1914	1919	1920	1921	1922	1923	1924	1925	1926	1927	1928	1929	1930	1931	1932	1933	1934	1935	1936	1937
West Indians								L																					DW					W			
South Africans				W		DD		L				DD										DD					DD				L						
Pakistanis																																					
New Zealanders																												D			D						D
Indians													W																			W			W		
Australians		DD		WL		LD			DD		DD		L		DL				DD			DL			D												
Oxford Univ.								D		W																			D	D	W	D	W	D	W	W	W
Cambridge Univ.	L	W	W	W	D	D	WW	W	W	L	W	W	L	L	L	L	D	W	D	W	L	W	W	W	D	D	D	D	W	D	D	L	W	W	D	A
MCC	LW	WD	WD	LW	WW	WL	DW	D	W	LW	DL	D	WD	WD	WD	D	WA	DD	W	D	W	D	W	D	W	DW	WD	DD	DD	DW	WW	WW	LW
Worcestershire			DD	WD	WW	DW	DD	DD	WL	LL	WL	WD	WW	WD	W			W		WD	DW		WW	WD	DW				WD	WW	WW	LW	WW
Warwickshire	DW	DD	WW	DD	WD	DW	WI	DW	WD	DW	DW	WL	DD	WD	DW	WW	WW	WW	WW	WD	WD	LD	DD	WD	DW	DD	DW	DD	DW	DL	LW	DW
Sussex	WL	WW	DD	WD	WD	LL	DD	DD	WD	LW	DD	WD	WW	DD	WD	LD	DL	WW	WW	WW	DW	DD	DL	DW	AW	DW	LL	LD	WD	DD	DW
Surrey	WD	WL	DD	DAD	LW	WD	DW	LW	WD	WW	WD	LD	AD	LW	LL	LD	DD	WD	DL	WD	WD	DD	DD	LD	WD	WW	WD	WD	WD
Somerset	WW	WW	WW	WL	LD	LD	WW	WW	DD	WD	DW	WW			WW	WW	WD		WW	WW			WW
Nottinghamshire	DD	DD	DW	DD	WD	WW	WD	DL	DA	DW	WD	DD	WW	WW	DW	LD	WD	LW	LD	WD	AD	DD	WD	DD	DW	DD	DD
Northamptonshire										WD	DW	WL	DL	DL	WW	WW	WW	WW	DD	WW	DW	WA	WD	WW	WW		
Middlesex	DD	WL	LD	WW	WD	LW	LD	WD	DW	WD	DD	WL	LD	LW	DW	WD	LD	WD	WD	WD	LD	DW	WD	WW	LW	DW	DW	LDW
Leicestershire	WD	WW	WW	WW	DA	WW	DD	DW	WD	WD	WL	DL	WL	WW	DD	WD	WD	DW	WW	WD	DD	WD	DD	WD	WW	WL	DW	DD	DW
Lancashire	DL	DW	LD	DD	WD	DW	DD	LW	WW	DW	WW	DL	WD	LLW	DDW	LD	DD	WD	DW	LD	DD	DW	DD	DD	LW	WD	DW	DD	WL
Kent	WW	WL	WL	WD	WW	WD	AD	LW	WD	DD	WD	LD	LL	DL	DW	DD	LL	DD	DL	WW	DW	DW	DD	DA	DD	WL	LW	DW	AW	WL	DW	WW
Hampshire	WW	WW	WD	WW		WW	WD	DD		DW	WL	DW	DD	WW	DW	LW	DW	WD	DD	DD	WD	DW	LW	DD	WD	WW	DD
Gloucestershire	WL	DW	WW	WW	WW	WW	DD	DL	WW			WL	WL	WW	WD	DW	WW	WW		WD	LW	WW	LL	WW	DD	WW
Glamorgan																		WW	WD	WD	WD	WD	DW	WW		DD	WD	WD	DW
Essex	LL	WW	WL	WW	WD	DW	WD	WD	WW	DD	WD	LD	LD	DW	WD	WW	DD	WW	WD	DD	DW	WD	WW	WW	WL	WL	DW	WW
Derbyshire	WW	DW	WW	DW	DD	WD	DW	WL	WW	AW	WW	WW		WW	WD	WW	WD	DW	WW	DD	DD	WW	DD	AD		AW	WD	DD	WW

254

1938	WW	WW	WW	DW	DW	DW	WW	WW	WL	WW	DD	...	WL	DW	WD	WD	DD	W	D	D	...	...	...	...	...
1939	WD	WL	WW	LL	WW	WW	WW	WW	WD	DW	DD	...	WD	WW	WW	LW	W	W	W	...	...	...	...	...	D
1945	...	...	...	...	...	...	D	...	...	...	...	...	...	...	...	...	...	...	...	...	...	...	...	...	...
1946	W	W	WW	DW	WL	WW	DD	DD	WD	W	WD	D	WW	W	WD	W	D	W	W	...	WD	...	...	...	...
1947	D	D	WW	LL	DD	LD	DD	DW	DL	W	LD	W	LD	L	WW	W	LL	D	W	...	...	...	...	D	...
1948	DD	WD	D	L	W	W	DD	L	WD	WW	WD	DD	WD	WL	L	WD	LD	...	D	LD	...	...	...	...	...
1949	WW	DD	W	W	W	W	DD	W	DD	WD	DD	WW	WL	WD	W	LW	D	W	L	...	...	DD	...	...	...
1950	LW	WD	D	DW	DW	W	LD	WD	DD	DW	WW	WW	DD	W	LW	W	L	...	...	...	...	...	...	...	LL
1951	WD	DW	W	WD	WW	W	DD	W	DD	DD	WW	WW	DD	DD	LL	L	DD	W	D	...	...	...	...	DD	...
1952	WL	W	DD	WW	W	WW	DD	WW	DW	D	WW	DW	LW	D	WD	WW	LD	D	D	...	D	...	...	...	...
1953	LW	D	DL	DW	W	WD	DD	DL	DD	L	DL	DD	LD	D	WD	WD	WD	D	D	LD	...	...	...	...	...
1954	DL	WW	D	WW	WW	D	DW	T	DL	WW	LD	WD	WD	WD	DW	D	DW	D	D	...	...	...	W	...	...
1955	WW	WW	L	WW	LW	W	WD	W	WL	WW	DW	WW	LW	LW	WW	W	WD	D	W	...	...	...	...	L	...
1956	LD	L	DD	WL	D	DD	LD	DD	DD	W	WD	WW	LL	D	WW	LW	DW	D	W	DD	...	...	...	...	...
1957	WL	W	LW	DL	W	WD	DD	DW	WD	D	WW	WW	LD	W	DD	WD	LW	W	W	...	...	...	...	...	DA
1958	DW	DW	D	LD	DD	W	LDL	D	DD	DL	AD	WW	WL	WL	DD	A	LL	W	W	...	...	D	...	...	...
1959	DW	WW	W	DL	WL	W	LWD	W	WW	DL	WD	DL	LL	WW	DW	W	LW	...	W	...	DD	...	...	...	...
1960	WW	DL	WL	WD	WD	WD	LL	WW	DD	WL	WW	WD	WD	LW	WW	WD	LD	D	W	...	...	...	...	D	...
1961	DW	WW	WD	LW	DWD	DL	WD	WL	LL	WW	WW	WD	DD	WD	WD	WW	WD	W	D	DD	...	...	...	...	...
1962	WD	DW	LW	WW	WD	WW	WD	WD	DL	LD	WD	WD	DD	DW	WL	DD	LD	W	W	...	...	...	D	...	...
1963	WW	D	WW	DD	L	DW	WD	WW	LD	W	DD	WD	DD	W	WW	DL	DD	D	...	...	...	...	...	...	WL
1964	DD	W	WW	DW	W	LW	DW	DD	WD	D	WW	DD	DL	D	LD	DW	DW	...	D	DL	...	...	...	...	...
1965	DD	DW	L	WD	LD	W	DW	W	DD	WL	DW	WW	LD	DD	DD	D	DW	W	...	...	...	W	...	D	...
1966	WW	WD	W	WD	DD	W	WW	W	DW	LL	WW	WW	LD	LD	WL	D	DL	W	A	...	...	...	...	...	D
1967	DD	L	DW	WW	L	DW	AD	AW	LD	W	WD	LD	WL	W	DW	WW	WW	W	...	...	W	...	D	...	...
1968	DD	L	LW	DD	D	DD	WD	WW	WW	D	DD	DW	WW	D	WL	WL	DD	W	...	W	...	...	...	...	...
1969	DD	D	D	WL	D	D	DD	DW	DD	L	DL	DD	DL	L	L	W	LD	...	W	...	...	D	...	...	D
1970	WW	W	L	LD	W	D	LD	DW	LD	D	DD	LW	DW	D	W	D	W	W	...	...	...	...	...	...	...
1971	DD	DD	D	L	L	LL	DD	D	WD	W	W	L	DL	D	WL	LD	...	...	W	...	D	...	D	...	...
1972	DD	L	W	W	D	L	DL	D	DW	L	D	D	LW	D	D	D	...	...	D	A	...	...	...		...
1973	DW	D	L	D	L	D	DD	D	LT	W	D	W	LL	D	D	D	...	D	...	...	...	...	...		D
1974	DW	L	D	W	A	D	DD	L	LL	L	W		DW	D	D	L	...	W	W	...	D	...	...		...
1975	DW	W	D	W	W	D	DD	D	LW	W	W	D	DW	W	W	D	...	...	...	...	...	...	...		...
1976	DD	L	W	D	D	W	DW	L	W	DL	LW	W	L	D	L	D	...	W	...	...	...	...	...		L
1977	DD	D	W	A	L	L	DW	D	DL	DW	DW	W	W	L	DD	L	...	W	...	D	...	...	...		...
1978	DD	D	W	D	D	D	WW	W	DD	WD	LW	D	W	D	LW	W	...	...	D	...	...	D	A		...
1979	DW	W	D	D	D	D	DW	D	DW	DD	AL	D	D	L	DW	L	...	W	...	...	...	...	...		...
1980	DD	D	D	D	D	W	DL	D	DL	DL	WW	D	D	D	WD	D	...	...	W	...	...	...	...		L
1981	DW	D	L	L	D	D	DL	W	LL	WW	DL	L	W	L	DD	L	...	...	D	...	...	...	...	D	...
1982	DW	D	D	L	D	D	DD	D	DD	DD	AW	D	D	W	WW	D	...	...	...	...	D	...	...	...	...
1983	LD	D	D	LD	W	D	DD	DL	AD	DL	DD	D	D	D	DL	D	...	...	...	...	...	...	...	...	...
1984	DW	L	DD	W	DD	D	DD	DD	L	W	WD	WD	L	DD	L	D	...	...	...	...	...	...	...	...	...
1985	DW	AL	W	L	D	LD	DD	DD	W	D	DD	D	LD	D	D	DD	...	...	D	D	...	...	...	...	...
1986	LD	L	D	DD	D	D	DD	DL	WD	DD	LD	W	W	W	DL	D	...	...	...	...	L	...	...	...	...
1987	WD	W	LD	W	WD	W	DD	WD	W	L	DL	D	D	AD	D	D	L	...	...	...	...	...	...	...	...
1988	LD	L	D	D	D	L	WD	W	DD	DD	DW	D	D	W	LL	L	...	W	...	...	...	...	...	D	...

Season-by-season record of all first-class matches

Season	Played	Won	Lost	Drawn	Abd§
1863	4	2	1	1	
1864	7	2	4	1	
1865	9	–	7	2	
1866	3	–	2	1	
1867	7	7	–	–	
1868	7	4	3	–	
1869	5	4	1	–	
1870	7	6	–	1	
1871	7	3	3	1	
1872	10	2	7	1	
1873	13	7	5	1	
1874	14	10	3	1	
1875	12	6	4	2	
1876	12	5	3	4	
1877	14	2	7	5	
1878	20	10	7	3	
1879	17	7	5	5	
1880	20	6	8	6	
1881	20	11	6	3	
1882	24	11	9	4	
1883	19	10	2	7	
1884	20	10	6	4	
1885	21	8	3	10	
1886	21	5	8	8	
1887	20	6	5	9	
1888	20	7	7	6	
1889	16	3	11	2	1
1890	20	10	4	6	
1891	17	5	11	1	2
1892	19	6	6	7	
1893	23	15	5	3	
1894	28	18	6	4	1
1895	31	15	10	6	
1896	32	17	6	9	
1897	30	14	7	9	
1898	30	18	3	9	
1899	34	17	4	13	
1900	32	19	1	12	
1901	35	23	2	10	1
1902	31	15	3	13	
1903	31	16	5	10	
1904	32	10	2	20	1
1905	33	21	4	8	
1906	33	19	6	8	
1907	31	14	5	12	
1908	38	19	5	14	
1909	33	12	8	13	
1910	32	11	9	12	
1911	32	16	9	7	
1912	35	14	3	18	
1913	32	16	5	11	1
1914	31	16	4	11	2
1919	31	12	5	14	
1920	30	17	6	7	
1921	30	17	5	8	
1922	33	20	2	11	
1923	35	26	1	8	
1924	35	18	4	13	
1925	36	22	–	14	1
1926	35	14	–	21	1
1927	34	11	3	20	
1928	32	9	–	23	
1929	35	11	2	22	
1930	34	13	3	18	2
1931	33	17	1	15	1
1932	32	21	2	9	2
1933	36	21	5	10	
1934	35	14	7	14	
1935	36	24	2	10	
1935–6	3	1	–	2	
1936	35	14	2	19	
1937	34	22	3	9	
1938	36	22	2	12	1
1939	34	23	4	7	
1945	2	–	–	2	
1946	31	19	1	11	
1947	32	10	9	13	
1948	31	11	6	14	
1949	33	16	3	14	1
1950	34	16	6	12	
1951	35	14	3	18	
1952	34	17	3	14	
1953	35	7	7	21	
1954	35	16	3	16*	
1955	33	23	6	4	
1956	35	11	7	17	
1957	34	16	5	13	1
1958	33	10	8	15	2
1959	35	18	8	9	
1960	38	19	7	12	
1961	39	19	5	15	
1962	37	16	5	16	
1963	33	14	4	15	
1964	33	12	4	17	
1965	33	12	4	17	
1966	32	16	6	10	
1967	31	16	5	10	1
1968	32	13	4	15	2
1969	29	4	7	18	
1970	26	10	5	11	
1971	27	5	8	14	
1972	21	4	5	12	1
1973	22	3	5	14*	
1974	22	6	7	9	1
1975	21	11	1	9	
1976	22	7	7	8	
1977	23	7	5	11	1
1978	24	9	2	13	1
1979	22	6	3	13	
1980	24	5	4	15	
1981	24	5	9	10	
1982	22	5	1	16	1
1983	23	1	5	17	
1984	24	5	4	15	
1985	25	3	4	18	1
1986	25	4	6	15	
1986–7	1	–	–	1	
1987	24	7	4	13	
1988	24	5	6	13	1
	3084	1352	527	1205	36

*Includes one tie in each season.

§All these matches were abandoned without a ball being bowled except Yorkshire v Kent at Harrogate, 1904, which was abandoned under Law 9. The two in 1914 were abandoned due to war. All these matches are excluded from the total played.

Of the 1352 matches won, 483 have been by an innings margin, 66 by 200 runs or more and 123 by ten wickets. Of the 527 matches lost, 93 have been by an innings margin, 7 by 200 runs or more and 27 by ten wickets.

Analysis of results versus all first-class counties

Opponents	Played	Won	Lost	Drawn	Tied	Abd
Derbyshire	181	95	15	71	–	3
Essex	141	75	21	45	–	1
Glamorgan	92	46	11	35	–	–
Gloucestershire	184	98	37	49	–	1
Hampshire	132	62	14	56	–	1
Kent	173	78	33	62	–	4
Lancashire	225	69	45	111	–	1
Leicestershire	145	77	11	56	1	2
Middlesex	210	79	45	85	1	1
Northamptonshire	117	60	18	39	–	1
Nottinghamshire	222	82	40	100	–	5
Somerset	134	79	12	43	–	–
Surrey	217	82	60	75	–	2
Sussex	172	78	24	70	–	2
Warwickshire	158	71	20	67	–	–
Worcestershire	117	58	17	42	–	1
Cambridgeshire	8	3	4	1	–	–
	2628	1192	427	1007	2	25

In addition to the above, Yorkshire played 20 matches regarded as first-class between 1833 and 1862. These were:
6 *v* Surrey (2 won, 4 lost), 5 *v* Norfolk (3 won, 2 lost), 4 *v* Lancashire (all won), 3 *v* Kent (1 won, 2 lost) and 2 *v* Sussex (1 won, 1 lost).

Analysis of results versus other first-class teams

Opponents	Played	Won	Lost	Drawn	Tied	Abd
Australians	55	6	19	30	–	1
Indians	13	5	1	7	–	–
New Zealanders	9	1	–	8	–	–
Pakistanis	4	1	–	3	–	1
South Africans	17	1	3	13	–	–
Sri Lankans	2	–	–	2	–	–
West Indians	15	3	6	6	–	1
Cambridge University	84	42	17	25	–	–
Canadians	1	1	–	–	–	–
Combined Services	1	–	–	1	–	–
England's XIs	6	1	2	3	–	1
Hon. M.B. Hawke's XI	1	–	1	–	–	–
International XI	1	1	–	–	–	–
Ireland	3	3	–	–	–	–
Jamaica	3	1	–	2	–	–
Liverpool & District	3	2	1	–	–	–
MCC	153	54	39	60	–	4
Minor Counties	1	1	–	–	–	–
Oxford University	40	20	3	17	–	1
Philadelphians	1	–	–	1	–	–
Rest of England	16	4	5	7	–	–
RAF	1	–	–	1	–	–
Scotland	11	7	–	4	–	–
South of England	2	1	–	1	–	–
C.I. Thornton's XI	5	2	–	3	–	–
United South of England	1	1	–	–	–	–
Windward Islands	1	–	–	1	–	–
I Zingari	6	2	3	1	–	–
	456	160	100	196	–	9

Lowest match aggregates – (1) under 225 runs in a completed match

Runs	Wkts	
165	30	Yorkshire (46 and 37:0) beat Nottinghamshire (24 and 58) by 10 wkts at Sheffield, 1888.
175	30	Yorkshire (104) beat Sussex (30 and 41) by an innings and 33 runs at Leyton, 1901.
182	15	Yorkshire (4:0 dec. and 88:5) beat Northampton (4:0 dec. and 86) by 5 wkts at Bradford, 1931.
193	29	Yorkshire (99) beat Worcester (43 and 51) by an innings and 5 runs at Bradford, 1900.
219	30	Yorkshire (113) beat Nottinghamshire (71 and 35) by an innings and 7 runs at Nottingham, 1881.
222	32	Yorkshire (98 and 14:2) beat Gloucestershire (68 and 42) by 8 wkts at Gloucester, 1924.
223	40	Yorkshire (58 and 51) lost to Lancashire (64 and 50) by 5 runs at Manchester, 1893.

Lowest match aggregates – (2) under 325 runs in a match in which all 40 wickets fell

Runs	Wkts	
223	40	Yorkshire (58 and 51) lost to Lancashire (64 and 50) by 5 runs at Manchester, 1893.
288	40	Yorkshire (55 and 68) lost to Lancashire (89 and 76) by 42 runs at Sheffield, 1872.
295	40	Yorkshire (71 and 63) lost to Surrey (56 and 105) by 27 runs at The Oval, 1886.
303	40	Yorkshire (109 and 77) beat Middlesex (63 and 54) by 69 runs at Lord's, 1891.
318	40	Yorkshire (96 and 96) beat Lancashire (39 and 87) by 66 runs at Manchester, 1874.
318	40	Yorkshire (94 and 104) beat Northampton-shire (61 and 59) by 78 runs at Bradford, 1955.
320	40	Yorkshire (98 and 91) beat Surrey (72 and 59) by 58 runs at Sheffield, 1893.
321	40	Yorkshire (88 and 37) lost to I Zingari (103 and 93) by 71 runs at Scarborough, 1877.
321	40	Yorkshire (80 and 67) lost to Derbyshire (129 and 45) by 27 runs at Sheffield, 1879.

Highest match aggregates – over 1250 runs

Runs	Wkts		Runs	Wkts	
1339	21	Yorkshire (352:8 and 318:3) beat Glamorgan (349:7 and 320:3 dec.) by 7 wkts at Middlesbrough, 1976.	1286	25	Yorkshire (557:8 dec.) drew with MCC (266 and 463:7) at Scarborough, 1933.
1313	37	Yorkshire (380 and 340:7 dec.) beat Nottinghamshire (296 and 297) by 127 runs at Nottingham, 1988.	1285	18	Yorkshire (463:3 dec. and 185:0 dec.) drew with Middlesex (315:6 dec. and 322:9) at Leeds, 1988.
1303	33	Yorkshire (241 and 492) drew with Kent (419 and 151:3) at Tunbridge Wells, 1904.	1262	39	Yorkshire (391 and 241:9) beat Somerset (349 and 281) by 1 wkt at Taunton, 1901.
1295	36	Yorkshire (259 and 388) lost to Middlesex (368 and 280:6) by 4 wkts at Lord's, 1889.	1261	33	Yorkshire (387 and 335:7 dec.) drew with Somerset (432:7 and 116:9) at Harrogate, 1975.
1291	33	Yorkshire (472:7 dec. and 240:5 dec.) beat Gloucestershire (404 and 175) by 133 runs at Bradford, 1932.	1255	17	Yorkshire (704) drew with Surrey (551:7) at The Oval, 1899.
1289	33	Yorkshire (398 and 247:5) beat Sussex (285 and 359:8 dec.) by 5 wkts at Hove, 1949.	1255	31	Yorkshire (309 and 369:9 dec.) drew with Middlesex (488 and 89:2) at Sheffield, 1904.

Large margins of victory – (1) by an innings and over 250 runs

Inns and 397 runs	Yorkshire (548:4 dec.) beat Northamptonshire (58 and 93) at Harrogate, 1921.		Inns and 284 runs	Yorkshire (467:7 dec.) beat Leicestershire (111 and 72) at Bradford, 1932.
Inns and 387 runs	Yorkshire (662) beat Derbyshire (118 and 157) at Chesterfield, 1898.		Inns and 282 runs	Yorkshire (481:8 dec.) beat Derbyshire (106 and 93) at Huddersfield, 1901.
Inns and 321 runs	Yorkshire (437) beat Leicestershire (58 and 58) at Leicester, 1908.		Inns and 280 runs	Yorkshire (562) beat Leicestershire (164 and 118) at Dewsbury, 1903.
Inns and 314 runs	Yorkshire (356:8 dec.) beat Northamptonshire (27 and 15) at Northampton, 1908. (Yorkshire's first match v Northamptonshire).		Inns and 271 runs	Yorkshire (460) beat Hampshire (128 and 61) at Hull, 1900.
			Inns and 271 runs	Yorkshire (495:5 dec.) beat Warwickshire (99 and 125) at Huddersfield, 1922.
Inns and 313 runs	Yorkshire (555:1 dec.) beat Essex (78 and 164) at Leyton, 1932.		Inns and 266 runs	Yorkshire (352) beat Cambridgeshire (40 and 46) at Hunslet, 1869.
Inns and 307 runs	Yorkshire (681:5 dec.) beat Sussex (164 and 210) at Sheffield, 1897.		Inns and 258 runs	Yorkshire (404:2 dec.) beat Glamorgan (78 and 68) at Cardiff, 1922. (Yorkshire's first match v Glamorgan)
Inns and 302 runs	Yorkshire (660) beat Leicestershire (165 and 193) at Leicester, 1896.			
Inns and 301 runs	Yorkshire (499) beat Somerset (125 and 73) at Bath, 1899.		Inns and 256 runs	Yorkshire (486) beat Leicestershire (137 and 93) at Sheffield, 1895.
Inns and 294 runs	Yorkshire (425:7 dec.) beat Gloucestershire (47 and 84) at Bristol, 1964.		Inns and 251 runs	Yorkshire (550) beat Leicestershire (154 and 145) at Leicester, 1933.

Large margins of victory – (2) by over 300 runs

389 runs	Yorkshire (368 and 280:1 dec.) beat Somerset (125 and 134) at Bath, 1906.		328 runs	Yorkshire (186 and 318:1 dec.) beat Somerset (43 and 133) at Bradford, 1930.
370 runs	Yorkshire (194 and 274) beat Hampshire (62 and 36) at Leeds, 1904.		308 runs	Yorkshire (89 and 420) beat Warwickshire (72 and 129) at Birmingham, 1921.
351 runs	Yorkshire (280 and 331) beat Northamptonshire (146 and 114) at Northampton, 1947.			

Large margins of victory – (3) by 10 wickets, with over 100 runs scored in the 4th innings

4th Innings

167:0 wkt Yorkshire (247 and 167:0) beat Northamptonshire (233 and 180) at Huddersfield, 1948.

147:0 wkt Yorkshire (381 and 147:0) beat Middlesex (384 and 142) at Lord's, 1896.

142:0 wkt Yorkshire (304 and 142:0) beat Sussex (254 and 188) at Bradford, 1887.

139:0 wkt Yorkshire (163:9 dec. and 139:0) beat Nottinghamshire (234 and 67) at Leeds, 1932.

138:0 wkt Yorkshire (293 and 138:0) beat Hampshire (251 and 179) at Southampton, 1897.

4th Innings

127:0 wkt Yorkshire (258 and 127:0) beat Cambridge University (127 and 257) at Cambridge, 1930.

119:0 wkt Yorkshire (109 and 119:0) beat Essex (108 and 119) at Leeds, 1931.

118:0 wkt Yorkshire (121 and 118:0) beat MCC (125 and 113) at Lord's, 1883.

116:0 wkt Yorkshire (147 and 116:0) beat Hampshire (141 and 120) at Bournemouth, 1930.

114:0 wkt Yorkshire (135 and 114:0) beat Hampshire (71 and 176) at Bournemouth, 1948.

Heavy defeats – (1) by an innings and over 250 runs

Inns and 272 runs Yorkshire (78 and 186) lost to Surrey (536) at The Oval, 1898.

Inns and 255 runs Yorkshire (125 and 144) lost to All-England XI (524) at Sheffield, 1865.

Heavy defeats – (2) by over 300 runs

305 runs Yorkshire (119 and 51) lost to Cambridge University (312 and 163) at Cambridge, 1906.

Heavy defeats – (3) by 10 wickets, with over 100 runs scored in the 4th innings

4th Innings

148:0 wkt Yorkshire (83 and 216) lost to Lancashire (154 and 148:0) at Manchester, 1875.

100:0 wkt Yorkshire (95 and 91) lost to Gloucestershire (88 and 100:0) at Bristol, 1956.

Narrow victories – (1) by 1 wicket

Yorkshire (70 and 91:9) beat Cambridgeshire (86 and 74) at Wisbech, 1867.

Yorkshire (91 and 145:9) beat MCC (73 and 161) at Lord's, 1870.

Yorkshire (265 and 154:9) beat Derbyshire (234 and 184) at Derby, 1897.

Yorkshire (177 and 197:9) beat MCC (188 and 185) at Lord's, 1899.

Yorkshire (391 and 241:9) beat Somerset (349 and 281) at Taunton, 1901.

Yorkshire (239 and 168:9) beat MCC (179 and 226) at Scarborough, 1935.

Yorkshire (152 and 90:9) beat Worcestershire (119 and 121) at Leeds, 1946.

Yorkshire (229 and 175:9) beat Glamorgan (194 and 207) at Bradford, 1960.

Yorkshire (265:9 dec. and 191:9) beat Worcestershire (227 and 227) at Worcester, 1961.

Yorkshire (329:6 dec. and 167:9) beat Essex (339:9 dec. and 154) at Scarborough, 1979.

Yorkshire (innings forfeited and 251:9 beat Sussex (195 and 55:1 dec.) at Leeds, 1986.

Narrow victories – (2) by 5 runs or less

By 1 run Yorkshire (228 and 214) beat Middlesex (206 and 235) at Bradford, 1976.

By 2 runs Yorkshire (108 and 122) beat Nottinghamshire (56 and 172) at Nottingham, 1870.

By 2 runs Yorkshire (304:9 dec. and 135) beat Middlesex (225:2 dec. and 212) at Leeds, 1985.

By 5 runs Yorkshire (271 and 147:6 dec.) beat Surrey (198 and 215) at Sheffield, 1950.

By 5 runs Yorkshire (151 and 176) beat Hampshire (165 and 157) at Bradford, 1962.

By 5 runs Yorkshire (376:4 and 106) beat Middlesex (325:8 and 152) at Lords, 1975.

By 5 runs Yorkshire (323:5 dec. and inns forfeited) beat Somerset (inns forfeited and 318) at Taunton, 1986.

Narrow defeats – (1) by 1 wicket

Yorkshire (224 and 210) lost to Australian Imperial Forces XI (265 and 170:9) at Sheffield, 1919.

Yorkshire (101 and 159) lost to Warwickshire (45 and 216:9) at Scarborough, 1934.

Yorkshire (239 and 184:9 dec.) lost to Warwickshire (125 and 302:9) at Birmingham, 1983.

Narrow defeats – (2) by 5 runs or less

By 1 run	Yorkshire (135 and 297) lost to Essex (139 and 294) at Huddersfield, 1897.
By 1 run	Yorkshire (159 and 232) lost to Gloucestershire (164 and 228) at Bristol, 1906.
By 1 run	Yorkshire (126 and 137) lost to Worcestershire (101 and 163) at Worcester, 1968.
By 2 runs	Yorkshire (172 and 107) lost to Gloucestershire (157 and 124) at Sheffield, 1913.
By 2 runs	Yorkshire (179:9 dec. and 144) lost to MCC (109 and 216) at Lord's, 1957.
By 3 runs	Yorkshire (126 and 181) lost to Sussex (182 and 128) at Sheffield, 1883.
By 3 runs	Yorkshire (160 and 71) lost to Lancashire (81 and 153) at Huddersfield, 1889.
By 3 runs	Yorkshire (134 and 158) lost to Nottinghamshire (200 and 95) at Leeds, 1923.
By 4 runs	Yorkshire (169 and 193) lost to Middlesex (105 and 261) at Bradford, 1920.
By 5 runs	Yorkshire (58 and 51) lost to Lancashire (64 and 50) at Manchester, 1893.
By 5 runs	Yorkshire (119 and 115) lost to Warwickshire (167 and 72) at Bradford, 1969.

High fourth-innings scores – 300 and over

By Yorkshire

To Win: 331:8 beat Middlesex by 2 wkts at Lord's, 1910.

323:5 beat Nottinghamshire by 5 wkts at Nottingham, 1977.

318:3 beat Glamorgan by 7 wkts at Middlesbrough, 1976.

309:7 beat Somerset by 3 wkts at Taunton, 1984.

305:8 beat Nottinghamshire by 2 wkts at Worksop, 1982.

304:4 beat Derbyshire by 6 wkts at Chesterfield, 1959.

300:4 beat Derbyshire by 6 wkts at Chesterfield, 1981.

To Draw: 316:6 (set 326) drew with Oxford University at Oxford, 1948.

To Lose: 380 (set 406) lost to MCC by 25 runs at Lord's, 1937.

309 (set 400) lost to Middlesex by 90 runs at Lord's, 1878.

By Opponents:

To Win: 392:4 Gloucestershire won by 6 wkts at Bristol, 1948.

334:6 Glamorgan won by 4 wkts at Harrogate, 1955.

329:5 Worcestershire won by 5 wkts at Worcester, 1979.

305:7 Lancashire won by 3 wkts at Manchester, 1980.

302:9 Warwickshire won by 1 wkt at Birmingham, 1983.

To Draw: 334:7 (set 339) MCC drew at Scarborough, 1911.

322:9 (set 334) Middlesex drew at Leeds, 1988.

317:6 (set 355) Nottinghamshire drew at Nottingham, 1910.

To Lose: 319 (set 364) Gloucestershire lost by 44 runs at Leeds, 1987.

318 (set 324) Somerset lost by 5 runs at Taunton, 1986.

310 (set 417) Warwickshire lost by 106 runs at Scarborough, 1939.

306 (set 413) Kent lost by 106 runs at Leeds, 1952.

300 (set 330) Middlesex lost by 29 runs at Sheffield, 1930.

Tied matches

Yorkshire (351:4 dec. and 113) tied with Leicestershire (328 and 136) at Huddersfield, 1954.

Yorkshire (106:9 dec. and 207) tied with Middlesex (102 and 211) at Bradford, 1973.

Highest scores by and against Yorkshire

Yorkshire *versus:-*

	By Yorkshire:	Against Yorkshire:
Derbyshire:		
In Yorkshire:	525:4 dec. at Sheffield, 1937	491 at Bradford, 1949
Away:	662 at Chesterfield, 1898	473 at Derby, 1982
Essex:		
In Yorkshire:	512:9 dec. at Sheffield, 1928	524:7 dec. at Leeds, 1984
Away:	555:1 dec. at Leyton, 1932	521 at Leyton, 1905
Glamorgan:		
In Yorkshire:	579:6 dec. at Huddersfield, 1925	349:7 at Middlesbrough, 1976
Away:	433 at Swansea, 1928	357:9 dec. at Cardiff, 1984
Gloucestershire:		
In Yorkshire:	504:7 dec. at Bradford, 1905	404 at Bradford, 1932
Away:	494 at Bristol, 1897	528 at Cheltenham, 1876
Hampshire:		
In Yorkshire:	493:1 dec. at Sheffield, 1939	456:2 dec. at Leeds, 1920
Away:	585:3 dec. at Portsmouth, 1920	521:8 dec. at Portsmouth, 1927
Kent:		
In Yorkshire:	459 at Leeds, 1896	424:5 dec. at Sheffield, 1983
Away:	559 at Canterbury, 1887	493 at Tonbridge, 1914
Lancashire:		
In Yorkshire:	590 at Bradford, 1887	450 at Leeds, 1948
Away:	528:8 dec. at Manchester, 1939	509:9 dec. at Manchester, 1926
Leicestershire:		
In Yorkshire:	562 { at Scarborough, 1901 / at Dewsbury, 1903	458 at Hull, 1937
Away:	660 at Leicester, 1896	425 at Leicester, 1906
Middlesex:		
In Yorkshire:	575:7 dec. at Bradford, 1899	527 at Huddersfield, 1887
Away:	538:6 dec. at Lord's, 1925	488 at Lord's, 1899
Northamptonshire:		
In Yorkshire:	548:4 dec. at Harrogate, 1921	422:8 dec. at Scarborough, 1986
Away:	523:8 dec. at Wellingborough, 1949	405:6 dec. at Northampton, 1952
Nottinghamshire:		
In Yorkshire:	562 at Bradford, 1899	492:5 dec. at Sheffield, 1949
Away:	520:7 dec. at Nottingham, 1928	490 at Nottingham, 1897
Somerset:		
In Yorkshire:	525:4 dec. at Leeds, 1953	630 at Leeds, 1901
Away:	549:9 dec. at Taunton, 1905	592 at Taunton, 1892
Surrey:		
In Yorkshire:	582:7 dec. at Sheffield, 1935	465 at Bradford, 1934
Away:	704 at The Oval, 1899	560:6 dec. at The Oval, 1933
Sussex:		
In Yorkshire:	681:5 dec. at Sheffield, 1897	566 at Sheffield, 1937
Away:	522:7 dec. at Hastings, 1911	560:5 dec. at Hove, 1901
Warwickshire:		
In Yorkshire:	540:7 dec. at Bradford, 1928	424:8 dec. at Dewsbury, 1914
Away:	887 at Birmingham, 1896	536:7 dec. at Birmingham, 1929

Worcestershire:
In Yorkshire: 500:9 dec. at Sheffield, 1933   402 at Scarborough, 1984
Away: 560:6 dec. at Worcester, 1928   456:8 at Worcester, 1904

Australians: **By Yorkshire:**   **Against Yorkshire:**
In Yorkshire: 377 at Sheffield, 1953   470 at Bradford, 1891

Indians:
In Yorkshire: 385 at Hull, 1911   490:5 dec. at Sheffield, 1946

New Zealanders:
In Yorkshire: 393:4 dec. at Bradford, 1969   370:7 dec. at Bradford, 1949

Pakistanis:
In Yorkshire: 433:9 dec. at Sheffield, 1954   356 at Sheffield, 1954

West Indians:
In Yorkshire: 312:5 dec. at Scarborough, 1973   358:9 dec. at Sheffield, 1963

Cambridge University:
In Yorkshire: 359 at Scarborough, 1967   284 at Sheffield, 1886
Away: 540 at Cambridge, 1938   425:7 at Cambridge, 1929

MCC
In Yorkshire: 557:8 dec. at Scarborough, 1933   478:8 at Scarborough, 1904
Away: 528:8 dec. at Lord's, 1919   488 at Lord's, 1919

Oxford University:
In Yorkshire: 190:6 dec. at Harrogate, 1972   173 at Harrogate, 1972
Away: 453 at Oxford, 1935   422:9 dec. at Oxford, 1953

Lowest scores by and against Yorkshire

Yorkshire *versus:-*
Derbyshire: **By Yorkshire:**   **Against Yorkshire**
In Yorkshire   50 at Sheffield, 1894   20 at Sheffield, 1939
Away: 44 at Chesterfield, 1948   26 at Derby, 1880

Essex:
In Yorkshire: 31 at Huddersfield, 1935   52 at Harrogate, 1900
Away: 98 at Leyton, 1905   30 at Leyton, 1901

Glamorgan:
In Yorkshire: 83 at Sheffield, 1946   52 at Hull, 1926
Away: 92 at Swansea, 1956   48 at Cardiff, 1924

Gloucestershire:
In Yorkshire: 61 at Leeds, 1894   36 at Sheffield, 1903
Away: 35 at Bristol, 1959   41 at Middlesbrough, 1969

Hampshire:
In Yorkshire: 23 at Middlesbrough, 1965   36 at Leeds, 1904
Away: 96 at Bournemouth, 1971   36 at Southampton, 1898

Kent:
In Yorkshire: 30 at Sheffield, 1865   39 at Sheffield, 1882
Away: 62 at Maidstone, 1889   63 at Canterbury, 1901

Lancashire:
In Yorkshire: 33 at Leeds, 1924   30 at Holbeck, 1868
Away: 51 { at Manchester, 1888 / at Manchester, 1893 }   39 at Manchester, 1874

Leicestershire
In Yorkshire: 93 at Leeds, 1935   34 at Leeds, 1906
Away: 47 at Leicester, 1911   57 at Leicester, 1898

Middlesex:
In Yorkshire: 45 at Leeds, 1898   45 at Huddersfield, 1879
Away: 43 at Lord's, 1888   49 at Lord's, 1890

Northamptonshire:
In Yorkshire: 85 at Sheffield, 1919   51 at Bradford, 1920
Away   64 at Northampton, 1959 15 at Northampton, 1908

Nottinghamshire:
In Yorkshire: 32 at Sheffield, 1876   24 at Sheffield, 1888
Away: 43 at Nottingham, 1869 13 at Nottingham, 1901

Somerset:
In Yorkshire: 73 at Leeds, 1895   43 at Bradford, 1930
Away: 83 at Wells, 1949   35 at Bath, 1898

Surrey:
In Yorkshire: 54 at Sheffield, 1873   31 at Holbeck, 1883
Away: 26 at The Oval, 1909   44 at The Oval, 1935

Sussex:
In Yorkshire: 61 at Dewsbury, 1891   20 at Hull, 1922
Away: 42 at Hove, 1922   24 at Hove, 1878

Warwickshire:
In Yorkshire: 49 at Huddersfield, 1951 35 at Sheffield, 1979
Away: 54 at Birmingham, 1964 35 at Birmingham, 1963

Worcestershire:
In Yorkshire: 62 at Bradford, 1907   24 at Huddersfield, 1903
Away: 72 at Worcester, 1977   65 at Worcester, 1925

Australians:
In Yorkshire: 48 at Leeds, 1893   23 at Leeds, 1902

Indians:
In Yorkshire: 146 at Bradford, 1959   66 at Harrogate, 1932

New Zealanders:
In Yorkshire: 189 at Harrogate, 1931   134 at Bradford, 1965

Pakistanis:
In Yorkshire: 137 at Bradford, 1962   150 at Leeds, 1967

West Indians:
In Yorkshire: 50 at Harrogate, 1906   58 at Leeds, 1928

Cambridge University:
In Yorkshire: 110 at Sheffield, 1903   39 at Sheffield, 1903
Away: 51 at Cambridge, 1906   30 at Cambridge, 1928

MCC
In Yorkshire;   46 { at Scarborough, 1876 31 at Scarborough, 1877
           { at Scarborough, 1877
Away: 44 at Lord's, 1880   27 at Lord's, 1902

Oxford University:
In Yorkshire: Have not been dismissed – lowest
          is 115:8 at Harrogate, 1972 133 at Harrogate, 1972
Away: 141 at Oxford, 1949   46 at Oxford, 1956

Centuries

Year		Score	Year		Score
	C.W.J. Athey (10)				
1976	Sussex	*131	1981	Northamptonshire	*123
1978	Somerset	131	1982	Glamorgan	100
1978	Northamptonshire	114	1982	Derbyshire	134
1980	Gloucestershire	*125	1982	Kent	100
1980	Warwickshire	114	1982	Surrey	*114
	D.L. Bairstow (8)				
1976	Glamorgan	106	1985	Derbyshire	*113
1980	Middlesex	145	1985	Derbyshire	*122
1983	Middlesex	*100	1987	Derbyshire	104
1985	Leicestershire	*100	1987	Leicestershire	128
	A.T. Barber				
1929	England XI				100
	W. Barber (27)				
1929	South Africans	108	1935	Glamorgan	120
1929	Glamorgan	114	1935	Surrey	255
1932	Middlesex	102	1936	Kent	158
1932	Middlesex	162	1937	Sussex	104
1932	Leicestershire	110	1937	Nottinghamshire	115
1933	Glamorgan	*120	1937	Gloucestershire	*107
1933	Warwickshire	124	1938	Surrey	157
1933	Nottinghamshire	*109	1938	Hampshire	111
1933	Essex	101	1938	Leicestershire	130
1934	Cambridge University	103	1939	Derbyshire	100
1934	MCC	168	1939	Northamptonshire	*128
1934	Kent	248	1939	Surrey	141
1935	Sussex	191	1946	Somerset	113
1935	Middlesex	107			
	W. Bates (8)				
1878	Nottinghamshire	102	1884	Nottinghamshire	116
1879	Lancashire	118	1886	Derbyshire	106
1881	Kent	108	1886	Sussex	136
1884	Cambridge University	133	1887	Derbyshire	103
	H.D. Bird				
1959	Glamorgan				*181
	J.T.D. Birtles				
1914	Lancashire				104
	R.J. Blakey (4)				
1987	Glamorgan	*101	1987	Northamptonshire	108
1987	Lancashire	*124	1987	Gloucestershire	*204
	J.B. Bolus (7)				
1960	Hampshire	*146	1961	Nottinghamshire	*102
1960	Rest of England	*103	1961	Hampshire	100
1961	Surrey	133	1962	Cambridge University	108
1961	Sussex	117			
	M.W. Booth (2)				
1911	Worcestershire	210	1913	Middlesex	*107

G. Boycott (103)

Year		Score	Year		Score
1963	Lancashire	145	1975	Nottinghamshire	139
1963	Lancashire	113	1975	Middlesex	*201
1963	Leicestershire	*165	1975	Lancashire	*105
1964	Middlesex	151	1976	Gloucestershire	*161
1964	Lancashire	131	1976	Cambridge University	*207
1964	Leicestershire	*151	1976	Nottinghamshire	141
1964	Australians	122	1976	Glamorgan	*156
1964	Gloucestershire	177	1976	Lancashire	*103
1966	MCC	123	1977	Somerset	*139
1966	Warwickshire	*136	1977	Australians	103
1966	Nottinghamshire	103	1977	Middlesex	117
1966	Nottinghamshire	105	1977	Nottinghamshire	154
1966	Sussex	164	1977	Warwickshire	104
1967	Glamorgan	102	1978	Warwickshire	115
1967	Northamptonshire	*220	1978	Northamptonshire	113
1967	Pakistanis	128	1978	New Zealanders	*103
1968	Leicestershire	*114	1978	Glamorgan	118
1968	Gloucestershire	125	1978	Nottinghamshire	129
1968	Warwickshire	*180	1979	Derbyshire	*151
1968	Leicestershire	132	1979	Somerset	*130
1968	Sussex	100	1979	Derbyshire	167
1968	MCC	*102	1979	Nottinghamshire	*175
1969	Somerset	*105	1980	Lancashire	135
1970	Kent	148	1980	Derbyshire	*154
1970	Essex	*260	1981	Nottinghamshire	124
1971	Warwickshire	110	1981	Derbyshire	*122
1971	Middlesex	*112	1982	Northamptonshire	138
1971	Nottinghamshire	169	1982	Glamorgan	134
1971	Essex	233	1982	Worcestershire	159
1971	Middlesex	*182	1982	Warwickshire	*152
1971	Derbyshire	133	1982	Sussex	*122
1971	Lancashire	169	1982	Somerset	129
1971	Leicestershire	151	1983	Derbyshire	*112
1971	Hampshire	111	1983	Kent	101
1971	Warwickshire	*138	1983	Nottinghamshire	*214
1971	Northamptonshire	*124	1983	Gloucestershire	*140
1972	Somerset	*122	1983	Nottinghamshire	163
1972	Nottinghamshire	100	1983	Nottinghamshire	*141
1972	Essex	121	1983	Derbyshire	*169
1972	Lancashire	105	1984	Kent	*104
1972	Leicestershire	*204	1984	Derbyshire	*153
1972	Hampshire	105	1984	Gloucestershire	*126
1973	Cambridge University	*141	1984	Glamorgan	*101
1973	Lancashire	101	1985	Somerset	*114
1973	Nottinghamshire	129	1985	Hampshire	115
1974	Cambridge University	140	1985	Worcestershire	*105
1974	Derbyshire	*149	1985	Worcestershire	184
1974	Sussex	117	1985	Warwickshire	*103
1974	Surrey	*142	1985	Nottinghamshire	*125
1975	Worcestershire	*152	1986	Leicestershire	127
1975	Gloucestershire	141	1986	Surrey	*135
1975	Middlesex	*175			

J. T. Brown (23)

Year		Score	Year		Score
1894	Liverpool & District	141	1896	Leicestershire	131
1894	Gloucestershire	100	1896	Hampshire	120
1895	Sussex	*168	1897	Nottinghamshire	119
1896	Middlesex	203	1897	Sussex	311
1896	Nottinghamshire	107	1897	Somerset	107

Year		Score

J. T. Brown (continued)

Year		Score	Year		Score
1898	Lancashire	144	1900	Cambridge University	129
1898	Derbyshire	300	1900	Leicestershire	128
1898	Sussex	150	1901	Warwickshire	121
1898	M.C.C.	100	1901	Warwickshire	*134
1899	Cambridge University	168	1901	Hampshire	110
1899	Derbyshire	192	1903	Gloucestershire	125
1899	Australians	167			

D.C.F. Burton (2)

Year		Score	Year		Score
1919	Hampshire	*142	1921	Leicestershire	110

D. Byas

Year		Score
1988	Gloucestershire	112

P. Carrick (3)

Year		Score	Year		Score
1978	Lancashire	105	1980	Northamptonshire	*131
1979	Gloucestershire	*128			

D.B. Close (23)

Year		Score	Year		Score
1954	Pakistanis	*123	1961	Glamorgan	103
1954	Combined Services	164	1961	Somerset	103
1955	Cambridge University	114	1961	Cambridge University	100
1955	Somerset	143	1962	Somerset	*121
1957	Derbyshire	108	1962	Warwickshire	*140
1957	Derbyshire	120	1962	Essex	*142
1957	Sussex	103	1963	Northamptonshire	161
1958	Glamorgan	120	1964	Surrey	*100
1959	Oxford University	*144	1965	New Zealanders	115
1959	Nottinghamshire	154	1965	South Africans	*117
1959	Lancashire	128	1965	Surrey	*101
1959	Somerset	128	1966	Cambridge University	103
1960	Hampshire	102	1966	Gloucestershire	105
1960	Surrey	198	1966	Nottinghamshire	*115
1960	Nottinghamshire	184	1969	New Zealanders	146
1961	Surrey	132	1970	Northamptonshire	128
1961	Lancashire	111			

A.J. Dalton (3)

Year		Score	Year		Score
1971	Oxford University	111	1972	Middlesex	128
1971	Worcestershire	*119			

K.R. Davidson (2)

Year		Score	Year		Score
1934	MCC	*101	1934	Kent	128

D. Denton (61)

Year		Score	Year		Score
1896	Derbyshire	113	1905	Gloucestershire	172
1897	Somerset	112	1905	Hampshire	*133
1897	Warwickshire	*141	1905	Essex	134
1899	Leicestershire	110	1905	Somerset	107
1899	Middlesex	113	1905	Warwickshire	132
1899	Lancashire	*101	1905	Middlesex	102
1901	C.I. Thornton's XI	132	1905	Australians	*153
1902	Essex	127	1906	Leicestershire	108
1902	Lancashire	*108	1906	Middlesex	127
1903	Cambridge University	101	1906	Nottinghamshire	107
1903	Leicestershire	133	1906	Nottinghamshire	*109
1903	Surrey	104	1906	West Indians	*112
1903	Surrey	105	1907	Gents. of Ireland	149
1904	Surrey	111	1908	Northamptonshire	110
1904	Somerset	119	1908	MCC	133
1904	South Africans	165	1908	MCC	121
1905	Hampshire				

Year		Score	Year		Score

D. Denton (continued)

Year		Score	Year		Score
1909	Warwickshire	140	1912	Kent	221
1909	Leicestershire	129	1912	Northamptonshire	111
1909	Australians	106	1912	Hampshire	191
1909	Nottinghamshire	184	1913	Nottinghamshire	148
1909	Derbyshire	130	1913	England XI	114
1910	Derbyshire	182	1914	Hampshire	*168
1911	Derbyshire	113	1914	Middlesex	129
1911	Somerset	120	1914	Sussex	124
1911	Leicestershire	*137	1919	Leicestershire	110
1911	All Indians	118	1919	Gloucestershire	122
1911	Nottinghamshire	*101	1919	Middlesex	120
1911	Lancashire	*101	1919	Kent	114
1912	Hampshire	107	1920	Worcestershire	*209
1912	Warwickshire	*200	1920	Kent	145
1912	Gloucestershire	182			

A. Drake (3)

Year		Score	Year		Score
1911	Derbyshire	*147	1913	Cambridge University	108
1911	Sussex	115			

T. Emmett

Year		Score
1873	Gloucestershire	104

P.A. Gibb (2)

Year		Score	Year		Score
1935	Nottinghamshire	*157	1946	Warwickshire	104

F.E. Greenwood

Year		Score
1929	Glamorgan	*104

I. Grimshaw (4)

Year		Score	Year		Score
1884	Cambridge University	115	1885	Nottinghamshire	114
1885	Cambridge University	*129	1886	Derbyshire	*122

S. Haigh (4)

Year		Score	Year		Score
1901	Nottinghamshire	159	1904	Derbyshire	104
1904	Warwickshire	138	1911	All Indians	111

L. Hall (9)

Year		Score	Year		Score
1883	Sussex	*124	1887	Lancashire	160
1884	Cambridge University	116	1887	Kent	110
1884	Kent	100	1887	Gloucestershire	*119
1884	Sussex	*128	1888	Gloucestershire	*129
1884	Middlesex	135			

H. Halliday (12)

Year		Score	Year		Score
1948	Gloucestershire	130	1951	Somerset	120
1948	Surrey	*105	1952	Oxford University	*126
1948	Northamptonshire	116	1952	Gloucestershire	118
1948	Worcestershire	102	1953	Gloucestershire	105
1949	Cambridge University	113	1953	Nottinghamshire	108
1950	Derbyshire	144	1953	Kent	100

J.H. Hampshire (34)

Year		Score	Year		Score
1963	Surrey	120	1965	Lancashire	*110
1964	Leicestershire	150	1965	MCC	*149
1964	Hampshire	110	1967	MCC	107
1965	Surrey	*105	1967	Warwickshire	102

Year		Score	Year		Score

J.H. Hampshire (continued)

Year		Score	Year		Score
1968	Derbyshire	100	1976	Gloucestershire	★155
1970	Leicestershire	107	1976	Surrey	133
1970	Derbyshire	★120	1976	Sussex	113
1971	Oxford University	★116	1977	Derbyshire	★100
1971	Sussex	★183	1978	Nottinghamshire	124
1971	Gloucestershire	★105	1978	Northamptonshire	109
1972	Glamorgan	111	1978	Warwickshire	132
1972	Middlesex	103	1980	Somerset	124
1974	Nottinghamshire	★157	1980	Warwickshire	★101
1974	Gloucestershire	158	1981	Leicestershire	112
1975	Gloucestershire	★106	1981	Surrey	127
1975	Somerset	115	1981	Hampshire	★118
1975	Surrey	127	1981	Northamptonshire	120

W.E. Harbord

Year		Score
1930	Oxford University	109

S.N. Hartley (4)

Year		Score	Year		Score
1981	Nottinghamshire	106	1984	Gloucestershire	★104
1982	Gloucestershire	114	1985	Oxford University	★108

Lord Hawke (10)

Year		Score	Year		Score
1886	Sussex	144	1898	Kent	★107
1887	Lancashire	125	1898	Warwickshire	134
1891	Somerset	126	1899	Hampshire	127
1896	Warwickshire	166	1902	Surrey	126
1896	Kent	★110	1904	Leicestershire	★100

G.H. Hirst (56)

Year		Score	Year		Score
1894	Gloucestershire	★115	1905	Leicestershire	341
1896	Leicestershire	107	1905	Cambridge University	★113
1897	Gloucestershire	134	1905	Sussex	★103
1898	Surrey	★130	1905	Surrey	★232
1899	Surrey	186	1906	Kent	101
1899	Hampshire	131	1906	Warwickshire	104
1899	Nottinghamshire	138	1906	Oxford University	169
1900	Somerset	106	1906	Sussex	122
1900	Nottinghamshire	155	1906	Somerset	111
1900	Gloucestershire	111	1906	Somerset	★117
1900	Gloucestershire	108	1908	Derbyshire	★128
1901	Worcestershire	214	1909	Northamptonshire	140
1901	Nottinghamshire	125	1910	Cambridge University	158
1902	Essex	134	1910	Middlesex	137
1902	Lancashire	★112	1910	Warwickshire	103
1903	Worcestershire	123	1911	Worcestershire	100
1903	Kent	120	1911	Lancashire	156
1903	Somerset	142	1911	Sussex	218
1903	Leicestershire	153	1912	Worcestershire	109
1904	Cambridge University	102	1913	Kent	★102
1904	Oxford University	153	1913	Surrey	★112
1904	Hampshire	152	1913	Sussex	★166
1904	Kent	157	1914	Hampshire	146
1904	Surrey	108	1914	Northamptonshire	★105
1904	Middlesex	103	1914	Somerset	107
1904	Essex	140	1919	MCC	★180
1904	Sussex	121	1919	Essex	120
1905	Worcestershire	★108	1919	Warwickshire	120

Year		Score	Year		Score
				P. Holmes (60)	
1919	Nottinghamshire	100	1925	Leicestershire	194
1919	Northamptonshire	133	1925	Hampshire	159
1919	Lancashire	123	1925	MCC	134
1919	Leicestershire	140	1926	Middlesex	128
1919	Middlesex	133	1926	Hampshire	108
1920	Middlesex	149	1926	Lancashire	143
1920	Essex	141	1926	Surrey	★127
1920	Derbyshire	104	1927	Gloucestershire	180
1920	Northamptonshire	★145	1927	Glamorgan	107
1920	Lancashire	126	1927	Somerset	126
1920	Lancashire	★111	1927	New Zealanders	★175
1920	Hampshire	★302	1928	Warwickshire	275
1921	Derbyshire	150	1928	Middlesex	★179
1921	Northamptonshire	★277	1928	Essex	136
1921	Lancashire	132	1928	Leicestershire	110
1922	Glamorgan	138	1928	Middlesex	105
1922	Warwickshire	209	1928	Nottinghamshire	★101
1922	Middlesex	129	1929	Northamptonshire	★110
1922	Kent	107	1929	Nottinghamshire	285
1922	Warwickshire	★220	1929	Derbyshire	100
1923	Cambridge University	★126	1929	Surrey	142
1923	Somerset	199	1930	Oxford University	★107
1923	Gloucestershire	★122	1930	Somerset	102
1924	Glamorgan	★118	1930	Gloucestershire	★132
1924	Nottinghamshire	112	1930	Glamorgan	130
1924	Derbyshire	107	1931	Warwickshire	250
1924	Kent	★105	1931	Nottinghamshire	133
1925	Derbyshire	125	1931	Lancashire	125
1925	Middlesex	★315	1932	Oxford University	110
1925	Glamorgan	130	1932	Essex	★224

Year		Score	Year		Score
				L. Hutton (85)	
1934	Worcestershire	196	1946	Northamptonshire	★171
1935	Middlesex	131	1946	Indians	★183
1936	Surrey	163	1947	Glamorgan	197
1937	Worcestershire	101	1947	Sussex	106
1937	Kent	136	1947	Leicestershire	137
1937	Derbyshire	★271	1947	Essex	197
1937	Leicestershire	153	1947	Essex	104
1937	Essex	124	1947	Hampshire	★270
1937	MCC	161	1947	Oxford University	103
1937	New Zealanders	135	1947	Cambridge University	★120
1937	Middlesex	121	1947	South Africans	137
1938	Sussex	107	1947	MCC	107
1938	Cambridge University	180	1948	Northamptonshire	★100
1938	Oxford University	141	1948	Lancashire	100
1939	MCC	★106	1948	Sussex	★176
1939	Cambridge University	102	1948	Middlesex	133
1939	Warwickshire	158	1948	Essex	103
1939	Hampshire	★280	1948	Lancashire	104
1939	Glamorgan	144	1948	Essex	★144
1939	Surrey	151	1948	Sussex	155
1939	Sussex	177	1948	MCC	★107
1939	Lancashire	★105	1949	New Zealanders	167
1939	Worcestershire	109	1949	Northamptonshire	104
1939	Kent	100	1949	Lancashire	201
1939	Sussex	103	1949	Middlesex	113
1946	Leicestershire	111	1949	Sussex	165
1946	Surrey	101	1949	Sussex	100

Year		Score	Year		Score
	L. Hutton (continued)				
1949	Scotland	★146	1952	Gloucestershire	108
1949	Northamptonshire	★269	1952	Middlesex	132
1949	MCC	147	1952	Kent	189
1950	Somerset	141	1952	Surrey	104
1950	Derbyshire	107	1952	Kent	120
1950	Essex	156	1952	MCC	103
1950	Nottinghamshire	153	1952	MCC	137
1950	West Indians	104	1953	Somerset	178
1951	Essex	141	1953	Worcestershire	100
1951	Middlesex	117	1953	Kent	★100
1951	Surrey	151	1953	Warwickshire	125
1951	Nottinghamshire	★194	1954	MCC	★101
1951	Gloucestershire	★110	1954	Combined Services	163
1951	South Africans	156	1954	Nottinghamshire	★149
1952	Somerset	119	1955	Nottinghamshire	194
1952	Lancashire	152			
	R. A. Hutton (4)				
1970	Derbyshire	104	1971	Pakistanis	189
1971	Oxford University	101	1974	Somerset	★102
	R. Iddison				
1869	Cambridgeshire				112
	R. Illingworth (14)				
1953	Essex	★146	1962	Warwickshire	107
1955	Essex	116	1962	Surrey	127
1955	MCC	138	1962	Hampshire	115
1959	Essex	150	1963	Warwickshire	★107
1959	Indians	162	1964	Kent	135
1959	Sussex	122	1964	MCC	103
1959	MCC	★105	1968	Leicestershire	★100
	Hon. F.S. Jackson (21)				
1893	MCC	★111	1898	Somerset	139
1894	Nottinghamshire	145	1898	Gloucestershire	160
1894	Sussex	131	1899	Cambridge University	133
1896	Warwickshire	117	1899	Middlesex	155
1896	Middlesex	115	1899	Nottinghamshire	114
1896	Sussex	102	1899	C.I. Thornton's XI	101
1897	Somerset	124	1902	Essex	★101
1897	Middlesex	101	1904	Surrey	158
1898	Middlesex	133	1904	Sussex	★110
1898	Leicestershire	147	1905	Derbyshire	111
1898	Lancashire	★134			
	C. Johnson (2)				
1973	Somerset	107	1976	Gloucestershire	102
	W. G. Keighley				
1951	Surrey				110
	N. Kilner (2)				
1921	Leicestershire	112	1923	Gloucestershire	★102
	R. Kilner (15)				
1913	Leicestershire	104	1919	MCC	120
1914	Gloucestershire	169	1919	Gloucestershire	★115
1919	Gloucestershire	112	1920	Derbyshire	★206

R. Kilner (continued)

Year		Score	Year		Score
1920	Warwickshire	121	1922	Northamptonshire	124
1920	Nottinghamshire	137	1925	Warwickshire	124
1921	Northamptonshire	166	1925	MCC	*100
1921	Northamptonshire	150	1926	Middlesex	150
1922	Worcestershire	117			

B. Leadbeater

Year		Score
1976	Hampshire	*140

F. Lee (3)

Year		Score	Year		Score
1885	Nottinghamshire	101	1887	Kent	119
1887	Lancashire	165			

E.I. Lester (24)

Year		Score	Year		Score
1947	Derbyshire	127	1952	Leicestershire	*130
1947	Northamptonshire	142	1952	Nottinghamshire	*101
1947	Northamptonshire	126	1952	Nottinghamshire	178
1948	Oxford University	149	1952	Indians	*110
1948	Gloucestershire	110	1952	Hampshire	109
1948	Lancashire	*125	1952	Surrey	*130
1948	Lancashire	132	1953	Cambridge University	157
1949	Sussex	112	1953	Surrey	*103
1949	Essex	102	1954	Oxford University	150
1949	Derbyshire	*140	1954	Derbyshire	*121
1949	Warwickshire	186	1954	Essex	163
1951	Nottinghamshire	118	1954	Surrey	142

M. Leyland (62)

Year		Score	Year		Score
1924	Lancashire	*133	1932	Rest of England	105
1924	Hampshire	*100	1933	Worcestershire	133
1925	Worcestershire	138	1933	Northamptonshire	192
1925	Middlesex	110	1933	Hampshire	133
1925	Gloucestershire	*131	1933	Nottinghamshire	134
1926	Surrey	133	1933	Kent	*210
1926	Hampshire	118	1933	Worcestershire	*117
1926	Leicestershire	116	1933	MCC	133
1926	Warwickshire	133	1934	MCC	*104
1926	Glamorgan	191	1934	Oxford University	100
1927	New Zealanders	118	1934	Glamorgan	135
1927	Middlesex	*204	1935	Oxford University	126
1927	Essex	127	1935	Rest of England	*133
1928	Worcestershire	247	1936	Jamaica	115
1928	Glamorgan	*189	1936	Essex	263
1928	Derbyshire	149	1936	Surrey	*163
1928	Surrey	139	1936	Middlesex	107
1928	Essex	*133	1936	Worcestershire	113
1929	Essex	134	1936	Surrey	107
1929	Hampshire	104	1936	Oxford University	141
1930	Kent	105	1936	Cambridge University	*110
1930	Lancashire	*211	1937	Worcestershire	167
1930	Middlesex	172	1937	Leicestershire	*118
1930	Derbyshire	186	1937	Sussex	101
1930	Kent	112	1938	Oxford University	100
1931	Surrey	124	1938	Essex	114
1932	Middlesex	189	1938	Glamorgan	127
1932	Leicestershire	153	1938	Lancashire	135
1932	Derbyshire	113	1939	Gloucestershire	112
1932	Leicestershire	166	1939	Middlesex	*180
1932	Hampshire	*153	1939	Surrey	114

Year		Score	Year		Score
		E. Lockwood (6)			
1869	Surrey	103	1881	Surrey	109
1872	Surrey	121	1882	I Zingari	★104
1878	Gloucestershire	107	1883	Kent	208
		J.D. Love (13)			
1976	Nottinghamshire	163	1981	Lancashire	154
1977	Warwickshire	129	1982	Derbyshire	110
1978	Oxford University	107	1982	Surrey	123
1979	Worcestershire	★170	1984	Somerset	112
1980	Warwickshire	104	1985	Oxford University	106
1980	Lancashire	★105	1986	Northamptonshire	109
1981	Warwickshire	161			
		F.A. Lowson (30)			
1949	Middlesex	104	1953	MCC	101
1950	Northamptonshire	112	1954	Somerset	115
1950	Essex	112	1954	Cambridge University	107
1950	Hampshire	104	1954	Middlesex	107
1950	Hampshire	103	1954	Sussex	165
1950	Northamptonshire	★141	1954	Essex	164
1951	Middlesex	113	1954	Kent	★150
1951	Kent	155	1955	Middlesex	116
1951	Oxford University	104	1956	Oxford University	★183
1951	South Africans	115	1956	Scotland	115
1952	Worcestershire	155	1956	Somerset	154
1952	Lancashire	120	1956	Nottinghamshire	★103
1953	Scotland	166	1957	Cambridge University	154
1953	Surrey	103	1957	Glamorgan	100
1953	Worcestershire	★259	1957	Middlesex	116
		R.G. Lumb (22)			
1973	Lancashire	114	1979	Northamptonshire	113
1973	Sussex	103	1979	Northamptonshire	★129
1973	West Indians	103	1979	Warwickshire	118
1974	Northamptonshire	★123	1979	Somerset	159
1974	Derbyshire	100	1979	Essex	110
1975	Gloucestershire	101	1980	Worcestershire	118
1975	Surrey	118	1980	Glamorgan	129
1976	Gloucestershire	132	1980	Gloucestershire	101
1976	Essex	118	1981	Derbyshire	145
1978	Oxford University	107	1984	Gloucestershire	★165
1978	Leicestershire	103	1984	Glamorgan	144
		G.G. Macaulay (3)			
1921	Nottinghamshire	★125	1926	Somerset	108
1922	Essex	★101			
		A.A. Metcalfe (12)			
1983	Nottinghamshire	122	1986	Lancashire	151
1985	Oxford University	109	1986	Glamorgan	149
1986	Worcestershire	108	1987	Sussex	113
1986	Northamptonshire	151	1987	MCC	152
1986	Kent	123	1988	Derbyshire	145
1986	Nottinghamshire	108	1988	Middlesex	★216
		A. Mitchell (39)			
1926	Northamptonshire	189	1928	Middlesex	105
1927	Leicestershire	105	1929	South Africans	126
1928	Kent	113	1929	Worcestershire	★122

A. Mitchell (continued)

Year		Score	Year		Score
1930	Leicestershire	*136	1934	Lancashire	121
1930	Somerset	*130	1934	Hampshire	152
1930	Middlesex	*105	1934	Middlesex	*102
1930	Nottinghamshire	176	1934	Surrey	181
1930	Kent	*101	1934	Northamptonshire	111
1931	Hampshire	*119	1936	Jamaica	*101
1931	Somerset	134	1936	Derbyshire	103
1932	Gloucestershire	140	1936	MCC	127
1932	Gloucestershire	*177	1937	Leicestershire	100
1932	MCC	102	1937	Glamorgan	105
1933	Glamorgan	*108	1938	Cambridge University	100
1933	Lancashire	123	1938	Northamptonshire	133
1933	Worcestershire	142	1938	Warwickshire	124
1933	Nottinghamshire	138	1938	Sussex	100
1933	Worcestershire	*150	1939	Lancashire	136
1933	MCC	158	1939	Northamptonshire	*102
1934	Glamorgan	104			

F. Mitchell (10)

Year		Score	Year		Score
1899	Gloucestershire	100	1901	Surrey	*106
1899	Leicestershire	194	1901	Warwickshire	*162
1899	Middlesex	121	1901	Leicestershire	122
1901	Hampshire	100	1901	Warwickshire	*116
1901	Middlesex	100	1901	Lancashire	106

R. Moorhouse (3)

Year		Score	Year		Score
1890	MCC	105	1896	Somerset	113
1895	Warwickshire	*102			

M.D. Moxon (17)

Year		Score	Year		Score
1981	Essex	116	1986	Indians	*112
1981	Derbyshire	111	1986	Lancashire	147
1983	Lancashire	153	1987	Windward Islands	105
1984	Kent	110	1987	Derbyshire	130
1984	Worcestershire	*126	1987	Essex	104
1985	Somerset	153	1988	Worcestershire	106
1985	Worcestershire	168	1988	Sri Lankans	132
1985	Lancashire	127	1988	Northamptonshire	191
1986	Indians	123			

J.T. Newstead

Year		Score
1908	Nottinghamshire	*100

C.M. Old (5)

Year		Score	Year		Score
1974	Indians	116	1977	Warwickshire	107
1975	Leicestershire	*115	1978	Lancashire	*100
1976	Northamptonshire	112			

E. Oldroyd (37)

Year		Score	Year		Score
1921	Warwickshire	125	1924	Essex	138
1921	Hampshire	*103	1924	Hampshire	*122
1921	Gloucestershire	*127	1924	Surrey	103
1921	Surrey	144	1925	Northamptonshire	*109
1922	Glamorgan	*151	1926	Warwickshire	104
1922	Worcestershire	121	1926	Sussex	135
1922	Warwickshire	*138	1926	Hampshire	109
1922	Glamorgan	143	1927	Cambridge University	114
1922	Leicestershire	128	1927	Gloucestershire	110
1923	Worcestershire	194	1927	Northamptonshire	110

Year		Score	Year		Score

E. Oldroyd (continued)

Year		Score	Year		Score
1927	Somerset	111	1929	MCC	147
1928	Glamorgan	*162	1929	Glamorgan	168
1928	Surrey	124	1929	England XI	143
1928	Nottinghamshire	119	1929	Hampshire	*100
1928	Worcestershire	119	1929	Surrey	140
1928	Essex	112	1930	Essex	*143
1928	Middlesex	108	1930	Somerset	*164
1928	Leicestershire	101	1930	Gloucestershire	127
1929	Cambridge University	111			

D.E.V. Padgett (29)

Year		Score	Year		Score
1955	Warwickshire	115	1962	Oxford University	*107
1956	Scotland	107	1962	Gloucestershire	*115
1959	Oxford University	*161	1962	Surrey	*125
1959	Lancashire	100	1963	Kent	101
1959	Somerset	122	1963	Derbyshire	142
1959	Nottinghamshire	*139	1964	Derbyshire	112
1960	Somerset	130	1964	Nottinghamshire	110
1960	Sussex	146	1967	Middlesex	111
1960	Surrey	117	1967	Nottinghamshire	139
1960	Northamptonshire	120	1968	Middlesex	*136
1960	Warwickshire	113	1968	Lancashire	105
1961	Nottinghamshire	114	1970	Hampshire	106
1961	Northamptonshire	*112	1970	Nottinghamshire	108
1961	Nottinghamshire	106	1971	Glamorgan	133
1961	Somerset	101			

R. Peel (6)

Year		Score	Year		Score
1889	Middlesex	158	1896	Sussex	111
1891	Sussex	128	1896	Sussex	106
1896	Warwickshire	*210	1897	Leicestershire	115

W. Rhodes (46)

Year		Score	Year		Score
1901	MCC	105	1912	Nottinghamshire	176
1904	Surrey	107	1913	Gloucestershire	110
1904	Worcestershire	196	1913	Cambridge University	102
1905	Somerset	201	1913	Northamptonshire	110
1905	Somerset	108	1913	Leicestershire	152
1906	Leicestershire	119	1914	Lancashire	*105
1906	Somerset	*115	1914	Sussex	113
1906	MCC	109	1919	Hampshire	135
1907	Leicestershire	112	1920	Nottinghamshire	*167
1908	Northamptonshire	140	1921	Leicestershire	*267
1908	Leicestershire	122	1921	Northamptonshire	*104
1908	Worcestershire	146	1921	Essex	*102
1909	Essex	114	1922	Glamorgan	110
1909	Kent	101	1922	Essex	*108
1909	Australians	108	1922	Middlesex	105
1909	Sussex	199	1922	Hampshire	106
1909	MCC	101	1923	Middlesex	126
1910	Sussex	111	1923	Essex	102
1911	Derbyshire	100	1924	Somerset	100
1911	Sussex	125	1925	Derbyshire	157
1911	MCC	128	1925	Somerset	*114
1911	MCC	115	1926	Essex	132
1912	Lancashire	107	1928	Worcestershire	*100

Year		Score	Year		Score

E. Robinson (7)

Year		Score	Year		Score
1921	Derbyshire	100	1925	Glamorgan	★108
1921	Sussex	115	1926	Glamorgan	★124
1921	Leicestershire	★135	1930	Hampshire	108
1925	Northamptonshire	★112			

P.E. Robinson (2)

1986	Kent	★104	1988	Nottinghamshire	★129

J.W. Rothery (3)

1905	Hampshire	118	1910	Derbyshire	134
1908	Kent	161			

J. Rowbotham (3)

1869	Surrey	101	1873	Surrey	113
1869	Nottinghamshire	100			

H. Rudston

1904	Leicestershire				164

A. Sellers (2)

1893	Middlesex	105	1893	Somerset	103

A.B. Sellers (4)

1934	Australians	104	1937	Kent	109
1936	Cambridge University	204	1937	Nottinghamshire	★103

K. Sharp (11)

1980	Middlesex	★100	1984	Glamorgan	132
1981	Sri Lankans	116	1984	Derbyshire	173
1982	Indians	115	1986	Gloucestershire	181
1983	Gloucestershire	121	1986	Warwickshire	★114
1983	Surrey	139	1988	Sri Lankans	128
1984	Derbyshire	104			

P.J. Sharpe (23)

1958	Somerset	141	1965	Warwickshire	100
1960	Cambridge University	★203	1967	Pakistanis	197
1960	Kent	152	1968	Nottinghamshire	★143
1962	Lancashire	★108	1968	Surrey	125
1962	Nottinghamshire	104	1968	Glamorgan	114
1962	Somerset	138	1969	MCC	101
1962	Surrey	132	1970	Kent	108
1962	Northamptonshire	110	1970	Middlesex	120
1962	Lancashire	112	1971	Glamorgan	★172
1962	Pakistanis	★136	1973	Somerset	133
1963	Derbyshire	★138	1973	Derbyshire	110
1963	Lancashire	106			

A. Sidebottom

1977	Glamorgan				116

T.F. Smailes (3)

1937	Warwickshire	109	1938	Surrey	116
1938	Glamorgan	117			

E. Smith (2)

1899	Hampshire	129	1900	Sussex	★116

Year		Score	Year		Score

G.A. Smithson (2)

| 1947 | Surrey | *107 | 1947 | Leicestershire | 169 |

G.B. Stevenson (2)

| 1980 | Derbyshire | 111 | 1982 | Warwickshire | *115 |

W.B. Stott (17)

1957	Essex	181	1960	Kent	116
1957	Leicestershire	139	1960	Hampshire	124
1957	Nottinghamshire	114	1960	Warwickshire	186
1958	Middlesex	126	1961	Hampshire	116
1958	Sussex	141	1961	Derbyshire	*114
1959	Lancashire	110	1961	Nottinghamshire	100
1959	Hampshire	*130	1962	Derbyshire	145
1959	Worcestershire	*144	1963	Lancashire	143
1960	Sussex	*138			

H. Sutcliffe (112)

1919	Northamptonshire	145	1928	Derbyshire	111
1919	Gloucestershire	118	1928	Nottinghamshire	111
1919	Lancashire	132	1928	Nottinghamshire	*100
1919	Middlesex	103	1928	Middlesex	104
1919	Kent	174	1929	South Africans	113
1920	Worcestershire	112	1929	Northamptonshire	150
1920	Nottinghamshire	107	1929	Essex	*133
1920	Essex	*125	1929	Lancashire	106
1920	Hampshire	131	1929	Surrey	*123
1922	Surrey	114	1930	Essex	*108
1922	Surrey	232	1930	Essex	*150
1922	MCC	*101	1930	Glamorgan	*132
1923	Cambridge University	*105	1930	Sussex	173
1923	Somerset	139	1930	MCC	*102
1924	Cambridge University	*108	1931	Cambridge University	*173
1924	Essex	*255	1931	Warwickshire	129
1924	Somerset	213	1931	Middlesex	*120
1924	Sussex	160	1931	Hampshire	107
1924	MCC	108	1931	Kent	230
1925	Middlesex	235	1931	Somerset	183
1925	Warwickshire	130	1931	Lancashire	195
1925	Glamorgan	121	1931	Leicestershire	187
1925	Warwickshire	206	1931	Surrey	*101
1925	Leicestershire	129	1932	Warwickshire	109
1925	MCC	171	1932	Hampshire	*104
1925	Rest of England	124	1932	Warwickshire	*153
1926	Warwickshire	102	1932	Essex	313
1926	Leicestershire	200	1932	Sussex	270
1926	Surrey	*131	1932	Gloucestershire	132
1926	MCC	107	1932	Lancashire	135
1926	MCC	*109	1932	Derbyshire	182
1927	Gloucestershire	134	1932	Essex	194
1927	Surrey	176	1932	Somerset	136
1927	Nottinghamshire	169	1932	Hampshire	112
1927	Lancashire	135	1932	Sussex	*122
1928	Sussex	228	1933	Warwickshire	205
1928	Glamorgan	*147	1933	Northamptonshire	113
1928	Lancashire	140	1933	Middlesex	177
1928	Derbyshire	138	1933	Leicestershire	174
1928	Essex	129	1933	MCC	107
1928	Lancashire	126	1933	Rest of England	*114
1928	Leicestershire	119	1934	Cambridge University	152

H. Sutcliffe (continued)

Year		Score	Year		Score
1934	Essex	166	1937	Surrey	138
1934	Surrey	203	1937	Lancashire	122
1934	Worcestershire	*187	1937	Leicestershire	109
1935	Glamorgan	*135	1938	Gloucestershire	110
1935	Worcestershire	*200	1938	Warwickshire	142
1935	Kent	110	1938	Northamptonshire	104
1935	Hampshire	100	1938	Leicestershire	105
1935	Glamorgan	121	1938	Nottinghamshire	100
1935	Nottinghamshire	135	1939	Oxford University	*125
1935	Leicestershire	212	1939	Lancashire	165
1935	Worcestershire	138	1939	Hampshire	116
1936	Surrey	129	1939	Leicestershire	*234
1936	Middlesex	202	1939	Middlesex	175
1937	Leicestershire	189	1939	Northamptonshire	*107

W.H.H. Sutcliffe (6)

Year		Score	Year		Score
1952	Worcestershire	*171	1955	Kent	107
1952	Kent	181	1955	Glamorgan	*161
1954	Northamptonshire	105	1955	Derbyshire	133

I.G. Swallow

Year		Score
1987	MCC	114

K. Taylor (16)

Year		Score	Year		Score
1956	Nottinghamshire	*168	1961	Worcestershire	141
1957	Nottinghamshire	*140	1961	Sussex	115
1958	Surrey	104	1962	Nottinghamshire	163
1959	Nottinghamshire	103	1962	Oxford University	*178
1959	Derbyshire	144	1964	Lancashire	153
1960	Sussex	*130	1964	Australians	160
1961	Warwickshire	*203	1966	MCC	106
1961	Leicestershire	159	1967	Worcestershire	162

T.L. Taylor (8)

Year		Score	Year		Score
1900	Surrey	147	1902	Derbyshire	106
1901	Leicestershire	113	1902	Derbyshire	*142
1901	Hampshire	156	1902	Leicestershire	114
1901	England XI	*135	1902	Nottinghamshire	120

J. Thewlis

Year		Score
1868	Surrey	108

F.S. Trueman (2)

Year		Score	Year		Score
1963	Northamptonshire	104	1965	Middlesex	101

J. Tunnicliffe (22)

Year		Score	Year		Score
1895	Nottinghamshire	104	1901	Derbyshire	145
1895	Middlesex	101	1902	Kent	127
1897	Sussex	147	1902	Nottinghamshire	105
1898	Gloucestershire	*107	1902	Nottinghamshire	104
1898	Kent	*108	1904	Nottinghamshire	119
1898	Lancashire	102	1904	Hampshire	128
1898	Derbyshire	243	1904	Kent	135
1900	Surrey	101	1904	Surrey	*139
1900	Hampshire	138	1905	Warwickshire	102
1900	Worcestershire	158	1907	Warwickshire	141
1900	Nottinghamshire	*100	1907	Surrey	*103

C. Turner (2)

Year		Score	Year		Score
1936	Somerset	*130	1936	Hampshire	*115

Year			Score	Year		Score

C. Tyson

| 1921 | Hampshire | | | | | ★100 |

G. Ulyett (15)

1878	Scotland		107	1887	Derbyshire	★199
1878	Gloucestershire		109	1887	Kent	124
1880	Surrey		141	1887	Gloucestershire	104
1881	Surrey		112	1890	Gloucestershire	107
1882	Surrey		120	1891	Somerset	118
1884	MCC		★146	1891	Sussex	109
1884	Middlesex		107	1892	Middlesex	111
1887	Sussex		★111			

H. Verity

| 1936 | Jamaica | | | | | 101 |

A. Waddington

| 1927 | Worcestershire | | | | | 114 |

E. Wainwright (18)

1888	Australians		105	1897	Nottinghamshire	103
1892	Sussex		104	1899	Leicestershire	153
1894	Warwickshire		107	1899	Surrey	228
1896	Warwickshire		126	1899	Kent	100
1896	Sussex		145	1900	Kent	116
1897	Gloucestershire		100	1900	Somerset	109
1897	Middlesex		171	1900	C.I. Thornton's XI	117
1897	Hampshire		★118	1901	Derbyshire	★108
1897	Sussex		★104	1901	South Africans	116

T.A. Wardall (2)

| 1892 | Gloucestershire | | 105 | 1893 | Gloucestershire | 106 |

I. Washington

| 1902 | Surrey | | | | | ★100 |

W. Watson (26)

1947	Surrey		★153	1953	Somerset	★162
1947	Worcestershire		147	1955	Sussex	163
1948	Northamptonshire		108	1955	Essex	105
1948	Derbyshire		172	1955	Lancashire	174
1949	Leicestershire		119	1955	Warwickshire	★214
1949	Warwickshire		115	1956	MCC	117
1950	Somerset		122	1956	Middlesex	149
1950	Northamptonshire		132	1956	Somerset	★139
1950	Kent		114	1956	Warwickshire	★103
1951	Derbyshire		108	1957	Scotland	134
1952	Nottinghamshire		★103	1957	Northamptonshire	162
1952	Gloucestershire		114	1957	Worcestershire	102
1952	Essex		★107	1957	Warwickshire	116

H. Wilkinson

| 1904 | MCC | | | | | 113 |

W.H. Wilkinson

| 1909 | Sussex | | | | | 103 |

Year		Score	Year		Score
			B.B. Wilson (15)		
1908	Derbyshire	109	1912	Warwickshire	150
1909	Warwickshire	102	1913	Gloucestershire	104
1909	Sussex	116	1913	Sussex	108
1909	Leicestershire	109	1914	Essex	106
1910	Nottinghamshire	108	1914	Derbyshire	101
1910	Worcestershire	115	1914	Gloucestershire	102
1910	Sussex	109	1914	Sussex	208
1911	Middlesex	125			
			E.R. Wilson		
1913	Essex				★104
			J.V. Wilson (29)		
1948	Surrey	111	1952	Surrey	121
1948	Derbyshire	140	1953	Hampshire	113
1949	Sussex	★157	1954	Leicestershire	138
1949	Scotland	★110	1954	Middlesex	111
1950	Gloucestershire	139	1954	Lancashire	★130
1950	Essex	157	1955	Cambridge University	110
1950	Nottinghamshire	142	1955	Somerset	★109
1951	Hampshire	139	1955	Warwickshire	★132
1951	Sussex	★166	1955	Essex	132
1951	Surrey	★114	1956	Oxford University	165
1951	Derbyshire	120	1957	Oxford University	132
1951	Leicestershire	107	1959	Rest of England	105
1951	Scotland	★223	1962	Warwickshire	134
1952	Oxford University	154	1962	Nottinghamshire	134
1952	Derbyshire	230			
			A. Wood		
1935	Worcestershire				★123
			J.D. Woodford		
1971	Warwickshire				101
			N.W.D. Yardley (17)		
1937	Surrey	101	1948	Surrey	114
1939	Cambridge University	★140	1949	New Zealanders	★134
1939	Warwickshire	108	1950	Surrey	104
1939	Sussex	108	1950	Somerset	★120
1946	Nottinghamshire	137	1950	Lancashire	119
1947	Glamorgan	137	1950	Scotland	101
1947	Leicestershire	100	1951	Hampshire	★183
1947	Derbyshire	177	1955	Gloucestershire	★100
1947	Hampshire	136			

★ signifies not out

Summary of centuries
for and against Yorkshire

Total	For Yorkshire In Yorkshire	Away		Total	Against Yorkshire In Yorkshire	Away
87	50	37	Derbyshire	41	19	22
62	28	34	Essex	30	16	14
54	31	23	Glamorgan	13	7	6
78	36	42	Gloucestershire	46	24	22
68	28	40	Hampshire	33	13	20
59	26	33	Kent	37	20	17
79	40	39	Lancashire	74	36	38
80	44	36	Leicestershire	32	17	15
83	43	40	Middlesex	71	28	43
64	25	39	Northamptonshire	32	18	14
103	48	55	Nottinghamshire	66	22	44
71	38	33	Somerset	28	11	17
93	42	51	Surrey	89	34	55
78	39	39	Sussex	48	19	29
82	25	57	Warwickshire	54	19	35
56	21	35	Worcestershire	32	10	22
1	1	–	Cambridgeshire	–	–	–
1198	565	633	Totals	726	313	413
9	9	–	Australians	16	16	–
9	9	–	Indians	6	6	–
8	8	–	New Zealanders	3	3	–
5	5	–	Pakistanis	1	1	–
9	9	–	South Africans	7	7	–
3	3	–	Sri Lankans	1	1	–
3	3	–	West Indians	3	3	–
41	1	40	Cambridge University	19	1	18
2	2	–	Combined Services	–	–	–
4	3	1	England XIs	3	2	1
–	–	–	International XI	1	1	–
1	–	1	Ireland	–	–	–
3	–	3	Jamaica	3	–	3
1	–	1	Liverpool & District	–	–	–
52	38	14	MCC	52	34	18
32	–	32	Oxford University	11	–	11
6	–	6	Rest of England	15	–	15
9	5	4	Scotland	1	–	1
3	3	–	C.I. Thornton's XI	4	4	–
1	1	–	I Zingari	1	1	–
201	99	102	Totals	147	80	67
1399	564	735	Grand Totals	873	393	480

Four centuries in one innings

	F.S. Jackson	117
	E. Wainwright	126
1896 *v.* Warwickshire	Lord Hawke	166
at Birmingham	R. Peel	*210

Three centuries in one innings

1884	*v.*	Cambridge University at Cambridge	L. Hall W. Bates I. Grimshaw	116 133 115
1887	*v.*	Kent at Canterbury	G. Ulyett L. Hall F. Lee	124 110 119
1897	*v.*	Sussex at Sheffield	J.T. Brown J. Tunnicliffe E. Wainwright	311 147 ★104
1899	*v.*	Middlesex at Bradford	F.S. Jackson D. Denton F. Mitchell	155 113 121
1904	*v.*	Surrey at The Oval	D. Denton G.H. Hirst J. Tunnicliffe	105 104 ★139
1919	*v.*	Gloucestershire at Leeds	H. Sutcliffe D. Denton R. Kilner	118 122 ★115
1925	*v.*	Glamorgan at Huddersfield	P. Holmes H. Sutcliffe E. Robinson	130 121 ★108
1928	*v.*	Middlesex at Lord's	P. Holmes E. Oldroyd A. Mitchell	105 108 105
1928	*v.*	Essex at Leyton	H. Sutcliffe P. Holmes M. Leyland	129 136 ★133
1929	*v.*	Glamorgan at Hull	E. Oldroyd W. Barber F.E. Greenwood	168 114 ★104
1933	*v.*	MCC at Scarborough	H. Sutcliffe A. Mitchell M. Leyland	107 158 133
1936	*v.*	Surrey at Leeds	H. Sutcliffe L. Hutton M. Leyland	129 163 ★163
1937	*v.*	Leicestershire at Hull	H. Sutcliffe L. Hutton M. Leyland	189 153 ★118
1947	*v.*	Leicestershire at Leicester	L. Hutton N.W.D. Yardley G.A. Smithson	137 100 169
1971	*v.*	Oxford University at Oxford	J.H. Hampshire R.A. Hutton A.J. Dalton	★116 101 111
1975	*v.*	Gloucestershire at Bristol	G. Boycott R.G. Lumb J.H. Hampshire	141 101 ★106

Century in each innings

D. Denton	107 and 109★	*v.* Nottinghamshire at Nottingham, 1906
G.H. Hirst	111 and 117★	*v.* Somerset at Bath, 1906
D. Denton	133 and 121	*v.* MCC at Scarborough, 1908
W. Rhodes	128 and 115	*v.* MCC at Scarborough, 1911
P. Holmes	126 and 111★	*v.* Lancashire at Manchester, 1920
H. Sutcliffe	107 and 109★	*v.* MCC at Scarborough, 1926
H. Sutcliffe	111 and 100★	*v.* Nottinghamshire at Nottingham, 1928
E.I. Lester	126 and 142	*v.* Northamptonshire at Northampton, 1947
L. Hutton	197 and 104	*v.* Essex at Southend, 1947
E.I. Lester	125★ and 132	*v.* Lancashire at Manchester, 1948
L. Hutton	165 and 100	*v.* Sussex at Hove, 1949
L. Hutton	103 and 137	*v.* MCC at Scarborough, 1952
G. Boycott	103 and 105	*v.* Nottinghamshire at Sheffield, 1966
G. Boycott	163 and 141★	*v.* Nottinghamshire at Bradford, 1983
M.D. Moxon	123 and 112★	*v.* Indians at Scarborough, 1986

The feat has been performed twelve times against Yorkshire

W.G. Grace scored 148 and 153 for Gloucestershire at Clifton, 1888.
W. Storer scored 100 and 100★ for Derbyshire, at Derby, 1896.
K.S. Ranjitsinhji scored 100 and 125★ for Sussex, at Hove, 1896.
G.L. Jessop scored 104 and 139 for Gloucestershire, at Bradford, 1900.
C.J.B. Wood scored 107★ and 117★ for Leicestershire, at Bradford, 1911.
G. Gunn scored 132 and 109★ for Nottinghamshire, at Nottingham, 1913.
D.J. Knight scored 114 and 101 for Surrey, at The Oval, 1919.
L. Fishlock scored 113 and 105 for Surrey, at The Oval, 1937.
P.B.H. May scored 174 and 100★ for MCC, at Scarborough, 1952.
Nawab of Pataudi scored 106 and 103★ for Oxford University, at Oxford, 1961.
A. Jones scored 132 and 156★ for Glamorgan, at Middlesbrough, 1976.
F.D. Stephenson scored 111 and 117 for Nottinghamshire, at Nottingham, 1988.

Highest individual scores
for and against Yorkshire

Yorkshire *versus:*

Derbyshire	*For Yorkshire:*	300–J.T. Brown at Chesterfield, 1898.
	Against:	219–J.D. Eggar at Bradford, 1949.
Most Centuries	*For Yorkshire:*	G. Boycott 9. *Against:* W. Storer 4.

Essex	*For Yorkshire:*	313–H. Sutcliffe at Leyton, 1932.
	Against:	219★–D.J. Insole at Colchester, 1949.
Most Centuries	*For Yorkshire:*	H. Sutcliffe 9. *Against:* F.L. Fane, K.W.R. Fletcher, G.A. Gooch and D.J. Insole 3 each.

Glamorgan	*For Yorkshire:*	197–L. Hutton at Swansea, 1947.
	Against:	156★–A. Jones at Middlesbrough, 1976.
Most Centuries	*For Yorkshire:*	G. Boycott, P. Holmes and H. Sutcliffe 5 each. *Against:* A. Jones and P.M. Walker 2 each.

Gloucestershire	*For Yorkshire:*	204★–R.J. Blakey at Leeds, 1987.
	Against:	318★–W.G. Grace at Cheltenham, 1876.
Most Centuries	*For Yorkshire:*	G. Boycott 6. *Against:* W.G. Grace 9.

Hampshire	*For Yorkshire:*	302★–P. Holmes at Portsmouth, 1920.
	Against:	268–Capt. E.G. Wynyard at Southampton, 1896.
Most Centuries	*For Yorkshire:*	H. Sutcliffe 6. *Against:* C.P. Mead 10.

Kent	*For Yorkshire:*	248–W. Barber at Leeds, 1934.
	Against:	188–F.E. Woolley at Bradford, 1931,
Most Centuries	*For Yorkshire:*	L. Hutton 5. *Against:* F.E. Woolley 5.

Yorkshire *versus:*

Lancashire	*For Yorkshire:*	211★–M. Leyland at Leeds, 1930.
	Against:	200★–R.H. Spooner at Manchester, 1910.
Most Centuries	*For Yorkshire:*	G. Boycott and H. Sutcliffe 9 each. *Against:* C.H. Lloyd 6.
Leicestershire	*For Yorkshire:*	341–G.H. Hirst at Leicester, 1905.
	Against:	186–N.F. Armstrong at Leicester, 1928.
Most Centuries	*For Yorkshire:*	H. Sutcliffe 10. *Against:* C.J.B. Wood 5.
Middlesex	*For Yorkshire:*	315★–P. Holmes at Lord's, 1925.
	Against:	243★–A.J. Webbe at Huddersfield, 1887.
Most Centuries	*For Yorkshire:*	P. Holmes and H. Sutcliffe 7 each. *Against:* M.W. Gatting and E.H. Hendren 6 each.
Northamptonshire	*For Yorkshire:*	277★–P. Holmes at Harrogate, 1921.
	Against:	203–G. Cook at Scarborough, 1988.
Most Centuries	*For Yorkshire:*	H. Sutcliffe 5. *Against:* W. Larkins 5.
Nottinghamshire	*For Yorkshire:*	285–P. Holmes at Nottingham, 1929.
	Against:	210–W.W. Keeton at Sheffield, 1949.
Most Centuries	*For Yorkshire:*	G. Boycott 15. *Against:* C.B. Harris, A. Shrewsbury and W. Whysall 4 each.
Somerset	*For Yorkshire:*	213–H. Sutcliffe at Dewsbury, 1924.
	Against:	217★–I.V.A. Richards at Harrogate, 1975.
Most Centuries	*For Yorkshire:*	G. Boycott 6. *Against:* L.C.H. Palairet and I.V.A. Richards 5 each.
Surrey	*For Yorkshire:*	255–W. Barber at Sheffield, 1935.
	Against:	273–T.W. Hayward at The Oval, 1899.
Most Centuries	*For Yorkshire:*	H. Sutcliffe 9. *Against:* J.B. Hobbs 8.
Sussex	*For Yorkshire:*	311–J.T. Brown at Sheffield, 1897.
	Against:	234–C.B. Fry at Bradford, 1903.
Most Centuries	*For Yorkshire:*	L. Hutton 8. *Against:* C.B. Fry 7.
Warwickshire	*For Yorkshire:*	275–P. Holmes at Bradford, 1928.
	Against:	206–C. Charlesworth at Dewsbury, 1914.
Most Centuries	*For Yorkshire:*	G. Boycott and H. Sutcliffe 8. *Against:* D.L. Amiss, H.E. Dollery, R.B. Kanhai and W.G. Quaife 4 each.
Worcestershire	*For Yorkshire:*	259★–F.A. Lowson at Worcester, 1953.
	Against:	259–D. Kenyon at Kidderminster, 1956.
Most Centuries	*For Yorkshire:*	M. Leyland 6. *Against:* D. Kenyon and G.M. Turner 5 each.
Australians	*For Yorkshire:*	167–J.T. Brown at Bradford, 1899.
	Against:	193★–B.C. Booth at Bradford, 1964.
Most Centuries	*For Yorkshire:*	G. Boycott and D. Denton 2 each. *Against:* N.C. O'Neill 2.
Indians	*For Yorkshire:*	183★–L. Hutton at Bradford, 1946.
	Against:	244★–V.S. Hazare at Sheffield, 1946.
Most Centuries	*For Yorkshire:*	M.D. Moxon 2. *Against:* V.S. Hazare, V. Mankad, P.R. Umrigar, D.K. Gaekwad, G.A. Parkar and R. Lamba 1 each.
New Zealanders	*For Yorkshire:*	175–P. Holmes at Bradford, 1927.
	Against:	126–W.M. Wallace at Bradford, 1949.
Most Centuries	*For Yorkshire:*	L. Hutton and D.B. Close 2 each. *Against:* H.G. Vivian, W.M. Wallace and J.G. Wright 1 each.

Yorkshire *versus:*

Pakistanis	*For Yorkshire:*	197–P.J. Sharpe at Leeds, 1967.
	Against:	139–A.H. Kardar at Sheffield, 1954.
Most Centuries	*For Yorkshire:*	P.J. Sharpe 2. *Against:* A.H. Kardar 1.

West Indians	*For Yorkshire:*	112★–D. Denton at Harrogate, 1906.
	Against:	164–S.F.A. Bacchus at Leeds, 1980.
Most Centuries	*For Yorkshire:*	D. Denton, L. Hutton and R.G. Lumb 1 each.
		Against: S.F.A. Bacchus, P.A. Goodman and G. St. A. Sobers 1 each.

Cambridge University	*For Yorkshire:*	207★–G. Boycott at Cambridge, 1976.
	Against:	171★–G.L. Jessop at Cambridge, 1899.
Most Centuries		171–P.B.H. May at Cambridge, 1952.
	For Yorkshire:	H. Sutcliffe 4. *Against:* G.M. Kemp 2.

MCC	*For Yorkshire:*	180★–G.H. Hirst at Lord's, 1919.
	Against:	214–E. Hendren at Lord's, 1919.
Most Centuries	*For Yorkshire:*	L. Hutton 8. *Against:* R.E.S. Wyatt 5.

Oxford University	*For Yorkshire:*	183★–F.A. Lowson at Oxford, 1956.
	Against:	201–J.E. Raphael at Oxford, 1904.
Most Centuries	*For Yorkshire:*	M. Leyland 4. *Against:* A.A. Baig and Nawab of Pataudi (Jun) 2 each.

J.B. Hobbs scored 11 centuries against Yorkshire – the highest by any individual (8 for Surrey and 3 for the Rest of England).

Three players have scored 10 centuries against Yorkshire – W.G. Grace (9 for Gloucestershire and 1 for MCC), E.H. Henderson (6 for Middlesex, 3 for MCC and 1 for the Rest of England) and C.P. Mead (all 10 for Hampshire).

Carrying bat through a completed innings

Batsman	Score	Total	Against	Season
G.R. Atkinson	30★	73	Nottinghamshire at Bradford	1865
L. Hall	31★	94	Sussex at Hove	1878
I. Grimshaw	36★	182	Kent at Maidstone	1881
L. Hall	124★	331	Sussex at Hove	1883
L. Hall	128★	285	Sussex at Huddersfield	1884
L. Hall	32★	81	Kent at Sheffield	1885
L. Hall	79★	285	Surrey at Sheffield	1885
L. Hall	37★	96	Derbyshire at Derby	1885
L. Hall	50★	173	Sussex at Huddersfield	1886
L. Hall	74★	172	Kent at Canterbury	1886
G. Ulyett	199★	399	Derbyshire at Sheffield	1887
L. Hall	119★	334	Gloucestershire at Dewsbury	1887
L. Hall	82★	218	Sussex at Hove	1887
L. Hall	34★	104	Surrey at The Oval	1888
L. Hall	129★	461	Gloucestershire at Clifton	1888
L. Hall	85★	259	Middlesex at Lord's	1889
L. Hall	41★	106	Nottinghamshire at Sheffield	1891
F.S. Jackson	59★	162	Cambridge University at Cambridge	1897
W. Rhodes	98★	184	MCC at Lord's	1903
J.W. Rothery	53★	258	Worcestershire at Worcester	1907
W. Rhodes	85★	152	Essex at Leyton	1910
P. Holmes	145★	270	Northamptonshire at Northampton	1920
H. Sutcliffe	125★	307	Essex at Southend	1920
P. Holmes	175★	377	New Zealanders at Bradford	1927
P. Holmes	110★	219	Northamptonshire at Bradford	1929
H. Sutcliffe	104★	170	Hampshire at Leeds	1932

Batsman	Score	Total	Against	Season
H. Sutcliffe	114★	202	Rest of England at The Oval	1933
H. Sutcliffe	187★	401	Worcestershire at Bradford	1934
H. Sutcliffe	135★	262	Glamorgan at Neath	1935
H. Sutcliffe	125★	322	Oxford University at Oxford	1939
L. Hutton	99★	200	Leicestershire at Sheffield	1948
L. Hutton	78★	153	Worcestershire at Sheffield	1949
F.A. Lowson	76★	218	MCC at Lord's	1951
W.B. Stott	144★	262	Worcestershire at Worcester	1959
D.E.V. Padgett	115★	230	Gloucestershire at Bristol	1962
G. Boycott	114★	297	Leicestershire at Sheffield	1968
G. Boycott	53★	119	Warwickshire at Bradford	1969
G. Boycott	182★	320	Middlesex at Lord's	1971
G. Boycott	138★	232	Warwickshire at Birmingham	1971
G. Boycott	175★	360	Nottinghamshire at Worksop	1979
G. Boycott	112★	233	Derbyshire at Sheffield	1983
G. Boycott	55★	183	Warwickshire at Leeds	1984
G. Boycott	55★	131	Surrey at Sheffield	1985

43 instances, of which L. Hall (14 times), G. Boycott (8) and H. Sutcliffe (6) account for 28 between them.

The highest percentage of an innings total is 61.17% by H. Sutcliffe (104★ *v.* Hampshire at Leeds in 1932) but P. Holmes was absent ill so only 9 wickets fell.

Other contributions exceeding 55% are:
59.48%   G. Boycott (138★ *v.* Warwickshire at Birmingham, 1971)
56.87%   G. Boycott (182★ *v.* Middlesex at Lord's, 1971)
56.43%   H. Sutcliffe (114★ *v.* Rest of England at The Oval, 1933)
55.92%   W. Rhodes (85 *v.* Essex at Leyton, 1910)

The lowest is by I. Grimshaw whose 36★ *v.* Kent at Maidstone in 1881 accounted for only 19.78% of the Yorkshire total.

Two thousand runs in a season

Batsman	Season	M	I	NO	Runs	HS	Avge	100s
G.H. Hirst	1904	32	44	3	2257	157	55.04	8
D. Denton	1905	33	52	2	2258	172	45.16	8
G.H. Hirst	1906	32	53	6	2164	169	46.04	6
D. Denton	1911	32	55	4	2161	137★	42.37	6
D. Denton	1912	36	51	4	2079	221	44.23	6
P. Holmes	1920	30	45	6	2144	302★	54.97	7
P. Holmes	1925	35	49	9	2351	315★	58.77	6
H. Sutcliffe	1925	34	48	8	2236	235	55.90	7
H. Sutcliffe	1928	27	35	5	2418	228	80.60	11
P. Holmes	1928	31	40	4	2093	275	58.13	6
H. Sutcliffe	1931	28	33	8	2351	230	94.04	9
H. Sutcliffe	1932	29	41	5	2883	313	80.08	12
M. Leyland	1933	31	44	4	2196	210★	54.90	7
A. Mitchell	1933	34	49	10	2100	158	53.84	6
H. Sutcliffe	1935	32	47	3	2183	212	49.61	8
L. Hutton	1937	28	45	6	2448	271★	62.76	8
H. Sutcliffe	1937	32	52	5	2054	189	43.70	4
L. Hutton	1939	29	44	5	2316	280★	59.38	10
L. Hutton	1947	19	31	2	2068	270★	71.31	10
L. Hutton	1949	26	44	6	2640	269★	69.47	9
F.A. Lowson	1950	31	54	5	2067	141★	42.18	5
D.E.V. Padgett	1959	35	60	8	2158	161★	41.50	4
W.B. Stott	1959	32	56	2	2034	144★	37.66	3
P.J. Sharpe	1962	36	62	8	2201	138	40.75	7
G. Boycott	1971	18	25	4	2221	233	105.76	11

A thousand runs in a season

Batsman	Runs scored	Runs scored	Runs scored
C.W.J. Athey	1113 in 1980	1339 in 1982	–
D.L. Bairstow	1083 in 1981	1102 in 1983	1163 in 1985
W. Barber	1000 in 1932	1595 in 1933	1930 in 1934
	1958 in 1935	1466 in 1937	1455 in 1938
	1501 in 1939	1170 in 1946	–
W. Bates	1093 in 1886	–	–
R.J. Blakey	1361 in 1987	–	–
J.B. Bolus	1245 in 1960	1970 in 1961	–
M.W. Booth	1202 in 1911	1076 in 1913	–
G. Boycott	1628 in 1963	1639 in 1964	1215 in 1965
	1388 in 1966	1530 in 1967	1004 in 1968
	1558 in 1970	2221 in 1971	1156 in 1972
	1478 in 1974	1915 in 1975	1288 in 1976
	1259 in 1977	1074 in 1978	1160 in 1979
	1913 in 1982	1941 in 1983	1567 in 1984
	1657 in 1985	–	–
J.T. Brown	1141 in 1893	1143 in 1894	1260 in 1895
	1755 in 1896	1634 in 1897	1693 in 1898
	1375 in 1899	1181 in 1900	1627 in 1901
	1291 in 1903	–	–
D.B. Close	1192 in 1952	1287 in 1954	1131 in 1955
	1315 in 1957	1335 in 1958	1740 in 1959
	1699 in 1960	1821 in 1961	1408 in 1962
	1145 in 1963	1281 in 1964	1127 in 1965
	1259 in 1966	–	–
K.R. Davidson	1241 in 1934	–	–
D. Denton	1099 in 1896	1357 in 1897	1595 in 1899
	1378 in 1900	1400 in 1901	1191 in 1902
	1562 in 1903	1919 in 1904	2258 in 1905
	1905 in 1906	1128 in 1907	1852 in 1908
	1765 in 1909	1183 in 1910	2161 in 1911
	2079 in 1912	1354 in 1913	1799 in 1914
	1213 in 1919	1324 in 1920	–
A. Drake	1502 in 1911	1029 in 1913	
S. Haigh	1031 in 1904	–	–
L. Hall	1004 in 1886	1400 in 1887	1013 in 1889
	1044 in 1891	–	–
H. Halliday	1357 in 1948	1484 in 1950	1351 in 1952
	1461 in 1953	–	–
J.H. Hampshire	1236 in 1963	1280 in 1964	1424 in 1965
	1105 in 1966	1244 in 1967	1133 in 1968
	1079 in 1970	1259 in 1971	1124 in 1975
	1303 in 1976	1596 in 1978	1425 in 1981
Lord Hawke	1055 in 1895	–	–
G.H. Hirst	1145 in 1896	1248 in 1897	1546 in 1899
	1752 in 1900	1669 in 1901	1113 in 1902
	1535 in 1903	2257 in 1904	1972 in 1905
	2164 in 1906	1167 in 1907	1513 in 1908
	1151 in 1909	1719 in 1910	1654 in 1911
	1119 in 1912	1414 in 1913	1655 in 1914
	1312 in 1919	–	–

Batsman	Runs scored	Runs scored	Runs scored
P. Holmes	1874 in 1919	2144 in 1920	1458 in 1921
	1614 in 1922	1884 in 1923	1610 in 1924
	2351 in 1925	1792 in 1926	1774 in 1927
	2093 in 1928	1724 in 1929	1957 in 1930
	1431 in 1931	1191 in 1932	–
L. Hutton	1282 in 1936	2448 in 1937	1171 in 1938
	2316 in 1939	1322 in 1946	2068 in 1947
	1792 in 1948	2640 in 1949	1578 in 1950
	1554 in 1951	1956 in 1952	1532 in 1953
R. Illingworth	1193 in 1957	1490 in 1959	1029 in 1961
	1610 in 1962	1301 in 1964	–
F.S. Jackson	1211 in 1896	1300 in 1897	1375 in 1898
	1468 in 1899	–	–
R. Kilner	1578 in 1913	1329 in 1914	1315 in 1919
	1240 in 1920	1137 in 1921	1125 in 1922
	1265 in 1923	1002 in 1925	1007 in 1927
E.I. Lester	1256 in 1948	1774 in 1949	1015 in 1950
	1786 in 1952	1380 in 1953	1330 in 1954
M. Leyland	1088 in 1923	1203 in 1924	1560 in 1925
	1561 in 1926	1479 in 1927	1554 in 1928
	1407 in 1929	1804 in 1930	1127 in 1931
	1821 in 1932	2196 in 1933	1228 in 1934
	1366 in 1935	1621 in 1936	1120 in 1937
	1660 in 1938	1239 in 1939	–
J.D. Love	1161 in 1981	1020 in 1983	–
F.A. Lowson	1678 in 1949	2067 in 1950	1607 in 1951
	1562 in 1952	1586 in 1953	1719 in 1954
	1082 in 1955	1428 in 1956	–
R.G. Lumb	1002 in 1973	1437 in 1975	1070 in 1978
	1465 in 1979	1223 in 1980	–
A.A. Metcalfe	1674 in 1986	1162 in 1987	1320 in 1988
A. Mitchell	1320 in 1928	1633 in 1930	1351 in 1932
	2100 in 1933	1854 in 1934	1530 in 1935
	1095 in 1936	1602 in 1937	1305 in 1938
	1218 in 1939	–	–
F. Mitchell	1678 in 1899	1801 in 1901	–
M.D. Moxon	1016 in 1984	1256 in 1985	1298 in 1987
	1430 in 1988	–	–
E. Oldroyd	1473 in 1921	1690 in 1922	1349 in 1923
	1607 in 1924	1262 in 1925	1197 in 1926
	1390 in 1927	1304 in 1928	1470 in 1929
	1285 in 1930	–	–
D.E.V. Padgett	1046 in 1956	2158 in 1959	1574 in 1960
	1865 in 1961	1750 in 1962	1380 in 1964
	1220 in 1965	1194 in 1966	1284 in 1967
	1163 in 1968	1078 in 1969	1042 in 1970
R. Peel	1193 in 1896	–	–
W. Rhodes	1251 in 1904	1353 in 1905	1618 in 1906
	1574 in 1908	1663 in 1909	1487 in 1910
	1961 in 1911	1030 in 1912	1747 in 1913
	1325 in 1914	1138 in 1919	1329 in 1921
	1368 in 1922	1168 in 1923	1030 in 1924
	1256 in 1925	1071 in 1926	–

Batsman	Runs scored	Runs scored	Runs scored
E. Robinson	1104 in 1921	1090 in 1929	–
P.E. Robinson	1173 in 1988	–	–
A. Sellers	1062 in 1893	–	–
A.B. Sellers	1109 in 1938	–	–
K. Sharp	1445 in 1984	–	–
P.J. Sharpe	1039 in 1960	1240 in 1961	2201 in 1962
	1273 in 1964	1091 in 1965	1352 in 1967
	1256 in 1968	1012 in 1969	1149 in 1970
	1320 in 1973	–	–
T.F. Smailes	1002 in 1938	–	–
W.B. Stott	1362 in 1957	1036 in 1958	2034 in 1959
	1790 in 1960	1409 in 1961	–
H. Sutcliffe	1839 in 1919	1393 in 1920	1235 in 1921
	1909 in 1922	1773 in 1923	1720 in 1924
	2236 in 1925	1672 in 1926	1814 in 1927
	2418 in 1928	1485 in 1929	1631 in 1930
	2351 in 1931	2883 in 1932	1985 in 1933
	1511 in 1934	2183 in 1935	1295 in 1936
	2054 in 1937	1660 in 1938	1416 in 1939
W.H.H. Sutcliffe	1193 in 1955	–	–
K. Taylor	1306 in 1959	1107 in 1960	1494 in 1961
	1372 in 1962	1149 in 1964	1044 in 1966
T.L. Taylor	1230 in 1901	1375 in 1902	–
J. Tunnicliffe	1029 in 1893	1311 in 1895	1350 in 1896
	1206 in 1897	1672 in 1898	1434 in 1899
	1496 in 1900	1295 in 1901	1274 in 1902
	1650 in 1904	1107 in 1905	1297 in 1906
	1195 in 1907	–	–
C. Turner	1153 in 1934	–	–
G. Ulyett	1074 in 1878	1158 in 1882	1220 in 1887
	1163 in 1891	–	–
E. Wainwright	1206 in 1892	1492 in 1897	1479 in 1899
	1044 in 1901	–	–
I. Washington	1022 in 1902	–	–
W. Watson	1331 in 1947	1352 in 1948	1586 in 1952
	1350 in 1953	1347 in 1954	1564 in 1955
	1464 in 1956	1455 in 1957	–
W.H. Wilkinson	1282 in 1908	–	–
B.B. Wilson	1054 in 1909	1478 in 1911	1453 in 1912
	1253 in 1913	1632 in 1914	–
J.V. Wilson	1460 in 1949	1548 in 1950	1985 in 1951
	1349 in 1952	1531 in 1953	1713 in 1954
	1799 in 1955	1602 in 1956	1268 in 1957
	1064 in 1960	1018 in 1961	1226 in 1962
A. Wood	1237 in 1935	–	–
N.W.D. Yardley	1208 in 1939	1299 in 1947	1413 in 1949
	1031 in 1950	–	–

Batsmen who have scored over 10,000 runs

Batsman	Runs	Completed innings	Average	Batsman	Runs	Completed innings	Average
H. Sutcliffe	38,558	768	50.20	W. Barber	15,289	443	34.51
D. Denton	33,282	997	33.38	R. Illingworth	14,986	537	27.90
G. Boycott	32,570	563	57.85	G. Ulyett	14,264	588	24.25
G.H. Hirst	32,024	922	34.73	W. Watson	14,049	367	38.28
W. Rhodes	31,098	1,035	30.04	F.A. Lowson	13,897	373	37.25
P. Holmes	26,220	625	41.95	Lord Hawke	13,124	648	20.25
M. Leyland	26,180	638	41.03	R. Kilner	13,104	435	29.91
L. Hutton	24,807	465	53.34	K. Taylor	12,864	480	26.80
D.B. Close	22,650	709	31.94	E. Wainwright	12,768	582	21.93
J.H. Hampshire	21,979	635	34.61	D.L. Bairstow	12,507	469	26.66
J.V. Wilson	20,539	658	31.21	L. Hall	12,079	501	24.10
D.E.V. Padgett	20,306	711	28.55	N.W.D. Yardley	11,632	364	31.95
J. Tunnicliffe	20,109	749	26.84	R.G. Lumb	11,525	365	31.57
A. Mitchell	18,034	479	37.64	R. Peel	11,131	523	21.28
P.J. Sharpe	17,685	595	29.72	S. Haigh	10,993	577	19.05
J.T. Brown	16,380	559	29.30	E.I. Lester	10,616	312	34.02
E. Oldroyd	15,876	458	34.66	Hon. F.S. Jackson	10,371	306	33.89

Record partnerships for Yorkshire

1st wkt	555	P. Holmes (224★) and H. Sutcliffe (313) v. Essex at Leyton, 1932.
2nd wkt	346	W. Barber (162) and M. Leyland (189) v Middlesex at Sheffield, 1932.
3rd wkt	323★	J. Sutcliffe (147★) and M. Leyland (189★) v. Glamorgan at Huddersfield, 1928.
4th wkt	312	D. Denton (168★) and G.H. Hirst (146) v. Hampshire at Southampton, 1914.
5th wkt	340	E. Wainwright (228) and G.H. Hirst (186) v. Surrey at The Oval, 1899.
6th wkt	276	M. Leyland (191) and E. Robinson (124★) v. Glamorgan at Swansea, 1926.
7th wkt	254	W. Rhodes (135) and D.C.F. Burton (142★) v. Hampshire at Dewsbury, 1979.
8th wkt	292	R. Peel (210★) and Lord Hawke (166) v. Warwickshire at Birmingham, 1896.
9th wkt	192	G.H. Hirst (130★) and S. Haigh (85) v. Surrey at Bradford, 1898.
10th wkt	149	G. Boycott (79) and G.B. Stevenson (115★) v. Warwickshire at Birmingham, 1982.

Record partnerships against Yorkshire

1st wkt	346	H.T. Hewitt (201) and L.C.H. Palairet (146) for Somerset at Taunton, 1892.
2nd wkt	349	C.B. Fry (209) and E.H. Killick (200) for Sussex at Hove, 1901.
3rd wkt	344	G. Brown (204) and C.P. Mead (183) for Hampshire at Portsmouth, 1927.
4th wkt	447	R. Abel (193) and T. Hayward (273) for Surrey at The Oval, 1899.
5th wkt	261	W.G. Grace (318★) and W.O. Moberley (103) for Gloucestershire at Cheltenham, 1876.
6th wkt	294	D.R. Jardine (157) and P.G.H. Fender (177) for Surrey at Bradford, 1928.
7th wkt	220★	J.T. Murray (111★) and D. Bennett (104★) for Middlesex at Leeds, 1964.
8th wkt	172	W.E. Astill (102) and A.E.R. Gilligan (100) for MCC at Scarborough, 1923.
9th wkt	160	D.R. Wilcox (64) and R. Smith (86★) for Essex at Southend, 1947.
10th wkt	128	F.R. Santall (105★) and W. Sanders (54) for Warwickshire at Birmingham, 1930.

Highest partnerships for each wicket

Qualification

First wicket 175 runs   Sixth wicket 150 runs
Second wicket 175 runs   Seventh wicket 125 runs
Third wicket 175 runs   Eighth wicket 125 runs
Fourth wicket 175 runs   Ninth wicket 100 runs
Fifth wicket 150 runs   Tenth wicket 100 runs

First wicket

555 P. Holmes (224*) and H. Sutcliffe (313)
     v. Essex at Leyton, 1932
554 J.T. Brown (300) and J. Tunnicliffe (243)
     v. Derbyshire at Chesterfield, 1898
378 J.T. Brown (311) and J. Tunnicliffe (147)
     v. Sussex at Sheffield, 1897
351 G. Boycott (184) and M.D. Moxon (168)
     v. Worcestershire at Worcester, 1985
347 P. Holmes (302*) and H. Sutcliffe (131)
     v. Hampshire at Portsmouth, 1920
323 P. Holmes (125) and H. Sutcliffe (195)
     v. Lancashire at Sheffield, 1931
315 H. Sutcliffe (189) and L. Hutton (153)
     v. Leicestershire at Hull, 1937
315 H. Sutcliffe (116) and L. Hutton (280*)
     v. Hampshire at Sheffield, 1939
309 P. Holmes (250) and H. Sutcliffe (129)
     v. Warwickshire at Birmingham, 1931
290 P. Holmes (179*) and H. Sutcliffe (104)
     v. Middlesex at Leeds, 1928
288 G. Boycott (130*) and R.G. Lumb (159)
     v. Somerset at Harrogate, 1979
286 L. Hutton (156) and F.A. Lowson (115)
     v. South Africans at Sheffield, 1951
282 M.D. Moxon (147) and A.A. Metcalfe (151)
     v. Lancashire at Manchester, 1986
281* W.B. Stott (138*) and K. Taylor (130*)
     v. Sussex at Hove, 1960
279 P. Holmes (133) and H. Sutcliffe (145)
     v. Northamptonshire at Northampton, 1919
274 P. Holmes (199) and H. Sutcliffe (139)
     v. Somerset at Hull, 1923
274 P. Holmes (180) and H. Sutcliffe (134)
     v. Gloucestershire at Gloucester, 1927
272 P. Holmes (194) and H. Sutcliffe (129)
     v. Leicestershire at Hull, 1925
268 P. Holmes (136) and H. Sutcliffe (129)
     v. Essex at Leyton, 1928
267 W. Barber (248) and L. Hutton (70) *v.* Kent
     at Leeds, 1934
265* P. Holmes (127*) and H. Sutcliffe (131*)
     v. Surrey at The Oval, 1926
264 G. Boycott (161*) and R.G. Lumb (132)
     v. Gloucestershire at Leeds, 1976
253 P. Holmes (123) and H. Sutcliffe (132)
     v. Lancashire at Sheffield, 1919
248 G. Boycott (163) and A.A. Metcalfe (122)
     v. Nottinghamshire at Bradford, 1983
245 L. Hutton (152) and F.A. Lowson (120)
     v. Lancashire at Leeds, 1952
241 P. Holmes (142) and H. Sutcliffe (123*)
     v. Surrey at The Oval, 1929

240 G. Boycott (233) and P.J. Sharpe (92)
     v. Essex at Colchester, 1971
238* P. Holmes (126*) and H. Sutcliffe (105*)
     v. Cambridge Univ. at Cambridge, 1923
236 G. Boycott (131) and K. Taylor (153)
     v. Lancashire at Manchester, 1964
235 P. Holmes (130) and H. Sutcliffe (132*)
     v. Glamorgan at Sheffield, 1930
233 G. Boycott (141*) and R.G. Lumb (90)
     v. Cambridge Univ. at Cambridge, 1973
233 H. Halliday (116) and W. Watson (108)
     v. Northamptonshire at Northampton, 1948
230 H. Sutcliffe (129) and L. Hutton (163)
     v. Surrey at Leeds, 1939
230 W.B. Stott (114) and K. Taylor (140*)
     v. Nottinghamshire at Nottingham, 1957
228 H. Halliday (90) and J.V. Wilson (223*)
     v. Scotland at Scarborough, 1951
228 G. Boycott (141) and R.G. Lumb (101)
     v. Gloucestershire at Bristol, 1975
227 P. Holmes (110) and H. Sutcliffe (119)
     v. Leicestershire at Leicester, 1928
225 R.G. Lumb (101) and C.W.J. Athey (125*)
     v. Gloucestershire at Sheffield, 1980
224 C.W.J. Athey (114) and J.D. Love (104)
     v. Warwickshire at Birmingham, 1980
222 W.B. Stott (141) and K. Taylor (90)
     v. Sussex at Bradford, 1958
221 P. Holmes (130) and H. Sutcliffe (121)
     v. Glamorgan at Huddersfield, 1925
219 P. Holmes (102) and A. Mitchell (130*)
     v. Somerset at Bradford, 1930
218 M. Leyland (110) and H. Sutcliffe (235)
     v. Middlesex at Leeds, 1925
218 R.G. Lumb (145) and M.D. Moxon (111)
     v. Derbyshire at Sheffield, 1981
210* P. Holmes (101*) and H. Sutcliffe (100*)
     v. Nottinghamshire at Nottingham, 1928
210 G. Boycott (128) and P.J. Sharpe (197)
     v. Pakistanis at Leeds, 1967
209 F.A. Lowson (115) and D.E.V. Padgett (107)
     v. Scotland at Hull, 1956
208 A. Mitchell (85) and E. Oldroyd (111)
     v. Cambridge Univ. at Cambridge, 1929
207 A. Mitchell (90) and W. Barber (107)
     v. Middlesex at Lord's, 1935
206 G. Boycott (118) and R.G. Lumb (87)
     v. Glamorgan at Sheffield, 1978
203 L. Hutton (119) and F.A. Lowson (83)
     v. Somerset at Huddersfield, 1952
200* P. Holmes (107*) and H. Sutcliffe (80*)
     v. Oxford University at Oxford, 1930

199 P. Holmes (79) and H. Sutcliffe (130)
   v. Warwickshire at Birmingham, 1925

199 P. Holmes (143) and H. Sutcliffe (89)
   v. Lancashire at Manchester, 1926

197 W. Rhodes (110) and B. B. Wilson (104)
   v. Gloucestershire at Bristol, 1913

197 P. Holmes (140) and H. Sutcliffe (88)
   v. Leicestershire at Leicester, 1919

197 L. Hutton (151) and F.A. Lowson (84)
   v. Surrey at The Oval, 1951

196 W.B. Stott (82) and P.J. Sharpe (203★),
   v. Cambridge Univ. at Cambridge, 1960

196 R.A. Hutton (101) and A.J. Dalton (111)
   v. Oxford University at Oxford, 1971

195 P. Holmes (83) and H. Sutcliffe (160)
   v. Sussex at Sheffield, 1924

194 F.A. Lowson (115) and J.V. Wilson (91)
   v. Somerset at Taunton, 1954

192 M. Leyland (133) and A. Mitchell (89)
   v. Surrey at Sheffield, 1926

191 P. Holmes (149) and H. Sutcliffe (70)
   v. Middlesex at Lord's, 1920

190 F.A. Lowson (90) and W. Watson (134)
   v. Scotland at Paisley, 1957

189 L. Hutton (104) and H. Halliday (80)
   v. Essex at Southend-on-Sea, 1947

189 R.G. Lumb (103) and C.W.J. Athey (87)
   v. Leicestershire at Leicester, 1978

186 L. Hall (92) and W. Bates (136)
   v. Sussex at Hove, 1886

186 G. Boycott (175★) and R.G. Lumb (88)
   v. Middlesex at Scarborough, 1975

185★ M.D. Moxon (89★) and A.A. Metcalfe (78★)
   v. Middlesex at Leeds, 1988

184 P. Holmes (83) and H. Sutcliffe (111)
   v. Nottinghamshire at Nottingham, 1928

182 G. Boycott (201★) and R.G. Lumb (77)
   v. Middlesex at Lord's, 1975

181 H. Sutcliffe (86) and L. Hutton (271★)
   v. Derbyshire at Sheffield, 1937

181 G. Boycott (105) and R.G. Lumb (70)
   v. Hampshire at Southampton, 1972

180 W. Rhodes (152) and B.B. Wilson (79)
   v. Leicestershire at Leicester, 1913

180 P. Holmes (99) and H. Sutcliffe (74)
   v. Rest of England at The Oval, 1923

178 G. Boycott (101) and R.G. Lumb (114)
   v. Lancashire at Manchester, 1973

178 G. Boycott (135) and R.G. Lumb (67)
   v. Lancashire at Manchester, 1980

178 G. Boycott (129) and R.G. Lumb (81)
   v. Somerset at Weston-super-Mare, 1982

177 G. Boycott (68) and K. Taylor (106)
   v. MCC at Lord's, 1966

176 E. Lockwood (91) and J. Thewlis (108)
   v. Surrey at The Oval, 1868

176 F.A. Lowson (154) and K. Taylor (57)
   v. Somerset at Taunton, 1956

176 G. Boycott (154) and B. Leadbeater (71)
   v. Nottinghamshire at Nottingham, 1977

175 F.S. Jackson (81) and J. Tunnicliffe (96)
   v. Warwickshire at Sheffield, 1897

Second wicket

346 W. Barber (162) and M. Leyland (189)
   v. Middlesex at Sheffield, 1932

343 F.A. Lowson (183★) and J.V. Wilson (165)
   v. Oxford University at Oxford, 1956

333 P. Holmes (209) and E. Oldroyd (138★)
   v. Warwickshire at Birmingham, 1922

314 H. Sutcliffe (255★) and E. Oldroyd (138)
   v. Essex at Southend-on-Sea, 1924

305 J.W. Rothery (134) and D. Denton (182)
   v. Derbyshire at Chesterfield, 1910

302 W. Watson (172) and J.V. Wilson (140)
   v. Derbyshire at Scarborough, 1948

301 P.J. Sharpe (172★) and D.E.V. Padgett (133)
   v. Glamorgan at Swansea, 1971

288 H. Sutcliffe (165) and A. Mitchell (136)
   v. Lancashire at Manchester, 1939

280 L. Hall (160) and F. Lee (165)
   v. Lancashire at Bradford, 1887

266★ K. Taylor (178★) and D.E.V. Padgett (107★)
   v. Oxford University at Oxford, 1962

261★ L. Hutton (146★) and J.V. Wilson (110★)
   v. Scotland at Hull, 1949

260 R.G. Lumb (144) and K. Sharp (132)
   v. Glamorgan at Cardiff, 1984

258 H. Sutcliffe (230) and E. Oldroyd (93)
   v. Kent at Folkestone, 1931

253 B.B. Wilson (150) and D. Denton (200★)
   v. Warwickshire at Birmingham, 1912

248 H. Sutcliffe (200) and M. Leyland (116)
   v. Leicestershire at Leicester, 1926

244 P. Holmes (138) and E. Oldroyd (151★)
   v. Glamorgan at Cardiff, 1922

243 G. Boycott (141) and J.D. Love (163)
   v. Nottinghamshire at Bradford, 1976

237 H. Sutcliffe (118) and D. Denton (122)
   v. Gloucestershire at Leeds, 1919

237 M.D. Moxon (132) and K. Sharp (128)
   v. Sri Lankans at Leeds, 1988

236 F.A. Lowson (112) and J.V. Wilson (157)
   v. Essex at Leeds, 1950

230 L. Hutton (180) and A. Mitchell (100)
   v. Cambridge Univ. at Cambridge, 1938

225 H. Sutcliffe (138) and E. Oldroyd (97)
   v. Derbyshire at Dewsbury, 1928

223 M.D. Moxon (153) and R.J. Blakey (90)
   v. Somerset at Leeds, 1985

222 H. Sutcliffe (174) and D. Denton (114)
   v. Kent at Dover, 1919

219 F.S. Jackson (155) and D. Denton (113)
   v. Middlesex at Bradford, 1899

217 R.G. Lumb (107) and J.D. Love (107)
   v. Oxford University at Oxford, 1978

206 J. Tunnicliffe (102) and F.S. Jackson (134★)
   v. Lancashire at Sheffield, 1898

206 H. Sutcliffe (187) and M. Leyland (90)
   v. Leicestershire at Leicester, 1931

205 H. Sutcliffe (174) and A. Mitchell (95)
   v. Leicestershire at Leicester, 1933

205 G. Boycott (148) and P.J. Sharpe (108)
   v. Kent at Sheffield, 1970

203 A.T. Barber (100) and E. Oldroyd (143)
   v. an England XI at Sheffield, 1929

202* W. Rhodes (115*) and G.H. Hirst (117*)
    v. Somerset at Bath, 1906

202 G. Boycott (113) and C.W.J. Athey (114)
    v. Northamptonshire at Northampton, 1978

199 W.B. Stott (100) and D.E.V. Padgett (106)
    v. Nottinghamshire at Nottingham, 1961

198 H. Sutcliffe (152) and W. Barber (103)
    v. Cambridge Univ. at Cambridge, 1934

197 B.B. Wilson (74) and D. Denton (191)
    v. Hampshire at Southampton, 1912

197 K. Taylor (160) and D.E.V. Padgett (70)
    v. Australians at Sheffield, 1964

196 H. Sutcliffe (232) and E. Oldroyd (83)
    v. Surrey at The Oval, 1922

196 L. Hutton (137) and G.A. Smithson (169)
    v. Leicestershire at Leicester, 1947

195 G. Boycott (126*) and K. Sharp (95)
    v. Gloucestershire at Bradford, 1984

194 J.T. Brown (168) and F.S. Jackson (133)
    v. Cambridge Univ. at Cambridge, 1899

194 L. Hutton (163) and R. Illingworth (56)
    v. Combined Services at Harrogate, 1954

193 H. Sutcliffe (112) and D. Denton (209*)
    v. Worcestershire at Worcester, 1920

192 P. Holmes (108) and E. Oldroyd (109)
    v. Hampshire at Bournemouth, 1926

192 P. Holmes (126) and E. Oldroyd (111)
    v. Somerset at Bradford, 1927

192 P.J. Sharpe (197) and D.E.V. Padgett (70)
    v. Pakistanis at Leeds, 1967

191 H. Sutcliffe (102) and E. Oldroyd (104)
    v. Warwickshire at Birmingham, 1926

191 D.B. Close (143) and J.V. Wilson (109*)
    v. Somerset at Taunton, 1955

190 G. Boycott (113) and P.J. Sharpe (106)
    v. Lancashire at Manchester, 1963

190 G. Boycott (136*) and D.E.V. Padgett (79)
    v. Warwickshire at Birmingham, 1966

188 H. Halliday (100) and J.V. Wilson (94)
    v. Kent at Scarborough, 1953

187 H. Halliday (130) and J.V. Wilson (80)
    v. Gloucestershire at Bristol, 1948

186 L. Hall (110) and F. Lee (119)
    v. Kent at Canterbury, 1887

185 L. Hutton (153) and J.V. Wilson (142)
    v. Nottinghamshire at Nottingham 1950

182 H. Sutcliffe (205) and A. Mitchell (52)
    v. Warwickshire at Birmingham, 1933

181 P. Holmes (97) and A. Mitchell (176)
    v. Nottinghamshire at Bradford, 1930

181 H. Sutcliffe (109) and A. Mitchell (100)
    v. Leicestershire at Leicester, 1937

181 G. Boycott (76) and A.A. Metcalfe (108)
    v. Worcestershire at Worcester, 1986

178* L. Hutton (280*) and W. Barber (91*)
    v. Hampshire at Sheffield, 1939

178 L. Hutton (141) and H. Halliday (97*)
    v. Somerset at Huddersfield, 1950

178 D.E.V. Padgett (142) and P.J. Sharpe (138*)
    v. Derbyshire at Chesterfield, 1963

177 L. Hutton (141) and W. Barber (70)
    v. Oxford University at Oxford, 1938

175 B.B. Wilson (102) and D. Denton (140)
    v. Warwickshire at Birmingham, 1909

175 G. Boycott (133) and D.E.V. Padgett (59)
    v. Derbyshire at Scarborough, 1971

Third wicket

323* H. Sutcliffe (147*) and M. Leyland (189*)
    v. Glamorgan at Huddersfield, 1928

301 H. Sutcliffe (175) and M. Leyland (180*)
    v. Middlesex at Lord's, 1939

258* J.T. Brown (134*) and F. Mitchell (116*)
    v. Warwickshire at Bradford, 1901

252 D.E.V. Padgett (139*) and D.B. Close (154)
    v. Nottinghamshire at Nottingham, 1959

249 D.E.V. Padgett (95) and D.B. Close (184)
    v. Nottinghamshire at Scarborough, 1960

248 C. Johnson (102) and J.H. Hampshire (155*)
    v. Gloucestershire at Leeds, 1976

247 P. Holmes (175*) and M. Leyland (118)
    v. New Zealanders at Bradford, 1927

244 D.E.V. Padgett (161*) and D.B. Close (144)
    v. Oxford University at Oxford, 1959

240 L. Hutton (151) and M. Leyland (95)
    v. Surrey at Leeds, 1939

236 H. Sutcliffe (107) and R. Kilner (137)
    v. Nottinghamshire at Nottingham, 1920

233 L. Hutton (101) and M. Leyland (167)
    v. Worcestershire at Stourbridge, 1937

229 L. Hall (86) and R. Peel (158)
    v. Middlesex at Lord's, 1889

228 A. Mitchell (142) and M. Leyland (133)
    v. Worcestershire at Sheffield, 1933

228 W. Barber (141) and M. Leyland (114)
    v. Surrey at The Oval, 1939

228 J.V. Wilson (132*) and D.E.V. Padgett (115)
    v. Warwickshire at Birmingham, 1955

226 D.E.V. Padgett (117) and D.B. Close (198)
    v. Surrey at The Oval, 1960

224 J.V. Wilson (110) and D.B. Close (114)
    v. Cambridge Univ. at Cambridge, 1955

224 G. Boycott (140*) and K. Sharp (121)
    v. Gloucestershire at Cheltenham, 1983

221 A. Mitchell (138) and M. Leyland (134)
    v. Nottinghamshire at Bradford, 1933

219 L. Hall (116) and W. Bates (133)
    v. Cambridge Univ. at Cambridge, 1884

216 R.G. Lumb (118) and J.H. Hampshire (127)
    v. Surrey at The Oval, 1975

215 A. Mitchell (73) and M. Leyland (139)
    v. Surrey at Bradford, 1928

213 E. Oldroyd (168) and W. Barber (114)
    v. Glamorgan at Hull, 1929

208 J.V. Wilson (157*) and E.I. Lester (112)
    v. Sussex at Leeds, 1949

205* E. Oldroyd (122*) and M. Leyland (100*)
    v. Hampshire at Harrogate, 1924

205 F.S. Jackson (124) and D. Denton (112)
    v. Somerset at Taunton, 1897

205 D.E.V. Padgett (83) and D.B. Close (128)
    v. Somerset at Bath, 1959

203 D. Denton (132) and J. Tunnicliffe (102)
    v. Warwickshire at Birmingham, 1905

203 A.A. Metcalfe (216*) and P.E. Robinson (88)
    v. Middlesex at Leeds, 1988

201 J. Tunnicliffe (101) and T.L. Taylor (147)
v. Surrey at The Oval, 1900

201 H. Sutcliffe (87) and W. Barber (130)
v. Leicestershire at Leicester, 1938

199 L. Hutton (194★) and E.I. Lester (83)
v. Nottinghamshire at Nottingham, 1951

199 P.J. Sharpe (132) and D.E.V. Padgett (125)
v. Surrey at Sheffield, 1962

197 H. Sutcliffe (202) and M. Leyland (107)
v. Middlesex at Scarborough, 1936

194 E. Oldroyd (100★) and M. Leyland (104)
v. Hampshire at Bournemouth, 1929

193 D. Denton (113) and A. Drake (147★)
v. Derbyshire at Chesterfield, 1911

192 L. Hutton (197) and W. Watson (71)
v. Essex at Southend-on-Sea, 1947

191 L. Hutton (163) and M. Leyland (163★)
v. Surrey at Leeds, 1936

191 G. Boycott (104) and D. Love (129)
v. Warwickshire at Birmingham, 1977

187 F.A. Lowson (98) and E.I. Lester (163)
v. Essex at Romford, 1954

187 J.B. Bolus (133) and D.B. Close (132)
v. Surrey at The Oval, 1961

186 G. Boycott (169) and J.H. Hampshire (83)
v. Lancashire at Sheffield, 1971

184 G. Boycott (122★) and J.H. Hampshire (84)
v. Derbyshire at Chesterfield, 1981

183 A. Mitchell (91) and M. Leyland (149)
v. Derbyshire at Derby, 1928

182 G. Boycott (151) and J.H. Hampshire (95)
v. Leicestershire at Bradford, 1971

181 D. Denton (119) and J. Tunnicliffe (80)
v. South Africans at Scarborough, 1904

180 G. Ulyett (109) and R. Peel (128)
v. Sussex at Hove, 1891

180 D.E.V. Padgett (72) and J.H. Hampshire (110★)
v. Lancashire at Sheffield, 1965

179 A. Mitchell (158) and M. Leyland (133)
v. MCC at Scarborough, 1933

177 D. Denton (124) and R. Kilner (88)
v. Sussex at Hove, 1914

177 A.B. Sellers (204) and H. Sutcliffe (49)
v. Cambridge Univ. at Cambridge, 1936

176 E. Oldroyd (82) and R. Kilney (90)
v. Derbyshire at Derby, 1922

176 G. Boycott (139★) and J.D. Love (89)
v. Somerset at Harrogate, 1977

Fourth wicket

312 D. Denton (168★) and G.H. Hirst (146)
v. Hampshire at Southampton, 1914

299 P. Holmes (277★) and R. Kilner (150)
v. Northamptonshire at Harrogate, 1921

271 B.B. Wilson (208) and W. Rhodes (113)
v. Sussex at Bradford, 1914

259 A. Drake (115) and G.H. Hirst (218)
v. Sussex at Hastings, 1911

258 J. Tunnicliffe (128) and G.H. Hirst (152)
v. Hampshire at Portsmouth, 1904

249 W.B. Stott (143) and G. Boycott (145)
v. Lancashire at Sheffield, 1963

247★ R.G. Lumb (165★) and S.N. Hartley (104★)
v. Gloucestershire at Bradford, 1984

247 M. Leyland (263) and L. Hutton (83)
v. Essex at Hull, 1936

226 W.H. Wilkinson (89) and G.H. Hirst (140)
v. Northamptonshire at Hull, 1909

225 C.H. Grimshaw (85) and G.H. Hirst (169)
v. Oxford University at Oxford, 1906

212 B. Wilson (108) and G.H. Hirst (166★)
v. Sussex at Hastings, 1913

212 G. Boycott (260★) and J.H. Hampshire (80)
v. Essex at Colchester, 1970

211 J.V. Wilson (120) and W. Watson (108)
v. Derbyshire at Harrogate, 1951

210★ A. Mitchell (150★) and M. Leyland (117★)
v. Worcestershire at Worcester, 1933

210 E.I. Lester (178) and W. Watson (97)
v. Nottinghamshire at Nottingham, 1952

205★ G. Boycott (151★) and P.J. Sharpe (79★)
v. Leicestershire at Leicester, 1964

205 E. Oldroyd (121) and R. Kilner (117)
v. Worcestershire at Dudley, 1922

205 W. Watson (162★) and E.I. Lester (98)
v. Somerset at Leeds, 1953

201★ J.H. Hampshire (105★) and D.B. Close (101★)
v. Surrey at Bradford, 1965

201 W.H.H. Sutcliffe (181) and L. Hutton (120)
v. Kent at Canterbury, 1952

200 J.V. Wilson (92) and W. Watson (122)
v. Somerset at Taunton, 1950

197 N.W.D. Yardley (177) and A. Coxon (58)
v. Derbyshire at Scarborough, 1947

196 M.D. Moxon (130) and D.L. Bairstow (104)
v. Derbyshire at Harrogate, 1987

193 A. Drake (85) and G.H. Hirst (156)
v. Lancashire at Manchester, 1911

192 J.V. Wilson (132) and W. Watson (105)
v. Essex at Bradford, 1955

191 M. Leyland (114) and C. Turner (63)
v. Essex at Ilford, 1938

188 H. Myers (60) and G.H. Hirst (158)
v. Cambridge Univ. at Cambridge, 1910

187 E. Oldroyd (168) and F.E. Greenwood (104★)
v. Glamorgan at Hull, 1929

187 K. Taylor (203★) and W.B. Stott (57)
v. Warwickshire at Birmingham, 1961

184 J.H. Hampshire (96) and R. Illingworth (100★)
v. Leicestershire at Sheffield, 1968

182★ E.I. Lester (101★) and W. Watson (103★)
v. Nottinghamshire at Bradford, 1952

180★ G. Boycott (207★) and B. Leadbeater (50★)
v. Cambridge Univ. at Cambridge, 1976

180 J. Tunnicliffe (139★) and G.H. Hirst (108)
v. Surrey at The Oval, 1904

179 J.H. Hampshire (179) and S.N. Hartley (63)
v. Surrey at Harrogate, 1981

178 E.I. Lester (186) and J.V. Wilson (71)
v. Warwickshire at Scarborough, 1949

177 J.D. Love (105★) and J.H. Hampshire (89)
v. Lancashire at Manchester, 1980

175 L. Hutton (177) and W. Barber (84)
v. Sussex at Scarborough, 1939

Fifth wicket

340 E. Wainwright (228) and G.H. Hirst (186)
   v. Surrey at The Oval, 1899
329 F. Mitchell (194) and E. Wainwright (153)
   v. Leicestershire at Leicester, 1899
276 W. Rhodes (104★) and R. Kilner (166)
   v. Northamptonshire at Northampton, 1921
273 L. Hutton (270★) and N.W.D. Yardley (136)
   v. Hampshire at Bournemouth, 1947
245★ H. Sutcliffe (107★) and W. Barber (128★)
   v. Northamptonshire at Northampton, 1939
217 D.B. Close (140★) and R. Illingworth (107)
   v. Warwickshire at Sheffield, 1962
198 E. Wainwright (145) and R. Peel (111)
   v. Sussex at Bradford, 1896
198 W. Barber (168) and K.R. Davidson (101★)
   v. MCC at Lord's, 1934
196★ R. Kilner (115★) and G.H. Hirst (82★)
   v. Gloucestershire at Leeds, 1919
193 A. Mitchell (189) and W. Rhodes (88)
   v. Northamptonshire at Northampton, 1926
193 J.D. Love (106) and S.N. Hartley (108)
   v. Oxford University at Oxford, 1985
192 C.W.J. Athey (114★) and J.D. Love (123)
   v. Surrey at The Oval, 1982
191★ L. Hutton (271★) and C. Turner (81★)
   v. Derbyshire at Sheffield, 1937
190★ R.J. Blakey (204★) and J.D. Love (79★)
   v. Gloucestershire at Leeds, 1987
188 D.E.V. Padgett (146) and J.V. Wilson (72)
   v. Sussex at Middlesbrough, 1960
187 J.V. Wilson (230) and H. Halliday (74)
   v. Derbyshire at Sheffield, 1952
185 G. Boycott (104★) and K. Sharp (99)
   v. Kent at Tunbridge Wells, 1984
182 E. Lockwood (208) and E. Lumb (40)
   v. Kent at Gravesend, 1882
182 B.B. Wilson (109) and W. Rhodes (111)
   v. Sussex at Hove, 1910
182 D.B. Close (164) and J.V. Wilson (55)
   v. Combined Services at Harrogate, 1954
181 A.A. Metcalfe (149) and J.D. Love (88)
   v. Glamorgan at Leeds, 1936
177 Hon. F.S. Jackson (87) and G.H. Hirst (232★)
   v. Surrey at The Oval, 1905
176 L. Hutton (176★) and A. Coxon (72)
   v. Sussex at Sheffield, 1948
175 A. Drake (108) and K. Kilner (77)
   v. Cambridge Univ. at Cambridge, 1913
173 H. Sutcliffe (206) and R. Kilner (124)
   v. Warwickshire at Dewsbury, 1925
170 W. Rhodes (157) and R. Kilner (87)
   v. Derbyshire at Leeds, 1925
170 J.V. Wilson (130★) and N.W.D. Yardley (67)
   v. Lancashire at Manchester, 1954
169 W. Watson (147) and A.B. Sellers (92)
   v. Worcestershire at Worcester, 1947
168 T. Barber (63) and A. Mitchell (122★)
   v. Worcestershire at Worcester, 1929
165 E. Oldroyd (143) and W. Rhodes (110)
   v. Glamorgan at Leeds, 1922
165 K. Sharp (100★) and P. Carrick (73)
   v. Middlesex at Lord's, 1980

164 A.A. Metcalfe (151) and D.L. Bairstow (88)
   v. Northamptonshire at Luton, 1986
159★ J.D. Love (170★) and D.L. Bairstow (52★)
   v. Worcestershire at Worcester, 1979
159 D.B. Close (128) and R. Illingworth (74)
   v. Lancashire at Sheffield, 1959
159 J.H. Hampshire (183★) and C. Johnson (53)
   v. Sussex at Hove, 1971
158★ G. Boycott (153★) and P.E. Robinson (74★)
   v. Derbyshire at Harrogate, 1984
157 T.L. Taylor (135★) and G.H. Hirst (72)
   v. an England XI at Hastings, 1901
157 G.H. Hirst (142) and F. Smith (51)
   v. Somerset at Bradford, 1903
157 W. Barber (87) and N.W.D. Yardley (101)
   v. Surrey at The Oval, 1937
153 S.N. Hartley (87) and M.D. Moxon (112★)
   v. Indians at Scarborough, 1986
152 J.H. Hampshire (83) and S.N. Hartley (106)
   v. Nottinghamshire at Nottingham, 1981
151★ G.H. Hirst (102★) and R. Kilner (50★)
   v. Kent at Bradford, 1913
151 G.H. Hirst (120) and F. Smith (55)
   v. Kent at Leeds, 1903
151 W. Rhodes (57) and R. Kilner (90)
   v. Nottinghamshire at Nottingham, 1925

Sixth wicket

276 M. Leyland (191) and E. Robinson (124★)
   v. Glamorgan at Swansea, 1926
233 M.W. Booth (210) and G.H. Hirst (100)
   v. Worcestershire at Worcester, 1911
229 W. Rhodes (267★) and N. Kilner (112)
   v. Leicestershire at Leeds, 1921
225 E. Wainwright (91) and Lord Hawke (127)
   v. Hampshire at Southampton, 1899
217★ H. Sutcliffe (200★) and A. Wood (123★)
   v. Worcestershire at Sheffield, 1935
214 W. Watson (214★) and N.W.D. Yardley (76)
   v. Worcestershire at Worcester, 1955
205 G.H. Hirst (125) and S. Haigh (159)
   v. Nottinghamshire at Sheffield, 1901
200 D. Denton (127) and G.H. Hirst (134)
   v. Essex at Bradford, 1902
198 M. Leyland (247) and W. Rhodes (100★)
   v. Worcestershire at Worcester, 1928
190 W. Rhodes (126) and M. Leyland (79)
   v. Middlesex at Bradford, 1923
188 W. Watson (174) and R. Illingworth (53)
   v. Lancashire at Sheffield, 1955
184 R. Kilner (104) and M.W. Booth (79)
   v. Leicestershire at Leeds, 1913
183 G.H. Hirst (131) and E. Smith (129)
   v. Hampshire at Bradford, 1899
183 W. Watson (139★) and R. Illingworth (78)
   v. Somerset at Harrogate, 1956
178★ D. Denton (108★) and G.H. Hirst (112★)
   v. Lancashire at Manchester, 1902
178★ N.W.D. Yardley (100★) and R. Illingworth (71★)
   v. Gloucestershire at Bristol, 1955
178 E. Robinson (100) and D.C.F. Burton (83)
   v. Derbyshire at Hull, 1921

178 H. Sutcliffe (135) and P.A. Gibb (157★)
    v. Nottinghamshire at Sheffield, 1935

172 A.J. Dalton (119★) and D.L. Bairstow (62)
    v. Worcestershire at Dudley, 1971

169 W. Barber (124) and H. Verity (78★)
    v. Warwickshire at Birmingham, 1933

169 R. Illingworth (162) and I. Birkenshaw (37)
    v. Indians at Sheffield, 1959

166 E. Wainwright (116) and E. Smith (61) *v.* Kent at
    Catford, 1900

166 D.B. Close (161) and F.S. Trueman (104)
    v. Northamptonshire at Northampton, 1963

162★ G. Boycott (220★) and J.G. Binks (70★)
    v. Northamptonshire at Sheffield, 1967

161★ D.L. Bairstow (100★) and P. Carrick (59★)
    v. Middlesex at Leeds, 1983

156 W. Rhodes (82★) and E. Robinson (94)
    v. Derbyshire at Chesterfield, 1919

154 C. Turner (84) and A. Wood (79)
    v. Glamorgan at Swansea, 1936

151 D. Denton (91) and W. Rhodes (76)
    v. Middlesex at Sheffield, 1904

151 G. Boycott (152★) and P. Carrick (75)
    v. Warwickshire at Leeds, 1982

150 G. Ulyett (199★) and J.M. Preston (93)
    v. Derbyshire at Sheffield, 1887

Seventh wicket

254 W. Rhodes (135) and D.C.F. Burton (142★)
    v. Hampshire at Dewsbury, 1919

247 P. Holmes (285) and W. Rhodes (79)
    v. Nottinghamshire at Nottingham, 1929

215 E. Robinson (135★) and D.C.F. Burton (110)
    v. Leicestershire at Leicester, 1921

185 E. Wainwright (100) and G.H. Hirst (134)
    v. Gloucestershire at Bristol, 1897

183 G.H. Hirst (341) and H. Myers (57)
    v. Leicestershire at Leicester, 1905

180 C. Turner (130) and A. Wood (97)
    v. Somerset at Sheffield, 1936

166 R. Peel (55) and I. Grimshaw (122★)
    v. Derbyshire at Holbeck, 1886

162 E. Wainwright (109) and S. Haigh (73)
    v. Somerset at Taunton, 1900

161 R.G. Lumb (118) and C.M. Old (89)
    v. Worcestershire at Bradford, 1980

160 J. Tunnicliffe (158) and D. Hunter (58★)
    v. Worcestershire at Worcester, 1900

157★ F.A. Lowson (259★) and R. Booth (53★)
    v. Worcestershire at Worcester, 1953

154★ G.H. Hirst (76★) and J.T. Newstead (100★)
    v. Nottinghamshire at Nottingham 1908

148 J. Rowbotham (113) and J. Thewlis (50)
    v. Surrey at The Oval, 1873

147 E. Wainwright (78) and G. Ulyett (73)
    v. Somerset at Taunton, 1893

141 G.H. Hirst (108★) and S. Haigh (48)
    v. Worcestershire at Worcester, 1905

141 J.H. Hampshire (149★) and J.G. Binks (72)
    v. MCC at Scarborough, 1965

140 E. Wainwright (117) and S. Haigh (54)
    v. C.I. Thornton's XI at Scarborough, 1900

138 D. Denton (78) and G.H. Hirst (103★)
    v. Sussex at Leeds, 1905

136 G.H. Hirst (93) and S. Haigh (138)
    v. Warwickshire at Birmingham, 1904

136 E. Robinson (77★) and A. Wood (65)
    v. Glamorgan at Scarborough, 1931

133★ W. Rhodes (267) and M. Leyland (52★)
    v. Leicestershire at Leeds, 1921

133★ E.I. Lester (86) and A.B. Sellers (73★)
    v. Northamptonshire at Northampton, 1948

132 W. Rhodes (196) and S. Haigh (59★)
    v. Worcestershire at Worcester, 1904

131★ D.L. Bairstow (79★) and A. Sidebottom (52★)
    v. Oxford University at Oxford, 1981

130 P.J. Sharpe (64) and J.V. Wilson (134)
    v. Warwickshire at Birmingham, 1962

128 W. Barber (66) and T.F. Smailes (86)
    v. Cambridge Univ. at Cambridge, 1938

128 D.B. Close (88★) and A. Coxon (59)
    v. Essex at Leeds, 1949

126 E. Wainwright (171) and R. Peel (46)
    v. Middlesex at Lord's, 1897

126 W. Rhodes (91) and G.G. Macaulay (63)
    v. Hampshire at Hull, 1925

126 J.C. Balderstone (58) and J.G. Binks (95)
    v. Middlesex at Lord's, 1964

125 A.B. Sellers (109) and T.F. Smailes (65)
    v. Kent at Bradford, 1937

Eighth wicket

292 R. Peel (210★) and Lord Hawke (166)
    v. Warwickshire at Birmingham, 1896

192★ W. Rhodes (108★) and G.G. Macaulay (101★)
    v. Essex at Harrogate, 1922

180 W. Barber (191) and T.F. Smailes (89)
    v. Sussex at Leeds, 1935

165 S. Haigh (62) and Lord Hawke (126)
    v. Surrey at The Oval, 1902

163 G.G. Macaulay (60) and A. Waddington (114)
    v. Worcestershire at Leeds, 1927

159 E. Smith (95) and W. Rhodes (105)
    v. MCC at Scarborough, 1901

152 W. Rhodes (98) and J.W. Rothery (70)
    v. Hampshire at Portsmouth, 1904

151 W. Rhodes (201) and Lord Hawke (51)
    v. Somerset at Taunton, 1905

147 J.P.G. Chadwick (59) and F.S. Trueman (101)
    v. Middlesex at Scarborough, 1965

146 S. Haigh (159) and Lord Hawke (89)
    v. Nottinghamshire at Sheffield, 1901

138 E. Wainwright (100) and Lord Hawke (81)
    v. Kent at Tonbridge, 1899

137 E. Wainwright (171) and Lord Hawke (75)
    v. Middlesex at Lord's, 1897

133 R. Illingworth (61) and F.S. Trueman (74)
    v. Leicestershire at Leicester, 1955

132 G.H. Hirst (103) and E. Smith (59)
    v. Middlesex at Sheffield, 1904

132 W. Watson (119) and J.H. Wardle (65)
    v. Leicestershire at Leicester, 1949

130 E. Smith (98) and Lord Hawke (54)
    v. Lancashire at Leeds, 1904

128   H. Verity (96★) and T.F. Smailes (77)
     v. Indians at Bradford, 1936
128   D.L. Bairstow (145) and J.H. Hampshire (67)
     v. Middlesex at Scarborough, 1980
127   E. Robinson (70★) and A. Wood (62)
     v. Middlesex at Leeds, 1928
126   R. Peel (74) and E. Peate (61)
     v. Gloucestershire at Bradford, 1883
126   M.W. Booth (56) and E.R. Wilson (104★)
     v. Essex at Bradford, 1913

Ninth wicket

192   G.H. Hirst (130★) and S. Haigh (85)
     v. Surrey at Bradford, 1898
179   R.A. Hutton (189) and G.A. Cope (30★)
     v. Pakistanis at Bradford, 1971
176★ R. Moorhouse (59★) and G.H. Hirst (115★)
     v. Gloucestershire at Bristol, 1894
173   S. Haigh (85) and W. Rhodes (92★)
     v. Sussex at Hove, 1902
167   H. Verity (89) and T.F. Smailes (80)
     v. Somerset at Bath, 1936
162   W. Rhodes (94★) and S. Haigh (84)
     v. Lancashire at Manchester, 1904
161   E. Smith (116★) and W. Rhodes (79)
     v. Sussex at Sheffield, 1900
149   G.H. Hirst (232★) and D. Hunter (40)
     v. Surrey at The Oval, 1905
146   G.H. Hirst (214) and W. Rhodes (53)
     v. Worcestershire at Worcester, 1901
136   R. Peel (210★) and G.H. Hirst (85)
     v. Warwickshire at Birmingham, 1896
125★ L. Hutton (269★) and A. Coxon (65★)
     v. Northamptonshire at Wellingborough, 1949
124   P.J. Hartley (87★) and P.W. Jarvis (47)
     v. Essex at Chelmsford, 1986
120   G.H. Hirst (138) and W. Rhodes (38)
     v. Nottinghamshire at Nottingham, 1899
119   A.B. Sellers (80★) and E.P. Robinson (66)
     v. Warwickshire at Birmingham, 1938
118   S. Haigh (96) and W. Rhodes (44)
     v. Somerset at Leeds, 1901

114   E. Oldroyd (194) and A. Dolphin (47)
     v. Worcestershire at Worcester, 1923
114   N. Kilner (102★) and G.G. Macaulay (60)
     v. Gloucestershire at Bristol, 1923
113   G.G. Macaulay (125★) and A. Waddington (44)
     v. Nottinghamshire at Nottingham, 1921
113   A. Wood (69) and H. Verity (45★)
     v. MCC at Lord's, 1938
112   G.H. Hirst (78) and Lord Hawke (61★)
     v. Essex at Leyton, 1907
109   L. Whitehead (60) and W. Rhodes (81★)
     v. Sussex at Harrogate, 1899
105   J.V. Wilson (134) and A.G. Nicholson (20★)
     v. Nottinghamshire at Leeds, 1962
105   C.M. Old (100★) and H.P. Cooper (30)
     v. Lancashire at Manchester, 1978
104   L. Hall (129★) and R. Moorhouse (86)
     v. Gloucestershire at Clifton, 1888
100   G. Pollitt (51) and L. Whitehead (54)
     v. Hampshire at Bradford, 1899

Tenth wicket

149   G. Boycott (79) and G.B. Stevenson (115★)
     v. Warwickshire at Birmingham, 1982
148   Lord Hawke (107★) and D. Hunter (47)
     v. Kent at Sheffield, 1898
144   A. Sidebottom (124) and A.L. Robinson (30★)
     v. Glamorgan at Cardiff, 1977
121   J.T. Brown (141) and D. Hunter (25★)
     v. Liverpool & District at Liverpool, 1894
118   Lord Hawke (110★) and D. Hunter (41)
     v. Kent at Leeds, 1896
108   Lord Hawke (79) and L. Whitehead (45★)
     v. Lancashire at Manchester, 1903
108   G. Boycott (129) and M.K. Bore (37★)
     v. Nottinghamshire at Bradford, 1973
106   A.B. Sellers (79) and D.V. Brennan (30)
     v. Worcestershire at Worcester, 1948
103   A. Dolphin (62★) and E. Smith (49)
     v. Essex at Leyton, 1919
102   D. Denton (77★) and D. Hunter (45)
     v. Cambridge Univ. at Cambridge, 1895

Most wickets in a match
(*Qualification:* twelve or more)

R. Appleyard (6)
12 for 94 (6 for 59 and 6 for 35) *v.* Somerset at Taunton, 1951
12 for 93 (5 for 36 and 7 for 57) *v.* Leicestershire at Leicester, 1951
12 for 43 (6 for 17 and 6 for 26) *v.* Essex at Bradford, 1951
12 for 88 (5 for 72 and 7 for 16) *v.* Somerset at Taunton, 1954
12 for 124 (7 for 44 and 5 for 80) *v.* MCC at Scarborough, 1954
12 for 106 (6 for 37 and 6 for 69) *v.* Derbyshire at Chesterfield, 1956

T. Armitage (1)
13 for 46 (6 for 20 and 7 for 26) *v.* Surrey at Sheffield, 1876

R. Aspinall (2)
14 for 65 (8 for 42 and 6 for 23) *v.* Northamptonshire at Northampton, 1947
13 for 100 (6 for 54 and 7 for 46) *v.* Somerset at Leeds, 1949

A.B. Bainbridge (1)
12 for 111 (6 for 58 and 6 for 53) *v.* Essex at Harrogate, 1961

M.W. Booth (3)
12 for 119 (7 for 50 and 5 for 69) *v.* Essex at Leyton, 1912
14 for 160 (6 for 96 and 8 for 64) *v.* Essex at Leyton, 1914
12 for 89 (6 for 48 and 6 for 41) *v.* Gloucestershire at Bristol, 1914

W.E. Bowes (10)

13 for 183 (9 for 121 and 4 for 62) *v.* Essex at Scarborough, 1932

12 for 96 (8 for 62 and 4 for 34) *v.* Sussex at Hove, 1932

12 for 117 (6 for 44 and 6 for 73) *v.* Kent at Leeds, 1933

13 for 176 (7 for 89 and 6 for 87) *v.* Nottinghamshire at Nottingham, 1933

12 for 140 (7 for 68 and 5 for 72) *v.* Surrey at Sheffield, 1933

13 for 88 (8 for 40 and 5 for 48) *v.* Worcestershire at Sheffield, 1935

16 for 35 (8 for 18 and 8 for 17) *v.* Northampton at Kettering, 1935

12 for 99 (6 for 16 and 6 for 83) *v.* Lancashire at Bradford, 1935

13 for 96 (8 for 56 and 5 for 40) *v.* Leicestershire at Scarborough, 1936

12 for 96 (7 for 50 and 5 for 46) *v.* Warwickshire at Birmingham, 1939

J.T. Brown (Darfield) (1)

12 for 109 (4 for 69 and 8 for 40) *v.* Gloucestershire at Huddersfield, 1899

P. Carrick (1)

12 for 89 (5 for 45 and 7 for 44) *v.* Derbyshire at Sheffield, 1983

R.O. Clayton (1)

12 for 104 (8 for 66 and 4 for 88) *v.* Lancashire at Manchester, 1877

G.A. Cope (1)

12 for 116 (7 for 42 and 5 for 74) *v.* Glamorgan at Cardiff, 1968

M.J. Cowan (1)

12 for 87 (3 for 44 and 9 for 43) *v.* Warwickshire at Birmingham, 1960

A. Drake (1)

15 for 51 (5 for 16 and 10 for 35) *v.* Somerset at Weston-super-Mare, 1914

T. Emmett (8)

13 for 97 (4 for 63 and 9 for 34) *v.* Nottinghamshire at Dewsbury, 1868

16 for 38 (7 for 15 and 9 for 23) *v.* Cambridgeshire at Hunslet, 1869

12 for 111 (5 for 76 and 7 for 35) *v.* Nottinghamshire at Sheffield, 1869

13 for 90 (5 for 59 and 8 for 31) *v.* Nottinghamshire at Sheffield, 1871

12 for 99 (6 for 57 and 6 for 42) *v.* Lancashire at Manchester, 1872

12 for 84 (6 for 38 and 6 for 46) *v.* Surrey at Sheffield, 1873

12 for 110 (6 for 21 and 6 for 89) *v.* Middlesex at Scarborough, 1874

13 for 83 (8 for 52 and 5 for 31) *v.* MCC at Scarborough, 1882

G. Freeman (4)

12 for 51 (7 for 10 and 5 for 41) *v.* Lancashire at Whalley, 1867

12 for 23 (8 for 11 and 4 for 12) *v.* Lancashire at Holbeck, 1868

12 for 62 (7 for 30 and 5 for 32) *v.* Middlesex at Sheffield, 1868

13 for 60 (8 for 29 and 5 for 31) *v.* Surrey at Sheffield, 1869

S. Haigh (10)

12 for 115 (6 for 45 and 6 for 70) *v.* Derbyshire at Sheffield, 1896

14 for 43 (8 for 21 and 6 for 22) *v.* Hampshire at Southampton, 1898

13 for 94 (6 for 61 and 7 for 33) *v.* Middlesex at Leeds, 1900

12 for 79 (5 for 39 and 7 for 40) *v.* Middlesex at Lord's, 1902

12 for 52 (6 for 30 and 6 for 22) *v.* Cambridge University at Sheffield, 1903

12 for 95 (6 for 36 and 6 for 59) *v.* Worcestershire at Leeds, 1905

12 for 55 (6 for 34 and 6 for 21) *v.* Nottinghamshire at Sheffield, 1905

12 for 105 (7 for 46 and 5 for 59) *v.* Middlesex at Lord's, 1906

13 for 40 (6 for 27 and 7 for 13) *v.* Warwickshire at Sheffield, 1907

14 for 65 (9 for 25 and 5 for 40) *v.* Gloucestershire at Leeds, 1912

A. Hill (1)

12 for 59 (6 for 35 and 6 for 24) *v.* Surrey at The Oval, 1871

G.H. Hirst (13)

12 for 48 (6 for 25 and 6 for 23) *v.* MCC at Lord's, 1893

12 for 89 (6 for 49) and 6 for 40) *v.* Middlesex at Leeds, 1895

13 for 149 (8 for 48 and 5 for 101) *v.* Australians at Bradford, 1899

12 for 77 (5 for 54 and 7 for 23) *v.* Lancashire at Manchester, 1901

12 for 29 (7 for 12 and 5 for 17) *v.* Essex at Leyton, 1901

12 for 66 (7 for 18 and 5 for 48) *v.* Leicestershire at Leeds, 1906

14 for 97 (7 for 27 and 7 for 70) *v.* Nottinghamshire at Dewsbury, 1906

12 for 137 (4 for 51 and 6 for 86) *v.* Gloucestershire at Harrogate, 1907

15 for 63 (8 for 25 and 7 for 38) *v.* Leicestershire at Hull, 1907

12 for 19 (6 for 12 and 6 for 7) *v.* Northamptonshire at Northampton, 1908

13 for 78 (4 for 55 and 9 for 23) *v.* Lancashire at Leeds, 1910

14 for 109 (5 for 40 and 9 for 69) *v.* MCC at Lord's, 1912

12 for 67 (6 for 30 and 6 for 37) *v.* Somerset at Taunton, 1912

R. Illingworth (5)

12 for 91 (3 for 49 and 9 for 42) *v.* Worcestershire at Worcester, 1957

15 for 123 (8 for 70 and 7 for 53) *v.* Glamorgan at Swansea, 1960

12 for 102 (7 for 39 and 5 for 63) *v.* Hampshire at Bournemouth, 1961

14 for 101 (7 for 49 and 7 for 52) *v.* Kent at Dover, 1964

14 for 64 (7 for 58 and 7 for 6) *v.* Gloucestershire at Harrogate, 1967

F. S. Jackson (2)
12 for 91 (5 for 28 and 7 for 63) *v*. Kent at Canterbury, 1895
12 for 80 (6 for 19 and 6 for 61) *v*. Hampshire at Southampton, 1897

R. Kilner (1)
12 for 55 (5 for 18 and 7 for 37) *v*. Sussex at Hove, 1924

G.G. Macaulay (8)
12 for 76 (7 for 47 and 5 for 29) *v*. Gloucestershire at Dewsbury, 1922
12 for 40 (5 for 19 and 7 for 21) *v*. Gloucestershire at Gloucester, 1924
12 for 71 (6 for 29 and 6 for 42) *v*. Glamorgan at Hull, 1926
14 for 92 (6 for 49 and 8 for 43) *v*. Gloucestershire at Bristol, 1926
12 for 50 (7 for 17 and 5 for 33) *v*. Worcestershire at Leeds, 1927
12 for 95 (5 for 73 and 7 for 22) *v*. MCC at Lord's, 1930
12 for 47 (6 for 25 and 6 for 22) *v*. Leicestershire at Bradford, 1933
12 for 49 (7 for 28 and 5 for 21) *v*. Lancashire at Manchester, 1933

F.W. Milligan (1)
12 for 110 (5 for 45 and 7 for 65) *v*. Sussex at Sheffield, 1897

H. Myers (1)
12 for 192 (8 for 81 and 4 for 111) *v*. Gloucestershire at Dewsbury, 1904

A.G. Nicholson (2)
12 for 73 (6 for 29 and 6 for 44) *v*. Glamorgan at Leeds, 1964
12 for 102 (9 for 62 and 3 for 40) *v*. Sussex at Eastbourne, 1967

E. Peate (6)
12 for 77 (6 for 39 and 6 for 38) *v*. Kent at Sheffield, 1879
12 for 108 (5 for 47 and 7 for 61) *v*. Kent at Maidstone, 1880
14 for 80 (6 for 56 and 8 for 24) *v*. Lancashire at Manchester, 1880
14 for 77 (6 for 47 and 8 for 30) *v*. Surrey at Huddersfield, 1881
14 for 130 (6 for 61 and 8 for 69) *v*. Sussex at Hove, 1881
12 for 95 (4 for 63 and 8 for 32) *v*. Middlesex at Sheffield, 1882

R. Peel (7)
12 for 62 (5 for 32 and 7 for 30) *v*. Lancashire at Manchester, 1888
14 for 33 (8 for 12 and 6 for 21) *v*. Nottinghamshire at Sheffield, 1888
13 for 84 (7 for 39 and 6 for 45) *v*. Gloucestershire at Halifax, 1888
13 for 118 (7 for 43 and 6 for 75) *v*. Sussex at Hove, 1889
12 for 69 (6 for 34 and 6 for 35) *v*. Australians at Sheffield, 1890
12 for 87 (6 for 65 and 6 for 22) *v*. Gloucestershire at Bristol, 1891
15 for 50 (9 for 22 and 6 for 28) *v*. Somerset at Leeds, 1895

D. Pickles (1)
12 for 133 (7 for 61 and 5 for 72) *v*. Somerset at Taunton, 1957

J.M. Preston (1)
13 for 63 (4 for 35 and 9 for 28) *v*. MCC at Scarborough, 1888

W. Rhodes (24)
13 for 45 (7 for 24 and 6 for 21) *v*. Somerset at Bath, 1898
12 for 70 (5 for 46 and 7 for 24) *v*. Surrey at Bradford, 1898
15 for 56 (9 for 28 and 6 for 28) *v*. Essex at Leyton, 1899
14 for 66 (6 for 43 and 8 for 23) *v*. Hampshire at Hull, 1900
14 for 192 (8 for 72 and 6 for 120) *v*. Gloucestershire at Bradford, 1900
14 for 68 (6 for 40 and 8 for 28) *v*. Essex at Harrogate, 1900
13 for 103 (6 for 36 and 7 for 67) *v*. Gloucestershire at Cheltenham, 1900
14 for 141 (7 for 78 and 7 for 63) *v*. Gloucestershire at Bristol, 1901
12 for 182 (6 for 115 and 6 for 67) *v*. Somerset at Taunton, 1901
13 for 96 (6 for 41 and 7 for 55) *v*. Leicestershire at Leicester, 1901
12 for 134 (8 for 53 and 4 for 81) *v*. Middlesex at Lord's, 1901
12 for 86 (7 for 20 and 5 for 66) *v*. Gloucestershire at Hull, 1901
12 for 195 (7 for 123 and 5 for 72) *v*. Essex at Bradford, 1902
12 for 58 (5 for 22 and 7 for 36) *v*. Gloucestershire at Leeds, 1902
12 for 52 (8 for 26 and 4 for 26) *v*. Kent at Catford, 1902
14 for 211 (8 for 87 and 6 for 124) *v*. Worcestershire at Worcester, 1903
13 for 152 (5 for 91 and 8 for 61) *v*. Lancashire at Bradford, 1903
12 for 128 (6 for 95 and 6 for 33) *v*. Warwickshire at Birmingham, 1904
12 for 130 (6 for 61 and 6 for 69) *v*. Somerset at Taunton, 1907
12 for 115 (6 for 68 and 6 for 47) *v*. Leicestershire at Dewsbury, 1909
13 for 108 (7 for 68 and 6 for 40) *v*. Lancashire at Bradford, 1909
14 for 139 (8 for 92 and 6 for 47) *v*. Northamptonshire at Northampton, 1911
14 for 77 (6 for 29 and 8 for 48) *v*. Somerset at Huddersfield, 1926
12 for 80 (3 for 41 and 9 for 39) *v*. Essex at Leyton, 1929

E. Robinson (1)
12 for 95 (8 for 32 and 4 for 63) *v*. Northamptonshire at Huddersfield, 1927

E.P. Robinson (3)
13 for 115 (5 for 80 and 8 for 35) *v*. Lancashire at Leeds, 1939
13 for 164 (8 for 76 and 5 for 88) *v*. Surrey at The Oval, 1946
12 for 53 (5 for 29 and 7 for 24) *v*. Hampshire at Scarborough, 1946

W. Slinn (1)
12 for 53 (6 for 19 and 6 for 34) *v*. Nottinghamshire at Nottingham, 1864

T.F. Smailes (2)

14 for 103 (6 for 35 and 8 for 68) v. Glamorgan at Hull, 1938
14 for 58 (4 for 11 and 10 for 47) v. Derbyshire at Sheffield, 1939

F.S. Trueman (5)

12 for 62 (6 for 34 and 6 for 28) v. Hampshire at Portsmouth, 1960
14 for 125 (7 for 60 and 7 for 65) v. Northamptonshire at Sheffield, 1960
14 for 123 (7 for 41 and 7 for 82) v. Surrey at The Oval, 1960
12 for 58 (7 for 45 and 5 for 13) v. Leicestershire at Sheffield, 1961
13 for 77 (8 for 36 and 5 for 41) v. Sussex at Hove, 1965

G. Ulyett (1)

12 for 102 (7 for 50 and 5 for 52) v. Lancashire at Huddersfield, 1889

H. Verity (24)

12 for 117 (3 for 57 and 9 for 60) v. Glamorgan at Swansea, 1930
13 for 83 (7 for 26 and 6 for 57) v. Hampshire at Bournemouth, 1930
13 for 97 (3 for 61 and 10 for 36) v. Warwickshire at Leeds, 1931
14 for 54 (6 for 21 and 8 for 33) v. Glamorgan at Swansea, 1931
13 for 145 (6 for 52 and 7 for 93) v. Sussex at Hove, 1931
12 for 74 (2 for 64 and 10 for 10) v. Nottinghamshire at Leeds, 1932
12 for 53 (6 for 12 and 6 for 41) v. Derbyshire at Hull, 1933
14 for 83 (7 for 29 and 7 for 54) v. West Indians at Harrogate, 1933
13 for 102 (7 for 35 and 6 for 67) v. Northamptonshire at Leeds, 1933
17 for 91 (8 for 47 and 9 for 44) v. Essex at Leyton, 1933
12 for 137 (3 for 78 and 9 for 59) v. Kent at Dover, 1933
12 for 96 (6 for 34 and 6 for 62) v. MCC at Lord's, 1935
14 for 78 (7 for 31 and 7 for 47) v. Hampshire at Hull, 1935
13 for 97 (5 for 69 and 8 for 28) v. Leicestershire at Leeds, 1935
13 for 107 (6 for 52 and 7 for 55) v. Hampshire at Portsmouth, 1935
15 for 129 (8 for 56 and 7 for 73) v. Oxford University at Oxford, 1936
13 for 88 (5 for 48 and 8 for 40) v. Worcestershire at Stourbridge, 1936
15 for 38 (6 for 26 and 9 for 12) v. Kent at Sheffield, 1936
15 for 100 (6 for 52 and 9 for 48) v. Essex at Westcliffe-on-Sea, 1936
14 for 92 (9 for 43 and 5 for 49) v. Warwickshire at Leeds, 1937
14 for 132 (8 for 80 and 6 for 52) v. Sussex at Eastbourne, 1937
12 for 85 (3 for 23 and 9 for 62) v. MCC at Lord's, 1939
12 for 114 (4 for 76 and 8 for 38) v. Leicestershire at Hull, 1939
14 for 68 (7 for 48 and 7 for 20) v. Glamorgan at Bradford, 1939

A. Waddington (3)

12 for 126 (6 for 58 and 6 for 68) v. Gloucestershire at Leeds, 1919
12 for 74 (5 for 49 and 7 for 25) v. Leicestershire at Hull, 1920
13 for 48 (6 for 30 and 7 for 18) v. Northamptonshire at Northampton, 1920

E. Wainwright (6)

12 for 96 (4 for 47 and 8 for 49) v. Middlesex at Sheffield, 1891
13 for 38 (6 for 18 and 7 for 20) v. Sussex at Dewsbury, 1894
12 for 108 (6 for 74 and 6 for 34) v. Surrey at Sheffield, 1894
12 for 103 (3 for 37 and 9 for 66) v. Middlesex at Sheffield, 1894
14 for 77 (6 for 43 and 8 for 34) v. Essex at Bradford, 1896
12 for 85 (5 for 31 and 7 for 54) v. Leicestershire at Dewsbury, 1898

J.H. Wardle (5)

12 for 160 (7 for 88 and 5 for 72) v. Essex at Westcliffe-on-Sea, 1948
12 for 122 (5 for 81 and 7 for 41) v. Surrey at The Oval, 1949
12 for 90 (4 for 64 and 8 for 26) v. Middlesex at Lord's, 1950
16 for 112 (9 for 48 and 7 for 64) v. Sussex at Hull, 1954
12 for 85 (9 for 25 and 3 for 60) v. Lancashire at Manchester, 1954

D. Wilson (1)

13 for 52 (6 for 31 and 7 for 21) v. Warwickshire at Middlesbrough, 1967

Ten wickets in an innings

Bowler		Year
A. Drake	10 for 35 v. Somerset at Weston-super-Mare	1914
H. Verity	10 for 36 v. Warwickshire at Leeds	1931
*H. Verity	10 for 10 v. Nottinghamshire at Leeds	1932
T.F. Smailes	10 for 47 v. Derbyshire at Sheffield	1939

*includes the hat-trick

Most wickets in an innings
(*Qualification:* seven or more)

R. Appleyard (9)
7 for 84 *v.* Gloucestershire at Bradford, 1951
7 for 57 *v.* Leicestershire at Leicester, 1951
8 for 76 *v.* Leicestershire at Leicester, 1951
7 for 16 *v.* Somerset at Taunton, 1954
7 for 35 *v.* Hampshire at Bradford, 1954
7 for 33 *v.* Lancashire at Manchester, 1954
7 for 44 *v.* MCC at Scarborough, 1954
7 for 29 *v.* Surrey at The Oval, 1955
7 for 48 *v.* Warwickshire at Bradford, 1956

T. Armitage (2)
7 for 26 *v.* Surrey at Sheffield, 1876
7 for 58 *v.* Surrey at Sheffield, 1877

R. Aspinall (2)
8 for 42 *v.* Northamptonshire at Northampton, 1947
7 for 46 *v.* Somerset at Leeds, 1949

G.R. Atkinson (1)
7 for 39 *v.* Surrey at The Oval, 1868

W. Bates (6)
7 for 38 *v.* Gloucestershire at Sheffield, 1878
8 for 45 *v.* Lancashire at Huddersfield, 1878
7 for 19 *v.* Sussex at Hove, 1878
7 for 47 *v.* MCC at Scarborough, 1878
8 for 21 *v.* Surrey at The Oval, 1879
7 for 43 *v.* Surrey at Sheffield, 1885

J. Birkenshaw (1)
7 for 76 *v.* Middlesex at Leeds, 1960

M.W. Booth (11)
7 for 30 *v.* Warwickshire at Birmingham 1910
8 for 52 *v.* Leicestershire at Sheffield, 1912
7 for 50 *v.* Essex at Leyton, 1912
8 for 47 *v.* Middlesex at Leeds, 1912
7 for 65 *v.* Leicestershire at Leicester, 1913
7 for 64 *v.* Northamptonshire at Leeds, 1913
7 for 77 *v.* Lancashire at Leeds, 1913
8 for 86 *v.* Middlesex at Sheffield, 1913
7 for 21 *v.* MCC at Lord's, 1914
8 for 64 *v.* Essex at Leyton, 1914
7 for 69 *v.* Northamptonshire at Huddersfield, 1914

M.K. Bore (1)
7 for 63 *v.* Derbyshire at Scarborough, 1977

W.E. Bowes (24)
8 for 77 *v.* Leicestershire at Dewsbury, 1929
8 for 69 *v.* Middlesex at Bradford, 1930
7 for 80 *v.* Nottinghamshire at Nottingham, 1931
7 for 71 *v.* Glamorgan at Scarborough, 1931
7 for 46 *v.* Middlesex at Lord's, 1932
9 for 121 *v.* Essex at Scarborough, 1932
8 for 62 *v.* Sussex at Hove, 1932
7 for 65 *v.* Rest of England at The Oval, 1932
8 for 69 *v.* Gloucestershire at Gloucester, 1933
7 for 89 *v.* Nottinghamshire at Nottingham, 1933

7 for 68 *v.* Surrey at Sheffield, 1933
7 for 39 *v.* Glamorgan at Scarborough, 1933
7 for 34 *v.* Northamptonshire at Northampton, 1934
7 for 100 *v.* Australians at Sheffield, 1934
7 for 85 *v.* Worcestershire at Worcester, 1934
7 for 89 *v.* Glamorgan at Neath, 1935
8 for 40 *v.* Worcestershire at Sheffield, 1935
8 for 18 *v.* Northamptonshire at Kettering, 1935
8 for 17 *v.* Northamptonshire at Kettering, 1935
7 for 58 *v.* Essex at Colchester, 1935
8 for 56 *v.* Leicestershire at Scarborough, 1936
7 for 56 *v.* Essex at Huddersfield, 1937
7 for 50 *v.* Warwickshire at Birmingham, 1939
7 for 54 *v.* Sussex at Scarborough, 1939

J.T. Brown (Darfield) (3)
7 for 78 *v.* Somerset at Hull, 1899
8 for 40 *v.* Gloucestershire at Huddersfield, 1899
7 for 54 *v.* Nottinghamshire at Sheffield, 1901

P. Carrick (5)
8 for 33 *v.* Cambridge University at Cambridge, 1973
8 for 72 *v.* Derbyshire at Scarborough, 1975
7 for 35 *v.* Glamorgan at Sheffield, 1978
7 for 44 *v.* Derbyshire at Sheffield, 1983
7 for 99 *v.* Glamorgan at Swansea, 1985

R.O. Clayton (2)
8 for 66 *v.* Lancashire at Manchester, 1877
7 for 35 *v.* Derbyshire at Derby, 1877

D.B. Close (24)
7 for 62 *v.* Essex at Bradford, 1955
8 for 41 *v.* Kent at Leeds, 1959
8 for 43 *v.* Essex at Leeds, 1960

H.P. Cooper (2)
8 for 62 *v.* Glamorgan at Cardiff, 1975
7 for 72 *v.* Northamptonshire at Northampton, 1976

G.A. Cope (4)
7 for 42 *v.* Glamorgan at Cardiff, 1968
7 for 36 *v.* Essex at Colchester, 1970
7 for 101 *v.* Middlesex at Middlesbrough, 1974
8 for 73 *v.* Gloucestershire at Bristol, 1975

M.J. Cowan (3)
7 for 44 *v.* Gloucestershire at Leeds, 1953
7 for 23 *v.* Scotland at Middlesbrough, 1958
9 for 43 *v.* Warwickshire at Birmingham 1960

A. Coxon (3)
8 for 31 *v.* Worcestershire at Leeds, 1946
7 for 62 *v.* Middlesex at Bradford, 1948
7 for 51 *v.* MCC at Scarborough, 1950

A. Drake (3)
8 for 59 *v.* Gloucestershire at Sheffield, 1913
7 for 69 *v.* Essex at Bradford, 1913
10 for 35 *v.* Somerset at Weston-super-Mare, 1914

T. Emmett (18)

9 for 34 v. Nottinghamshire at Dewsbury, 1868
7 for 43 v. Middlesex at Islington, 1868
7 for 15 v. Cambridgeshire at Hunslet, 1869
9 for 23 v. Cambridgeshire at Hunslet, 1869
7 for 35 v. Nottinghamshire at Sheffield, 1869
8 for 31 v. Nottinghamshire at Sheffield, 1871
7 for 29 v. Lancashire at Manchester, 1873
8 for 46 v. Gloucestershire at Chilton, 1877
8 for 16 v. MCC at Scarborough, 1877
7 for 9 v. Sussex at Hove, 1878
8 for 22 v. Surrey at The Oval, 1881
7 for 68 v. I Zingari at Scarborough, 1881
8 for 52 v. MCC at Scarborough, 1882
8 for 32 v. Sussex at Huddersfield, 1884
7 for 20 v. Derbyshire at Derby, 1884
7 for 50 v. Lancashire at Manchester, 1885
7 for 33 v. Lancashire at Manchester, 1886
7 for 46 v. Middlesex at Bradford, 1886

S.D. Fletcher (1)

8 for 58 v. Essex at Sheffield, 1988

T.W. Foster (2)

9 for 59 v. MCC at Lord's, 1894
7 for 56 v. Warwickshire at Birmingham, 1894

G. Freeman (7)

7 for 10 v. Lancashire at Whalley, 1867
7 for 29 v. Surrey at Sheffield, 1867
8 for 11 v. Lancashire at Holbeck, 1868
7 for 30 v. Middlesex at Sheffield, 1868
8 for 29 v. Surrey at Sheffield, 1869
7 for 74 v. Surrey at Sheffield, 1871
7 for 30 v. Nottinghamshire at Nottingham, 1871

K. Gillhouley (1)

7 for 82 v. Middlesex at Bradford, 1961

L. Greenwood (2)

7 for 43 v. Nottinghamshire at Nottingham, 1865
8 for 35 v. Cambridgeshire at Dewsbury, 1867

S. Haigh (26)

8 for 78 v. Australians at Bradford, 1896
7 for 49 v. Warwickshire at Leeds, 1896
8 for 35 v. Hampshire at Harrogate, 1896
7 for 17 v. Surrey at Leeds, 1897
7 for 46 v. MCC at Scarborough, 1897
8 for 21 v. Hampshire at Southampton, 1898
7 for 60 v. Middlesex at Lord's, 1898
8 for 33 v. Warwickshire at Scarborough, 1899
7 for 33 v. Middlesex at Leeds, 1900
7 for 47 v. Middlesex at Bradford, 1902
7 for 38 v. Worcestershire at Harrogate, 1902
7 for 40 v. Middlesex at Lord's, 1902
7 for 56 v. MCC at Scarborough, 1904
7 for 35 v. Oxford University at Oxford, 1906
7 for 46 v. Middlesex at Lord's, 1906
7 for 13 v. Warwickshire at Sheffield, 1907
7 for 44 v. MCC at Lord's, 1908
7 for 23 v. Cambridge University at Cambridge, 1908
7 for 32 v. Essex at Leeds, 1909

7 for 25 v. Lancashire at Manchester, 1909
7 for 43 v. Leicestershire at Leicester, 1909
7 for 46 v. Worcestershire at Harrogate, 1909
7 for 65 v. Surrey at The Oval, 1909
7 for 65 v. Kent at Maidstone, 1910
7 for 20 v. Sussex at Leeds, 1911
9 for 25 v. Gloucestershire at Leeds, 1912

J.H. Hampshire (1)

7 for 52 v. Glamorgan at Cardiff, 1963

G.P. Harrison (1)

7 for 43 v. Lancashire at Manchester, 1883

A. Hill (3)

7 for 62 v. Surrey at Sheffield, 1874
7 for 39 v. MCC at Scarborough, 1875
7 for 14 v. Surrey at Hull, 1879

G.H. Hirst (35)

7 for 38 v. MCC at Scarborough, 1893
7 for 25 v. Lancashire at Manchester, 1894
7 for 32 v. Somerset at Taunton, 1894
7 for 16 v. Essex at Harrogate, 1895
8 for 59 v. Warwickshire at Birmingham, 1896
7 for 47 v. MCC at Lord's, 1899
8 for 48 v. Australians at Bradford, 1899
7 for 55 v. MCC at Lord's, 1901
7 for 43 v. Derbyshire at Huddersfield, 1901
7 for 23 v. Lancashire at Manchester, 1901
7 for 78 v. Surrey at Bradford, 1901
7 for 21 v. Leicestershire at Scarborough, 1901
7 for 12 v. Essex at Leyton, 1901
7 for 24 v. Kent at Canterbury, 1901
7 for 68 v. Nottinghamshire at Hull, 1902
7 for 36 v. Nottinghamshire at Leeds, 1903
7 for 48 v. Somerset at Taunton, 1905
7 for 33 v. Kent at Catford, 1906
7 for 18 v. Leicestershire at Leeds, 1906
7 for 27 v. Nottinghamshire at Dewsbury, 1906
7 for 70 v. Nottinghamshire at Dewsbury, 1906
8 for 86 v. Gloucestershire at Harrogate, 1907
7 for 22 v. Derbyshire at Glossop, 1907
8 for 25 v. Leicestershire at Hull, 1907
7 for 38 v. Leicestershire at Hull, 1907
9 for 45 v. Middlesex at Sheffield, 1907
7 for 51 v. Nottinghamshire at Leeds, 1908
7 for 95 v. Middlesex at Leeds, 1909
9 for 23 v. Lancashire at Leeds, 1910
8 for 80 v. Somerset at Sheffield, 1910
7 for 28 v. Worcestershire at Leeds, 1910
7 for 56 v. Hampshire at Portsmouth, 1910
9 for 41 v. Worcestershire at Worcester, 1911
9 for 69 v. MCC at Lord's, 1912
7 for 33 v. Leicestershire at Leeds, 1913

R.A. Hutton (1)

7 for 39 v. Somerset at Leeds, 1969

R. Iddison (1)

7 for 30 v. Nottinghamshire at Bradford, 1863

R. Illingworth (18)

7 for 22 *v*. Hampshire at Bournemouth, 1953
8 for 69 *v*. Surrey at The Oval, 1954
9 for 42 *v*. Worcestershire at Worcester, 1957
7 for 49 *v*. Essex at Middlesbrough, 1958
8 for 70 *v*. Glamorgan at Swansea, 1960
7 for 53 *v*. Glamorgan at Swansea, 1960
8 for 50 *v*. Lancashire at Manchester, 1961
7 for 54 *v*. Warwickshire at Middlesbrough, 1961
7 for 39 *v*. Hampshire at Bournemouth, 1961
7 for 40 *v*. Northamptonshire at Northampton, 1962
7 for 89 *v*. Nottinghamshire at Scarborough, 1964
7 for 49 *v*. Kent at Dover, 1964
7 for 52 *v*. Kent at Dover, 1964
7 for 62 *v*. Surrey at The Oval, 1964
8 for 20 *v*. Worcestershire at Leeds, 1965
7 for 58 *v*. Gloucestershire at Harrogate, 1967
7 for 6 *v*. Gloucestershire at Harrogate, 1967
7 for 73 *v*. MCC at Scarborough, 1968

Hon. F.S. Jackson (4)

7 for 63 *v*. Kent at Canterbury, 1895
7 for 78 *v*. Kent at Canterbury, 1897
7 for 42 *v*. Middlesex at Leeds, 1898
7 for 61 *v*. Lancashire at Manchester, 1903

P.W. Jarvis (3)

7 for 105 *v*. Kent at Maidstone, 1985
7 for 55 *v*. Surrey at Leeds, 1986
7 for 82 *v*. Gloucestershire at Leeds, 1987

R. Kilner (3)

8 for 26 *v*. Glamorgan at Cardiff, 1923
7 for 37 *v*. Sussex at Hove, 1924
8 for 40 *v*. Middlesex at Bradford, 1926

E. Leadbeater (2)

8 for 83 *v*. Worcestershire at Worcester, 1950
7 for 131 *v*. Nottinghamshire at Nottingham, 1951

M. Leyland (3)

7 for 52 *v*. Lancashire at Bradford, 1929
8 for 63 *v*. Hampshire at Huddersfield, 1938
7 for 36 *v*. Warwickshire at Birmingham, 1946

G.G. Macaulay (29)

7 for 47 *v*. Gloucestershire at Dewsbury, 1922
7 for 13 *v*. Glamorgan at Cardiff, 1923
7 for 111 *v*. MCC at Scarborough, 1923
7 for 21 *v*. Gloucestershire at Gloucester, 1924
7 for 66 *v*. Warwickshire at Sheffield, 1924
7 for 31 *v*. Leicestershire at Bradford, 1924
7 for 20 *v*. Worcestershire at Worcester, 1925
7 for 13 *v*. Derbyshire at Chesterfield, 1925
7 for 76 *v*. Nottinghamshire at Sheffield, 1925
7 for 81 *v*. Glamorgan at Huddersfield, 1925
7 for 67 *v*. Sussex at Bradford, 1925
7 for 39 *v*. MCC at Lord's, 1925
7 for 135 *v*. Rest of England at The Oval, 1925
8 for 43 *v*. Gloucestershire at Bristol, 1926
7 for 32 *v*. Glamorgan at Swansea, 1926
7 for 40 *v*. Glamorgan at Cardiff, 1927
7 for 17 *v*. Worcestershire at Leeds, 1927

8 for 37 *v*. Derbyshire at Hull, 1927
7 for 76 *v*. MCC at Scarborough, 1927
7 for 57 *v*. Glamorgan at Swansea, 1928
7 for 22 *v*. MCC at Lord's, 1930
7 for 63 *v*. Gloucestershire at Hull, 1930
7 for 24 *v*. Essex at Leeds, 1931
7 for 66 *v*. Northamptonshire at Northampton, 1932
8 for 21 *v*. Indians at Harrogate, 1932
7 for 41 *v*. MCC at Lord's, 1933
7 for 28 *v*. Lancashire at Manchester, 1933
7 for 9 *v*. Northamptonshire at Kettering, 1933
7 for 52 *v*. Middlesex at Bradford, 1933

F.W. Milligan (1)

7 for 65 *v*. Sussex at Sheffield, 1897

H. Myers (1)

8 for 81 *v*. Gloucestershire at Dewsbury, 1904

J.T. Newstead (5)

7 for 10 *v*. Worcestershire at Bradford, 1907
7 for 18 *v*. Leicestershire at Leicester, 1908
7 for 68 *v*. Nottinghamshire at Nottingham, 1908
7 for 66 *v*. Gloucestershire at Cheltenham, 1908
7 for 77 *v*. Sussex at Hove, 1909

A.G. Nicholson (4)

7 for 32 *v*. Lancashire at Leeds, 1964
9 for 62 *v*. Sussex at Eastbourne, 1967
8 for 22 *v*. Kent at Canterbury, 1968
7 for 49 *v*. Lancashire at Leeds, 1972

C.M. Old (2)

7 for 20 *v*. Gloucestershire at Middlesbrough, 1969
7 for 42 *v*. West Indians at Sheffield, 1976

E. Peate (13)

7 for 61 *v*. Kent at Maidstone, 1880
8 for 24 *v*. Lancashire at Manchester, 1880
7 for 35 *v*. MCC at Scarborough, 1880
8 for 30 *v*. Surrey at Huddersfield, 1881
7 for 59 *v*. Derbyshire at Derby, 1881
8 for 69 *v*. Sussex at Hove, 1881
7 for 31 *v*. Kent at Sheffield, 1882
7 for 31 *v*. Australians at Sheffield, 1882
7 for 68 *v*. Nottinghamshire at Sheffield, 1882
8 for 32 *v*. Middlesex at Sheffield, 1882
8 for 5 *v*. Surrey at Holbeck, 1883
7 for 46 *v*. Lancashire at Sheffield, 1884
8 for 63 *v*. Kent at Gravesend

R. Peel (24)

7 for 51 *v*. Kent at Sheffield, 1885
7 for 72 *v*. Sussex at Hove, 1887
7 for 30 *v*. Lancashire at Manchester, 1888
8 for 12 *v*. Nottinghamshire at Sheffield, 1888
7 for 39 *v*. Gloucestershire at Halifax, 1888
7 for 43 *v*. Sussex at Hove, 1889
7 for 35 *v*. Liverpool and District at Liverpool, 1890
8 for 60 *v*. Surrey at Sheffield, 1890
7 for 27 *v*. Gloucestershire at Dewsbury, 1890
7 for 25 *v*. Sussex at Hove, 1890

7 for 90 *v.* Lancashire at Bradford, 1891
7 for 106 *v.* Surrey at Sheffield, 1891
7 for 43 *v.* Surrey at Leeds, 1892
7 for 133 *v.* Somerset at Taunton, 1892
7 for 60 *v.* MCC at Scarborough, 1892
8 for 54 *v.* Cambridge University at Cambridge, 1893
7 for 55 *v.* Sussex at Leeds, 1893
7 for 116 *v.* Australians at Bradford, 1893
7 for 60 *v.* Kent at Sheffield, 1893
7 for 58 *v.* Nottinghamshire at Nottingham, 1894
7 for 30 *v.* Leicestershire at Harrogate, 1894
9 for 22 *v.* Somerset at Leeds, 1895
8 for 27 *v.* South of England XI at Scarborough, 1896
8 for 53 *v.* Kent at Halifax, 1897

D. Pickles (1)
7 for 61 *v.* Somerset at Taunton, 1957

R.K. Platt (2)
7 for 70 *v.* Sussex at Bradford, 1956
7 for 40 *v.* Gloucestershire at Bristol, 1956

J.M. Preston (4)
7 for 55 *v.* Middlesex at Huddersfield, 1887
7 for 82 *v.* Gloucestershire at Clifton, 1888
8 for 27 *v.* Sussex at Hove, 1888
9 for 28 *v.* MCC at Scarborough, 1888

W. Rhodes (60)
7 for 24 *v.* Somerset at Bath, 1898
7 for 24 *v.* Surrey at Bradford, 1898
9 for 28 *v.* Essex at Leyton, 1899
7 for 147 *v.* Middlesex at Lord's, 1899
8 for 38 *v.* Nottinghamshire at Nottingham, 1899
7 for 56 *v.* C.T. Thornton's XI at Scarborough, 1899
7 for 20 *v.* Worcestershire at Bradford, 1900
8 for 68 *v.* Cambridge University at Cambridge, 1900
7 for 72 *v.* Derbyshire at Sheffield, 1900
8 for 43 *v.* Lancashire at Bradford, 1900
7 for 46 *v.* Essex at Leyton, 1900
8 for 23 *v.* Hampshire at Hull, 1900
7 for 32 *v.* Derbyshire at Derby, 1900
7 for 59 *v.* Sussex at Sheffield, 1900
8 for 72 *v.* Gloucestershire at Bradford, 1900
8 for 28 *v.* Essex at Harrogate, 1900
7 for 67 *v.* Gloucestershire at Cheltenham, 1900
7 for 115 *v.* Sussex at Hove, 1900
7 for 78 *v.* Gloucestershire at Bristol, 1901
7 for 63 *v.* Gloucestershire at Bristol, 1901
7 for 55 *v.* Leicestershire at Leicester, 1901
8 for 53 *v.* Middlesex at Lord's, 1901
7 for 20 *v.* Gloucestershire at Hull, 1901
8 for 55 *v.* Kent at Canterbury, 1901
7 for 24 *v.* Middlesex at Bradford, 1902
7 for 123 *v.* Essex at Bradford, 1902
7 for 36 *v.* Gloucestershire at Leeds, 1902
8 for 26 *v.* Kent at Catford, 1902
8 for 87 *v.* Worcestershire at Worcester, 1903
7 for 40 *v.* Nottinghamshire at Nottingham, 1903
8 for 61 *v.* Lancashire at Bradford, 1903
8 for 90 *v.* Warwickshire at Birmingham, 1905
7 for 45 *v.* Middlesex at Bradford, 1905

7 for 83 *v.* Warwickshire at Birmingham, 1909
7 for 87 *v.* Nottinghamshire at Bradford, 1909
7 for 68 *v.* Lancashire at Bradford, 1909
7 for 16 *v.* Derbyshire at Chesterfield, 1911
8 for 92 *v.* Northamptonshire at Northampton, 1911
7 for 98 *v.* Cambridge University at Cambridge, 1913
7 for 45 *v.* Northamptonshire at Northampton, 1913
7 for 19 *v.* Derbyshire at Leeds, 1914
7 for 47 *v.* Gloucestershire at Gloucester, 1919
7 for 74 *v.* Nottinghamshire at Sheffield, 1919
8 for 44 *v.* Warwickshire at Bradford, 1919
7 for 36 *v.* Cambridge University at Cambridge, 1920
7 for 24 *v.* Derbyshire at Derby, 1920
8 for 39 *v.* Sussex at Leeds, 1920
7 for 53 *v.* Middlesex at Bradford, 1920
7 for 80 *v.* Lancashire at Manchester, 1921
7 for 15 *v.* Gloucestershire at Bristol, 1923
7 for 60 *v.* Derbyshire at Bradford, 1923
8 for 48 *v.* Somerset at Huddersfield, 1926
7 for 102 *v.* Northamptonshire at Northampton, 1926
7 for 116 *v.* Lancashire at Manchester, 1926
7 for 39 *v.* Middlesex at Lord's, 1928
7 for 55 *v.* Derbyshire at Dewsbury, 1928
9 for 39 *v.* Essex at Leyton, 1929
7 for 38 *v.* Nottinghamshire at Sheffield, 1929
7 for 116 *v.* Kent at Tunbridge, 1929
7 for 35 *v.* Cambridge University at Cambridge, 1930

W. Ringrose (2)
9 for 76 *v.* Australians at Bradford, 1905
7 for 51 *v.* Leicestershire at Sheffield, 1905

E. Robinson (8)
9 for 36 *v.* Lancashire at Bradford, 1920
7 for 26 *v.* Kent at Tonbridge, 1923
8 for 32 *v.* Northamptonshire at Huddersfield, 1927
8 for 13 *v.* Cambridge University at Cambridge, 1928
7 for 110 *v.* Hampshire at Southampton, 1928
7 for 63 *v.* Hampshire at Bradford, 1928
7 for 25 *v.* Hampshire at Bradford, 1930
7 for 27 *v.* Nottinghamshire at Nottingham, 1931

E.P. Robinson (10)
7 for 45 *v.* Gloucestershire at Leeds, 1937
7 for 122 *v.* Nottinghamshire at Nottingham, 1938
7 for 32 *v.* MCC at Lord's, 1939
8 for 35 *v.* Lancashire at Leeds, 1939
7 for 22 *v.* Glamorgan at Cardiff, 1946
7 for 60 *v.* Oxford University at Oxford, 1946
7 for 41 *v.* Worcestershire at Leeds, 1946
8 for 76 *v.* Surrey at The Oval, 1946
7 for 24 *v.* Hampshire at Scarborough, 1946
7 for 82 *v.* MCC at Scarborough, 1947

M. Ryan (1)
7 for 45 *v.* Warwickshire at Birmingham, 1958

A. Sidebottom (3)
7 for 18 *v.* Oxford University at Oxford, 1980
8 for 72 *v.* Leicestershire at Middlesbrough, 1986
7 for 89 *v.* Nottinghamshire at Nottingham, 1988

T.F. Smailes (6)

7 for 47 *v*. Sussex at Hove, 1935
7 for 72 *v*. Middlesex at Scarborough, 1936
7 for 24 *v*. Worcestershire at Leeds, 1936
8 for 68 *v*. Glamorgan at Hull, 1938
7 for 24 *v*. Scotland at Harrogate, 1938
10 for 47 *v*. Derbyshire at Sheffield, 1939

E. Smith (1)

7 for 40 *v*. MCC at Scarborough, 1893

B. Stead (1)

7 for 76 *v*. Indians at Bradford, 1959

G.B. Stevenson (4)

8 for 65 *v*. Lancashire at Leeds, 1978
7 for 48 *v*. Nottinghamshire at Nottingham, 1980
8 for 57 *v*. Northamptonshire at Leeds, 1980
7 for 46 *v*. Northamptonshire at Leeds, 1981

I.G. Swallow (1)

7 for 95 *v*. Nottinghamshire at Nottingham, 1987

F.S. Trueman (21)

8 for 70 *v*. Minor Counties at Lord's, 1949
8 for 68 *v*. Nottinghamshire at Sheffield, 1951
8 for 53 *v*. Nottinghamshire at Nottingham, 1951
7 for 46 *v*. Worcestershire at Bradford, 1952
7 for 67 *v*. Warwickshire at Coventry, 1954
7 for 15 *v*. Glamorgan at Neath, 1954
8 for 28 *v*. Kent at Dover, 1954
7 for 23 *v*. Nottinghamshire at Scarborough, 1955
7 for 30 *v*. Gloucestershire at Huddersfield, 1955
7 for 37 *v*. Cambridge University at Cambridge, 1957
7 for 57 *v*. Nottinghamshire at Middlesbrough, 1959
7 for 60 *v*. Northamptonshire at Sheffield, 1960
7 for 65 *v*. Northamptonshire at Sheffield, 1960
7 for 41 *v*. Surrey at The Oval, 1960
7 for 82 *v*. Surrey at The Oval, 1960
7 for 42 *v*. Warwickshire at Bradford, 1960
7 for 45 *v*. Leicestershire at Leicester, 1961
8 for 84 *v*. Nottinghamshire at Worksop, 1962
8 for 45 *v*. Gloucestershire at Bradford, 1963
8 for 36 *v*. Sussex at Hove, 1965
8 for 37 *v*. Essex at Bradford, 1966

C. Turner (1)

7 for 54 *v*. Gloucestershire at Gloucester, 1935

G. Ulyett (6)

7 for 82 *v*. United South of England XI at Bradford, 1874
7 for 40 *v*. Surrey at Sheffield, 1875
7 for 30 *v*. Surrey at Sheffield, 1878
7 for 32 *v*. Lancashire at Sheffield, 1879
7 for 33 *v*. Kent at Sheffield, 1884
7 for 50 *v*. Lancashire at Huddersfield, 1889

H. Verity (48)

9 for 60 *v*. Glamorgan at Swansea, 1930
7 for 26 *v*. Hampshire at Bournemouth, 1930
7 for 77 *v*. Essex at Leyton, 1931
10 for 36 *v*. Warwickshire at Leeds, 1931
7 for 64 *v*. Gloucestershire at Sheffield, 1931
8 for 33 *v*. Glamorgan at Swansea, 1931
7 for 62 *v*. Northamptonshire at Bradford, 1931
7 for 93 *v*. Sussex at Hove, 1931
8 for 107 *v*. Lancashire at Bradford, 1932
8 for 39 *v*. Northamptonshire at Northampton, 1932
10 for 10 *v*. Nottinghamshire at Leeds, 1932
7 for 29 *v*. West Indians at Harrogate, 1933
7 for 54 *v*. West Indians at Harrogate, 1933
7 for 35 *v*. Northamptonshire at Leeds, 1933
8 for 47 *v*. Essex at Leyton, 1933
9 for 44 *v*. Essex at Leyton, 1933
9 for 59 *v*. Kent at Dover, 1933
7 for 75 *v*. Essex at Hull, 1934
7 for 39 *v*. Cambridge University at Cambridge, 1935
7 for 31 *v*. Hampshire at Hull, 1935
7 for 47 *v*. Hampshire at Hull, 1935
8 for 28 *v*. Leicestershire at Leeds, 1935
7 for 53 *v*. Kent at Tonbridge, 1935
7 for 55 *v*. Hampshire at Portsmouth, 1935
8 for 56 *v*. Oxford University at Oxford, 1936
7 for 73 *v*. Oxford University at Oxford, 1936
8 for 40 *v*. Worcestershire at Stourbridge, 1936
7 for 55 *v*. Glamorgan at Swansea, 1936
9 for 12 *v*. Kent at Sheffield, 1936
9 for 48 *v*. Essex at Westcliffe-on-Sea, 1936
7 for 35 *v*. Glamorgan at Hull, 1936
8 for 42 *v*. Nottinghamshire at Bradford, 1936
7 for 74 *v*. Warwickshire at Bradford, 1936
9 for 43 *v*. Warwickshire at Leeds, 1937
7 for 38 *v*. Worcestershire at Bradford, 1937
8 for 80 *v*. Sussex at Eastbourne, 1937
8 for 43 *v*. Middlesex at The Oval, 1937
7 for 39 *v*. Cambridge University at Cambridge, 1938
7 for 40 *v*. Essex at Sheffield, 1938
7 for 63 *v*. Glamorgan at Cardiff, 1938
7 for 18 *v*. Leicestershire at Bradford, 1938
9 for 62 *v*. MCC at Lord's, 1939
8 for 38 *v*. Leicestershire at Hull, 1939
7 for 48 *v*. Glamorgan at Bradford, 1939
7 for 20 *v*. Glamorgan at Bradford, 1939
7 for 47 *v*. Gloucestershire at Bristol, 1939
7 for 35 *v*. Warwickshire at Scarborough, 1939
7 for 9 *v*. Sussex at Hove, 1939

A. Waddington (10)

7 for 25 *v*. Leicestershire at Hull, 1920
7 for 18 *v*. Northamptonshire at Northampton, 1920
7 for 21 *v*. Warwickshire at Harrogate, 1920
7 for 31 *v*. Derbyshire at Derby, 1922
8 for 34 *v*. Northamptonshire at Leeds, 1922
8 for 39 *v*. Kent at Leeds, 1922
7 for 6 *v*. Sussex at Hull, 1922
8 for 35 *v*. Hampshire at Bradford, 1922
7 for 43 *v*. Leicestershire at Leicester, 1924
7 for 96 *v*. Glamorgan at Huddersfield, 1925

S. Wade (1)

7 for 28 *v*. Gloucestershire at Cheltenham, 1886

E. Wainwright (14)

7 for 47 *v*. Gloucestershire at Sheffield, 1891
7 for 73 *v*. Somerset at Bradford, 1891
8 for 49 *v*. Middlesex at Sheffield, 1891

7 for 66 *v.* Sussex at Sheffield, 1892
7 for 20 *v.* Sussex at Dewsbury, 1894
7 for 34 *v.* Gloucestershire at Leeds, 1894
9 for 66 *v.* Middlesex at Sheffield, 1894
8 for 34 *v.* Essex at Bradford, 1896
7 for 55 *v.* Hampshire at Harrogate, 1896
7 for 43 *v.* Leicestershire at Scarborough, 1896
7 for 24 *v.* Hampshire at Huddersfield, 1898
7 for 54 *v.* Leicestershire at Dewsbury, 1898
7 for 114 *v.* C.I. Thornton's XI at Scarborough, 1898
7 for 38 *v.* Derbyshire at Derby, 1899

J.H. Wardle (15)
7 for 66 *v.* Middlesex at Leeds, 1947
8 for 87 *v.* Derbyshire at Chesterfield, 1948
7 for 88 *v.* Essex at Westcliffe-on-Sea, 1948
7 for 41 *v.* Surrey at The Oval, 1949
7 for 65 *v.* Worcestershire at Worcester, 1950
8 for 26 *v.* Middlesex at Lord's, 1950
7 for 49 *v.* Middlesex at Sheffield, 1952
7 for 119 *v.* Surrey at Leeds, 1952
7 for 56 *v.* Worcestershire at Huddersfield, 1953
7 for 74 *v.* Leicestershire at Leicester, 1953
9 for 48 *v.* Sussex at Hull, 1954
7 for 64 *v.* Sussex at Hull, 1954
9 for 25 *v.* Lancashire at Manchester, 1954
7 for 72 *v.* Worcestershire at Worcester, 1955
7 for 34 *v.* Somerset at Leeds, 1957

J. Waring (1)
7 for 40 *v.* Lancashire at Leeds, 1966

F. Wilkinson (1)
7 for 68 *v.* Hampshire at Bournemouth, 1938

A.C. Williams (1)
9 for 29 *v.* Hampshire at Dewsbury, 1919

D. Wilson (6)
7 for 92 *v.* MCC at Scarborough, 1963
7 for 50 *v.* Somerset at Bath, 1967
7 for 21 *v.* Warwickshire at Middlesbrough, 1967
7 for 50 *v.* Leicestershire at Leicester, 1968
7 for 36 *v.* Middlesex at Leeds, 1968
7 for 19 *v.* MCC at Scarborough, 1969

E.R. Wilson (3)
7 for 46 *v.* MCC at Scarborough, 1919
7 for 32 *v.* Middlesex at Sheffield, 1921
7 for 67 *v.* Sussex at Hove, 1921

R. Wood (1)
8 for 45 *v.* Scotland at Glasgow, 1952

Other outstanding bowling performances
(*Qualification:* five and six wickets in an innings at less than 4 runs each)

R. Appleyard (3)
6 for 17 *v.* Essex at Bradford, 1951
6 for 12 *v.* Hampshire at Bournemouth, 1954
5 for 18 *v.* Glamorgan at Cardiff, 1957

T. Armitage (2)
5 for 8 *v.* Nottinghamshire at Nottingham, 1875
6 for 20 *v.* Surrey at Sheffield, 1876

R. Aspinall (2)
6 for 23 *v.* Northamptonshire at Northampton, 1947
5 for 19 *v.* Somerset at Wells, 1949

W. Bates (7)
5 for 17 *v.* Nottinghamshire at Sheffield, 1878
6 for 11 *v.* Middlesex at Huddersfield, 1879
5 for 15 *v.* Derbyshire at Derby, 1880
6 for 22 *v.* Kent at Bradford, 1881
6 for 17 *v.* Nottinghamshire at Nottingham, 1881
6 for 12 *v.* Kent at Sheffield, 1882
6 for 19 *v.* Lancashire at Dewsbury, 1886

W.E. Blackburn (1)
5 for 17 *v.* Derbyshire at Bradford, 1919

A. Booth (2)
5 for 16 *v.* Cambridge University at Cambridge, 1946
6 for 21 *v.* Warwickshire at Birmingham, 1946

W.E. Bowes (6)
6 for 17 *v.* Middlesex at Lord's, 1934
6 for 16 *v.* Lancashire at Bradford, 1935
6 for 20 *v.* Gloucestershire at Sheffield, 1936
5 for 14 *v.* Warwickshire at Birmingham, 1938
5 for 17 *v.* Kent at Bradford, 1946
6 for 23 *v.* Warwickshire at Birmingham, 1947

J.T. Brown (Darfield) (1)
6 for 19 *v.* Worcestershire at Worcester, 1899

R.O. Clayton (1)
6 for 20 *v.* Nottinghamshire at Sheffield, 1876

D.B. Close (1)
5 for 12 *v.* Warwickshire at Sheffield, 1959

G.A. Cope (2)
5 for 19 *v.* Oxford University at Oxford, 1974
5 for 10 *v.* Cambridge University at Cambridge, 1977

M.J. Cowan (1)
5 for 15 *v.* Surrey at Leeds, 1955

A. Coxon (3)
6 for 17 *v.* Surrey at Sheffield, 1948
5 for 17 *v.* Glamorgan at Newport, 1949
5 for 13 *v.* Leicestershire at Harrogate, 1950

F. Dennis (1)
5 for 12 v. Northamptonshire at Northampton, 1929

A. Drake (2)
5 for 16 v. Derbyshire at Chesterfield, 1914
5 for 16 v. Somerset at Weston-super-Mare, 1914

T. Emmett (11)
6 for 17 v. Surrey at Sheffield, 1867
6 for 13 v. Lancashire at Holbeck, 1868
5 for 19 v. Lancashire at Sheffield, 1873
5 for 18 v. Sussex at Sheffield, 1874
6 for 21 v. Middlesex at Scarborough, 1874
5 for 3 v. Scotland at Edinburgh, 1878
6 for 12 v. Derbyshire at Sheffield, 1878
6 for 19 v. Derbyshire at Bradford, 1881
5 for 10 v. Australians at Bradford, 1882
6 for 22 v. Australians at Bradford, 1882
5 for 18 v. Middlesex at Lord's, 1885

H. Fisher (2)
6 for 11 v. Leicestershire at Bradford, 1932
5 for 12 v. Somerset at Sheffield, 1932

G. Freeman (2)
5 for 14 v. Kent at Dewsbury, 1870
5 for 15 v. Surrey at The Oval, 1870

S. Haigh (16)
6 for 18 v. Derbyshire at Bradford, 1897
6 for 22 v. Hampshire at Southampton, 1898
6 for 21 v. Surrey at The Oval, 1900
6 for 23 v. Cambridge University at Cambridge, 1902
6 for 19 v. Somerset at Sheffield, 1902
5 for 18 v. Warwickshire at Birmingham, 1902
6 for 22 v. Cambridge University at Sheffield, 1903
5 for 13 v. Essex at Sheffield, 1903
6 for 21 v. Hampshire at Leeds, 1904
6 for 21 v. Nottinghamshire at Sheffield, 1905
5 for 13 v. Cambridge University at Cambridge, 1907
5 for 9 v. Essex at Leyton, 1907
6 for 13 v. Surrey at Leeds, 1908
5 for 19 v. Gloucestershire at Sheffield, 1908
5 for 14 v. Somerset at Dewsbury, 1912
6 for 14 v. Australians at Bradford, 1912

G.P. Harrison (1)
5 for 14 v. Middlesex at Lord's, 1891

A. Hill (4)
6 for 9 v. United South of England XI at Bradford, 1874
5 for 17 v. Middlesex at Sheffield, 1878
5 for 16 v. Derbyshire at Sheffield, 1879
6 for 18 v. MCC at Lord's, 1881

G. H. Hirst (14)
5 for 16 v. Sussex at Sheffield, 1892
6 for 23 v. MCC at Lord's, 1893
5 for 9 v. Somerset at Huddersfield, 1894
5 for 11 v. Sussex at Bradford, 1901
5 for 17 v. Essex at Leyton, 1901
5 for 9 v. Australians at Bradford, 1902
5 for 18 v. Worcestershire at Huddersfield, 1903
6 for 20 v. Lancashire at Bradford, 1906

5 for 15 v. Worcestershire at Hull, 1906
6 for 12 v. Northamptonshire at Northampton, 1908
6 for 7 v. Northamptonshire at Northampton, 1908
6 for 23 v. Surrey at Leeds, 1908
6 for 23 v. Lancashire at Manchester, 1909
6 for 20 v. Surrey at Sheffield, 1909

R. Illingworth (5)
6 for 15 v. Scotland at Hull, 1956
5 for 12 v. Cambridge University at Cambridge, 1961
5 for 10 v. Sussex at Scarborough, 1962
5 for 13 v. Leicestershire at Scarborough, 1963
6 for 13 v. Leicestershire at Leicester, 1963

F.S. Jackson (3)
6 for 19 v. Hampshire at Southampton, 1897
5 for 8 v. Lancashire at Sheffield, 1902
5 for 12 v. Australians at Leeds, 1902

J. Johnson (1)
5 for 16 v. Leicestershire at Leicester, 1939

R. Kilner (8)
6 for 22 v. Essex at Harrogate, 1922
6 for 13 v. Hampshire at Bournemouth, 1922
6 for 14 v. Middlesex at Bradford, 1923
6 for 22 v. Surrey at Sheffield, 1923
6 for 15 v. Hampshire at Portsmouth, 1924
5 for 18 v. Sussex at Hove, 1924
5 for 14 v. Lancashire at Sheffield, 1925
5 for 14 v. Sussex at Bradford, 1925

G.G. Macaulay (15)
6 for 10 v. Warwickshire at Birmingham, 1921
6 for 3 v. Derbyshire at Hull, 1921
6 for 8 v. Northamptonshire at Northampton, 1922
6 for 12 v. Glamorgan at Cardiff, 1922
6 for 18 v. Northamptonshire at Bradford, 1923
5 for 11 v. Worcestershire at Harrogate, 1923
5 for 15 v. Glamorgan at Cardiff, 1924
5 for 19 v. Gloucestershire at Gloucester, 1924
6 for 19 v. Northamptonshire at Northampton, 1925
6 for 22 v. Leicestershire at Leeds, 1926
5 for 15 v. Leicestershire at Leeds, 1926
5 for 17 v. Essex at Harrogate, 1926
6 for 11 v. Leicestershire at Hull, 1930
6 for 22 v. Leicestershire at Bradford, 1933
6 for 22 v. Middlesex at Leeds, 1934

H. Myers (1)
5 for 17 v. Kent at Hull, 1905

A.G. Nicholson (3)
5 for 7 v. Middlesex at Leeds, 1963
5 for 19 v. Gloucestershire at Harrogate, 1965
5 for 12 v. Derbyshire at Sheffield, 1966

C.M. Old (1)
5 for 14 v. Derbyshire at Bradford, 1970

E. Peate(9)
6 for 14 *v.* Middlesex at Huddersfield, 1879
5 for 11 *v.* Derbyshire at Derby, 1880
6 for 12 *v.* Derbyshire at Derby, 1882
5 for 17 *v.* Nottinghamshire at Sheffield, 1883
6 for 13 *v.* Gloucestershire at Moreton-in-Marsh, 1884
5 for 12 *v.* Cambridge University at Cambridge, 1885
5 for 19 *v.* Derbyshire at Huddersfield, 1885
6 for 16 *v.* Sussex at Huddersfield, 1886
6 for 16 *v.* Cambridge University at Sheffield, 1886

R. Peel (7)
5 for 14 *v.* Kent at Sheffield, 1887
6 for 21 *v.* Nottinghamshire at Sheffield, 1888
6 for 19 *v.* Australians at Huddersfield, 1888
5 for 16 *v.* Middlesex at Lord's, 1890
5 for 19 *v.* Middlesex at Lord's, 1891
6 for 22 *v.* Gloucestershire at Bristol, 1891
6 for 19 *v.* Leicestershire at Scarborough, 1896

D. Pickles (1)
5 for 19 *v.* Oxford University at Oxford, 1958

J. M. Preston (1)
5 for 10 *v.* Nottinghamshire at Sheffield, 1887

A. C. Rhodes (1)
6 for 19 *v.* Cambridge University at Cambridge, 1932

W. Rhodes(19)
6 for 21 *v.* Somerset at Bath, 1898
5 for 11 *v.* Somerset at Bath, 1899
6 for 16 *v.* Gloucestershire at Bristol, 1899
6 for 4 *v.* Nottinghamshire at Nottingham, 1901
6 for 15 *v.* MCC at Lord's, 1902
5 for 4 *v.* Worcestershire at Huddersfield, 1903
6 for 16 *v.* Cambridge University at Cambridge, 1905
6 for 9 *v.* Essex at Huddersfield, 1905
6 for 22 *v.* Derbyshire at Glossop, 1907
6 for 17 *v.* Leicestershire at Leicester, 1908
5 for 5 *v.* Derbyshire at Bradford, 1910
5 for 16 *v.* Warwickshire at Birmingham, 1919
5 for 16 *v.* Northamptonshire at Bradford, 1920
5 for 12 *v.* Warwickshire at Birmingham, 1922
6 for 13 *v.* Sussex at Hove, 1922
6 for 23 *v.* Nottinghamshire at Leeds, 1923
5 for 8 *v.* Essex at Leyton, 1923
6 for 22 *v.* Cambridge University at Cambridge, 1924
6 for 20 *v.* Gloucestershire at Dewsbury, 1927

W. Ringrose (1)
6 for 20 *v.* Leicestershire at Dewsbury, 1903

E. Robinson (1)
5 for 16 *v.* Derbyshire at Chesterfield, 1921

H. Sedgwick (1)
5 for 8 *v.* Worcestershire at Hull, 1906

A. Sidebottom (1)
5 for 6 *v.* Hampshire at Southampton, 1983

W. Slinn (1)
6 for 19 *v.* Nottinghamshire at Nottingham, 1864

T. F. Smailes (3)
5 for 16 *v.* Kent at Bradford, 1937
5 for 16 *v.* Warwickshire at Bradford, 1946
5 for 16 *v.* Sussex at Eastbourne, 1946

J. Smurthwaite (1)
5 for 7 *v.* Derbyshire at Sheffield, 1939

G. B. Stevenson (1)
6 for 14 *v.* Warwickshire at Sheffield, 1979

F. S. Trueman (10)
5 for 19 *v.* South Africans at Bradford, 1951
5 for 8 *v.* Oxford University at Oxford, 1954
6 for 23 *v.* Oxford University at Oxford, 1955
6 for 23 *v.* Oxford University at Oxford, 1958
5 for 19 *v.* Surrey at Sheffield, 1958
5 for 13 *v.* Leicestershire at Sheffield, 1961
6 for 18 *v.* Warwickshire at Birmingham, 1963
5 for 18 *v.* Lancashire at Leeds, 1966
5 for 18 *v.* Cambridge University at Cambridge, 1968
6 for 20 *v.* Leicestershire at Sheffield, 1968

G. Ulyett (2)
5 for 17 *v.* Nottinghamshire at Huddersfield, 1873
5 for 16 *v.* Lancashire at Sheffield, 1883

H. Verity (8)
5 for 18 *v.* Gloucestershire at Bristol, 1930
6 for 11 *v.* Surrey at Bradford, 1931
6 for 21 *v.* Glamorgan at Swansea, 1931
5 for 8 *v.* Essex at Leyton, 1932
6 for 12 *v.* Derbyshire at Hull, 1933
5 for 17 *v.* Essex at Colchester, 1935
6 for 10 *v.* Essex at Ilford, 1937
6 for 22 *v.* Hampshire at Bournemouth 1939

A. Waddington (3)
6 for 21 *v.* Northamptonshire at Harrogate, 1921
5 for 14 *v.* Nottinghamshire at Nottingham, 1922
6 for 21 *v.* Northamptonshire at Northampton, 1923

S. Wade (1)
6 for 18 *v.* Gloucestershire at Dewsbury, 1887

E. Wainwright (6)
5 for 11 *v.* Middlesex at Lord's, 1890
6 for 16 *v.* Sussex at Leeds, 1893
6 for 23 *v.* Sussex at Hove, 1893
6 for 18 *v.* Sussex at Dewsbury, 1894
6 for 22 *v.* MCC at Scarborough, 1894
5 for 19 *v.* Sussex at Bradford, 1901

T. A. Wardall (1)
5 for 13 *v.* Surrey at Sheffield, 1893

J.H. Wardle (10)
6 for 17 *v.* Sussex at Sheffield, 1948
5 for 15 *v.* Glamorgan at Newport, 1949
6 for 10 *v.* Scotland at Edinburgh, 1950
6 for 12 *v.* Gloucestershire at Hull, 1950
6 for 20 *v.* Kent at Scarborough, 1950
6 for 23 *v.* Somerset at Sheffield, 1951

J.H. Wardle (continued)
6 for 21 *v*. Glamorgan at Leeds, 1951
6 for 18 *v*. Gloucestershire at Bristol, 1951
6 for 6 *v*. Gloucestershire at Bristol, 1955
5 for 18 *v*. Oxford University at Oxford, 1956

J. West (1)
5 for 3 *v*. Surrey at Sheffield, 1870

D. Wilson (4)
6 for 22 *v*. Sussex at Bradford, 1963
6 for 15 *v*. Gloucestershire at Middlesbrough, 1966
6 for 22 *v*. Middlesex at Sheffield, 1966
5 for 17 *v*. Middlesex at Lord's, 1968

Four wickets in four balls
A. Drake *v*. Derbyshire at Chesterfield 1914

Hat-tricks

G. Freeman *v*. Lancashire at Holbeck, 1868
G. Freeman *v*. Middlesex at Sheffield, 1868
A. Hill *v*. United South of England XI at Bradford, 1874
A. Hill *v*. Surrey at The Oval, 1880
E. Peate *v*. Kent at Sheffield, 1882
G. Ulyett *v*. Lancashire at Sheffield, 1883
E. Peate *v*. Gloucestershire at Moreton-in-Marsh, 1884
W. Fletcher *v*. MCC at Lord's, 1892
E. Wainwright *v*. Sussex at Dewsbury, 1894
G.H. Hirst *v*. Leicestershire at Leicester, 1895
J.T. Brown *v*. Derbyshire at Derby, 1896
R. Peel *v*. Kent at Halifax, 1897
S. Haigh *v*. Derbyshire at Bradford, 1897
S. Haigh *v*. Somerset at Sheffield, 1902
H.A. Sedgwick *v*. Worcestershire at Hull, 1906
G. Deyes *v*. Gentlemen of Ireland at Bray, 1907
G.H. Hirst *v*. Leicester at Hull, 1907
J.T. Newstead *v*. Worcestershire at Bradford, 1907
S. Haigh *v*. Lancashire at Manchester, 1909
M.W. Booth *v*. Worcestershire at Bradford, 1911
A. Drake *v*. Essex at Huddersfield, 1912
M.W. Booth *v*. Essex at Leyton, 1912
A. Drake *v*. Derbyshire at Chesterfield, 1914 (4 in 4)
W. Rhodes *v*. Derbyshire at Derby, 1920

A. Waddington *v*. Northamptonshire at Northampton, 1920 (4 in 5)
G.G. Macaulay *v*. Warwickshire at Birmingham, 1923
E. Robinson *v*. Sussex at Hull, 1928
G.G. Macaulay *v*. Leicestershire at Hull, 1930
E. Robinson *v*. Kent at Gravesend, 1930
H. Verity *v*. Nottinghamshire at Leeds, 1932
H. Fisher *v*. Somerset at Sheffield, 1932 (all lbw)
G.G. Macaulay *v*. Glamorgan at Cardiff, 1933
G.G. Macaulay *v*. Lancashire at Manchester, 1933 (4 in 5)
M. Leyland *v*. Surrey at Sheffield, 1935
E.P. Robinson *v*. Kent at Leeds, 1939
A. Coxon *v*. Worcestershire at Leeds, 1946
F.S. Trueman *v*. Nottinghamshire at Nottingham, 1951
F.S. Trueman *v*. Nottinghamshire at Scarborough, 1955
R. Appleyard *v*. Gloucestershire at Sheffield, 1956
F.S. Trueman *v*. MCC at Lord's, 1958
D. Wilson *v*. Nottinghamshire at Middlesbrough, 1959
F.S. Trueman *v*. Nottinghamshire at Bradford, 1963
D. Wilson *v*. Nottinghamshire at Worksop, 1966
D. Wilson *v*. Kent at Harrogate, 1966
G.A. Cope *v*. Essex at Colchester, 1970
A.L. Robinson *v*. Nottinghamshire at Worksop, 1974
P.W. Jarvis *v*. Derbyshire at Chesterfield, 1985

47 hat-tricks: G.G. Macaulay and F.S. Trueman took four each, S. Haigh and D. Wilson three each. There have been 7 hat-tricks *versus* Nottinghamshire and 5 each *versus* Derbyshire and Kent.

Two hundred wickets in a season

Bowler	Season	Overs	Maidens	Runs	Wickets	Average
W. Rhodes	1900	1366.4	411	3054	240	12.72
W. Rhodes	1901	1455.3	474	3497	233	15.00
G.H. Hirst	1906	1111.1	262	3089	201	15.36
G.G. Macaulay	1925	1241.2	291	2986	200	14.93
R. Appleyard	1951	1323.2	394	2829	200	14.14

A hundred wickets in a season

Bowler	Wickets taken	Wickets taken	Wickets taken
R. Appleyard	200 in 1951	141 in 1954	110 in 1956
A. Booth	111 in 1946	–	–
M.W. Booth	104 in 1912	167 in 1913	155 in 1914
W.E. Bowes	117 in 1931	168 in 1932	130 in 1933
	109 in 1934	154 in 1935	113 in 1936
	106 in 1938	107 in 1939	–
D.B. Close	105 in 1949	114 in 1952	–
A. Coxon	101 in 1949	129 in 1950	–
A. Drake	115 in 1913	158 in 1914	–
T. Emmett	112 in 1886	–	–
S. Haigh	160 in 1900	154 in 1902	102 in 1903
	118 in 1904	124 in 1905	161 in 1906
	120 in 1909	100 in 1911	125 in 1912
G.H. Hirst	124 in 1893	150 in 1895	–
	171 in 1901	121 in 1903	114 in 1904
	100 in 1905	201 in 1906	169 in 1907
	164 in 1908	138 in 1910	130 in 1911
	113 in 1912	–	–
R. Illingworth	103 in 1956	120 in 1961	116 in 1962
	122 in 1964	105 in 1968	–
R. Kilner	107 in 1922	143 in 1923	134 in 1924
	123 in 1925	–	–
G.G. Macaulay	101 in 1921	130 in 1922	163 in 1923
	184 in 1924	200 in 1925	133 in 1926
	130 in 1927	117 in 1928	102 in 1929
	141 in 1933	–	–
J.T. Newstead	131 in 1908	–	–
A.G. Nicholson	113 in 1966	101 in 1967	–
E. Peate	131 in 1880	133 in 1881	165 in 1882
R. Peel	118 in 1888	132 in 1890	114 in 1891
	106 in 1892	134 in 1894	155 in 1895
	108 in 1896	–	–
W. Rhodes	141 in 1898	153 in 1899	240 in 1900
	233 in 1901	174 in 1902	169 in 1903
	118 in 1904	158 in 1905	113 in 1906
	164 in 1907	100 in 1908	115 in 1909
	105 in 1911	117 in 1914	155 in 1919
	156 in 1920	128 in 1921	100 in 1922
	127 in 1923	102 in 1926	112 in 1928
	100 in 1929	–	–
E. Robinson	111 in 1928	–	–
E.P. Robinson	104 in 1938	120 in 1939	149 in 1946
	108 in 1947	–	–
T.F. Smailes	105 in 1934	125 in 1936	120 in 1937
	104 in 1938	–	–
F.S. Trueman	129 in 1954	140 in 1955	104 in 1959
	150 in 1960	124 in 1961	106 in 1962
	121 in 1965	107 in 1966	–
H. Verity	169 in 1931	146 in 1932	168 in 1933
	100 in 1934	199 in 1935	185 in 1936
	185 in 1937	137 in 1938	189 in 1939
A. Waddington	100 in 1919	140 in 1920	105 in 1921
	132 in 1928	105 in 1925	–
E. Wainwright	107 in 1891	124 in 1892	114 in 1893
	157 in 1894	108 in 1896	–
J.H. Wardle	148 in 1948	100 in 1949	172 in 1950
	122 in 1951	169 in 1952	126 in 1953
	122 in 1954	159 in 1955	146 in 1956
	104 in 1957	–	–
D. Wilson	100 in 1966	107 in 1968	101 in 1969

Bowlers who have taken over 500 wickets

Bowler	Wickets	Runs	Average
W. Rhodes	3,597	57,634	16.02
G.H. Hirst	2,481	44,716	18.02
S. Haigh	1,876	29,289	15.61
G.G. Macaulay	1,773	30,292	17.08
F.S. Trueman	1,745	29,980	17.13
H. Verity	1,558	21,353	13.70
J.H. Wardle	1,539	27,917	18.13
R. Illingworth	1,431	26,806	18.73
W.E. Bowes	1,351	21,227	15.71
R. Peel	1,311	20,638	15.74
T. Emmett	1,216	15,465	12.71
E. Wainwright	1,183	20,230	17.24
D. Wilson	1,104	22,626	20.49
D.B. Close	967	23,489	24.29
E. Robinson	892	19,607	21.98
A.G. Nicholson	876	17,296	19.74
R. Kilner	858	14,873	17.33
A. Waddington	831	16,095	19.36
T.F. Smailes	802	16.622	20.72
P. Carrick	797	23,998	30.11
E. Peate	794	9,986	12.57
E.P. Robinson	735	15,135	20.59
W. Bates	660	11,024	16.70
C.M. Old	647	13,409	20.72
R. Appleyard	637	9,813	15.40
G.A. Cope	630	15,627	24.80
A. Hill	563	7,151	12.70
M.W. Booth	558	10,632	19.05
Hon. F.S. Jackson	506	9,690	19.15

Bowling unchanged in a match
in which the opponents were dismissed twice

L. Greenwood (11 for 71) and G. Freeman (8 for 73)
v. Surrey at The Oval, 1867
Yorkshire won by an innings and 111 runs

L. Greenwood (7 for 76) and G. Freeman (12 for 51)
v. Lancashire at Whalley, 1867
Yorkshire won by an innings and 56 runs

G. Freeman (12 for 23) and T. Emmett (8 for 24)
v. Lancashire at Holbeck, 1868
Yorkshire won by an innings and 186 runs

G. Freeman (12 for 62) and T. Emmett (6 for 57)
v. Middlesex at Sheffield, 1868
Yorkshire won by an innings and 24 runs

G. Freeman (13 for 60) and T. Emmett (5 for 55) *v.* Surrey
at Sheffield, 1869
Yorkshire won by 6 wickets

G. Freeman (4 for 31) and T. Emmett (16 for 38)
v. Cambridgeshire at Hunslet, 1869
Yorkshire won by an innings and 266 runs

G. Freeman (10 for 43) and T. Emmett (9 for 92) *v.* Surrey
at The Oval, 1870
Yorkshire won by 137 runs

G. Freeman (7 for 84) and T. Emmett (11 for 82)
v. Lancashire at Manchester, 1871
Yorkshire won by 222 runs

T. Emmett (8 for 111) and A. Hill (12 for 59) v. Surrey at
The Oval, 1871
Yorkshire won by 10 wickets

T. Emmett (11 for 82) and A. Hill (8 for 47) v. Lancashire at
Manchester, 1873
Yorkshire won by 9 wickets

A. Hill (8 for 55) and T. Emmett (12 for 84) v. Surrey at
Sheffield, 1873
Yorkshire won by 8 wickets

A. Hill (10 for 96) and T. Emmett (9 for 87)
v. Nottinghamshire at Nottingham, 1874
Yorkshire won by an innings and 13 runs

A. Hill (9 for 67) and G. Ulyett (10 for 107) v. United
South of England XI at Bradford, 1874
Yorkshire won by 26 runs

A. Hill (10 for 38) and T. Emmett (8 for 74) v. Lancashire at
Manchester, 1874
Yorkshire won by 66 runs

W. Bates (9 for 34) and T. Emmett (10 for 21) v. Sussex at
Hove, 1878
Yorkshire won by 226 runs

A. Hill (6 for 85) and E. Peate (14 for 77) v. Surrey at
Huddersfield, 1881
Yorkshire won by an innings and 217 runs

E. Peate (8 for 57) and W. Bates (11 for 47)
v. Nottinghamshire at Nottingham, 1881
Yorkshire won by an innings and 17 runs

G.P. Harrison (11 for 76) and E. Peate (8 for 59) v. Kent at
Dewsbury, 1883
Yorkshire won by an innings and 131 runs

E. Wainwright (13 for 38) and R. Peel (7 for 60) v. Sussex at
Dewsbury, 1894
Yorkshire won by 166 runs

W. Rhodes (11 for 36) and S. Haigh (7 for 49)
v. Worcestershire at Bradford, 1900
Yorkshire won by an innings and 5 runs

G.H. Hirst (12 for 29) and W. Rhodes (6 for 37) v. Essex at
Leyton, 1901
Yorkshire won by an innings and 33 runs

S. Haigh (12 for 52) and W. Rhodes (7 for 55)
v. Cambridge University at Sheffield, 1903
Yorkshire won by 206 runs

G.H. Hirst (10 for 67) and W. Rhodes (10 for 81) v. Surrey
at The Oval, 1903
Yorkshire won by an innings and 97 runs

W. Rhodes (10 for 39) and S. Haigh (10 for 49)
v. Hampshire at Leeds, 1904
Yorkshire won by 370 runs

G.H. Hirst (11 for 44) and W. Rhodes (8 for 71)
v. Derbyshire at Glossop, 1907
Yorkshire won by an innings and 130 runs

G.H. Hirst (12 for 19) and S. Haigh (6 for 19)
v. Northamptonshire at Northampton, 1908
Yorkshire won by an innings and 314 runs

M.W. Booth (12 for 89) and A. Drake (8 for 81)
v. Gloucestershire at Bristol, 1914
Yorkshire won by an innings and 227 runs

M.W. Booth (5 for 77) and A. Drake (15 for 51)
v. Somerset at Weston-super-Mare, 1914
Yorkshire won by 140 runs

A. Waddington (13 for 48) and E. Robinson (6 for 34)
v. Northamptonshire at Northampton, 1920
Yorkshire won by an innings and 173 runs

E. Robinson (10 for 70) and A. Waddington (9 for 61)
v. Northamptonshire at Harrogate, 1921
Yorkshire won by an innings and 397 runs

E. Robinson (8 for 65) and G.G. Macaulay (12 for 50)
v. Worcestershire at Leeds, 1927
Yorkshire won by an innings and 106 runs

Most catches in an innings

6 E.P. Robinson v. Leicestershire at Bradford, 1938
5 J. Tunnicliffe v. Leicestershire at Leeds, 1897
5 J. Tunnicliffe v. Leicestershire at Leicester, 1900
5 J. Tunnicliffe v. Leicestershire at Scarborough, 1901
5 A.B. Sellers v. Essex at Leyton, 1933
5 D. Wilson v. Surrey at The Oval, 1969
5 R.G. Lumb v. Gloucestershire at Middlesbrough, 1972

Most catches in a match

7 J. Tunnicliffe v. Leicestershire at Leeds, 1897
7 J. Tunnicliffe v. Leicestershire at Leicester, 1900
7 A.B. Sellers v. Essex at Leyton, 1933
7 E.P. Robinson v. Leicestershire at Bradford, 1938

Most catches in a season

70 J. Tunnicliffe in 1901
70 P.J. Sharpe in 1962
61 J. Tunnicliffe in 1895
60 J. Tunnicliffe in 1904
59 J. Tunnicliffe in 1896
57 J.V. Wilson in 1955
54 J.V. Wilson in 1961
53 J.V. Wilson in 1957
51 J.V. Wilson in 1951

Most catches in a career

665 J. Tunnicliffe (1.41 per match)
572 W. Rhodes (0.64 per match)
564 D.B. Close (1.05 per match)
525 P.J. Sharpe (1.27 per match)
521 J.v. Wilson (1.08 per match)
500 G. Hirst (0.69 per match)

Most dismissals in an innings

7	(7ct)	D.L. Bairstow v. Derbyshire at Scarborough, 1982
6	(6ct)	J. Hunter v. Gloucestershire at Gloucester, 1887
6	(5ct, 1st)	D. Hunter v. Surrey at Sheffield, 1891
6	(6ct)	D. Hunter v. Middlesex at Leeds, 1909
6	(2ct, 4st)	W.R. Allen v. Sussex at Hove, 1921
6	(5ct, 1st)	J.G. Binks v. Lancashire at Leeds, 1962
6	(6ct)	D.L. Bairstow v. Lancashire at Manchester, 1971
6	(6ct)	D.L. Bairstow v. Warwickshire at Bradford, 1978
6	(5ct, 1st)	D.L. Bairstow v. Lancashire at Leeds, 1980
6	(6ct)	D.L. Bairstow v. Derbyshire at Chesterfield, 1984

Most dismissals in a match

11 (11ct)	D.L. Bairstow v. Derbyshire at Scarborough, 1982	
9 (9ct)	J. Hunter v. Gloucestershire at Gloucester, 1887	
9 (8ct, 1st)	A. Dolphin v. Derbyshire at Bradford, 1919	
9 (9ct)	D.L. Bairstow v. Lancashire at Manchester, 1971	
8 (2ct, 6st)	G. Pinder v. Lancashire at Sheffield, 1872	
8 (2ct, 6st)	D. Hunter v. Surrey at Bradford, 1898	
8 (7ct, 1st)	A. Bairstow v. Cambridge University at Cambridge, 1899	
8 (8ct)	A. Wood v. Northamptonshire at Huddersfield, 1932	
8 (8ct)	D.L. Bairstow v. Lancashire at Leeds, 1978	
8 (7ct, 1st)	D.L. Bairstow v. Derbyshire at Chesterfield, 1984	
8 (6ct, 2st)	D.L. Bairstow v. Derbyshire at Chesterfield, 1985	

Most dismissals in a season

107 (96ct, 11st)	J.G. Binks, 1960
94 (81ct, 13st)	J.G. Binks, 1961
89 (75ct, 14st)	A. Wood, 1934
88 (80ct, 8st)	J.G. Binks, 1963
86 (70ct, 16st)	J.G. Binks, 1962
82 (52ct, 30st)	A. Dolphin, 1919
80 (57ct, 23st)	A. Wood, 1935

Most dismissals in a career

1190 (863ct, 327st)	D. Hunter (2.30 per match)
1044 (872ct, 172st)	J.G. Binks (2.12 per match)
1004 (874ct, 130st)	D.L. Bairstow (2.34 per match)
855 (612ct, 243st)	A. Wood (2.09 per match)
828 (568ct, 260st)	A. Dolphin (1.93 per match)

The "double"

Player	Year	Runs	Average	Wickets	Average	Player	Year	Runs	Average	Wickets	Average
M.W. Booth	1913	1228	27.28	181	18.46	F.S. Jackson	1898	1566	41.21	104	15.67
D.B. Close	1949	1098	27.45	113	27.87	R. Kilner	1922	1198	27.22	122	14.73
	1952	1192	33.11	114	24.08		1923	1404	32.24	158	12.91
A. Drake	1913	1056	23.46	116	16.93		1925	1068	30.51	131	17.92
S. Haigh	1904	1055	26.37	121	19.85		1926	1187	37.09	107	22.52
G.H. Hirst	1896	1122	28.20	104	21.64	R. Peel	1896	1206	30.60	128	17.64
	1897	1535	35.30	101	23.23	W. Rhodes	1903	1137	27.07	193	14.57
	1901	1950	42.39	183	16.38		1904	1537	35.74	131	21.59
	1903	1844	47.28	128	14.94		1905	1581	35.93	182	16.95
	1904	2501	54.36	132	21.09		1906	1721	29.16	128	23.57
	1905	2266	53.95	110	19.94		1907	1055	22.93	177	15.57
	1906	2385	45.86	208	16.50		1908	1673	31.56	115	16.13
	1907	1344	28.38	188	15.20		1909	2094	40.26	141	15.89
	1908	1598	38.97	114	14.05		1911	2261	38.32	117	24.07
	1909	1256	27.30	115	20.05		1914	1377	29.29	118	18.27
	1910	1840	32.85	164	14.79		1919	1237	34.36	164	14.42
	1911	1789	33.12	137	20.40		1920	1123	28.07	161	13.18
	1912	1133	25.75	118	17.37		1921	1474	39.83	141	13.27
	1913	1540	35.81	101	20.13		1922	1511	39.76	119	12.19
R. Illingworth	1957	1213	28.20	106	18.40		1923	1321	33.02	134	11.54
	1959	1726	46.64	110	21.46		1924	1126	26.18	109	14.46
	1960	1006	25.79	109	17.55		1926	1132	34.30	115	14.86
	1961	1153	24.53	128	17.90	T.F. Smailes	1938	1002	25.05	113	20.84
	1962	1612	34.29	117	19.45	E. Wainwright	1897	1612	35.75	101	23.70
	1964	1301	37.17	122	17.45						

Other feats

Yorkshire, in their match against Warwickshire at Birmingham, 7, 8 and 9 May 1896, scored 887 runs, the highest total ever obtained in a first-class county match in England. In this innings of Yorkshire four individual hundreds were scored, a feat which had never previously been accomplished in first-class cricket.

It is interesting to note that H. Sutcliffe and P. Holmes scored 100 or more for the first wicket for Yorkshire on 69 occasions, and 74 times in all. G. Boycott and R.G. Lumb shared 29 century partnerships for Yorkshire's first wicket; L. Hutton and F.A. Lowson 22; J.T. Brown and J. Tunnicliffe 19; H. Sutcliffe and L. Hutton 15; and L. Hall and G. Ulyett 12.

In first-class matches H. Sutcliffe shared in 145 first-wicket partnerships of 100 runs or more.

H. Sutcliffe (194) and M. Leyland (45) hit 102 off consecutive overs for Yorkshire v. Essex at Scarborough in 1932.

The second-smallest total in a first-class county match is 13, scored by Nottinghamshire v. Yorkshire at Nottingham, 20 and 21 June 1901.

The smallest aggregate total for which a first-class county has ever been twice dismissed is 42 (innings of 27 and 15), for which total Yorkshire dismissed Northamptonshire at Northampton, 7 and 8 May 1908.

In 1902, at Leeds, Yorkshire dismissed the Australians in their second innings for 23 runs. G.H. Hirst took five wickets for 9 runs and Sir F.S. Jackson five wickets for 12 runs.

G.H. Hirst, in 1906, performed the unparalleled feat of scoring over two thousand runs and taking over two hundred wickets in first-class matches, his record being:

	Matches	Innings	Times not out	Total Runs	Most in an innings	Average
Batting	35	58	6	2385	169	45.86

	Overs	Maidens	Runs	Wickets	Average
Bowling	1306.1	271	3434	208	16.50

The highest individual score for Yorkshire in first-class cricket is 341 by G.H. Hirst v. Leicestershire, at Leicester, 19 and 20 May 1905.

The highest individual score against Yorkshire in first-class cricket is 318 not out, by Dr W.G. Grace, for Gloucestershire, at Cheltenham, 17 and 18 August 1876.

In 1932 P. Holmes and H. Sutcliffe scored 555 for the first wicket v. Essex, at Leyton, thus breaking the world's record of 554, also made by two Yorkshiremen, J. Tunnicliffe and J.T. Brown v. Derbyshire at Chesterfield, in 1898.

In Yorkshire matches J. Tunnicliffe caught 678. He also kept wicket in six matches, one in 1891 and five in 1892 when he stumped nine and caught seven.

In 1962 P.J. Sharpe took 71 catches in first-class matches, the highest in a season by any Yorkshireman (excluding wicket-keepers).

From 1898 to 1930 inclusive, Wilfred Rhodes took no less than 4187 wickets, and scored 39,969 runs in first-class cricket at home and abroad, a remarkable record. He also took a hundred wickets and scored a thousand in a season sixteen times, and G.H. Hirst fourteen times.

Wilfred Rhodes was the first England player to have taken over a hundred wickets and scored a thousand runs in Test matches against Australia.

Of players with a qualification of not less than fifty wickets, Wilfred Rhodes was first in bowling in first-class cricket in 1900, 1901, 1919, 1920, 1922, 1923 and 1926, Schofield Haigh in 1902, 1905, 1908 and 1909, Mr E.R. Wilson in 1921, G.G. Macaulay in 1924, Hedley Verity in 1930, 1933, 1935, 1937 and 1939, W.E. Bowes in 1938, A. Booth in 1946, R. Appleyard in 1951 and 1955, and F.S. Trueman in 1952 and 1963.

In 1951, his first full season in first-class cricket, R. Appleyard took 200 wickets at a cost of 14.14 each.

In scoring 132 v. Gloucestershire at Bradford in 1932, H. Sutcliffe obtained his hundredth century, being the first Yorkshireman to accomplish the feat. He obtained his hundredth century for his county when scoring 122 v. Lancashire at Sheffield in 1937. L. Hutton obtained his hundredth century in first-class cricket when he scored 151 v. Surrey at The Oval in 1951.

G. Boycott became the eighteenth player (and the third Yorkshireman) to score a hundred first-class centuries when he made 191 for England v. Australia on 11 August 1977. He was the first player to score his hundredth hundred in a Test match.

The highest aggregate of runs made in one season in first-class cricket by a Yorkshire player is 3429 by L. Hutton in 1949. This total has been exceeded three times, viz. D.C.S. Compton (3816), W.J. Edrich (3539, both 1947), and 3518 by T. Hayward in 1906. H. Sutcliffe scored 3336 in 1932.

C.M. Old's century in 37 minutes v. Warwickshire at Edgbaston on 9 August 1977 is the third fastest in first-class cricket.

Three players have taken all ten Yorkshire wickets in an innings. G. Wootton playing for All England at Sheffield in 1865 took all ten wickets for 54 runs; H. Howell performed the feat for Warwickshire at Edgbaston in 1923 at a cost of 51 runs, and C.V. Grimmett, Australia, took all ten wickets for 37 runs at Sheffield in 1930.

The match against Sussex at Dewsbury, 7 and 8 June 1894, was brought to a summary conclusion by a remarkable bowling performance on the part of Edward Wainwright. In the second innings of Sussex he took the last five wickets in seven balls, including the performance of the hat-trick. In the whole match he obtained thirteen wickets for only 38 runs.

At Sheffield on 17 August 1932 v. Somerset, H. Fisher accomplished the hat-trick, all three batsmen being out lbw. This was the first occasion in first-class cricket of a leg-before-wicket hat-trick.

The greatest number of wickets taken in one season in first-class cricket by a Yorkshireman is 261, by W. Rhodes in 1900.

J.G. Binks kept wicket for Yorkshire in 412 consecutive County Championship matches (1955–1969). A. Wood kept wicket for Yorkshire in 222 consecutive County Championship matches (1928–1935).

M.D. Moxon has the unique distinction of scoring a century in each of his first two first-class matches in Yorkshire (116 (2nd inns) v. Essex at Leeds and 111 (1st inns) v. Derbyshire at Sheffield, June 1981).

A.A. Metcalfe became only the second Yorkshire player to score a century in his first first-class innings when he made 122 v. Nottinghamshire at Bradford in 1983. (C. Tyson was the first when he scored 100* v. Hampshire at Southampton in 1921.)

P.W. Jarvis made his first-class debut v. Sussex at Hove on 12 September 1981 and so, at 16 years 75 days, became the youngest ever to appear for Yorkshire in first-class cricket.

D.L. Bairstow held eleven catches v. Derbyshire at Scarborough in September 1982 and so equalled the world record for catches taken in a match by a wicket-keeper. His seven catches in the first innings of that match created a Yorkshire record for the number of catches in an innings.

In the Yorkshire v. Norfolk match played on the Hyde Park ground at Sheffield, 14 to 18 July 1834, 851 runs were scored in the four innings, of which no fewer than 128 were extras, 75 byes and 53 wides. At that time wides were not run out, so that every wide included in the above total represents a wide actually bowled. This particular achievement has never been surpassed in the annals of county cricket.

The following first-wicket partnerships of over 100 runs in both innings of a match have been scored for Yorkshire:

G. Ulyett and L. Hall *v*. Sussex at Hove, 1885	123 and 108
J.T. Brown and J. Tunnicliffe *v*. Middlesex at Lord's 1896	139 and 147
P. Holmes and H. Sutcliffe *v*. Surrey at The Oval, 1926	105 and 265
P. Holmes and H. Sutcliffe *v*. Nottinghamshire at Trent Bridge, 1928	184 and 210
L. Hutton and W. Watson *v*. Lancashire at Old Trafford, 1947	110 and 117
W.B. Stott and K. Taylor *v*. Nottinghamshire at Trent Bridge, 1957	122 and 230
J.B. Bolus and K. Taylor *v*. Cambridge University at Cambridge, 1962	136 and 138
G. Boycott and K. Taylor *v*. Leicestershire at Leicester, 1963	105 and 105
K. Taylor and J.H. Hampshire *v*. Oxford University at Oxford, 1964	116 and 112
G. Boycott and R.G. Lumb *v*. Sussex at Leeds, 1974	104 and 104

L. Hutton reached his thousand runs in first-class cricket in 1949 as early as 9 June. W. Barber reached his thousand runs in 1925 on 13 June. P. Holmes reached his in 1925 on 16 June, as also did H. Sutcliffe in 1932. J.T. Brown reached his in 1899 on 22 June. In 1905 D. Denton reached his thousand runs on 26 June; and in 1906 G.H. Hirst gained the same total on 27 June.

In 1912 D. Denton scored over a thousand runs during the month of July, while M. Leyland and H. Sutcliffe both scored over a thousand runs in August 1932.

L. Hutton scored over a thousand runs in June, and then again in August in 1949.

H. Verity took his hundredth wicket in first-class cricket as early as 19 June in 1936 and on 27 June in 1935. In 1900 W. Rhodes obtained his hundredth wicket on 21 June and again on the same date in 1901, while G.H. Hirst obtained his hundredth wicket on 28 June 1906.

In 1930 Yorkshiremen (H. Sutcliffe and H. Verity) occupied the first places by English players in the batting and the bowling averages of first-class cricket, which is a record without precedent. H. Sutcliffe was also first in the batting averages in 1931 and 1932.

G. Boycott is the only player to have achieved an average of over 100 in each of two English seasons. In 1971 he scored 2503 runs at an average of 100.12 and in 1979 he scored 1538 runs at an average of 102.53.

First-class matches begun and finished in one day

Yorkshire *v*. Somerset, at Huddersfield, 9 July 1894

Yorkshire *v*. Hampshire, at Southampton, 27 May 1898

Yorkshire *v*. Worcestershire, at Bradford, 7 May 1900

★Yorkshire *v*. Gloucestershire, at Sheffield, 5 June 1931

★Yorkshire *v*. Northamptonshire, at Bradford, 11 August 1931

★After the first innings had been declared closed without a wicket falling.

Yorkshire Test cricketers 1877–1988

The England eleven that played the first Test match at Melbourne, in March 1877, contained five Yorkshiremen, and in the subsequent years of Test cricket few England sides have taken the field without at least one Yorkshire representative.

Below are complete figures of the sixty-six Yorkshire cricketers who have appeared in Test matches up to 31 December 1988.

	No. of Tests	Runs	100s	Aver.	Wkts	Aver.	Ct/St
Appleyard, R. (1954–56)	9	51	–	17.00	31	17.87	4
Armitage, T. (1877)	2	33	–	11.00	–	–	
Athey, C.W.J. (1980–88)	23	919	1	22.97	–	–	13
Bairstow, D.L. (1979–81)	4	125	–	20.83	–	–	12/1
Barber, W. (1935)	2	83	–	20.75	1	0	1
Bates, W. (1882–87)	15	656	–	27.33	50	16.42	9
Binks, J.G. (1964)	2	91	–	22.75	–	–	8/-
Booth, M.W. (1913–14)	2	46	–	23.00	7	18.57	–
Bowes, W.E. (1932–46)	15	28	–	4.66	68	22.33	2
§Boycott, G. (1964–82)	108	8114	22	47.72	7	54.57	33
Brennan, D.V. (1951)	2	16	–	8.00	–	–	-/1
Brown, J.T. (1894–99)	8	470	1	36.15	–	–	7
§Close, D.B. (1949–76)	22	887	–	25.34	18	29.55	24
Cope, G.A. (1977)	3	40	–	13.33	8	34.62	1
Coxon, A. (1948)	1	19	–	9.50	3	57.33	–
Denton, D. (1905–10)	11	424	1	20.19	–	–	8
Dolphin, A. (1921)	1	1	–	0.50	–	–	1/-
Emmett, T. (1877–82)	7	160	–	13.33	9	31.55	9
Gibb, P.A. (1938–46)	8	581	2	44.69	–	–	3/1
Greenwood, A. (1877)	2	77	–	19.25	–	–	2
Haigh, S. (1899–1912)	11	113	–	7.53	24	25.91	8

	No. of Tests	Runs	100s	Aver.	Wkts	Aver.	Ct/St
Hampshire, J.H. (1969–75)	8	403	1	26.86	–	–	9
§Hawke, Lord (1896–99)	5	55	–	7.85	–	–	3
Hill, A. (1877)	2	101	–	50.50	7	18.57	1
Hirst G.H. (1899–1909)	24	790	–	22.57	59	30.00	18
Holmes, P. (1921–32)	7	357	–	27.46	–	–	3
Hunter, J. (1884–85)	5	93	–	18.60	–	–	8/3
§§Hutton, L. (1937–55)	79	6971	19	56.67	3	77.33	57
Hutton, R.A. (1971)	5	219	–	36.50	9	28.55	9
§Illingworth, R. (1958–73)	61	1836	2	23.24	122	31.20	45
§Jackson, Hon. F.S. (1893–1905)	20	1415	5	48.79	24	33.29	10
Jarvis, P.W. (1988)	4	76	–	19.00	12	34.83	–
Kilner, R. (1924–26)	9	233	–	33.28	24	30.58	6
Leadbeater, E. (1951–52)	2	40	–	20.00	2	109.00	3
Leyland, M. (1928–38)	41	2764	9	46.06	6	97.50	13
Lowson, F.A. (1951–55)	7	245	–	18.84	–	–	5
Macaulay, G.G. (1923–33)	8	112	–	18.66	24	27.58	5
Milligan, F.W. (1899)	2	58	–	14.50	–	–	1
Mitchell, A. (1933–38)	6	298	–	29.80	–	–	9
★Mitchell, F. (1899)	2	88	–	22.00	–	–	2
Moxon, M.D. (1986–88)	9	437	–	31.21	–	–	10
Old, C.M. (1972–81)	46	845	–	14.82	143	28.11	22
Padgett, D.E.V. (1960)	2	51	–	12.75	–	–	–
Peate, E. (1882–86)	9	70	–	11.66	31	22.00	2
Peel, R. (1884–96)	20	427	–	14.72	102	16.81	17
Rhodes, W. (1899–1930)	58	2325	2	30.19	127	26.96	60
Sharpe, P.J. (1963–69)	12	786	1	46.23	–	–	17
Sidebottom, A. (1985)	1	2	–	2.00	1	65.00	–
Smailes, T.F. (1946)	1	25	–	25.00	3	20.66	–
Smithson, G.A. (1948)	2	70	–	23.33	–	–	–
§Stanyforth, R.T. (1927–28)	4	13	–	2.60	–	–	7/2
Stevenson, G.B. (1980–81)	2	28	–	28.00	5	36.60	–
Sutcliffe, H. (1924–35)	54	4555	16	60.73	–	–	23
Taylor, K. (1959–64)	3	57	–	11.40	–	–	1
Trueman, F.S. (1952–65)	67	981	–	13.81	307	21.57	64
Ulyett, G. (1877–90)	25	949	1	24.33	50	20.40	19
Verity, H. (1931–39)	40	669	–	20.90	144	24.37	30
Waddington, A. (1920–21)	2	16	–	4.00	1	119.00	1
Wainwright, E. (1893–98)	5	132	–	14.66	–	–	2
Wardle, J.H. (1948–57)	28	653	–	19.78	102	20.39	12
Watson, W. (1951–59)	23	879	2	25.85	–	–	8
Wilson, C.E.M. (1899)	2	42	–	14.00	–	–	–
Wilson, D. (1964–71)	6	75	–	12.50	11	42.36	1
Wilson, E.R. (1921)	1	10	–	5.00	3	12.00	–
Wood, A. (1938–39)	4	80	–	20.00	–	–	10/1
§Yardley, N.W.D. (1938–50)	20	812	–	25.37	21	33.66	14

§ captained England
§§ first professional captain of England to be appointed by MCC
★ also represented and captained South Africa

Test centuries

C.W.J. Athey (1)

1987	Pakistan				123

G. Boycott (22)

1964	Australia	113	1973/74	West Indies	112
1964/5	South Africa	117	1977	Australia	107
1967	India	★246	1977	Australia	191
1967/68	West Indies	116	1977/78	Pakistan	★100
1969	West Indies	128	1978	New Zealand	131
1969	West Indies	106	1979	India	125
1970/71	Australia	★142	1979	India	155

1970/71	Australia	*119	1980	Australia	*128
1971	Pakistan	112	1980/81	West Indies	*104
1971	Pakistan	*121	1981	Australia	137
1973	New Zealand	115	1981/2	India	105

J. T. Brown (1)

| 1894/95 | Australia | | | | 140 |

D. Denton (1)

| 1909/10 | South Africa | | | | 104 |

P. A. Gibb (2)

| 1938/39 | South Africa | 106 | 1938/39 | South Africa | 120 |

J. H. Hampshire (1)

| 1969 | West Indies | | | | 107 |

L. Hutton (19)

1937	New Zealand	100	1949	New Zealand	206
1938	Australia	100	1950	West Indies	*202
1938	Australia	364	1950/51	Australia	*156
1939	West Indies	196	1951	South Africa	100
1939	West Indies	*165	1952	India	150
1946/47	Australia	*122	1952	India	104
1947	South Africa	100	1953	Australia	145
1948/49	South Africa	158	1953/54	West Indies	169
1948/49	South Africa	123	1953/54	West Indies	205
1949	New Zealand	101			

R. Illingworth (2)

| 1969 | West Indies | 113 | 1971 | India | 107 |

Hon. F. S. Jackson (5)

1893	Australia	103	1905	Australia	*144
1899	Australia	118	1905	Australia	113
1902	Australia	128			

M. Leyland (9)

1928/29	Australia	137	1935	South Africa	161
1929	South Africa	102	1936/37	Australia	126
1934	Australia	109	1936/37	Australia	*111
1934	Australia	153	1938	Australia	187
1934	Australia	110			

W. Rhodes (2)

| 1911/12 | Australia | 179 | 1913/14 | South Africa | 152 |

P. J. Sharpe (1)

| 1969 | New Zealand | | | | 111 |

H. Sutcliffe (16)

1924	South Africa	122	1929	South Africa	114
1924/25	Australia	115	1929	South Africa	100
1924/25	Australia	{ 176 / 127	1929	South Africa	{ 104 / *109
1924/25	Australia	143	1930	Australia	161
1926	Australia	161	1931	New Zealand	117
1927/28	South Africa	102	1931	New Zealand	*109
1928/29	Australia	135	1932/33	Australia	194

G. Ulyett (1)

| 1881/82 | Australia | | | | 149 |

W. Watson (2)

| 1953 | Australia | 109 | 1953/54 | West Indies | 116 |

*denotes not out

Test cricket feats
(Revised by Bill Frindall)

W. Bates
Was the first England cricketer to achieve a hat-trick in Test cricket (Second Test, Melbourne, 1882–83).

G. Boycott
1. Scored 657 runs (average 93.85) *v.* Australia in the 1970–71 series.
2. Became the first England player to bat on each day of a five-day Test match (*v.* Australia at Nottingham, 1977).
3. Became only the third England player (after R. Abel and L. Hutton) to carry his bat through an innings *versus* Australia, when he scored 99★ at Perth in 1979.
4. Scored more runs (8114) in Test cricket than any other England player.
5. Reached fifty in Test cricket more times than any other England player (64 – 22 hundreds and 42 fifties).
6. Played more innings (193) in Test cricket than any other England player.
7. Was only the second England player to score five hundreds against Australia in England (see Hon. F.S. Jackson).
8. Remains the only batsman to score 99 and a century in the same Test (*v.* West Indies at Port of Spain in 1974).

D.B. Close
Is the only cricketer to represent England before he was nineteen (*v.* New Zealand at Manchester, 1949).

P.A. Gibb
Enjoyed a record England debut, scoring 93 and 106, and sharing partnerships of 184 and 168 for the second wicket with E. Paynter (Johannesburg, 1938).

J.H. Hampshire
The only England batsman to score a hundred in his first Test, that match being at Lord's (*v.* West Indies, 1969).

L. Hutton
1. The highest (364) and longest (13 hours 17 minutes) innings in Test matches *versus* Australia (The Oval, 1938).
2. Is the only cricketer who has shared partnerships of 300 and 200 runs in the same innings of a Test match (The Oval, 1938).
3. With C. Washbrook twice shared century first-wicket partnerships in each innings of a Test match.
4. Carried his bat through two Test innings in six months – 202 not out *v.* West Indies, The Oval, August 1950, and 156 not out *v.* Australia, Adelaide, February 1951.
5. Is the only cricketer given out "obstructing the field" in a Test match.
6. In 1952 Hutton became the first professional to be appointed England captain for a full series of Test matches.

Hon. F.S. Jackson
Was the first England player to score five hundreds against Australia in England (see G. Boycott).

M. Leyland
1. Was the first England batsman to score three hundreds in a series against Australia in England (1934).

2. Is the only cricketer whose first and last innings in England–Australia matches were hundreds (137 at Melbourne, 1929; 187 at The Oval, 1938).

G.G. Macaulay
Took a wicket with his first ball in Test cricket and, batting number eleven, made the winning hit in the same match (*v.* South Africa at Cape Town, 1923).

C.M. Old
Was the second bowler to take four wickets in five balls in Test cricket (*v.* Pakistan at Birmingham, 1978).

W. Rhodes
1. Shared record England partnerships against Australia for the first (323) and last (130) wickets.
2. The first bowler to take a hundred wickets against Australia.
3. The oldest Test cricketer: he was 52 years and 165 days old when his career ended at Kingston, Jamaica, in 1930.
4. Enjoyed the longest Test career, a period of 30 years 315 days (1899–1930).

H. Sutcliffe
1. Is the only English cricketer to (a) score two separate hundreds in a Test match twice (*v.* Australia at Melbourne, 1925 and *v.* South Africa at The Oval, 1929); (b) average over 500 runs per innings in six consecutive series against Australia; (c) score four hundreds in a series twice (*v.* Australia, 1924–25 and South Africa, 1929).
2. Set record for scoring a thousand runs in the fewest Test innings (12 – subsequently equalled by E. de C. Weekes for West Indies).
3. Shared with J.B. Hobbs three first-wicket partnerships exceeding a hundred runs in consecutive innings (*v.* Australia, 1924–25).
4. With J.B. Hobbs, shared in the first Test-match partnership to endure throughout a full day's play (third day *v.* Australia, Melbourne, 1925).

F.S. Trueman
1. Took 29 wickets (average 13.31) in his first Test series – against India in 1952.
2. The first bowler to take 300 wickets in Test cricket.

H. Verity
Is the only bowler to take fourteen wickets in a day in a Test match against Australia (Lord's, 1934).

N.W.D. Yardley
1. In three consecutive innings in 1946–47 dismissed D.G. Bradman without assistance from the field.
2. Was the first England cricketer to score fifty runs in each innings of a Test match, and take five wickets in the same match (Melbourne, 1947).

Yorkshire
Is the only county which has had five representatives in a Test team five times (twice at Melbourne in 1877, at Johannesburg and Cape Town in 1899 and at The Oval in 1938).

List of players who have played for Yorkshire since 1863 in all representative matches

It has been confirmed that 29 players were born outside Yorkshire and these are denoted in this list by a §.

Name	First played	Last played	Date of birth	Date of death (if known)
Ackroyd, Mr Alfred	1879	1879	Aug. 29, 1858	Oct. 3, 1927
Allen, Mr S.	1924	1924	Dec. 20, 1893	Oct 9, 1978
Allen, W.R.	1921	1925	Apr. 14, 1893	Oct. 14, 1950
Ambler, Joseph	1886	1886	Feb. 12, 1860	
Anderson, George	1851	1869	Jan. 20, 1826	Nov. 27, 1902
Anderson, P.N.	1988	1988	Apr. 28, 1966	
Anson, Mr C.E.	1924	1924	Oct. 14, 1889	Mar. 26, 1969
Appleton, Mr Charles	1865	1865	May 15, 1844	Feb. 26, 1925
Appleyard, R.	1950	1958	June 27, 1924	
Armitage, Mr Charles Ingram	1873	1878	Apr. 24, 1849	Apr. 24, 1917
Armitage, Thomas	1872	1878	Apr. 25, 1848	Sept. 21, 1922
Ash, D.L.	1965	1965	Feb. 18, 1944	
Ashman, J.R.	1951	1951	May 20, 1926	
Aspinall, R.	1946	1950	Oct. 26, 1918	
Aspinall, Walter	1880	1880	Mar. 24, 1858	
Asquith, Fred T.	1903	1903	Feb. 5, 1870	Jan. 11, 1916
Athey, C.W.J.	1976	1983	Sept. 27, 1957	
Atkinson, George Robert	1861	1870	Sept. 21, 1830	May 3, 1906
Atkinson, H.	1907	1907	Feb. 1, 1881	Dec. 22, 1959
Backhouse, E.N.	1931	1931	May 13, 1901	Nov. 1, 1936
Badger, Mr H.D.	1921	1922	Mar. 7, 1900	Aug. 10, 1975
Bainbridge, A.B.	1961	1963	Oct. 15, 1932	
Baines, Mr F.E.	1888	1888	June 18, 1864	Nov. 17, 1948
Bairstow, Arthur	1896	1900	Aug. 14, 1868	Dec. 7, 1945
Bairstow, D.L.	1970	1988	Sept. 1, 1951	
Baker, George Robert	1884	1884	Apr. 18, 1862	Feb. 6, 1938
Baker, Mr Robert	1874	1875	July 13, 1849	June 21, 1896
Balderstone, J.C.	1961	1969	Nov. 16, 1940	
Barber, Mr A.T.	1929	1930	June 17, 1905	Mar. 10, 1985
Barber, W.	1926	1947	Apr. 18, 1901	Sept. 10, 1968
Barraclough, E.S.	1949	1950	Mar. 30, 1923	
Bates, William	1877	1887	Nov. 19, 1855	Jan. 8, 1900
Bates, William Edric	1907	1913	Mar. 5, 1884	Jan. 17, 1957
Bayes, George W.	1910	1921	Feb. 27, 1884	Dec. 6, 1960
Beaumont, H.	1946	1947	Oct. 14, 1916	
Beaumont, John	1877	1878	Sept. 16, 1855	May 1, 1920
Bedford, H.	1928	1928	July 17, 1907	July 5, 1968
Bedford, Walter H.	1903	1903	Feb. 24, 1879	Jan. 1, 1946
Bell, J.T.	1921	1923	June 16, 1895	Aug. 8, 1974
Berry, John	1849	1867	Jan. 10, 1823	Feb. 26, 1895
Berry, Joseph	1861	1874	Nov. 29, 1829	Apr. 20, 1894
Berry, P.J.	1986	1988	Dec. 28, 1966	
Betts, George	1873	1874	Sept. 19, 1843	Sept. 26, 1902
Binks, J.G.	1955	1969	Oct. 5, 1935	
Binns, John	1898	1898	Mar. 31, 1870	Dec. 8, 1934
Bird, H.D.	1956	1959	Apr. 19, 1933	
Birkenshaw, J.	1958	1960	Nov. 13, 1940	
Birtles, J.T.D.	1913	1924	Oct. 26, 1886	Jan. 13, 1971
Blackburn, Joseph S.	1876	1877	Sept. 24, 1852	July 8, 1922
Blackburn, Mr J.D.H.	1956	1956	Oct. 27, 1924	Feb. 19, 1987
§Blackburn, Mr W.E.	1919	1920	Nov. 24, 1888	June 3, 1941
Blake, F.	1880	1880		
Blakey, R.J.	1985	1988	Jan. 15, 1967	
Blamires, Emanuel	1877	1877	July 31, 1850	Mar. 22, 1886
Bloom, G.R.	1964	1964	Sept. 13, 1941	
Bocking, Henry	1865	1865	Dec. 10, 1835	Feb. 22, 1907
Boden, Mr John George	1878	1878	Dec. 27, 1848	Jan 3, 1928
Bolton, Mr Benjamin Charles	1890	1891	Sept. 23, 1862	Nov. 18, 1910
Bolus, J.B.	1956	1962	Jan. 31, 1934	
Booth, A.	1931	1947	Nov. 3, 1902	Aug. 17, 1974
Booth, Major William	1908	1914	Dec. 10, 1886	July 1, 1916
Booth, P.A.	1982	1988	Sept. 5, 1965	
Booth, R.	1951	1955	Oct. 1, 1926	
Bore, M.K.	1969	1977	June 2, 1947	
Borril, D.	1971	1971	July 4, 1951	
Bosomworth, William Edward	1872	1880	Mar. 8, 1847	June 7, 1891
Bottomley, Mr Isaac Henry	1878	1880	Apr. 9, 1855	Apr. 23, 1922
Bottomley, T.	1934	1935	Dec. 26, 1910	Feb. 19, 1977
Bower, W.H.	1883	1883	Oct. 17, 1857	June 1942
Bowes, W.E.	1929	1947	July 25, 1908	Sept. 4, 1987
Boycott, G.	1962	1986	Oct. 21, 1940	
Brackin, Thomas	1882	1882	Jan. 5, 1859	1928
Brayshaw, Mr P.B.	1952	1952	Oct. 14, 1916	
Brearley, Mr H.	1937	1937	June 26, 1913	
Brennan, Mr D.V.	1947	1953	Feb. 10, 1920	Jan. 9, 1985
Britton, George	1867	1867	Feb. 7, 1843	Jan. 3, 1910
Broadbent, Arthur S.	1909	1910	June 7, 1879	July 1958
Broadhead, W.B.	1929	1929	May 31, 1903	Apr. 2, 1986
Brook, J.W.	1923	1923	Feb. 1, 1897	
Brooke, B.	1950	1950	Mar. 3, 1930	
Broughton, P.N.	1956	1956	Oct. 22, 1935	
Brown, Alfred	1872	1872	June 10, 1854	Nov. 2, 1900
Brown, John Thomas	1889	1904	Aug. 20, 1869	Nov. 4, 1904
Brown, J.T. (Darfield)	1897	1903	Nov. 24, 1874	Apr. 12, 1950
Brown, W.	1902	1908	Nov. 19, 1878	July 26, 1945
Brownhill, Thomas	1861	1871	Oct. 10, 1938	Jan. 6, 1915
Brumfitt, Mr J.	1938	1938	Feb. 18, 1917	Mar. 16, 1987
Buller, J.S.	1930	1930	Aug. 23, 1909	Aug. 7, 1970
Bulmer, J.R.L.	1891	1891	Dec. 28, 1867	1917
Burgess, Thomas	1895	1895	1861	Feb. 22, 1922
Burgin, E.	1952	1953	Jan. 4, 1924	
Burman, J.	1867	1867	Oct. 5, 1838	May 14, 1900
Burnett, Mr J.R.	1958	1959	Oct. 11, 1918	
§Burrows, Matthew	1880	1880	Aug. 18, 1855	May 29, 1893
Burton, Mr D.C.F.	1907	1924	Sept. 13, 1887	Sept. 24, 1971
Burton, Mr R.C.	1914	1914	Apr. 11, 1891	Apr. 30, 1971
Butterfield, Mr E.B.	1870	1870	Oct. 22, 1848	May 6, 1899
Byas, D.	1986	1988	Aug. 16, 1963	
Byrom, Mr John Lewis	1874	1874	July 20, 1851	Aug. 24, 1931
Cammish, J.	1954	1954	May 21, 1921	1975
Carrick, P.	1970	1988	July 16, 1952	
Carter, Rev. Edmund Sardinson	1876	1881	Feb. 3, 1845	May 23, 1923
Cartman, W.	1891	1891	June 20, 1861	Jan. 16, 1935
Cawthray, G.	1939	1952	Sept. 28, 1913	
Chadwick, J.P.G.	1960	1965	Nov. 8, 1934	
Champion, Albert	1876	1879	Dec. 27, 1851	June 30, 1909
Charlesworth, A.P.	1894	1895	Feb. 19, 1865	May, 1926
Clarkson, A.	1963	1963	Sept. 5, 1939	
Claughton, H.M.	1914	1919	Dec. 24, 1891	Oct. 17, 1980
Clayton, Robert Owen	1870	1879	Jan. 1, 1844	Nov. 26, 1901
Clegg, H.	1881	1881	Dec. 8, 1850	Dec. 30, 1920
Clifford, C.C.	1972	1972	July 5, 1942	
Close, D.B.	1949	1970	Feb. 24, 1931	
Collinson, Mr Robert Whiteley	1897	1897	Nov. 6, 1875	Dec. 26, 1963
§Constable, R.C. Chichester	1919	1919	Dec. 21, 1890	May 26, 1963
Cooper, H.P.	1971	1980	Apr. 17, 1949	
Cooper, Mr Philip Edward	1910	1910	Feb. 19, 1885	May 22, 1950
Cope, G.A.	1966	1980	Feb. 23, 1947	
Corbett, A.M.	1881	1881	Nov. 25, 1854	Oct. 7, 1934
Coverdale, S.P.	1973	1980	Nov. 20, 1954	
Coverdale, Mr W.	1888	1888	July 8, 1862	Sept. 23, 1934
Cowan, M.J.	1953	1962	June 10, 1933	
Cownley, J.M.	1952	1952	Feb. 24, 1929	
Coxon, A.	1945	1950	Jan. 18, 1916	
Crawford, G.H.	1914	1926	Dec. 15, 1890	June 28, 1975
Crawford, Mr M.G.	1951	1951	July 30, 1920	
Creighton, E.	1888	1888	July 9, 1859	July, 1933

Name	First played	Last played	Date of birth	Date of death (if known)
Crick, H.	1937	1947	Jan. 29, 1910	Feb. 10, 1960
Crookes, Ralph	1879	1879	Oct. 9, 1846	Feb. 15, 1897
Crossland, S.M.	1883	1886	Aug. 16, 1853	April 11, 1906
Crowther, Arthur	1905	1905	Aug. 1, 1878	June 4, 1946
Cuttell, William	1862	1871	Jan. 28, 1835	June 10, 1896
Dalton, A.J.	1969	1972	Mar. 14, 1947	
§Darnton, Thomas	1864	1868	Feb. 12, 1836	Oct. 25, 1874
Davidson, K.R.	1933	1935	Dec. 24, 1905	Dec. 24, 1954
Dawes, Joseph	1865	1865	Feb. 14, 1836	
Dawson, Edwin	1863	1874	May 1, 1835	Dec. 1, 1888
Dawson, Mr William Arthur	1870	1870	Dec. 3, 1850	Mar. 6, 1916
Day, Mr Albert G.	1885	1888	Sept. 20, 1865	Oct. 16, 1908
Dennis, F.	1928	1933	June 11, 1907	Oct. 16, 1908
Dennis, S.J.	1980	1988	Oct. 18, 1960	
Denton, David	1894	1920	July 4, 1874	Feb. 17, 1950
Denton, Joseph	1887	1888	Feb. 3, 1865	July 19, 1946
Dewse, Harry	1873	1873	Feb. 23, 1836	July 8, 1910
Deyes, George	1905	1907	Feb. 11, 1879	Jan. 1963
Dick, Mr R.D.	1911	1911	Apr. 16, 1889	Dec. 14, 1983
Dobson, Arthur	1879	1879	Feb. 22, 1854	Sept. 17, 1932
Dolphin, Arthur	1905	1927	Dec. 24, 1885	Oct. 23, 1942
Douglas, J.S.	1925	1934	Apr. 4, 1903	Dec. 27, 1971
Drake, Alonzo	1909	1914	Apr. 16, 1884	Feb. 14, 1919
Drake, John	1923	1924	Sept. 1, 1893	May 22, 1967
Driver, Jeremiah	1889	1889	May 16, 1861	Dec. 10, 1946
Dury, Mr Theodore Seaton	1878	1881	June 12, 1854	Mar. 20, 1932
Dyson, W.L.	1887	1887	Dec. 11, 1857	May 1, 1936
Earnshaw, Wilson	1893	1896	Sept. 20, 1867	Nov. 24, 1941
Eastwood, David	1870	1877	Mar. 30, 1848	May 17, 1903
Eckersley, R.	1945	1945	Sept. 4, 1925	
Elam, Mr Fred W.	1900	1902	Sept. 13, 1871	Mar. 19, 1943
Ellis, J.E.	1888	1892	Nov. 12, 1864	Dec. 1, 1927
Ellis, Mr S	1880	1880	Nov. 23, 1851	Oct. 28, 1930
Elms, J.E.	1905	1905	Nov. 10, 1864	Nov. 7, 1951
Emmett, Thomas	1866	1888	Sept. 3, 1841	June 30, 1904
Farrar, Albert	1906	1906	Apr. 29, 1884	Dec. 25, 1954
Fearnley, M.C.	1962	1964	Aug. 21, 1936	July 7, 1979
Featherby, W.D.	1920	1920	Aug. 18, 1888	Nov. 20, 1985
Fiddling, K.	1938	1946	Oct. 13, 1917	
Firth, Mr Alfred	1869	1869	Sept. 3, 1847	Jan. 16, 1927
Firth, Rev. E. Beckwith	1894	1894	Apr. 11, 1863	July 25, 1905
Firth, J.	1949	1950	June 27, 1918	Sept. 7, 1981
Fisher, H.	1928	1936	Aug. 3, 1903	Apr. 16, 1974
Flaxington, Samuel	1882	1882	Oct. 14, 1860	Mar. 10, 1895
Fletcher, S.D.	1983	1988	June 8, 1964	
Fletcher, W.	1892	1892	Feb. 16, 1866	June 1, 1935
Foord, C.W.	1947	1953	June 11, 1924	
Foster, M.E.	1901	1901	Nov. 23, 1873	Apr. 16, 1956
§Foster, Thomas W.	1894	1895	Nov. 12, 1871	Jan. 31, 1947
Frank, Mr Joseph	1881	1881	Dec. 17, 1857	Oct. 22, 1940
Frank, Mr Robert W.	1889	1903	May 29, 1864	Sept. 9, 1950
Freeman, George	1865	1880	July 28, 1843	Nov. 18, 1895
Gibb, Mr P.A.	1935	1946	July 11, 1913	Dec. 7, 1977
§Gilkins, Mr C.J.	1880	1880	Feb. 19, 1856	
Gill, Fairfax	1906	1906	Sept. 3, 1883	Nov. 1, 1917
Gillhouley, K.	1961	1961	Aug. 8, 1934	
Goulder, A.E.	1929	1929	Aug. 16, 1907	
Greenwood, Andrew	1869	1880	Aug. 20, 1847	Feb. 12, 1889
Greenwood, Mr F.E.	1929	1932	Sept. 28, 1905	July 30, 1963
Greenwood, Luke	1861	1874	July 13, 1834	Nov. 1, 1909
Grimshaw, Charles H.	1904	1908	May 12, 1880	Sept. 25, 1947
Grimshaw, Irwin	1880	1887	May 4, 1857	Jan. 18, 1911
Haggas, Stell	1878	1882	Apr. 18, 1856	Mar. 14, 1926
Haigh, Schofield	1895	1913	Mar. 19, 1871	Feb. 27, 1921
Hall, Brian	1952	1952	Sept. 16, 1929	Feb. 27, 1989
Hall, C.H.	1928	1934	Apr. 5, 1906	Dec. 11, 1976

Name	First played	Last played	Date of birth	Date of death (if known)
§Hall, John	1844	1863	Nov. 11, 1815	Apr. 17, 1888
Hall, Louis	1873	1894	Nov. 1, 1852	Nov. 19, 1915
Halliday, H.	1938	1953	Feb. 9, 1920	Aug. 27, 1967
Halliley, Charles	1872	1872	Dec. 5, 1852	1929
Hamer, A.	1938	1938	Dec. 8, 1916	
Hampshire, A.W.	1975	1975	Oct. 18, 1950	
Hampshire, J.	1937	1937	Oct. 5, 1913	
Hampshire, J.H.	1961	1981	Feb. 10, 1941	
§Harbord, Mr W.E.	1929	1935	Dec. 15, 1908	
Hardisty, Charles H.	1906	1909	Dec. 10, 1885	Mar. 2, 1968
Hargreaves, H.S.	1934	1938	Mar. 22, 1913	
Harris, William	1884	1887	Nov. 21, 1861	May 23, 1923
Harrison, George Puckrin	1883	1892	Feb. 11, 1862	Sept. 14, 1940
Harrison, Harold	1907	1907	Jan. 24, 1885	Feb. 11, 1962
Harrison, W.H.	1888	1888	May 27, 1863	July 15, 1939
Hart, Mr H.W.	1888	1888	Sept. 21, 1859	Nov. 2, 1895
Hart, P.R.	1981	1981	Jan. 12, 1947	
Hartington, H.E.	1910	1911	Sept. 18, 1881	Feb. 16, 1950
Hartley, P.J.	1985	1988	Apr. 18, 1960	
Hartley, S.N.	1978	1988	Mar. 18, 1956	
Hatton, A.G.	1960	1961	Mar. 25, 1937	
§Hawke, Lord	1881	1911	Aug. 16, 1860	Oct. 10, 1938
Hayley, Harry	1884	1898	Feb. 22, 1860	June 3, 1922
Haywood, William John	1878	1878	Feb. 25, 1842	1912
Hicks, John	1872	1876	Dec. 10, 1850	June 10, 1912
Higgins, James	1901	1905	Mar. 13, 1877	July 19, 1954
Hill, Allen	1871	1882	Nov. 14, 1843	Aug. 29, 1910
Hill, Mr Henry	1888	1891	Nov. 29, 1858	Aug. 14, 1935
Hill, Mr L.G.	1882	1882	Nov. 2, 1860	Aug. 27, 1940
Hirst, Mr Edward Theodore	1877	1888	May 6, 1857	Oct. 26, 1914
Hirst, Mr E.W.	1881	1881	Feb. 27, 1855	Oct. 24, 1933
Hirst, George Herbert	1891	1921★	Sept. 7, 1871	May 10, 1954
Hirst, Thomas Henry	1899	1899	May 21, 1865	Apr. 3, 1927
Hodgson, G.	1964	1964	July 24, 1938	
Hodgson, Isaac	1855	1866	Nov. 15, 1828	Nov. 24, 1867
Hodgson, P.	1954	1956	Sept. 1935	
Holdsworth, W.E.N.	1952	1953	Sept. 17, 1928	
Holgate, Gideon	1865	1867	June 23, 1839	July 11, 1895
Holmes, Percy	1913	1933	Nov. 25, 1886	Sept. 3, 1971
Horner, N.F.	1950	1950	May 10, 1926	
Hoyle, T.H.	1919	1919	Mar. 10, 1884	June 2, 1953
Hudson, Bennett	1880	1880	June 29, 1852	Nov. 11, 1901
Hunter, David	1888	1909	Feb. 23, 1860	Jan. 11, 1927
Hunter, Joseph	1878	1888	Oct. 21, 1856	Jan. 4, 1891
Hutton, Leonard	1934	1955	June 23, 1916	
Hutton, Richard A.	1962	1974	Sept. 6, 1942	
Iddison, Roger	1855	1876	Sept. 15, 1834	Mar. 19, 1890
Illingworth, R.	1951	1983	June 8, 1932	
Ingham, P.G.	1979	1981	Sept. 28, 1956	
Jackson, Hon. F.S.	1890	1907	Nov. 21, 1870	Mar. 9, 1947
Jackson, Mr S.R.	1891	1891	July 15, 1859	July 19, 1941
Jacques, T.A.	1927	1936	Feb. 19, 1905	
Jakeman, F.	1946	1947	Jan. 10, 1920	May 18, 1986
James, B.	1954	1954	Apr. 23, 1934	
Jarvis, P.W.	1981	1988	June 29, 1965	
Johnson, C.	1969	1979	Sept. 5, 1947	
Johnson, J.	1936	1939	May 16, 1916	
Johnson, M.	1981	1981	Apr. 23, 1958	
Joy, Jonathan	1849	1867	Sept. 29, 1826	Sept. 27, 1889
Judson, A.	1920	1920	July 10, 1885	Apr. 8, 1975
Kaye, Mr Harold S.	1907	1908	May 9, 1882	Nov. 6, 1953
Kaye, Haven	1872	1873	June 11, 1846	1892
§Keighley, Mr W.G.	1947	1951	Jan. 10, 1925	
Kennie, G.	1927	1927	May 19, 1904	
Kilburn, Sam	1896	1896	Oct. 16, 1868	Sept. 25, 1940
Kilner, Norman	1919	1923	July 21, 1895	Apr. 28, 1979
Kilner, R.	1911	1927	Oct. 17, 1890	Apr. 6, 1928
King, A.M.	1955	1955	Oct. 8, 1932	
Kippax, P.J.	1961	1962	Oct. 15, 1940	

Name	First played	Last played	Date of birth	Date of death (if known)
Lancaster, W.W.	1895	1895	Feb. 4, 1873	Dec. 30, 1938
§Landon, Mr Ch. Whittington	1878	1882	May 30, 1850	Mar. 5, 1903
§Law, Mr William	1871	1873	Apr. 9, 1851	Dec. 20, 1892
Leadbeater, B.	1966	1979	Aug. 14, 1943	
Leadbeater, E.	1949	1956	Aug. 15, 1927	
Leadbeater, Mr Harry	1884	1890	Dec. 31, 1863	Oct. 9, 1928
Leatham, Mr Gerald Arthur Buxton	1874	1886	Apr. 30, 1851	June 19, 1932
Leather, Mr Roland Sutcliffe	1906	1906	Aug. 17, 1880	Jan. 3, 1913
Lee, Charles	1952	1952	Mar. 17, 1924	
Lee, Fred	1882	1890	Nov. 18, 1856	Sept. 12, 1896
Lee, G.H.	1879	1879	Aug. 24, 1854	Oct. 4, 1919
Lee, Herbert	1885	1885	July 2, 1856	Feb. 4, 1908
Lee, Mr J.E.	1867	1867	1838	Apr. 2, 1880
Legard, Mr Alfred Digby	1910	1910	June 19, 1878	Aug. 15, 1939
Lester, E.I.	1945	1956	Feb. 18, 1923	
Leyland, M.	1920	1947	July 20, 1900	Jan. 1, 1967
Linaker, L.	1909	1909	Apr. 8, 1885	Nov. 17, 1961
Lister, Benjamin	1874	1878	Dec. 9, 1850	Dec. 3, 1918
Lister, Mr J.	1954	1954	May 14, 1930	
§Lister-Kaye, Mr K.	1928	1928	Mar. 27, 1892	Feb. 28, 1955
Lockwood, Ephraim	1868	1884	Apr. 4, 1845	Dec. 19, 1921
Lockwood, Henry	1877	1882	Oct. 20, 1855	Feb. 18, 1930
Lodge, J.T.	1948	1948	Apr. 16, 1921	
Love, J.D.	1975	1988	Apr. 22, 1955	
Lowe, George Emanuel	1902	1902	Jan. 12, 1878	Aug. 15, 1932
Lowson, F.A.	1949	1958	July 1, 1925	Sept. 8, 1984
§Loxley-Firth, Mr Edward	1912	1912	Mar. 7, 1886	Jan. 8, 1949
Lumb, Mr Edward	1872	1886	Sept. 12, 1852	Apr. 5, 1891
Lumb, R.G.	1970	1984	Feb. 27, 1950	
Lupton, Mr A.W.	1908	1927	Feb. 23, 1879	Apr. 14, 1944
Lynas, George Goulton	1867	1867	Sept. 7, 1832	Dec. 8, 1896
Macauley, G.G.	1920	1935	Dec. 7, 1897	Dec. 13, 1940
McHugh, F.P.	1949	1949	Nov. 15, 1925	
Marshall, Amos	1874	1874	July 10, 1849	Aug. 3, 1891
Mason, A.	1947	1950	May 2, 1921	
Maude, Mr E.	1866	1866	Dec. 31, 1839	July 2, 1876
Metcalfe, A.A.	1983	1988	Dec. 25, 1963	
Micklethwait, Mr W.H.	1911	1911	Dec. 13, 1885	Oct. 7, 1947
Middlebrook, Willie	1888	1889	May 23, 1858	Apr. 26, 1919
Midgley, Mr C.A.	1906	1906	Nov. 11, 1877	June 24, 1942
§Milligan, Mr F.W.	1894	1898	Mar. 19, 1870	Mar. 31, 1900
Mitchell, A.	1922	1945	Sept. 13, 1902	Dec. 25, 1976
Mitchell, Mr Frank	1894	1904	Aug. 13, 1872	Oct. 11, 1935
Monks, G.D.	1952	1952	Sept. 3, 1929	
Moorhouse, Robert	1888	1899	Sept. 7, 1866	Jan. 7, 1921
Mosley, H.	1881	1881	Mar. 8, 1852	1933
Motley, Mr A.	1879	1879	Feb. 5, 1858	Sept. 28, 1897
Mounsey, Joseph Thomas	1891	1897	Aug. 30, 1871	Apr. 6, 1949
Moxon, M.D.	1981	1988	May 4, 1960	
Myers, Hubert	1901	1910	Jan. 2, 1875	June 12, 1944
Myers, Matthew	1876	1878	Apr. 12, 1847	Dec. 8, 1919
Naylor, J.E.	1953	1953	Dec. 11, 1930	
Newstead, John Thomas	1903	1913	Sept. 8, 1877	Mar. 25, 1952
Nicholson, A.G.	1962	1975	June 25, 1938	Nov. 3, 1985
Nicholson, N.G.	1988	1988	Oct. 17, 1963	
Oates, W.F.	1956	1956	June 11, 1929	
Oates, William	1874	1875	Jan. 2, 1852	Dec. 9, 1940
Old, C.M.	1966	1982	Dec. 22, 1948	
Oldham, S.	1974	1984	July 26, 1948	
Oldroyd, Edgar	1910	1931	Oct. 1, 1888	Dec. 29, 1964
Oyston, Charles	1900	1909	May 12, 1869	July 15, 1942
Padgett, D.E.V.	1951	1971	July 20, 1934	
Padgett, G.H.	1952	1952	Oct. 9, 1931	
Padgett, John	1882	1889	Nov. 21, 1860	
§Parkin, C.H.	1906	1906	Feb. 18, 1886	June 15, 1943
Parratt, John	1888	1890	Mar. 24, 1859	May 6, 1905
§Parton, J.W.	1889	1889	Jan. 31, 1863	Jan. 30, 1906
Pearson, Harry Eyre	1878	1880	Aug. 7, 1851	July 8, 1903
Pearson, J.H.	1934	1936	May 14, 1915	
Peate, Edmund	1879	1887	Mar. 2, 1855	Mar. 11, 1900
Peel, Robert	1882	1897	Feb. 12, 1857	Aug. 12, 1941
Penny, J.H.	1891	1891	Sept. 29, 1856	1902
Pickles, C.S.	1985	1988	Jan. 30, 1966	
Pickles, D.	1957	1960	Nov. 16, 1935	
Pinder, George	1867	1880	July 15, 1841	Jan. 15, 1903
Platt, R.K.	1955	1963	Dec. 26, 1932	
Pollard, David	1865	1865	Aug. 7, 1835	Mar. 26, 1909
Pollitt, George	1899	1899	June 3, 1875	
Prest, Mr Charles Henry	1864	1864	Dec. 9, 1841	Mar. 4, 1875
Preston, Joseph M.	1885	1889	Aug. 23, 1864	Nov. 26, 1890
Pride, Thomas	1887	1887	July 23, 1864	Feb. 16, 1919
Pullan, Peter	1884	1884	Mar. 29, 1857	1901
§Radcliffe, Mr E.J.	1909	1911	Jan. 27, 1884	Nov. 23, 1969
Ramage, A.	1979	1983	Nov. 29, 1957	
Raper, Mr J.R.S.	1936	1947	Aug. 9, 1909	
Rawlin, E.R.	1927	1936	Oct. 4, 1897	Jan. 11, 1943
Rawlin, John Thomas	1880	1885	Nov. 10, 1856	Jan. 22, 1924
Rawlinson, Elisha Barker	1867	1875	Apr. 10, 1837	Feb. 17, 1892
Redfern, Joseph	1890	1890	May 13, 1862	Jan. 14, 1931
Render, George W.A.	1919	1919	Jan. 5, 1887	Sept. 17, 1922
Rhodes, A.C.	1932	1934	Oct. 14, 1906	May 21, 1957
§Rhodes, Mr Herbert Edward	1878	1883	Jan. 11, 1852	Sept. 1, 1889
Rhodes, S.J.	1981	1984	June 17, 1964	
Rhodes, Wilfred	1898	1930	Oct. 29, 1877	July 8, 1973
Rhodes, William	1911	1911	Mar. 4, 1883	Aug. 5, 1941
Richardson, Mr J.A.	1936	1947	Aug. 4, 1908	Apr. 2, 1985
Riley, Henry	1895	1900	Aug. 17, 1875	Nov. 6, 1922
Riley, Mr Martin	1878	1882	Apr. 5, 1851	June 1, 1899
Ringrose, William	1901	1906	Sept. 2, 1871	Sept. 14, 1943
Robinson, A.L.	1971	1977	Aug. 17, 1946	
Robinson, Mr Edward	1887	1887	Dec. 27, 1862	Sept. 3, 1942
Robinson, Emmott	1919	1931	Nov. 16, 1883	Nov. 17, 1969
Robinson, E.P.	1934	1949	Aug. 10, 1911	
Robinson, H.	1879	1879	May 12, 1858	Dec. 14, 1909
Robinson, P.E.	1984	1988	Aug. 3, 1963	
Robinson, Walter	1876	1877	Nov. 29, 1851	Aug. 14, 1919
Roper, Mr Edward	1878	1880	Apr. 8, 1851	Apr. 26, 1921
Rothery, James William	1903	1910	Sept. 5, 1877	June 2, 1919
Rowbotham, Joseph	1861	1876	July 8, 1831	Dec. 22, 1899
Rudston, Horace	1902	1907	Nov. 22, 1879	Apr. 14, 1962
Ryan, M.	1954	1965	June 23, 1933	
Ryder, L.	1924	1924	Aug. 28, 1899	Jan. 24, 1955
Savile, Mr George	1867	1874	Apr. 26, 1847	Sept. 4, 1904
Schofield, D.	1970	1974	Oct. 9, 1947	
Scott, Emanuel	1864	1864	July 6, 1834	Dec. 13, 1898
Sedgwick, H.	1906	1906	Apr. 8, 1883	Dec. 28, 1957
Sellers, Mr Arthur	1890	1899	May 31, 1870	Sept. 25, 1941
Sellers, Mr A.B.	1932	1948	Mar. 5, 1907	Feb. 20, 1981
Shackleton, W.A.	1928	1934	Mar. 9, 1908	Nov. 16, 1971
Sharp, K.	1976	1988	Apr. 6, 1959	
§Sharpe, Mr Charles Molesworth	1875	1875	Sept. 6, 1851	June 25, 1935
Sharpe, P.J.	1958	1974	Dec. 27, 1936	
Shaw, C.	1984	1988	Feb. 17, 1964	
Shaw, James	1896	1897	Mar. 12, 1865	Jan. 22, 1921
Sheepshanks, Mr E.R.	1929	1929	Mar. 22, 1910	Dec. 31, 1937
Shepherd, Mr D.A.	1938	1938	Mar. 10, 1916	

Name	First played	Last played	Date of birth	Date of death (if known)
Shotton, William	1865	1874	Dec. 1, 1840	May 26, 1909
Sidebottom, A.	1973	1988	Apr. 1, 1954	
Sidgwick, Mr R.	1882	1882	Aug. 7, 1851	1934
Silvester, S.	1976	1977	Mar. 12, 1951	
Simpson, Mr E.T.B.	1889	1889	Mar. 5, 1867	Mar. 20, 1944
§Sims, Rev. Herbert Marsh	1875	1877	Mar. 15, 1853	Oct. 5, 1885
Slinn, William	1861	1864	Dec. 13, 1826	June 19, 1888
Smailes, T.F.	1932	1948	Mar. 27, 1910	Dec. 1, 1970
Smales, K.	1948	1950	Sept. 15, 1927	
Smith, Alfred Farrer	1868	1874	Mar. 7, 1847	Jan. 6, 1915
Smith, Mr Ernest	1888	1907	Oct. 19, 1869	Apr. 12, 1945
Smith, E.	1914	1926	July 11, 1888	Jan. 2, 1972
Smith, Fred (Idle)	1911	1911	Dec. 26, 1885	
Smith, Fred (Yeadon)	1903	1903	Dec. 18, 1879	Oct. 20, 1905
Smith, George	1901	1901	Jan. 13, 1876	Jan. 16, 1929
Smith, John	1865	1865	Mar. 23, 1833	Feb. 12, 1909
Smith, Neil	1970	1971	Apr. 1, 1949	
Smith, R.	1969	1970	Apr. 6, 1944	
Smith, Walker (Bradford)	1874	1874	Aug. 14, 1847	1900
§Smith, William	1865	1874	Nov. 1, 1839	
Smithson, G.A.	1946	1950	Nov. 1, 1926	Sept. 6, 1970
Smurthwaite, J.	1938	1939	Oct. 17, 1916	
Sowden, Abram	1878	1887	Dec. 1, 1853	July 5, 1921
Squire, D.	1893	1893	Dec. 31, 1864	Apr. 28, 1922
Squires, P.J.	1972	1976	Aug. 4, 1951	
Stanley, Mr H.C.	1911	1913	Feb. 16, 1888	May 18, 1934
§Stanyforth, Mr R.T.	1928	1928	May 30, 1892	Feb. 21, 1964
Stead, B.	1959	1959	June 21, 1939	Apr. 15, 1980
Stephenson, Edwin	1861	1873	June 5, 1832	July 5, 1898
Stephenson, Mr J.S.	1923	1926	Nov. 10, 1903	Oct. 7, 1975
Stevenson, G.B.	1973	1986	Dec. 16, 1955	
Stott, W.B.	1952	1963	July 18, 1934	
Stringer, P.	1967	1969	Feb. 23, 1943	
Stuchbury, S.	1978	1981	June 22, 1954	
§Sugg, Frank Howe	1883	1883	Jan. 11, 1862	May 30, 1933
§Sugg, Walter	1881	1881	May 21, 1860	May 23, 1933
Sullivan, Mr J. Hubert Baron	1912	1912	Sept. 21, 1890	Feb. 8, 1932
Sutcliffe, H.	1919	1945	Nov. 24, 1894	Jan. 22, 1978
Sutcliffe, Mr W.H.H.	1948	1957	Oct. 10, 1926	
Swallow, I.G.	1983	1987	Dec. 18, 1962	
§Tait, Thomas	1898	1899	Oct. 7, 1872	Sept. 6, 1954
Tasker, Mr J.	1912	1913	Feb. 4, 1887	Aug. 24, 1975
Tattersall, Mr Geoffrey	1905	1905	Apr. 21, 1882	June 29, 1972
Taylor, H.S.	1879	1879	Dec. 11, 1856	Nov. 16, 1896
Taylor, Harry	1924	1925	Dec. 18, 1900	
Taylor, John	1880	1881	Apr. 2, 1850	May 27, 1924
Taylor, K.	1953	1968	Aug. 21, 1935	
Taylor, N.S.	1982	1983	June 2, 1963	
Taylor, Mr Tom Launcelot	1899	1906	May 25, 1878	Mar. 16, 1960
Thewlis, Herbert	1888	1888	Aug. 31, 1865	Nov. 20, 1920
Thewlis, John Jnr	1879	1879	Sept. 21, 1850	Aug. 9, 1901
Thewlis, John Snr	1861	1875	June 30, 1828	Dec. 29, 1899
Thornton, A.	1881	1881	July 20, 1854	Apr. 19, 1915
Thornton, Mr George	1891	1891	Dec. 24, 1867	Jan. 31, 1939
Thorpe, George	1864	1864	Feb. 20, 1834	1899
Threapleton, Joseph William	1881	1881	July 20, 1857	1918
Tinsley, H.J.	1890	1891	Feb. 20, 1865	Dec. 10, 1938
Townsley, R.A.J.	1974	1975	June 24, 1952	
Towse, D.A.	1988	1988		
Trueman, F.S.	1949	1968	Feb. 6, 1931	
Tunnicliffe, John	1891	1907	Aug. 26, 1866	July 11, 1948
Turner, Alban	1910	1911	Sept. 2, 1885	Aug. 29, 1951
Turner, Brian	1960	1961	July 25, 1938	
Turner, C.	1925	1946	Jan. 11, 1902	Nov. 19, 1968
Turner, F.I.	1924	1924	Sept. 3, 1894	Oct. 18, 1954
Tyson, C.	1921	1921	Jan. 24, 1889	Apr. 4, 1940

Name	First played	Last played	Date of birth	Date of death (if known)
Ullathorne, Charles Edward	1868	1875	Apr. 11, 1845	May 3, 1904
Ulyett, George	1873	1893	Oct. 21, 1851	June 18, 1898
Usher, John	1888	1888	Feb. 26, 1859	Aug. 10, 1905
van Geloven, J.	1955	1955	Jan. 4, 1934	
§Verelst, Mr Henry William	1868	1869	July 2, 1846	Feb. 5, 1918
Verity, Hedley	1930	1939	May 18, 1905	July 31, 1943
Waddington, A.	1919	1927	Feb. 4, 1893	Oct. 27, 1959
Wade, Saul	1886	1890	Feb. 8, 1858	Nov. 5, 1931
Wainwright, Edward	1888	1902	Apr. 8, 1865	Oct. 28, 1919
Wainwright, Walker	1903	1905	Jan. 21, 1882	Dec. 31, 1961
Wake, Mr W.R.	1881	1881	May 21, 1852	Mar. 14, 1896
Walker, Mr Ashley	1863	1870	June 22, 1844	May 26, 1927
Walker, Clifford	1947	1948	June 7, 1920	
Walker, Thomas	1879	1880	Apr. 3, 1854	Aug. 28, 1925
Waller, George	1893	1894	Dec. 3, 1864	Dec. 10, 1937
Wallgate, Mr L.W.	1875	1878	Nov. 12, 1849	May 9, 1887
Ward, Albert	1886	1886	Nov. 21, 1865	Jan. 6, 1939
Ward, F.	1903	1903	Aug. 31, 1881	Feb. 28, 1948
Ward, Mr Humphrey P.	1920	1920	Jan. 20, 1899	Dec. 1946
Wardall, Thomas A.	1884	1894	Apr. 19, 1862	Dec. 20, 1932
Wardle, J.H.	1946	1958	Jan. 8, 1923	July 23, 1985
Waring, J.S.	1963	1966	Oct. 1, 1942	
Waring, Seth	1870	1870	Nov. 4, 1838	Apr. 17, 1919
Washington, Irving	1900	1902	Dec. 11, 1879	Oct. 20, 1927
Watson, Howarth	1908	1914	Sept. 26, 1880	Nov. 24, 1951
Watson, W.	1939	1957	Mar. 7, 1920	
Waud, Mr Brian Wilkes	1862	1864	June 4, 1837	May 30, 1889
Webster, Charles	1861	1868	June 9, 1838	Jan. 6, 1881
Webster, Henry Heywood	1868	1868	May 8, 1844	1914
West, John	1868	1876	Oct. 16, 1844	Jan. 27, 1890
Whatmuff, Francis John	1878	1882	Dec. 4, 1856	June 4, 1904
Wheater, Mr C.H.	1880	1880	Mar. 4, 1860	May 11, 1885
White, Sir Archibald Woolaston, Bart	1908	1920	Oct. 14, 1877	Dec. 16, 1945
Whitehead, J.P.	1946	1951	Sept. 3, 1925	
Whitehead, Lees	1889	1904	Mar. 14, 1864	Nov. 22, 1913
Whitehead, Luther	1893	1893	June 25, 1869	Jan. 16, 1931
Whiteley, J.P.	1978	1982	Feb. 28, 1955	
Whiting, C.P.	1914	1920	Apr. 18, 1888	Jan. 14, 1959
Whitwell, Mr J.F.	1890	1890	Feb. 22, 1869	Nov. 6, 1932
§Whitwell, Mr William Fry	1890	1890	Dec. 12, 1867	Apr. 12, 1942
§Wilkinson, Mr A.J.A.	1865	1868	May 28, 1835	Dec. 11, 1905
Wilkinson, Frank	1937	1939	May 23, 1914	Mar. 26, 1984
Wilkinson, Mr H.	1903	1905	Dec. 11, 1877	Apr. 15, 1967
Wilkinson, W.H.	1903	1910	Mar. 12, 1881	June 4, 1961
Williams, A.C.	1911	1919	Mar. 1, 1887	1966
Wilson, Benjamin B.	1906	1914	Dec. 11, 1879	Sept. 14, 1957
Wilson, Mr C.E.M.	1896	1899	May 15, 1875	Feb. 8, 1944
Wilson, D.	1974	1974	Aug. 7, 1937	
Wilson, Mr E. Rockley	1899	1923	Mar. 25, 1879	July 21, 1957
Wilson, Mr G.A.	1936	1939	Feb. 2, 1916	
Wilson, Mr Geoffrey	1919	1924	Aug. 21, 1895	Nov. 29, 1960
Wilson, Mr John	1887	1888	June 30, 1857	Nov. 11, 1931
Wilson, Mr J.P.	1911	1912	Apr. 3, 1889	Oct. 3, 1959
Wilson, J.V.	1946	1962	Jan. 17, 1921	
Wood, Arthur	1927	1946	Aug. 25, 1898	Apr. 1, 1973
Wood, B.	1964	1964	Dec. 26, 1942	
Wood, C.H.	1959	1959	July 23, 1934	
Wood, George William	1895	1895	Nov. 18, 1862	Dec. 4, 1948
Wood, Mr Hugh	1879	1880	Mar. 22, 1855	July 31, 1941
Wood, Mr J.H.	1881	1881		
Wood, R.	1952	1956	June 3, 1929	
Woodford, J.D.	1968	1972	Sept. 9, 1943	

Name	First played	Last Played	Date of birth	Date of death (if known)
Woodhead, Mr Frank Ellis	1893	1894	May 29, 1868	Aug. 25, 1943
Woodhouse, Mr W.H.	1884	1885	Apr. 16, 1856	Mar. 4, 1938
Wormald, Alfred	1885	1891	May 10, 1855	Feb. 6, 1940
Worsley, Mr W.A.	1928	1929	Apr. 5, 1890	Dec. 4, 1973
Wrathmell, L.F.	1886	1886	Jan. 22, 1855	Sept. 16, 1928
Wright, Robert	1877	1877	July 19, 1852	
Wright, Mr T.J.	1919	1919	Mar. 5, 1900	
Yardley, Mr N.W.D.	1936	1955	Mar. 19, 1915	
Yeadon, James	1888	1888	Dec. 10, 1861	May 30, 1914

*Also played in one match in 1929

Most appearances

Matches	Player	Matches	Player
881	W. Rhodes (1898–1930)	480	J.V. Wilson (1946–1962)
715	G.H. Hirst (1891–1929)	471	J. Tunnicliffe (1891–1907)
677	D. Denton (1894–1920)	459	F.S. Trueman (1949–1968)
602	H. Sutcliffe (1919–1945)	456	J.H. Hampshire (1961–1981)
548	M. Leyland (1920–1947)	444	G.G. Macaulay (1920–1935)
536	D.B. Close (1949–1970)	428	A. Dolphin (1905–1927)
512	D. Hunter (1888–1909)	428	D.L. Bairstow (1970–1988)
510	Lord Hawke (1881–1911)	414	G. Boycott (1962–1986)
505	S. Haigh (1895–1913)	412	E. Robinson (1919–1931)
496	R. Illingworth (1951–1983)	411	P.J. Sharpe (1958–1974)
491	J.G. Binks (1955–1969)	408	A. Wood (1927–1946)
487	D.E.V. Padgett (1951–1971)	400	A. Mitchell (1922–1945)
485	P. Holmes (1913–1933)		

Career averages

(Note: Names of professionals are indented)

Name	Comp. innings	Runs	Aver.	Runs	Wickets	Aver.
Ackroyd, A.	0	2	—	7	0	—
Allen, S.	2	8	4.00	116	2	58.00
Allen, W.R.	22	474	21.54	—	—	—
Ambler, Joseph	8	72	9.00	22	0	—
Anderson, G.	25	520	20.80	—	—	—
Anderson, P.N.	1	0	0.00	47	1	47.00
Anson, C.E.	3	29	9.66	—	—	—
Appleton, C.	5	56	11.20	—	—	—
Appleyard, R.	78	679	8.70	9,813	637	15.40
Armitage, C.I.	7	38	5.42	73	4	18.25
Armitage, T.	79	1,074	13.59	1,676	119	14.08
Ash, D.L.	3	22	7.33	22	0	—
Ashman, J.R.	1	0	—	116	4	29.00
Aspinall, R.	40	763	19.07	2,620	131	20.38
Aspinall, W.	3	16	5.33	—	—	—
Asquith, F.	1	0	0.00	—	—	—
Athey, C.W.J.	225	6,320	28.08	1,003	21	47.76
Atkinson, G.R.	30	399	13.30	1,144	57	20.07
Atkinson, H.	2	0	—	17	0	—
Backhouse, E.N.	1	2	2.00	4	0	—
Badger, H.D.	2	56	28.00	145	6	24.16
Bainbridge, A.B.	10	93	9.30	358	20	17.90
Baines, F.E.	1	0	0.00	—	—	—
Bairstow, A.	16	111	6.93	—	—	—
Bairstow, D.L.	469	12,507	26.66	192	6	32.00
Baker, G.R.	10	42	4.20	—	—	—
Baker, R.	4	45	11.25	43	0	—
Balderstone, J.C.	75	1,332	17.76	790	37	21.35
Barber, A.T.	51	1,050	20.58	—	—	—
Barber, W.	443	15,289	34.51	405	14	28.92
Barraclough, E.S.	2	43	21.50	136	4	34.00
Bates, W.	329	6,877	20.90	11,024	660	16.70
Bates, W.E.	152	2,634	17.32	57	0	—
Bayes, G.	14	165	11.78	1,545	39	39.61
Beaumont, H.	40	716	17.90	214	8	26.75
Beaumont, J.	6	60	10.00	50	2	25.00
Bedford, H.	4	57	14.25	179	9	19.88
Bedford, W.M.	1	38	38.00	117	2	58.50
Bell, J.T.	7	125	17.85	—	—	—
Berry, John	30	492	16.40	150	8	18.75
Berry, Joseph	4	68	17.00	—	—	—
Berry, P.J.	1	31	31.00	229	5	45.80

Name	Comp. innings	Runs	Aver.	Runs	Wickets	Aver.
Betts, G.	3	56	18.66	—	—	—
Binks, J.G.	459	6,742	14.69	66	0	—
Binns, J.	1	4	4.00	—	—	—
Bird, H.D.	23	613	26.65	—	—	—
Birkenshaw, J.	35	588	16.80	1,819	69	26.36
Birtles, J.T.D.	46	876	19.04	20	0	—
Blackburn, J.	10	102	10.20	173	7	24.71
Blackburn, J.D.H.	2	18	9.00	—	—	—
Blackburn, W.E.	7	26	3.71	1,113	45	24.73
Blake, F.	5	47	9.40	19	1	19.00
Blakey, R.J.	79	2,563	32.44	68	1	68.00
Blamires, Emanuel	2	23	11.50	82	5	16.40
Bloom, G.R.	1	2	2.00	—	—	—
Bocking, Henry	2	14	7.00	—	—	—
Boden, J.G.	1	6	6.00	—	—	—
Bolton, B.C.	9	40	4.44	401	27	14.85
Bolus, J.B.	161	4,712	29.26	407	13	31.30
Booth, A.	20	114	5.70	1,684	122	13.80
Booth, M.W.	170	3,649	21.46	10,632	558	19.05
Booth, P.A.	20	178	8.90	1,470	34	43.23
Booth, R.	48	730	15.20	—	—	—
Bore, M.K.	57	483	8.47	4,866	162	30.03
Borrill, D.	—	—	—	61	5	12.20
Bosomworth, W.E.	6	20	3.33	139	9	15.44
Bottomley, I.H.	12	166	13.83	75	1	75.00
Bottomley, T.	7	142	20.28	188	1	188.00
Bower, W.H.	5	51	10.20	—	—	—
Bowes, W.E.	140	1,251	8.93	21,227	1,351	15.71
Boycott, G.	563	32,570	57.85	665	28	23.75
Brackin, T.	6	12	2.00	—	—	—
Brayshaw, P.B.	3	20	6.66	104	3	34.66
Brearley, H.	2	17	8.50	—	—	—
Brennan, D.V.	155	1,653	10.66	—	—	—
Britton, G.	2	3	1.50	—	—	—
Broadbent, A.S.	5	66	13.20	133	1	133.00
Broadhead, W.B.	2	5	2.50	—	—	—
Brook, J.W.	1	0	—	—	—	—
Brooke, B.	4	16	4.00	191	2	95.50
Broughton, P.N.	3	19	6.33	365	16	22.81
Brown, A.	3	9	3.00	47	3	15.66
Brown, J.T.	559	16,380	29.30	5,612	196	28.63
Brown, J.T. (Darfield)	31	351	11.32	2,141	102	20.99
Brown, W.	1	2	2.00	61	3	20.33
Brownhill, T.	17	185	10.88	—	—	—
Brumfitt, J.	1	9	9.00	—	—	—
Buller, J.S.	2	5	2.50	—	—	—
Bulmer, J.R.	2	0	—	79	1	79.00
Burgess, T.	1	1	1.00	—	—	—
Burgin, E.	7	92	13.14	795	31	25.64
Burman, J.	1	1	1.00	—	—	—
Burnet, J.R.	69	889	12.88	26	1	26.00
Burrows, M.	10	82	8.20	—	—	—
Burton, D.C.F.	115	2,273	19.76	—	—	—
Burton, R.C.	2	47	23.50	73	6	12.16
Butterfield, E.B.	2	18	9.00	—	—	—
Byas, D.	25	592	23.68	64	0	—
Byrom, J.L.	4	19	4.75	—	—	—
Cammish, J.	1	0	—	155	3	51.66
Carrick, P.	346	8,021	23.18	23,998	797	30.11
Carter, Rev. E.S.	19	210	11.05	104	8	13.00

Name	Comp. innings	Runs	Aver.	Runs	Wickets	Aver.
Cartman, W.	11	238	21.63	—	—	—
Cawthray, G.	6	114	19.00	304	4	76.00
Chadwick, J.P.G.	6	106	17.66	67	2	33.50
Champion, A.	21	149	7.09	17	1	17.00
Charlesworth, A.P.	13	258	19.84	—	—	—
Clarkson, A.	7	80	11.42	92	5	18.40
Claughton, H.M.	6	39	6.50	176	3	58.66
Clayton, R.O.	93	996	10.70	2,528	154	16.41
Clegg, H.	9	69	7.66	—	—	—
Clifford, C.C.	8	39	4.87	666	26	25.61
Close, D.B.	709	22,650	31.94	23,489	967	24.29
Collinson, R.W.	7	172	24.57	—	—	—
Constable, R.C. Chichester	1	0	0.00	6	0	—
Cooper, H.P.	78	1,159	14.85	6,327	227	27.87
Cooper, P.E.	2	0	0.00	—	—	—
Cope, G.A.	160	2,241	14.00	15,627	630	24.80
Corbett, A.M.	2	0	0.00	—	—	—
Coverdale, S.P.	4	31	7.75	—	—	—
Coverdale, W.	2	2	1.00	—	—	—
Cowan, M.J.	37	170	4.59	6,271	263	23.84
Cownley, J.M.	1	19	19.00	119	1	119.00
Coxon, A.	149	2,747	18.43	9,428	464	20.31
Crawford, G.H.	8	46	5.75	541	21	25.76
Crawford, M.G.	2	22	11.00	—	—	—
Creighton, E.	7	38	5.42	215	16	13.43
Crick, H.	10	88	8.80	—	—	—
Crookes, R.	1	2	2.00	14	0	—
Crossland, S.M.	4	32	8.00	—	—	—
Crowther, A.	2	0	0.00	—	—	—
Cutell, W.	21	271	12.90	597	38	15.71
Dalton, A.J.	29	710	24.48	—	—	—
Darnton, T.	21	314	14.95	350	12	29.16
Davidson, K.R.	41	1,331	32.46	—	—	—
Dawes, J.	7	93	13.28	195	5	39.00
Dawson, W.A.	2	0	0.00	—	—	—
Dawson, E.	24	224	9.33	—	—	—
Day, A.G.	17	163	9.58	—	—	—
Dennis, F.	72	1,331	18.48	4,517	154	29.33
Dennis, S.J.	38	5,548	8.89	5,548	173	32.06
Denton, D.	997	33,282	33.38	957	34	28.14
Denton, J.	30	377	12.56	—	—	—
Dewse, H.	2	14	7.00	15	0	—
Deyes, G.	20	44	2.20	944	41	23.02
Dick, R.D.	1	2	2.00	37	2	18.50
Dobson, A.	3	1	0.33	—	—	—
Dolphin, A.	300	3,325	11.08	28	1	28.00
Douglas, J.S.	19	125	6.57	1,310	49	26.73
Drake, A.	221	4,804	21.73	8,626	482	17.88
Drake, J.	3	21	7.00	111	1	111.00
Driver, J.	3	24	8.00	—	—	—
Dury, T.S.	23	328	14.26	21	0	—
Dyson, W.L.	5	11	2.20	—	—	—
Earnshaw, W.	8	54	6.75	—	—	—
Eastwood, D.	49	591	12.06	349	11	31.72
Eckersley, R.	0	9	—	62	0	—
Elam, F.W.	2	48	24.00	—	—	—
Ellis, J.E.	13	56	4.30	—	—	—
Ellis, S.	5	30	6.00	—	—	—
Elms, J.E.	2	20	10.00	28	1	28.00
Emmett, T.	419	6,315	15.07	15,465	1,216	12.71

Name	Comp. innings	Runs	Aver.	Runs	Wickets	Aver.
Farrar, A.	1	2	2.00	—	—	—
Fearnley, M.C.	2	19	9.50	133	6	22.16
Featherby, W.D.	—	—	—	12	0	—
Fiddling, K.	18	182	10.11	—	—	—
Firth, A.	1	4	4.00	—	—	—
Firth, Rev. E.B.	1	1	1.00	—	—	—
Firth, J.	3	134	44.66	—	—	—
Fisher, H.	44	680	15.45	2,560	93	27.52
Flaxington, S.	8	121	15.12	—	—	—
Fletcher, S.D.	34	294	8.64	5,394	170	31.72
Fletcher, W.	13	213	16.38	366	16	22.87
Foord, C.W.	17	112	6.58	3,412	126	27.07
Foster, E.	1	2	2.00	27	0	—
Foster, T.W.	15	138	9.20	952	58	16.41
Frank, J.	2	10	5.00	17	1	17.00
Frank, R.W.	44	830	18.86	54	2	27.00
Freeman, G.	52	752	14.46	2,085	209	9.97
Gibb, P.A.	47	1,545	32.87	82	3	27.33
Gifkins, C.J.	3	30	10.00	—	—	—
Gill, F.	4	18	4.50	—	—	—
Gillhouley, K.	24	323	13.45	1,702	77	22.10
Goulder, A.	—	—	—	90	3	30.00
Greenwood, A.	156	2,780	17.82	9	0	—
Greenwood, F.E.	58	1,458	25.13	36	2	18.00
Greenwood, L.	72	886	12.30	1,615	85	19.00
Grimshaw, C.H.	68	1,219	17.92	212	7	30.28
Grimshaw, I.	193	3,544	18.36	12	1	12.00
Haggas, S.	44	478	10.86	—	—	—
Haigh, S.	577	10,993	19.05	29,289	1,876	15.61
Hall, B.	2	14	7.00	55	1	55.00
Hall, C.H.	12	67	5.58	1,200	45	26.80
Hall, J.	2	4	2.00	—	—	—
Hall, L.	501	12,079	24.10	1,124	33	34.06
Halliday, H.	261	8,361	32.03	3,138	101	31.06
Halilley, C.	5	27	5.40	—	—	—
Hamer, A.	2	3	1.50	64	1	64.00
Hampshire, A.W.	2	18	9.00	—	—	—
Hampshire, J.	2	5	2.50	109	5	21.80
Hampshire, J.H.	635	21,979	34.61	1,108	24	46.16
Harbord, W.E.	20	411	20.55	—	—	—
Hardisty, C.H.	50	991	19.82	—	—	—
Hargreaves, H.S.	14	51	3.64	1,146	55	20.83
Harris, W.	7	45	6.42	21	0	—
Harrison, G.P.	77	536	6.96	4,272	295	14.48
Harrison, H.	0	4	—	—	—	—
Harrison, W.H.	9	47	5.22	39	2	19.50
Hart, H.W.	8	40	5.00	181	9	20.11
Hart, P.R.	5	23	4.60	140	2	70.00
Hartington, H.E.	6	51	8.50	764	23	33.21
Hartley, P.J.	52	1,323	25.44	5,285	154	34.31
Hartley, S.N.	172	4,193	24.37	2,052	42	48.85
Hatton, A.G.	0	4	—	202	6	33.66
Hawke, Lord	648	13,124	20.25	16	0	—
Hayley, H.	16	186	11.62	110	2	55.00
Haywood, W.J.	2	7	3.50	14	1	14.00
Hicks, J.	22	313	14.22	17	0	—
Higgins, J.	7	43	6.14	—	—	—
Hill, A.	203	1,786	8.79	7,151	563	12.70
Hill, H.	36	565	15.69	—	—	—

Name	Comp. innings	Runs	Aver.	Runs	Wickets	Aver.
Hill, L.G.	2	13	6.50	—	—	—
Hirst, E.T.	34	387	11.38	—	—	—
Hirst, E.W.	3	33	11.00	3	0	—
Hirst, G.H.	922	32,024	34.73	44,716	2,481	18.02
Hirst, T.H.	0	5	—	27	0	—
Hodgson, G.	1	4	4.00	—	—	—
Hodgson, I.	21	164	7.80	1,544	87	17.74
Hodgson, P.	4	33	8.25	648	22	29.45
Holdsworth, W.E.N.	15	111	7.40	1,598	53	30.15
Holgate, G.	19	174	9.15	—	—	—
Holmes, P.	625	26,220	41.95	124	1	124.00
Horner, N.F.	4	114	28.50	—	—	—
Hoyle, T.H.	2	15	7.50	—	—	—
Hudson, B.	4	13	3.25	—	—	—
Hunter, D.	358	4,177	11.86	43	0	—
Hunter, J.	162	1,318	8.13	—	—	—
Hutton, L.	465	24,807	53.34	4,220	154	27.40
Hutton, R.A.	247	4,986	20.18	10,254	468	21.91
Iddison, R.	93	1,916	20.60	1,545	104	14.85
Illingworth, R.	537	14,986	27.90	26,806	1,431	18.73
Ingham, P.G.	14	290	20.71	—	—	—
Jackson, Hon. F.S.	306	10,371	33.89	9,690	506	19.15
Jackson, S.R.	3	78	26.00	—	—	—
Jacques, T.A.	13	162	12.46	1,786	57	31.33
Jakeman, F.	14	262	18.71	—	—	—
James, B.	2	22	11.00	228	8	28.50
Jarvis, P.W.	59	788	13.35	6,859	260	26.38
Johnson, C.	138	2,960	21.44	265	4	66.25
Johnson, J.	1	5	5.00	27	5	5.40
Johnson, M.	2	2	1.00	301	7	43.00
Joy, J.	5	107	21.40	5	0	—
Judson, A.	—	—	—	5	0	—
Kaye, H.S.	24	243	10.12	—	—	—
Kaye, H.	14	117	8.35	—	—	—
Keighley, W.G.	46	1,227	26.67	18	0	—
Kennie, G.	2	6	3.00	—	—	—
Kilburn, S.	2	16	8.00	—	—	—
Kilner, N.	67	1,259	18.79	—	—	—
Kilner, R.	435	13,014	29.91	14,873	858	17.33
King, A.M.	1	12	12.00	—	—	—
Kippax, P.J.	5	37	7.40	279	8	34.87
Lancaster, W.W.	10	163	16.30	29	0	—
Landon, C.W.	13	51	3.92	74	0	—
Law, W.	7	51	7.28	—	—	—
Leadbeater, B.	209	5,247	25.10	5	1	5.00
Leadbeater, E.	65	898	13.81	5,655	202	27.99
Leadbeater, H.	8	141	17.62	11	0	—
Leatham, G.A.B.	13	61	4.69	—	—	—
Leather, R.S.	2	19	9.50	—	—	—
Legard, A.D.	5	50	10.00	26	0	—
Lee, C.	4	98	24.50	—	—	—
Lee, F.	211	4,992	23.65	4	1	4.00
Lee, G.H.	2	13	6.50	—	—	—
Lee, H.	6	20	3.33	—	—	—
Lee, J.E.	3	9	3.00	—	—	—
Lester, E.I.	312	10,616	34.02	160	3	53.33
Leyland, M.	638	26,180	41.03	11,079	409	27.08

Name	Comp. innings	Runs	Aver.	Runs	Wickets	Aver.
Linaker, L.	2	0	0.00	28	1	28.00
Lister, B.	10	36	3.60	—	—	—
Lister, J.	4	35	8.75	—	—	—
Lister-Kaye, K.	1	13	13.00	64	1	64.00
Lockwood, E.	338	7,868	23.27	2,273	141	16.12
Lockwood, H.	25	408	16.32	37	0	—
Lodge, J.T.	3	48	16.00	17	0	—
Love, J.D.	317	9,999	31.54	815	10	81.50
Lowe, G.E.	0	5	—	—	—	—
Lowson, F.A.	373	13,897	37.25	15	0	—
Loxley-Firth, E.	4	43	10.75	—	—	—
Lumb, E.	23	489	21.26	—	—	—
Lumb, R.G.	365	11,525	31.57	5	0	—
Lupton, A.W.	65	668	10.27	77	0	—
Lynas, G.G.	2	4	2.00	—	—	—
Macaulay, G.G.	318	5,579	18.11	30,292	1,773	17.08
McHugh, F.P.	1	0	0.00	147	4	36.75
Marshall, Amos	2	2	1.00	11	0	—
Mason, A.	16	105	6.56	1,473	51	28.88
Maude, E.	2	17	8.50	—	—	—
Metcalfe, A.A.	139	4,769	34.30	154	3	51.33
Micklethwait, W.H.	1	44	44.00	—	—	—
Middlebrook, W.	27	139	5.14	1,270	77	16.49
Midgley, C.A.	4	115	28.75	149	8	18.62
Milligan, F.W.	103	1,879	18.24	2,736	112	24.42
Mitchell, A.	479	18,034	37.64	289	5	57.80
Mitchell, F.	119	4,090	34.36	16	1	16.00
Monks, G.D.	1	3	3.00	—	—	—
Moorhouse, R.	332	6,232	18.77	1,751	65	26.93
Mosley, H.	4	1	0.25	34	3	11.33
Motley, A.	1	10	10.00	133	7	19.00
Mounsey, J.	141	2,357	16.71	582	19	30.63
Moxon, M.D.	196	7,546	38.50	832	12	69.33
Myers, H.	243	4,450	18.31	7,095	282	25.15
Myers, M.	38	586	15.42	20	0	—
Naylor, J.E.	—	—	—	88	0	—
Newstead, J.T.	107	1,742	16.28	5,555	297	18.70
Nicholson, A.G.	142	1,667	11.73	17,296	876	19.74
Nicholson, N.G.	3	47	15.66	—	—	—
Oates, W.F.	3	20	6.66	—	—	—
Oates, W.	6	34	5.66	—	—	—
Old, C.M.	206	4,785	23.22	13,409	647	20.72
Oldham, S.	20	204	10.20	3,747	126	29.73
Oldroyd, E.	458	15,876	34.66	1,668	42	39.71
Oyston, C.	13	96	7.38	657	22	29.86
Padgett, D.E.V.	711	20,306	28.55	208	6	34.66
Padgett, G.H.	3	56	18.66	336	4	84.00
Padgett, J.	9	92	10.22	—	—	—
Parkin, C.H.	1	0	0.00	25	2	12.50
Parratt, J.	6	45	7.50	166	6	27.66
Parton, J.W.	4	22	5.50	13	1	13.00
Pearson, H.E.	4	36	9.00	132	7	18.85
Pearson, J.H.	3	54	18.00	—	—	—
Peate, E.	165	1,793	10.86	9,986	794	12.57
Peel, R.	468	9,322	19.86	20,638	1,311	15.74
Penny, J.H.	1	10	10.00	89	5	17.80
Pickles, C.S.	3	55	18.33	443	6	73.83
Pickles, D.	18	60	3.33	2,062	96	21.47

Name	Comp. innings	Runs	Aver.	Runs	Wickets	Aver.
Pinder, G.	158	1,650	10.44	357	19	18.78
Platt, R.K.	55	405	7.36	6,218	281	22.12
Pollard, D.	2	3	1.50	19	0	—
Pollitt, G.	1	51	51.00	—	—	—
Prest, C.H.	4	57	14.25	—	—	—
Preston, J.M.	150	2,392	15.94	3,872	228	16.98
Pride, T.	3	28	9.33	—	—	—
Pullan, P.	3	15	5.00	32	3	10.66
Radcliffe, E.J.	76	826	10.86	134	2	67.00
Ramage, A.	13	219	16.84	1,649	44	37.47
Raper, J.R.S.	4	24	6.00	—	—	—
Rawlin, E.R.	9	72	8.00	498	21	23.71
Rawlin, J.T.	35	364	10.40	284	12	23.66
Rawlinson, E.B.	63	991	15.73	62	5	12.40
Redfern, J.	11	156	14.18	17	0	—
Render, G.	1	5	5.00	—	—	—
Rhodes, A.C.	51	917	17.98	3,026	107	28.28
Rhodes, H.E.	15	269	17.93	—	—	—
Rhodes, S.J.	1	41	41.00	—	—	—
Rhodes, Wilfred	1,035	31,098	30.04	57,634	3,597	16.02
Rhodes, William	0	1	—	40	0	—
Richardson, J.A.	10	308	30.80	90	2	45.00
Riley, H.	4	36	9.00	54	1	54.00
Riley, M.	25	349	13.96	10	0	—
Ringrose, W.	36	234	6.50	3,224	155	20.80
Robinson, A.L.	38	363	9.55	4,927	196	25.13
Robinson, Emmott	385	9,444	24.53	19,607	892	21.98
Robinson, E.	1	23	23.00	—	—	—
Robinson, E.P.	208	2,596	12.48	15,135	735	20.59
Robinson, H.	2	5	2.50	20	1	20.00
Robinson, P.E.	93	3,192	34.32	139	0	—
Robinson, W.	13	151	11.61	—	—	—
Roper, E.	6	85	14.16	—	—	—
Rothery, J.W.	218	4,613	21.16	44	2	22.00
Rowbotham, J.	153	2,625	17.15	37	3	12.33
Rudston, H.	30	609	20.30	—	—	—
Ryan, M.	90	673	7.47	9,460	413	22.90
Ryder, I.	1	1	1.00	151	4	37.75
Savile, G.	7	140	20.00	—	—	—
Schofield, D.	0	13	—	112	5	22.40
Scott, E.	1	8	8.00	27	2	13.50
Sedgwick, H.	3	53	17.66	327	16	20.43
Sellers, A.	107	1,971	18.42	187	8	23.37
Sellers, A.B.	386	8,949	23.18	653	8	81.62
Shackleton, W.A.	6	49	8.16	121	6	20.16
Sharp, K.	262	7,596	28.99	751	12	62.58
Sharpe, C.M.	1	15	15.00	17	0	—
Sharpe, P.J.	595	17,685	29.72	140	2	70.00
Shaw, C.	31	340	10.96	4,101	123	33.34
Shaw, J.	3	14	4.66	291	16	18.18
Sheepshanks, E.R.	1	26	26.00	—	—	—
Shepherd, D.A.	1	0	0.00	—	—	—
Shotton, W.	4	13	3.25	—	—	—
Sidebottom, A.	167	3,777	22.61	12,046	485	24.83
Sidgwick, R.	13	64	4.92	—	—	—
Silvester, S.	3	30	10.00	313	12	26.08
Simpson, E.T.B.	5	23	4.60	—	—	—
Sims, Rev. H.M.	9	109	12.11	—	—	—
Slinn, W.	11	22	2.00	740	48	15.41

Name	Comp. innings	Runs	Aver.	Runs	Wickets	Aver.
Smailes, T.F.	296	5,683	19.19	16,622	802	20.72
Smales, K.	16	165	10.31	766	22	34.81
Smith, A.F.	45	692	15.37	–	–	–
Smith, E.	230	4,787	20.81	6,780	284	23.87
Smith, E.	16	269	16.81	1,090	46	23.69
Smith, F. (Idle)	1	11	11.00	45	2	22.50
Smith, F. (Yeadon)	18	292	16.22	–	–	–
Smith, G.	1	7	7.00	62	0	–
Smith, J.	3	28	9.33	71	6	11.83
Smith, Neil	6	82	13.66	–	–	–
Smith, R.	5	99	19.80	–	–	–
Smith, Walker	9	152	16.88	–	–	–
Smith, William	16	260	16.25	–	–	–
Smithson, G.A.	55	1,449	26.34	84	1	84.00
Smurthwaite, J.	4	29	7.25	237	12	19.75
Sowden, A.	12	140	11.66	22	0	–
Squire, D.	2	0	–	25	0	–
Squires, P.J.	76	1,271	16.72	32	0	–
Stanley, H.C.	13	155	11.92	–	–	–
Stanyforth, R.T.	3	26	8.66	–	–	–
Stead, B.	2	8	4.00	115	7	16.42
Stephenson, E.	56	803	14.33	–	–	–
Stephenson, J.S.	17	182	10.70	65	0	–
Stevenson, G.B.	185	3,856	20.84	13,254	464	28.56
Stott, W.B.	290	9,168	31.61	94	6	15.66
Stringer, P.	9	101	11.22	696	32	21.75
Stuchbury, S.	1	7	7.00	236	8	29.50
Sugg, F.H.	8	80	10.00	–	–	–
Sugg, W.	1	9	9.00	–	–	–
Sullivan, J.H.B.	2	41	20.50	43	0	–
Sutcliffe, H.	768	38,558	50.20	381	8	47.62
Sutcliffe, W.H.H.	239	6,247	26.13	152	6	25.33
Swallow, I.G.	33	657	19.90	2,231	46	48.50
Tait, T.	2	7	3.50	–	–	–
Tasker, J.	39	586	15.02	–	–	–
Tattersall, G.	2	26	13.00	–	–	–
Taylor, H.	5	36	7.20	–	–	–
Taylor, Harry	13	153	11.76	–	–	–
Taylor, J.	12	107	8.91	–	–	–
Taylor, K.	480	12,864	26.80	3,672	129	28.46
Taylor, N.S.	5	10	2.00	720	22	32.72
Taylor, T.L.	112	3,951	35.27	–	–	–
Thewlis, H.	7	78	11.14	–	–	–
Thewlis, J. Jnr	4	21	5.25	–	–	–
Thewlis, J. Snr	77	1,280	16.62	–	–	–
Thornton, A.	4	21	5.25	–	–	–
Thornton, G.	4	21	5.25	74	2	37.00
Thorpe, G.	1	14	14.00	–	–	–
Threapleton, J.W.	0	8	–	–	–	–
Tinsley, H.J.	28	340	12.14	220	15	14.66
Townsley, R.A.J.	4	22	5.50	0	0	–
Towse, A.D.	1	1	1.00	50	3	16.66
Trueman, F.S.	452	6,852	15.15	29,890	1,745	17.13
Tunnicliffe, J.	749	20,109	26.84	401	7	57.28
Turner, A.	15	163	10.86	–	–	–
Turner, B.	2	7	3.50	47	4	11.75
Turner, C.	234	6,117	26.14	5,320	173	30.75
Turner, F.I.	7	33	4.71	–	–	–
Tyson, C.	3	232	77.33	–	–	–

Name	Comp. innings	Runs	Aver.	Runs	Wickets	Aver.
Ullathorne, C.E.	38	283	7.44	—	—	—
Ulyett, G.	588	14,264	24.25	8.181	457	17.90
Usher, J.	2	7	3.50	50	3	16.66
van Geloven, J.	2	17	8.50	224	6	37.33
Verelst, H.W.	3	66	22.00	—	—	—
Verity, H.	217	3,898	17.96	21,353	1,558	13.70
Waddington, A.	184	2,261	12.28	16,095	831	19.36
Wade, S.	118	2,029	17.19	3,392	207	16.38
Wainwright, E.	582	12,768	21.93	20,230	1,173	17.24
Wainwright, W.	33	648	19.63	582	19	30.63
Wake, W.R.	3	13	4.33	—	—	—
Walker, A.	15	138	9.20	74	1	74.00
Walker, C.	7	268	38.28	71	2	35.50
Walker, G.	8	26	3.25	143	8	17.87
Walker, T.	20	179	8.95	7	0	—
Wallgate, L.W.	3	9	3.00	17	1	17.00
Ward, A.	6	67	11.16	1	0	—
Ward, F.	1	0	0.00	16	0	—
Ward, H.P.	0	10	—	—	—	—
Wardall, T.A.	100	2,009	20.09	1,150	54	21.29
Wardle, J.H.	361	5,756	15.96	27,917	1,539	18.13
Waring, J.S.	12	137	11.41	1,122	53	21.16
Waring, S.	1	9	9.00	—	—	—
Washington, I.	56	1,290	23.03	—	—	—
Watson, H.	23	141	6.13	—	—	—
Watson, W.	367	14,049	38.28	66	0	—
Waud, B.W.	9	165	18.33	—	—	—
Webster, C.	4	30	7.50	—	—	—
Webster, H.H.	3	10	3.33	—	—	—
West, J.	51	461	9.03	818	53	15.43
Whatmuff, F.J.	10	51	5.10	111	5	22.20
Wheater, C.H.	3	45	15.00	—	—	—
White, Sir A.W., Bart	100	1,457	14.57	7	0	—
Whitehead, J.P.	19	364	19.15	2,165	79	27.40
Whiteley, J.P.	21	231	11.00	2,410	70	34.42
Whitehead, Lees	158	2,314	14.64	3,106	141	22.02
Whitehead, Luther	4	21	5.25	—	—	—
Whiting, C.P.	8	92	11.50	416	15	27.73
Whitwell, J.F.	3	54	18.00	35	4	8.75
Whitwell, W.F.	12	67	5.58	518	25	20.72
Wilkinson, A.J.A.	6	129	21.50	57	0	—
Wilkinson, F.	13	73	5.61	590	26	22.69
Wilkinson, H.	72	1,382	19.19	121	3	40.33
Wilkinson, W.H.	178	3,812	21.41	971	31	31.32
Williams, A.C.	4	95	23.75	678	30	22.60
Wilson, B.B.	288	6,934	24.07	278	2	139.00
Wilson, C.E.M.	10	256	25.60	257	12	21.41
Wilson, D.	417	5,788	13.88	22,626	1,104	20.49
Wilson, E.R.	55	902	16.40	3,078	196	15.70
Wilson, G.A.	20	352	17.60	138	1	138.00
Wilson, G.	80	985	12.31	11	0	—
Wilson, J.	11	172	15.63	304	24	12.66
Wilson, J.P.	13	81	6.23	24	1	24.00
Wilson, J.V.	658	20,539	31.21	305	3	101.66
Wood, A.	406	8,579	21.13	33	1	33.00
Wood, C.H.	3	22	7.33	319	11	29.00
Wood, B.	5	63	12.60	—	—	—
Wood, G.	2	2	1.00	—	—	—
Wood, H.	15	156	10.40	212	10	21.20
Wood, J.H.	1	14	14.00	—	—	—

Wood, R.	14	60	4.28	1,326	51	26.00
Woodford, J.D.	59	1,204	20.40	185	4	46.25
Woodhead, F.E.	11	129	11.72	–	–	–
Woodhouse, W.H.	13	218	16.76	–	–	–
Wormald, A.	9	162	18.00	–	–	–
Worsley, W.A.	45	733	16.28	–	–	–
Wrathmell, L.F.	3	18	6.00	–	–	–
Wright, R.	3	28	9.33	–	–	–
Wright, T.J.	1	12	12.00	–	–	–
Yardley, N.W.D.	364	11,632	31.95	5,816	192	30.29
Yeadon, J.	4	41	10.25	–	–	–

Gillette Cup and NatWest Trophy records (1963–1988)

Opponents	Played	Won	Lost
Derbyshire	1	1	0
Essex	1	1	0
Glamorgan	1	1	0
Gloucestershire	1	0	1
Hampshire	3	2	1
Kent	3	1	2
Lancashire	3	1	2
Leicestershire	3	1	2
Middlesex	4	1	3
Northamptonshire	1	0	1
Nottinghamshire	3	3	0
Somerset	3	1	2
Surrey	4	2	2
Sussex	3	0	3
Warwickshire	4	1	3
Worcestershire	1	1	0
Berkshire	2	2	0
Cambridgeshire	2	2	0
Cheshire	1	1	0
Durham	3	2	1
Norfolk	1	1	0
Shropshire	2	1	1
Wiltshire	1	1	0
	51	27	24

Benson and Hedges Cup records (1972–1988)

Opponents	Played	Won	Lost	No result
Derbyshire	7	5	1	1
Essex	3	2	1	0
Gloucestershire	1	1	0	0
Hampshire	1	1	0	0
Kent	3	2	1	0
Lancashire	9	3	5	1
Leicestershire	4	2	2	0
Middlesex	4	1	2	1
Northamptonshire	5	2	2	1
Nottinghamshire	9	3	4	2
Somerset	1	0	1	0
Surrey	4	1	3	0
Sussex	3	3	0	0
Warwickshire	7	3	4	0
Worcestershire	6	1	5	0
Oxford & Cambridge Universities	2	1	1	0
Minor Counties	1	1	0	0
Minor Counties (East)	1	1	0	0
Minor Counties (North)	5	5	0	0
Scotland	4	4	0	0
	81	43	32	6

John Player League and Refuge Assurance League records (1969–1988)

Opponents	Played	Won	Lost	Tied	No result
Derbyshire	20	11	7		2
Essex	20	9	9		2
Glamorgan	20	7	12		1
Gloucestershire	20	7	8		5
Hampshire	20	6	13		1
Kent	20	9	8		3
Lancashire	20	5	10		5
Leicestershire	20	12	6		2
Middlesex	20	9	7		4
Northamptonshire	20	13	5		2
Nottinghamshire	20	10	8	1	1
Somerset	20	6	12		2
Surrey	20	9	9		2
Sussex	20	6	11		3
Warwickshire	20	7	7	1	5
Worcestershire	20	9	10		1
	320	135	142	2	41

Bibliography

Books and other publications used in the preparation of this History.

'Talks with Old Yorkshire Cricketers' ('Old Ebor', *Yorkshire Post*, 1898)

History of Yorkshire County Cricket, 1833–1903, Rev. R.S. Holmes (Constable and Co., 1904)

History of Yorkshire County Cricket, 1903–1923, A.W. Pullin (Chorley and Pickersgill, 1924)

History of Yorkshire County Cricket, 1924–49, J.M. Kilburn (Yorkshire CCC, 1950)

The Book of Cricket, Pelham Warner (Dent, 1922)

Cricket Memories, 'A Country Vicar' (Methuen, 1930)

The Happy Cricketer, 'A Country Vicar' (Frederick Muller, 1946)

A History of Cricket, Altham and Swanton (Allen and Unwin, 1947)

Yorkshire, J.M. Kilburn (Convoy, 1950)

Cricket: A History, Roland Bowen (Eyre and Spottiswoode, 1970)

Recollections and Reminiscences, Lord Hawke (Williams and Norgate, 1924)

Parkin on Cricket, Cecil Parkin (Hodder and Stoughton)

Laughter at the Wicket, Harry East (Whitehorn, 1980)

Hedley Verity, Alan Hill (Kingswood, 1986)

Hirst and Rhodes, A.A. Thomson (Epworth, 1959)

Holmes and Sutcliffe, Leslie Duckworth (Hutchinson, 1970)

Carr's Illustrated Dictionary of Extra-Ordinary Cricketers (Quartet, 1983)

The Roses Matches, 1919–39, Neville Cardus (Souvenir, 1982)

Yorkshire Cricketers, 1839–1939, Peter Thomas (Hodgson, 1973)

Boycott, Geoffrey Boycott (Macmillan, 1987)

A History of Yorkshire Cricket, J.M. Kilburn (Stanley Paul, 1970)

Cricket Heroes, The Cricket Writers' Club (Queen Anne, 1984)

Just – My Story, Len Hutton (Hutchinson, 1956)

Cricket Campaigns, Norman Yardley (Stanley Paul, 1950)

Len Hutton, Gerald Howat (Heinemann Kingswood, 1988)

Yorkshire's Pride, John Callaghan (Pelham, 1984)

A Yorkshire Diary, David Bairstow (Sidgwick and Jackson, 1984)

Boycott, Don Mosey (Methuen, 1985)

We Don't Play it for Fun, Don Mosey (Methuen, 1988)

Family Argument, John Hampshire (Allen and Unwin, 1983)

Illy, Mike Stevenson (Midas, 1978)

Fred, John Arlott (Eyre and Spottiswoode, 1973)

Opening Up, Geoffrey Boycott (Arthur Barker, 1980)

Overthrows, J.M. Kilburn (Stanley Paul, 1975)

Put to the Test, Geoffrey Boycott (Arthur Barker, 1979)

I Don't Bruise Easily, Brian Close (MacDonald and Jane's, 1978)

Thanks to Cricket, J.M. Kilburn (Stanley Paul, 1972)

Boycott, John Callaghan (Pelham, 1982)

Jackson's Year, Alan Gibson (Cassell, 1965)

Cricket Choice, Alec Bedser (Pelham, 1981)

Cricket's Silver Lining, David Rayvern Allen (Collins, 1987)

Jubilee Book of Cricket, Prince Ranjitsinhji (Blackwood, 1897)

The County Cricket Championship, Roy Webber (Sportsmen's, 1958)

Express Deliveries, Bill Bowes (Sportsmen's, 1958)

Cricket All the Year, Neville Cardus (Collins, 1952)

Crusoe on Cricket, R.C. Robertson-Glasgow (Pavilion, 1985)

Days in the Sun, Neville Cardus (Hart-Davis, 1948)

The Summer Game, Neville Cardus (Hart-Davis, 1948)

A Fourth Innings with Cardus (Souvenir, 1981)

From Bradman to Boycott, Ted Dexter (Queen Anne, 1981)

John Arlott's Book of Cricketers (Lutterworth, 1979)

The Spinner's Turn, Patrick Murphy (Dent, 1982)

Vintage Cricketers, E.M. Wellings (Allen and Unwin, 1983)

The Slow Men, David Frith (Allen and Unwin, 1984)

Neil Lloyd (Wombwell Cricket Lovers, 1982)

Wisden Cricketers' Almanac (various)

Yorkshire CCC Yearbook (various)

Cricketer International (various)

Wisden Cricket Monthly (various)

Cricket Conjuror, Alan Hill (David and Charles, 1988)

The Tempestuous Years, Ray Illingworth (Sidgwick and Jackson, 1987)

The Boundary Book, Leslie Frewin (Pelham, 1986)

The Spinners' Web, Bailey and Trueman (Willow, 1988)

The White Rose (Yorkshire CCC) various

Yorkshire Post Benefit Book (1987)

Cricket Hotch-Potch, Tom Naylor (Fretwell and Brian, 1984)

Before and After Bramall Lane, Keith Farnsworth (private publication, 1988)

Yorkshire Cricketers 1863–1985 (Cricket Statisticians, 1986)

Index